THE CRAFTSMAN AND THE CRITIC

The Craftsman and the Critic

Defining Usefulness and Beauty
in Arts and Crafts–Era Boston

Beverly K. Brandt

UNIVERSITY OF MASSACHUSETTS PRESS
Amherst

Copyright © 2009 by Beverly K. Brandt
All rights reserved
Printed in the United States of America

LC 2008035411
ISBN 978-1-55849-677-4

Designed by Sally Nichols
Set in Janson Text and Poetica
Printed and bound by Sheridan Books, Inc.

Library of Congress Cataloging-in-Publication Data

Brandt, Beverly Kay.
　The craftsman and the critic : defining usefulness and beauty in arts and crafts–era Boston / Beverly K. Brandt.
　　p. cm.
　Includes bibliographical references and index.
　ISBN 978-1-55849-677-4 (cloth : alk. paper)
　1. Arts and crafts movement—Massachusetts—Boston—History—19th century. 2. Decorative arts—Massachusetts—Boston—History—19th century. I. Title.
　NK1141.B73 2008
　745.09744′61—dc22
　　　　　　　　　　　　2008035411

British Library Cataloguing in Publication data are available.

To Mark, Barbara, Richard, Carol, Stephen, and Kristen
And in memory of Edith

Contents

Illustrations ix

Preface xvii

Acknowledgments xxvii

INTRODUCTION. *In Quest of Usefulness and Beauty* 1
The Evolution of the Discipline of Design Criticism in the Nineteenth Century

CHAPTER ONE. *Boston in the Gilded Age* 57
Embracing Design Criticism and the Reform Movement

CHAPTER TWO. *By Word, Deed, or Example* 109
Promoting Design Reform in Boston

CHAPTER THREE. *Adviser, Promoter, Tormentor, and Midwife* 141
The Multiple Roles of Boston's Design Critics

CHAPTER FOUR. *Models and Methodologies* 185
Guidelines for Achieving "Good Design"

CHAPTER FIVE. *The Boston Diaspora* 225
Promoting Boston's Standards of Usefulness and Beauty Nationwide

Afterword 275

EPILOGUE. *Usefulness and Beauty in the New Millennium* 281
The Legacy of the Society of Arts and Crafts, Boston

APPENDIXES.

A. *Members of the SACB Jury, 1900–1917* 293

B. *Survey of the SACB Membership by Craft Category, 1916* 295

C. *List of Books in the SACB Library, Compiled 1917–1918* 297

D. *Works Commended by the SACB Jury as Listed in the*
   ANNUAL REPORTS, *1913–1918* 301

E. *Architect Members of the SACB, 1897–1917* 311

Notes 313

Bibliography 359

Index 381

Illustrations

COLOR PLATES follow page 224.

Plate 1. Bedstead and hangings in Renaissance Revival style, 1851
Plate 2. Interior of Wedgwood salesroom, London, 1809
Plate 3. Plate XXVIII, from R. Ackermann, *Repository of Arts, Literature, Commerce, Manufactures, Fashions, and Politics*, 1811
Plate 4. "Engraved Muslins," exhibited at the Crystal Palace, *Journal of Design and Manufactures*, 1851
Plate 5. "My Lady's Chamber," frontispiece to Clarence Cook, *The House Beautiful*, 1881
Plate 6. "The Craftsman Look," illustration from advertising brochure, undated
Plate 7. Trade card illustrating "Aesthetic" vignette
Plate 8. Cover of a trade catalogue for Daniel Low & Co., Salem, Mass., 1926
Plate 9. Cover of a trade catalogue for Bunkio Matsuki, Boston, undated
Plate 10. Book cover, by Amy Sacker, 1903
Plate 11. Book cover, by Alice Morse, 1899
Plate 12. Book cover, by Alice Morse, 1898
Plate 13. Study of a marsh scene, by Arthur Wesley Dow, undated
Plate 14. Study of a lily, by Arthur Wesley Dow, undated
Plate 15. "Lily," by Arthur Wesley Dow, 1901
Plate 16. Architectural illustration, by Alexander Hoyle, ca. 1916
Plate 17. Mr. and Mrs. Ralph Adams Cram's Christmas card, 1909
Plate 18. "Willow Boughs" wallpaper, Morris & Co., ca. 1887
Plate 19. Cover, *Home, The Remodeling and Decorating Resource*, September 1994

FIGURES

1.	Exterior view of Crystal Palace, 1851	3
2.	Interior view of Crystal Palace, 1851	4
3.	Ralph Nicholson Wornum	7
4.	Tea service and breakfast service, showing French influence, 1851	8
5.	French Department at the Great Exhibition, 1851	9
6.	William Hogarth	13
7.	Engraving, Plate 1, Third State, from Hogarth, *Analysis of Beauty*, 1757	13
8.	David Hume	14
9.	Edmund Burke	15
10.	"Design for a State-Bed," from Thomas Chippendale, *The Gentleman and Cabinet-Maker's Director*, 1754	22
11.	Secretary-Bookcase, from George Hepplewhite, *The Gentleman and Cabinet-Maker's Guide*, 1788	23
12.	"Design for a Four-Poster Bed," from Thomas Sheraton, *The Cabinet Encyclopedia*, 1804	24
13.	Three carved wood plates, from *Journal of Design and Manufactures*, 1850	27
14a and b.	Cover and interior illustration from Barstow Stove Co. trade catalogue, *Fireside and Kitchen*	30
15.	Trade card, Physical Culture Restaurant, Boston	35
16.	Business card, Professor J. J. Foley, ca. 1894	35

17.	Page from sketchbook of Mary Ware Dennett, ca. 1897	37
18.	"Pattern Plans and Motifs," from Walter Crane, *Bases of Design*, 1892	37
19.	Announcement by Daniel Berkeley Updike (?), for meeting of the Society of Arts and Crafts, Boston, 1898	38
20.	Advertisement for Paine's Furniture Manufactory, Boston, undated	40
21.	"Dining Room Fireplace," from Robert W. Edis, *Decoration & Furniture of Town Houses*, 1881	42
22.	Slipper case, from W. N. Swett & Co. trade catalogue	43
23.	Silver trophy, ca. 1886–99, Reed & Barton Manufactory	44
24a.	Trade card, Glenwood Ranges & Parlor Stoves, 1887)	45
24b.	Front parlor, 39 Beacon Street, Boston, ca. 1885	45
25.	Diagram showing proper proportion in pouring vessels, from Frank Jackson, *Theory and Practice of Design*, 1894	46
26.	Calendar illustration, "The New England of Years Ago; The New England of Today," New England Mutual Life Insurance Co., Boston, 1885	49
27a.	"Honeysuckle" chintz, Morris & Co., 1876	50
27b.	Drawing of tunic, from Alexander Speltz, *The Styles of Ornament*, 1904	50
28.	"Adaptation of the Horned Poppy in Design," from Walter Crane, *Line & Form*, 1900	51
29.	Residence of Henry D. Sleeper, 336 Beacon Street, Boston, undated	52
30.	Business card, for Jones, McDufee & Stratton, Boston, showing influence of Aesthetic movement	53
31.	Charles Eliot Norton	56
32.	Herbert Langford Warren	56
33.	Denman Waldo Ross	56
34.	Charles Howard Walker	56
35a.	George Edward Barton	58
35b.	Invitation to the First Exhibition of the Arts and Crafts, 1897	58
36.	Alexander Wadsworth Longfellow, Jr.	58
37a.	George R. Shaw	59
37b.	Design for a fireplace, by George R. and R. G. Shaw, 1880	59
38.	Advertisement for Hugh Cairns, Architectural Sculptor, Modeler, and Stone Carver	59
39.	John A. Evans	60
40.	Johannes Kirchmayer	60
41.	Advertisement for Goodnow & Jenks, Stanhope Street, Boston	60
42.	Design for a tea set in solid silver, by Barton P. Jenks	60
43.	John Templeman Coolidge, Jr.	61
44.	Cover of *Arts and Crafts in the Middle Ages* by Julia de Wolf Addison	61
45.	Sarah Wyman Whitman	61
46.	Daniel Berkeley Updike	61
47.	Henry Lewis Johnson	62
48.	Morris Gray	62
49.	Arthur Astor Carey	62
50.	Samuel Dennis Warren II	62
51a.	Postcard, Museum of Fine Arts, Boston, undated	63
51b.	Postcard, View of Copley Square, and Museum of Fine Arts, undated	63
52.	Guy Lowell	63
53.	Richard Clipston Sturgis	63
54.	Edmund March Wheelwright	64
55a.	Wharves near Custom House Tower, Boston, ca. 1913–15	64

55b. Immigration quarters, Cunard Line Pier, East Boston, ca. 1910	64
56. Paper sample, "Warren's Cameo Plate Coated Book," from *The Plimpton Press Yearbook*, 1911	66
57. Governor Benning Wentworth House, New Castle, N.H., 1916 or earlier	67
58. Postcard, View of Commonwealth Avenue, Boston, undated	68
59. Interior view, Boston Foreign Fair, from *Scrapbook of [Gen.] Charles B. Norton*, 1884	69
60. Advertisement for Bigelow Kennard & Co., Inc., Washington Street, Boston, ca. 1916	70
61. Advertisement for J. F. Bumstead & Co., ca. 1890	70
62. Advertisement for John H. Pray, Sons & Co., Washington Street, Boston	70
63a. View of 155–189 Washington Street, illustrating facade of Joel Goldthwait & Co., ca. 1880	71
63b. Bill head for Joel Goldthwait & Co., Carpet Dealers, 1878	71
64. Postcard, Shopping District, Washington Street, Boston, undated	71
65a. View of 4–60 School Street, illustrating exterior of Richard Briggs, 1870s	72
65b. Business card for Richard Briggs, 137 Washington Street, Boston	72
66. Interior, 348 Beacon Street, Boston, 1886 (?)	73
67. Bedroom, 200 Beacon Street, Boston, ca. 1885	73
68. Corner of Antique Room, Jordan Marsh Co. (?), ca. 1926	74
69. Announcement of "Farewell Lecture on Decorative Art" by Oscar Wilde, ca. 1882–83	74
70. Edward Henry Clement	76
71. Advertisement for the Heliotype Printing Co., Tremont Street, Boston	77
72a. Postcard, Old State House, Boston, undated	78
72b. Postcard, Old South Meeting House, Boston, undated	78
73a. Postcard, Tremont Street and Park Street Church, Boston, ca. 1909	79
73b. Building subway beneath corner of Tremont and Park Streets, Boston, ca. 1890s	79
74. 135 Marlborough Street, Boston, 1880 (?), by Cabot & Chandler, architects	79
75a. Interior of home in Brookline, showing sculpture of Winged Victory of Samothrace	80
75b. Arthur Little residence, 2 Raleigh Street, Boston, undated, showing sculpture of Winged Victory of Samothrace	80
75c. Cover of trade catalogue, Alandale Studios, Boston, featuring image of Winged Victory of Samothrace, ca. 1922	80
75d. Arts and Crafts exhibition at Deerfield, Mass., undated	80
76. Interior, 3 Autumn Street (?), Roxbury, Mass., ca. 1882	81
77. Studio, T. Quincy Browne House, 98 Beacon Street, Boston, undated	82
78. Advertisements from *Our Homes and How To Heat & Ventilate Them*, 1886	83
79a. Amory-Ticknor House, Park and Beacon Streets, Boston, after renovations, undated	84
79b. Amory-Ticknor House, prior to renovations, undated	84
80a. Exterior, Normal School of Art, Newbury Street, Boston, ca. 1897	85
80b. Life class, Cowles Art School, Dartmouth Street, Boston, ca. 1897	85
81. Announcement, "Hallowe'en at the Tavern," Tavern Club, 1910	86
82. Postcard, Trinity Church, Boston, ca. 1905	87
83. H. H. Richardson's office, Brookline, ca. 1881	87
84. John Ruskin and Constance Hilliard, October 1879	88
85. Susan Ridley Sedgwick Norton, photographic copy of a portrait by Rouse, ca. 1862	89
86a. Sir Edward Burne-Jones, 1882 (?)	89

86b. Lady Georgina Burne-Jones, 1882 (?)   89
87. Margaret Burne-Jones, Sally Norton, and Lily Norton, 1890   91
88a and b. Interiors, South Kensington Museum, South Court and North Court, from Moncure Conway, *Travels in South Kensington*, 1882   92–93
89. Interior showing kindergarten class, Denison House, Boston, 1900   95
90. Prospectus pamphlet, "Exhibition of the Arts and Crafts, Copley Hall, Boston," by Theodore Brown Hapgood, Jr., 1896   97
91. Pamphlet with border design, by Bertram Grosvenor Goodhue, ca. March 1897   97
92. Interior, Copley Hall, Boston, First Exhibition of the Arts and Crafts, 1897   99
93. Cover of program for concert at Chickering Hall, undated   99
94. Ednah D. Cheney   99
95. Lois Lilley Howe   100
96. Catalogue for First Exhibition, by Bertram Grosvenor Goodhue, 1897   102
97. Bertram Grosvenor Goodhue in Persian dress, 1891   102
98. "The First Car Through the Subway Yesterday," from *Boston Globe*, 1897   104
99. Japanese Corridor, Museum of Fine Arts, Copley Square, Boston, undated   104
100. Advertisement for *Bradley His Book*, ca. 1896–97   105
101. Cover of *The Yellow Book*, illustration by Ethel Reed, 1897   105
102. Original study for seal of the SACB, by Bertram Grosvenor Goodhue, ca. 1897   106
103. Wall hanging, by Mary Ware Dennett, illustrating the Society's seal, 1900–1920   106
104. Mrs. Joshua Montgomery [Sarah Choate] Sears, by John Singer Sargent, 1899   110
105. *Untitled (A Poet)*, by Sarah Choate Sears, ca. 1892–ca. 1905   111
106. Office of Frank Gair Macomber, 115 Water Street, Boston   115
107. Joseph Lindon Smith   116
108a. Design for an oval table in Hepplewhite style, by John Endicott Peabody, ca. 1906–1921   116
108b. Design for a tea table with saltire stretcher in Hepplewhite style, by John Endicott Peabody, ca. 1906–1921   116
108c. Signature of John Endicott Peabody, ca. 1906–1921   116
109. Postcard, Mrs. Jack Gardner's Venetian Palace, Boston, undated   117
110. Interior, Allston Hall, Exhibition of the Society of Arts and Crafts, 1899   117
111. Interior, Copley Hall, Exhibition of the Society of Arts and Crafts, 1899   118
112. Catalogue cover, by William Porter Jenkins, for 1899 Exhibition   119
113. Somerset Street looking toward Hampton Place Church, undated   122
114. Frederick Allen Whiting   122
115. Olive Elizabeth Whiting   123
116. Watchmaking factory in Waltham, from *Appleton's Journal*, 1870   125
117. Sterling silver salt cellars and spoons, by Mary C. Knight and Karl F. Leinonen, Handicraft Shop, ca. 1902   126
118. Promotional pamphlet, "A Declaration of Economic Independence," 1904   131
119. Mary Ware Dennett   132
120. Laurin Hovey Martin   144
121. Copper tazza, by Laurin Hovey Martin   144
122. Henry Hunt Clark   145
123. Grueby vase, by George P. Kendrick   145
124a. Frank Gardner Hale   146
124b. Broach, by Frank Gardner Hale   146
125. Studio of Madeline Yale Wynne and Annie Cabot Putnam   147
126. Hermann Dudley Murphy, self-portrait   148
127. "Apse of the Cathedral at Pisa," drawing, by Joseph Lindon Smith   148
128. Plate, trial glaze design, by Joseph Lindon Smith   149

129.	"The Princess Who Never Laughed," illustration, by Amy Sacker	149
130.	Chestnut Street, Boston, 1917 (?)	153
131.	Medal, the Society of Arts and Crafts, Boston	156
132.	Henry Chapman Mercer	160
133.	"The Apostles," stained glass window, by Margaret Redmond	161
134.	Exhibition of the Society of Arts and Crafts, Copley Hall, Boston, 1907	163
135a and b.	Metalwork and silver shown at the 1907 Exhibition	164
136.	Exterior, Society salesroom, 9 Park Street	166
137.	Interior, Society salesroom, 9 Park Street	166
138.	Plate, silver and enamel, by Mary C. Knight, undated	178
139.	Altar vase, by Julia de Wolf Addison, ca. 1890–1920	179
140.	"General Rules for Consignors" of SACB	180
141.	Studio of Arthur J. Stone, Gardner, Mass., ca. 1908	182
142.	Silver patch box, by Arthur J. Stone, ca. 1905–12	183
143.	Interior, T. Quincy Browne house, 98 Beacon Street, undated	187
144.	Bedroom, 200 Beacon Street, 1885	187
145.	Pulpit door from Cairo in Wood Carving Room, Museum of Fine Arts, Copley Square, undated	188
146.	Greek Vase Room, Museum of Fine Arts, Copley Square, undated	189
147.	Belgian wrought iron work in Metal Room, Museum of Fine Arts, Copley Square, undated	190
148.	Illustration of metalwork, trade catalogue, F. Krasser & Company	190
149.	Studio at Massachusetts Institute of Technology, 1889	191
150.	Design for a silver sugar server, by Arthur John Stone, ca. 1914	193
151.	Sketch for "Early Georgian" side chair in the Chippendale style, ca. 1897	195
152a and b.	Living room, unidentified residence, undated	196
153.	Sketch of All Saints, Brookline, by Bertram Grosvenor Goodhue, undated	197
154.	Anonymous, Rookwood Pottery, "Corn Mug," 1903	199
155.	Illustration, by H. M. O'Kane, from *Sonnets from the Portuguese*, 1900	200
156.	Tenney (?) residence, Manchester, Mass., undated	201
157.	"Convolvulus," from *Art-Studies from Nature, as Applied to Design*, 1872	202
158.	Book cover, by Thomas B. Meteyard, for Bliss Carman, *A Winter Holiday*, 1899	203
159.	"The American Drawing-Cards," Nos. 1 and 2, Second Series, published 1873	204
160.	Examples of conventionalized ornament: border motifs, from Alexander Speltz, *The Styles of Ornament*, 1904	205
161.	Foyer, unidentified residence, ca. 1925	206
162.	Examples of conventionalized ornament: strapwork, from Alexander Speltz, *The Styles of Ornament*, 1904	207
163.	Book cover, by Theodore Brown Hapgood, Jr., for Jennie Hall, *Weavers and Other Workers*, 1917	207
164.	Detail of architectural metalwork, showing acanthus leafage, by Louis Sullivan, architect, 1889–1901, 1903–04	208
165.	Graphic design, by Will Dwiggins, for Harriet Mason Kilburn, *Calendar of The Fellowship, A.D. 1910*	208
166.	Illustration from trade catalogue, *Sterling Hollow Ware*, Reed & Barton, ca. 1909	209
167.	348 Beacon Street, 1886 (?), Allen & Kenway, architects	210
168a.	Illustration of stained glass treatment, from Walter Crane, *Line and Form* (1900)	211
168b.	Stained glass and wrought iron fire screen, by Sarah Wyman Whitman, 1896	211
169a.	Illustration of the "Sorrel," from *Art-Studies from Nature, as Applied to Design*, 1872	212

169b.	Living room, unidentified residence, undated	212
170.	Illustration of "Cresting and Finials," from trade catalogue, W. A. Snow & Co., Boston	213
171.	Book cover, by Bertram Grosvenor Goodhue, for Craigie's *An Old Man's Romance*, 1895	213
172a.	Chimney detail, 54 Boutwell Avenue (?), Dorchester, Mass., Cabot & Chandler, architects, ca. 1882	214
172b.	Book cover, by Theodore Brown Hapgood, Jr., for Guy Wetmore Carryl, *Far from the Maddening Girls*, 1904	214
173.	Advertisement, "Grueby Pottery for the Holidays," 1900	215
174.	Example of a smoking-room from Jordan Marsh Company, Boston, ca. 1906	216
175.	Book cover, by Sarah Wyman Whitman, for Edna Dean Proctor, *Song of the Ancient People*, 1898	216
176a.	Finishing tools, used for book binding by Mary Crease Sears	217
176b.	Book binding, by Mary Crease Sears, for the *Commonplace Book*, ca. 1917	217
176c.	Sanborn-Raymond House, 125 Magazine Street, Cambridge, Mass., undated	218
177.	Thompson House, 161 Brattle Street, Cambridge, Mass., Cram, Goodhue & Ferguson, architects (?), undated	220
178.	Book cover, by Sarah Wyman Whitman, for S. Weir Mitchell, *In War-Time*, 1884	221
179.	Book cover, by Sarah Wyman Whitman, for Percival Lowell, *The Soul of the Far East*, 1888	221
180.	Advertisement featuring a Craftsman-type interior, for the Cobb-Eastman Co., ca. 1902	222
181.	Fourth Presbyterian Church, Chicago, Cram, Ferguson & Goodhue, architects, ca. 1914	223
182.	"Landscape Vase," by Edward Diers, for Rookwood Pottery, 1919	223
183.	Howe residence, Manchester Cove, Mass., Edmund M. Wheelwright, architect, undated	224
184.	Advertisement, Bigelow, Kennard & Co., featuring Grueby pottery, 1901	226
185.	Exterior, Palace of Fine Arts, Louisiana Purchase Exposition, 1904	227
186.	Electricity Building, Festival Hall, and Grand Basin, Louisiana Purchase Exposition, 1904	228
187.	Halsey C. Ives	229
188.	Charles M. Kurtz	232
189.	William Morris, *Pre-Raphaelite Ballads*, with illustrations by H. M. O'Kane, 1900	233
190.	Pages from Tacitus, *Minor Works*, printed at the Merrymount Press by Daniel Berkeley Updike, 1904	234
191.	Anne and Artus Van Briggle in their studio, ca. 1902–04	235
192.	Ernest Allen Batchelder	236
193.	*What Lies Beyond*, by Dawson Dawson-Watson, oil on canvas, 1936	239
194.	Palace of Varied Industries, Louisiana Purchase Exposition, 1904	240
195.	Trade card, Charles R. Yandell & Co., Art Leather Manufacturers, New York	240
196a and b.	Interior views, Palace of Art, International Sculpture Hall, 1904	241
197.	Stained glass window, "America," or "Courage, Love, Patience," by Sarah Wyman Whitman, 1904	242
198.	Advertisement, The Harry Eldredge Goodhue Co., Cambridge, Mass., 1908	242
199.	Vase with "Volcanic" glaze, by Hugh C. Robertson, ca. 1896–1908	243
200.	Tile, Grueby Faience Pottery Company, 1900	244
201.	Writing table in Art Nouveau style, by William C. Codman, ca. 1904	245
202.	Trade catalogue, cover, Union Glass Co., Somerville, Mass., undated	247
203.	"Fern" and "Morning Glory" vases from trade catalogue for the Union Glass Co.	247
204.	Decorative sketch, "Jeanne D'Arc," by George H. Hallowell, 1902	251

205.	Book cover, by George H. Hallowell, for *Low Tide on Grand Pré*, 1894	251
206.	Decorated bowl, by Maud Masson, ca. 1907	253
207.	Candlestick, silver with enamel, by Elizabeth Copeland, ca. 1917	253
208.	Design for a chapel, by Bertram Grosvenor Goodhue, undated	255
209.	Design for a house in Bar Harbor, Me., Andrews, Jaques & Rantoul, architects, 1897	256
210.	Houses at Cohasset and Milton, Mass., Andrews, Jaques & Rantoul, architects, 1908	256
211.	Japanese Room, Longfellow House, Cambridge, undated	256
212.	Design for The Hall, Renfrew Park, Newport, R.I., by H. Langford Warren, architect, 1890	257
213a.	Charles J. Page House, 90 Westland Avenue, Boston, H. Langford Warren, architect, ca. 1888	257
213b.	Interior, dining room with inglenook, Charles J. Page House	257
214.	Residence in Brookline, H. Langford Warren, architect, undated	257
215.	Design for store on Farnham Street, Omaha, Neb., by Walker & Best, architects, 1890	258
216.	Edward Robinson residence, Manchester, Mass., C. Howard Walker, architect, ca. 1888	258
217.	Book plate, for C. Howard Walker, 1922	259
218.	Frank C. Brown	259
219.	Business card for Frank C. Brown, architect, ca. 1920s	260
220.	"Proposal for a Brick Cottage Bungalow," by Frank C. Brown, architect, 1912	260
221.	Sketches for set design for *The Merchant of Venice*, by Frank C. Brown, ca. 1907	260
222.	Fountain in Garden Room in a house by Ripley, Fisher & LeBoutillier, architects, 1916	261
223.	"Elevation of North End of Living Room," by Fisher, Ripley & LeBoutillier, architects, 1916	261
224.	Interior perspective rendering, "Chapel, Tabor Academy, Marion, Mass." by Addison B. LeBoutillier, 1916	261
225.	Country house, Lois L. Howe, architect, 1906	262
226.	Two views in house, Lois L. Howe, architect, undated	262
227.	Portrait of Guy Lowell, by John Singer Sargent, 1917	263
228a–c.	Museum of Fine Arts, Boston: Three views	263
229a and b.	Working-men's cottages at Bridgeport, Conn., R. Clipston Sturgis, architect, 1917	264
230.	Banking Room, First National Bank, Boston, R. Clipston Sturgis, architect, 1908	264
231.	Book illustrations, by R. Clipston Sturgis, for Mrs. R. Clipston Sturgis, *Random Reflections of a Grandmother*, 1917	265
232.	Invitation to an exhibition by The Weavers' Guild at the Society of Arts and Crafts, 1922	266
233.	Postcard, Charles River Basin, Boston, ca. 1916	268
234.	Postcard, "New England Views on Boston & Maine R.R., Deerfield Valley, Mass.," undated	268
235.	Cross pendant with chain, by Janet Payne Bowles, ca. 1907–11	270
236.	Madeline Yale Wynne	271
237.	Box lid with rabbit motif, by Madeline Yale Wynne	271
238.	Ellen Gates Starr, by Frances Allen and Mary Allen, ca. 1905	272
239.	Fireplace with Batchelder tiles, Charlevoix Public Library, Charlevoix, Mich., ca. 1927	273
240.	Residence in Arts and Crafts Revival style, Rick Neumann, architect (Petoskey, Mich.), 2004	289

Preface

> Just let us consult our own desires and needs, and refuse to be governed by those of other people. And, let us refuse to take what is offered to us, if it does not suit our needs and purses, and learn not to fear being sent to Conventry for our refusal.
> —Clarence Cook, *The House Beautiful* (1877)

When I was visiting the San Francisco Bay Area in December 1999, I was thrilled to pick up the year-end Home & Garden section of the *San Francisco Chronicle* and to read its list of the "Top 10 Home and Garden Events of the [20th] Century." There, among the electric washing machine, the refrigerator, the television, household bleach, cat litter, and hybrid bulbs, was none other than the "Arts and Crafts Style," the sole entry on that list that was not a product or a laborsaving device.[1]

That tiny sidebar on the front page of the Home & Garden section started me thinking about the long-term implications of this Anglo-American design reform movement, begun nearly 150 years ago. Why did this movement prove to be more durable than myriad other movements and styles that were also born during the last half of the nineteenth century? Why did this movement make a graceful transition as historicism gave way to early modernism? Why did the original design reform movement fuel a full-blown Arts and Crafts Revival in the 1990s, while we did not experience, say, a parallel "Rococo Revival Revival" or "Aesthetic Movement Revival"? And why, in the aftermath of modernism, minimalism, postmodernism, neo-modernism, deconstructivism, and even millennialism has the Arts and Crafts movement prevailed, when other "-isms" have, to quote the editor and columnist David Shribman, become "was-ims"?[2]

We can, I believe, attribute the enduring nature of the Arts and Crafts movement to the quality of ideas that gave rise to it in the first place. William Morris summarized those best when he urged his followers: "Have nothing in your houses that you do not know to be useful or believe to be beautiful." Morris empowered consumers to take control of their own environments by choosing only those products that they deemed functional or attractive. He urged consumers to take responsibility for the quality of their homes and workplaces, and to decide for themselves what the concepts Usefulness and Beauty really meant.[3]

If the design reform movement prevailed during the period 1860–1920, it may be because Morris left definitions of those concepts open to personal interpretation. Thus, Beauty might imply variously a brightly colored Morris & Co. chintz, a W. H. Grueby vase with a watermelon-rind glaze, a C. R. Mackintosh stencil of a Glasgow rose, or a Greene & Greene chair blending Asian and American influences. And Usefulness might suggest alternately a simple brass teakettle by C. F. A. Voysey, an ebonized rush-seat "Sussex" chair, or a woolen "Craftsman" rug with a bold, geometric design. By upholding Usefulness and Beauty as ideals but not prescribing what either *must be* according to a single theory, Morris—along with his contemporaries and his followers—ensured that the products of the design reform movement would transcend the particulars of style and thus age gracefully, as they have into the twenty-first century.

The downside to such openness to interpretation was this: at the time, the Arts and Crafts ideal was not always easy to comprehend or to assimilate. Where did one begin in one's quest for Usefulness and Beauty? How might one recognize them on the pages of a sketchbook, at the potter's wheel or jeweler's bench, at an art exhibition, in a store window, or within the confines of one's own home? Where might one turn to find an example of so-called good design, something that would enhance one's quality of life, escape the clutches of historicism, revivalism, and eclecticism, and ensure that Usefulness and Beauty were ever-present at every scale? As these questions suggest, many consumers—and the craftspeople whom they patronized—must have struggled as they sought to determine what William Morris *really* meant.

Enter the design critic—that arbiter of taste, midwife to the creative process, champion of integrity and truth in the designed environment. It was the critic who sought to answer such questions and to define Usefulness and Beauty in a way that would enlighten both maker and user on all matters functional and aesthetic. It was the critic who hoped to inspire craftspeople to "do common things uncommonly well," so that consumers might find an ample supply of products that bespoke the Arts and Crafts ideal.[4]

Design reform was not the product of craftspeople working in isolation. Critics were as essential to craftsworkers' growth and development as they were to refining consumers' tastes and raising their expectations. Critics played an integral role in the production/consumption cycle. Providing inspiration at its beginning and passing judgment upon finished products at its end, critics functioned as important intermediaries between theory and practice, between makers and users.

For that reason, the all-important critic is the subject of this book, which offers a new perspective on a dynamic—and essential—contributor to the campaign to reform design.

Uniquely qualified to ascertain Usefulness and Beauty throughout the built environment, design critics played an increasingly important role as the nineteenth century evolved. Serving as intermediaries between product makers, on the one hand, and product users on the other, they provided guidelines for discerning "good design" in buildings, interiors, furnishings—broadly defined—and finishing materials. They considered carefully all aspects of the built environment, passing judgment on relative merits or flaws and making their views known in person or in print. In this way, design critics inspired makers to produce works that excelled conceptually, aesthetically, and technically, while enabling users to make informed decisions in the marketplace, in the manner that Morris himself had advocated. Without these critics, the design reform movement would not have occurred: for inherent in the concept of reform is the need for thoughtful appraisal of the status quo and suggestions for ways to improve it. Reform could not have taken place without these critics' input.

The purpose of this book is to explore the impact of design criticism—which emerged as a discipline in its own right in the mid-nineteenth century—upon the campaign to reform design as it evolved internationally between 1860 and 1920. It focuses upon the quest for Usefulness and Beauty—which in part constituted the arts and crafts ideal and guided the creative process of architects, designers, and craftspeople. It seeks to clarify how such individuals defined Usefulness and Beauty and then strove to manifest both in their work. It stresses the interaction of such individuals with design critics, who functioned as their advisers, promoters, and even, on occasion, tormentors, while serving as midwives to their creative process.

The setting for this exploration is Boston during the Gilded Age. A leader in all things cultural and artistic, Boston wholeheartedly embraced the Arts and Crafts movement as a means for improving the quality of the daily living and working environment. Its Society of Arts and Crafts (SACB)—one of the first such organizations established in the United States in the manner of the English Arts and Crafts Exhibition Society—had a large and active membership. Its most prominent supporters were influential well beyond the city or region. Architects and craftspeople, connoisseurs and educators, theorists and journalists, many were known nationwide. Most important to this discussion was the quality of design criticism associated with the SACB and emanating from its writers, lecturers, and spokespersons. By the time of its twentieth anniversary in 1917, standards of Usefulness and Beauty upheld by the SACB were accepted nationwide and contributed to shaping the American arts and crafts ideal.

This book determines how Boston's design critics defined Usefulness and Beauty, while simultaneously surveying the many ways in which both traits were manifest at different scales and in assorted media. It examines representative examples within the large body of work produced by members of the SACB, as well as graphic designs that reflect the impact of the Aesthetic and Arts and Crafts movements more broadly throughout the community. It questions whether or not these critics—many of whom were architects, designers, and educators—practiced what they preached, and how craftspeople working within their sphere of influence applied, or challenged, their recommendations. What these works make clear is how diversely these makers interpreted critics' recommendations about Usefulness and Beauty, and how eclectic the American arts and crafts oeuvre truly was.

This is a regional study having national and even international implications. It traces the influence of an idea articulated by one individual living and working in England, as that idea—the concept of Usefulness and Beauty—captured the imaginations of makers and users at home and abroad. By exploring how critics interpreted that idea, it demonstrates the complexity of Morris's seemingly simple recommendation. It documents the myriad ways that critics defined Usefulness and Beauty for their audiences, resulting in clarification as well as obfuscation of his intent. It examines definitions of Usefulness and Beauty in a particular place, at a specific time, and within the context of a single organization. Yet in the end it demonstrates how universality arises from such specificity: Boston's interpretation of Morris's maxim shaped the look and feel of reformed products nationwide, to an extent that they were culturally relevant at the time and have remained so today.

With that in mind, this account closes with an examination of the legacy of Boston's arts and crafts in the twenty-first century, viewed in the context of the Arts and Crafts Revival. It chronicles the ways in which these works have been celebrated since the 1970s. The subject of theses, dissertations, monographs, exhibition catalogues, centenary reviews, and articles, the works of the members of the SACB exemplify the American arts and crafts ideal, while demonstrating how broadly it might be interpreted. The inclusion of works of the SACB in articles in the popular press, on the Internet, and on television programs such as *Antiques Roadshow* bespeaks these objects' widespread appeal to a mass audience and justifies national interest in learning more about their background and how they came to be.

The book is organized as follows: The Introduction highlights the origins of the profession of design criticism that thrived in the nineteenth and early twentieth centuries, evolving from the eighteenth-century philosophy of aesthetics. Chapter One focuses upon Boston in the Gilded Age as a context within which the Arts and Crafts movement flourished, culminating with the founding of the Society of Arts and Crafts, Boston. Chapter Two explores the formative years of the SACB, and how critics functioned within the confines of the organization and used its activities, exhibitions, publications, and outreach to the community as arenas in which to express critical opinions. Chapter Three focuses upon the SACB Jury—an elite body that functioned as the organization's collective arbiter of taste—offering selected critics' opinions on what constituted Usefulness and Beauty in the everyday arts. It considers their advice on conceptual, aesthetic, and technical matters, while discussing the effects of such advice upon craftsman members. Of interest is not only the content of these critics' views, but also the style in which they expressed them. Like Morris, many turn-of-the-century critics were eloquent writers and speakers about design whose impassioned language served their reformist purpose as well as their insightful observations. One of Boston's finest arbiters of taste, and a feature of this chapter's discussion, is the architect and educator Charles Howard Walker.

Chapter Four discusses the link between design criticism and design theory, especially as the latter articulated models and methodologies for achieving so-called good design. It examines how craftsworkers turned to history and nature as models, and considers how they transformed such models into statements, both personal and original, through the process of conventionalization. Conventionalization was a topic of great debate among period critics, and it still interests practitioners, educators, and theorists today.

Chapter Five examines the SACB's contributions nationwide by considering the phenomenon of the Boston diaspora. It discusses world's fairs—especially the Louisiana Purchase Exposition (St. Louis, 1904)—and the variety of ways in which Bostonians contributed to its noteworthy display of American arts and crafts. It highlights the work of architect-members of the SACB who taught, lectured, published, and practiced across the nation and internationally. It explores how SACB craftsworkers gained broad exposure by showing their work at important exhibitions, selling it at galleries across the United States, and having it purchased by museums at home and abroad. It demonstrates how the SACB became a model for similar organizations nationwide and how its members were recruited for important positions elsewhere. It considers how members of the SACB—who shared a common construct of an arts and crafts ideal—left the city, either intermittently or permanently, to promote that ideal elsewhere.

The Epilogue explores the concepts of Usefulness and Beauty in the present day, by considering the phenomenon of the Arts and Crafts Revival that began in the 1970s and continues to this day. It asks why the arts and crafts ideal seems to resonate among today's consumers, while considering how expressions of Usefulness and Beauty created by members of the SACB over a hundred years ago have fared in the antiques and collectibles marketplace.

Simply stated, this book examines, in succession, a profession, a place, an organization, a group, a theory and its manifestation, a dispersal of a shared ideal, and a revival. Each chapter explores the impact of one of these topics upon definitions of Usefulness and Beauty and establishes interconnections among ideas, persons, and places.

Within the growing body of literature devoted to the Arts and Crafts movement, this study is more an intellectual history than a reflection of connoisseurship or material culture studies. It traces the evolution of an idea that inspired a group of works—including buildings, gardens, interiors, furnishings, and objects—focusing more upon the expression of that idea than the works themselves. Though regional in focus, it is truly American in scope. It draws upon the paper trail generated by the SACB, in the form of internal documents—memoranda, minutes, bulletins, and correspondence—and those intended for public consumption, including annual reports, exhibition catalogues, publications, promotional materials, and texts of public lectures. Throughout, articles in the period press provide an independent point of view.

While some illustrations included here feature exquisite objects drawn from museums or private collections, most fall within the realm of popular culture, celebrating the paper paraphernalia—period photographs, postcards, stereopticon slides, business cards, trade cards, trade catalogues, magazine advertisements, posters, and brochures—that captured the essence of everyday life in turn-of-the-century Boston. Striving to place into a broad cultural context the beautiful and useful objects produced by members of the SACB (amply illustrated in numerous exhibition catalogues published during the past two decades), I have chosen to include many images of period interiors that reflect the impact of the Aesthetic movement, Arts and Crafts movement, and/or Art Nouveau. (This reflects my bias as an interior design historian, while calling attention to the eclecticism that prevailed throughout Boston—reform notwithstanding.) When discussing the work of local architects—who played an essential role in the founding and administration of the SACB—I have similarly selected more images of the interiors of their structures than exterior views. My intention is to demonstrate their concern for combining fine finishes, exquisite art, and elegant furnishings produced in collaboration with local artists and craftspeople. Wherever possible, I have made an effort to illustrate points with images drawn from Boston, from Massachusetts, or from New England to make obvious how widely the campaign for design reform permeated the region. Equally evident in some of these images (chosen with tongue firmly in cheek) is the *need* for design reform—to improve both products and interiors that violate every principle of "good design" espoused by William Morris and his followers.

This work draws upon my background, education, training, and passions, as they have evolved since the 1970s; yet, it also is a product of serendipity. My love affair with the Arts and Crafts movement began in 1973, when I enrolled in my first design history course as part of a Master's Program at Michigan State University. There, in a darkened lecture hall, I saw slides of jewel-toned Morris chintzes for the first time. I enjoyed Nikolaus Pevsner's description of them—"brimful of life," "crisp," and "essentially original"—as put forth in his book *The Sources of Modern Architecture & Design* (1968). That text, like the course content, exposed me to the major figures and beliefs of the movement.

I spent the summer of 1975 in London on an overseas studies program that expanded my knowledge of the movement by highlighting its products, personalities, and propaganda. I was privileged to see the Victoria and Albert Museum's exhibition commemorating Liberty & Co.'s centenary, resplendent with Arthur Silver textiles, Archibald Knox metalwork, and svelte furnishings with mortarboard finials. As part of our program based at Bedford College, I also heard a riveting talk on arts and crafts architecture by the late John Brandon-Jones. His manner of lecturing was as mesmerizing as were his comments about architects Philip Webb, William R. Lethaby, Charles F. A. Voysey, and their colleagues. Our esteemed lecturer took snuff throughout, his left thumb and forefinger deftly moving from tweedy vest pocket to horn snuffbox to nostrils in one fluid motion. Though this happened repeatedly during the seventy-five-minute lecture, Professor Brandon-Jones never lost his concentration. My classmates and I, on the other hand, sat breathlessly on the edges of our seats, anticipating an enormous sneeze that seemed inevitable, yet never came. In an effort to stay focused, I made copious notes and sketched furiously.

My exposure via John Brandon-Jones to the work of Voysey led to a graduate research project on the latter. That research project in turn introduced me to *The Studio* magazine, with its firsthand interviews and captivating illustrations. Those interviews, images, and quotable quotes—which I now pass on to my own design history students—made the movement come alive.

Between 1977 and 1980, I taught design history courses, perhaps emphasizing the turn-of-the-century era more than either syllabus or current scholarship warranted. (Our text, Sherill Whiton's *Elements of Interior Design and Decoration* [1974], dismissed most of the Victorian era as unworthy of contemplation, though it regarded Morris, Arthur Heygate Mackmurdo, Voysey, and their colleagues as "pioneers of modernism" in the Pevsnerian sense.) Inspired by that teaching experience, I decided to pursue an academic career, enrolling in Boston University's American and New England Studies Program in fall semester 1980.

During my first months in the program, I learned of the existence of the SACB, discovered its extensive archives—most of which had been microfilmed conveniently by the Smithsonian Institution Archives of American Art—and decided to devote my dissertation to writing an institutional history of its first twenty years. Professors Keith Morgan, Jonathan Fairbanks, and the late William Vance recognized my interest in the SACB during my first semester, and encouraged me to undertake research on Boston's arts and crafts architects, the work of silversmith Arthur J. Stone, and the role of Charles Eliot Norton in the founding of the SACB as part of their respective course requirements. One outcome of that research was my first scholarly publication on the SACB, "The Essential Link: Boston Architects and The Society of Arts and Crafts," which appeared in *Tiller*, Robert Edwards's handsome publication in the arts and crafts style.

This book is, thus, a culmination of two-and-a-half decades of researching the Arts and Crafts movement. It draws upon my general interest in the English origins of the movement and how its ideals came to inspire supporters across the Atlantic. It builds upon my doctoral dissertation, "'Mutually Helpful Relations': Architects, Craftspeople, and The Society of Arts and Crafts, Boston, 1897–1917" (Boston University, 1985). It incorporates subsequent research on that topic conducted over the past two decades, which has delved further into such topics as the role of architects in the organization, style and the persistence of the Colonial Revival as one manifestation of Boston's arts and crafts aesthetic, the role of the SACB Jury and its critics, and their collective influence at the Louisiana Purchase Exposition. In 2005, I had the good fortune to spend three months in Boston under the auspices of the New England Research Fellowship Consortium, which enabled me to hunt down missing facts and secure illustrations.

This book incorporates, as well, my research on the evolution of the profession of design criticism as it relates to the development of the design reform movement, inspired in part by a graduate seminar on the subject that I have been teaching since 1989. Finally, it reflects my fascination with the Arts and Crafts Revival. This trend has stimulated among consumers a heightened interest in arts and crafts artifacts from the turn of the century, alongside a taste for line-for-line recreations, sympathetic approximations, and all manner of arts and crafts kitsch—if that phrase is not an oxymoron.

An artist and designer by training, I have evolved into a design historian, critic, and educator. Schooled in the fine and applied arts in my undergraduate and master's programs, I intended to be a practitioner—a maker—but changed plans when fate intervened. Today, I teach a new generation of would-be makers from among the architecture, fine arts, and applied arts majors who enroll in my courses.

For this reason, my interest in the Arts and Crafts movement has always been more process- than product-oriented. What intrigues me most are the processes by which arts and crafts products came to be, and the ideas that informed them. Equally relevant is the interdisciplinary and collaborative nature of the movement, which attracted the sorts of faculty and students with whom I work today in Arizona State University's College of Design. My curiosity about the role of the critic has as much relevancy for my work as a professor of design as it has for my work as a scholar of the Arts and Crafts movement. Just as the products of the movement continue to captivate, the struggle of critics working between 1850 and 1920—to define what was truly Useful and Beautiful and to offer guidelines for achieving both—is equally applicable today, and just as enduring.

Today, I spend my summers in a midwestern Chautauqua called "Bay View," one of the few anti-urban summer communities devoted to physical, intellectual, and spiritual renewal, that has operated continuously since its founding in 1875. Only recently have I learned that it had a strong arts and crafts program in the early 1900s, attracting faculty from Chicago, Detroit, and Indianapolis who taught china painting, Sloyd woodcrafting, and metalwork.[5]

The *Bay View Magazine* (published between 1893 and 1921 with a monthly distribution of 125,000 issues) attracted readers—including members of nearly 1,000 women's clubs—from across the nation. Boston was a frequent subject of articles in the magazine (especially in 1907–08, the year of the Jamestown Exposition). Supporters of the SACB—the ethnologist George Wharton James, the poet Bliss Perry, and the critic William Howe Downes, to name just three—contributed articles to the magazine, while SACB founders such as Sarah Wyman Whitman and Denman W. Ross were mentioned in its pages. That Bay View—like Boston—was a hotbed of reform at the turn of the century is evident from the following statement (which may be the only instance in print in which these two locations are mentioned in the same sentence). Speaking of an early national conference of the Woman's Christian Temperance Union (Fort Worth, 1901), Fanny L. Armstrong, president of the Texas branch of the WCTU (1891–1907) and secretary of the board of regents for the College of Industrial Arts of Texas (1901–07), wrote: "I often meet delegates who attended that convention, and whether in St. Louis, Mississippi, Bay View, Boston, or Portland, each smiles and exclaims, 'I'm glad I went to Texas, I am, I am.'" By linking Bay View and Boston, Armstrong suggests that they were part of the same reformist circuit that attracted enthusiastic visionaries hoping to change the status quo.[6]

Learning more about that branch of the movement and its connection to Boston, while researching the Arts and Crafts movement in the Southwest (which had numerous Boston ties as well), are interests that will continue for decades to come. Such historical research complements my ongoing work as a critic: I jury shows and exhibitions and write on contemporary craft for such publications as *American Craft*, *Metalsmith*, and *American Ceramics*. As I do so, I continue to ponder evolving definitions of Usefulness and Beauty, while I question what William Morris *really* meant.

This book is thus a manifestation of strong planning coupled with serendipitous intervention. In its portrayal of the interaction of craftsman and critic, I have tried to be as accurate as possible, adding new insights while strengthening—and even correcting—arguments presented in earlier papers and publications. Despite my desire to produce a flawless manuscript, I accept the human impossibility of doing so, a philosophy of tolerance that I have learned from the Navajo culture to which I have been exposed during my tenure in the American Southwest. I suspect that William Morris would have appreciated the Navajo aspiration to "walk in beauty."[7]

Acknowledgments

This work reflects the influence and support of numerous individuals to whom I am indebted. Chief among these are mentors, past and present, who shaped my knowledge of the Arts and Crafts movement and my evolution as a scholar. Richard L. Graham introduced me to the movement and to the discipline of design history; Jonathan Fairbanks, Keith N. Morgan, and the late William Vance encouraged my early research on the Arts and Crafts movement in Boston; the late Margaret Henderson Floyd provided initial opportunities to present papers on that subject at professional conferences; and Robert L. Edwards published my first articles in his handsome periodical, *Tiller*. My late colleague Donald Bush shared his passion for William Morris, the Pre-Raphaelite Brotherhood, design history, and teaching excellence during my years as a junior faculty member in the School of Design at Arizona State University. Robert L. Wolf, former Director of the School, ensured that I would couple an emerging interest in the discipline of design criticism with a continuing fascination with the Arts and Crafts movement. He presented me with challenges, opportunities, and encouragement during my academic career that have proven invaluable.

Colleagues—many of whom have become friends—constitute a supportive, ever-expanding arts and crafts network. I have enjoyed consultation, collaboration, or conversation with: Kenneth L. Ames, William S. Ayres, Jim Benjamin, Eileen Boris, Edward R. Bosley, Nicola G. Bowe, W. Scott Braznell, Elenita Chickering, Robert Judson Clark, Edward S. Cooke, Donald and Suze Davidoff, Paul Duchscherer, Jeannine Falino, Jean France, Stephen Gray, Ken Hafertepe, David A. Hanks, Bruce Kahler, Bruce Kamerling, Patricia Kane, Wendy Kaplan, Lisa Koenigsberg, Maureen Meister, Marilee Boyd Meyer, Susan J. Montgomery, Jeffrey Ochsner, James O'Gorman, Cleota Reed, Cheryl Robertson, Barry Shifman, Bruce Smith, Neville Thompson, Kenneth Trapp, the late Sir George Trevelyan, Gerald W. R. Ward, Richard Guy Wilson, Robert Winter, and Catherine Zusy, among others. Many thanks to each individual who provided feed-back, called my attention to a source, provided encouragement, or shared ideas.

Other supportive friends and colleagues beyond the arts and crafts sphere include Cigdem Akkurt, Geoffrey Beard, Neil Dennis, Mary Jane Doerr, Tom Eckert, the late Helena Hayward, Jan Jennings, Toni and Joe Junken, Beth Krase, Sara and David Lieberman, Sandra Luehrsen, Jill Marderness, Mary Alice Molloy, Sandra Perkins, Jim and Joanne Rapp, Martha Shattuck, Pamela Shippey, Mary Corbin Sies, Lynn Timmons, Diane Upchurch, Mary Waits, and Laura Welch. Friends within the Bay View Association have provided constant motivation over the past five summers by asking whenever our paths have crossed, "How's the book coming along?"

Former graduate students whose research has informed this book are Christina Lindeman and Kent Boese. Others who provided valuable advice and direction in the 1980s included Herta Loeser and Meryl Zassman (the Society of Arts and Crafts, Boston), Robert Brown, Joyce Tyler, Erica Ell, and Heather Munro (the New England office of the Smithsonian Institution Archives of American Art), John Carmichael (the School of the Museum of Fine Arts), Teresa D. Cederholm (the Fine Arts Department of the Boston Public Library), Warren Seamans (MIT Historical Collections), Michael W. Yeates (MIT Museum), Cathy Marquis (MIT Archives), Nancy Carlson Schrock (Massachusetts Committee for the Preservation of Architectural Records, Inc.), Tom Sexton (Pusey Library of Harvard University), Cathleen Catalano (Longfellow National Historical Site), Ellie Reichlin and Lorna Condon (Historic New England, formerly the Society for the Preservation of New England Antiquities), Masahiko Kawahara (Kyoto National Museum), Hideki Matsumoto (Kyoto Furitsu Sogo Shiryokan), Kojiro Uchiyama (Consulate General of Japan), Else Roth (Consulate General of Denmark), and Melissa R. Katz (Davis Museum and Cultural Center).

Faculty and administrators of Arizona State University have played a critical role in enabling me to undertake and complete this project. The opportunity to be on sabbatical for a full academic year in 2002–03 allowed me to complete the first draft. For facilitating my ongoing research efforts and professional development, I am grateful to Lattie Coor, Milton Glick, John Meunier, Mary Kihl, and Cheryl McNab. Colleagues Tom Witt, José Bernardi, and Michael Kroelinger each ensured in their own way that I stayed focused for the project's duration. Marilyn Wurzburger, Dennis Madden, Deborah H. Koshinsky, and Beth Luey all offered archival or methodological support. John Turpin was an outstanding research associate in 2004, whose energy and persistence in tracking down obscure facts and locating illustrations was invaluable. ASU's Graduate College underwrote that research assistance. More recently, Donna Atwood helped to integrate illustrations with captions during the manuscript's final stages.

A Travel to Collections Grant provided by the National Endowment for the Humanities (1986) enabled me to delve into archives and repositories and to uncover materials pertaining to architect members of the Society of Arts and Crafts, Boston. Many of the archival collections listed in the bibliography indicate which repositories I visited. I am grateful to the staff members at those institutions for their gracious assistance and interest in the project.

The New England Regional Fellowship Consortium allowed me a semester free of teaching responsibilities (Spring 2005) and firsthand access to important archives at the following institutions: the Massachusetts Historical Society, the Boston Athenaeum, Baker Library (Harvard Business School), Schlesinger Library

(Radcliffe Institute for Advanced Study), New England Historic Genealogical Society, and Historic Deerfield. At those institutions, the assistance of the following individuals (and their capable staff) was invaluable: Conrad E. Wright, Cherylinne Pina, Carrie Supple, and Kim Nusco (MHS), Stephen Z. Nonack, Patricia Boulos, and Sally Pierce (Boston Athenaeum), Kathy Jacobs and Jacalyn Blume (Schlesinger Library), Laura Linard and Timothy Mahoney (Baker Library), David C. Bosse (Historic Deerfield/Pocumtuck Valley Memorial Association Library), Suzanne L. Flynt (Memorial Hall Museum), and Michael Leclerc and Christopher Childs (NEHGS). Participating in the fellowship was a great privilege and motivator as this project began drawing to a close.

Following the conclusion of the fellowship, I spent additional time at the Boston Public Library and Historic New England, where the following energetic individuals helped me track down missing facts and locate potential illustrations: Janice Chadbourne, Kim Tenney, Evelyn Lannon (Fine Arts Department, BPL), Roberta Zonghi, Stuart Walker, and Eric P. Frazier (Rare Books and Manuscripts, BPL), Jane Winton, Karen Shaff, and Jamie McGlone (Print Department, BPL), Lorna Condon, Emily Novak, and Sally Hinkle (Historic New England). I much appreciate their support, persistence, and enthusiasm.

Others who assisted with securing illustrations are Michelle Gachette (Harvard University Archives), Laura Knott (MIT Museum), Leslie Cade and Kathleen Kornell (Cleveland Museum of Art), Margaret Daley (British National Gallery), Anthony Wornum, Margaret Gardiner (Episcopal Diocese of Massachusetts), Maryalice Mohr (New England Conservatory of Music), David Killian (Rector, All Saints Brookline), Robert Spindler, Marilyn Wurzberger, and Elizabeth Bentley (Arizona State University Libraries), Peter Held, Anne Sullivan, and Laura Wenzel (Arizona State University Art Museum), Robert Winter, Erin Schleigh (Museum of Fine Arts, Boston), Maureen Melton, Aubrey Baer, Jessica Goehner (School of the Museum of Fine Arts), Barry Shifman and Ruth Roberts (Indianapolis Art Museum), W. Scott Braznell, Susan J. Tarlow and Donald A. Davidoff, Richard Hunter (Stark Museum of Art), Jim Kaufman (Dedham Historical Society), Laura Dye Lang (*Home* magazine), Lance Hidy, Anita Israel (Longfellow National Historic Site), Matthew Robinson, Richard Neumann, Patricia Hurley (Trinity Church, Boston), Ward Miller (Richard Nickle Committee), Kelly Murphy (Colorado Springs Pioneers Museum), Margaret McKee (Museum of Fine Arts, Houston), Michelle Lamuniere (Fogg Museum, Harvard University), and Beth Lander (Mercer Museum).

Arizona State University supported my recent fellowship by covering transportation costs (courtesy of the Hildegard Streuffert Endowment) and providing affordable housing in the Boston area (many thanks to Dean Wellington Reiter and Patti Reiter). Dean Reiter also provided generous financial support for subvention fees as this project neared completion.

The Craft Research Fund, administered by the University of North Carolina Center for Craft, Creativity and Design, generously provided a grant (2005–06) to cover the costs of high-quality illustrations, reproduction, publication, copyright, and subvention fees. I am extraordinarily grateful to the Center, the Fund, and its National Advisory Board for awarding me this wonderful grant in its inaugural year.

The University of Massachusetts Press expressed interest in this project early on and supported my efforts through its completion. I much appreciate the help and insights offered by Bruce Wilcox (Press Director), Paul Wright (Senior Editor), Jack Harrison (Production and Design Manager), Carol Betsch (Managing Editor) and others. Special thanks to Katherine D. Scheuer for her superb copyediting.

Lastly, I am grateful to close friends and family members, who remained helpful and optimistic even as the exigencies of the creative process took their toll and isolated me during too many evenings, weekends, holidays, and summers. All writers should have such an enduring support system.

THE CRAFTSMAN AND THE CRITIC

INTRODUCTION

In Quest of Usefulness and Beauty
The Evolution of the Discipline of Design Criticism
in the Nineteenth Century

[Lady Bertram] was a woman who spent her days in sitting, nicely dressed, on a sofa, doing some long piece of needlework, of little use and no beauty. . . .
—Jane Austen, *Mansfield Park* (1814)

Beauty had existed long before 1880.
—Max Beerbohm, *The Yellow Book* (1894)

The quest for Usefulness and Beauty that characterizes the Arts and Crafts movement was not exclusively a concern of nineteenth-century design reformers and design critics. That quest had proven equally compelling to philosophers of aesthetics who wrote about taste—and related issues—in the eighteenth century, laying the groundwork for the reformers and critics who followed.

Among the catalysts for the arguments in favor of Usefulness and Beauty were world's fairs, or international exhibitions, that took place regularly during the 1800s, evolving from regional events held at the end of the eighteenth century. These events presented an overview of the output of industrialized nations, highlighting their raw materials, new technologies, and latest products. Chief among these was the "Great Exhibition of Works of Industry" (London, 1851). Attracting a broad cross-section of society—ranging from royalty to household servants—it fueled a debate among producers, consumers, and critics regarding the condition of design at mid-century.

Because of its importance, that exhibition—and the criticism that it provoked—is the focus of this chapter, which explores the event and its impact upon two mid-nineteenth-century English critics, Mary Philadelphia Merrifield (1804/5–85) and Ralph Nicholson Wornum (1812–77). Their essays form an important nexus between the criticism of the eighteenth century and that of the design reform movement, written between the 1860s and the 1920s.[1]

The first section surveys the work of some of Merrifield and Wornum's eighteenth-century predecessors, considering how it served as a basis for the profession of design criticism, which burgeoned in the 1800s. It summarizes the criticism of both periods, highlighting major issues and themes that both pondered, and concludes by examining the profession of design criticism in general as it evolved in the aftermath of the Great Exhibition, fueling a debate among design reformers, who ultimately championed the cause of "good design" under the aegis of the Arts and Crafts movement. This introduction provides a general overview of such topics as who design critics were, how they functioned and their modus operandi, their spheres of influence, and the challenges that they faced.

The Great Exhibition of Works of Industry

The quest for Usefulness and Beauty gathered momentum in England in the 1850s in response to the "Great Exhibition of Works of Industry," held in London's Hyde Park during the spring and summer of 1851. This first world's fair celebrated the products of the Industrial Revolution along with raw materials and machinery, putting them on display for all to see. Reaction to these products' Usefulness and Beauty—or lack thereof—stimulated critical debate among those involved with their design, fabrication, merchandising, and consumption. The exhibition invited assessment by professional design critics, who gave formal lectures and published erudite essays on the event's strengths, weaknesses, and implications. Among these were Merrifield and Wornum.[2]

The Great Exhibition was a watershed moment in the history of design—and the design reform movement—because of its scope, size, duration, and accessibility. It was equally influential upon the evolution of design criticism as a profession because of the wrath it provoked among critics. Most agreed that British products fared poorly in comparison to those produced abroad. This realization prompted them to seek alternatives. Their efforts gave rise to the design reform movement—epitomized by the Arts and Crafts movement, but embracing as well the shorter-lived Aesthetic movement, and the English Domestic Revival in architecture. It heightened the level of debate about Usefulness and Beauty among critics, who began proposing changes to every aspect of life affecting design.

The history of the design reform movement and the evolution of the profession of design criticism would have been very different had the Great Exhibition not taken place. The event revealed a problem needing attention, while providing a model for future exhibitions that would serve as testing grounds for regular assessment of the state of the applied arts. Merrifield's and Wornum's essays similarly provide insight into the minds of design critics, while serving as examples for their successors' works in terms of content, organization, style, and methodology—roadmaps for those who followed.

When the Great Exhibition of Works of Industry opened in the spring of 1851, it enabled anyone able to pay the nominal entry fee an opportunity to view raw materials, machinery, and products representing the industrialized nations of the world. A competition as well as an exhibition, this event invited comparison and judgment among products across national boundaries.[3]

What set the Great Exhibition apart from others that had preceded it was its international flavor. Many exhibitions of the decorative—or applied—arts had taken place in France, Belgium, Bavaria, and England starting in the mid-eighteenth century; but these had been restricted to works of a single nation shown

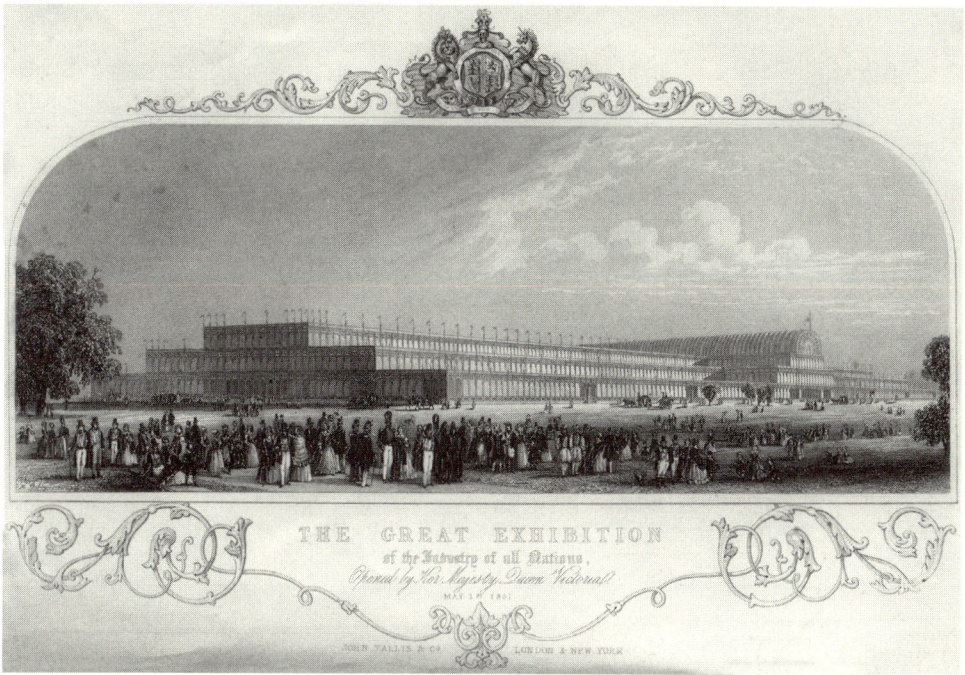

1. "Great Exhibition of the Industry of all Nations, Opened by Her Majesty Queen Victoria May 1st, 1851." From *Tallis's History and Description of the Crystal Palace and the Exhibition of the World's Industry in 1851*, vol. 1. (Courtesy Special Collections, University Libraries, Arizona State University) Designed by a landscape architect, the innovative iron-and-glass Crystal Palace resembled a giant green house. It was far more forward-looking than were the derivative and eclectic products displayed within. Queen Victoria may be the figure above the "R" holding a parasol.

within its own borders. Most of these were competitions as well as exhibitions, administered by juries of review that awarded prizes. Jurors used as criteria for making awards publications by philosophers of aesthetics who outlined principles of "good taste" or "good design."[4]

What distinguished early French exhibitions from those held in other countries was their sponsorship by the Society of Arts and Manufactures, founded ca. 1802. That society promoted unification of the fine and the applied arts, and as such served as a model for similar organizations established elsewhere in Britain and Europe later in the century. By contrast, England's "Society of Arts"—an organization that was just beginning to recognize the existence of so-called Art manufacturing and its challenges—sponsored the Great Exhibition.[5]

That the Great Exhibition was international in scope may be attributed to the influence of England's Prince Albert (1819–61), who hoped to stimulate healthy international rivalry with a spirit of "exhibition, competition, and encouragement." He and other supporters of the event viewed it as "a true test of the point of development at which the whole of mankind [had] arrived in this great task" to date, that is, the task of blending Art with Industry, believing that the exhibition would mark "a starting point from which all nations would be able to direct their further exertions." It was that designation of the Great Exhibition as a "starting point" for critical, competitive assessment of the applied arts worldwide that made it a watershed event in the history of design, design reform, and design criticism.[6]

IN QUEST OF USEFULNESS AND BEAUTY

2. "The Transept of the Great Exhibition, Looking South. Engraved by W. Lacey from a Daguerreotype by Mayall." From *Tallis's History and Description of the Crystal Palace and the Exhibition of the World's Industry in 1851*, vol. 1. (Courtesy Special Collections, University Libraries, Arizona State University) The Crystal Palace flooded displays with natural light, while accommodating thousands of products and crowds of visitors within a colorfully painted framework, conceived by architect, decorator, and author Owen Jones.

The event was also important architecturally, due to the innovative building designed by Joseph Paxton (1803–65), the nearly 1,851-foot-long, iron-and-glass structure, erected quickly from prefabricated, modular parts (Fig. 1). Dubbed by the editors of *Punch* the "Crystal Palace" for its resemblance to a huge greenhouse (and the "Crystal Humbug" by its detractors), the structure flooded the displays with natural light, while accommodating thousands of objects and crowds of visitors within a colorfully painted framework, conceived by the architect, decorator, and author Owen Jones (1809–74).[7]

The plethora of products on display represented approximately 25 nations and their colonies, hundreds of styles and time periods, diverse methods of construction—some traditional, others threateningly new and unfamiliar—and materials ranging from natural to synthetic. An essay on the history of the exhibition published by *The Art-Journal*—founded in 1846, specifically "to connect the Fine Arts with the Industrial Arts" and to "promote the interests of the manufacturer" and art education—provides a description of the interior (Fig. 2) that only begins to suggest the bewildering effect. "Traversing the gallery for naval architecture, by the organ," the account begins," we have philosophical instruments, civil engineering, architecture and building models, musical instruments, anatomical models, glass chandeliers, decorations, etc." Added to this were "china, cutlery, and animal and vegetable manufactures." Augmenting these were "perfumery, toys, fishing materials, miscellaneous articles, wax flowers, stained glass, British, French, Austrian, Belgian, Prussian, Bavarian, and American products." What the "animal and vegetable manufactures" might be, the writer did not explain. What is clear is that the Crystal Palace was an eclectic jumble that even the seasoned observer found difficult to fathom. How could visitors glean from this display the all-important lessons they might learn from a thoughtful analysis of all that it offered? Where did one begin the process of assimilating this awesome assemblage and making sense of what it said about mid-Victorian culture and society?[8]

Design Criticism at the Great Exhibition

Aiding consumers' analysis of what they saw were catalogues documenting the exhibition. Some merely listed what was on display, while others provided intricately detailed engravings or chromolithographs of furnishings and machinery. Many included commentary by critics, describing selected displays, pointing out their relative merits—and flaws—urging consumers to be discerning as they toured the acres of displays.

Editors of *The Art-Journal* anticipated attendees' angst when it published an illustrated catalogue that included essays analyzing numerous aspects of the display. One covered science, another raw materials (specifically the "Vegetable World as Contributing to the Great Exhibition"), and a third discussed machinery. Two essays offered appraisals of products and the overall display within the Crystal Palace. One, by Merrifield, addressed "Color Harmony as Exemplified by the Exhibition," while the other, by Wornum, was more general, focusing upon the issue of "Taste." Their purpose was to interpret the displays and their inherent lessons for the benefit of British manufacturers, their primary audience, but these essays offered something for anyone who wished to learn more about the exhibition's contents and implications. Each exemplifies mid-nineteenth-century British design criticism, and, as such, both are excellent introductions to the state of the profession at that time. Both comment upon Usefulness and Beauty and provide insight into period definitions of each.[9]

The need for critical assessment of the displays was something that most visitors acknowledged. Writers for *The Art-Journal* predicted that the "benefits arising out of the Exhibition [would] prove both important and permanent" provided that British manufacturers applied its lessons assiduously. "It will encourage us in the prosecution of those arts in which we are in the ascendant"—there were few—"and show us our weaknesses in those branches of industry in which we may be behind our neighbors"; here there were many. "To be aware of our deficiencies is the first step towards amending them," the writer concluded, inviting the input of critics.[10]

Wornum's, the prize-winning essay, is probably the more significant, both historically and in terms of scholarship. Merrifield's has much to recommend it from the standpoint of design criticism, however, and thus deserves some elaboration. Together the two essays provide a snapshot of what constituted—in the eyes of *The Art-Journal*—the best design criticism at mid-century. They are as important for what they say as for how they say it. They are as quick to point out flaws as they are to offer praise. Both attempt to be as objective as possible, offering their critiques within a framework of history or theory. They strive to make design criticism as exacting as was the precision-machinery that manufactured the glittering products that they analyzed.

Merrifield, an art historian, early feminist, and author, connects her topic, "The Harmony of Colors as Exemplified in the Exhibition," with the theories of Michel Eugène Chevreul (1786–1889), a French professor of chemistry, consultant to the great textile manufactories Gobelins, Beauvais, and Savonnerie, and author of *The Principles of Harmony and Contrast of Colors* (1839), which had strongly influenced Owen Jones's color scheme for the interior of the Crystal Palace. Her immediate conclusion is that foreign displays demonstrate a "more pleasing and tasteful arrangement of colors" than do either the British or American. Here, she refers not only to individual products—specifically textiles and related artifacts—but also to their manner of installation within the sections of the Crystal Place assigned to particular countries and their manufacturers.[11]

She attributes some of this to design education, pointing out that where it is strong, excellence prevails. She admits, however, that countries lacking a formal program in design education, but possessing an established apprenticeship tradition—the Near and Far East, specifically—are equally adept at achieving color harmony in individual products and the overall ensemble.

She argues that education ensures "knowledge of the laws governing" color usage, "in the same manner as the other branches of natural philosophy." She warns that good taste alone is insufficient to guarantee color harmony, stating: "A 'good eye,' as it is called, may, indeed, greatly assist, but nine times out of ten the *good eye* will be found to mean the *educated eye*. All persons have not equal power of analyzing their thoughts, so as to perceive accurately the whole chain of ideas which have led to certain conclusions." Hinting at the trait that separates the true critic from the rest, she concludes: "They are scarcely conscious of the intermediate state between the first impressions and the ultimate decision, and the 'good eye' frequently receives credit for what has been, in fact, a mental operation."[12]

Here Merrifield makes a case for why professional critics are important. Like others practicing this discipline in the nineteenth century, she is eager to demonstrate that her "ultimate decisions" are intellectual rather than emotional, objective not subjective, reasoned not intuitive.

To do so, she enlists the theories of Chevreul, indicating that color harmony depends upon specific principles: symmetry, value, contrast, fitness, repetition, and variety. She analyzes products and their installation throughout the Great Exhibition, pointing out their relative merits and demerits. Faults evident within the British displays she attributes to "the nature of the materials employed, to the deficient education of the artisan, or to a false taste in the manufacturers." She does not condemn the public taste, but proposes ways to elevate it, namely by "presenting to it only what is good and excellent of its kind," by "placing good examples constantly before the eyes," and by force of "habit," ensuring that the public will "not tolerate [works] of an inferior order." She also advocates "studying the principles of design and color observed in the ancient and medieval works," thus enlisting both contemporary theory and history as her allies.[13]

As she discusses "good" and "bad design," Merrifield indicates that beauty results from a judicious application of the principles of color harmony. She notes that repetition and variety are essential to a beautiful scheme. In her conclusion, she suggests that British manufacturers are more adept at the "production of what is useful" than at creating what is beautiful. Some critics, she indicates, believe that British manufacturers "*cannot* attain eminence in the ornamental arts" because of their overemphasis upon utility. She disagrees with such a blanket condemnation, however, holding out hope that the development of "good taste" and a "good eye" will elevate British Art manufacturing through a process of "comparing and analyzing," and learning the "fixed laws" of good design "after long and assiduous study." She is hopeful for the future, believing that the "mediocrity" and "defects" evident at the Great Exhibition will no longer be apparent at similar future events.[14]

3. Ralph Nicholson Wornum. (Reproduced by kind permission of Anthony Wornum)

In his lengthy essay "The Exhibition as a Lesson in Taste," Wornum (Fig. 3)—a son of an English piano manufacturer, a teacher in government-sponsored schools of design, who would later become chief curator at London's National Gallery—drew some of the same conclusions, but offered different remedies for improving the state of British design. Twenty-two pages long, this essay epitomizes the state of design criticism in the 1850s, and is as much a lesson in organization, style, and tone practiced by critics, as it is a primer on what Wornum deemed to be "good design". In it, Wornum describes in great detail how British manufactures compare to those representing other industrialized nations. He is not impressed by what he sees. At the essay's conclusion, he implores British manufacturers to pay closer attention to the lessons of the past, while striving to create a new style for a new industrial era, one that might be both nationalistic and original.[15]

Wornum's subtitle, "An Essay On Ornamental Art As Displayed In The Industrial Exhibition In Hyde Park, In Which The Different Styles Are Compared With A View To The Improvement Of Taste In Home Manufacturers," identifies the essay's major thrust. Wornum begins by discussing taste—"the paramount agent in all competitions involving ornamental design, where the means

4. "[Left] California Gilt Tea Service. Presented by the Mayor & Citizens of New York to C. R. Collins, Esq. Manufactured by Messers. Ball, Thompson & Black, New York. Engraved by G. Greatbach, from a drawing by Mason. [Right] Silver Breakfast Service. Manufactured by Reid of Newcastle. Engraved by G. Greatbach from a Drawing by Mason." From *Tallis's History and Description of the Crystal Palace and the Exhibition of the World's Industry in 1851*, vol. 2. (Courtesy Special Collections, University Libraries, Arizona State University) Both examples demonstrate the widespread influence of French taste at the Great Exhibition.

of production are equally advanced"—but moves quickly to the subject of ornament (his particular area of expertise—he would later publish a book on the subject, *An Analysis of Ornament*), claiming: "Ornament is one of the mind's necessities." He then summarizes his intended methodology: to analyze the "principles and styles of ornament" as they had evolved from the ancient world, and then question "how far our manufacturers might improve their taste" by "testing the works exhibited [British and otherwise] by these principles [in order] that any sound or useful conclusions can be drawn." In this way, the achievements of the past would provide guidelines for the present.[16]

The second section of his essay, titled simply "The Styles," Wornum intended to demonstrate his credentials as a historian and arbiter of taste. At the same time, he provides readers with a brief refresher course on ornament that might enable them to confront the exhibition's prevalent historicism and revivalism more competently. Arguing that nine styles—three ancient, three medieval, and three "modern"—were the primary influences upon European civilization (European nations were the chief contributors to the Great Exhibition), Wornum neatly summarizes each, stressing its symbolism and character. He speaks of the conventionalism, symbolism, symmetry, and "sumptuousness" of the Egyptian,

5. "Gobelin and Sevres Room. French Department." From *The Illustrated Exhibitor, Tribute to the World's Industrial Jubilee comprising sketches, by Pen and Pencil, of the Principle Objects, in the Great Exhibition of the Industry of All Nations, 1851* (London: John Cassell, [1851]). (Courtesy Special Collections, University Libraries, Arizona State University) The "Louis" Revivals—recalling the eras of Louis XIV, XV, and XVI—dominated the displays within the Crystal Palace, although catalogues documenting the exhibition list about eighty varied styles and cultural influences evident in products displayed.

the "great simplicity" of the Greek, the "gorgeous magnificence" of the Roman, and a move away from "pagan" influences during the Middle Ages. He characterizes Byzantine ornament as "rich" and "gorgeous," but founded upon a "rude symbolism." He comments upon the anti-naturalism of the Islamic in contrast with the foliated verticality of the Gothic.[17]

Wornum's generalizations regarding ornament of the ancient and medieval worlds shift to scholarly hair-splitting as he addresses the "modern" era, which he defines as the fifteenth through the eighteenth centuries. This discussion suggests that Wornum's particular area of expertise within the history of ornament may have been the Renaissance, as his comments border on the obsessive. He reviews "the Trecento, the Quattrocento, the pure Cinquecento, the mixed Cinquecento, or Renaissance," the French Renaissance ("the same," he points out, "as the mixed cinquecento of Italy"), and the "Elizabethan, or English Renaissance." His comment "minor modifications it is unnecessary to notice here" indicates that he had far more to say on the subject than the essay's limitations, and his readers' patience, may have permitted.[18]

Wornum betrays here a patriotic fervor bordering upon xenophobia. His acknowledgment of national distinctions in the interpretation of Renaissance ornament permits him to mention similar national distinctions in the contemporary interpretation of ornament at the Great Exhibition. Claiming "The [Italian] Cinquecento is considered the culminating style in Ornamental Art," he notes its formal link to the French Louis Quatorze, to its derivation, the Louis Quinze, and to "its final debasement, the Rococo" (Fig. 4). Wornum establishes his thorough dislike of most things French, and he uses his discussion of the evolution of historical ornament to suggest that a similar debasement in British ornamental art is currently taking place because of a persistent French influence.[19]

Wornum brings to light a Francophobia prompted by rivalries among French and British manufacturers at mid-century, and exemplified by the domination of the "Louis Revival" styles at the exhibition (Fig. 5). Products exhibited there reflected the influence of hundreds of styles interpreted with wildly varying degrees of accuracy; yet, French-based styles—reflecting the prevailing aesthetics of the sixteenth, seventeenth, and eighteenth centuries—were in the majority. "The influence of France," Wornum lamented, "is paramount," noting that French Renaissance, Louis Quinze, and Rococo were highly visible, while "the Louis Quatorze varieties perhaps prevail in quantity." Designers' tendencies to combine these into one work led to such invented styles as the Barococo Revival, an eclectic blending of elements drawn from the seventeenth and eighteenth centuries into gilded and veneered confections.[20]

Such French influence notwithstanding, Wornum was pleased to note that the "best understood" revival style was the Italian Renaissance. It was evident throughout the Great Exhibition and remained an important influence on both sides of the Atlantic in architecture, landscape, interiors, and products during the last half of the nineteenth century. Despite this, Wornum concluded famously, "there is nothing new in the Exhibition in ornamental design," a condemnation which others shared, and which fueled the belief that a new nationwide program of design reform was essential.[21]

In addition to Wornum's comments on the state of design in general are those on particular media categories that he provides in sections 4 through 8, where he covers "the precious Metals," "Carving and Modelling, etc.," "Bronzes, Hardware, etc.," "Pottery, Porcelain, and Glass," and "Woven and Printed Fabrics." By addressing these categories, Wornum provides a model for critics who followed. He focuses upon the five major media divisions—defined broadly as metal, wood, clay, glass, and fiber—that epitomized the arts and crafts in the nineteenth century, and continue to do so today.

Wornum's approach to critiquing each category also informed the work of his successors. Striving to define "good taste" and "good design," he analyzes the conceptual, aesthetic, and technical merits and demerits of the products he evaluates, reacting to line, form, color, texture, pattern, surface finish, materials, construction, and expression. He suggests that no trait is unimportant in the quest for Usefulness and Beauty in design.

Of particular interest is his attention to models that influence designers' concepts for their works, concepts that dictate a work's meaning or expression. One model that Wornum addresses is history. He questions which styles or time periods designers *should* choose to emulate, as well as their methods for doing so—

approximation, or line-for-line duplication. He notes as well the influence of naturalism, pondering the correct approach to basing a work upon nature, and suggesting that conventionalization is the key. He also raises the issue of national character and how designers might instill that desirable trait in their works through the selection of appropriate models and development of apt concepts.[22]

As Wornum moves his critique from the exhibition in general to specific media categories, he presents a series of conclusions about the state of the industrial arts, justifying a need for implementing a nationwide program of design reform. He questions the "wide-spread influence of France" despite, in his considered opinion, the "most debased taste in design ever tolerated." He bemoans the "very general mistake that quantity of ornament implies beauty." He notes the contrast offered by Asian works, which he describes as both "simple and rich" in expression. He discerns a general "disregard to usefulness" in the "more magnificent foreign productions." He questions England's ability to design well for the masses rather than for the "few who command vast means." He concludes this section of his remarks by lobbying for "a key or standard by which mere ordinary works may be tested" and their relationship to the concept of "good taste" (Plate 1).[23]

These conclusions remained important topics of debate among critics who championed design reform in the exhibition's aftermath. Many questioned designers' reliance upon the past and their tendency to revive historical styles from foreign countries that had little relevancy to their own indigenous design history. Most viewed the overwrought, ornament-encrusted products of the industrial age with suspicion, concluding that they were neither attractive nor functional. For this reason, the simplicity of Asian works—especially Japanese and Chinese—seemed to offer an intriguing alternative worth exploring in the West. Like Wornum, many critics argued for the democratization of "good design," believing that expense was unrelated to taste. Finally, all critics pondered the issue of "keys" to determining "good design," or "standards" of "good taste," hoping to define them for the benefit of designers, manufacturers, and consumers alike.

In writing his essay, Wornum also strives to define what he believes to be the critic's role. "It is not so much the business of criticism to create taste," he writes, "as to destroy what is vicious in it; the critic judges, and he fulfils his functions if only he condemn the bad without lauding the good.... To laud the good and pass over the bad in silence may be more generous, but it is certainly less sure; and if the critic be not allowed to freely criticize what is exposed to public criticism, better that his functions cease altogether; for of all evil genii, the most mischievous are those who only flatter or bepraise our follies and our vices." Advocating a degree of fearlessness on the part of critics, he urges them to tackle difficult issues head-on as they advise designers, manufacturers, and consumers.[24]

Wornum's was but one essay among many evaluating the displays at the "Great Exhibition," but it is a useful summary of that event and an introduction to British design criticism at mid-century. Insightful in its commentary, comprehensive in scope, erudite in tone, and stylistically dense—Wornum's writing style approaches in complexity the over-ornamented objects that he bemoaned in his lengthy critique—it epitomized critics' concerns and methodology at the time.

Wornum was only one of myriad detractors who concluded that British manufactured goods had declined to a woeful state and compared poorly to those from other nations. Together, these mid-century critics established a need for contemplation of the status quo that might lead to suggestions on how to improve it. Concerned with the present state of design as exemplified by the Great Exhibition, and outraged by dramatic changes to home and work environment wrought by the Industrial Revolution—with its division of labor, machine-assisted fabrication, and rapid production techniques—Merrifield, Wornum and their contemporaries were among those who ensured that design criticism quickly took hold.

The Eighteenth-Century Philosophy of Aesthetics

Mid-nineteenth-century design critics did not operate without precedent. Their concern for Usefulness and Beauty in daily life emerged from the contemplation of the sublime, the beautiful, and the picturesque that had occurred in the eighteenth century, under the auspices of the philosophy of aesthetics. To some degree, the issues that they addressed, the themes enriching their work, and their methodologies derived from their eighteenth-century predecessors.

During the eighteenth century, choices for middle-class consumers had increased dramatically as styles changed from Baroque to Rococo to Neo-Classical, and as cabinet-makers expanded their services to include the specification of upholstery and drapery and suggestions for interior decoration. The Industrial Revolution first affected the textile industry—especially the type, quantity, and cost of fabrics available for fashions and furnishing—eventually influencing the production of the decorative arts, especially ceramics. This was due, in part, to the willingness of entrepreneurs such as Josiah Wedgwood (1730–95) to introduce steam power into manufactories (Plate 2). Pattern books—engraved picture books with a brief commentary meant to enlighten furniture makers and their clients—offered bewildering alternatives in furniture design, ranging from the classical, to "Gothick," to French- or Asian-influenced, eventually shifting to the Neo-Classical or Classical Revival. Key authors of such pattern books included Thomas Chippendale, George Hepplewhite, Thomas Sheraton, and others. Advising consumers on their selections were architects, cabinet-makers, drapers and upholsterers, merchants, and entrepreneurs, guided by philosophers of aesthetics who sought to define what was tasteful and appropriate.

The 1750s were as important for the publication of pattern books on furniture and ornament as they were for treatises on the philosophy of aesthetics. This decade marked the appearance of Chippendale's seminal *The Gentleman and Cabinet-Maker's Director* (1754), as well as four key essays on Beauty and Taste whose influence would be far-reaching. These included William Hogarth's *Analysis of Beauty. Written in a view of fixing the fluctuating Ideas of Taste* (1757), David Hume's *Of the Standard of Taste* (1757), Edmund Burke's *A Philosophical Enquiry into the Origin of our Ideas of the Sublime and Beautiful* (1757), and Alexander

Gerard's *An Essay on Taste* (1759). English consumers dealt with myriad choices in the market place, during this decade when London was the largest city in Europe. At the same time, these writers—none of whom were professional critics—debated Beauty, Taste, criticism, standards, and human perception in an effort to inform consumers' choices.

Artist William Hogarth (1697–1764) explored the expressive potential of line and form, arguing that the "S"-curve—so prevalent in furnishings during the first three-quarters of the century—was truly the "line of beauty" (Figs. 6 and 7). He credited Lambert Hermanson Ten Kate, author of *Beau Ideal* (ca. 1732), for inspiring his own musings upon the serpentine line in the 1740s. Hogarth expanded his theory of Beauty to

6. William Hogarth. From International Portrait Gallery, Gale Research Co., 1968. (Boston Public Library/Department of Fine Arts. Courtesy of the Trustees)

7. Plate 1, Third State, 14 5/6 by 19 5/16 in. From William Hogarth, *Analysis of Beauty*. (Boston Public Library/Print Department. Courtesy of the Trustees) This plate illustrates Hogarth's theory of beauty. Marginalia document the prevalence of the "S" curve in everyday life and culture, demonstrating—though it constituted the "line of beauty"—that some "S" curves were more pleasing than others.

8. David Hume. From International Portrait Gallery, Gale Research Co., 1968. (Boston Public Library/ Department of Fine Arts. Courtesy of the Trustees)

incorporate the following principles: fitness, variety (exemplified by the serpentine line and the spiral form), uniformity, simplicity, intricacy, and quantity, all of which he derived from the natural world.[25]

Hogarth explained how each principle contributed to Beauty, especially Beauty in paintings, and might lead any reader—not just "painters and connoisseurs"—to ascertain "the elegant and beautiful in artificial as well as natural forms." Despite the firmness of his conviction regarding the superiority of the serpentine line specifically and the six principles of Beauty generally, Hogarth admitted—citing Ten Kate as justification—that a certain *je ne sais quoi* characterized the greatest works of art, and that theories of Beauty and Taste could only go so far in explaining how or why such works attracted the connoisseur.[26]

The Scotsman David Hume (1711–76) lacked Hogarth's artistic training, bringing to his discussion of taste a varied background in law, merchandising, writing, and editing (Fig. 8). By the time he wrote *Of the Standard of Taste* in 1757, he was, according to the historian David W. Lenz, "one of the leading literary figures of Great Britain." In contrast to Hogarth, who focused upon the six principles comprising Beauty, Hume stressed the importance of "seeking a Standard of Taste" that might ensure that the judgments of critics, connoisseurs, and consumers regarding Beauty were uniform. He discussed the critic's character and credentials—arguing that true critics were rare—as well as proposing a methodology for making critical appraisals. Hume is less concerned with defining Beauty, Taste, and their components than he is with establishing "a rule by which the various sentiments of man may be reconciled." The historian Dabney Townsend notes: "Hume's reliance on the uniformity of human nature leads him to formulate general rules in aesthetics and morals," though he cautions, "The question of what kind of rules is a thorny one." This link between aesthetics and morality was an issue upon which nineteenth-century critics would build, just as they would ponder the role of rules in the critical process.[27]

If Hogarth and Hume shared a belief, it was that a certain indescribable something distinguishes Beauty, or at least one's perceptions of Beauty. "But besides all the agreeable qualities the origin of whose beauty we can, in some degree, explain and account for," Hume argues, "there still remains something mysterious and inexplicable, which conveys an immediate satisfaction to the spectator, but how, or why or for what reason, he cannot pretend to determine. There is a manner, a grace, an ease, a genteelness, an I-know-not-what . . . which is very different from external beauty and comeliness, and which, however, catches our affection almost as suddenly and as powerfully." This quality complicated the job of eighteenth-century philosophers just as it would that of their nineteenth-century successors.²⁸

In the same year that Hume wrote *Of the Standard of Taste*, the British statesman and political writer Edmund Burke (1729–97) published anonymously *A Philosophical Enquiry into the Origin of our Ideas of the Sublime and the Beautiful*, equating each quality with Nature, while noting gender distinctions (Fig. 9). (The Sublime represented the masculine, the Beautiful the feminine.) The Sublime, Burke argued, engendered astonishment in the beholder, whereas Beauty evoked "love, or some passion similar to it." Such qualities as power,

9. Edmund Burke. From International Portrait Gallery, Gale Research Co., 1968. (Boston Public Library/ Department of Fine Arts. Courtesy of the Trustees)

privation, vastness, and infinity caused one to experience the Sublime. Conversely, smallness, smoothness, variation, fluidity (of form), delicacy, clarity and brightness (of color) led one to perceive Beauty. By listing and discussing those traits, Burke paralleled Hogarth's approach. The former, however, focused more upon what modern theorists call design *elements*, the latter on design *principles*.²⁹

Two years later, a second edition of Burke's *Enquiry* appeared, augmented by a new introduction. Historian James T. Boulton notes that Burke, like Hume, is "convinced of the existence of general laws governing human behavior; he can also be accurately described as an investigative critic fascinated by the nature of psychological reactions to the external world." Burke's essay builds upon Hume's pondering why human reactions to a work of Art or Nature can vary—even when that work possesses traits or reflects principles that critics collectively regard as excellent. Burke ponders the issue of taste, drawing a cautious conclusion: "What is called Taste, in its most general acceptation, is not a simple idea, but is partly made up of a perception of the primary pleasures of sense," and, he adds, "of the secondary pleasures of the imagination, and of the conclusions of the reasoning faculty, concerning the various relations of these, and concerning the human passions, manners and actions."³⁰

In the same year that Burke's new introduction appeared, Alexander Gerard (1728–95) produced the similarly titled *An Essay on Taste*, ostensibly "inspired by Hume himself," according to Dabney Townsend. A professor and cleric, Gerard differed in both background and approach from Hogarth, Hume, and Burke. Rather than addressing principles or traits that contributed to the Beautiful and the Sublime or pondering a standard of taste, or the effects of taste upon perception (or vice-versa), Gerard focused upon the critic.³¹

Gerard, a Professor of Moral Philosophy and Logic (1752), and then of Divinity

(1759) at Marichal College, and subsequently Professor of Divinity (1773) at King's College, both in Aberdeen, analyzes "the influence of Taste on criticism," arguing that it is the "fundamental ingredient in the character of the critic." Stressing the necessity of objectivity, he warns, "A critic must not only feel, but possess that accuracy of discernment, which enables a person to reflect upon his feelings with distinctness, and to explain them to others." This quality was essential for critics but sometimes lacking in theorists.[32]

Gerard argues that critics must be rigorous in their observations: "In order therefore to form an able critic, taste must be attended with a philosophical genius, which may subject [its observations] to a regular induction, reduce them into classes, and determine the general rules that govern them." Gerard suggests that critics should employ a scientific methodology. Yet, he warns that "perfect criticism . . . requires . . . the greatest philosophical acuteness, united with the most exquisite perfection of taste. If taste is wanting, our conclusions must be defective, faulty, or precarious: if philosophical genius [is lacking], our observations will be trifling, superficial, unconnected, and perplexed with too great particularity." The best criticism, he insists, "arrives at the most universal distinctions that can be made," those that resonate with the "invariable principles of human nature." That striving to ascertain the universal truth was a quality that eighteenth-century critics passed on to their nineteenth-century followers.[33]

Books written in the 1750s and 1760s as primers, or "how-to" guides for would-be critics, are proof that criticism of the everyday environment was evolving into a profession. One of these was the *Elements of Criticism* (ca. 1762), written by the Scottish philosopher and judge Henry Home (Lord Kames, 1696–1782). In it, Home addresses "good" and "bad design" in such disciplines as "gardening and architecture" (chapter 24). He discusses as well the "Standards of Taste" (chapter 25).[34]

He argues that standards of taste are difficult to establish in gardening and architecture (and presumably the applied arts) precisely because they combine Usefulness and Beauty. The outcome of such disciplines "may be destined for use solely, for beauty solely, or for both"; thus, it is more difficult to determine tastefulness in either discipline than it is "in any art that has but a single destination." When the useful arts become beautiful, he suggests, the task for their critic becomes more challenging.[35]

Home complicates the critic's task further by suggesting that Beauty falls into two distinct subcategories: *intrinsic beauty*, found in a work "intended solely for pleasure," and *relative beauty*, found in a work "destined for use." He argues that these distinctions pose fewer challenges for the gardener than for the architect because "intrinsic and relative beauty must often be blended in the same building," making it "difficult . . . to attain both in any perfection," whereas most gardeners stress either one quality or the other, in, say, a pleasure garden or a kitchen garden.[36]

To aid designers in achieving a perfect blending of these two subcomponents of Beauty, Home offers Nature as a model. To approximate Nature's "richness and variety" requires, he suggests, absorbing those principles illustrated in her creations: regularity, uniformity, variety, proportion, concord or harmony, and congruity. He devotes the bulk of his discussion to proportion, or the relationship of parts to the whole. But, he concludes, "Proportion of parts is not only itself a beauty, but is inseparably connected with a beauty of the highest relish, that of concord or harmony." In doing so, he relates achievement of Beauty to key design elements and principles, arguing that each and all contribute to the desired effect, "good design."[37]

While Home emphasizes Beauty throughout his essay, he also acknowledges the importance of Usefulness. "Regularity and proportion are essential in buildings destined chiefly or solely to please the eye," he writes, "because they are the means to produce intrinsic beauty. But a skilful artist will not confine his view to regularity and proportion." The artist "will also study congruity, which is perceived when the form and ornaments of a structure are suited to the purpose for which it is appointed." In this passage, which might be written of any of the applied arts, Home is discussing utility, function, or usefulness, without identifying it as such. "The sense of congruity dictates the following rule," he concludes: "That every building ought to have an expression corresponding to its destination." Use, he suggests, is an important determinant in expression, or the way in which an artifact communicates a message from maker to user.[38]

By mentioning expression, Home introduces an issue that critics would continue to address—and obsess over—for the next hundred years and more. Expression was a trait that, critics believed, transcended Usefulness and Beauty, though it depended upon them. It communicated the designer's concept while appealing to the user's most acute sensibilities. Thus it was an intermediary among maker, object, and user. Effective expression was a quality that critics prized even more than Usefulness or Beauty. It made a statement that was, at best, of its time, yet timeless. Expression and its definition would remain essential to the discussion of Usefulness and Beauty into the twentieth century.

Critics like Home took exception to the maxim "There is no accounting for taste." Demystifying taste was one of their chief goals. Their profession depended upon the existence of a standard of taste, the topic of Home's ensuing essay by the same name. In it, he refutes the conventional wisdom, arguing: "What is universal must have a foundation in [human] nature. If we can reach that foundation, the standard of taste will no longer be a secret."[39]

Home equates the perception of "good" or "bad" in the arts—here, once again, he refers specifically to the fine arts, though his comments apply equally to the applied—to a sense of "right" or "wrong" in morals. Individuals who have no notion of either deviate from, what Homes terms "the common standard." By the "conviction of a common standard being made a part of our nature," he concludes, "we intuitively conceive a taste to be right or good if conformable to the common standard, and wrong or bad if disconformable." To deviate from a common standard, he indicates, could only yield the "disgust" of any critics subscribing to it. This linking of taste to morality would inspire generations of design reformers, who believed, in a Darwinian fashion, that environment molded character.[40]

Home indicates that a common or "uniform" standard of taste might be inspirational to architects, artists, and designers. "Uniformity of taste gives opportunity for sumptuous and elegant buildings, for fine gardens, and extensive embellishments, which please universally," he notes. "And the reason is that without uniformity of taste, there could not be any suitable reward, either of profit or honor, to encourage [persons] of genius to labor in such works, and to advance them toward perfection." Uniformity was a prerequisite, he stated, for ensuring the continuing health of the arts. A uniform standard of taste gives makers and users alike something to strive toward. As such, it has the potential to unite the different social classes. This concept remained attractive to design reformers in the nineteenth century, who hoped to draw together diverse social groups by democratizing "good design."[41]

Home insists that this standard of taste—like a standard in morality—must not be "local or transitory." Instead, it must be based upon "what is most universal and the most lasting among polite nations." That comment foreshadows what mid-nineteenth-century critics like Merrifield and Wornum hoped events such as the Great Exhibition would establish. Home warns against a standard that is ostentatious, or, in his terms, "voluptuous." Instead, he advocates championing such qualities as "simplicity, elegance, propriety, and things natural, sweet, or amiable"—the same qualities that design reformers prized a hundred years later, and that often contributed to definitions of Usefulness and Beauty into the 1920s.[42]

Having made his case in favor of establishing a standard of taste, Home concludes his essay by defining the sort of person who might work to enforce it, by assuming the role of critic. He admits that a "narrow compass" defines those who "are qualified to be judges in the fine arts. . . . Many circumstances are necessary to form a judge of this sort. There must be a good natural taste . . . . This taste," he continues, "must be improved by education, reflection, and experience: it must be preserved alive; by a regular course of life, by using the goods of fortune with moderation, and by following the dictates of improved [human] nature, which gives welcome to every rational pleasure without deviating into excess. This is the tenor of life," he concludes, "which of all contributes the most to the refinement of taste." It avoids any influence that might contribute to its becoming, in his words, "defective" or "depraved."[43]

Here again, Home is perspicacious: recognizing that refinement of taste requires "education, reflection, and experience," he anticipates remarks made by nineteenth-century design reformers on both sides of the Atlantic. Those with socialistic political leanings, especially, argued that such advantages were essential for those wishing to cultivate "good taste" and "good design." They lamented that most workers lacked education in design fundamentals, and had no leisure time for contemplating how they might improve themselves and their skills to advance the standards of design. They promoted adult education programs (held evenings and weekends), and arts and crafts societies as a way of rectifying this situation.[44]

Nearly a decade passed between publication of Hogarth's *Analysis of Beauty* and Home's *Elements of Criticism*. The period from the early 1750s to the early 1760s was an unusually fertile one for quickening the debate regarding aesthetics, taste, standards, critics, and criticism. The key contributors raised issues that their successors continued to ponder, while demonstrating a need for professional arbiters of taste.

The 1770s witnessed the application of their theories, as gentleman-amateurs appropriated their ideas and applied them to a critique of the fine arts. One of these was "Roger Shanhagan." Shanhagan, a pseudonym under which three critics wrote, was an eighteenth-century prototype for those, such as Merrifield and Wornum, who critiqued works at exhibitions. His essay *The Exhibition, or a Second Anticipation: Being Remarks on the Principal Works to be Exhibited next Month, at the Royal Academy* (1779) exemplifies the foundation that eighteenth-century critics provided for those who followed. In it, Shanhagan comments on architecture, painting, and sculpture—that is, the fine arts, only. But, he does so in a way that informs critiques of the applied arts that would become prevalent in the nineteenth century, as the Industrial Revolution burgeoned.[45]

Shanhagan presents his credentials in the opening paragraphs, and then allies himself with the "science of criticism" as a theoretical position. He declares himself "the guardian and protector of the Arts," one who is worthy of judging works shown under the auspices of the Royal Academy, and distinguishes himself from other critics whom he dismisses as "monsters," given their "meager unprincipled Criticism," their "venom," and their "destruction of Genius and Taste." He undertakes his role of critic as if a warrior going into battle against his enemies, who are not the public, the press, artists, or architects, but instead rival critics.[46]

As a proponent of the "science of criticism," Shanhagan turns to history and theory to support his observations. "We have long considered the remains of ancient magnificence, as the sources from whence every Architect must derive his ideas of excellence," he argues, "and the rules drawn from them, as laws positive and permanent, from which no deviation could be permitted." This is Shanhagan's introduction to a discussion of the works of the Scottish architects Robert and James Adam, the chief proponents of Neo-Classicism in Britain in the 1760s–1770s. Their adherence to these "rules" and "laws" enables Shanhagan to pronounce their works-on-display "excellent," "great," and "novel."[47]

Shanhagan did not regard another exhibitor, the English architect Sir William Chambers, rival to the Adam brothers, in the same favorable light. He condemns him as "an Architect of inferior merit, when compared with the Adams," and uses his discussion of Chambers's entries as an opportunity to provide a tutorial on "bad" and "good design," specifically Beauty. Though his remarks pertain to Beauty in architecture, they seem applicable to definitions of Beauty in the lesser arts, and provide a basis for comparison with later definitions. "Beauty is the result of an artful combination of many parts which are themselves esteemed Beautiful," he begins, "because experience has proved that they are properly formed to answer the end required." Beauty arises, at least in part, from Usefulness.[48]

Architectural Beauty results as well, he continues, from "Ornaments, which, by contrasting with Plainness, give alternate action and repose to the eye." Beauty is perfect "when parts, well formed and proportioned in themselves, are so combined and proportioned to each other and to the size of the Building, that those parts which are apparently most necessary shall first attract notice; and the rest, preserving a proper subordination, all together form an harmonious whole." This was the formula for "good design" in a nutshell during the last quarter of the eighteenth century. What Shanhagan implied by offering it was that Chambers's work was inferior and the Adam brothers' superior because of adherence to these principles.[49]

Yet, he admits "true genius brooks no control, and needs no instruction," unlike "inferior ability," which requires an "implicit obedience to rules and laws." Herein lay a paradox that plagued critics of the eighteenth and nineteenth centuries: the vast majority of their readers benefited from prescribed principles of "good design," and of Usefulness and Beauty. But the handful of truly great designers could willfully violate them, often achieving inspired results. "Their works," Shanhagan writes, referring to the Adam brothers, "are not only erected without Rules, but from them no Rules can be drawn." Determining the principles of "good design" was, thus, no easy matter.[50]

This was the sort of genius that inspired—and frustrated—critics. "The man who would criticize them as he ought, or would imitate them, must possess a portion of the same fire which animates the Artists," Shanhagan advised. This last point is important because it illustrates how critics struggled to define what their own credentials—and their criteria—should be. The angst in Shanhagan's tone foreshadows the uneasiness professed by critics who followed. The old query "who knows who knows best?" dogged even the most conscientious critics in the eighteenth century and continues to unsettle their successors today.[51]

Significant contributions to the literature of aesthetics, taste, and criticism at the end of the eighteenth century included George Hepplewhite's *Cabinet-Maker and Upholsterer's Guide* (1788), Sir Uvedale Price's *Dialogue on The Distinct Characters of the Picturesque and the Beautiful* (1801), Thomas Sheraton's *Cabinet-maker and Upholsterer's Drawing-Book* (ca. 1802), and Richard Payne Knight's *Analytical Inquiry into the Principles of Taste* (1805). Each of these in its own way built upon the treatises of the 1750s, often quoting from them directly or referring to their authors. Price, for example, expanded upon Burke's ideas by introducing the concept of "the Picturesque," a descriptor that applied "when there are any marked irregularities in the features combined with the qualities of beauty, although such combinations have often a wild variety and playfulness, more attractive perhaps than even beauty of a more pure and unmixed kind." Knight challenged Price's distinctions between the Picturesque and the Beautiful, while rejecting Burke's emphasis upon the importance of sensation to perception.[52]

The essays of Hogarth, Hume, Burke, Gerard, Home, Shanhagan, Price, and Knight appealed to members of the social elite, who had the education and experience to appreciate their sophisticated theories. They suggested how a cultured individual might apply those theories to analyzing art, architecture, garden, and landscape. By contrast, pattern books compiled by eighteenth-century entrepreneurs illustrated furnishings in the latest taste in a way that would inform busy consumers who needed a more practical guide to infusing their homes with the Useful and the Beautiful.

Entrepreneurs as Design Critics: Chippendale, Hepplewhite, Sheraton

Entrepreneurs such as Thomas Chippendale (1718–79) applied suggestions from contemporary theorists to designs "suited to the fancy and circumstances of persons in all degrees of life." Though he was a cabinet-maker and not a professional critic, he nevertheless offered suggestions on décor in *The Gentleman and Cabinet-Maker's Director*. He wrote it for the benefit of gentlepersons who perused his engravings of "elegant and useful" designs, and, by doing so, hoped to "improve and refine the present taste." In the time-honored manner of pattern book authors dating back to the Renaissance, Chippendale was a trendsetter and a tastemaker. He and colleagues who emulated him—Hepplewhite, Sheraton, and others—were entrepreneurs first and arbiters of taste second. Still, they were highly visible and influential upon generations of consumers, and their comments on Usefulness and Beauty are worth noting as a foundation for individuals like Merrifield and Wornum.[53]

That critics were active watchdogs of taste during the eighteenth century is evident from Chippendale's "Preface" to the third edition of *The Director*. Here he makes clear that he has no patience for the "pointless Abuse" of critics who are mere faultfinders, but welcomes constructive criticism from workers or clients using his designs. Such comments were not uncommon in pattern books. Most went through multiple revisions or reprintings. (*The Director*, for example, which first appeared in 1754, was reprinted with few alterations in 1755, and reissued in 1762 with extensive updates.)[54]

One bridge between the criticism of the Age of Enlightenment and that of the mid-Victorian Age of Industry was the acceptance—among critics, designers, and consumers—of history as a model for "good design." Just as Wornum began his analysis of the Great Exhibition with a synopsis of the history of ornament, so too did Chippendale begin *The Director* with annotated illustrations of the Orders of ancient architecture. Ironically, these are evident in few of his furniture designs; yet, he included them in his book, arguing: "These, therefore, ought to be carefully studied by every one who would excel in this Branch [cabinet-making], since they are the very Soul and Basis of his Art." The Orders of ancient architecture, the Doric, Ionic, and Corinthian, were a touchstone for tastefulness among successive generations—understood universally, though applied differently.[55]

Chippendale's subsequent commentary is succinct as he discusses each of his new designs in terms of some or all of the following: dimensions, proportion, scale; required and optional parts; materials ranging from wood to fabric, gilding, japanning, mirror, glass, and metal; cost and potential cost-cutting measures; and symbolism. Desirous of, above all, a "Good Effect" in each design—as, for example, in his "Design of a State-Bed" (Fig. 10), where he strives for "magnificence, proportion, and harmony"—Chippendale discusses and critiques his designs, pointing out to his readers what "looks well" or "badly," what is "proper,"

10. A "Design for a State-Bed," from Thomas Chippendale, *The Gentleman and Cabinet-Maker's Director* (1754), as reproduced in Frederick Litchfield, *Illustrated History of Furniture*, 2nd ed. (London: Truslove & Shirley, 1892). (Author's collection) Though Chippendale argued that he had achieved "magnificence, proportion, and harmony," it is an overwrought, Rococo confection "in the French taste," which has had less lasting influence than have his more restrained designs for seat furniture, tables, and cabinets.

and "not unbecoming." A purveyor of taste, he is his own worst critic, and, in that respect, not too different from the practitioner-critics who would abound in the nineteenth century.[56]

Chippendale's successor George Hepplewhite—whose background is obscure—died two years before his wife, Alice, published his *Cabinet-maker and Upholsterer's Guide* in 1788. "The *Guide*," writes his biographer Simon Jervis, "was the first major furniture pattern-book to appear after the third edition of Chippendale's *Director* . . . , and the first to exhibit the Neo-Classical style. The gap from 1762 to 1788 was filled by the first two volumes (1773–9) of the *Works* of Robert and James Adam, whose influence on the *Guide* was immense, many of its designs being elegant artisan variations on Adam themes." Unlike Chippendale, Hepplewhite showed little awareness of history in compiling his pattern book. But, like many designers and purveyors of furnishings who would follow, he considered himself a judge of eighteenth-century "elegance and utility," or qualities that would become Beauty and Usefulness in the nineteenth century (Fig. 11). His preface addresses the issue of taste, specifically "English taste in the various articles of household furniture," which, he notes, "has been much sought for by surrounding nations of late years." He defines "useful" as "such articles as are generally serviceable in genteel life." He advises his readers—"residents of London," gentlemen, countrymen, and "artizans"—that his designs "follow the latest or most prevailing fashion only," and that he has "purposely omit[ted] such articles, whose recommendation was mere novelty, and perhaps a violation of all established rule, [and] the production of whim at the instance of caprice." Hepplewhite's mention of a "rule," or standard ties his comments to earlier writers.[57]

He indicates that "novelty" and "caprice" do not ensure a beautiful result. In this and other ways, his comments foreshadow many of Wornum's expressed sixty-three years later. Both are concerned with Usefulness and Beauty. Each disassociates those qualities from novelty, whim, or caprice. Both acknowledge that designers must follow rules to achieve good taste. Each is nationalistic, seeking to view his country's productions positively. Yet, Hepplewhite's obvious pride in the desirability of English furnishings beyond its shores contrasts markedly with Wornum's dismay at how English products were faring in international competition in the nineteenth century. (A second edition of the *Guide* appeared in 1789, as did a third in 1794. Both included revisions, possibly made by someone in Hepplewhite's firm, although the identity of the contributor remains a mystery.)

By the time the drawing master and furniture maker Thomas Sheraton (1751–1806) published the third edition of his *Cabinet-maker and Upholsterer's Drawing-Book* (ca.1802), so many similar pattern books had appeared that he found it necessary to include a brief literature review and critique at the front of his own. Among these were Ince & Mayhew's *Universal System of Household Furniture* (1759); Robert Sayer's *Household Furniture in Genteel Taste* (1760, with later editions); and Thomas Shearer's *The Cabinet-Makers' London Book of Prices* (1788, with later editions). Dismissing Chippendale's *Director* as "wholly antiquated and laid aside," and Hepplewhite's *Guide* as "already having caught the decline," Sheraton proves himself a literary critic as well as a designer and arbiter of taste. He distinguishes the *Drawing Book* (which appeared in parts between 1791 and 1793) from works of his predecessors, pointing out that it is less a pattern book than it is a guide to geometry, perspective, and drawing—three subjects in

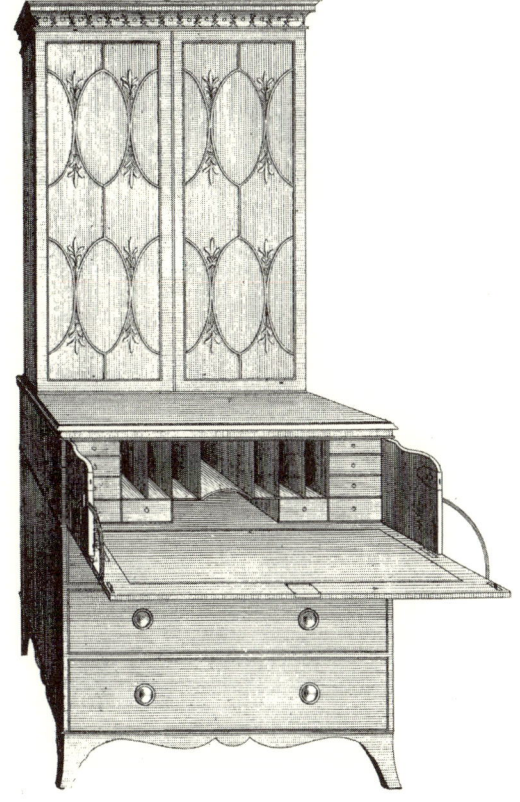

11. Secretary-Bookcase, from George Hepplewhite, *The Gentleman and Cabinet-Maker's Guide* (1788); facsimile ed., comp. and ed. N. I. Bienenstock (New York: Towse, 1942). (Author's collection) This secretary-bookcase illustrates the qualities to which Hepplewhite aspired. The crisp lines and restrained ornament are typical of Classical Revival "elegance." The fall-front writing surface with pigeon holes provides ample storage and bespeaks "utility." Overall, the design demonstrates a love of gadgetry that was ubiquitous in eighteenth-century pattern books.

which he regarded himself an expert. He downplays its importance in setting a standard for middle-class consumers who preferred the Neo-Classical and newly emerging Greco-Roman Revival styles. In a self-effacing fashion, he regards his designs as only "somewhat elegant" and credits a friend with one of the more mechanically ingenious designs, a "Harlequin Pembroke Table." Sheraton's designs, writes biographer Simon Jervis, "are competent and elegant, but display that tendency to over-ornament so common in the artisan designer."[58]

Sheraton published his second book, *The Cabinet Dictionary*, in 1803. A useful reference for anyone interested in cabinet-making, it presents "original" and "novel" designs, instructions and technical tips for the "good mechanic," and snippets of furniture history. (Of particular interest is his brief history of the bed.) Sheraton the critic provides a running commentary on the fashions of the day: The latest

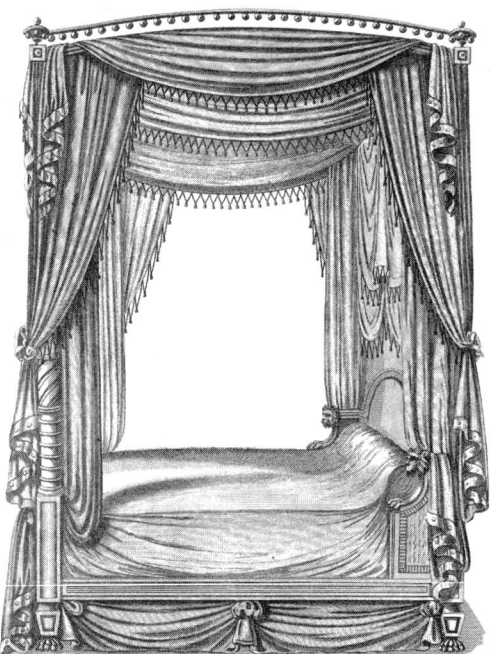

12. "Design for a Four-Poster Bed," from Thomas Sheraton, *The Cabinet Encyclopedia* (1804), as reproduced in N. I. Bienenstock, comp. and ed., *Thomas Sheraton's Complete Furniture Works* (New York: Towse, 1946), plate 3 of Beds. (Author's collection) Neither the unity nor the simplicity that Sheraton thought he had captured in this design are concepts that most readers would associate with it today.

French chairs are "not without proper effect," he notes, "when due restraint is laid on the quantity [of ornament]." Drawing-room chairs, he indicates, "should always be the produce [*sic*] of studied elegance," a piece of advice that, ironically, he seldom followed. Yet, the bolster-shaped cushion or "squab" of a Grecian couch sofa (illustrated in his plate 49), he warns, "requires upholsterers of taste and ability." These were scarce commodities, evidently, in this era when the draper and upholsterer were becoming key decision-makers in home decoration, more so than either cabinetmakers or architects. Regarding a writing tambour table (such as that shown in his plate 38), he cautions his readers that it "is both insecure and very liable to injury," and, what is more, is falling out of fashion. Always diffident, Sheraton was highly self-critical; his eccentric work attracted the wrath of myriad others as well.[59]

Sheraton died while writing *The Cabinet Encyclopedia* (begun 1804), for which he completed only thirty of the planned 125 sections. Entries provide a description of the component parts of each design, along with notes on construction and suggestions for finishes. Ever the critic, he comments upon what is "useful and elegant," or what is no longer fashionable. He describes with particular pride a design for a draped four-poster bed (Fig. 12): "In my opinion, [it] exceeds in beauty because of its unity and simplicity. This is my constant aim in designing, and constitutes the perfection of the art." He was fortunate to have believed that he had reached "perfection," given the timing of that comment just preceding his death in 1806. But it was surprising that he associated unity and simplicity with his own work, which was more often eccentric, overwrought, and drowning in fabric.[60]

Together, Chippendale, Hepplewhite, and Sheraton reflected the prevailing theories of the time, although they did not always allude to them. At the same time, they anticipated the approach that their successors, such as writers of advice manuals on home furnishings or treatises on taste, would take in decades to follow. They established their credentials as trendsetters; they discussed their designs in detail, offering insights on everything from materials and dimensions to broader issues of relevancy and symbolism; they identified what was out of fashion, while introducing the latest taste; they suggested that rules governed products in the market place; they attempted to define—in pictures and with words—what constituted the "elegant and useful"; they bemoaned the decline of British influence upon European production; they even engaged in meta-criticism, as they critiqued critics' comments regarding their work.

Taken as a group, eighteenth-century critics, whether theorists or entrepreneurs, explored common topics and themes. They pondered taste—what it was and why it was important; critics and their credentials; criticism per se and what constituted it; the science of criticism; how taste influenced criticism; and influences upon "good taste." They contemplated contemporary theories of the sublime, the picturesque, the beautiful, and the useful. They considered models offered by history or nature. They addressed morality and its relationship to design. They demonstrated knowledge of design fundamentals, stressing the importance of principles, rules, or laws. Recurring themes included: taste as an expression of morality; a common or universal standard of taste that was permanent; expression; and the paradox of genius that could avoid laws or rules and yet produce something tasteful. All were issues and themes that would inform the work of critics in decades to follow. Significantly, Ralph Nicholson Wornum quotes Edmund Burke at the start of his essay "The Exhibition as a Lesson in Taste," and speaks of "elegance and fitness," thus showing his awareness of and comfort with the language of his predecessors. And, like Chippendale, Wornum discusses the Orders of classical architecture on page two, as a way of establishing his credentials as an arbiter of taste.

Design Criticism, 1800–1850: Foundation for the Design Reform Movement

Successors to the critics of the eighteenth century carried on enthusiastically during the first five decades of the nineteenth. Men and women, professionals and amateurs, fueled debates on both sides of the Atlantic, as they pertained to issues of taste, definitions of beauty, and, most important, the increasing urgency of reforming the arts—especially the industrial arts. At one end of the spectrum were publications such as *The Director, A Weekly Literary Journal*, which published chatty letters from readers regarding the latest taste in home furnishings purveyed by fashionable shops in London. In 1807, for example, a rural housewife visiting the city complained to her husband of the preponderance of furnishings "*a l'antique*," or in the "monstrous Egyptian fashion," condemning them as indicative of a "ludicrous mania. . . . The imitation of the arts in their 'rudest' state," she concluded, "neither contributes to just decoration, nor evinces a correct taste in those who adopt it." At the other end of the spectrum were erudite studies that built upon—but refuted—popular theories espoused by eighteenth-century philosophers. Works such as Alexander Walker's *Beauty* (London, 1836) and M. V. Cousin's *Lectures on the True, The Beautiful, and The Good* (Paris, ca. 1854) fell into this latter category. Significantly, both addressed the beauty of useful objects and the usefulness of beautiful objects, pondering whether both qualities could be present simultaneously.[61]

The eclectic, but short-lived *Repository of the Arts, Literature, Commerce, Manu-*

factures, Fashions [and] Politics, published by Rudolph Ackermann (ca. 1809–18), combined elements of both the conversational and the philosophic. Resembling what twenty-first-century readers would call a "lifestyle magazine," Ackermann's *Repository* interspersed essays with colored engravings of architecture, interior décor, furnishings, and fashion. A distinctive feature was the inclusion of elaborate engraved plates to which were affixed tiny samples of woven and printed fabrics (Plate 3). Though published in England, and reflecting a bias toward English textile manufacturing, the *Repository* illustrated myriad designs having strong French influence.

Design was not the *Repository*'s sole focus, though, since it included as well poetry, matters of public record—marriages, births, bankruptcies—an almanac of weather statistics and tidal charts, and information on stocks, bonds, and commodities. Musical reviews and articles on sport, geography, and hobbies—such as "Directions for the Breeding and General Treatment of Canary Birds" (July 1809)—ensured that the *Repository* offered something for every reader, in the manner of today's *Martha Stewart Living* written for protagonists of a Jane Austen novel.[62]

In the September 1813 issue, an article titled "Fashionable Furniture" advised young artists and "artizans" to consult nature and "monuments of antiquity" to improve their taste, while advocating improved education, better "models of the perfections in art," and greater energy on the part of professionals who must "point out and correct" designs so that they might suit the English climate and client. The *Repository* went so far in its quest for reform as to offer a medal for the best essay submitted by a reader providing a "historical account of the progressive Improvements in the Arts, Agriculture, Commerce, and Manufactures, of this country; their effect upon the morals and manners of the people; and stating the best means for their future advancement." In this way, the *Repository* promoted design reform while maintaining the position held by eighteenth-century philosophers that a nation's industrial production reflected—and indeed affected—its inhabitants' collective character.[63]

That Americans bought this argument is evident in contemporaneous publications, such as *The Mirror of the Graces* (New York, 1813), published by an otherwise anonymous "Lady of Distinction." In the introduction to this Francophobe narrative on the history of fashion, the author asserts: "Fine taste in apparel I have ever seen the companion of pure morals; while a licentious style of dress is as certainly the token of the like laxity in manners and conduct." She advised her readers to "correct" this "dangerous" state of affairs. Such publications on taste and fashion were vehicles for women to express critical views on design despite their reticence to reveal their identities and lack of opportunity to discuss weightier issues of architecture and interior décor.[64]

In the years leading up to the Great Exhibition, one of the most important publications ever produced on design criticism appeared, the *Journal of Design and Manufactures* (London, 1849–52). Dedicated to Prince Albert, and compiled by his advisers on the upcoming Exhibition—Richard Redgrave, Digby Wyatt, Henry Cole, Owen Jones, and others—it had as its mission to reform Britain's schools of design, improve copyright legislation as it pertained to design, advocate a system of elementary drawing, and establish recognized principles of good design. Small in

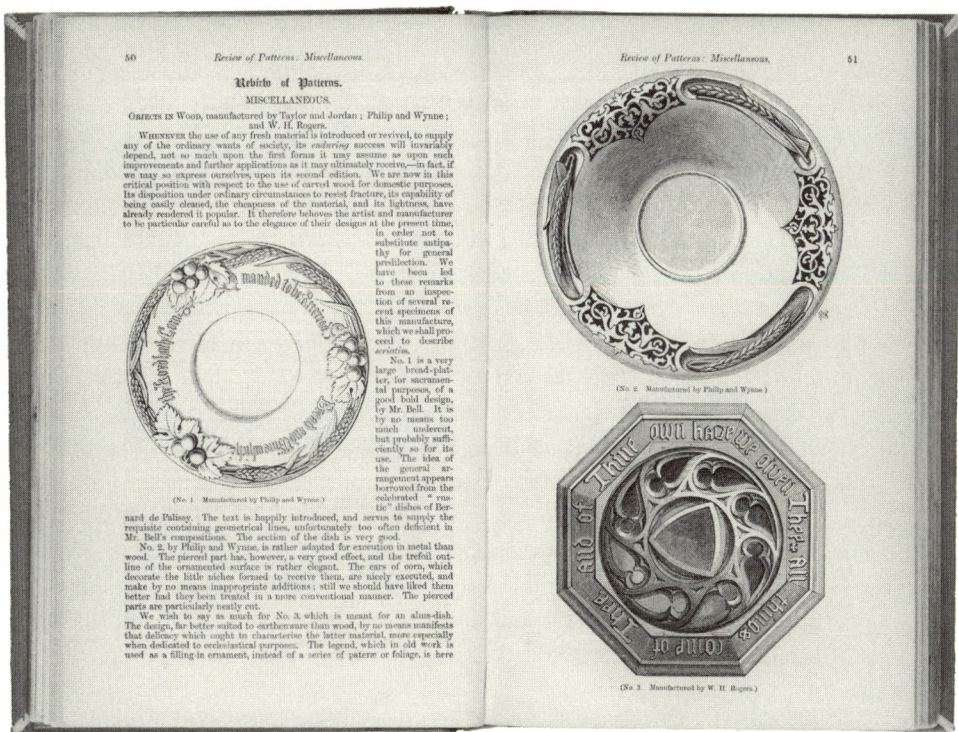

13. Three carved wood plates, *Journal of Design and Manufactures*, 3 (March–August 1850): 50–51. (Courtesy Baker Library, Harvard Business School) This "Review of Patterns" critiques the work of manufacturers Philip and Wynne and W. H. Rogers. Editors praise plates 1 and 2, but write of 3: "The whole border is too heavy, the tracery ill-drawn, the escutcheon-shaped triangle sadly out of place."

format (about six inches by eight) and printed in miniscule type, it resembled Ackermann's *Repository* in that it also included actual textile and wallpaper samples. (In the issues published after the opening of the Great Exhibition, many of these were examples of products shown in the Crystal Palace) (Plate 4). Appealing to professionals, who appreciated its reviews of books, lectures, and exhibitions, or periodic evaluations of activities at the schools of design, the *Journal* also reached out to "that large public who are interested in the progress of the Decorative Manufactures" in England. Its comprehensive scope, passionate tone, and forthright writing style made it useful to professionals as well as lay readers. "Until we make every object of design tell its own straightforward tale," writes a contributor to the September 1849 issue, "we can never be 'great' or even respectable; . . . art, in fact, must be truth."[65]

Among those critiqued by the *Journal* were Merrifield, Wornum, A. W. N. Pugin, Ruskin, and Carlyle. Wornum and Ruskin received the *Journal*'s harshest criticism, the former for his "dry" lectures at the schools of design, the latter for the romantic impracticality of much of what he advised in *The Seven Lamps of Architecture* and *The Stones of Venice*. The *Journal* disliked imitations of any sort, which it dismissed as "shams," promoting instead an honesty that resulted from utility, unity of style, and fitness—all qualities championed by later supporters of the Arts and Crafts movement.[66]

When not critiquing theorists or products, the *Journal* (Fig. 13) weighed in on the qualifications of the critic. Knowing that the upcoming Great Exhibition would also be a competition requiring juries of review, the *Journal* provided a definition of who such persons might be. "Those who constitute a committee for selecting a work," it began, "should not only know what they want, but should be acquainted with what has been done, and who have done it; they should have an acquaintance with the department of art on which they are to adjudicate, and should have time and inclination to pay the utmost attention to their judgment. Further than this," it went on to argue, "they should be conversant, to a considerable degree, with the comparative merits of the present professors of those arts which are intended to be employed. They should know what has been and what can be done in this country, and by whom. Unless they have this knowledge, they are not fitted to be the adjudicators." Like Hume, the *Journal* had an idealistic view of the perfect critic.[67]

Its last issue appeared in February 1852, shortly after the Great Exhibition closed. Believing their goals to have been met and mission accomplished, the *Journal*'s editors dissolved the publication and moved on to other endeavors. Among the Great Exhibition's strongest boosters prior to its opening, they were among its most vocal detractors once it was underway. Owen Jones called it "a fruitless struggle to produce art novelty without beauty—beauty without intelligence; all work without faith." In other essays, his colleagues concurred, as did critics writing for the *Times* and the *Morning Chronicle*, whom the *Journal* quoted. Acknowledging that such criticism was "sometimes more honest than was politic," the outspoken contributors to the *Journal* left their readers with the following advice: "True simple beauty . . . is modest and unobtrusive, but when we see her we are never wearied of gazing." Their promotion of an ideal, their belief in principles of good design, their confidence that the British could, in fact, change the status quo laid the groundwork for the design reform movement that followed.[68]

The Influence of the Design Reform Movement, 1850–1900

The literature of design criticism that evolved between 1850 and 1900 addressed many of the same broad issues and themes first contemplated in the eighteenth century, and raised by Merrifield, Wornum, and their colleagues in the 1850s. As critical writing about design reform became more prolific, it also became more specialized. Two movements that paralleled each other and occasionally overlapped were the Aesthetic movement and the Arts and Crafts movement. Both attracted enthusiastic, opinionated critics who aligned themselves with particular theories or approaches to architecture and interiors.

Design Criticism and the Aesthetic Movement

During the 1870s and 1880s, supporters of the Aesthetic movement, called "aesthetes," focused upon living well among beautiful things—art, *objets d'art*, antiques, exotic collectibles—as a way of improving consumers' quality of life.

They believed that the character of the environment sets a standard for the individual. Beautiful surroundings, they advised, can instill within each person a corresponding beauty of demeanor, thought, and deed. Aesthetes argued that Beauty was generally absent from Victorian life in part because it had been hampered by needless restrictions. Nineteenth-century conventions considered Beauty a means to an end whose purpose was primarily didactic. Aesthetes defined Beauty, conversely, as a relatively free spirit whose existence required no justification. Beauty, they said, was its own excuse for being.

The Aesthetic movement promoted a general attitude more than a specific style. By the 1890s, that attitude had become international, evident throughout Britain, Europe, and North America. It affected diverse aspects of culture, from literature, music and theater, to fashion and standards of feminine beauty. In addition, it transformed the appearance of gardens, architecture, and interiors as well as that of furnishings, decorative arts, and finishing materials. As aesthetes averted their gaze from the grim realities of the present, they looked back with nostalgia at the past (Figs. 14a and b). Seeking refuge in the gentility of the pre-industrial era, they created tasteful, comfortable surroundings as shelter from the exigencies of modern living. They fled from the noise and soot of the city to cottages and estates in suburb and countryside. Attracted by the promise of fresh air and sunshine, verdant lawns, flowering trees, and protected gardens, they searched for an atmosphere of what the English poet and critic Matthew Arnold termed "sweetness and light." They built quaint houses with doll's-house–like proportions in styles—the "Olde English" and the "Queen Anne"—loosely adapted from the Elizabethan Age or the eighteenth century. They filled their homes with artful clutter, striving for a blending of the antique, the exotic, and the hand-made, all of which contributed to their definition of Beauty. It was, in fact, the eclecticism of the Queen Anne that made it so appealing to aesthetes. The American critic, author, and editor Clarence Cook remarked upon "its freedom from pedantry, its willingness to admit into its scheme of ornamentation almost anything that is intrinsically pretty or graceful."[69]

As these examples suggest, exclusivity lay at the heart of Aestheticism. While eighteenth-century critics believed in the existence of a universal standard of good taste, aesthetes viewed their quest for Beauty as a way to set themselves apart from the rest of the world. Criticism associated with the Aesthetic movement was distinctive for its belief that the quest for Beauty was sufficient unto itself. Like Henry Home, aesthetes promoted the concept of *intrinsic beauty*, or "beauty intended solely for pleasure." But there, all parallels with his work—and that of other eighteenth-century philosophers of aesthetics—ended.[70]

Aesthetes did not necessarily link Beauty with Usefulness. And, unlike their eighteenth-century predecessors, they uncoupled taste from morality. They believed neither that contemplation of Beauty must have a didactic purpose, nor that it must improve the moral fiber of the beholder. They did, however, recommend that individuals aspire to seek out Beauty, and to consort with beautiful things as an antidote to the exigencies of life in an industrial age. "The experience of art was held to be not only equal in value to the experiences in life, but in

14a and b. *Fireside and Kitchen: Ancient and Modern*, cover and page from a trade catalogue for the Barstow Stove Co., Providence, 1886. (Courtesy Historic New England) This catalogue illustrates the eclecticism of the Aesthetic movement: the cover, with its spinning wheel and large fireplace, alludes to the Colonial era, while the interior contrasts the functionalism of the Barstow Furnace in the cellar with the dainty fussiness of the first-floor parlor. The young mother pouring tea might have stepped off the cover of Clarence Cook's *House Beautiful*. The child on the fur pelt plays with the heat register grill, while a guest perches on a Turkish-influenced divan.

some cases even capable of transcending them," writes one historian of the movement, Ian Small. "'To experience life in the manner of art' was the definition of spiritual success in terms of Aestheticism." And the term "experience" was essential. Aesthetes did not merely behold Beauty; they immersed themselves in it.[71]

Those aspiring to live beautifully among beautiful things turned to a variety of critics for advice and inspiration: from Matthew Arnold, they learned of "sweetness and light" and to avoid the "philistine." From English writer and philosopher Walter Pater, they learned to trust their impressions when contemplating beauty, to "see an object as it really is," and to believe in "art for art's sake." From Anglo-Irish author and playwright Oscar Wilde, they gained permission to uncouple morality from art: "To discern the beauty of a thing is more important in the development of the individual than a sense of right and wrong," Wilde proclaimed. The American expatriate painter James A. M. Whistler concurred, stating: "Art should be independent of all claptrap . . . [such] as devotion, pity, love, patriotism and the like." Others providing philosophical underpinnings for aestheticism included the feminist Violet Paget, who wrote under the pseudonym Vernon Lee, the American philosopher George Santayana, and Clarence Cook. From these and others, supporters of aestheticism learned how to create *The House Beautiful* (Plate 5), as Cook's influential advice manual of 1877 was called, and to live accordingly. The interior of such a house comprised "an eclectic mix of antique and modern, with furniture, decorative arts and textiles perhaps imported from the East or made in Britain" or America. These were used, advises the design historian David Dewing, "together with family heirlooms, souvenirs and personalia, selected and placed with an eye for colour and harmony to form a pleasing whole."[72]

With its emphasis upon Beauty and its appeal to consumers of means—upper-middle-class, upper-class, and aristocratic—the Aesthetic movement's critical writing reflected the eighteenth-century philosophy of aesthetics, which had appealed to the social elite. Given its goal of spreading the doctrine of "good design," the criticism written by supporters of the Arts and Crafts movement, by contrast, addressed the realities of life in an industrial age, and considered how each aspect must change in order to ameliorate the situation for all through improved design. If anything, the Aesthetic movement shunned the exigencies of modern living, while the Arts and Crafts movement viewed hardship as inspirational. It was democratic to the point of being socialistic.

Design Criticism and the Arts and Crafts Movement

From the 1850s to the 1920s, supporters of the Arts and Crafts movement, in contrast to the aesthetes, stressed the importance of Usefulness equally with that of Beauty, if not more so. The literature of design criticism associated with the Arts and Crafts movement had a longer-lasting impact than that of the Aesthetic movement. Critics associated with the Arts and Crafts movement addressed diverse subjects including: theories that might yield Usefulness and Beauty; design fundamentals; the history of craft and ornament; the art and mystery of specific media and craft techniques; design education for workers and consumers;

working and living conditions of laborers; the relationship between socio-economics and design reform; the potential of different political systems to improve everyday life; the production/consumption cycle and its influence; and the home—its design, construction, materials, contents, and siting. "Because of the decline of all the arts, especially the arts of use," wrote Arthur Clutton-Brock, critic for the London *Times*, in 1920, "which began at the end of the eighteenth century and has continued up to our own time, we are more interested in art than any people of the past, with the interest of a sick man in health." Critics hoped that design reform might be the remedy for the ailing applied arts.[73]

Supporters of the Arts and Crafts movement argued that the character of the environment molds that of the individual. Believing design to be a means to an end rather than an end in itself, design reformers set about creating surroundings that would benefit inhabitants (Plate 6). They argued that Beauty arose from something more than a stylish manipulation of facade or plan. They concluded that it was the manifestation of an integrity or inner strength. This may explain their preference for plans, shapes, and motifs that were simple and direct, for joinery that was exaggerated, and for ornamentation that was essentially structural. It may justify as well their selection of colors that were bright and strong, for flat, crisply delineated, naturalistic patterns, and for materials that were practical and capable of aging gracefully. In their eyes, Useful meant pragmatic or rational, and Beautiful was synonymous with truthful, natural, or ingenuous.

Writers outlining such altruistic motives included architect and designer Augustus W. N. Pugin (1812–52), Oxford professor John Ruskin (1819–1900), and William Morris. As a group, they acknowledged the vital interconnection of design and society. They placed high expectations upon the former, believing that design had the potential to strengthen society's moral fiber. They were convinced that attractive, efficient surroundings had the capacity to teach individuals how to lead better lives.

In books such as *Contrasts* (1836) and *The True Principles of Pointed or Christian Architecture* (1841), Pugin argued that architecture mirrors the morality of society. Accordingly, he urged English architects to abandon Greco-Roman models (such as those promoted by Sheraton) in favor of medieval examples, claiming that the former were pagan (and therefore inappropriate) while the latter suitably reflected mid-Victorian—and especially Christian—beliefs. In *The Seven Lamps of Architecture* (1849) and *The Stones of Venice* (1851–53), Ruskin concluded that architecture must reflect the spirit of each individual involved in its creation. He noted the presence of that spirit in medieval architecture and deplored its absence from contemporary examples. Consequently, he advised mid-Victorian architects to focus less upon the finished product than on the process by which it was made, and to cultivate among workers an atmosphere of "healthy and ennobling labor." Morris placed a high expectation upon every stage of the design process, from the conception of an idea to its completion. In essays such as "The Beauty of Life" (ca. 1880), he admonished consumers to take personal responsibility for the standards evident in their immediate surroundings. Together, Pugin, Ruskin, and Morris launched the campaign for design reform. Their writings publicized the cause and marshaled a generation of enthusiastic supporters, while establishing the philosophical tone of the movement as serious and earnest.[74]

The necessarily moralistic and weighty tone of arts and crafts critics contrasted with the *joie-de-vivre* of those writing on "The House Beautiful." Its concern for the relationship of design to the broadest aspects of culture and society may explain why the Arts and Crafts movement outlasted the Aesthetic movement by several decades, and why the tasks of its critics were especially comprehensive.

While making these distinctions, it is important to note, however, that the Aesthetic and the Arts and Crafts movements paralleled each other and frequently overlapped. Both had links to Pre-Raphaelitism, a mid-century art movement that celebrated the Middle Ages—its romance, chivalry, mysticism, and subject matter. English writers such as Walter Crane, an artist and illustrator, (1845–1915), and the designer and educator Lewis Foreman Day (1845–1910) served as theorists for both movements. Indeed, a joint publication, *Moot Points, Friendly Disputes upon Art and Industry between Walter Crane and Lewis F. Day* (Batsford, 1903) recalled Oscar Wilde's earlier essay *The Artist as Critic*, a duologue (published in *The Nineteenth Century* in July and September of 1890). The latter debated whether the artist could, in fact, be a critic, and which was the more creative activity—art-making or the writing of criticism. The former pondered whether or not industry could be artistic, and the impact of commercialism on the creative process.

John Ruskin addressed the issue of Beauty in a manner that appealed to supporters of both movements (though he himself took umbrage at the approach of some aesthetes, J. A. M Whistler specifically). In his book *Decoration and Furniture of Town Houses* (1881), the English aesthete/architect Robert W. Edis quoted Ruskin on the importance of Beauty for all individuals. "'Beautiful art can only be produced by people,' Ruskin states, 'who have beautiful things about them, and leisure to look at them; and unless you provide some elements of beauty for your workmen to be surrounded by, you will find that no elements of beauty can be invented by them.'" Such comments influenced design reformers to consider not just the appearance of consumers' homes but also the working environment for laborers.[75]

Most critics of the time championed the causes of Usefulness and Beauty regardless of their loyalty to one movement versus the other. Tastefully appointed interiors from the era might reflect, to some degree, the influence of both movements. Traits found in these interiors include color schemes of green and gold—spoofed by Gilbert and Sullivan as "greenery-yallery" in *Patience* (1881)—collections of blue-and-white Asian porcelains, antique furnishings from the 1690s through the 1820s, textiles ranging from hand-knotted rugs to brightly colored chintzes to pseudo-medieval tapestries, and minor works of original art, such as drawings, prints, and watercolors (Plate 7).[76]

One great distinction between critical writings of the eighteenth century and those of the nineteenth is that the latter addressed the applied arts more than the fine arts. Nineteenth-century critics found every aspect of the built environment fair game for their analysis. No aspect of an interior was too insignificant for their consideration. As critics associated with a cause—whether the Aesthetic movement or Arts and Crafts movement—they turned their attention from buildings and their contents to such issues as fashion, jewelry, millinery, coiffeur, children, their dress and belongings, and even food. Mary Philadelphia Merrifield, for example, was an adamant proponent of dress reform, especially the elimination of corsets. Culinary reform—as consumers became more aware of the benefits of eating right, exercising, and enjoying fresh air and sunshine—was a byproduct of the design reform movement, broadly defined (Figs. 15 and 16). "Health and aestheticism ran in tandem," writes design historian Charlotte Gere, "both promoting lightness and absence of [certain types of] clutter, even if for different reasons." Lifestyle publications of the era—including advice columns, articles on the household arts, "how-to" books, and shelter magazines—demonstrated that living well in tasteful surroundings required reform not only of the physical environment, but also of the physiological, intellectual, emotional, and even spiritual aspects of each consumer's daily life.[77]

Critics Promoting the Arts and Crafts Movement

Critics who promoted design reform varied in background, training, and approach. Many combined a firsthand knowledge of aesthetics, some practical experience in art, craft, or trade, and a firm grounding in history, theory, or methodology with the ability to write, and lecture, convincingly.

John Ruskin advocated such a blending of traits in critics, makers, and users. He blamed the separation of thought and action in the design process upon the division of labor in factories, arguing in favor of change. "We want one man to be always thinking, and another to be always working," he wrote in his seminal essay "The Nature of Gothic," which first appeared in *The Stones of Venice*, "and we call one a gentleman, and the other an operative; whereas the workman ought often to be thinking, and the thinker often to be working, and both should be gentlemen, in the best sense." In this era when divorce was on the rise and the number of single women living in urban areas burgeoned, his advice applied equally to many genteel craftswomen, whether they engaged in handicraft as an avocation or a primary means of supporting themselves.[78]

In light of recommendations such as Ruskin's, it is not surprising that most critics who succeeded him were practicing artists, architects, designers, or craftspeople. Architects—on both sides of the Atlantic—were particularly vocal. They understood that the quality of the various crafts and trades directly affected the quality of any building that they might design. Eager for the best possible results—that would reflect well upon themselves, their clients, and the craftspeople whom they employed—they threw themselves into a critique of the built environment.

This was increasingly important, as architecture grew from an avocation practiced by self-trained amateurs of the eighteenth century into a full-fledged profession, whose practitioners enrolled in specialized educational programs. The legitimization of architecture as a profession paralleled the founding of support organizations such as the Royal Institute of British Architects (1837) and the

15. Obverse and reverse of trade card, Physical Culture Restaurant, Boston. Advertising Ephemera Box 17, f. :873. (Courtesy Baker Library, Harvard Business School) The motto of this establishment, "It is your duty to be energetic and strong," is one that proponents of the moralistic Arts and Crafts movement would have supported.

16. Business card, Boston, ca. 1894. Advertising Ephemera Box 41. (Courtesy Baker Library, Harvard Business School) In an era of spindly furnishings and aesthetic clutter, clients of Prof. Foley may have appreciated his proviso that instruction in their homes would involve "no hard hitting."

American Institute of Architects (1857). Concurrent with this was the establishment of professional schools of architecture. Within a short time most offered courses on architectural history and theory, and a few included those on the history of ornament and the decorative arts. Such training enabled architects to become knowledgeable critics, who took advantage of the thriving architectural press to express their opinions.

Eloquent, educated practitioners may have comprised ideal critics, but other less conventionally qualified individuals got into the act as well, including skilled amateurs, well-heeled connoisseurs, educators, journalists, retailers, administrators, and social reformers. Among the most meaningful criticism was that written by craftspersons for craftspersons. The English émigré ceramist Charles Fergus Binns (1857–1934), who settled in upstate New York, wrote his book *The Potter's Craft* (1897) for the benefit of other "artist critics," sharing his expertise in ceramics along with his "enthusiasm, skill, discrimination and infinite patience" as a worker.[79]

In addition to documenting techniques that he had perfected during his career, Binns offered a critique of the craft to which he owed his livelihood, proposing numerous ways to improve it. He urged his colleagues to join him in demonstrating the "courage to destroy that which is below standard" and the "self-denial to resist the temptation to sell an unworthy product." Treating his readers as equals, Binns offered to them his "counsel as a fellow craftsman," hoping that they might be "stimulated, guided, helped and encouraged" by his insight and his example.[80]

"Artist critics" such as Binns clearly offered one another good advice. But amateurs questioned the critical ability of such practitioners, arguing that they lacked the objectivity that an outsider might provide. "The worker in any branch of the arts, as well as in anything that man's hand or brain can be occupied with," stated Edith (Mrs. Nelson) Dawson (1860–1928), author, metalsmith, and enamelist, "is surely not the best person to write or talk on that particular subject. As Benvenuto Cellini so truly put it, 'they of the craft are for the most part better at work than at talk.'" Both underestimated the verbal skills of many of their colleagues.[81]

While "artist critics" and amateurs argued the relative merits of practical experience, others dismissed such discussions as irrelevant: "The question to be asked about the critic," asserted Arthur Clutton-Brock, "is not whether he is an amateur as an artist, but whether he is an amateur as a critic." What these differing opinions suggest is that critics' qualifications were as much a topic of concern as were their criteria and recommendations. Yet all critics shared a desire to elevate tastes among makers and users of everyday items by setting and enforcing the highest conceptual, aesthetic, and technical standards.[82]

The literature of the history of craft, ornament, design, and the decorative arts burgeoned during the course of the nineteenth century, as scholars, professionals, collectors, and amateurs demanded illustrated reference books and instruction manuals. The literature grew as programs in art, architecture, and their respective histories were established to serve the needs of emerging professions. Critics also gained knowledge of historical examples through travel and study, often making notes and sketches on site (Fig. 17). Books such as Ruskin's

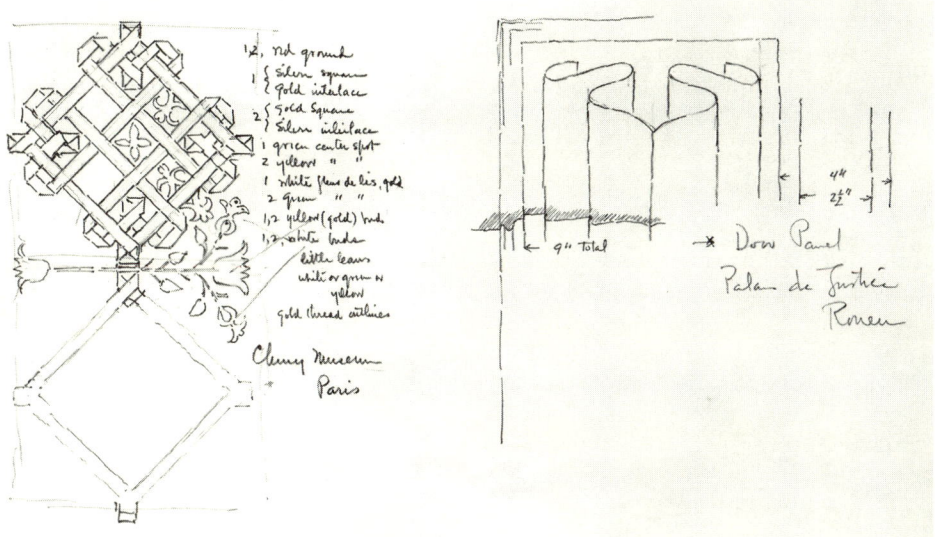

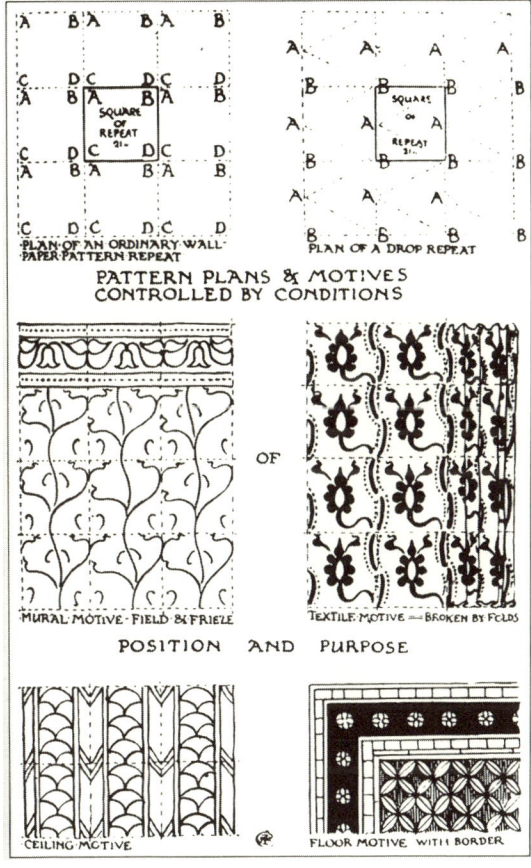

17. Page from sketchbook of Mary Ware Dennett, completed during European trip, ca. 1897. (Courtesy Schlesinger Library, Radcliffe Institute, Harvard University) This page shows designs from the Cluny Museum, Paris, and the Palais de Justice, Rouen. The diagram on the left appears to be an analysis of a textile with notes about color, motifs, and materials. The sketch on the right is of a door, carved with linenfold paneling.

18. Image from Walter Crane, *Bases of Design* (1892). (Courtesy University Libraries, Arizona State University) This array of "pattern plans and motifs" shows Crane's concern for the application of two-dimensional designs to varying surfaces. The pattern at center right is based upon the blossom and trailing stem motif of the late Middle Ages and Renaissance, often used by William Morris in his textile and wallpaper designs.

Stones of Venice (1853), and Crane's *Bases of Design* (1892) included these sorts of drawings. They presented arguments that a careful study of historical examples revealed timeless principles—such as balance, proportion, rhythm, and harmony—and, thus, were invaluable to present-day designers (Fig. 18). Supple-

19. Announcement, likely by Daniel Berkeley, for an upcoming meeting of Society of Arts and Crafts, Boston. (Courtesy SACB Archives) This announcement of a speech by Denman Ross was printed in black with a red Neo-Classical accent motif.

menting or generating such publications were museums of decorative or applied arts; these became more common during the latter half of the century, offering visitors—whether collectors, designers, or students—a chance to view antiquities directly. By the 1870s, for example, museums of applied art had opened in Paris, London, Edinburgh, Moscow, Berlin, Stuttgart, Munich, Weimar, Gotha, Limoges, and Lyons, to mention only British and European examples.[83]

Along with studying design history and potential models, critics became increasingly familiar with design theory. Some were aware of established or emerging theories only secondhand, but others were theorists in their own right. Americans in this group included Arthur Wesley Dow, who published the influencing book *Composition* (1899); Ernest Batchelder, author of *The Principles of Design* (1904); and Denman Ross, who wrote *A Theory of Pure Design* (1907, Fig. 19). Theories of particular interest to nineteenth-century critics included those dealing with utility or functionalism, aesthetics, those that addressed structural integrity, the nature of materials and tools used to shape them, culminating in treatises on the Machine and its potential, its drawbacks, and its limitations. Others pondered the issue of expression, or the way in which artifacts communicated from maker to user. As they had done with history, all sought to extract from these theories timeless principles appropriate to creating or evaluating design in an industrial age.[84]

In their quest to define "good design" and to determine how to achieve it, these critics addressed a variety of issues. Some of these had arisen in the eighteenth century; others still inform the work of their successors today. First, they considered the character of the product, along with that of its maker and its user. They believed that these were inextricably linked, so that "bad design" adversely affected anyone coming into contact with its impracticality or ugliness. Second, they debated the issue of design education and how it might improve both the public's expectations and the craftsperson's capabilities. Critics in Europe, Britain, and the United States argued in favor of teaching drawing and design fundamentals in the public schools. They deemed this method of training eye and hand to be essential to increasing sensitivity to one's surroundings. Third, critics questioned the criteria according to which products should be judged, and they discussed the credentials of the critic. As Wornum had suggested when he raised the issue of a key or standard, critics sought specific guidelines that might help them determine "good design." Fourth, they questioned what models, if any, could inspire originality in design. Most supported turning to history or to nature; yet, they knew that those models were insufficient to inspire truly innovative designs. Fifth, critics pondered the impact of the Machine upon form, ornament, construction, and finish. Some accepted machine-assisted labor as a helpmate whose time had come. Others feared that new technology would obliterate the human touch altogether and render handicraft obsolete. A few realized that this was not an either/or proposition. Lastly, critics addressed the issue of taste, debating what it was, who determined it, and what caused it to change.[85]

Critics' breadth of vision extended ultimately to everyone associated in any way with making or using objects common to daily living. This included individuals whose involvement in the design process—the whole cycle that began with a designer's inspiration, carried through to an artifact's completion, included utilization by consumers, and ultimately the critic's evaluation—fell somewhere between those of producer or consumer, namely manufacturers and merchants, or students and teachers. Many reformers viewed the educated consumer as a sort of lay critic whose purchases—or lack thereof—directly affected decisions made by designers and craftspeople. The whole production/consumption cycle, professional critics believed, was a finely tuned mechanism in which the opinions of all participants were equally important.[86]

Design criticism thus became inextricably linked with the design reform movement, inspiring new institutions such as museums of industrial arts, schools of practical design or mechanical arts, compulsory programs in art education, public exhibitions, and numerous publications devoted to design. Improving the character of work processes and products through education and debate—the goal of the design reform movement—demanded evaluation of both from an objective, theoretical perspective, which was the role of design criticism.

Critics in the Design Reform Movement

Critics spread the gospel of "good design" by word, deed, and example. They joined arts and crafts organizations, where they served on juries-of-review for local, national, or international exhibitions, or screened craftsmen's submissions to salesrooms. They presented public lectures, and taught in trade schools, art programs, and universities. Most important, they published books and articles. Many of these became standard texts in schools and libraries, and appeared on recommended reading lists published by other critics, educators, design magazines, or reform organizations.[87]

In disseminating their ideas, critics suited their tone to the sophistication of their audiences: some wrote books intended for practitioners on specialized subjects, such as the historical, theoretical, or practical aspects of a particular craft; aesthetics or art appreciation; educational reform or manual training. Others, following on the heels of Shanhagan, Merrifield, and Wornum, contributed evaluative essays to exhibition catalogues aimed at consumers. A select few wrote

CABINET CUSTOM WORK DEPARTMENT,
At Paine's Manufactory,
48 CANAL, and 141 FRIEND STS., BOSTON,

columns and reviews for local newspapers on a regular basis. Many published their work in magazines having a national or international readership, expanding their scope from coverage of the fine or performing arts to the applied arts. These ranged from general interest publications, to women's journals, to specialty magazines dedicated to the arts and crafts.

Altruistic motives drove these critics: one was to arm makers and users with a heightened power of discrimination in the face of what many viewed as having too many options. Critics blamed this condition on the over-abundance of goods available in the market place, advertised in the press, and sold in department stores and specialty shops run by overly zealous sales people (Fig. 20). Similarly, designers and producers functioned in a world where eclecticism, historicism, revivalism, and an ever-present quest for novelty provided no single clear direction. What is more, the ease of manufacturing complex forms encrusted with ornamentation, using rapid-production methods, and a plethora of materials complicated the process of decision-making for designers and manufacturers. If anything seemed possible—even desirable—who was to say which was the correct approach to take?

Another motivation among critics was to reform work processes to a point where they once again engaged, in Ernest Batchelder's words, the "mind, eye, hand, heart, and soul" of the maker, which, in turn, would result in products that would appeal to the same faculties of users. Restoring a Ruskinian "joyfulness in labor," they proposed, might result in production of things of beauty that would, indeed, be a joy forever.[88]

A third motivation was to acknowledge the effect that the built environment had upon the character of both maker and user, in the manner that Pugin, Ruskin, and Morris had suggested. Most critics viewed the character of buildings, interiors, and their contents as a reflection of the character of the nation that had produced them. They feared that living and working environments filled with the cheap, meretricious, and tawdry would produce persons bereft of moral fiber, and a nation poised on the proverbial "slippery slope."[89]

One manifestation of this was interiors, furnishings, textiles, and objects inscribed with mottoes, instructing inhabitants on how they should live (Fig. 21). The frieze above the fireplace in the parlor at William Morris's comfortable home, Red House (1859), warned: "Ars longa, vita brevis," suggesting that life lasts but a short time while art endures, or, as Morris interpreted it: "The life so short, the craft so long to learn." The "Battye Hanging," an embroidery completed by May Morris (1862–1938) shortly after her father's death in 1896, approximates a medieval tapestry, ornamented with maxims of the sort popularized in *Poor Richard's Almanac* and other sources. One phrase, "The tree remayneth

---

20. (Opposite) Advertisement for Paine's Furniture Manufactory, Canal and Friend Streets, Boston, undated. Showing exterior, interior of salesroom, and interior of Cabinet Custom Work Department. (Courtesy Historic New England) American manufacturers enjoyed flaunting their state-of-the-art facilities. Here, views of the exterior and factory floor flank one salesroom, which displays an eclectic array of furnishings, including those in the Renaissance Revival and "naturalistic" styles.

21. "A Dining Room Fireplace," from Robert W. Edis, *Decoration & Furniture of Town Houses* (London: Kegan & Paul, 1881). (Courtesy Boston Athenaeum) Images from Edis's book influenced aesthetes in Britain and abroad. The "hang" of pictures and porcelain-encrusted overmantle are typical features of the Aesthetic movement. But the motto on the frieze—"The friend thou hast and their adoption tried, grapple them to thy soul with hooks of steel. Welcome ever smiles and farewell goes out sighing"—is more in sympathy with the moralism of the Arts and Crafts movement.

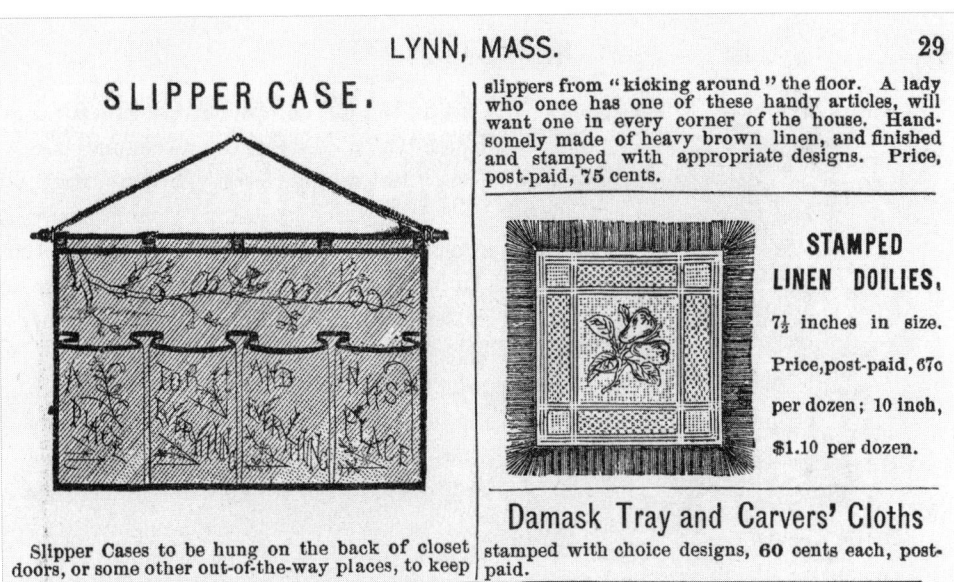

22. Slipper case, W. N. Swett & Co. trade catalogue, Boston. (Courtesy Baker Library, Harvard Business School) This reflects the importance of hobbies and handicraft in late-nineteenth-century Boston, coupled with an obsession with organization and controlling clutter.

but not ye handes ye planted itt," may be a subtle, bittersweet tribute from May to her father, a reference to the legacy of design reform that was to endure long after his death. In Boston, W. N. Swett & Co., a hobby and toy store, sold a kit with all necessary materials for stitching a hanging "slipper case" stamped with artistic lettering proclaiming: "A Place For Everything and Everything in its Place" (Fig. 22). These mottoes were but one manifestation of the moralism that characterized the Arts and Crafts movement. Just as critics pronounced products "good" or "bad," so too did those products suggest to their users that there was an appropriate way to live.[90]

Criticism in the Arts and Crafts Movement
Theory and Methodology

The sobriety with which critics approached their task in part explains the degree to which they relied upon design theory as a foundation for their judgments. They wanted to show that criticism was less intuitive than it was scientific. They hoped to prove that their pronouncements on "good design" were neither arbitrary nor subject to personal whim. Thus, they turned to theories—pragmatism, moralism, functionalism, naturalism, historicism, revivalism, and so on—for justification. They believed each theory to be founded upon strict principles, referring to these principles variously: as rules or laws, conventions or canons, precedents or standards, conditions, or even "recipes." Critics used such principles as check sheets for determining "good" or "bad design." Few critics ever produced

23. "Egg Trophy with Chicken Claw Tripod Base, and Putto with Wreath Finial, Silver." From Reed & Barton (Taunton, Mass.), *Scrapbook of Silver Designs, Sterling*, No. 1, ca. 1886–99. Reed & Barton Collection, vol. C-10. (Courtesy Baker Library, Harvard Business School) Objects such as this exemplify the overwrought excess promoted by major American manufacturers in the late nineteenth century. The chaste Colonial Revival designs executed by Boston's arts and crafts silversmiths, on the other hand, contrast markedly with the high-style, effusive works made by their colleagues in Taunton.

anything as explicit as a list, but a careful reading of their comments reveals what they deemed to be desirable or unwelcome traits.[91]

Critics' nomenclature differed, but all regarded principles as being fundamental, universal, and timeless. They insisted that principles must inform every opinion a critic rendered regarding a finished product. Similarly, they urged craftspeople to keep those guidelines in mind in the process of making, and likewise instructed consumers to employ those guidelines when selecting purchases for their homes. Morris's maxim regarding Usefulness and Beauty is the most famous of these.[92]

Critics believed that the application of theory founded upon principles might ensure a uniform standard of excellence among the crafts while eliminating the "artistic anarchy" caused by apostasy. According to William Morris, such artistic anarchy had led not to Usefulness and Beauty, but instead to the production of what he termed "masses of sordidness, filth, and squalor, embroidered with patches of pompous and utter hideousness." These were the sorts of items displayed at the Great Exhibition or sold by department stores and mail order catalogues that subsequently filled late-nineteenth-century homes (Fig. 23). They were the antithesis of those purveyed by Morris & Company, the eponymous business established in 1861 by Morris and several partners to offer Victorian consumers alternative household furnishings.[93]

A man cut from the same cloth as Morris, and equally incapable of mincing words, was the American Charles DeGarmo (1849–1934), who served as principal of the Grammar School at Illinois State Normal University from 1886 to 1890, and later wrote on the subject of industrial design. He represented the second generation of design reformers, who built upon the legacy of Pugin, Ruskin, and Morris. He described what ignorance of the principles of "good design" had wrought within the home in his book *Aesthetic Education* (1913). "Let us not delude ourselves by imagining that it is because these things are made by machinery that they are so hideous," he stated, referring to items in the average middle-class American interior. "The whole matter is purely psychological—an uneducated public to which commerce caters, either with greater ignorance or with a moral culpability, whose lightest punishment should be condemnation to live in houses furnished with the aesthetic corruptions they invent. The decoration on stoves, sewing-machines, rugs, wall-papers, bedsteads, table-coverings, etc. which these [firms] furnish are of the same order, varying only with the possibilities of distortion [Fig. 24a]. Why should one seem to be walking on a flamboyant flowerbed when one steps upon a rug, or behold a horticultural garden upon the walls? [Fig. 24b] Will the miseries of cold-storage eggs and poultry be alleviated by cooking them upon a stove that is a mass of senseless curlicues, projections, and depressions? Such articles should be consigned to the scrap-heap, or hidden in museums along with other instruments of torture. . . . Let us then," he said, concluding on a positive note, "make a bonfire of all meaningless, foolish, or atrocious decorations and replace them with what is fitting, chaste, and beautiful, and a part of the world will be there by transformed from a nightmare of ugliness into a dream of beauty." DeGarmo's choice of the word "hideous" parallels Morris's use of nearly the same word decades earlier.[94]

In this passage, DeGarmo speaks of "aesthetic corruptions" just as others of his day referred to "artistic anarchy." He makes clear that such "aesthetic corruption" leads to results that are "meaningless, foolish, and atrocious," and contrasts it with what is good: that which is "fitting, chaste, and beautiful." DeGarmo, who was an early functionalist, thus provides three guidelines for determining what is "good," whether he

24a. Trade card, Glenwood Ranges & Parlor Stoves (Boston, 1887). Advertising Ephemera Box 18, f. :527. (Courtesy Baker Library, Harvard Business School) "Made in All Desirable Styles," these stoves incorporate decorative motifs favored by aesthetes: the Japanese "pie" or rosette, fretwork, and spooled trellis work. The vine border sprouting Tudor roses is more arts and crafts in taste. The decorative nature of such utilitarian appliances bothered functionalist design reformers like Charles DeGarmo.

24b. Front parlor, William Sumner Appleton residence, 39 Beacon Street, Boston, ca. 1885. (Courtesy Historic New England) The carpet epitomizes the "flamboyant flowerbed" pattern that Charles DeGarmo detested. It is in keeping with other Rococo Revival features in the room, such as the étagère and chandeliers. Other furnishings date to the era of the Greco-Roman Revival, and may be contemporary with the house, built ca. 1818. Appleton was the founder of the Society for the Preservation of New England Antiquities.

IN QUEST OF USEFULNESS AND BEAUTY

25. Diagram showing "the proper relationship of [handles to] the lips and spouts [of pouring vessels]." From Frank Jackson, *Theory and Practice of Design* (1894). (Courtesy University Libraries, Arizona State University) The caption, typifying the advice of design reformers, continues: This ensures that "the weight of the vessel and its contents may not be against the action of the pouring."

addressed makers, users, or critics. In this manner, writers identified not only their theoretical framework, but also the criteria derived from it.

Criteria for Determining Usefulness and Beauty

Generally speaking, these sets of criteria addressed any or all of three categories: when critics discussed Beauty, they focused upon aesthetic issues, or in essence how something looked. In doing so, they examined the basic design elements—shape, color, and texture—and their component parts, namely line or form; hue, value, and intensity; pattern and surface finish. Equally, they considered the basic design principles—balance, scale, proportion, harmony, rhythm, unity, and the like. These building blocks of design had been present for millennia, dating back to a time when humans had first crafted objects and had had the luxury of evaluating them. They were still the fundamental traits analyzed by critics in the nineteenth century, despite the onset of an industrial age.[95]

Critics also addressed Usefulness, turning to technical issues, such as how something functioned, how it was constructed, or the materials from which it was made. Here they might consider, for example, the overall weight of a pitcher when full, the heft of its handle, ease in pouring facilitated by relationships among lip, spout, and handle, or its stability when set upon a flat surface (Fig. 25). Critics might ask if this form filled a real need, or question if it seemed a frivolous response to a short-lived want. They considered the appropriateness of the material to its task: did it dissipate or retain heat, was it porous, and easy to clean? Was the chosen material traditional to this craft, or imported from another, unrelated medium? Was the material integrated throughout the object, or merely superficial?[96]

Often, critics were less concerned with how something appeared or functioned than with its meaning or significance. Here, they turned to conceptual issues, such as where craftspersons got their ideas in the first place, what they tried to express in the finished product, or what that product said about the culture that it represented. In doing so, they considered all of the cultural influences affecting maker and product, and they evaluated the maker's degree of success in putting it all together.

In evaluating individual products—a chair, a vase, a textile—critics tended to focus more upon the technical, or conceptual aspects than upon the aesthetic. This was particularly true among design reformers intent upon changing the status quo and encouraging originality. They did not hesitate to say exactly how an individual might construct or finish an object—and finish was an almost obsessive preoccupation—but they avoided dictating how that object should look. What is more, most resisted promoting a specific style. This is one reason why manifestations of the American Arts and Crafts movement vary from region to region.[97]

Armed with a particular theory as justification (many of which today's scholars might label proto-modern or early-modern), critics dispensed advice of all sorts on how craftspeople might achieve "good design." Much of this was very general and conceptual. Most advocated infusing the handicrafts with originality; yet, to a person, they decried "novelty for novelty's sake." They questioned works that seemed fashionable or short-lived in appeal. They denounced elements in any creation that were, in their words, inconsistent or incongruous, startling to the mind, or confounding to the senses. They condemned any aspect of a work seeming false or ingenuous, or that might be construed, according to their criteria, as cunning or smug.[98]

Achieving "Good Design"
The Precedents of History and Nature

If nineteenth-century critics were anti-novelty, they were pro-precedent. They believed that precedent might help to stock designers' brains with suitable ideas, and argued that the foundation for "good design" in the present lay upon precedents established by the exemplary craftsmanship of the past. In this respect, they built upon the work of Chippendale, who began his *Director* with an overview of the Orders of ancient architecture, and Wornum, who tied the success of products displayed in 1851 to their interpretation of nine historic styles. In the mid-nineteenth century, Ruskin, Morris, and their followers began promoting preservation and restoration of historic buildings and studied them to ascertain what secrets they might reveal about materials or craft. On both sides of the Atlantic, architects collected building fragments for their offices, studios, and classrooms. Professionals, educators, and critics urged their constituents to study historical examples and to analyze how they looked, how they functioned, their materials and construction, and, most important, what they said about the culture, time, or person(s) that had produced them. "For your teachers, they must be Nature and History," William Morris had advocated simply in the 1880s. Decades later, his followers were still promoting the same models.[99]

Critics' promotion of the benefits of studying historical precedent paralleled the late-nineteenth-century flourishing of the antiques trade (Plate 8), which had grown out of the taste for antiquarianism that evolved a century earlier. In Britain and Europe, antiquarianism emerged in the eighteenth century with the discovery and excavation of the ancient cities of Pompeii and Herculaneum, the founding of groups of "cognoscenti" who studied ancient artifacts, the Grand Tour as a means of examining them firsthand, and the subsequent rise of Neo-Classicism. "The only way of knowing is to study, to look at good work, old work by preference," wrote Lewis F. Day, nearly a century after antiquarianism had peaked. "Measure yourself with the best, not with the common run of work," he advised. Like many critics, he believed that historic artifacts provided a standard for the present.[100]

In the United States, nostalgia for the Colonial past paralleled the first great world's fair held on American soil, the Centennial Exhibition (Philadelphia, 1876). Two decades later, when members of the Society of Arts and Crafts, Boston, held their second major Exhi-bition of the Arts and Crafts (1899), it consisted not just of new handcrafted works in all media, but also of a roomful of antiques gathered from private collections. Such pairings of old and new continued to be a feature of arts and crafts exhibitions, affording visitors a chance to drink in the "ripe flavor of antiquity." Such public events, along with the proliferation of antiques shops, the growth of museums of applied arts, and the expanding literature of the history of decorative arts, available in an increasing number of public libraries, enabled craftspeople, critics, and consumers alike to ponder the old as they critiqued the new (Fig. 26).[101]

In the same breath that Morris suggested History as a teacher, he upheld Nature as a muse, not only because she had inspired makers for millennia, but also because she was perceived as a constantly regenerating font of originality. In America, where critics decried the degree to which designers mimicked foreign—

26. "The New England of Years Ago; The New England of Today." Calendar for New England Mutual Life Insurance Co. of Boston, 1885. (Courtesy Historic New England) This illustration contrasts a bleak, snowy landscape and isolated figure from the Late Colonial–Early Federal era with a scene of a bustling downtown Boston, framed by multistory office blocks in the French Second Empire Style, and crowded with vehicles. The young woman's costume in the top image betrays traces of the Aesthetic movement through its slim silhouette and Kate Greenaway–type bonnet.

especially European—examples, nature, which abounded in a virgin, unsullied state, seemed the perfect inspiration for something fresh and new.

Note that the positive label "new" differed from the derogatory "novel." Critics advised their constituents to strive for the former while avoiding the latter. "Novelty and freshness are not always easily distinguished at first sight," wrote the British jewelry maker and silversmith Bernard Cuzner (1877–1956). "The first is usually cheap and alluring to shallow minds. The last is the exact opposite." The challenge for craftspersons, critics warned, was not to copy from history or nature directly, but instead to abstract from and to interpret each in a way that was personal and appropriate to the modern age.[102]

A case in point was William Morris himself, whose exuberant flat patterns—designed for textiles and wallpapers sold by Morris & Co.—interpret both historical and naturalistic sources in a stylized manner as recognizable as his signature. For example, the ogival-shaped blossom with trailing, "S"-curved stem, characteristic of so many of his wallpapers and fabrics, derives from similar motifs found in fifteenth-

27a. "Honeysuckle" hand-blocked chintz, Morris & Company, 1876. (Courtesy Special Collections, University Libraries, Arizona State University) The use of the honeysuckle—or ancient anthemion—reflects Morris's historicism, as do the trailing, "S" curved-stems. The strong outlines, juxtaposed warm and cool hues, and range of scales among the floral motifs are typical of Morris's flat patterns.

27b. Drawing of tunic from the Museo Civico, Turin, Plate 181, Figure 1. From Alexander Speltz, *The Styles of Ornament* (New York: Dover, reprint of 1904 edition,), p. 302. (Courtesy Dover Pictorial Archives) This tunic is made of "carmine-red velvet on a gold ground." Despite the large-scale repeat, the garment shows off the pattern to full advantage. The Asian lotus flower may have inspired the exotic blossom motif. The trailing "S"-curved stem creates a sinuous rhythm..

century Italian brocaded velvets (Figs. 27a and b). And the pairs of birds that give Morris's "Strawberry Thief" chintz (1896) its name mimic the confronting or addorsing animals that appear in early Middle Eastern and Byzantine textiles.

Morris was the rare exception, who practiced what he (and other critics) preached. Most designers encountered great difficulty adapting a historical or naturalistic model in a way that was suitable for a two- or three-dimensional application. Replicating the spirit of such models without resorting to line-for-line duplication was a challenge. Lewis Day said it best when he wrote: "Nature does not provide for us ornament ready made; were that so, our occupation would be gone. Nature is the starting point, but by no means the end of ornament. . . . Refreshing as it may be to refer to his studies, or to Nature herself, [the craftsperson] cannot *design* with either in front of him." The art of "good design," Morris, Day, and many others suggested, lay in transforming any model in a way that was both personal and appropriate to the end result. It required passing one's perceptions of reality through the filter of abstraction.[103]

The Methodology of Conventionalization

There was a name for this process, which was *conventionalization*. In advocating this, critics were proposing not a model, but rather a methodology for working.

Conventionalization was a means of translating what a designer saw into a two- or three-dimensional interpretation that was successful—conceptually, aesthetically, and technically (Fig. 28). At the least, to conventionalize was to make something less representational and more abstract to the point of becoming generic. At the most, to conventionalize made something specific to a culture, time, and place more universal, timeless, and enduring.

Evidently, this methodology was difficult for most workers to grasp, and thus the art of conventionalizing figured prominently in most nineteenth-century primers on "good design." Lewis Day wrote exhaustively on the subject throughout his career, explaining that it implied "modification," "repetition," and "omission of the superfluous." He likened conventionalization in design to "shorthand" in writing. "Conventionality in ornament," he stressed, "is the natural consequence of reticence or restraint, of doing not all that the artist could have done, but just what is called for by the occasion."[104]

Such advice cleared the way for early twentieth-century Modernism, which advocated the methodology of design by subtraction. Ultimately, this led to the theory espoused by architect Ludwig Mies van der Rohe that "less is more," resulting in an even more extreme mid-century

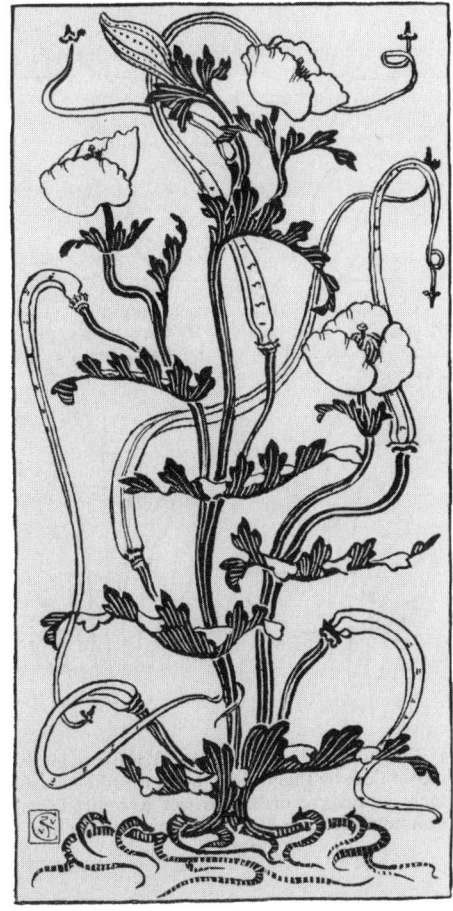

28. "Adaptation of the Horned Poppy in Design," from Walter Crane, *Line and Form* (1900). (Courtesy Boston Athenaeum) Modeled after eighteenth-century botanical illustrations, this poppy reflects the influence of Art Nouveau through its whiplash curves and attenuation. Crane has incorporated flatness, repetition, and strong outlines to conventionalize this flower, according to the tenets of the day.

Minimalism. But, in the nineteenth century, advocating reticence or restraint must have been perplexing to craftspeople living in what Mark Twain termed the "Gilded Age." Those promoting the conventional wisdom of the day espoused design by addition and the theory that more is more, or Thorstein Veblen's "conspicuous consumption" (Fig. 29). In doing so, they thwarted everything that design reformers hoped to promote.[105]

This growing appreciation among a select group of reformers for "reticence or restraint" in ornament paralleled a taste for empty space in compositions, or even furniture arrangements. They rejected conspicuous consumption, favoring what Thomas B. Macaulay termed "ostentatious simplicity." In Western design, this

29. Henry Davis Sleeper residence, 336 Beacon Street, Boston. (Courtesy Historic New England) A Veblenesque "conspicuous consumption" characterizes this vignette of a sitting room. Ancient Greece, eighteenth-century France and England, and Asia have all influenced this cluttered interior, where every surface has been draped, layered, or cushioned.

came about especially through contact with Asian products (Fig. 30). Commenting upon the incidence of empty space in Chinese and Japanese paintings, British author Laurence Binyon wrote: "Even the emptiness, the blankness of great solitudes were not shrunk from, but were sought out in their due time as spaces where the spirit could roam in freedom." Extrapolating that to the "House Beautiful," Clarence Cook argued: "There is hardly anything this time of ours enjoys less, less knows how to value than a clear space of blank wall. Yet, there are few things so pleasant to the eye." By the 1900s, the English architect Charles F. A. Voysey noted how the same quality could enhance an arts and crafts interior. "Try the effect of a well proportioned room," he wrote, "with white washed walls, plain carpet, and simple oak furniture, and nothing in it but necessary articles of use . . . , and you will then find reflections begin to dance in your brain." A room filled with eloquent empty space, Voysey suggested, might enable a beleaguered late-Victorian consumer to think clearly. Critics seemed to recognize that too much clutter compromised one's spiritual and intellectual engagement with one's possessions, one's surroundings, or the world beyond.[106]

Usefulness, Beauty, and Expression

While critics never passed up an opportunity to tell their audience exactly what constituted "good design," and to suggest strategies for achieving it, they were equally wary of offering what might be misconstrued as a foolproof formula.

30. Business card, showing influence of Aesthetic movement. Advertising Ephemera Box 7, f. :605. (Courtesy Baker Library, Harvard Business School) The ivory-and-brown platter featuring the "Warwick" pattern reflects a love for things both English and Asian. The platter's composition, with its broad, plain areas, illustrates the eloquent emptiness that Westerners were learning to appreciate as a result of contact with the Far East.

There were, as a result, few critics who did not include disclaimers alongside their advice. They wanted the creative process to seem logical and sound. But they knew that a certain intangible quality separated good work from great. They avoided offering "rigid rules as of cast iron" that would ensure "good design" every time. Above all, they cautioned that novices might benefit from such rules, while master craftspeople could, most likely, violate them with great success. When Lewis Day wrote: "It is only a master that can reconcile us to something which, until he did it, we did not think could properly be done," he conceded that rules did not apply equally to everyone—a conclusion similar to Roger Shanhagan's in regard to the Adam brothers.[107]

Ultimately, the goal of most critics in offering theories, guidelines, methodologies, and disclaimers was to encourage the manifestation of "good design" in all things, characterized by what they termed "expression." It was not enough for a work merely to be Useful and Beautiful. It was not sufficient for it just to satisfy high conceptual, aesthetic, and technical standards. In the end, what mattered most was what the work said—about the maker, its user, and its time. Expression, thus, was communication, and what any great work conveyed transcended its appearance, function, fabrication, or concept.

Critics often described expression of exemplary design with the same terms used to discuss the qualifications of outstanding craftspersons. Viewing the hand-made object as a mirror of its creator, critics vowed that the principles shaping the former dictated a way of life for the latter. "A noble vase, like nobility of character," wrote the New England photographer and ceramic artist E. E. Soderholtz, "carries its conviction even to those who cannot understand it. It identifies itself to the observer with the ideas and ideals of its owner, and bespeaks to him its owner's sense of the value and dignity of objects of purely ornamental use and being." Here, the "owner" might be the maker or the consumer. Expression, Soderholtz implies, was a complicated phenomenon, communicating from the inanimate to the living, from maker to user, and from maker or user to the observer.[108]

For some, the link between the two was transparent. Voysey, for example, wrote: "Simplicity, sincerity, directness, repose, and frankness are moral qualities as essential to good architecture as to good [persons]." Here he is not describing how his houses or their contents looked, so much as what they reflected about themselves and their inhabitants. Voysey was arguing that design—especially "good design"—was a language capable of making powerful statements about architects, craftspeople, their clients, and the culture that they represented.[109]

The Linguistic Model

Critics often used linguistic metaphors when they described "good design" and powerful "expression." They advised their constituents against producing objects "having nothing meaningful to say," or that made statements which might be denounced as elaborate, affected, pretentious, artificial, or strained (all their words). In addition, they often defined abstract concepts, which were difficult to comprehend, by means of a linguistic metaphor: For example: "Fit treatment," wrote Day, addressing a chief concern of design reformers, "is, in fact, the translation of natural or other form, not merely into the language of art, but into the dialect of some particular handicraft. We detect in it the homely accent of sincere workmanship. . . . It is because we find in it no turn of native or vernacular expression," he concluded, "that modern manufacture is so dull."[110]

As Day's comments indicate, critics who employed a linguistic model rejected high-toned rhetoric in favor of simple everyday speech. Similarly, when they advised their constituents to turn to history for inspiration, they recommended that they favor models that were domestic, unstudied, and vernacular: these included folk motifs based upon local flora and fauna, forms produced by self-trained anonymous craftspersons of the past, works executed in indigenous materials, and those using traditional construction techniques particular to a geographical region. The vernacular thus served as a model whether one sought inspiration from history, nature, or language.

This obsession with language extended to critics' judgment of their own work. They sought to render opinions that were constructive and comprehensible, but admitted that discrepancies in language jeopardized their statements' effectiveness: "Beware of catch words and phrases," warned Bernard Cuzner. "To say a thing is 'fit for purpose' is far better than the newer 'functional.' Each generation will use different terms, just as each generation sees things from a different point of view. What matters is that terms really mean something and that the views are broad and true." Evidently critics sought within their discipline the same refinement of expression that they hoped to instill within the arts and crafts. And their wish to be frank and direct in their pronouncements was as proto-Modern as was the aesthetic of simplicity that they promoted.[111]

The relative newness of their discipline compromised the effectiveness of critics espousing design reform during the second half of the nineteenth century. For they struggled to define their own discipline—determining its objectives, methods, and merits—even as they sought to apply it to others' professions or avocations. In the process, they came to realize that criticism faced some of the same challenges as did the handicrafts. "Criticism has value for mankind and not merely for artists or critics," explained Clutton-Brock. "But the value of it does not lie in the judgment of the critic anymore than the value of art lies in the judgment, taste, or preference of the artist. The value in both cases lies in the power of expression; and by that art and criticism are to be judged." Thus critics could not begin strengthening the "power of expression" of art, craft, or design without first enhancing the expressive capabilities of the criticism that they offered. Only then could they truly restore Usefulness and Beauty to architecture, interiors, and their contents.[112]

In the end, many reformers looked forward to a time when everyone involved in any way with the creative process might function as a critic in his or her own right. Yet, they recognized with some regret the irony of that situation: as the critical thinking of others improved, the need for an outside opinion diminished—and the job of the professional critic might become obsolete.

It is in this context that critics flourished in and around Boston in the period between the Civil War and the First World War. Believing their city to be the hub of American culture, they sought to ensure the highest standards possible in all aspects of the built environment. Receptive to the teachings of Ruskin and Morris in the 1850s and 1860s, these critics encouraged Bostonians to embrace design reform, first by exploring the Aesthetic movement, and then the Arts and Crafts movement, and founding their own Society of Arts and Crafts in 1897. Boston's historical connections to England facilitated acceptance of its theories of design reform. Boston's critics—functioning in a stimulating intellectual and artistic milieu—regarded themselves as arbiters of taste for the city, region, and indeed the entire nation, and found the quest for Usefulness and Beauty a cause worth championing.

31. Charles Eliot Norton. From *Harper's Magazine* (1881). (Courtesy Historic New England)

33. Denman Waldo Ross. (Courtesy Harvard University Archives)

32. Herbert Langford Warren. (Courtesy Harvard University Archives)

34. Charles Howard Walker. (Courtesy Harvard University Archives)

CHAPTER ONE

Boston in the Gilded Age

Embracing Design Criticism and the Reform Movement

I have found that all ugly things are made by those who strive to make something beautiful, and that all beautiful things are made by those who strive to make something useful.

Oscar Wilde, "The Value of Art in Modern Life" (1880s)

On June 28, 1897, twenty-one individuals signed the articles of incorporation founding the Society of Arts and Crafts in Boston (SACB). This small group represented a microcosm of Boston's cultural elite, bringing together architects and craftspeople, educators and connoisseurs, all of whom pledged to "develop and encourage higher artistic standards in the handicrafts." Their coming together to found an organization was the culmination of decades of interest in design reform evident throughout the city. For this reason, the formation of the SACB was both a summation and a starting point. The organization made visible efforts that had been ongoing, but unfocused, in diverse segments of the community since the 1860s.[1]

These twenty-one people had ties to major components of Boston's thriving economy, embracing education and manufacturing, publishing, the arts, architecture, and the building trades. Their diversity of background, vision, and breadth of experience represented everything that was best about Boston in the 1890s, and had made it a leader among cities nationwide. Boston was an ideal environment in which a campaign for design reform might take hold. Its traditional dedication to Emersonian "plain living and high thinking," its progressivism and commitment to social reform, its energetic "Boston Women" and "institution men," its intellectual and spiritual idealism, combined with its belief in its ability to reshape itself in a new image, provided a culture in which design reform could thrive.[2]

The Founders: A Group Portrait

A group portrait of SACB founders makes clear why the American campaign for design reform took hold so firmly in that city under their aegis. The nucleus of the group was Charles Eliot Norton (1827–1908), Professor of Fine Arts at

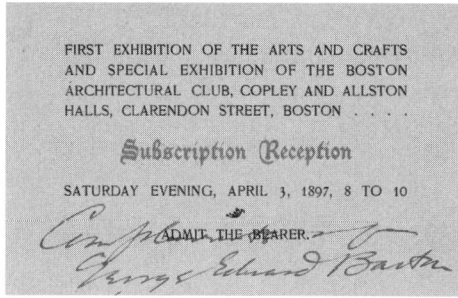

35a. George Edward Barton. (Courtesy Historic New England) This image bears the label, "August 17–18, 1907. We go a-fishing at Tyson [Vermont]. George Edward Barton. I studied architecture in his office. K.A.P."

35b. Invitation to the First Exhibition of the Arts and Crafts, signed by George Edward Barton, 1897. (Boston Public Library/Department of Fine Arts. Courtesy of the Trustees)

36. Alexander Wadsworth Longfellow, Jr. (Courtesy Harvard University Archives)

Harvard, personal friend of John Ruskin (he was executor of Ruskin's estate), social do-gooder, author, and critic; he was considered a "senator of Boston culture" (Fig. 31). Joining Norton were other Harvard faculty: Herbert Langford Warren (1857–1917), dean of Harvard's School of Architecture (Fig. 32), and Denman Waldo Ross (1853–1935), who lectured and wrote on design theory, principles, and practice (Fig. 33). Another architect-educator—who taught at the Massachusetts Institute of Technology, Harvard, and other institutions in the city—was Charles Howard Walker (1857–1936), whose reputation as a formidable critic earned him the label "watchdog of Boston taste" (Fig. 34).[3]

Along with Warren and Walker were four other architects: Robert D. Andrews (1857–1928), George E. Barton (d. ca. 1920), Alexander Wadsworth (Waddy) Longfellow, Jr. (1854–1934), and George R. Shaw (1848–1937) (Figs. 35a and b, 36). Barton combined interests in architecture and utopian societies with social reform. Shaw (Figs. 37a and b) was an elder statesman among Boston architects with a reputation for tasteful interiors filled with "art produce" purveyed by local merchants. Andrews, Longfellow, and Warren were all products of Henry Hobson Richardson's (1838–1886) Brookline studio, and as such brought with them a shared appreciation for historicism, fine interior finishing, and artistic

37a. George R. Shaw. (Courtesy Harvard University Archives) Shaw later took up leatherwork, which he exhibited under the Society's auspices. He also authored a series of books on conifers.

37b. Illustration of a fireplace designed by George R. and R. G. Shaw. Plate XLIV, from *Our Homes and How To Heat & Ventilate Them*, Smith & Anthony Stove Co., 1886. (Courtesy Historic New England) George Russell Shaw practiced briefly with his relative Robert Gould Shaw before going into a partnership with Henry Hunnewell. This fireplace design with spindled overmantle reflects the Aesthetic movement. Notable is the Japanesque carved panel above the mantle with its asymmetrical composition of twigs, leaves, and birds.

38. Advertisement for Hugh Cairns. From *Catalogue of the Boston Architectural Club Exhibition 1906*, p. 143. (Courtesy Boston Athenaeum) This fierce griffin bracket is medieval in feeling, though the rosette, arabesque, and leaf border are more Greco-Roman in origin. Fenway Studios was a prime location for many of Boston's most prolific craftspeople.

collaboration. They embodied the values that the SACB promoted, especially its goal of bringing together fine and applied artists.[4]

Their artist colleagues included three sculptors: Scottish-trained Hugh Cairns (1862–1949), Welsh-trained John Evans (1847–1923), and the German John (Johannes) Kirchmayer (1860–1930). Cairns (Fig. 38) carved architectural embellishments in stone. Due to the influence of Henry Hobson Richardson, these were often in the Romanesque style. John Evans & Co. provided carvings and castings in diverse materials and produced architectural scale models. Evans (Fig. 39) and Cairns had collaborated on sculpture for the porch of Richardson's Trinity Church. Evans's firm was influential well beyond Boston, having produced carvings for some of the 1893 World's Fair buildings in Chicago. Kirchmayer (Fig. 40) emigrated from Oberammergau, Germany, to Cambridge. He was renown for his "American Gothic" style carvings in wood and stone, produced for architects including Richard Morris Hunt, and Stanford White. He specialized in ecclesiastical work, featured in churches across the nation.[5]

39. John A. Evans. Photograph by Elmer Chickering. John Evans Collection. (Boston Public Library/Department of Fine Arts. Courtesy of the Trustees)

40. Johannes Kirchmayer. Ralph Adams Cram Personal Papers. (Boston Public Library/Department of Fine Arts. Courtesy of the Trustees) This photograph bears the inscription: "A Happy New Year. J. Kirchmayer."

41. Advertisement for Goodnow & Jenks. From *Exhibition of The Society of Arts and Crafts, Copley Hall, Boston, February 5–26, 1907*. (Courtesy SACB Archives) Barton P. Jenks was a principal in this firm, and known for designs for silver hollowware.

42. Design for a tea set in solid silver, by Barton P. Jenks. From "Things of Beauty. Masterpieces of Handwork Put on Exhibition," *Boston Herald*, April 5, 1897. (Courtesy SACB Archives) This sketch reflects the continuing popularity of the Rococo Revival style, with its characteristic "C" curves, shells, and foliage. Jenks also exhibited work in the Colonial Revival style.

Those associated with the applied arts were George P. Kendrick (1850–1919), architectural draftsman and designer of pottery, metalwork, and graphics; Barton P. Jenks (1871–1941), designer for the eponymous metalworking concern Goodnow & Jenks (Figs. 41, 42); J. Templeman Coolidge, Jr. (1856–1945), artist, art patron, antiquarian, furniture designer, and Colonial Revival enthusiast (Fig. 43); Julia de

43. John Templeman Coolidge, Jr. (Courtesy Harvard University Archives)

44. Cover of book by Julia de Wolf Addison. (Courtesy Boston Athenaeum) The cover is olive-green with gold embossing. The background of the roundels varies from red to blue-gray. The central figure may be Tubal Cain (who appears on the official seal of the Society of Arts and Crafts.)

45. Sarah Wyman Whitman. (Schlesinger Library, Radcliffe Institute, Harvard University) Whitman was the founder of the Lily Glass Works (184 Boylston Street, Boston) and a graphic designer for commercial publishers including Houghton Mifflin.

46. Daniel Berkeley Updike. From Daniel Berkeley Bianchi, *The Merrymount Press, A Centenary Keepsake* (Bridgewater, Conn., 1993). Updike's style varied from the Morrisian to the Colonial Revival. His office décor reflected his penchant for Colonial artifacts.

Wolf Addison (1866–1952), author, artist, craftswoman, composer, and collector, (Fig. 44); and Sarah Wyman Whitman (1842–1904), painter, craftsperson, patron, and socialite (Fig. 45). Like a majority of the SACB founders, these craft workers were multi-talented.[6]

Addison, Kendrick, and Whitman were engaged in the book arts, in which

DESIGN CRITICISM AND THE REFORM MOVEMENT   61

Boston was a leader—designing for the local publisher Houghton Mifflin & Co., among others. Joining them was Daniel Berkeley Updike (1860–1941), who worked for Houghton Mifflin before founding his own Merrymount Press in 1893 in Cambridge (Fig. 46), and the distinguished graphic designer, author, and editor Henry Lewis Johnson (1867–1937, Fig. 47). These individuals' work was distinct and eclectic, reflecting the influences of the Gothic Revival, Aesthetic movement, Arts and Crafts movement (epitomized by Morris's Kelmscott Press), and Art Nouveau. Yet recurring motifs in their work—the rosette and Tudor rose, the abstract blossom atop an elongated stem, the windblown poppy—reflected their close collaboration.[7]

Those remaining provided a connection with the business community and lent financial support to the new organization. Morris Gray (1856–1931, Fig. 48), Arthur Astor Carey (1857–1923, Fig. 49), and Samuel Dennis Warren II (1852–1910, Fig. 50) were Associate members of the Society. They were patrons—versus practitioners—of the arts and crafts. Each had graduated from Harvard in the 1870s, and all played important roles in the Museum of Fine Arts.

Sam Warren's support was especially important. Head of the family paper firm begun by his father, Samuel Dennis Warren, Sr.—a firm that supplied high-quality paper to local publishers of books and periodicals—Sam was an attorney and partner of Louis Brandeis. A trustee of Massachusetts General Hospital and president of the board of trustees of the Museum of Fine Arts, he was privy to the innermost circles of Boston society. A visionary and idealist,

47. Henry Lewis Johnson. From *The Graphic Arts*, ca. 1916. Johnson was an editor of *The Printing Art, An Illustrated Monthly Magazine of the Art of Printing and of the Allied Arts* and a driving force behind the First Exhibition of the Arts & Crafts.

48. Morris Gray. (Harvard University Archives) Attorney and private trustee, Gray graduated from Harvard in 1877. He was an active supporter of the Museum of Fine Arts, serving as president of its Board of Trustees from 1914 to 1924.

49. Arthur Astor Carey. (Harvard University Archives) Carey helped in the founding of the SACB and later served as its second president. A social do-gooder who suffered from fragile health, he devoted his life to volunteering with the Boy Scouts of America and writing books on nervous disorders and rest cures.

50. Samuel Dennis Warren II. (Harvard University Archives)

Warren was known for hard work and perfectionism, values consistent with the Arts and Crafts ethos. His wife, Mabel Bayard Warren (1860/61–1924), later joined the SACB, as did his sister-in-law, Gretchen Osgood (Mrs. Fiske) Warren (1871–1961). Such endorsement by a highly visible social elite—many SACB founders and members represented Boston's "first families"—added to the new organization's legitimacy and connections.[8]

Like Sam Warren, other SACB founders had supported the Museum of Fine Arts for years (Figs. 51a and b). Norton served as an adviser, while Ross, Longfellow, Carey, Gray, and Coolidge were also on the board of trustees. Gray acted both as treasurer and as president. Walker was "instructor in charge" of the museum's School of Drawing and Painting in the 1880s and 1890s. Whitman was the first female member of the Council of the Museum School. Langford Warren, Whitman, and Coolidge were Museum School administrators at various times. Some of the founders showed their art, architectural designs, or handicrafts at museum-sponsored exhibitions. Sam Warren would be instrumental in the campaign to construct a new museum building on Huntington Avenue—a focus for the city's cultural institutions—in 1901. He would commission three future SACB members to design the structure, specifically architect Guy Lowell (1870–1927, Fig. 52), working in collaboration with R. Clipston Sturgis (1860–1951, Fig. 53) and Edmund M. Wheelwright

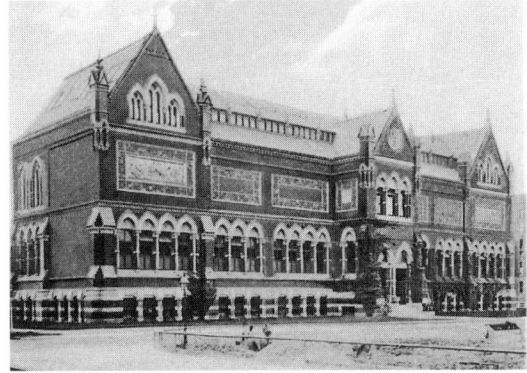

51a. Postcard, Museum of Fine Arts. Published by the Photograph Co., New York City; printed in Germany. (Author's collection) Members of the Society of Arts and Crafts supported the Museum of Fine Arts in myriad ways, by serving on its boards, teaching and taking classes, donating to its collections, and even designing its new headquarters when it moved from Copley Square (seen here) to Huntington Avenue in the early twentieth century.

51b. Postcard, View of Copley Square and Museum of Fine Arts. Published by Reichner Brothers, Germany. (Author's collection) This view shows the proximity of the original museum building (1876, Sturgis and Brigham) to other monuments in Copley Square, such as Trinity Church (1877) and New Old South Church (1875).

52. Guy Lowell. (Courtesy Harvard University Archives) Lowell was a product of the École des Beaux Arts in Paris.

53. Richard Clipston Sturgis. (Courtesy Harvard University Archives) A graduate of Harvard (1881), Sturgis studied architecture in London before beginning his practice in Boston. He served on the SACB Council, eventually becoming president in 1917.

54. Edmund March Wheelwright. (Courtesy Harvard University Archives) Wheelwright worked for the Boston firm Peabody & Stearns from 1870 to 1917. He was a member of the SACB from 1899 until 1911.

55a. Wharves near the Custom House Tower, Boston. (Author's collection.) The date of this hand-colored photograph may be ca. 1913–15, taken shortly after the tower's completion by Peabody & Stearns. The image is testimony to the importance of the harbor, wharves, and shipping to Boston's economy, and to the expansion of its population through immigration.

55b. Immigration quarters, Cunard Line Pier, East Boston, 1910. Photograph by the Boston and Albany Railroad Collection. (Courtesy Historic New England). This empty waiting room lacks the flocks of immigrants that swelled Boston's ranks, comprising 72 percent of the city's population by 1900.

(1854–1912, Fig. 54). Many of these individuals supported the museum financially. Among the collections housed there were those given by Sam and other members of the Warren family, along with Whitman and Ross. The museum was a magnet for the city's cultural elite who supported it in a spirit of volunteerism and philanthropy.[9]

As a group, these twenty-one founders were well traveled and well educated. Carey was born in Rome, Langford Warren in Manchester, England. Addison lived in England until adolescence. Whitman had studied painting in France in the atelier of Thomas Couture in the 1870s, while Coolidge had done the same under the direction of Carolus Duran in the late '70s–early '80s. Longfellow and Shaw had attended the École des Beaux Arts in Paris. Many founders studied abroad, undertook a "Grand Tour," and continued to make trips to Britain, Europe, and the Near or Far East on a regular basis. Most had earned at least one degree from Harvard or MIT; Addison had spent one semester at the latter studying English.[10]

These founders of a new organization were, not surprisingly, already active members of other clubs, societies, and associations. Many in fact belonged to the same ones: their network was concentrated and overlapping. Some of these clubs were strictly social, while others were professional in nature. A few—in what Elizabeth Dwight Cabot termed this "most moral of all cities"—were devoted to social activism and reform. The latter addressed swelling ranks of immigrant laborers—by 1900, immigrants comprised 72 percent of Boston's population—whom Boston's industries employed, and their diverse needs: safe working conditions, fair pay, affordable housing, education, and acculturation (Fig. 55a and b).[11]

To some degree, the SACB addressed all of these: it stimulated social interaction among like-minded individuals, whether patron of the arts and crafts or craftsworker—drawing together representatives of the architectural profession, the arts, crafts, and trades. It embraced the ideals of social reform, which some members (and a few founders) addressed with fervor. It was an appropriate addition to the list of already extant organizations, reflecting Boston's well-established reputation as a city of joiners.[21]

What Boston's club culture only begins to suggest is the closely knit, though unofficial network that operated within the city. These philanthropists, educators, architects, artists, and craftspeople crossed one another's paths in a variety of contexts. They drew together into homogeneous groups as immigration diversified Boston's greater population. Many knew writers, such as Henry Adams, George Santayana, Henry and William James, reading their books, attending their lectures, espousing their theories, socializing with them informally. Those who shared an appreciation for good books, music, and art were likely to be connected in some way with local painters—such as "The 10" (a group also founded in 1897), and members of the so-called Boston School—and to know the connoisseur, critic and writer Bernard Berenson. Few painters who did not already practice the applied arts or writers joined the SACB. They were thus one step removed from that organization's inner circle; yet their influence within it was still evident.[13]

One important figure in Boston's literary-artistic circle—who epitomized the multivalent abilities and widespread social connections of this network—was F. Holland Day (b. 1864). Aesthete and collector, photographer and publisher (Copeland & Day), he belonged to the Society of Arts and Crafts briefly in the 1890s. Despite his short tenure as a member, he influenced the organization as only a "Renaissance man" of his aptitudes might: he published SACB members' works in books and periodicals, such as *The Hobby Horse* and *The Knight Errant*; he collaborated with architect-members Ralph Adams Cram and Bertram G. Goodhue on publications and hired Louis C. Newhall to design his summer retreat in Maine; he rubbed elbows with SACB members at meetings of the Club of Odd Volumes and the Visionists; he pioneered the "New School" of American pictorial photography, which influenced many SACB members working in that

56. Paper sample, "Warren's Cameo Plate Coated Book." From *The Plimpton Press Year Book. An Exhibit of Versatility* (1911). (Courtesy Baker Library, Harvard Business School) This sample shows an embossed cameo surrounded by a border of lettering. A swag below bears the initials "SDW," for Samuel Dennis Warren II, whose papers were among those used by Boston's publishers.

medium. Day thus contributed to the same quest for Usefulness and Beauty in the city that inspired his friends to found the SACB.[14]

That group reflected Boston's intelligentsia at a time when the city was regarded as the "intellectual and cultural hub" of the United States. Most founders held at least one college degree. A few were educators, several lectured in the city and across the nation, and many were internationally known in their fields. Most wrote books and articles, while several were editors. As writers, many of these individuals functioned as historians, theorists, or critics. Their interests were often specific to a profession, craft, or trade; but many reflected widespread interests and a catholicity of taste that characterized Boston's past and its worldview.[15]

Those in the book arts designed their own or others' works. Some—S. W. Whitman is the best example—designed trade bindings for major publishing houses, while others produced one-of-a-kind custom bindings. They made their colleagues' ideas visible and tangible by creating new type faces, manufacturing suitable papers (Fig. 56), selecting binding materials, or developing graphic images that complemented the ideas presented in their colleagues' books.[16]

Closely tied to the city's publishing industry, this group thus contributed to the life of the mind by forging new ideas or debating those promoted by distinguished authors, including Ralph Waldo Emerson, Henry David Thoreau, and Walt Whitman. Surely, these founders of the SACB took to heart Emerson's thoughts on art, the topic of a lecture in which he argued: "Beauty must come back to the useful arts, and the distinction between the fine and the useful arts be forgotten. If history were truly told, if life were nobly spent, it would be no longer easy or possible to distinguish the one from the other. In nature, all is useful, all is beautiful. It is therefore beautiful because it is alive, moving, reproductive; it is therefore useful because it is symmetrical and fair. Beauty will not come at the call of a legislature," he warned, "nor will it repeat in England and America its history in Greece. It will come, as always, unannounced, and spring up between the feet of brave and earnest men." That description applied equally to the individuals founding this new organization, who dedicated it to promoting Usefulness and Beauty.[17]

A shared interest in the past is another theme uniting this group and linking it

57. Governor Benning Wentworth House, New Castle, N.H., 1916 or earlier. Photograph by Halliday Historic Photograph Co. (Courtesy Historic New England)

to the city as a whole. Several of the founders were historians of architecture, art, craft, or ornament, who lectured and published on their subject. Among their works were: Julia de W. Addison, *Arts and Crafts in the Middle Ages* (1908), J. Templeman Coolidge, Jr., "A Few Considerations of Japanese Wood-carving" (1903), Henry Lewis Johnson, *Historic Design in Printing* (1923), Charles Eliot Norton, *Historical Studies of Church Building in the Middle Ages, Venice, Siena, Florence* (1880), Daniel Berkeley Updike, *Printing Types, Their History, Forms and Uses* (1922), Charles Howard Walker, "Classical Architecture" (1923), and Herbert Langford Warren, *The Foundations of Classical Architecture* (1919). As a group, these works explored the art and mystery of traditional craft categories, analyzed historical building types, styles, and time periods, and addressed the importance of art, craft, and architecture to society as a whole. Having written such works gave these individuals, and the group as a whole, credibility as critics of the arts and crafts.[18]

Several of the founder-architects worked in a historicist or revivalist mode, turning to foreign as well as domestic models. Many employed the Colonial Revival style or the more innovative Shingle style. Longfellow and Andrews embraced preservation and restoration as part of their professional work. Longfellow was an early member of the Society for the Preservation of New England Antiquities (SPNEA). This linked Boston architects to British colleagues (such as William Morris) who were also design reformers and founders of organizations such as the Society for the Protection of Ancient Buildings. In the same manner, Boston's architects revived and reinterpreted historical styles even as they engaged in building conservation, preservation, and restoration.

Though not an architect, Coolidge—a close acquaintance of the founder of the SPNEA, William Sumner Appleton—was restoring the fifty-room Governor Benning Wentworth Mansion (Fig. 57) in New Castle (near Little Harbor), New Hampshire, which he had purchased in 1886. Others members of this coastal summer community were Carey, Longfellow, and two local architects, R. C. Sturgis

58. Postcard, View of Commonwealth Avenue. Published by the Leighton & Valentine Co., New York. (Author's collection) The main thoroughfare of the Back Bay was traversed by streetcars and flanked by handsome townhouses, hotels, and clubs.

and E. M. Wheelwright. (The latter would become members of the SACB and would collaborate on the new Museum of Fine Arts building with Guy Lowell.) Coolidge functioned as the nucleus of this "Little Harbor" group.[19]

Many of these founders were also collectors, who incorporated antiques into their own homes and workplaces or those of their clients. Others were serious connoisseurs who sought rarities worldwide—sometimes seeking advice of Bernard Berenson—with the intention of leaving (or selling) their collections to the Museum of Fine Arts or other of the city's institutions. Most were interested in handicraft and in ensuring that traditional techniques and material usage would not become obsolete in the face of industrialization. They viewed their historicist interests as an antidote to Boston's post–Civil War expansion and manufacturing boom. They regarded historicism and revivalism as reflections of the city's pre-industrial heritage, and its link with fine hand-craftsmanship during the Colonial era.

With this as background, it is easy to see why these individuals coalesced as a group, and why their new organization had relevancy to the life of the city. Nearly forty years after they had formed the SACB, a member recalled the founders, saying: "Their outlook was wide-visioned, scholastic, versed in traditional backgrounds, with full consciousness that something was being lost by the substitution of the quicker methods of the machine for the craft of the hand." Connected to Boston's social elite; linked with education and the intelligentsia, the architectural profession, the crafts and trades, publishing, and manufacturing; tied to the MFA and the arts community; related to but different from other existing organizations; aware of historical precedent but wishing to advance the industrial age in part by improving the lives of newly arrived, immigrant laborers, the SACB and its founders reflected interests within the city at large.[20]

The Roots of Design Reform in Gilded Age Boston

During the last quarter of the nineteenth century, Boston was a city of innovation and reform, which had successfully undertaken a variety of precedent-setting ventures: the filling of the Back Bay, the development of the park system, and the rapid growth of commuter suburbs linked by streetcars and subways had altered the topography of the city on a grand scale (Fig. 58). The growth of public schools, universities, hospitals, the city's police force, and new social institutions supported the education and welfare of Boston's residents. The founding of the Museum of Fine Arts (incorporated 1870) and the Symphony Orchestra (1881) were among the city's cultural achievements. Even as the landscape and urban fabric changed, residents became increasingly aware of a need for preservation of Colonial-era monuments, such as the Paul Revere House (1676) and the Craigie-Longfellow House (1759). It was in that dynamic climate—where a progressive and reformist spirit challenged the status quo—that the Society of Arts and Crafts arose.[21]

59. Interior view, Boston Foreign Fair. From *Scrapbook of [Gen.] Charles B. Norton (Secretary of the Boston Foreign Fair), June 19th, 1884,* p. 60. (Boston Public Library/Department of Rare Books. Courtesy of the Trustees) The caption for this newspaper illustration reads: "Massachusetts. The opening of the Foreign Exhibition of Arts, Manufactures and Products at Boston, Sept. 3d."

Between 1860 and 1890, Bostonians became familiar with the English Arts and Crafts movement by direct exposure. They viewed fine and applied arts at exhibitions, both at home and abroad. As early as 1857, a show of British paintings in Boston featured the work of the Pre-Raphaelite Brotherhood. Their images of russet-haired maidens and armor-clad knights on horseback recalled the culture of the late Middle Ages, stressing idealized romance and chivalry. In 1883, the American Exhibition of Products, Arts and Manufactures of Foreign Nations, otherwise known as the Boston Foreign Fair (Fig. 59), included stained glass windows handcrafted by Morris & Co. that reflected Morris's early collaboration with the Pre-Raphaelites, as well as six rooms of wall papers, printed and woven textiles, and tapestries. A reviewer for the *Transcript* admired the display for its "well-bred unobtrusiveness, depth and richness, and repose." In 1895, a display of posters in Brookline highlighted the work of British and European graphic artists—such as the Swiss Eugène Grasset and the Moravian Alphonse Mucha—and the impact of the Aesthetic movement, the Arts and Crafts movement, and Art Nouveau.[22]

Bostonians also viewed "art produce" at world's fairs, in which local architects, artisans, and manufacturers participated. These included fairs held at home and abroad in London (1851), Vienna (1873), Philadelphia (1876), and Chicago (1893). The impact of Boston's products upon visitors to these events was probably less enduring than was that of works by foreign architects, designers, and manufacturers upon Bostonians. Through these events, they became exposed to Asian goods, European and British "art manufactures," to use a term coined by Sir Henry Cole, architectural styles such as the Olde English and the Queen Anne, and traditional Japanese building methods—all of which later influenced their work. Business cards, trade cards, and trade catalogues for local companies—promoting every-

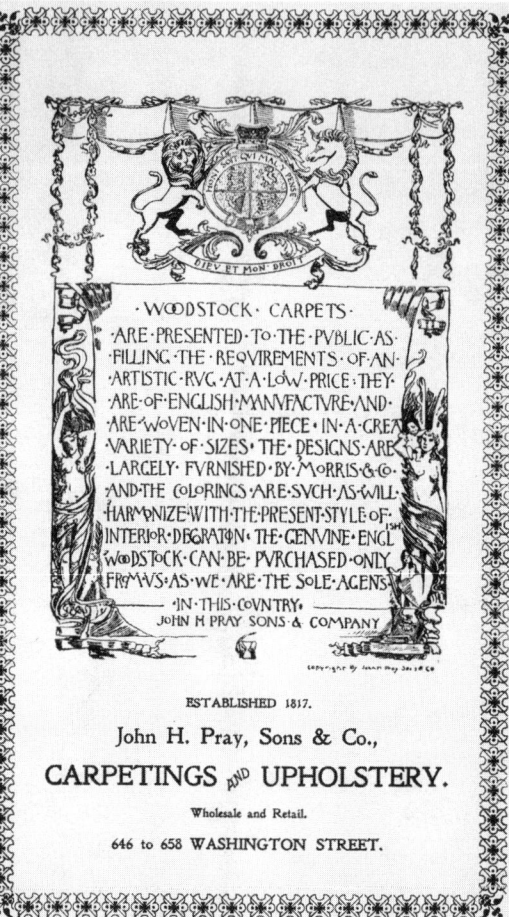

60. Advertisement for Bigelow Kennard & Co., Inc., ca. 1916. From *Current Architecture. Joint Exhibition, Architecture, Landscape Architecture, and the Allied Arts* (Boston Architectural Club, 1916). (Courtesy Boston Athenaeum) This shows the store's Washington street facade, and the border contains designs for lighting fixtures. Of particular interest is the sconce in the Arts and Crafts style in the upper right, for which Harvard University, Baker Library, Historical Collections holds the original working drawings.

61. Advertisement for J. F. Bumstead & Co., ca. 1890. From *Boston Architectural Club Catalogue of the First Annual Exhibition, May 1890* (Boston: R. Clipston Sturgis, 1890). (Courtesy Boston Athenaeum) This scene of craftspeople block-printing wallpaper stresses handcraftsmanship. The wallpaper designs are less innovative than they are traditional, featuring a large-scale ogival motif, typical of Renaissance, Baroque, and nineteenth-century revival designs.

62. Advertisement for John H. Pray, Sons & Co. (Courtesy Historic New England) The copy emphasizes Pray's exclusive rights to sell Morris & Co.'s "Woodstock" carpets in the United States. The presence of the British royal crest demonstrates Boston's characteristic Anglophilia.

thing from food stuffs and pharmaceuticals, to "Artistic" pianos and "Morris" chairs—featured "Aesthetic," japanesque, and "Arts and Crafts" motifs, color schemes, and fonts, demonstrating the pervasiveness of these new influences.[23]

At home, Bostonians patronized specialty shops that imported foreign goods, including Bigelow, Kennard & Co. (Fig. 60), Josiah E. Bumstead & Co. (Fig. 61), John H. Pray Sons & Co. (Fig. 62), and Joel Goldthwait & Co. (Figs. 63a and b). Many of these were located within blocks of each other on Washington Street,

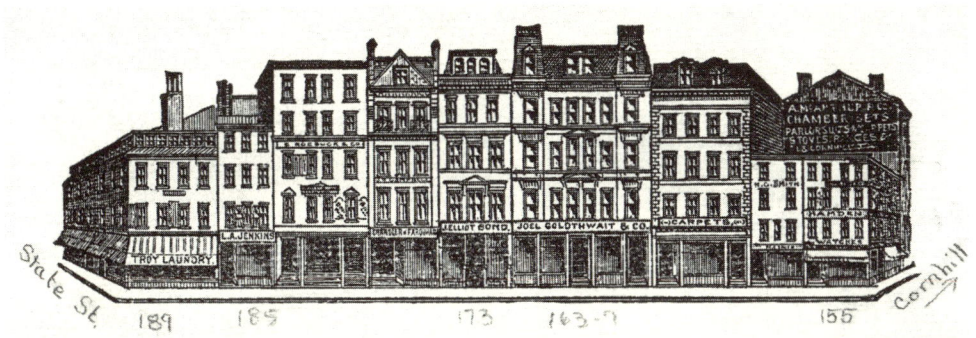

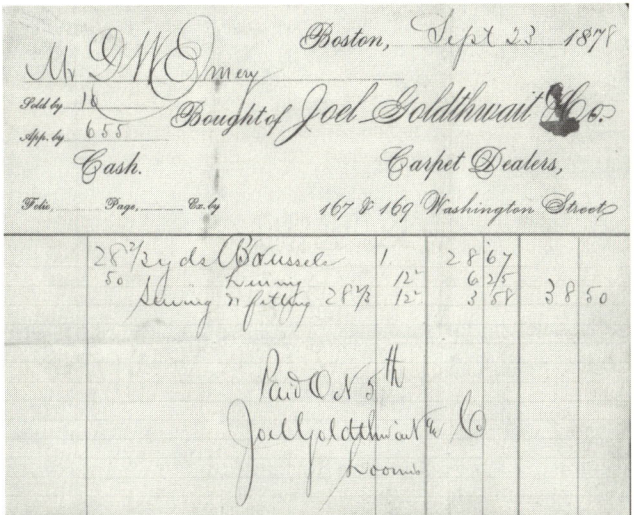

63a. View of 155–189 Washington Street, between State Street and Cornhill, showing the facade of Joel Goldthwait & Co., ca. 1880. Boston File. (Boston Public Library/Department of Fine Arts. Courtesy of the Trustees) The mansard-roofed Goldthwait building is the tallest structure on the block. Dr. Joel E. Goldthwait was an Associate member of the SACB between 1912 and 1927.

63b. Bill head, Joel Goldthwait & Co., 1878. (Courtesy Historic New England) This is one of several invoices for Mr. Willard Emery, who evidently patronized Goldthwait & Co. over a period of years.

64. Postcard, Shopping District, Washington Street, Boston. (Author's collection) This card—sent from Boston on August 28, 1919—says, "Had a fine time here."

situated at the crossroads of the city's mercantile district and deemed by a local guidebook the "most crowded thorofare in the World" (Fig. 64). Pray sold "Artistic" and expensive "English Woodstock carpets" designed by Morris & Co., while Goldthwait advertised "a full line of William Morris Carpets and Hammersmith rugs for which [it was] the sole [Boston] agent." Richard Briggs (located in the "Old Corner Store" building, also on Washington Street) specialized in glass and ceramics (Figs. 65a and b), while the Household Art Tile Company (later, the Household Art Company) offered wares by some of England's most celebrated art potteries, such as Minton, Worcester, Wedgwood, and Doulton. Frank B. Norris was the sole source for gilded wooden bowls imported from Russia. Norris, Household Art, Briggs, and Bumstead's all figured prominently in Clarence Cook's *The House Beautiful*, as sources for unusual and, therefore, desirable furnishings and accessories. W. H. Davis & Co.—located on rival

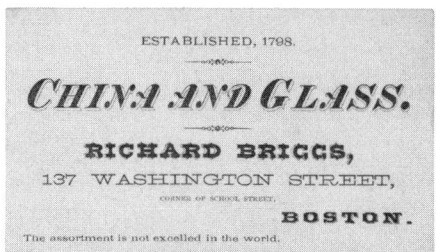

65a. View of 4–60 School Street, illustrating exterior of Richard Briggs, 1870s. Boston File. (Boston Public Library/Department of Fine Arts. Courtesy of the Trustees) Richard Briggs occupied a four-story building at the corner of Washington Street and School Street. The company began at that location in 1798 and remained there until 1902. It then moved to 116 Boylston Street and later to Newbury Street All three streets were important to the retail trade in Boston.

65b. Business card for Richard Briggs, Inc., 137 Washington Street, Boston. Advertising Ephemera Box 42 (Courtesy Baker Library, Harvard Business School) This card advertises the wares for which the company was renowned specifically glassware and ceramics.

Boylston Street—were agents for London's Liberty & Co., which catered to both Aesthetic and Arts and Crafts tastes.[24]

Bunkio Matsuki, an Asian art dealer married to Martha Meacom of Salem, Massachusetts, sold Japanese imports, first at Salem's Almy, Bigelow & Washburn, and then at his White Rabbit Store at 380 Boylston Street in Boston. A charming trade catalogue—printed in color on silk—explains: "All our Japanese goods are genuine used by natives themselves, therefore are more interesting and artistic than those made for American markets." Matsuki's inventory included Japanese antiques and prints, artists' materials, and "ornaments for summer resorts" (Plate 9). Such Asian imports were extraordinarily popular in Boston during the second half of the nineteenth century, in part because they had become more readily available following the reopening of Japan to foreign trade in the 1850s. In addition, Asian products had never really lost favor due to Boston's flourishing China Trade, ca. 1790–1860. Cook, among others, promoted the excellence of Asian *objets d'art* in *The House Beautiful*. Edward S. Morse augmented consumers' knowledge of Japanese architecture, interiors, and furnishings in his important book *Japanese Homes and their Surroundings* (1886). *Japonisme* and *japonaiserie* permeated the arts and crafts after the 1860s due, in part, to the influence of Japanese prints. They continued to do so into the early twentieth century, thanks to artist-educator Arthur Wesley Dow, director of the Ipswich summer school, who argued in favor of Japanese principles in his influential book *Composition* (1899).[25]

This taste for Asian art was an expression not only of Boston's earlier China Trade but also of the contemporary Aesthetic movement, which flourished during the last quarter of the century (Figs. 66, 67). Many aesthetes in Britain and America collected Asian—especially Japanese—art, or assimilated its traits into their work. Boston was a center for aestheticism for many of the same reasons that it championed design reform and the arts and crafts. Historian Martin Green goes so far as to argue that Boston, "the city of culture[, was] the world

66. Interior, 348 Beacon Street, Boston, 1886 (?), Allen & Kenway, Architects. Photography by Soule Art Co. (Courtesy Historic New England) This interior incorporates Asian elements—most evident is the wall covering with a flying crane motif—comfortably overstuffed seat furniture, a ceramic-encrusted overmantle in the Aesthetic taste, a tiger pelt, musical instruments, and assorted artistic bric-a-brac. Despite the clutter, the Asian wall covering dominates.

67. Bedroom, 200 Beacon Street, Boston, 1885. (Courtesy Historic New England) This charming vignette combines chintz fabrics, wicker furniture, peacock feathers, art prints, and odd bits of pottery and glass with the sort of palm leaf fan sold by stores such as Bunkio Matsuki. The wallpaper may be an example purveyed by Morris & Co. The diffused lighting enhances the Aesthetic mood.

capital" of the movement. Bostonians combined their "old-fashioned idealism," their obsession with politics and history, and their renewed interest in the built environment with wanderlust and a penchant for collecting and creating public institutions such as the Museum of Fine Arts and elegant private houses that reflected the movement's infatuation with Beauty. They did so intelligently, having read—or heard—the ideas of the movement's key theorists, or having been exposed to aesthetic art, architecture, and products through their travels.[26]

Purveyors of "art produce" surely enhanced Boston's tasteful interiors, as they whetted consumers' appetites for similar, locally produced examples. In recognizing the merits of combining aestheticism and merchandising, these late-nineteenth-century entrepreneurs proved that they had overcome the "merchant's traditional distrust of artistic pursuits" that had characterized Boston retailers during earlier decades.[27]

In addition to purchasing new merchandise—local or imported—from Boston's shopkeepers, consumers also incorporated antiques into their homes. A strong impetus to do so was the wave of nostalgia brought about by the Centennial Exhibition (Philadelphia, 1876). Following on its heels, Clarence Cook, among others, advised them of the unusual beauty that antiques offered relative to their functionality and low cost. He recognized that gently used furnishings from the seventeenth, eighteenth, and early nineteenth centuries added warmth to interiors, noting "old furniture is 'the fashion' in some parts of our country. In Boston a polite internecine warfare has for some time raged between rival searchers after 'old pieces' . . . ." What is more, he realized that buying items secondhand

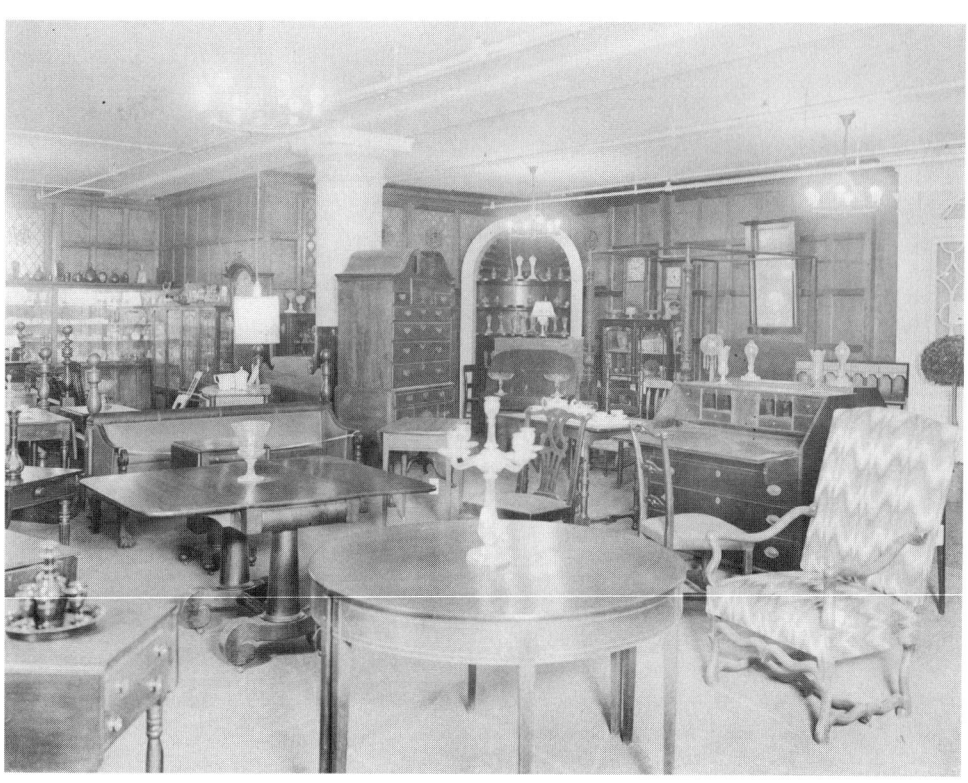

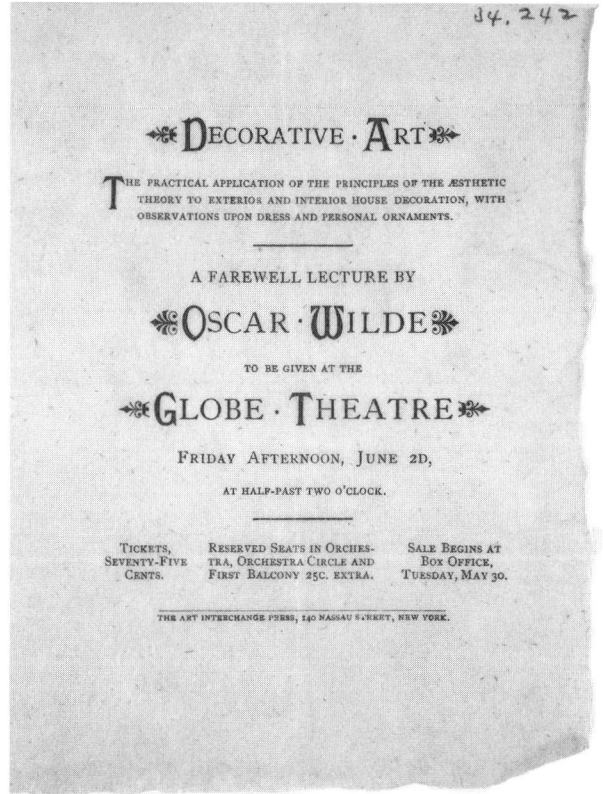

68. Corner of Antique Room, Jordan Marsh Co. (?), Boston, 1926. (Courtesy Historic New England) The importance of antiques to Boston interior décor is evident at this department store, probably Jordan Marsh Co. located at Washington and Avon Streets. Here English influences predominate, including examples in the Queen Anne, Chippendale, Hepplewhite, and pillar-and-scroll styles.

69. Announcement of "Farewell Lecture on Decorative Art" by Oscar Wilde, ca. 1882–83. (Boston Public Library/Department of Rare Books. Courtesy of the Trustees) The original announcement is on tea-stained tissue paper, printed in scarlet red ink. The second page features a portrait sketch of Wilde.

appealed to Bostonians' characteristic "retail penury" (Cleveland Amory's term), and to their instinct to "use it up, wear it out, and make it do." (Fig. 68)[28]

In addition to viewing or purchasing reformist products, Bostonians immersed themselves in the theories that had shaped them. They read books and essays by Carlyle, Ruskin, Morris, and their followers and, in doing so, acknowledged the seminal contributions of these British theorists to the design reform effort, hoping to build upon their ideas in America.

At the same time, their late-nineteenth-century enthusiasm for all things English reflected the city and region's historical link to that country during the Colonial era. Bostonians' Anglophilia stemmed from a desire to strengthen ties with the mother country, ties that seemed threatened as Western expansion turned America's collective attention increasingly toward the Pacific and the Far East. In this regard, Boston was like the Roman god Janus, looking back to its English roots even as Boston's industrialists and entrepreneurs extended their influence into the Midwest and West.[29]

Bostonians attended lectures by prominent British design reformers making American speaking tours, including Christopher Dresser (1876), Oscar Wilde (1882–83), Walter Crane (1891), Charles Robert Ashbee (1896), and T. J. Cobden-Sanderson (1907). Dr. Dresser (1834–1904), a botanist trained in design by Owen Jones and the author of *The Principles of Decorative Design* (1873), promoted functionalism and conventionalization in ornament with a view that was truly protomodern. Wilde lectured on such varied topics as "The Renaissance in English Art," "Art and the Handicraftsman" (in which he quoted Morris's famous maxim on Usefulness and Beauty almost exactly), "House Decoration," and "The House Beautiful . . . ," while astounding frontier America with his foppish dress (Fig. 69). In doing so, he appealed to aesthetes in the crowd, who shared Emerson's belief that "if eyes were made for seeing, then beauty is its own excuse for being."[30]

Crane (1845–1915)—an illustrator, designer, author, and avowed Socialist—spoke on political and social reform, and made important contacts with Boston's publishers, creating numerous illustrations for their books. He mentored Bernard Berenson, who in turn guided many of Boston's key art patrons. In 1891, Crane spoke at a meeting of the Boston Society of Architects, discussing "his artistic career, and his aims and methods, especially in decorative work," and exhibited several water-colors and "designs for wall-papers, glass work and mosaic," on loan from a show of his work then taking place at the Museum of Fine Arts.[31]

The architect and designer Ashbee (1863–1942) visited New York and Philadelphia in 1896, but not Boston. He pondered the relationship of the handicrafts and the Machine. His trips in later years generally used Boston as a point of arrival or departure as he forged strong friendships with residents and members of the SACB. A lawyer-turned-bookbinder and printer, Thomas James Cobden-Sanderson (1840–1922), came to Boston for an extensive lecture series in December 1907, showing books created by the Doves Press and Doves Bindery. He was one of 1,300 speakers to address the Twentieth Century Club, a group of progressive men and women, during its first two decades. These visitors lent a face and a voice to otherwise abstract theories of "good design," making the

70. Edward Henry Clement. From *Men of Massachusetts* (Boston: Boston Press Club, 1903). (Courtesy Historic New England) Clement was editor-in-chief of the *Boston Transcript* from 1881 to 1906, and from 1901 to 1920 wrote "The Listener" column, which often commented upon SACB exhibitions.

campaign for design reform more personal through direct connections with Britain.[32]

To supplement what they had learned from these visitors, Bostonians perused an ever-increasing number of periodicals, published at home or abroad, and devoted to design reform. Among these were the *Woman's Home Companion* (1873), the *Magazine of Art* (London, 1878), the *Ladies' Home Journal* (1883), the *House Beautiful* (1896), the *Studio* (London, 1893) and its American edition, the *International Studio* (New York, 1897), and *Brush and Pencil* (1897). They also read a local publication, *The New England Magazine* (1831), on related issues concerning social and economic reform.[33]

The SACB benefited from international connections from its inception; such links were, in fact, partially responsible for its success. Many of its founders and members had first become aware of the design reform movement while traveling abroad, and their experiences ranged from studying architecture in France at the École des Beaux Arts, or in Italy courtesy of MIT's Rotch Traveling Scholarship, to working in the studios of such preeminent English artists and craftspeople as Ashbee and Cobden-Sanderson, jeweler-enamelist Frederick Partridge, who designed occasionally for Liberty & Co., and sculptor, silversmith, and enamelist Alexander Fisher. And many of the SACB's most prominent members were British immigrants who settled in the Boston area. These included architect H. Langford Warren and his younger brother, painter Harold Broadfield Warren, silversmith Arthur J. Stone, and potters Hugh Cornwall Robertson and Charles Fergus Binns. Additionally, Europeans played important roles within the organization, including Cairns, Evans, Kirchmayer, Finnish silversmith Karl F. Leinonen, and printer Carl H. Heintzemann.[34]

Influenced by such reformist products, propaganda, and people, Bostonians took to heart Morris's oft-quoted maxim: "Have nothing in your houses that you do not know to be useful or believe to be beautiful." When they formed the SACB, they would incorporate some of those words into their official seal as a reflection of their commitment to Morris's ideals.[35]

Making it easier for consumers to assimilate that advice were critics who wrote for local newspapers. Among these were Sylvester Baxter (1850–1927), Frederick William Coburn (b. 1870), Grant Hyde Code (1896–1974), Joseph Edgar Chamberlin (1851–1935), Edward H. Clement (1843–1920, Fig. 70), William Howe Downes (1854–1941), Anthony J. Philpott (ca. 1861–1952), and physician W. Henry Winslow (1840–1917). "The mediating function of the critic, between the creative artist on the one hand and the public on the other, is hard to define," wrote Downes, art critic for the *Transcript*, "but his continued existence, in Boston as in other centers of production, offers at least *prima facie* evidence that he exerts a stimulating influence in both directions." These individuals functioned variously as art critics, historians, journalists, and editors. Contributing feature articles, reviews, and opinion-

71. Advertisement for The Heliotype Printing Co., Tremont Street, Boston. From *Art Gems from The American Architect*, 1886. (Courtesy Historic New England) "J.E.H." was the graphic designer.

editorial pieces to the Boston *Transcript*, *Globe*, and *Herald*, they wrote on city cultural affairs, discussing matters affecting architecture, arts, and crafts, and publicized Boston efforts to champion design reform. They also published books and articles in national magazines, such as *The Nation*, the *Atlantic Monthly*, the *New York Times Literary Supplement*, *Handicraft* and *The International Studio*. Some of these were general interest publications, while others were specific to the arts and crafts.³⁶

Boston's Architects and the Quest for Usefulness and Beauty

Members of Boston's architectural community were particularly receptive to the concept of design reform. They believed that it might benefit their profession, which was flourishing in the aftermath of the fire of 1872 and the rebuilding effort that followed. They reconstructed the heart of the city's mercantile and commercial district, developed Copley Square into a religious and cultural hub, and constructed a new residential district on reclaimed land in the Back Bay. In doing so, many incorporated innovations reflecting the Arts and Crafts movement or the English Domestic Revival.

Such Boston-based periodicals as *American Architect and Building News* (1876–1908), *Architectural Review* (1891–1910), and *Architectural Sketchbook* (1873–1876) chronicled their efforts. These periodicals were a small but important part of Boston's publishing industry. The city was the center for a new heliotype process (Fig. 71), enabling these publications to incorporate crisp illustrations—photography, lithography, and engraving—to great advantage. Much of the impact of

72a. Postcard, Old State House. Published by The Leighton & Valentine Co., New York. (Author's collection)
72b. Postcard, Old South Meeting House. Published by the Detroit Publishing Co. (Author's collection)

Boston's architectural community in the late nineteenth century depended upon the presence of its strong architectural press, which flourished until the First World War and made the work of Boston's architects influential internationally.[37]

Photographers enhanced these publications with images of both historic structures and new ones. Especially gifted were those—including A. H. Folsom, William T. Clark, the Soule Art Company, Mary Northend, Elmer Chickering, Baldwin Coolidge, Lois L. Howe—who specialized in interior photography. Their sensitive and detailed images, generally photographed without occupants, illustrate architectural features enhanced by furnishings, textiles, lighting, *objets d'art*, and personalia. These images record key features of historic structures or the stylish idiosyncrasies of Boston's artistic homes and work places. Architectural photography was a small subcategory of the larger field of both professional and amateur photography, which had become increasingly prevalent in the aftermath of the Civil War.

That publishing was Boston's largest industry enabled architects not only to promote their current work, but also to express an editorial opinion or to present research on design history, theory, or methodology. It also offered them the opportunity to design book covers, illustrations, brochures, and advertisements. So great was the demand for beautiful books and periodicals in Boston that architects, and even landscape architects, worked as designers alongside artists trained specifically in the graphic and fine arts.[38]

The desire among Boston's architects to implement a program of design reform reflected in part their awareness of international trends, their concern for

73a. Postcard, Tremont Street and Park Street Church. Published by Reichner Bros., Boston, Munich, Leipzig. (Author's collection) The postmark on this card is January 17, 1909. The serene profile of Park Street Church belies the presence of the bustling subway system that lies beneath the intersection.

73b. Construction of the Tremont Street Subway, Park and Tremont Streets, 1896. (Courtesy Historic New England) The steel framing for the Park Street Station contrasts markedly with the traditional brick-and-wood construction of historic Park Street Church.

74. 135 Marlborough Street, Boston, 1880 (?), Cabot & Chandler, architects. (Courtesy Historic New England) This handsome brick residence shows the influence of the English Domestic Revival. The slender, linear chimney, pseudo-half-timbering in the gable, rosettes, and sunflower ornamentation were equally popular with aesthetes who patronized English architect Richard Norman Shaw.

innovation, and their appreciation for the city's artistic heritage. Since the Colonial period, Boston had been a leader in art, artisanry, and craftsmanship. Accordingly, at the turn of the century, architects demonstrated awareness of its legacy by producing measured drawings of extant Colonial architecture and preserving monuments from the seventeenth and eighteenth centuries (Figs. 72a and b), including the Fairbanks House in Dedham (1636), the Old South Meeting House (1729–30), and the Boston State-house (1795–98). They did so even as they erected new structures, demonstrating the latest advances in materials and technology (Figs. 73a and b).[39]

Consumers shared these architects' sensitivity to the past. They enjoyed living in proximity to historical monuments and in established neighborhoods. In newer sections of the city, such as the Back Bay, which burgeoned with house-building activity during the period 1899–1902, they commissioned houses in revival styles (Fig. 74). These reflected their appreciation for the past and their desire to enhance the city's extant urban fabric. They did so to make a substantive

DESIGN CRITICISM AND THE REFORM MOVEMENT   79

75a. Interior of a home in Brookline, showing sculpture of the Winged Victory of Samothrace. From *Catalogue of the Architectural Exhibition, Boston Architectural Club and Boston Society of Architects, St. Botolph Club, 2 Newbury Street, 1899.* (Courtesy Boston Athenaeum) This was an advertisement for Wheeler, Osgood & Co. (Boston), supplier of red cedar for the inglenook. Note the Chippendale side and corner chairs, combined with the Morris chair, just visible in the right foreground.

75b. Arthur Little residence, 2 Raleigh Street, Boston, undated. (Courtesy Historic New England) The sculpture of the Winged Victory of Samothrace appears here to the left of the grand piano. This interior—restrained in comparison to other spaces in Little's house—appears to function as a gallery, music room, and library. The groin-vaulted ceiling contrasts with the delicate, Hepplewhite-type side table and the heavy, fully upholstered sofa.

75c. Arts and Crafts exhibition at Deerfield, Mass. Photograph by the Allen Sisters, undated. (Courtesy of the Pocumtuck Valley Memorial Association, Memorial Hall Museum, Deerfield, Mass.) Even at Deerfield, a reproduction of the Winged Victory of Samothrace presides over one of the annual Arts and Crafts exhibitions, at which textiles, metalwork, jewelry, basketry, and other crafts were on display.

75d. Cover of trade catalogue for Alandale Studios, Boston, ca. 1922, featuring an image of the Winged Victory of Samothrace. (Courtesy Historic New England) Alandale Studios was a commercial art school.

76. Interior, 3 Autumn Street (?), Roxbury, 1882. Photograph by A. H. Folsom. (Courtesy Historic New England) This suite of rooms exemplifies the layered busyness that characterizes late-nineteenth-century interiors. A distinguishing feature of this home is a series of preserved animals—birds and a cat—that appear in many rooms. Aesthetic touches include the row of Japanese fans resting on the door frame.

statement, while distancing themselves from the floods of immigrants who were infiltrating older neighborhoods.[40]

They collected antiques acquired at home or abroad to furnish their houses in a fashion that paid homage to the past. Among Boston's "first families" such items were either "an heirloom," as Cleveland Amory points out, "or a wedding present." Advising them in their quest were authors such as Alice Morse Earle, whose book *Customs and Fashions in Old New England* (1899) chronicled the layout, usage, and furnishing of each room in the Colonial home.[41]

Boston's *nouveau riche*, by contrast, tended to acquire these antiques at local shops or while traveling on their European "Grand Tours." Such antiquities and *objets d'art* represented myriad time periods and styles. Those that were classical were always popular. Writing on "Culture" in *The Future in America: A Search after Realities* (1906), English author H. G. Wells spoke, for example, of the prevalence of reproductions of the "Winged Victory of Samothrace" as a sculptural accent in Boston households (Figs. 75a–d). "It is incredible how many people in Boston have selected her for their aesthetic symbol and expression. Always that lady was in evidence about me, unobtrusively persistent." Her lithe, dynamic form, symbolic of triumph and evocative of female beauty in ancient times, must have appealed to cultured Boston households, which eagerly purchased reproductions—ranging in size from statuettes to full scale—from two local companies, P. P. Caproni & Bro., or A. Da Prato & Co.[42]

DESIGN CRITICISM AND THE REFORM MOVEMENT   81

77. Studio, T. Quincy Browne House, 98 Beacon Street, undated. (Courtesy Historic New England) Herbert Browne, the client's brother, made alterations to this residence in 1882. This studio is indicative of the eclectic influences upon Boston's design community in the 1880s and 1890s. The Arts and Crafts movement has informed the sturdy fireplace with built-in settle, and the *sgraffito* plasterwork that enlivens the tall chimney stack. On the other hand, the Aesthetic movement is seen in the pokerwork (or pyrography) panel (to the left of the fireplace) embellished with an asymmetrical composition of flowers and leaves, the wicker armchair, and the surfaces strewn with tasteful bric-a-brac.

Writing on "The Decorative Arts in Boston" from the perspective of the 1930s, Grant Hyde Code, who served as SACB director between 1928 and 1930, commented upon the stylistic hodge-podge of the turn-of-the-century Boston interior, with its antiquities, Colonial hand-me-downs, Asian *objets d'art*, and Aesthetic touches: "In the more superficial aspects of decoration the period was imitative and eclectic. The result was confusion and ugliness except in a wealth of details and a few large forms" (Fig. 76). This setting was ripe for intervention by design reformers.[43]

Indicative of this eclecticism was an exhibition sponsored by the Massachusetts Charitable Mechanic Association in the fall of 1898, which featured only those displays that were "instructive and educational" vis-à-vis the "useful arts." These included a recreated "Japanese Garden," an "Oriental Smoking-Room furnished by and in care of a native Turk," a "loan collection of rare articles" accumulated by the MCMA over a century and representing the work or possessions of early members, a "Colonial Tea" featuring table furnishings from Historic Deerfield, and instruction in "the latest fancy in China Decoration." This exhibit was a microcosm of influences affecting architecture and design in turn-of-the-century Boston (Fig. 77).[44]

By taking an interest in interior appointments, Boston's architects hoped to ensure that allied trades and manufactures—sometimes referred to as "art indus-

78. Advertisements from *Our Homes and How To Heat & Ventilate Them*, Smith & Anthony Stove Company, (1886). (Courtesy Historic New England) Key suppliers of interior furnishings and finishes represented here include Low Art Tile Works, Wakefield Rattan, Irving & Casson, and James S. Conant. Note the use of the word "Artistic."

tries"—would advance and mature at the same rate as architecture, painting, sculpture, and urban planning. More important, they wished to elevate in all art forms conceptual, aesthetic, and technical standards, so that they might one day equal, or surpass, those established by Boston's Colonial artisans and craftspeople.

Of particular interest were those trades and manufactures—a small subset of the approximately 2,500 industries operating in Boston in the 1880s—upon which the architectural profession relied. Among these were carpentry, turning and carving, masonry, and plastering as well as the production of hardware, ironwork and light fixtures, brick, tile, and terra cotta, and stained and ornamental glass (Fig. 78). Associated home furnishings were also produced in abundance, since Boston's furniture industry held a leading position among eastern cities. Advertisements, business cards, trade cards, and trade catalogues—representing companies throughout Boston and Massachusetts—reflect the eclectic influences to which these companies were responding during the 1880s and 1890s.[45]

In Boston, as in Britain, architects led the design reform effort in part because of their professional solidarity. This evolved as a result of shared experiences that seemed to be unique to Boston's architectural community: many architects received their education in professional programs at the Massachusetts Institute of Technology (established in 1866) and Harvard (established twenty-five years later). After completing their studies, some graduates traveled together at home or abroad; they were particularly active doing so in the 1860s, 1870s, and 1880s. Some combined travel with study as they attended the American Academy in Rome (founded 1895). In these ways, Boston's architects became familiar with the monuments of American and European culture as well as with the work of contemporary design reformers.[46]

As professionals, many architects worked in close proximity within the same offices, or in buildings that seemed to attract architectural partnerships and

DESIGN CRITICISM AND THE REFORM MOVEMENT

79a. Amory-Ticknor House, Park and Beacon Streets, after renovations, undated. Photograph by William T. Clark. (Courtesy Historic New England) Renovations reflect the impact of the Queen Anne style, popularized in the Bedford Park district (London) by Richard Norman Shaw, the architect-of-choice for aesthetes. The triple gable, oriel windows, and vitrines accommodated a variety of businesses. These include Harry F. Estabrook, Thomas Strahan, the Enos Co., the Elson Co., and various purveyors of antiques.

79b. Amory-Ticknor House, prior to renovations. 19th century. Boston Photograph Collection Box 1, f. 9. (Courtesy Baker Library, Harvard Business School) This undated photograph shows the Amory and Ticknor Houses prior to the Queen Anne renovations that took place in the 1880s.

workers in the allied arts. One of these was the Amory-Ticknor House at 9 Park Street (Figs. 79a and b), near the Boston Statehouse, the offices of Houghton, Mifflin & Co., exclusive galleries, and social clubs. Once the "home of the gifted publisher whose name it [bore]," in F. A. Whiting's words, it later became headquarters for the SACB. Serving as a nucleus for Boston's design professionals, it was not unlike Chicago's Steinway Hall, where, Wendy Kaplan notes, many members of the Prairie School shared office space in the 1890s. This group, which included Frank Lloyd Wright (1869–1959), Myron Hunt (1868–1952), Dwight H. Perkins (1867–1941), and Robert C. Spencer, Jr. (1864–1953), "was linked in other ways as well," Kaplan explains. The architects "met with other reform-minded colleagues for monthly discussions over lunch," became loosely organized as "the Eighteen," and helped to found architectural and arts organizations throughout the city. This was not dissimilar from the situation in Boston.[47]

Most architects belonged to the same professional organizations, such as the Boston Society of Architects (founded 1867) or the Boston Architectural Club (founded 1889). Several architects who later joined the SACB were also members of the Tavern Club. United professionally as well as socially, they occupied a prominent position within the design community. "The city was growing, full of life and exercised a [great] influence upon the country financially, artistically and in every way," reminisced architect Walter H. Kilham of the period 1885–93. "The preponderance of New York had not begun, and Boston was the artistic, literary and musical capital of the country." Its influence on architecture, he might have added, was equally strong.[48]

To stimulate a similar camaraderie among the city's artisans and craftspeople, architects actively promoted programs in design education for workers in the

80a. Life class, Cowles Art School, Dartmouth Street. From George W. Englehardt, *Boston, Massachusetts* (1897), p. 63. (Courtesy Boston Athenaeum) Frank M. Cowles was the manager of the school. Note that this life drawing class comprised men only.

80b. Normal School of Art, Newbury Street. From Englehardt, *Boston, Massachusetts*, p. 54. (Courtesy Boston Athenaeum) The facade incorporates some elements of the Richardsonian Romanesque, epitomized by Trinity Church.

applied arts. Education had been something of a "regional specialty" in the city and the commonwealth since the days of the Puritans. Programs took place at the Massachusetts Charitable Mechanic Association (1795), which had sponsored the Boston Foreign Fair, and the Women's Educational and Industrial Union (1877). The New England School of Design for Women (1851), the Lowell School of Practical Design (1872), the Massachusetts Normal School of Art (1873, Fig. 80b), the Cowles Art School (1873, Fig. 80a), and the Museum's School of Drawing and Painting (1876) offered design education and technical training as early as the 1870s. The School of the Museum of Fine Arts later founded a Department of Design and Decoration (ca. 1884). Other institutions augmented these programs in the decades following, such as the Eric Pape School of Art (1890s), Arthur Wesley Dow's summer school in Ipswich (1900), The School of Miss Amy Sacker (1901), and C. Howard Walker's School of Fine Arts, Crafts, and Decorative Design,

Boston (1913). Flourishing art industries required well-educated workers; Boston's design educators—many of whom were architects—were happy to oblige.⁴⁹

In addition to enhancing the education of art workers, architects hoped to establish professional and social organizations for them—the Society of Arts and Crafts was one of these—to counteract the isolation that laborers experienced in factories using a division of labor. Boston's architects recognized a need for design and social reform in the city in general and viewed the Arts and Crafts movement as a means to achieve it. Among those organizations to which SACB founders and members belonged were: the Boston Art Club (1855), the Boston Art Students' Association (founded 1879 and renamed the Copley Society in 1901), St. Botolph Club (1880), the Boston Camera Club (1882), the Boston Water Color Club (founded in 1887 for women only), and its male-only counterpart, the Boston Society of Water Color Artists (1885), the Society of Printers

81. Announcement, "Hallowe'en at the Tavern," 1910. (Courtesy Historic New England) The bear was the Tavern Club's mascot. Members of the SACB who are listed on this poster include Robert Andrews, Herbert Jaques, and Howard Walker, all architects. The Tavern Club attracted a literary/artistic crowd.

(1905), the Society for the Preservation of New England Antiquities (1910), the Dante Society of America (1881), the Tavern Club (1884, Fig. 81), the Decadents (ca. 1886), the Visionists (1890s), the Saturday Club (1857), and the Twentieth Century Club (1894), which was devoted to "the free and frank discussion of social reform." Open to men and women alike, the last-named organized a "notable series of lectures on beauty in the home." As their names suggest, these organizations reflected a diversity of interests. Some focused upon a particular art or craft, while others were more devoted to ideas. Social clubs never lost popularity.⁵⁰

Architects' familiarity with the design reform movement may have come in part through exposure to Henry Hobson Richardson and his work. His masterpiece of the 1870s, Trinity Church (Fig. 82), located in the city's urbane Back Bay and presided over by the imposing pastor Phillips Brooks (1835–93), introduced many parishioners firsthand to products of the Arts and Crafts movement. These included stained glass windows furnished by the firm of William Morris, and designed by the Pre-Raphaelite Edward Burne-Jones (1833–98). (Richardson had met both during a European trip in 1882, viewing Morris & Co. products at Merton Abbey, taking tea with the Morris family at Kelmscott House, and dining at Burne-Jones's home.) The American painter and decorative artist John La Farge (1835–1910) contributed murals that enhanced Trinity's rich interior color scheme, as well as several opalescent stained glass windows. Others represented in Trinity, who would play a significant role in the Arts and Crafts movement in Boston, included stained glass artists Sarah Wyman Whitman and Margaret Redmond (1867–1948), and sculptors John Evans and Hugh Cairns. Stylistically, Trinity reflected Richardson's love for the Middle Ages, and the Romanesque style specifically. Though not an arts and crafts structure *per se*, in part as well as in whole Trinity exuded the spirit of the Arts and Crafts movement, standing as testimony to the unification of the fine and the applied arts.[51]

82. Postcard, Trinity Church, Boston, ca. 1905. Published by Metropolitan News Co., Boston. (Author's collection) Trinity Church's imposing Romanesque facade influenced American civic, commercial, and residential architecture for decades after its architect's untimely death in 1886. Its colorful interior was a model of the successful unification of the fine and allied arts, and many future members of the SACB contributed to its completion.

83. H. H. Richardson's office, Brookline, 1881. (Courtesy Historic New England) Books, prints, photographs, busts, relief sculpture, arts and crafts portières, oriental rugs, and an eclectic assortment of furniture and light fixtures littered Richardson's cozy office. Note the photograph of the Winged Victory of Samothrace atop the rear bookcase. In the foreground is a framed photo of the interior of Istanbul's great religious edifice Hagia Sophia.

Richardson influenced members of Boston's architectural community not only through completed projects such as Trinity Church, but also through direct exposure to his work process. He employed as assistants several of those who would later stand at the forefront of the design reform effort within the city, among these Langford Warren, Waddy Longfellow, Robert Andrews, and Herbert Jaques (1857–1916). (Jaques traveled with Richardson on his European trip in 1882.) They learned from Richardson's works as well as from his methodology, thriving in an atmosphere of artistic cooperation and mutual respect that characterized his Brookline studio (Fig. 83). Writing of his experience in Richardson's office, ca. 1880–82, Waddy Longfellow reported to his mother: "The atmosphere of the place is exceed-

84. John Ruskin and Constance Hilliard, October 1879. (Courtesy Historic New England) An inscription reads: "C.E.N. with Connie's love," explaining, "I am sending you this photo tho' it is far too melancholy for a Christmas card! Please do not think I always look so dreary!! It is rather good of Cuzzie as he is now the Stereoscope."

ingly artistic" and the "system of personal superintendence. . . excellent." A year or so later, he asserted to her, this "is as strong an office as there is in town and things are [run] about as promptly, but how can you say when drawings and designs are to be done when they require invention and artistic treatment. Richardson has imagination & he sees things in his mind & keeps up his interest wonderfully, even in small work." This same atmosphere, breadth of vision, and attention to detail was that which Boston's architects hoped to instill in the design community in the years that followed Richardson's untimely death.[52]

The Influence of Charles Eliot Norton

An equally influential figure among Boston's intellectual elite was Charles Eliot Norton (Fig. 31), whose role in linking the British and American sectors of the movement was crucial. Just as John Ruskin was one of the founders of the movement in England, Norton was his counterpart in Boston. They were contemporaries and kindred spirits for forty-five years, whose occupations and avocations were similar. As a founder and the first president of the SACB, Norton stands as a distinctive link between the British and the American branches of the movement, whose participation ensured that it took hold forcefully in Boston.

Born in Hingham, just south of Boston, Norton attended Harvard, graduating Phi Beta Kappa in 1846. During the next five years, he worked for Bullard & Lee, the Boston-based merchants of the East India Trade, on whose behalf he took his first trip abroad. Travel to India terminated in visits to Rome, Paris, and London. Sailing for New York in January 1851, Norton missed firsthand exposure to the Great Exhibition.[53]

He began his literary career shortly after his return with publication of his first book, *Considerations of Some Recent Social Theories* (1853). Shortly after, he became a regular contributor to the newly established *Atlantic Monthly* (1858), eventually assuming editorship of the *North American Review*. His contributions to Boston's architectural press were more limited, however, due to philosophical differences between Norton, his Harvard colleague Charles H. Moore (1840–1930), and the editors of the *American Architect & Building News*.[54]

It was during his second European sojourn (1855–57) that Norton first met

Ruskin (Fig. 84), whom he would later describe as "*mi magister dulcissime, homo honestissime et rarissime, suavitas et caritas mea.*" Their friendship was immediate, fueled by a variety of mutual concerns and shared passions. Among these were respect for the culture of the Middle Ages, dedication to the preservation of ancient architecture, and belief in the restorative powers of nature. Their horror at the encroachment of industrialization paralleled their concern for improving the working conditions of the contemporary craftsperson. For both, early Italian cathedrals were symbolic of a more joyous and productive age. And, as an antidote to the exigencies of modern life, each surrounded himself with the art and artifacts of the past. (In a city perceived by Henry James to be dominated by strong women, Norton, for example, collected paintings of Madonnas.) Contact with Ruskin honed Norton's sensibilities, culminating in an attitude that embraced the tenets of the English Arts and Crafts movement.[55]

Ruskin's was not the sole British influence upon Norton. Between 1868 and 1873, Norton lived abroad with his wife, Susan Ridley Sedgwick Norton (1838–72, Fig. 85), and their young children, dividing their time between England and the continent. During this period, Norton not only strengthened his friendship with Ruskin, but became acquainted with Thomas Carlyle, William Morris, and Pre-Raphaelites Dante Gabriel Rossetti and Edward Burne-Jones. The influence of each was as important as was their cumulative effect. Among Norton's personal pos-

85. Photographic copy of a portrait of Susan Ridley Sedgwick Norton, by Rouse, ca. 1862. (Courtesy Historic New England) This exquisite portrait of the wife of Charles Eliot Norton conveys the sensitivity of both the subject and the artist.

86a. Sir Edward Burne-Jones, 1882 (?). Photograph by Fred Hollyer, London. (Courtesy Historic New England) This photograph was among Charles Eliot Norton's personal possessions.

86b. Lady Georgina Burne-Jones, 1882 (?). Photograph by Fred Hollyer, London. (Courtesy Historic New England) This portrait echoes the "woman reading" motif that was so popular among Boston graphic designers.

sessions were inscribed photographic portraits of Ruskin and Burne-Jones (Figs. 86a and b).

Norton's connection with these men was only one link between the intelligentsia of England and Boston. Lionel Lambourne argues that Emerson, Thoreau, and Whitman—ever present on Bostonians' reading lists—were "constantly reiterating concerns of Carlyle, Ruskin, and Morris." The trans-Atlantic exchange of ideas was thus bi-directional, and Norton trod an already well-worn path.[56]

The relationship between Norton and the Scotsman Carlyle was truly symbiotic. Carlyle described Norton as "amiable, very friendly, sincere and cultivated," and he extended affection toward Norton, his wife, and his family. Norton summarized his impression of Carlyle in a letter of December 1872 written toward the end of his trip: "I think the chief pleasure of my stay in London this year has been the frequent walks and talks I have had with Carlyle. I see him often enough to have grown familiar in some sort with him, and sincerely attached to him. He is, though seventy-seven years old, in excellent health, and vigorous for his years. Age has tempered whatever once may have been hard in him, and yet has taken from him nothing of keenness of intelligence or richness of humour and imagination. . . . He is," Norton concludes, "the most striking figure in London,—and when he dies there will be a bigger gap than the death of any other man could make." That dreaded event would occur just nine years later.[57]

Norton appreciated Carlyle as friend, author, intellectual, humanitarian, and champion for the rights of the common person. Later in his life, Norton was instrumental in persuading Carlyle to leave his library and personal papers to Harvard. Norton subsequently edited several volumes of Carlyle's letters, including *The Correspondence of Thomas Carlyle and Ralph Waldo Emerson, 1834–1872* (1883) and *The Letters of Thomas Carlyle, 1826–1836* (1889).[58]

Norton's exposure to the works of the Pre-Raphaelite Brotherhood (founded 1848) came during his second trip to London in 1857, when he visited the same exhibition of paintings—assembled by British publisher and art dealer Ernest Gambart—that traveled to Boston later that year. His appreciation for their work was immediate and lasting, and he argued that "great good will [would] come out of [the] school of the Pre-Raphaelites and that its influence [would] do much for the art of the next generation." One of his favorite possessions was a painting by Rossetti, given to him by Ruskin.[59]

Norton generally spoke of Edward Burne-Jones and William Morris in the same breath, noting that "with curiously differing temperaments they [were] curiously similar in certain spiritual and artistic gifts." Here Norton may have been reacting to those qualities that had first drawn Morris and Burne-Jones together when they both attended Exeter College, Oxford, in the early 1850s. Norton characterized Burne-Jones as the personification of "sweetness and light," a quality that Norton perceived in his work and attitude toward life. "Sweetness and light," a phrase attributed to Matthew Arnold, was associated with the Aesthetic movement; but, there was much crossover among the Pre-Raphaelites, aesthetes, and supporters of design reform, so this appellation seems appropriate. A testimony to Norton's friendship with Burne-Jones is the exquisite portrait of Norton's daughter Sarah—or Sally, as Norton called her—painted by the artist. In keeping with the theme of sweetness and light is the name "Lily," given to another of Norton's daughters (Fig. 87).⁶⁰

Norton described Morris, by contrast, as combining "in a wonderful measure the solid earthly qualities of the man of practical affairs, with the fine perceptions and quick fancy of the poet." In saying so, Norton—the former employee of the East India traders Bullard & Lee—belied the Boston merchant's traditional disbelief that art and commerce might mix. Norton's initial appreciation of Morris as a poet and craftsman eventually developed into a broader respect for him as a reformer, preservationist, and political activist. Direct exposure to Morris's work and theories must have contributed to development of Norton's own sympathies.⁶¹

87. Margaret Burne-Jones, Sally Norton, Lily Norton, September 1890. Photograph by Naudin and Company, London. (Courtesy Historic New England) This triple portrait expresses the closeness between the Norton and Burne-Jones families. The kitten is unidentified.

A passion for the culture of the Middle Ages was another commonality of these men, which culminated for Norton in the publication *Historical Studies of Church Building in the Middle Ages* (1880). The volume extended his sphere of influence well beyond Harvard Yard, though it never achieved the international influence of Ruskin's work, despite a common subject: unification of the fine and applied arts in thirteenth-century Italy. This interest may explain Norton's enthusiasm for Richardson's Trinity Church, whose exterior and interior epitomized such artistic unification and collaboration.

Norton's lyrical descriptions of that place and time revealed his vision of what the present might be like given restoration of social and artistic cooperation: "The spirit of art penetrated every department of life," Norton wrote, "and gave form to all the products of design. There is a solidarity in the Arts. They do not flourish in isolated independence. So at this time art exhibited itself in the least no less than in the great things, in objects of common use," he went on to explain, "as well as of display—in the weaving and embroidery of stuffs; in the shape and ornament of dress; in metalwork of all sorts; in the work of blacksmith no less than of goldsmith; in armor; in jewelry; in articles of the table or the altar; in the woodwork of the carpenter and the joiner; in the calligraphy and illumination of manuscripts. Whatever the hand found to do," he concluded, "that it did under guidance of artistic fancy and feeling." It was this spirit that Norton hoped to revive in late-nineteenth-century Boston, by founding and then leading the SACB.⁶²

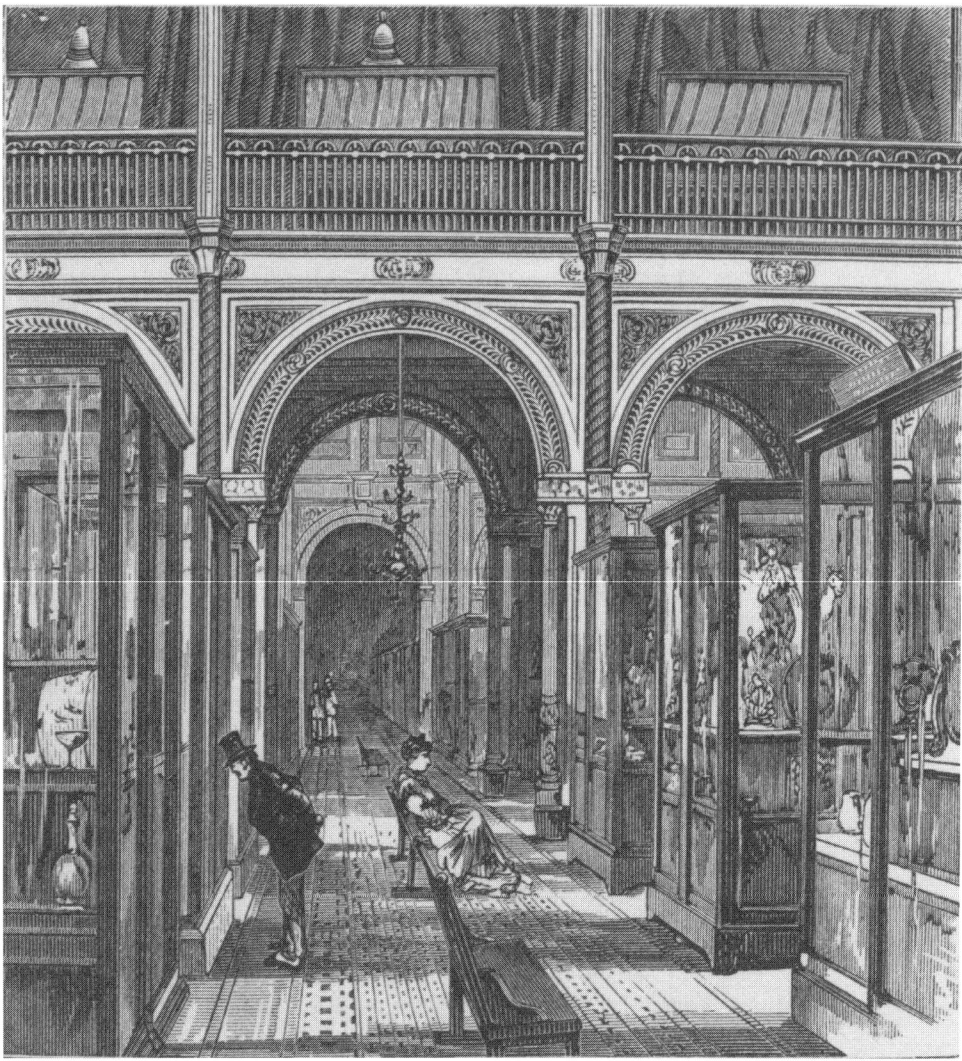

88a. Interior, South Kensington Museum, South Court, showing the Prince Consort's Gallery. From Moncure Conway, *Travels in South Kensington* (New York: Harper Bros., 1882). (Courtesy Boston Athenaeum)

The tragic death in childbirth of Norton's wife Susan prompted his return to Boston in May 1873. The following year, he became Professor of Fine Arts at Harvard, a post that he held until retirement in 1899. Ruskin had held a similar position as Slade Professor of Art at Oxford since 1870, so this gave Norton an opportunity to parallel his mentor's.

Norton's appointment as art educator occurred in the same decade as the founding of the Lowell School of Practical Design, construction of the new Museum of Fine Arts on Copley Square, and the Museum's own School of Drawing and Painting. Efforts to improve art education paralleled those undertaken in Britain and Europe, as world's fairs such as the Crystal Palace Exhibition identified a need for increased awareness of the arts among consumers, craftspeople, and manufacturers. The South Kensington Museum (Figs. 88a and b), known

88b. Interior, South Kensington Museum. From Conway, *Travels in South Kensington*. (Courtesy Boston Athenaeum) The caption reads: "North Court, North-West Corner, Showing casts of the Biga (or Two-horse Chariot) from the original in marble at the Vatican, and of the Pulpit by Giovanni Pisano, formerly in the Cathedral at Pisa."

today as the Victoria and Albert Museum, and its School of Design (1863) were products of that greater awareness.[63]

Boston played an important role in the movement for art education in America, and Norton occupied a unique position as the first Professor of Fine Arts in an American university. He was, said H. L. Johnson, the one who "taught an unseeing age to see." Appointments such as Norton's (and Ruskin's) were rare at the time: "Nowhere in English-speaking lands had culture in the arts been admitted as an essential portion of education," wrote John Stuart Mill. "They had been regarded as of trivial concern; the study of them had been relegated to professional artists or mere dilettanti, and the idea that a complete and satisfactory education could not be obtained without some knowledge of their character and history, and without such culture of the aesthetic faculties as the study of these might afford appeared strange and unacceptable to many of the most enlightened thinkers on the subject of the education of youth." Both Norton and Ruskin regarded themselves as just such enlightened thinkers. They accepted the challenge of integrating art into university curricula with relish. Norton often quoted Mill's observation as a way of explaining the rarity of his own position and its challenges.[64]

As a result of his lectures on fine arts, which most certainly betrayed the theories of his British friends, Norton molded the sensibilities of a generation of Harvard graduates. "He, if any man . . . ," said C. Howard Walker of his revered teacher, "did his utmost to encourage appreciation of the best." What is more, as Keith Morgan and Richard Cheek point out, Norton "was the first academic to join his architect-historian colleagues in creating the scholarly atmosphere in Boston and Cambridge that would nourish [architecture] students from the 1870s on." This earned Norton the role of arbiter of taste in late-nineteenth-century Boston, as he became an eloquent advocate of the quest for Usefulness and Beauty. "As always with him," reminisced Edward W. Emerson, "the ethical [went] hand in hand with the aesthetic."[65]

Norton's dedication to design education and reform extended beyond Harvard's confines and into the greater community. He argued "the character of the population depends upon the nature of its habitations," and implemented a model lodging house project in Boston in the 1850s. The example of low-cost, alternative housing for the poor that Norton provided earned the approbation of both the project's residents and its board of directors. The venture prompted others to erect similar low-cost housing for those whom Norton termed the "honest and self-supporting poor."[66]

Norton's efforts inspired colleagues and followers to become involved with the college settlement house movement. Among these were the feminist, scholar, and reformer Vida Scudder (1861–1951), the philosopher, reformer, and author of *English Social Movements* Robert Archey Woods (1865–1925), professor Frank Parsons (1854–1908), *New England Magazine* editor and Twentieth Century Club founder Edwin Doak Mead (1849–1937), Wellesley College president Alice Freeman Palmer (1855–1902), and the author, philanthropist, and sister of Samuel D. Warren, Jr., Cornelia Warren (1857–1921).

This movement resulted in the establishment of Toynbee Hall, which was founded in London's East End (1884) and served as the prototype for such American equivalents as 95 Rivington Street (New York, 1889), Hull House—founded by Jane Addams and Ellen Gates Starr (Chicago, 1889)—and Denison House (Boston, 1890–91, Fig. 89). These college settlement houses enabled university students to live in working-class neighborhoods where they were exposed directly to the exigencies of their neighbors' daily lives. Students regarded these settlement houses as laboratories where they might experience myriad social problems and then propose ways to ameliorate them, "materially, morally, and spiritually." Such ventures allowed members of Boston's social elite to interact with the disadvantaged and to witness firsthand the results of philanthropy, educational programs, and social activism. Their commitment continued for de-

89. Interior showing kindergarten class, Denison House, Boston, 1900. (Schlesinger Library, Radcliffe Institute, Harvard University) The rooms of Denison House were hung with paintings and low-relief sculpture. On a pedestal to the left of the fireplace stands a reproduction of the Venus de Milo. Teaching children fell within the purview of settlement houses such as Denison House.

cades. Even as late as the 1920s, the SACB regularly showed displays of "Folk Handicrafts" made under the auspices of programs at Denison House.[67]

During this period, Norton became involved with art education for women, serving as administrator for the short-lived New England School of Design for Women (founded in 1851 by Ednah Cheney). His participation in that and other schools demonstrated his awareness of the need to extend art education beyond the confines of the university. His involvement parallels that of Ruskin, Rossetti, and Burne-Jones, who were drawing instructors at the Workingmen's College in London during the 1850s, and C. R. Ashbee, who taught classes in drawing and decoration and lectured on Ruskin's works at Toynbee Hall in the 1880s. This dedication to design education for the working classes was only one interest that Norton shared with his English colleagues.[68]

Writer, critic, educator, social reformer, Norton had made a commitment to improving the state of the fine and applied arts through education at all levels of society. Commenting on Norton's work at Harvard, Michael W. Brooks argues that Norton's goal was to produce a graduate who was "critical, urbane, genteel, someone who would look on the Gilded Age with disdain but would work to transform it." The same might be said of the sorts of individuals who joined Norton in founding the SACB and supported him as its leader. By the late 1890s, he was highly visible within the Boston cultural community, had earned the esteem of his peers, and had forged the international social and intellectual connections to make the movement for design reform a reality in Boston. As such, Norton played a key role in the transmission of the Arts and Crafts movement from England to America, and guaranteed its ultimate acceptance.[69]

The First Exhibition of the Arts and Crafts

The SACB was among the first American organizations to pattern itself after England's Arts and Crafts Exhibition Society (ACES). Organized between 1885 and 1888, the latter gave its name to the design reform movement, which was dubbed the Arts and Crafts movement from the late 1880s on, a label coined by Cobden-Sanderson. As its name suggests, one of its chief activities was organizing public exhibitions of handicrafts as a way of promoting the goals of design reform. It had held five such exhibitions between 1888 and 1896, as an alternative to the more traditional fine arts exhibitions sponsored by the Royal Academy. Supporters of the ACES included Crane, Morris, Cobden-Sanderson, ceramist William de Morgan (1839–1917), whom H. H. Richardson had visited during a trip to England in 1882, engraver and printer Emery Walker (1851–1933), architect William R. Lethaby (1857–1931), and others with whom Bostonians would have been familiar.[70]

In the manner of the English society that it emulated, the SACB evolved from an exhibition of handicrafts held in April 1897. H. L. Johnson was the impetus behind the show. As early as December 1896, he began promoting the idea of holding such an exhibition, and issued a series of handsome brochures to promote the idea to potential participants and supporters. Theodore Brown Hapgood, Jr. (1871–1938) designed the first prospectus (ca. December 1896), printed on brown craft paper in red and black ink. A second brochure—designed by architect Bertram Grosvenor Goodhue (1869–1924) and "showing a touch of the Morris revival" in its elaborate border—included endorsements from the press and from individual supporters. These pamphlets (Figs. 90 and 91) invited members of the regional arts community to participate. Thirty-seven of Boston's social and intellectual leaders signed the prospectus, many of whom later served as the organization's founders. Endorsement by these highly respected members of the community gave an air of distinction to the proposed exhibition. Architects, painters, sculptors, educators, writers, and social reformers, artisans, craftsmen, and patrons rallied behind Johnson's cause, demonstrating its multidisciplinary appeal.[71]

Such exhibitions were not entirely unfamiliar in Boston. The Massachusetts Charitable Mechanic Association had been holding similar displays regularly since its founding in 1795, though it placed less emphasis upon handicraft. "All the doubts of the usefulness of these exhibitions in bringing to public notice the latest mechanical inventions and improvements," noted one historian, commenting upon the historic role of these displays, "their power to educate public taste, and to stimulate [manufacturers] to further triumphs in changing rude materials into forms of beauty and utility were dispelled." Such mechanics' fairs demon-

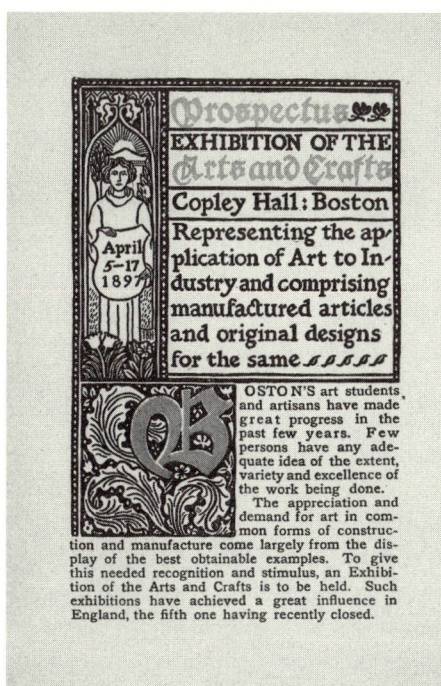 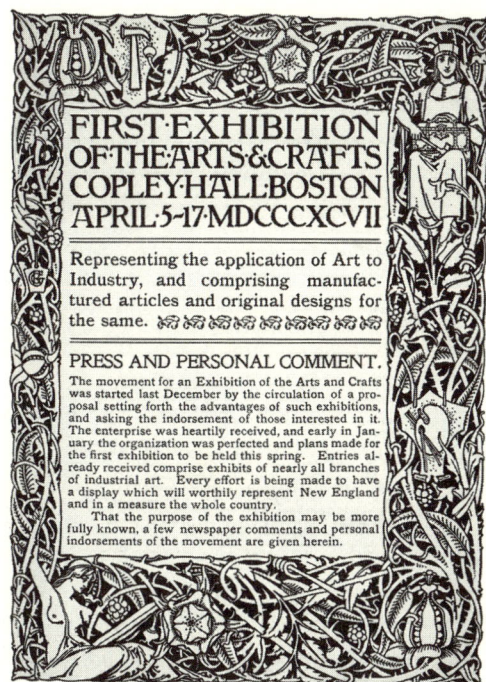

90. Prospectus pamphlet, "Exhibition of the Arts and Crafts, Copley Hall," by Theodore Brown Hapgood, Jr., ca. December 1896, SACB Archives. (Boston Public Library/Department of Fine Arts. Courtesy of the Trustees) This pamphlet conveys the spirit of the English Arts and Crafts movement. The Gothic arch and robed figure add a touch of medievalism, evident in the work of the Pre-Raphaelites.

91. Pamphlet advertising the First Exhibition of the Arts and Crafts, by Bertram Grosvenor Goodhue, ca. March 1897. SACB Archives. (Boston Public Library/Department of Fine Arts. Courtesy of the Trustees) A note in the margin indicates that this was reproduced in the "Transcript Friday a.m." A version of Goodhue's pamphlet includes endorsements from major Boston newspapers and graphic designer Will Bradley. Typical of Goodhue's work is the complex border of intertwined vines, figures, the Tudor rose, and pomegranate.

strated that, in Boston, the quest for Beauty and Usefulness was popular well before the founding of the SACB.[72]

Writers for the *Herald* and *Globe* agreed that Boston was the logical place for such an event to take place, given its nationally recognized commitment to educational and cultural excellence. One of the most persuasive supporters was Candace Wheeler (1827–1923), president of Associated Artists (New York), associate of Louis Comfort Tiffany, and one of the nation's leading designers. In a letter to Johnson, Wheeler stated: "I have made an attempt for several years to organize such an exhibit in New York, but, as usual, found that Boston is more ready to act in matters which are purely in the interests of art than New York." The press quoted her comments extensively.[73]

The press also discussed Boston's accomplishments in the area of design reform and education at length in the days leading up to the exhibition's opening. Critics viewed the event as a sort of cultural report card that would permit attendees to judge the state of design and design education in the city and region. Writers described the history of design education, the backgrounds of local and national schools, their curricula, faculty, and facilities, and their status as compared to

British and European schools. They closely scrutinized Boston craftsmen's training. Writing on "American Decorative Art" in the *Boston Herald*, one journalist noted: "The ultimate effect of broad decorative art education in this country would be harmony between society and its surroundings, between the family and the dwelling, the individual and the room, the picture and the frame." Evidently, the idealism of the exhibition's organizers extended to the local press.[74]

Many articles addressed the issue of taste, and who affected it most—designers or consumers. They asked what the forthcoming display would reveal about taste-making in the city. One writer predicted that the First Exhibition of the Arts and Crafts would be a triumph of American innovation, and that it would mark a break from British and European influence.[75]

The author of the article "American Decorative Art" was less certain of that, however, noting that many citizens who traveled abroad had returned as "eclectic[s] with a taste for a little of everything." This resulted, the writer continued, offering as an example, a "modern parlor that was kaleidoscopic, a little bewildering, and generally fantastic. . . . The United States began with a good century of simplicity and plainness, the almost sacred plainness of the Puritans, and it has experienced a round century of experimenting, of imitating, of looking to other countries for all things commendable in decorative art." Here the writer expressed a bias toward the Colonial era, which endured long after the era of the Centennial Exhibition. This was "a century of sampling both bad and good, the appropriate and the inappropriate, the ugly and the beautiful, indiscriminately. And now . . . America has had its fill of ugliness," the writer declared optimistically, as if to forecast the effect that the upcoming exhibition might have. "It is getting rid of what is very bad. We are . . . appreciating more and more the virtue of originality—of American originality." With such comments, analysts of the forthcoming exhibition voiced concerns that critics had been debating internationally since the time of the Great Exhibition, showing that many of Wornum's concerns of the 1850s continued to be current in an international arena.[76]

The First Exhibition of the Arts and Crafts opened in Copley and Allston Halls in the Grundmann Studios Building near Copley Square to great fanfare on the evening of Saturday, April 3, 1897 (Fig. 92). Boston's social elite turned out *en masse*. The exhibition consisted of about 400 displays comprising over 1,000 objects, divided into twenty-four broad categories. Over 160 individuals contributed objects for display. The most extensive categories consisted of textiles, metalwork, jewelry, and printing. Augmenting the display of professional works were those representing students enrolled in regional design schools, such as the School of the Museum of Fine Arts, the Cowles Art School, and the Rhode Island School of Design. Showing professional solidarity with New England's art workers were architect-members of the Boston Architectural Club who filled Allston Hall with sketches, drawings, renderings, and photographs of their work. International exhibits included sixteen carpets by Morris, twelve wallpapers by Voysey, and metalwork representing the British ACES.[77]

92. Interior, Copley Hall, First Exhibition of the Arts and Crafts, 1897. Photograph by N. L. Stebbins. (Courtesy SACB Archives) Topiary trees, wreaths, and swags of greenery complement works in two and three dimensions—free-standing, wall-hung, or crammed into glass showcases. The door at left led to Allston Hall's display of works submitted by members of the Boston Architectural Club.

93. Program for concert at Chickering Hall, undated. (Courtesy Historic New England) A young girl holds a scroll from which a woman reads music while strumming a lyre—a variation upon the motif of the "woman reading." Both figures in their flowing robes might have stepped out of a painting by one of the Pre-Raphaelite Brotherhood.

94. Ednah D. Cheney, ca.1905. (Schlesinger Library, Radcliffe Institute, Harvard University)

Women in Boston's Arts and Crafts Movement

Nearly one-third of the objects on display represented the work of women. They had always been active in the arts in Boston, producing their own drawings, prints, paintings, and sculpture, or posing as models in others' work. Many were immortalized in the paintings of "The 10." Receiving training at the schools operating within the city, they quickly embraced the arts and crafts both as a means of artistic expression and, for many, a livelihood. Some, like S. W. Whitman, practiced both the fine and the applied arts, and thus embraced the Arts and Crafts movement wholeheartedly.[78]

Women's dedication to the arts and crafts may explain why the image of the intellectual "Boston Woman" figured prominently in the graphic arts of this era. The "woman reading" motif (Fig. 93) was popular in posters, book covers, and advertising, and was an expression of all that women had accomplished within the city's vibrant cultural milieu.[79]

Their proclivity for the arts and crafts figures in essays in Justin Winsor's *Memorial History*, compiled in the 1880s. Writing on women's issues, contributing editor Ednah D. Cheney (1824–1904, Fig. 94) mentioned the "rapid advances" that women had made in the "plastic arts" as a result of their educational opportunities in and around the city. Cheney was familiar with these firsthand, having

95. Lois Lilley How, undated. Photograph by Florence Maynard. (Courtesy MIT Museum)

established the Boston School of Design for Women. Describing their collective aesthetic nature as "serious and refined," Cheney noted that the interest women showed in "decorative art had gone beyond all possibility of measurement." She indicated as well that these students of the arts and crafts regarded their education seriously and sought actively to sell their work so that they "might be classed as artists, not as amateurs." The opportunity to do so offered by the First Exhibition in part explains what drew women to it and ultimately to the SACB in such numbers.[80]

Addison and Whitman's involvement as founders of the SACB, and the subsequent membership of women such as Mabel Bayard Warren and Gretchen Osgood Warren (painted with her daughter by John Singer Sargent in 1903), illustrates how important Boston's women were to the design reform movement. Some worked quietly behind the scenes as philanthropists and social do-gooders. Others were more visible as professionals and accomplished amateurs.

Women studied architecture and landscape architecture at MIT, for example, soon after its programs were established. Sophia Hayden (1868–1953), MIT's first alumna of the two-year architecture program (1890), won the competition for the Women's Building at the World's Columbian Exposition in 1893. Marion L. Mahoney (1871–1961), who became one of Frank Lloyd Wright's principal designers in Oak Park, Illinois, graduated in 1894. Marian C. Coffin (1876–1957) and Mabel Keyes Babcock (1862–ca. 1930s) were the first female graduates in landscape architecture, matriculating in the early 1900s. Lois Lilley Howe (1864–1964, Fig. 95), another early graduate of the architecture program (1890), launched an active career in Boston and Cambridge, eventually branching out to include architectural history. She was one of the first women in the United States to publish in that field, and one of the first women architects to join the SACB, ca. 1900.[81]

Howe was also a photographer, one of numerous women working in Boston and around Massachusetts who demonstrated the fascination that photography held for American women—both professionals and amateurs—in the aftermath of the Civil War. The introduction of the Kodak camera and roll film in 1889 enticed increasing numbers of American women to try their hand at a medium that demanded close attention to detail, a critical eye, and a delicate touch. By 1900, more than 3,500 women across the United States worked as professional photographers. In Boston, many of those became members of local camera clubs and exhibitors at displays of photographic works. Along with Howe, the sisters Frances S. Allen and Mary E. Allen showed their works under the auspices of the SACB. Their prominence led Boston's male photographers, such as F. Holland Day, to question whether or not the gradual feminization of profession might lower its prestige.[82]

In *The American Scene* (1907), Henry James commented upon the domination of Boston culture by women. Well educated, traveled, and connected, Boston's women—whom Cleveland Amory called "Boston Amazons"—"went on to great things." They were active in the cultural life of their community, whether architecture, landscape architecture, art or craft was a vocation or a livelihood. They were highly visible at the First Exhibition and continued to make their collective presence known under the auspices of the SACB.[83]

The First Exhibition and the Society's Founding

Contributed by exceptional women, men, and foreign invitees, the works shown at the First Exhibition represented a variety of styles, interpreted with scholarly accuracy or willful negligence. Catalogue descriptions mention stylistic influences from the Near and Far East, ranging from Moorish to eighteenth-century Arabian, Hindu, Egyptian, Algerian, Indian, and Chinese. Western influences included the Gothic, "Old Spanish," and Italian Renaissance. Many artifacts reflected the impact of eighteenth-century France or England, and representatives of the Colonial Revival style abounded. Naturalism was also evident in objects based upon floral, foliate, or vegetal forms and ornament.[84]

Visitors to the exhibition received a copy of a handsome catalogue whose cover was designed by B. G. Goodhue (Figs. 96 and 97). Its bold block print of a stylized Tudor rose and pomegranate captured the essence of the arts and crafts aesthetic, and recalled his design for the exhibition prospectus. The rose may have symbolized the movement's English origins, while the pomegranate—an organic whole comprised of multiple discrete parts—may have represented the unification of the fine and applied arts under the auspices of the Arts and Crafts movement. The rose may also have hinted at Goodhue's participation in a Jacobite organization, the Order of the White Rose, which was inspired by seventeenth-century British culture and devoted to restoration of the Stuart monarchy. The rose figured prominently in the work of other Boston graphic artists, as did the pomegranate, which Bruce Rogers (1870–1957) and Theodore Brown Hapgood, Jr., also favored.[85]

Following a precedent established by the Arts and Crafts Exhibition Society, the catalogue listed designer, executor, and exhibitor for each item. In some cases, all three were the same person; in other cases, each was different. These catalogue entries document the professional interrelationships among designer and craftsperson, manufacturer, and purveyor. Exhibition planners strove to identify each individual responsible for designing or fabricating the items on display. By doing so, they hoped to banish the anonymity that industrialization and the division of labor had imparted to the design process.[86]

96. Catalogue, First Exhibition of the Arts and Crafts. (Courtesy SACB Archives) The Tudor rose may have symbolized the English origins of the Arts and Crafts movement, while the pomegranate may have represented the unification of the fine and applied arts under the movement's auspices. The sinuous stems and roots were influenced equally by eighteenth-century botanical prints and Art Nouveau.

97. Bertram Grosvenor Goodhue in Persian dress, February 14, 1891. Notman Photo Co., Boston. Ralph Adams Cram Personal Papers. (Boston Public Library/Department of Fine Arts. Courtesy of the Trustees) It was not unusual to see Boston's architects and art students in fancy dress. H. H. Richardson appears in photographs dressed in monk's robes. New York architect Richard Morris Hunt posed in a photo as the Renaissance artist Cimabue. The Boston Art Students Association—to which many SACB members belonged—held costume pageants.

Catalogue entries, photographs, and newspaper descriptions of the First Exhibition—though enthusiastic—give the impression that the objects on display were hardly progressive. *The House Beautiful* magazine dismissed the exhibition as "too much like a fancy bazar," though it concurred that "the general standard was good." Technical execution was often masterful; yet, aesthetic sensibility seemed weak. Overall the displays reflected a prevalent conservatism that continued to dominate handicrafts produced in Boston and New England for decades to follow. "The furniture will be found wanting in originality and simplicity," wrote W. Henry Winslow for the *Transcript*, "for which the public must be held principally responsible. The best things on the whole, are literal reproductions of fixed historic styles." Reliance upon historical precedent and dependency upon accepted models indicated a distance between British and American proponents of the movement that was more conceptual than geographical.[87]

As critics of the Great Exhibition had done forty-six years earlier, analysts of the First Exhibition of the Arts and Crafts identified a need for improvement.

"We may be able to live without splendor," stated a newspaper journalist. "But, we cannot live without beauty, and it is by such arts that whatever refined taste is latent in the American will be awakened and satisfied."[88]

From the perspective of its promoters, the First Exhibition of the Arts and Crafts was a success. Attendance was high, publicity extensive. Manufacturers, merchants, patrons, and consumers had an opportunity to become better acquainted with members of the design community. Craftspeople benefited from competition with their peers. Architects, painters, and sculptors recognized the potential of expanding their own *oeuvre* by working in the applied arts. Visitors had a chance to assess the applied arts in terms of conceptual, aesthetic, and technical standards. The First Exhibition set the tone for the formalization of the design reform movement in Boston that followed. Architects, who had been active in the show as both promoters and exhibitors, continued to lead the movement for decades. Women supported it in growing numbers, while many of the craftsmen who had been involved remained dedicated to the movement's ideals throughout their lives.

So enthusiastic were supporters of the First Exhibition that—within days of dismantling it—they announced plans for a sequel in 1898. "Continued annual exhibitions," argued C. Howard Walker forcefully, "if they are as good as the present one, will keep the matter before the public and stimulate craftsmen." Over the period of the next two months, however, support for holding annual exhibitions shifted in favor of creating a permanent organization. With a sense of purpose and in a spirit of optimism, Robert D. Andrews commented that "the opportunity of the society was certainly extraordinary, even phenomenal," and predicted that "the movement was likely to be one of the biggest projects of the kind undertaken in Boston for a long time." Six weeks later, the founding members of the SACB incorporated officially, by drawing up and signing articles of agreement. They followed by electing Charles Eliot Norton as their president, Carey, Whitman, and Evans as vice-presidents, and Morris Gray as treasurer.[89]

The *Boston Herald* commented upon the composition of the new organization's "provisional governing committee" (later replaced by the SACB Council): It is "broad and liberal; representing the arts and crafts equally; and composed of [persons] of recognized position." The article noted as well that this group included members of the Boston Society of Architects, the Boston Architectural Club, the Master Builders' Association, the Museum of Fine Arts, MIT, Harvard, and the Boston Art Students' Association, implying that the new organization's link to an established network was important.[90]

The *Boston Transcript* pronounced Norton's appointment "most fitting," declaring: "It is to be hoped that the famous critic of the arts may find it possible to lend his taste and judgment to the beginnings of an institution which should prove an Alma mater of good craftsmanship and also appreciation." The *Boston Journal* stated hopefully: "If the Society of Arts and Crafts could make the words [art and craft] again synonymous, the names of the founders of the Society should be carved on a wall of the Public Library." This apotheosis of the founders, it warned, would not come easily: "In this country, which claims to be a democracy, working

THE FIRST CAR THROUGH THE SUBWAY YESTERDAY.

98. "The First Car Through the Subway Yesterday," *Boston Globe*, September 2, 1897. (Courtesy Historic New England)

99. Japanese Corridor, Museum of Fine Arts, Copley Square, undated. Photograph by Baldwin Coolidge. (Courtesy Historic New England) Ernest Fenollosa may have been responsible for the museum's acquisition of some of the objects displayed in the Japanese Corridor during 1890–97.

with one's hands is thought by many Americans a pitiable occupation." This was only one of many challenges that the twenty-one SACB founders faced when they convened the following fall to launch their new campaign for design reform.[91]

Postscript: 1897: An Auspicious Year

Boston was the logical place to found a new American arts and crafts organization. Its twenty-one founders were the appropriate visionaries to conceive it. Charles Eliot Norton was its quintessential leader. And, 1897 was a serendipitous time in which to incorporate. Following the year in which William Morris had died, and the Arts and Crafts Exhibition Society had held its most recent show, 1897 was a year of intellectual and creative ferment locally, nationally, and internationally.

In 1897, Boston continued to augment its infrastructure, completing construction of the Commonwealth Pier on the South Boston Flats, which was the "largest of its type on the East Coast at the time." It was also the year when the city's—and, in fact, the nation's—first subway system opened beneath Boylston and Tremont Streets, after only one-and-a-half years of construction (Fig. 98). This expanded Boston's capacity as an international port, while introducing an innovative means of moving its residents and visitors around the ever-growing city.[92]

In that year, architecture students at MIT and Harvard first entered into interscholastic competition with those from the University of Pennsylvania, Columbia, and Cornell at the recommendation of the AIA. This annual competition highlighting work from the nation's premier architectural programs enhanced the students' and programs' awareness of one another. It also introduced the students to the sort of competition they would experience as professionals, while honing their appreciation of Usefulness and Beauty.[93]

In this year, one of Boston's elite women's clubs, the 1897 Sewing Circle, was founded, strengthening the city's social club infrastructure. Its members devoted "money, personal time, and labor" toward charitable works throughout the city. American impressionist painters—many with Boston ties—formed "The 10" and showed their work under the auspices of the St. Botolph Club. The Twentieth Century Club hired a social reformer and alumnus of Toynbee Hall, Harold Estabrook (1870–1953), to study the conditions of Boston's slums, demonstrating its commitment to social reform. The club also sponsored seven lectures on "Beauty in the Home," at which C. Howard Walker, William Emerson, Edith Brown, Edward Morse, and Alice Palmer, among others, spoke. Fiske and Gretchen Warren made a grandest of "Grand Tours," traveling around the globe and collecting many choice *objets d'art* in the Far East. Professor Ernest Francisco Fenollosa (1853–1908), who had functioned as curator of oriental art at the Museum of Fine Arts from 1890 to 1897 and had helped to stimulate an appreciation for such Asian artifacts, left the MFA to take a teaching position in Japan (Fig. 99). The Decorative Designers (New York) began creating covers for Houghton Mifflin & Co.[94]

On a related note, publisher Louis Prang, a prominent supporter of Boston's book artists and graphic designers, sold his business, and, the Plimpton Press—devoted to "perfect book-making in its entirety"—moved from Boston to Norwood. Nevertheless, graphic design in the city made great strides. Joseph M. Bowles (1860–1934) went to work for Carl Heintzemann. Will Bradley (1868–1962) strengthened his reputation as "the most original American typographer of his time" by issuing seven numbers of *Bradley—His Book* between 1896 and 1897 (Fig. 100). Bostonian Ethel Reed (b. 1874) succeeded the notorious Englishman Aubrey Beardsley as illustrator for the *Yellow Book* in 1897, a signal accomplishment given her nationality and gender (Fig. 101). Reed's work was reproduced in *The Studio Magazine* that year to great acclaim.[95]

Other Boston book artists and poets—Thomas Buford Meteyard (1865–1928), Dawson Dawson-Watson (1864–1939), Richard Hovey (1864–1900), Bliss Carmen (1861–1929) and

100. Advertisement for *Bradley His Book*, ca. 1896–97. (Courtesy Historic New England) The conventionalized cover motif resembles an espaliered grape vine.

101. Cover, *The Yellow Book, An Illustrated Quarterly*, January 1897, illustration by Ethel Reed. (Boston Public Library/Department of Rare Books. Courtesy of the Trustees) Reed's designs often juxtaposed innocence with decadence. Here the youthful profile with enormous hair bows belies the sophistication of the low décolletage and feather fan.

102. Original study for seal of the Society of Arts and Crafts, Boston, by Bertram Grosvenor Goodhue, ca. 1897. (Courtesy MIT Museum) The Tudor rose and pomegranate appear once again at the seal's center, along with tools of the art-craftsperson's trade. On the left, Saint Luke holds an artist's palette and brushes. On the right, Tubal Cain, the "First Artificer," holds a hammer. Acanthus leafage links these figures to the motto *Pulchritudo cum Utilitate*, or "Beauty with Usefulness."

103. Wall hanging, tooled, painted, and gilded leather, by Mary Ware Dennett, ca. 1900–1920. Photography by Percy Rainford. (Schlesinger Library, Radcliffe Institute, Harvard University) Ware Dennett's interpretation of Goodhue's design is faithful to the original. She studied the techniques of medieval and Renaissance leatherworking abroad, often incorporating embossing with varnished gold or silver leaf.

his colleague B. G. Goodhue—met in Scituate, Massachusetts, to produce two issues of the *Courrier Innocent*. This reflected their ongoing artistic and social collaboration in the context of clubs like the Pewter Mugs and the Visionists. In this and other ways, Boston's book artists and publishers demonstrated their international influence, innovation, and interconnectedness.[96]

Nationally, 1897 marked publication of John Dewey's *Pedagogic Creed*, stressing the important psychological and sociological aspects of children's education, and promoting an active pedagogy that included manual training. The founding of the Chicago Arts and Crafts Society in October followed the lead of the SACB earlier that year. Photographer Gertrude Kasebier opened her first public studio in New York City. Frank Lloyd Wright's dining room within his Shingle style home and studio in Oak Park, Illinois, was published in *House Beautiful* magazine in February, while Edith Wharton and Ogden Codman, Jr.'s *The Decoration of Houses* appeared in December. With Wharton's links to the Berkshires, Codman's reputation as "a clever young Boston architect," and graphic designs provided by D. B. Updike, that book's appearance was of local as well as a national importance.[97]

These events are significant for illustrating how the Arts and Crafts movement specifically and the quest for Usefulness and Beauty more generally had become national phenomena. Dewey's credo of "learning by doing" continued to inform the approach of manual training programs throughout the nation and around the world. (It was, for example, a slogan for the Evening Trade School sponsored by the Massachusetts Charitable Mechanic Association.) The founding of the Boston and the Chicago Arts and Crafts societies in 1897 led quickly to the establishment of at least seventy others throughout the country. Within ten years, forty-five of these received an invitation to join together to form the National League of Handicraft Societies.[98]

House Beautiful magazine became one of the leading voices for design reform in the country, and F. L. Wright epitomized the arts and crafts ideal in his early residential work. *The Decoration of Houses* had less influence upon the movement *per se*; but it proved that design reform transcended a particular movement and as such was less a style than an attitude. When Wharton, in the book's introduction, bemoaned the "piling up of heterogeneous ornament, [and] a multiplication of incongruous effects imposed upon interiors by the upholsterer untrained in architectural principles," her tirade recalled Morris's ranting against "masses of sordidness, filth, and squalor, embroidered with patches of pompous and utter hideousness." Certainly, *The Decoration of Houses* was important in heightening the level of critical discourse among tastemakers in the early twentieth century. It proved that Usefulness and Beauty were as important to Beaux-Arts interiors as to the more radical Prairie style, or Arts and Crafts versions.[99]

These local and national events reflected those taking place on the broader international scene. The year 1897 saw the beginning or completion of important works by architect-supporters of design reform in Britain: among these were Ernest Gimson's The White House (Leicester) built for his half-brother Arthur; Edwin Lutyen's Tigbourne Court (Surrey), described by Pevsner as "Lutyen's gayest and most elegant building and probably his best"; and C. R. Mackintosh's School of Art and the first of his tea rooms for the Misses Cranston (Glasgow). For one of these, he created his enduring "Argyle" chair. In the same year, the London publisher B. T. Batsford reprinted Hepplewhite's *Guide*, ushering in a taste for the "Georgian Revival."[100]

In 1897, Pilkington's, the English maker of lusterwares and art pottery, first began manufacturing tiles and other ceramics designed by Crane, Day, and Voysey. The American Albert Stickley (1862–1928) established a factory and showroom marketing Stickley Brothers' furniture in London. He also hired British designers to work at the Stickley establishment in Grand Rapids, Michigan. C. F. Binns immigrated to the United States and published *The Potter's Craft*. Thus, the trans-Atlantic exchange of reformist people, products, and ideas continued.[101]

The impact of the Anglo-American design reform movement became evident in reformist activities taking place throughout Europe in 1897. The year marked the founding of the Secession movement in Vienna, the culmination of decades of concern for the state of the applied arts, following the international exhibition that had taken place there in 1873. (Bostonians had attended that important event.) In 1897, reformers in Munich started the Deutsche Werkstätten fur Kunst und Handwerk, a cooperative workshop modeled after English handicraft guilds, and those in Darmstadt published *Deutsche Kunst und Dekoration*. Even the conservative École des Beaux Arts in Paris progressed during this year by admitting its first women students.[102]

Germany had acknowledged a need for design reform relatively late in comparison to other countries, but when it did so, it did enthusiastically. The Germans established artists' colonies, cooperative workshops, and exhibition societies, invited design reformers from elsewhere to visit, live, lecture, and teach within its borders, and eventually sent its own critics abroad to witness firsthand and report on what British design reformers were doing. One of these was Hermann Muthesius, who wrote *Das englische Haus* (*The English House*, 1904) as a result of his trip.

The year 1897 was an auspicious one for design reform in Scandinavia as well. An international exhibition in Brussels included a display of Swedish arts and crafts. The writer and feminist Ellen Key (1849–1926) completed pamphlets on the theme "Beauty for All." Artist Carl Larsson showed charming watercolors of Lilla Hyttnäs—his home and studio in Sundborn—at the Art and Industry Exhibition in Stockholm. Two years later, he would publish these images in the influential book *Ett Hem*, or *A Home*, which blended together arts and crafts influences in an atmosphere of "sweetness and light," filled with antiques, aesthetic touches, bright painted finishes, pots of geraniums and ivy, and his wife Karin's lovely textiles. Such events demonstrated that the quest for Usefulness and Beauty was truly international and open to diverse interpretations.[103]

It was serendipitous that the SACB appeared in 1897, and that it would include on its official seal (Figs. 102 and 103)—designed by B. G. Goodhue—the phrase "Pulchritudo cum Utilitate." Declaring "Beauty with Usefulness," the new organization proclaimed its dedication to excellence in all aspects of the built environment, represented in its seal by an architect's ruling pen, a designer's calipers, an artist's brushes and palette, and a craftsperson's claw hammer.

Incorporating these terms in the official seal established a direct link between the Boston and English branches of the Arts and Crafts movement, and paid homage to the movement's founder, William Morris, who had died a year earlier. Reflecting upon those terms, the *Boston Transcript* remarked: "There is an effect upon a community, upon municipal and national life to be gained by the appreciation of good workers and good handiwork which is inestimable. The use of beauty and the beauty of use are good masters for all concerned to serve." Defining what those terms meant, however, posed a special challenge: Only by doing so could supporters of the SACB cultivate such qualities in their work, or begin to appreciate them in the work of others. These were among the chief tasks of the new organization, the subject of Chapter Two.[104]

CHAPTER TWO

By Word, Deed, or Example

Promoting Design Reform in Boston

It is but one incident in the long history of the career of Use and Beauty through the world, hand in hand, undivorceable. All our science is engaged in spelling out their story.
—Moncure Conway, *Travels in South Kensington* (1882)

Beauty has as many meanings as man has moods. Beauty is the symbol of symbols. Beauty reveals everything, because it expresses nothing. When it shows us itself, it shows us the whole fiery-coloured world.
—Oscar Wilde, *The Critic as Artist* (1890)

From October 1897 until December 1898, the members of the SACB focused upon two goals: developing an organizational structure and recruiting active members. In doing so, they established an identity and a direction that steered the organization during its first decades. Both the organizational and membership structures provided contexts within which critics operated as they implemented their quest for Usefulness and Beauty. Three key activities during the Society's formative months were the creation of the Council—the governing body of the SACB—the writing of the by-laws, and the crafting of a mission statement.

The new society held its first meeting on October 13, 1897, at which time—following a plan developed during the previous May—members appointed representatives to the Council. In the years that followed, the Council controlled every action taken by the new organization. Those serving as Councilors during the first year included recently elected officers—C. E. Norton (president), A. A. Carey, S. W. Whitman, and J. Evans (vice-presidents), M. Gray (treasurer)—and eight others: R. D. Andrews, J. T. Coolidge, Jr., H. L. Johnson, J. Kirchmayer, A. W. Longfellow, Jr., Sarah Choate Sears (1858–1935), C. H. Walker, and H. L. Warren. Seven individuals had functioned as founders. Sears (Figs. 104 and 105) was an award-winning painter, photographer, and craftsworker in metals and textiles. The wife of Boston realtor J. Montgomery Sears, she exhibited both nationally and internationally.[1]

By November 1897, by-laws for the SACB appeared in print. They consisted of fourteen articles, preceded by the same pledge—"to develop and encourage higher artistic standards in the handicrafts"—that had been included in the charter written the previous June. It took the new organization several months to draw up the official by-laws, which then remained effectively unchanged for twenty years.[2]

Of particular interest was the description of the membership hierarchy. From the beginning, the SACB attracted a heterogeneous group of supporters: these

104. Mrs. Joshua Montgomery [Sarah Choate] Sears, 1899, by John Singer Sargent, oil on canvas, 58 1/8 x 38 1/8 in. (The Museum of Fine Arts, Houston; Gift of George R. Brown in honor of his wife, Alice Pratt Brown)

included professionals who, after years of education, training, and practice, had achieved a reputation for excellence in their fields. Others worked at a craft, as an occupation or avocation, but were novices, striving to achieve expertise and visibility. Finally, there were connoisseurs, who practiced neither art nor craft, but wished to aid the organization by means of financial support or social connections.

To recognize these distinctions, the by-laws provided for three membership classifications. Connoisseurs joined the "Patron" category (a term that later became "Associate"), and paid the highest annual dues of the three groups ($10.00/year) for the privilege of being members. Working architects, designers, and craftspeople fell into either the "Master" or the "Apprentice" (later called "Craftsman") categories, depending upon training, years of experience, and level of expertise. (Dues for these groups ranged from $5 to $2–3 respectively.) In this way, the SACB's organizational structure recalled that of a medieval guild, where masters trained apprentices and journeymen in the art and mystery of a craft or trade, working under the patronage of church and nobility. After some debate,

105. *Untitled (A Poet)*, by Sarah Choate Sears, ca. 1892–ca. 1905. (Courtesy Harvard University Art Museums, Fogg Art Museum, Gift of Montgomery S. Bradley and Cameron Bradley, P1984.73) This three-quarter-length portrait photo shows the unidentified subject standing against a tapestry and near a paneled seating piece. The sharply focused figure contrasts with the softly focused furnishings.

the founders of the SACB—who were aware of the Socialist connections of many of the British reform organizations—chose to incorporate the term "Society" rather than "Guild" into the new organization's name, believing the former to be less political. The similarity between the organization's structure and that of a medieval guild was, nevertheless, strong.[3]

The number of Patrons and Masters was always smaller than was the number of Craftsman members; yet, the collective voice of the Patrons and Masters prevailed over the Craftsman members in the day-to-day running of the organization, in determining its policies, and ultimately in defining what the organization deemed Useful or Beautiful. Not surprisingly, this led to dissension within the group.

It is worth noting that the designation "Craftsman" pertained equally to men and women, and never changed to a less gender-specific designation. It may be that members regarded the "Craftsman" designation as being derived not from the term "man," meaning "male," but instead from an abbreviation of the Latin term *manus*, meaning "hand." Thus, a Craftsman member was any person engaged in handmade crafts, regardless of gender.[4]

A prospectus that appeared on December 9, 1897, outlined non-administrative activities for the SACB's first eighteen months. In this brochure, the organization proposed to "open a room in a central position where Artists and Craftsmen [might] meet for consultation and discussion." This was important, since meetings during the first months took place wherever space was available—at members' homes, in artists' studios, or in buildings around town. The brochure indicated that "workmen desirous of advice and instruction [might] at stated times find competent and sympathetic advisers" under the SACB's auspices. Implied, but unspoken, was the presence of critics who were willing to function in this role. Keeping the importance of design education in mind, the brochure also outlined a plan to "open Workshops and Classes where young Craftsmen [might] receive instruction." Such ambitious plans suggested that establishing a permanent headquarters would soon be a priority.[5]

Third and perhaps most important, the brochure indicated that the SACB would "from time to time to hold Exhibitions of exemplary work in metal, wood, stone, glass, clay, textile and other materials, and in every branch of industry in which Art and Craft are combined." It anticipated holding such an event in the "early Spring of 1899" provided that such a venture were financially viable, and explained the rules that would control the selection of exhibits. "Objects may be offered for exhibition by members of the Society only," it began, "but designers and craftsmen, living beyond a limit of 40 miles from Boston, may be invited by members of the Council to send in objects for exhibition." Even at this early date, the brochure makes clear the power of the Council as an administrative body and as an arbiter of taste. "No work," the brochure cautioned, "shall be accepted which is not deemed worthy according to the best standards." After outlining the plans by which the Society would determine exactly what those standards would be, the brochure concluded with a plea: "Such are the immediate aims of The Society of Arts and Crafts and to enable it to carry them out, it asks for the help and co-operation of all Workmen, Artists, and Lovers of Art,—of all men and women who are interested in improving the quality and raising the standards of Handicraft." With this final statement, the brochure indicated that the SACB welcomed anyone who would support its campaign for design reform and its promotion of excellence.

The inclusion of the capital T, as in "The Society," reveals something about the SACB's self-image even at an early stage. Its founders always regarded the organization not as one society among many, but instead as "The Society," first among equals. "The fact that our Society was the first organized," stated the Council in a report of January 1903, "makes it the natural leader in the movement and should give us still further incentive to make our plans as progressive and sound as possible, both from the economic and artistic standpoints . . . after earnest study of the underlying principles."[6]

During the first year and a half, the SACB worked quietly but with purpose. Members kept busy with meetings, craft demonstrations, lectures, and classes—held at Mechanics Hall—that were "of practical service to Workmen, quickening the spirit of invention in design and encouraging technical excellence."

Advertising these events were striking announcements, designed by D. B. Updike and printed crisply in black ink on creamy, deckle-edged paper (Fig. 19). In contrast to B. G. Goodhue's bold Morrisian design for the catalogue cover for the First Exhibition of the Arts and Crafts, these announcements were conservatively classical in nature, embellished with delicate motifs—swags, urns, finials, birds, anthemia, and grotesques—printed in bright red. For an organization in which book artists were so prominent, it is surprising that the SACB never really developed a consistent and recognizable graphic identity. Designers and printers changed frequently as did the appearance of the organization's announcements and publications.[7]

In character, Updike's announcements were consistent with the SACB's formal statement of purpose, drafted sometime during the spring or summer of 1897 by an unidentified author who may have been Norton, H. L. Warren, or the two working together. Thereafter, it appeared in every important document published by the SACB. "This Society was incorporated," it began, "for the purpose of promoting artistic work in all branches of handicraft. It hopes to bring Designers and Workmen into mutually helpful relations, and to encourage workmen to execute designs of their own. It endeavors to stimulate in workmen an appreciation of the dignity and value of good design," it went on, "to counteract the popular impatience of Law and Form, and the desire for over-ornamentation and specious originality. It will insist upon the necessity of sobriety and restraint, of ordered arrangement, of due regard for the relation between the form of an object and its use, and," it concluded, "of harmony and fitness in the decoration put upon it."[8]

This statement encapsulated the Society's emerging definition of "good design." It does not mention Beauty per se, but it offers suggestions of what aesthetic traits contribute to it. It argues that a little ornament or decoration goes a long way. It indicates that Usefulness results when aesthetic and functional considerations coincide. It promotes originality provided that it is genuine. It implies that the design process is deliberate and time-consuming, while arguing that laws are important to keep in mind at all times. This last point links the SACB's definition of "good design" to that of other critics—national and international—who emphasized the importance of laws, principles, rules, canons, or even recipes.

At the core of this statement of purpose were commitments to artistic and social cooperation, and a dedication to design reform. "Sobriety and restraint" influenced not only the aesthetic approach of most members in the years that followed, but also characterized their attitude toward design reform, which most regarded not as a leisure-time pursuit but as a serious, life-long mission.

Promoting Sobriety and Restraint: The Society's 1899 Exhibition

During 1899, the SACB continued to create a context for promoting its campaign for design reform. Several significant events took place that year, each of which affected in some way critics' ability to function under the organization's auspices or to achieve greater visibility within the community. The first was a change in administration, as Arthur Astor Carey took over the presidency from the aging Charles Eliot Norton. The second was the opening of a second major exhibition of arts and crafts. The third was a dramatic increase in membership, due in part to a requirement that individuals be SACB members to be eligible to participate in the show.

Carey (Fig. 49) was forty-two years old when he replaced the seventy-one-year-old Norton as president. A graduate of Harvard (1879), Carey had traveled and studied in Europe in the 1880s, at which time he responded to Ruskin's influence. Between 1890–and 1893, he had taught English at Harvard, eventually leaving academia to devote himself to social reform. He was also an active committee member and trustee of the Museum of Fine Arts, and treasurer of the Boston Public School Art League, which helped install pictures, casts, and photographs in schoolrooms. By the time he became SACB president, his social and professional acquaintances included many of Boston's artists, architects, art administrators, social reformers, and connoisseurs. Highly visible both beyond and within the organization, Carey was a logical choice to succeed Norton.[9]

Most important, he was able to bring a level of financial support to the fledgling organization through his connections with the city's social elite, and his own philanthropy. Few SACB members realized that Carey financed the 1899 Exhibition, anonymously and almost single-handedly, and would continue to infuse the organization with funds for the duration of his presidency, which lasted until November 1903.[10]

It required more than money, though, to guarantee the success of the 1899 Exhibition. This was an opportunity to put the SACB's newly drafted credo of "good design" to the test. To ensure high standards among the works exhibited, the Council appointed an executive committee composed exclusively of founders: H. L. Warren, S. W. Whitman, A. W. Longfellow, J. T. Coolidge Jr., H. L. Johnson, and J. Kirchmayer. The executive committee enlisted the help of others—again a majority had been founders—to select items within specific media categories, including metalwork and jewelry (R. D. Andrews); cabinetry, modeling, and carving (Edmund Wheelwright (1854–1912, architect for the City of Boston); pottery and glassware (A. W. Longfellow); stained glass and decorations (S. W. Whitman); illustrations, printing, bookbinding, engraving, and photography (D. B. Updike); textiles, embroidery, and leatherwork (G. R. Shaw); and carpets and wallpaper (Mrs. William Stone, representing the School of the Museum of Fine Arts). It is significant that four of these seven were architects, reflecting the control as a group that they had exerted over the organization in its formative months, and would continue to wield for decades to follow. Together, these committee members solicited objects for display, and then reviewed and accepted or rejected them, installing the chosen entries in time for the April 4th opening.[11]

"I hope this second display," stated H. L. Johnson, "will in a small degree mark a turning point in public attention to industrial art in this community. If we could only have transported to Boston or New York one of the German or English Exhibitions or museums of applied art, the American public, with its ready and keen power of observation, and its faculty for determining differences and making comparisons, would be a little chagrined to find out how limited our applied art is, except in the houses of well-to-do people who have been abroad." Thus Johnson appealed to the public's critical eye, while suggesting that design reform in Boston still had a long way to go.[12]

These exhibition planners used the First Exhibition of the Arts and Crafts of 1897 as a model for the second, but made improvements to the conceptual, aesthetic, and technical quality of works on display. They selected these with care, restricting contributors to SACB members or invited guests. They increased publicity to appeal to a broad audience, and extended the hours of operation to attract working people. They stressed the educational function of the show by including lectures and live demonstrations of craft techniques.

What is more, they compiled a special display of antiques, loaned by SACB members and a few local collectors. Contributors included A. A. Carey, J. T. Coolidge, Jr., D. W. Ross, and C. E. Norton, as well as Associate member Frank Gair Macomber (1883–1929), who was an insurance agent, collector of Chinese pottery, and honorary curator of the Museum of Fine Arts (Fig. 106), the painter, bookbinder, and designer Joseph Lindon Smith (1863–1950, Fig. 107), interior decorator and designer John Endicott Peabody (1853–1921, Figs. 108a, b, and c), and connoisseur Isabella Stewart Gardner (1840–1924, Fig. 109). Mrs. Gardner was not an SACB member; yet she had been a long-time friend of founders Norton, Coolidge, and Whitman and a patron of Smith's, and remained a strong supporter of the organization for years.[13]

OFFICE OF FRANK GAIR MACOMBER,
115 Water Street.

Fire, Marine, and Liability Insurance. Agency of the British and Foreign Marine Insurance Company, Limited, of Liverpool, London, and Boston. Marine Agency of the Delaware Insurance Company of Philadelphia.

106. Advertisement for Frank Gair Macomber. From George W. Englehardt, *Boston, Massachusetts* (1897). (Courtesy Boston Athenaeum)

By compiling this loan collection, the exhibit planners gave those attending the show "an opportunity for instructive comparison of some of the best examples of craftsmanship of past times with the most promising work of the present." This was one of the first major public displays of *objets d'art* from private collections to

PROMOTING DESIGN REFORM IN BOSTON   115

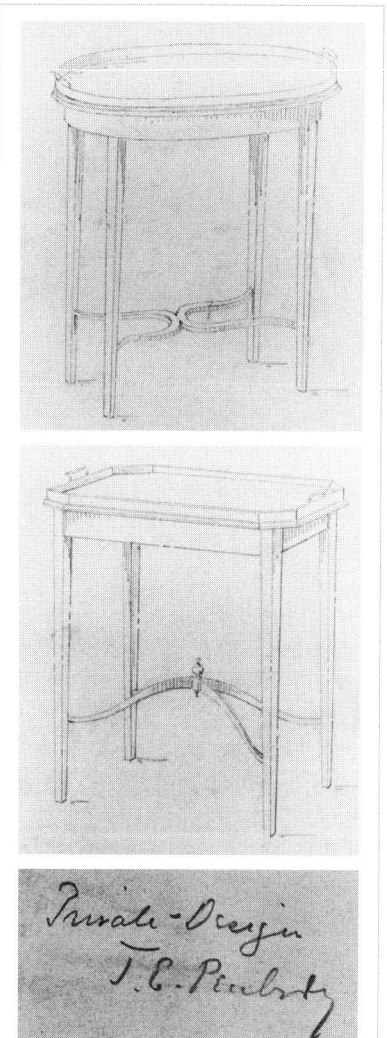

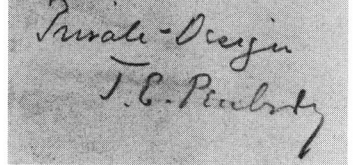

be held in the United States, and thus offered attendees an unprecedented opportunity (Fig. 110). It also made clear that the SACB viewed the past as an important model for "good design" in the present (a topic addressed more fully in Chapter Four).[14]

The goal of the exhibition planners was to assuage concerns expressed by local critics such as Frederick W. Coburn (b. 1870), who wrote for the *Boston Herald* as well as other papers. A supporter of the plans for the 1899 Exhibition, Coburn nevertheless pointed out the limitations of the First Exhibition: "Held in Copley Hall," he wrote years later, "it was successful in a popular sense, but the time was not ripe for maintaining a very high standard." Here Coburn stressed a point emphasized in the SACB's newly drafted statement of purpose. "I recall," he continued, "the criticism made of the show by a distinguished New York painter who went over to Boston especially to see the exhibits and who told a group of art students on his return that his really strong belief in the arts and crafts revival had been put to a severe test." Coburn did not identify this individual (who most likely chose to remain anonymous due to

107. Joseph Lindon Smith, ca. 1910. (Schlesinger Library, Radcliffe Institute, Harvard University) A multi-talented painter and graphic designer, Smith was known to members of the Tavern Club as "JoJo."

108a. "Private-Design" for an oval table in Hepplewhite style, by John Endicott Peabody, ca. 1906–21. (Courtesy SACB Archives) Peabody was an interior decorator, collector of antiques, and occasional designer of furniture in the Colonial Revival style. This design may have been for one of his clients or for sale in the SACB salesroom. The price of the table, listed on the reverse side of the drawing, was $30.

108b. "Private-Design" for a tea table with saltire stretcher in Hepplewhite style, by John Endicott Peabody, ca. 1906–21. (Courtesy SACB Archives)

108c. Signature of J. E. Peabody. (Courtesy SACB Archives) This appears on the reverse side of the drawings of the two tables.

109. Postcard, Mrs. Jack Gardner's Venetian Palace, Boston. Published by The Leighton & Valentine Co., New York. (Author's collection)

110. Allston Hall, Exhibition of the Society of Arts and Crafts, 1899. Photograph by Chickering. (Courtesy SACB Archives) The exhibition catalogue notes that this display, "drawn entirely from the private collections of Boston," represents primarily the fifteenth through the seventeenth centuries. "It has been extremely difficult to arrange in a satisfactory manner, . . ." and the "many pieces of such various styles . . . have been grouped . . . to please the eye rather than to maintain historic sequence."

the vitriol of his comments), but nevertheless went on to share his critique: "'Many of the things were uglier than the machine could have made them—misshapen pots all aswim with molasses; sprawling hinges and eccentric fireirons. Other exhibits were of course better, but our craftsmen have not yet reached the point where they can be original without being bizarre.'" By raising the issue of originality and noting the difficulty of achieving it, both the artist and Coburn reinforced one of the Council's chief concerns.[15]

When the exhibition, held once again in the Grundmann Studios Building near Copley Square, opened on the evening of April 4th, visitors were able to judge for themselves the progress made by the SACB during its formative years. Copley Hall was the repository for contemporary handicrafts (Fig. 111), while Allston Hall held the loan collection. Newspaper accounts indicated that the combined value of items in both rooms—approximately 4,000 works—approached one million dollars.[16]

Journalists seemed uniformly impressed by what they saw, though they differed regarding which hall held the most noteworthy contents. One reviewer considered the loan collection "to be the prime attraction," while another preferred the display of contemporary handicrafts, describing it in superlatives as "the most diversified, the most valuable and the most beautiful display of industrial art ever presented in the United States." Such praise must have been welcome to the exhibition planners.[17]

111. Copley Hall, Exhibition of the Society of Arts and Crafts, 1899. Photograph by Chickering. (Courtesy SACB Archives) This installation followed the precedent set at the 1897 First Exhibition, once again including topiary trees, wreaths, and swags of greenery. But the overall effect is less cluttered.

Several journalists regarded the accompanying catalogue as one of the exhibition's most notable products, calling it "one of the most important descriptive catalogues of foreign and American industrial art ever published in the United States." Its handsome cover—designed by book artist William Porter Jenkins (b. ca. 1860)—featured a full-blown poppy surmounting asymmetrical scrolled acanthus leafage in the Art Nouveau style, framing an open book with ornamental clasps inscribed with a quotation from William Morris (Fig. 112). It is," the writer continued, "brimful of historical annotations, with regard to the superb loan collection of examples of old crafts in Allston Hall—a capital little reference book for medieval craftsmanship; it contains a carefully edited list of 3,000 Boston, New England and New York examples of art craftsmanship for 1898 and 1899, and is prefaced with a brief essay written especially for the catalogue by Professor H. Langford Warren of Harvard University."[18]

Warren's essay, like the statement of purpose drafted in 1898, justifies the role played by the SACB in the community and summarizes its emerging philosophy of "good design." Warren begins by emphasizing the educational nature of the exhibition that might benefit both consumers and design practitioners. He stresses that the loan collection provides visitors with an opportunity for comparison of old to new. He warns that the vitality and very existence of the applied arts are presently in jeopardy, stating: "The century now drawing to a close has been marvelous for its mechanical and scientific development; but the

112. Catalogue cover, by William Porter Jenkins. (Courtesy SACB Archives) Like the installation of contemporary handicrafts, this cover design shows a greater restraint than that produced by Goodhue for the 1897 First Exhibition.

very rapidity of this development and the conditions that made it possible have been adverse to the development of the Fine Arts. Indeed, with regard to the lesser arts of handicraft," he points out, "we almost reached the condition of forgetting that they might be fine arts at all,—they have, in fact, for the most part, ceased to be such." Warren then commends the current revival of public interest in the applied arts both in the United States and abroad, but warns that the public must work to implement reforms by "demanding what is good and refusing what is base." He challenges the public to encourage—not "crush, stunt, or misdirect"—the latent talents within Boston's design community.[19]

Justifying the importance of design reform to the community in this way, Warren then presents a series of guidelines that might enable anyone—maker, manufacturer, retailer, consumer, critic—to determine "good design." In doing so, he assumes the role of critic and adviser. First, he states, "every form must be perfectly adapted to the use for which it is intended: it must be fitting and suitable,—recognition of purpose must be the dominant idea in the design." Second, he cautions that "eccentricity of form is to be avoided as vulgar." Third, he states, "every form should be in harmony with the material in which it is executed." To ensure this, he warns, requires "a thorough knowledge and sensitive appreciation of the habits of the materials used, and of the methods of the particular craft employed." In a Ruskinian tone, Warren says: "Out of these will grow beauty and grace of proportion and outline,—the expression of the delight which the workman takes in his work." Fourth, he states, "the decoration put upon any object must be in harmony with its form and appropriate to its use," as "the more intimate [this] relation . . . the more beautiful it will be." Finally, he advises that simplicity is preferable to meretricious or vulgar decoration, calling the former "one of the highest qualities in artistic work.".[20]

In the next section of his essay, Warren argues that the present system of factory production—with its division of labor—discourages the application of these five guidelines. He condemns the division of labor as segregating designer from craftsworker, thus creating what he terms an "unnatural divorce." Ideally, Warren stresses, the two should be one in the same, allowing conceptualization and execution of a design to be controlled by one mind and a single pair of hands. "Good design is organic and living," Warren argues, "and finds expression in the thing itself, not merely in paper to be unsympathetically translated by another." The theory of organic design was an important contribution of the nineteenth century, espoused by Ruskin and adopted by such midwestern architects as Louis Sullivan and his apprentice Frank Lloyd Wright.

Warren warns against "machine-executed designs." He acknowledges that machinery has the capacity to relieve workers from tedious processes, but he cautions against executing ornament mechanically, stating: "artistic character and quality can only be given by handiwork." Here Warren reiterates themes popularized by Carlyle, Ruskin, and Morris in earlier decades. In doing so, he aims the SACB's reformist efforts directly at Boston's thriving manufacturers.[21]

In conclusion, Warren reminds consumers—or "all those who sincerely love beauty"—that "public demand really controls the quality of design." He advises buyers to heed Morris's words: "Have nothing in your houses that you do not know to be useful or believe to be beautiful." He stresses that the exhibition provides models for the public to follow as they learn to be more discriminating in their selection of goods for home or workplace.

He ends his essay with a challenge to every reader: "It remains to be seen whether the encouraging signs of an awakening interest in things artistic and of the growing appreciation of the supreme importance of beauty to the welfare and happiness of mankind is as yet sufficiently strong to carry the movement forward to an abiding success." He implies that such success depends upon forces beyond his organization, that the SACB can do only so much in championing the cause of Usefulness and Beauty.[22]

Despite the challenges facing design reformers generally, the 1899 Exhibition was a success. To satisfy popular demand, the exhibition committee extended the show's duration by one week, enabling more visitors to attend. The committee made arrangements for art students from throughout New England to attend at special times when the show was closed to the general public. It organized lectures, by S. W. Whitman and others, and live demonstrations of lace-making and rug-weaving to supplement the displays. As a result of its efforts, by the exhibition's conclusion, SACB membership had more than doubled.[23]

Journalists interpreted the exhibition's success as having myriad implications.

A writer for the *Transcript* believed that the show was a "decided refutation" of the argument that Boston could not mount two outstanding shows within two years' time. Another "noted expert on industrial design" called the exhibition "the most comprehensive, most costly and most beautiful ever seen in the United States." Yet, though he pronounced it "distinctly admirable as a new educational feature in this country," the expert nevertheless found the show to be "very inferior to European exhibitions." A third noted a positive outcome of the exhibition, indicating that, through such events, "industrial and moneyed people" were becoming increasingly aware of the "right of the one beautiful thing" to exist. They might, the journalist argued, thus "cease to pin their faith wholly to the stock type of things . . . that can be turned out in a million exact duplicates." In addition, the writer noted, corporations or companies were beginning to "acknowledge the dependence of industry on the individual artist" who had designed or executed these beautiful things. This might lead to artists' receiving greater recognition from manufacturers and the public.[24]

A last reviewer praised the SACB—and the exhibition—as "established force[s] for the promotion of a higher standard of beauty in our manufactured goods." But, this writer cautioned, the social elite alone could not bring about a renaissance of the industrial arts. "The arts are co-equal," he stated, "and in no country can they flourish for long without the backing of the plain people." The writer advised a "rehabilitation of the artistic trades and manufacturers" as one way of achieving this. Such comments allowed critics both within and outside the SACB to render opinions on the present state of the allied arts in the city and region, and on the progress made by the SACB thus far.[25]

Establishing a Headquarters: The Permanent Exhibition and Salesroom

At the conclusion of the 1899 Exhibition, A. A. Carey set out to solidify the SACB's presence in the community by establishing a permanent headquarters, made possible by his annual gift to the organization of $2,000. By the autumn of 1900, those headquarters—which had been leased in the spring from the Twentieth Century Club—were open for business at 14 Somerset Street (Fig. 113). The link with the reformist Twentieth Century Club—where both C. Howard Walker and Sarah Wyman Whitman served on the Art Committee—and the proximity to the Boston Society of Architects and the Boston Architectural Club seemed appropriate for the SACB, which remained at that location for four years.[26]

At the same time, Carey set out as well to find a paid employee to function as secretary and treasurer, duties performed until then by SACB officers on a volunteer basis. In June 1900, Carey hired Frederick Allen Whiting (1873–1959), a native of Tennessee, who had grown up and had received his education in the Boston vicinity (Fig. 114). A twenty-seven-year-old bachelor, Whiting began his new job shortly after returning from a trip to England. He had met Howard Walker aboard ship on his trip home, and also knew SACB members Mary Ware

113. Somerset Street toward Hampton Place Church, Boston, undated. (Courtesy Historic New England) The lighter brick, four-story structure stands at the intersection of Somerset and Ashburton Place, close to the location of the Twentieth Century Club.

114. Frederick Allen Whiting. (Courtesy Cleveland Museum of Art)

Dennett (1872–1947) and her husband, architect Hartley Dennett (1870–1936). Together, they may have convinced Whiting to apply for the job. He served as SACB secretary and treasurer for twelve years, during which time he married Olive Elizabeth Cook (b. ca. 1873, Fig. 115) and established his reputation as a promoter of design reform as well as a writer, critic, and lecturer. Neither artist nor craftsperson, Whiting was nevertheless a passionate spokesman for the Arts and Crafts movement.[27]

In part because of these activities and the success of the 1899 Exhibition, membership in the SACB grew to over 200 by the end of 1900. Such support and suitable accommodations enabled Whiting—as a full-time administrator—to under-take establishing a "permanent exhibition and salesroom" shortly after his arrival.[28]

By displaying and selling members'

work, the SACB hoped, as Whiting noted in a pamphlet, to "draw the public into closer and more sympathetic relations with [its] craftsmen members." It strove to attract "the intelligent support of those who desire[d] to secure better made and more beautiful things for their own homes or for gifts." The salesroom was only modestly successful in its first years, but its presence led to the establishment of a Jury—composed of a select group of the SACB's elite—to review all work submitted by members for display or sale. That, in turn, required the Jury members to develop criteria according to which they would judge submissions. The Jury used as a basis for those criteria references to "good design" given in the organization's early pledge, its statement of purpose, and some of the guidelines articulated by Langford Warren in his introduction to the *1899 Exhibition Catalogue*. So important

115. Olive Elizabeth Whiting, taken after 1922. (Courtesy Cleveland Museum of Art)

was the Jury in determining the organization's evolving definition of Usefulness and Beauty, that its composition, activities, and criticism are the subject of Chapter Three.[29]

Whiting recalled with some wistfulness the ambience of the early days of the SACB salesroom. "There comes to me tonight," he reminisced in later years, "a picture of the old rooms in Somerset Street where we started our salesrooms. The great oak table made by one of our members and lent by Mr. Carey, lamplighted for the cheerful evening consultations. The sparkling comments of Mrs. Henry [Sarah Wyman] Whitman (always a devoted friend to the Society) and the continuous flow of epigrams by Dr. Ross. These bespoke a sense of leisureliness impossible in the more strenuous later days." Here Whiting referred to the SACB's increasingly ambitious agenda and to political strife that erupted within the organization a few years later.[30]

Whiting's recollections contrast with those of Elizabeth Bent Eaton Stone (1858–1942), wife and business partner of English émigré silversmith Arthur J. Stone (1847–1938), whose works were among the salesroom's best sellers over the ensuing decades. Mrs. Stone's comments give a vivid—if not always flattering—impression of the salesroom's appearance in its early years: "Eight years ago in that little Somerset room, which took quite a deal of finding," she began, pointing out one of its several demerits, "I recall the tiny wall cupboard just on the left as we entered in which the silver was kept. There was wont to be displayed a child's mug or two, a sugar and cream, a porringer, some bowls and a few lonesome spoons. . . . I never left in a covetous frame of mind. There was little variety to be found, and a depressing sparseness about it all that laid hold of the spirit. Mind you, the germ was there," she pointed out, "a thoroughly active culture as it proves. Such textiles as there were suggest[ed] bungaloes . . . of the simple life. Something more in accord with urban life was to be found in the pottery. . . . I liked the textiles and the leather but I am bound to say that my recollection of the jewelry," she concluded humorously, "carried with it visions of wearers never less than 6–2, moving with theatrical imperturbability to the fixed gaze of their fellow creatures." Because the SACB salesroom was so important to her husband's career, New Englander Elizabeth Stone was always one of its staunchest critics, evaluating not only the merchandise, but also the shop's ambience, staff, and business practices.[31]

Whiting was critical of the salesroom as well. At the end of his first year, he provided Carey with a self-evaluation that included plans for the future and an assessment of the SACB's situation. He felt that he must become more knowledgeable about workers and craft techniques to represent them fully. He strove to "facilitate cooperation of the most helpful kind among craftsmen, and also between craftsmen and the public." With that in mind, he established a "Bureau of Information," a repository of biographical materials on SACB craftsworkers, and a growing reference library of books on craft history and techniques.[32]

Most important, Whiting promoted expanding the SACB membership to strengthen the organization's visibility and effectiveness in the community, and to increase sales. But he cautioned Carey that any new members should include Masters and Craftsmen only, since many believed the SACB to be "run by a lot of connoisseurs," and accordingly felt disenfranchised. They were probably reacting to the power of the founders—many of whom were Associate members—who held key decision-making positions as officers, Councilors, Jurors, and committee chairs.[33]

Articulating a Philosophy of Design Reform

In the fall of 1901, Carey offered some of his own observations to the entire membership in a lecture entitled "The Past Year and Its Lessons." On this occasion, he proved himself to be a powerful critic of the organization and a visionary with a controversial point of view.

He began his talk by reviewing the history of the Society, condensing the events of the first years into a few broad and highly critical statements. "During the first three years," he indicated, "we made the mistake of relying too much upon our good intentions, and not organizing the work closely enough to make it practically effective." By 1900, he said, the organization had grown "a little afraid of abstract principles and somewhat hungry for concrete and tangible facts. We had pleasant social meetings, charming and scholarly addresses, and widely attended public exhibitions of works of varying quality. But," he concluded sternly, ". . . far too little of Art and Craft."[34]

He then reiterated the Society's statement of purpose, questioning the meaning of each section. "The reason why designers and workmen are so rarely working

116. "Scenes of the Watch Making Factory in Waltham," from *Appleton's Journal*, 1870, pp. 29–30. (Schlesinger Library, Radcliffe Institute, Harvard University) A "division of labor" meant that most workers performed only one part of the fabrication process, repetitively. Women, for example, though they worked side-by-side with men, were responsible for the gilded finishes of these watches.

together in mutually helpful relations," he began, "and why workmen do not execute designs of their own, is because employers of artistic labor are for the most part business concerns that care more for the profit they can make on the product than they do for the beauty or use of the product itself." Carey attributed the current state of the handicrafts to a variety of evils, reiterating many of Langford Warren's points from his *1899 Exhibition Catalogue* introduction. These included the factory-method of production, which "subjected the craftsman to artistically stultifying conditions" by enforcing an artificial division of labor (Fig. 116); manufacturers' quest for low costs and high profits, which, in his view, proved "antagonistic to the requirements to making things beautifully"; pervasive commercialism that supported a market in which "inferior" products survived at the expense of the "genuine" article; the practice of thwarting healthy competition in the market place by offering bribes to obtain commissions; and the system of vocational training and design education in general.

Together, he concluded, these had created a situation in which it was impossible for individual handicrafts persons to survive. To illustrate his point, he presented several case studies of SACB members—leatherworkers, metalworkers, and tile makers—who had been unable to operate profitably an independent workshop or studio.

Carey offered a solution for ensuring a "strong, lasting revival of the arts of beauty in connection with use": he proposed starting a series of cooperative workshops in Boston that would bring together independent workers in a collaborative atmosphere. Such workshops, he believed, would "preserve and protect the [handicrafts] until such time as the conditions of society at large [would] be more hospitabl[e]." Carey hoped these workshops might eventually relocate to a rural setting "where the principles of true craftsmanship could be lived and practiced as a matter of course," and, he added, "where space, air, light and quiet" would contribute to a congenial communal work environment.

Such anti-urban, cooperative enterprises were consistent with regional, national, and international trends, as utopian craft communities sprang up throughout

117. Coin or sterling silver salt cellars and spoons, produced at the Handicraft Shop, by Mary C. Knight, and Karl F. Leinonen. From *Handicraft*, ca. April 1902. (Courtesy SACB Archives) These simple forms with restrained ornament were typical of the hollowware and flatware produced at the Handicraft Shop.

the United States and Great Britain. American examples included Rose Valley, which operated in Moylan, Pennsylvania, between 1901 and 1908, the Roycrofters, who lived and worked in East Aurora, New York, ca. 1895–1916, the Elverhoj Artist's and Craftsman's Colony, located along the Hudson River, and Byrdcliffe (founded ca. 1903) in Ulster County, New York. But, Carey cautioned, "it would not be necessary for a member of this community to be eccentric, to wear long hair, or to do any of the things which rob such movements of their dignity, while adding to their notoriety in the eyes of the world."[35]

One manifestation of Carey's vision was the Handicraft Shop, a true cooperative workshop, which encouraged the artistic interaction of several members of the SACB who were guided in their venture by three directors: a business manager, a financial backer, and an artistic director. The Handicraft Shop produced "beautiful and appropriate" articles in silver, copper and brass, and other materials (Fig. 117). Metalworkers Mary C. Knight (b. 1876, active until 1927), Seth Ek (active 1906–12), and Karl F. Leinonen (1866–1957)—the latter two both Finnish immigrants—designed and executed coin or sterling silver coffee services and flatware in a restrained Colonial Revival style. Enameling embellished some pieces. As the shop grew, the metalworkers also provided a service to "convert old silver which is either too ugly or too worn for use, into ware which is both useful and beautiful." Mary Ware Dennett, the shop's artistic director who also sold work under its auspices, produced leather wall hangings and wallpapers, printed from blocks designed by Lockwood de Forest (1850–1932), the former associate of Louis Comfort Tiffany, Candace Wheeler, and Samuel Coleman.[36]

Carey provided financial support for the Handicraft Shop, where craftspeople labored, as he said, with "single-minded devotion to their work" in an atmosphere that was "friendly, reciprocally helpful, broadening and pleasure-giving." The shop was a living embodiment of the principle of "mutually helpful relations." Carey viewed the experimental workshop as an alternative where independent craftspeople might earn a living. He believed that the Handicraft Shop—if a success—could serve as a model for other similar shops throughout Boston. By working in a small cooperative situation, craftspeople could avoid the debilitating isolation from their co-workers that they experienced in the typical factory, using a system of divided labor. They could learn, Carey argued, from each other's conceptual, aesthetic, and technical expertise. They could produce more artifacts as a group than they might if working alone, and thus realize a greater profit. They could, he concluded, benefit from the guidance of business managers.[37]

Carey ended his remarks by urging SACB members to be "discriminating in their purchases" and to patronize only those craftspeople whose work reflected a "love of truth and beauty carried out in useful work"; this would "tend to develop individual character, to dignify skill in the worker, to raise the standard of public taste and," he concluded idealistically, "to add vastly to the sum of human happiness." Above all, Carey urged all craftspeople to work "for the love of [their] work and of useful service first and only as a secondary matter for the money that [they might] earn." He ended his speech with an exhortation: "The cause we are trying to uphold lies deeper than at first appears; it is far broader than Art itself, and underlies all human action whenever effort rises above the mere animal plane." Carey's talk—and its socio-economic overtones—may have reflected recent actions of Boston's trade unions, described in articles published at the time of the 1899 Exhibition. The *American Architect and Building News*, for example, identified trade unions as the SACB's "principal enemy" in "carrying out its beneficent purposes." Trade unions strove to limit the number of apprentices in shops in order "to restrict the possible number of competitors." Trade unions, the article went on to explain, would strike against any shop exceeding a set limit, but they could not strike against trade schools, institutions that the SACB supported as a means of improving design education. Graduates of such schools, the writer argued, were "as a rule so intelligent and skilful" that employers and unions competed to employ them, driving up wages. In defiance of such efforts, Boston trade unions had recently lobbied against the Franklin Fund, which had dedicated $350,000 to supporting trade schools.[38]

As long as such funds were "diverted to other uses," H. L. Johnson argued in another article in the *Boston Herald*, existing American schools would always compare poorly to European schools. The result of this, Johnson pointed out, was that the "best workmen" in the city and the nation would continue to be "foreign . . . artisans who have secured a thorough training abroad." This was an ongoing problem—antithetical to the SACB's efforts—and continued to be debated in the local press for years to come.[39]

Motivated by this and other pressing issues, Carey's vision for the SACB was necessarily political. He was more concerned with socio-economic reform than with aesthetic issues. His comments presented a strategic plan for the Society's activities that was focused, but to some members alienating.

In the same month that Carey delivered his talk, Whiting began lecturing on behalf of the SACB, traveling around the commonwealth, the region, and the nation. While Carey's "The Past Year and Its Lessons" was intended initially for SACB members only—he was essentially "preaching to the choir"—Whiting's standard speech was aimed at a broad lay audience. His topic, "The Development and Meaning of the Arts and Crafts Movement," presented a consistent overall philosophy of Usefulness and Beauty.

Whiting generally began his talk with a historical overview, tracing how the lives of craftspeople and methods of production had changed over time. He spoke of the close relationship between maker and user during the Middle Ages, and the "rise and fall of the guilds." He followed with an account of the introduction of labor-saving devices and the transformation of the worker to a mere "hand." He discussed the intervention of the Machine and changes to the production process resulting in the division of labor—"the one thing which is most to blame for the mass of uninteresting, ill-constructed, thoughtless work which confronts us today"—that came with the Industrial Revolution.[40]

He contrasted the situation of the pre-industrial worker, who "was interested in his work for its own sake, who believed that everything has an inherent beauty which it is the craftsman's duty and privilege to bring forth," with the plight of the late-nineteenth-century factory employee restricted to replicating a single task monotonously. The result of that system, Whiting argued, using chairs as examples, was: "100 or 1000 of them—as identical and as perfect as accurate machinery can make them, with hardly a touch of human interest left by one of the many hands through which [the chairs] have passed." As a remedy, he took the path of Warren and Carey, admonishing his listeners to invest in products—even though they might be more expensive than commercial examples—made by the "struggling, earnest company of Craftsmen." He viewed this as a way of improving the quality of available goods, while restoring these craftspeople' sense of worth, dignity, and interest in work. Whiting suggested that Usefulness and Beauty were expressions of these three factors.

Whether addressing makers, manufacturers, patrons, or users, Whiting provided a brief overview of the origins of the Arts and Crafts movement, quoting liberally from Carlyle, Ruskin, and Morris. "Mr. Morris successfully proved," Whiting stated, "that in our day, under the right conditions, people without artistic training can produce artistic results when directed by those who inspire them with a vital interest in the production of beauty." He made clear that writers, critics, educators, and even reformist organizations might be inspirationally instructive to novices, amateurs, factory workers, manufacturers, or consumers. Whiting then went on to discuss the SACB, its background, and its mission.

He ended his talks offering a philosophy of "good design," in keeping with the aesthetic bias of the SACB. "Our country," he said switching from the role of historian and administrator to critic, "has been suffering from a plague of applied decoration.... This is apparently a terrible craving, usually irresistible, and in most cases the result is far from appropriate." Sounding like a doctor diagnosing an ill patient, Whiting then offered a threefold remedy. "In all art," he explained, "constraint is essential—appropriateness is necessary, [and] consistency is most desirable." These three traits comprised his tonic for "good design."

He then became more specific about methodology, promoting the "learning by doing" approach popularized in the writings of John Dewey, and adapted by the German architect and educator Walter Gropius – at the Bauhaus in the 'teens and 'twenties. He advised individuals to learn to "design through work in the material itself," appealing directly to the craftsworker. "Learn the nature of your material first—its possibilities and limitations," he began, anticipating a phrase used by Frank Lloyd Wright. "Then learn the traditions of the craft, which you will usually find to be closely related to the limitations of the material itself." Here Whiting touched upon points stressed in the works of Walter Crane, such as *The Bases of Design* (1898).

"Trying to realize the organic,—the structural—nature of the thing you wish to create," Whiting continued, "and bearing always in mind the necessary requirements for its most complete usefulness, work out the most perfect combination of lines you can conceive as adapted to the purpose." Here he appealed to the craftsworker's understanding of basic design principles while evoking Sullivan's theory of organic architecture. Then try "to make the *thing itself* so beautiful . . . that mere *applied* ornament will not only be unnecessary but superfluous. And remember always," he concluded, "that the thing shall be perfectly adapted to its use, and that beauty is, after all, a second consideration." In drawing this conclusion, Whiting seems to have returned to Morris's earlier ordering of the two concepts—Usefulness before Beauty—in his famous maxim.[41]

Whiting quoted that maxim, reminding his audience: "reform begins in the home." He explained that such consumer activism would "purge [our houses] of quantities of trash which [had] accumulated through the changing fashions of the last decades." His reference to "trash" recalls Morris's exhortation against "masses of sordidness, filth, and squalor," and Wharton's condemnation of combining "heterogeneous ornament" with "incongruous effects." He ended by encouraging his listeners to live "simply," unhampered by "anything which retards our freedom and makes us subject to false and merely transitory standards." Always in these critical diatribes, Whiting raised the issue of standards (as Langford Warren had done in his introduction to the *1899 Exhibition Catalogue*). Many of the views that Whiting expressed in these lectures were less original than they were impassioned, as he borrowed ideas from the great theorists of his time. His views were, nevertheless, consistent with Carey's. Both despised current factory production methods. Both championed the rights of individual crafts-persons. Both found the paradox of commercialism frustrating. Neither had patience for those who misinterpreted or exploited the aims of the movement for their own gain.

Despite such similarities in outlook, Whiting and Carey voiced differing opinions regarding anti-urbanism, the potential of rural cooperative workshops, and the viability of a salesroom located in the city. These distinctions became increasingly pronounced in 1901, '02, and '03, as Whiting, Carey, and other SACB members aired their philosophical differences in yet another new venture for the SACB, a small periodical called *Handicraft*. In it, critical diatribes moved from the confines of the SACB to the printed page, where they received national—and even international—visibility, and inspired heated debate.

A Forum for Debating Design Reform: HANDICRAFT Magazine

When it was launched in the spring of 1902, the mission of *Handicraft* (as outlined in the SACB's *Annual Report*) was to "increase clearness of thought and community of sentiment among followers of the Arts and Crafts Movement." In stating that *Handicraft* was not intended to "compete with any other magazine now in existence," the *Report* might have been referring indirectly to Gustav Stickley's (1857–1942) *The Craftsman*, introduced in 1901 and available in Boston at the Cobb-Eastman Co., and further afield in Pittsfield (at Rice & Kelly) as well as Worcester (at Flint & Barker). The new magazine—edited by Carey, Norton, and H. L. Warren—would "offer an opportunity for public discussion of the artistic and economic problems involved" in implementing design reform. In addition, it would be a "constant reminder of the strong and wholesome principles which must necessarily underlie permanent success in genuine handicraft." These principles demonstrated that the Society's credo of "good design" was evolving into a theory, supported by specific rules or guidelines.[42]

The first issue of *Handicraft* outlined these "strong and wholesome principles" (Fig. 118), a summarization of the SACB's emerging aesthetic and, now, economic positions. Section I, "Principles of Handicraft," indicated that the "motives of the true Craftsman are the love of good and beautiful work as applied to useful service, and the need of making an adequate livelihood." Section II outlined the "conditions of true Handicraft," indicating that they are "natural aptitude, thorough technical training, and a just appreciation of standards," the final phrase implying a level of excellence. "The unit[s] of labor," the section continued, condemning the factory system and its division of labor, "should be intelligent [persons], whose ability is used as a whole, and not subdivided for commercial purposes." They should, the section concluded, evoking the methodology of "learning by doing," "exercise the faculty of design in connection with manual work, and manual work should be part of [their] training in design."[43]

Section III addressed a chief aim of the SACB, namely "Artistic Co-operation," arguing "when the designer and the workman are not united in the same person, they should work together." Section IV, "Social Co-operation," raised a similar issue aimed at the SACB's Associate members. It advised that "reciprocal service and co-operation" should "supersede the idea of patronage." Finally, the "Principles of Handicraft" concluded, "The results aimed at are the training of true craftsmen, the developing of individual character in connection with artistic work, and the raising of standards of beauty in the objects of use." Consistent with the motto on the Society's seal, the statement focused upon ways to combine "pulchritudo cum utilitate." These principles highlight critical issues that the SACB and its membership were confronting at the time. Some individuals in the

118. Promotional pamphlet, 1904. (Photograph courtesy of Pocumtuck Valley Memorial Association, Memorial Hall Museum, Deerfield) This handsome pamphlet reproduces the "Principles of Handicraft" first published in *Handicraft* in 1902. That the Deerfield, Greenfield, and New Clairvaux Arts and Crafts Societies adopted these principles within two years is testimony to the SACB's growing influence.

organization were strongly socialistic in their views, and hoped to steer the SACB in a more political direction. As Whiting had indicated in his fiscal-year summary for 1900–1901, Craftsman members of the organization clearly felt disenfranchised by the power wielded by Associates. The attack on patronage in section IV of the "Principles of Handicraft" attempted to assuage their concerns and to assure workers in the SACB greater influence. Prevailing from the time of the SACB's initial statement of purpose, was the concept of artistic cooperation. And the organization's dedication to furthering the quest for Usefulness and Beauty remained unchanged.

During the two-year period of *Handicraft*'s publication by the SACB, these "Principles of Handicraft" continued to inspire analysis and debate. Some contributors addressed them directly, while others avoided them altogether, preferring instead to provide general-interest articles on topics ranging from the theoretical to practical. Twenty or so SACB members—respected experts in particular media—wrote articles on their specialty areas, presenting an overview of the history of their craft, discussing the training process for workers in that field, and highlighting the conceptual, aesthetic, or technical challenges inherent in that medium. A few contributors chose to focus upon the handicrafts in other cultures, including Native American, Japanese, and East Indian. Local

119. Mary Ware Dennett, ca. 1892–96. (Schlesinger Library, Radcliffe Institute, Harvard University) This photo dates to the period just before Mary Ware went to Europe to study and sketch.

critics—Sylvester Baxter was one of these—contributed work to the magazine as well, thus broadening the range and perspective of writers and topics.[44]

Five of the most outspoken contributors during the period 1902–04 were SACB members who wrote personal and controversial opinion pieces. These included founders and officers Carey, Ross, Walker, and H. L. Warren, and one Master craftsman member, Mary Ware Dennett (Fig. 119), a well-to-do feminist, educator, leatherworker (in business with her sister, Clara), and artistic director of the Handicraft Shop. Niece of social reformer Edwin D. Mead (1849–1937), she was married to SACB member Hartley Dennett, an architect-preservationist who worked in the Colonial Revival style. (Both had taken credit for finding Whiting, when Carey was looking for a new SACB secretary. They divorced a decade after her articles appeared.)[45]

Carey reprinted his speech "The Past Year and Its Lessons" in the first issue of *Handicraft*. Langford Warren followed suit, reprinting his first speech as SACB president (given in December 1903) shortly after he succeeded Carey in that post. Between the appearances of these two, Ware Dennett contributed two pieces, "Aesthetics and Ethics" (May 1902) and "The Arts and Crafts: An Outlook" (April 1903). Ross published "Arts and Crafts: A Diagnosis" (January 1903), and Walker contributed "The Museum and the School" (May 1903). Taken as a group, these articles demonstrate that the path toward achieving Usefulness and Beauty was divided and full of pitfalls.

Inspired by the varied political positions of John Ruskin, Prince Peter A. Kropotkin, the Russian geographer, philosophical anarchist, and author of *Field, Factory and Workshop*, her uncle Edwin Mead, and his colleague, Boston University professor and economic reformer Frank Parsons (1854–1908), Ware Dennett promoted socio-economic reform as the chief means of achieving aesthetic change. In "Aesthetics and Ethics," she argued in favor of uniting two groups of reformers who, in her opinion, often worked at cross-purposes. These were connoisseurs, concerned primarily with the "aesthetic value of a material thing," and humanitarians, whom she described as valuing the "happiness, the physical, mental, moral and even spiritual well-being of the person who makes the material thing." Allying herself with the latter group, Ware Dennett suggested that Usefulness and Beauty were by-products of a healthy lifestyle and working conditions, of the union of aesthetics with ethics.[46]

Ware Dennett regarded educators and critics—in fact, she mentions Denman Ross by name—as those who might unite these two groups. But she questioned how successful they might be ultimately in "elevating the public taste." Will "purchasers and admirers" of the arts and crafts, that is, connoisseurs, ever become true "producers of beauty" as well, she asked. She felt that creators alone could guarantee that the arts and crafts would thrive.[47]

"The man who is interested in art," she argued, "in its completion rather than its process, in its ownership rather than in its creation, the connoisseur, the critic, the teacher, will always have a certain very strong and valuable influence on opinion and public taste." Here she described many of her fellow SACB members. "There will always be a man," she continued, "who has a sure instinct that appreciates not only a beautiful effect, but also fine workmanship, and that vital personal something which defies description, but without which nothing can be a work of art." Here she raised the issue of an indescribable quality, a *je ne sais quoi* that critics attributed to the best, most expressive examples of handicraft. "This man's verdict will be passed along and accepted by many people who have faith in him, but," she stressed, "who lack his perception." That lack of perception in the general public, she explained, "renders buyers powerless" in the face of exploitative industrialists and unscrupulous merchants. The example of the connoisseur and the advice of the critic—no matter how well intentioned—could not ensure the vitality of the arts and crafts.[48]

With this description of the "connoisseur, critic, teacher," Ware Dennett was making a subtle jab at the SACB founders and administrators with whom she found herself increasingly at odds philosophically. Associate members who read her essay must have felt unfairly marginalized. She characterized these elite consumers as "not so easily satisfied" as the general public, suggesting that they "must have original objects of art or none at all," and that they were those who "know the difference between true and spurious work, who have a genuine appreciation of beauty, and probably also of fitness, who have had the opportunities of study and travel, and who have been able to collect beautiful things and use them in their own homes in such a way that . . . they form a suitable and useful part of the furnishing or decoration of the house." This statement described many of those who had contributed to the loan collection at the 1899 Exhibition of the Arts and Crafts.[49]

Her purpose in satirizing her friends and colleagues may have been to suggest that no amount of education and appreciation could enable such connoisseurs to ensure the welfare of contemporary arts and crafts. In Ware Dennett's eyes, regardless of their wealth and social position, they could not guarantee that handicrafts would remain vital and prosper for generations to come. That responsibility lay with the creator, the worker.

She went on to describe the plight of the modern factory worker who had little control over the outcome of the production process—in determining whether results were "fine instead of shabby, beautiful instead of ugly." Independent craftsworkers, she explained, did not fare much better, since they had to spend too much time selling their work and too little time creating it. She then went on to attack profit-seeking "middlemen," referring obliquely to Whiting and the SACB Salesroom.[50]

As a remedy, she suggested that variety in work, a return to an agrarian lifestyle, a "subsistence annuity" such as Parsons proposed in his theory of "Mutualism," along with greater opportunities for "education, refinement and leisure," would ameliorate the life of craftsworkers and the quality of their work. "What else can we conclude," she asked, "than that the man who is to produce beauty must have these things, too . . . ? Such a worker might then, she suggested, be able to modify Morris's famous words, "*mak[ing]* only those things which we knew to be useful or believed to be beautiful."[51]

Ware Dennett's reformist activities in 1902 extended beyond the SACB and her article in *Handicraft*. She played an integral part in organizing the "Women's Department" of the 21st Exhibition of the Massachusetts Charitable Mechanic Association, under the auspices of the Women's Educational and Industrial Union. At that event, she gave lectures each Friday from September 21 to November 1 on the Handicraft Shop, and collaborated with SACB members Ross Turner, Amy Sacker, and Lois Howe to organized a display of "Arts and Crafts."[52]

Eight months after Ware Dennett's article appeared, Denman Ross offered an alternative viewpoint. In "The Arts and Crafts: A Diagnosis," he suggested that increased communication and improved design education were keys to ameliorating the state of the applied arts. He lamented that in the United States, few craftsworkers possessed a high level of technical skill, a firm grounding in basic design theory, and a degree of originality. He attributed this to the separation of critic from craftsworker. He argued in favor of uniting the critic's "idealism with its love of righteousness, truth and beauty" and the craftsperson's "technical ability, with its standard of perfection." The remedy was to meld theory into practice by teaching art and design together, along with technical training.[53]

The product of such a comprehensive approach to design education, Ross indicated, would be "the all-round, complete artist with his knowledge of fine things, his determination and judgment, his standard and ideals, his knowledge of tools and materials, of ways, means and methods." In this way, Ross envisioned an artist-craftsman hybrid, who would possess the "finest possible impulses—those which come from a knowledge of the best work that has been done in the world and the best thought that has been put into it." This hybrid's partner in reform was to be the critic-craftsman, versed in theoretical as well as practical matters. He imagined a "critic [who would have] all the knowledge of the workman." Ross reiterates Ruskin's theories, advocating "thinking and doing," by imagining a scenario in which "the philosopher goes to work and the working man becomes a philosopher."

Broadly speaking, Ross's views paralleled those of Ware Dennett. Both regarded education as integral to implementing design reform. Both viewed the Arts and Crafts movement as a cause divided. Yet Ross's views were essentially exclusive, while Ware Dennett's were all-embracing. Ross proposed that an elite group of hybrids would serve as leaders in the reform movement. Ware Dennett, by contrast, believed that socio-economic reorganization alone would initiate design reform. Ross's paradigm presented design reform as an active force in society, while Ware Dennett's viewed reform as a by-product of greater socio-economic change. Surprisingly, neither had confidence in the arts and crafts society per se as a vehicle to implement such change.

Four months following publication of Ross's article, Ware Dennett wrote a second essay as rebuttal. In "The Arts and Crafts: An Outlook," she reiterated points made in her earlier essay and challenged Ross's argument. Inspired by her opponent, she presented her ideas with strength and clarity.

Improved education and technical training were not cure-alls for the malaise of the arts and crafts, she began. Nor would these improve the lot of the independent craftsworker. She offered herself as an example, explaining that a combination of social position, education, financial security, and a degree of the "refinement" that she had advocated in her previous essay had not enabled her to make a success of her and her sister's Cordova leatherworking venture. She had been forced—as a result of their failure as entrepreneurs—to join Carey's cooperative Handicraft Shop.[54]

Ware Dennett also questioned whether design education, such as Ross proposed, would have any effect upon consumers or manufacturers. She argued that the factory system would resist change brought about by such a sophisticated proposal. What is more, she speculated that better education and training among factory workers would not result in artist-worker hybrids, but instead would tend to inspire their upward mobility, prompting them to abandon the stifling conditions of the factory altogether.

In "Aesthetics and Ethics," Ware Dennett had spoken of the split between connoisseurs and humanitarians, or those concerned with the object versus the object's maker. Now she expanded her tirade. She saw the former group as mere aesthetes, concerned only with "art for art's sake," in contrast to the latter group, who promoted "art for life's sake." Illustrating her point, she argued: "It should startle every Arts and Crafts Society to realize . . . that the employed craftsman can almost never use in his own home things similar to those he works on every day." In this statement, she implied that SACB Craftsman members could not afford to shop in the salesroom as Associate members could do. This was one of the ironies of the British Arts and Crafts movement, which American design reformers had hoped to remedy through the democratization of "good design."

Like Carey, Ware Dennett warned that the SACB must stand behind its principles and not function merely as "a pastime masquerading in the name of Art." Like Ross, who accused the SACB of "playing at Arts and Crafts," Ware Dennett believed the Society's efforts to be misguided. It should serve an "educational and missionary" purpose first, she claimed, and an aesthetic purpose last. "One cannot avoid the conclusion," she wrote, "that the Arts and Crafts Problem is at bottom, not an educational, so much as an economic, moral, and religious problem." Taking a final jab at Ross's proposal, she concluded: "its solution is ultimately a matter not of school curriculum, but of life itself." She had been a member of the SACB since 1899, and had served on the Council and the

Jury; but, to reinforce her points Ware Dennett resigned from the organization for philosophical reasons in 1905.[55]

Howard Walker did not agree with Ware Dennett's critique of Ross's views. In a lucid and at times humorous article published five months later in May 1903, he concurred with Ross that education could change each step of the design process positively, and ensure Usefulness and Beauty. In "The Museum and the School," he argued that such institutions—along with libraries—could replace what "tradition, long apprenticeships and a focused environment" had supplied in the past. Studying examples from the past, he urged confidently, could elevate equally the tastes of maker, seller, and consumer, by providing a standard of good taste to which all might aspire.[56]

Walker believed that a firm foundation in the best works of the past was a requirement for improving standards in the present. Knowledge of the history of architecture, decorative arts, and ornament was essential, he noted, for craftsworkers, merchants, and buyers alike. Contemporary craftspeople should study the methods of their predecessors, he advised, so they might reinterpret them appropriately for application in the twentieth century. He urged workers to examine objects from the past—not with the intention of copying them literally, but instead in order to ascertain the thought process, or the conceptualization, that had led to their creation. By making these remarks, Walker reinforced the obsession with history and historical precedent already evident in the city at large, and present in the work of Boston's historicist architects, promoted at local educational institutions, and exemplified by exhibitions of antiquities (such as that shown at the SACB's Exhibition of 1899).

"Having lived in the art of the past," he wrote, the pupils "build up as worthy an art of the present—founded on the past, as all things must be, but on the best of the past, and permeated by the life of the present, as all active workers must be." As a result, he concluded, "the art of the past [would] suffer a change which [would] make it the art of the present." As those of someone who taught courses throughout Boston and Cambridge in all of these areas, Walker's views are predictable.[57]

In this article, Walker demonstrated the "clarity of thought" to which its editors had dedicated *Handicraft*. His ability to express complex ideas simply—and humorously—led to his appointment as the official "Critic of the Jury" shortly thereafter.

The published debate among Arthur Carey, Mary Ware Dennett, Denman Ross, and Howard Walker did not reach any conclusion in the pages of *Handicraft*. But it called attention to ideological differences inherent in the SACB. By doing so, *Handicraft* thwarted Carey's attempt to "increase community of sentiment" among its readers. They continued to contest interpretations of the "Principles of Handicraft," as divisions between aesthetes and humanitarians, craftsmen and critics increased.

Like Ware Dennett, Carey resigned from the SACB in November 1903. He had suffered a "protracted illness" that might have been related to ongoing "nervous difficulties." He left the organization both for health reasons and because of philosophical differences. Perhaps unbeknownst to his SACB colleagues, Carey had joined the Swedenborgian church in April 1901, having become familiar with it in the 1890s. Responding in part to a sense of obligation stemming from having undertaken marriage and fatherhood late in life, Carey became a lay reader and then an ordained minister in the church. In March 1902, he began making plans to move his new family to Waltham, to manage the "New Church School" and to assist its elderly minister. To facilitate that move, he hired Ware Dennett and her husband to build a modest cottage in Waltham that would serve as living quarters for his wife and family.[58]

Langford Warren succeeded him in the office of president, a post he kept until his premature death in 1917. Warren was forty-six when he became SACB president. As a professional architect and educator, he was determined to avoid politics at all costs, focusing instead upon making the SACB a successful educational and business venture. That he took an aggressive stance from the beginning of his tenure is documented in his inaugural address, "Our Work and Our Prospects," delivered to the SACB just five days after Carey's resignation. A reprint of the speech appeared in *Handicraft* in December 1903. It provided yet another opinion on some of the same issues that Carey, Ware Dennett, Ross, and Walker had debated, while providing a new direction for the organization and a calming effect upon its members.

Warren divided his speech into four sections. In the first part, he discussed the controversial "Principles of Handicraft" and provided a personal interpretation of them. In the second, he questioned how the SACB should, as an organization, try to exemplify those principles. In the third part, he provided a critical review of the Society's history to date. Finally, he turned his attention to the salesroom, which he regarded as the organization's best achievement, one worthy of support.

In his discussion of the "Principles of Handicraft," Warren reiterated many points that he had made in his introduction to the *1899 Exhibition Catalogue*. In doing so, he made clear that he had not changed his definitions of Usefulness and Beauty over time. "Good design" was the result of functionality blended with simplicity and economy. He advised using materials with integrity and applying ornamentation with discretion. Usefulness and Beauty were, he indicated, the direct expression of the "maker's delight in his work."[59]

Warren cautioned his readers to apply the "Principles of Handicraft" only to the design process. To seek to apply them to the "whole production of the world at the present time," he warned, was damaging. Unlike Carey and Ware Dennett, he did not condemn the factory system and the division of labor, arguing instead that mass production had "accomplished great things for the benefit" of humans. Provided that factory conditions were "wholesome," he pointed out, divided labor was not necessarily "inconsistent with high development of character in the individual." Warren seemed to accept machine production and the factory system as necessary evils.

Warren's opinions were not dissimilar from those previously expressed in the pages of *Handicraft*. He, too, identified commercialism, the subdivision of labor, and the Machine as "things which chiefly affect the condition of handicraft in the modern world adversely." But he realized that any problems caused by these factors resulted from their "abuse," not their "proper use."

Warren took issue with Ware Dennett's interpretation of the principle of social cooperation, which she used to attack patrons generally and SACB Associate members specifically. Patrons, she had claimed, did not make or inspire creative work; they only appreciated it or acquired it after the fact—like parasites. Warren, by contrast, insisted that patrons made craftspeople' work possible from the start and took pleasure in the completed product. As an architect, he would have known firsthand the benefits of collaborating with his patron/clients, or promoting "participatory design." He argued that patrons were a necessary link in the design process, participating in and facilitating its conception, completion, utilization, and evaluation stages. In his mind, patrons and craftspeople provided a reciprocal service—a symbiosis—and thus played invaluable roles in design reform.

Having raised this issue, Warren then went on to address what he termed the "social question." He believed that the Arts and Crafts movement had "suffered" from association with Socialism, a philosophy that had, in his eyes, prejudiced the modern world against the movement. He argued that the SACB should avoid politics altogether, concentrating its efforts instead upon design education, design reform, and sales of exemplary goods. "One of the strong things in the Society," he stated, "is that we have succeeded thus far in keeping these questions entirely out of our midst, in disassociating ourselves from such questions, and in attending to our own proper concerns." Like a stern father, he attempted to quell the ideological squabbles within his organizational "family" that had erupted during 1902–03.

Warren had mixed feelings about the accomplishments of the organization to date. In his opinion, the handicraft exhibitions of 1897 and 1899 might have caused more harm than good because of a lack of uniform excellence among the displays. Workshops and classes he labeled a "dead failure," since most Craftsman members had too little time and energy after a full day of working to participate enthusiastically. For the present, Warren believed that the SACB should direct all of its efforts toward developing the salesroom, calling it the "one successful thing the Society had undertaken."

It was useful to makers and users, he argued, "giving [consumers] an opportunity to get good things and helping to raise the standards of taste." The salesroom, in turn, had made it possible for Craftsman members to "make a living by having an outlet for [their] work." He argued that it must become self-supporting (its financing had become a challenge without underwriting from Carey, something he had withdrawn at the time of his resignation). Warren actually looked forward to a time when the SACB salesroom would become obsolete, due to competition from other enlightened businesses that operated similarly. This, he projected, would enable the SACB to "go forth and accomplish greater and larger things." He did not outline specifically what those might be.

Warren's speech commemorated more than just a change in administration;

it marked the end of the developmental stage in the Society's history. During the next four years, the SACB achieved its greatest success, developing a strong national reputation for promoting Usefulness and Beauty under Warren's direction and with Whiting's support. It was a period of maturity and relative stability, but it was not untouched by dissension.

In 1907, at the time of the Society's decennial anniversary, F. W. Coburn summarized the calming effect that Warren had upon the organization, implying that his leadership had allowed it to "go forth and accomplish greater and larger things," in a manner that Warren himself had predicted. "No effort to reconstruct society as a whole has ever been included in the scope of the Society of Arts and Crafts," Coburn began, somewhat understating the debate that had raged in the pages of *Handicraft*, "fortunately, no doubt, for the material success of the enterprise." From the discussions and publications of the Society, he continued, "comment on current themes of socialism, philosophical anarchism and other cults has been invariably excluded." (This referred directly to some of the influences that Ware Dennett had hoped to introduce.) "Individual members of the Society hold, of course, various opinions as to the stability of the present social organization," he explained, implying that supporters of Carey's and Ware Dennett's points of view still remained in the SACB, "but, since the association to which they belong exists for the sake of work and not of talk, they aim to attend to the duty which lies nearest."[60]

This, he indicated, was "to demonstrate that in this as in every age he who skillfully and lovingly fashions objects of usefulness, personally following all the processes of production, is certain to have created something which the world will see to be beautiful." Whether the status of today is or is not the "best possible for the average worker," he concluded, "good work, nevertheless, can always be done by the determined craftsman." In this passage, Coburn suggested that the Society's commitment to Usefulness and Beauty had not wavered, despite the internal debate regarding connoisseurs versus humanitarians, or aesthetics versus ethics.

This brief overview of the SACB's formative years highlights multiple contexts within which critics operated—officially and unofficially. The membership hierarchy separated patrons from makers, and may have inadvertently fueled the debates about patronage versus cooperation, and "thinking" versus "doing," but it also raised issues of how makers and users might collaborate to raise standards of taste.

The administrative structure—with its officers, Council, Jury, committees, and paid secretary-treasurer—defined arenas within which a group or individual might present ideas that represented the organization as a whole. Examples would be Warren's introduction to the *1899 Exhibition Catalogue*, Carey's speech "The Past Year and Its Lessons," and Whiting's lecture "The Development and Meaning of the Arts and Crafts Movement." Each of these offered definitions of Usefulness and Beauty, viewing both as the result of healthy working conditions.

The Council and the Jury generated official statements—such as the brochure (dated December 9, 1899), the *1899 Exhibition Catalogue*, the "Principles of Handicraft," and *Handicraft* magazine—that enabled the SACB to spread its emerging aesthetic, and in some cases socioeconomic, philosophy. Public exhibitions, whether they occurred in Copley and Allston Halls, or the SACB headquarters on Somerset Street, enabled members as well as the independent press to critique physical expressions of that emerging philosophy.

Whiting's "Bureau of Information" was a repository of files and printed materials that enabled individuals—members, the buying public, and critics—to become more knowledgeable about craftsworkers, materials, techniques, and products, and thus to be more discriminating in their choices.

Public lectures, reprints of addresses, and articles on diverse subjects heightened the level of discourse, and publicized diverse points of view regarding the movement as a whole, and the SACB's mission within it, along with the place of Usefulness and Beauty in the crafts at the turn of the twentieth century.

As important as these were singly and collectively, none had as much impact upon defining Usefulness and Beauty in Boston as did the SACB Jury, and C. Howard Walker, its appointed spokesperson. Both espoused a philosophy of Usefulness and Beauty within the organization that became influential throughout the United States, from 1904 through the ensuing decades. The all-important Jury and its critic are the focus of Chapter Three.

CHAPTER THREE

Adviser, Promoter, Tormentor, and Midwife
The Multiple Roles of Boston's Design Critics

With ever deepening interest and conviction, I have taken part in an important movement initiated within the museum, directed . . . to quicken the sense of beauty and promote a sound standard of taste among the people.
—Samuel D. Warren II (1906)

I seek till I find what is truly useful and then I try to make it beautiful. I believe that this cannot be done by copying old work, no matter how beautiful . . . . The Romans made Rome and the Americans—well! They are making America.
—Charles Sumner Greene (1907)

The masterworks of the Arts and Crafts movement did not spring fully formed from the brains of craftspeople. They were the products of a lifelong struggle to put theories of design reform into practice, the result of years of experimentation, of trial and error, of countless returns to the drawing board or the bench. Yet their restrained forms, subdued finishes, and chaste ornamentation belie the long and arduous labor that led to their creation.

As they evolved from novices to masters, craftspeople strove to improve their work conceptually, aesthetically, and technically, and, in doing so, sought advice from critics whose judgment they deemed superior to their own. The challenge for the critic was to promote high standards while remaining ever mindful of the craftsperson's limitations in achieving them. Successful design reform thus depended upon close interaction between the craftsman and the critic. The most effective critic was generally a blending of a practitioner—someone who could relate, by virtue of experience, to the craftsman's challenges—and theorist, an individual who could view the craftsman's work within a broad intellectual framework.

In his essay "The Arts and Crafts: A Diagnosis" (1903), Denman Ross described best the sort of hybrid who functioned in this capacity. "To be a real critic," he wrote, "you must have studied the masterpieces in a way which the man of words cannot understand. You must have analyzed the fine things. You must know exactly what they are made of, and how the materials were put together. To make sure of your knowledge," he argued, "you must have put similar materials together in the same way with approximately the same results. . . . To be a real critic, you must have all the knowledge of the workman." The critic, Ross suggested, could learn as much from the craftsman as the craftsman might from the critic. Having served on the SACB Jury for three years, Ross spoke from experience. This sort of reciprocal relationship was the goal of all critics serving on the Jury who hoped to instruct their constituents on the best methods for achieving Usefulness and Beauty. Among those with whom he collaborated was Hugh C. Robertson (1845–1908), founder of the Dedham Pottery, for which Ross developed a "tapestry lion" motif.[1]

Identifying how critics functioned—either overtly or covertly—in the context of the SACB is this chapter's focus. It examines the Jury—why it came about, its purpose, and how it functioned during the organization's first two decades. It reviews its composition—initially and as it evolved over a decade and a half—arguing that a small core group within the Jury dominated its decisions and its evolving philosophy of "good design." It briefly analyzes the body's policies and procedures as a way of showing how the Jury functioned within the larger Society. And it surveys the range of criticism offered by the Jury, as revealed in the minutes of its meetings in 1900–1905, its "Report of the Jury" published in the Society's annual reports after 1906, and the "Report of the Critic of the Jury," namely C. Howard Walker, written after 1911. Inherent in these minutes and reports are definitions of what the Jury deemed to be Usefulness and Beauty.

This chapter also explores the interaction of Jurors with their constituents, chronicling some of the Craftsman members' reactions to the Jury's suggestions. It argues that the complexity of these Jurors' roles affected their interaction with constituents and the types of criticism that they offered. Sometimes these critics functioned simply as advisers, especially to Master members, whose acknowledged level of expertise required little guidance. At other times they served as promoters, especially when they represented SACB members beyond the organization to the city, region, and nation. Occasionally these critics served as tormentors, especially in the eyes of those receiving severe—and repeated—tongue-lashings. Those most sensitive to criticism resented it, protesting the Jury's comments and actions, though others acknowledged—albeit grudgingly—that they had grown professionally as a result of the Jury's input. Most craftspeople regarded critics who served on the Jury as "midwives" to the creative process, believing that they benefited from the critics' efforts to, in the words of Charles F. Binns, "stimulate, guide, help, and encourage" their colleagues and constituents.[2]

An Overview of Jury Membership

The Jury of the SACB was established in the wake of the Society's exhibition of 1899 and the subsequent opening of its salesroom in September 1900. Increased participation in displays and exhibitions, coupled with the salesroom's growth, precipitated the Jury's formation. Its charge was to develop and implement a consistent policy regarding the conceptual, aesthetic, and technical merits of handicrafts put on display or offered for sale. In that capacity, it served as both a definer of Usefulness and Beauty and an arbiter of taste within the organization and beyond, as the SACB's influence extended nationwide.

One of the first of its kind in the country, the Jury influenced craftsmen and consumers throughout the United States and elsewhere, in part because of the organization's growing international membership. By 1917, members emanated from 30 states and nine foreign countries: England, Ireland, Canada, Norway, Denmark, Switzerland, Italy, the Philippines, and Mexico. The Jury became a model for others nationwide, ultimately serving as a prototype for review boards at events such as international expositions. In 1907, at the time of the Society's tenth anniversary, Frederick W. Coburn wrote: "The 'Boston branch' . . . , from which the movement has radiated, maintains its high standard through the ministrations of an unemotional jury, which weeds out much that is good to make room for all that is best." Those standards extended not only to a product's appearance and style but also to its materials and manner of construction.[3]

When the Jury first met, on November 7, 1900, it consisted of twelve members. (See Appendix A.) Six of these had been founders of the organization: A. A. Carey, J. T. Coolidge, Jr., A. W. Longfellow, Jr., D. W. Ross, H. L. Warren, and S. W. Whitman. Some of these also served as officers, Councilors, and committee members. Joining them was F. A. Whiting, in his capacity as clerk and recorder of the meeting minutes. Completing this distinguished group were Henry Hunt Clark, Mary Ware Dennett, Nils Kjellstrom, and Laurin Hovey Martin, all respected craftsworkers. The twelfth was the architect Richard Clipston Sturgis of the firm Sturgis and Barton, though because he attended only one meeting of the Jury that year, his impact was negligible. Significantly, many of these people would contribute articles to *Handicraft*, and their participation on the Jury may have fueled some of the ensuing debate. Several were concurrently members of the board for the School of the Museum of Fine Arts.[4]

During the first five years, others joined this group, coming and going as their schedules allowed, or as they were needed to form a quorum or to add to the Jury's diversity. (It appears that Sarah Wyman Whitman, Mary Ware Dennett, and Sarah Choate Sears worked together to ensure that at least one woman was present for most Jury meetings.) Those augmenting the group in later years included founder George Prentiss Kendrick, councilor Mary Crease Sears, and two respected artists/designers, Joseph Lindon Smith and Amy Sacker. C. Howard Walker—whose participation on the Jury would become so essential after 1909—attended only two meetings in the period 1900–1905, in part because of extensive travel in England, and also because of his involvement with the 1904 Louisiana Purchase Exposition in St. Louis as planner, architect, exhibitor, juror, and judge.[5]

The group was even more select during this early period than the membership roster might indicate. Only a handful of Jurors attended a majority of meetings, constituting the core of the Jury. They included A. A. Carey, who took a particular interest in the activities of the group during his years as president; J. T. Coolidge, Jr., who served as chair of the Jury continuously until 1914 (when he enrolled in the ambulance corps for the First World War); A. W. Longfellow, Jr., who served as vice-chairman, eventually succeeding Coolidge as chair; Ross, Kjellstrom, Martin, and Whitman. F. A. Whiting seldom missed a meeting until

120. Laurin Hovey Martin. (Courtesy of Matthew Robinson) Martin was in his twenties at the time of this photograph.

121. Copper tazza, by Laurin Hovey Martin, as published in *The Studio* magazine. Martin supplied the calligraphic label. (Courtesy Matthew Robinson)

he resigned from the SACB in 1912, but his participation was limited to record keeping.[6]

Initially, the Jury met weekly, but members soon cut their meetings to once or twice a month from fall through spring. At the start, all twelve tried to attend every meeting; but this soon proved unwieldy, and by 1902 a few began casting their votes in absentia. By 1903, a small subgroup, or "examining committee," was formed to vet the hundred or so entries submitted by craftsmen every few weeks for the Jury's consideration. Members of the examining committee generally included Coolidge, Longfellow, Whiting, who kept the minutes, and two or so others who cast votes in absentia to constitute a quorum of five.[7]

Four Jurors, who were neither founders nor Councilors during the Society's first years, deserve elaboration given the importance of their role in the Jury's early years. Laurin Hovey Martin (1875–1939) was first a Craftsman member (1900–1903), later promoted to Master, who fabricated silver services, covered caskets (or boxes), and jewelry, among other items, often embellishing them with enamel (Figs. 120 and 121). Educated in Boston, he had studied in England with Alexander Fisher (1864–1936) at the Birmingham Art School. He received numerous honors, and his work had been published in magazines—*The Studio* and *Brush and Pencil*. Joining Martin was Craftsman member Henry Hunt Clark (1875–1962, Fig. 122). Educated in Boston, Clark had studied at MIT with Denman Ross. Showing proficiency for teaching, he first functioned as Ross's assistant, eventually leaving Boston in 1902 to take charge of the Department of Design at the Rhode Island School of Design. In 1913, he returned to Boston to succeed C. H. Walker as an administrator at the MFA School. Though his service on the Jury was short-lived, he remained an SACB member through 1927, eventually moving to Cleveland, where he became the director of the Cleveland School of Art. Swedish-trained Nils J. Kjellstrom (1860–1922) was among those immigrant wood-carvers who made their living working in cooperation with local architects. A respected Master craftsman member, he joined the SACB in 1899 and remained a member into the 1920s. He was one of the most diligent members of the Jury. Kendrick, an SACB founder, also participated. In the years before joining the Society, he had worked variously as an architect (Andrews, Jaques & Rantoul), designer, and metalworker. When he joined the Jury, he held the position for which he is best remembered today—first designer for the Grueby Faience Company, credited with developing its distinctive organic shapes (Fig. 123).[8]

Over the years, others—representing both the Master and Craftsman levels—joined the original core group. Master craftsman Frank Gardner Hale (1876–1945), Craftsman member Carl Forssen (active 1903–10), who was promoted to Master in 1908, and Craftsman member Annie C. Putnam (1850–1924) demonstrated the growing influence of metalworkers and jewelers within the organization. All three were quite vocal and frequently expressed dissenting views; but Hale was especially formidable (Figs. 124a and b). He had studied with Ross and H. H. Clark in Boston, and then had honed his skills in enameling in England at the Guild of Handicraft in Chipping Camden, and with Frederick Partridge (1877–1942) in London. Recipient of numerous awards—including the SACB's prestigious medal—and the frequent subject of articles in the press, he lectured on craftsmanship, jewelry and enamels, and was outspoken to the point of being "dictatorial."[9]

Annie Cabot Putnam was among the important female members of the Jury in its first decade. Raised in a Brahmin household, where her father and brothers were physicians, she was an accomplished painter and musician. While living in Florence in the 1880s, she met the irrepressible artist, teacher and philanthropist Madeline Yale Wynne (1847–1918), becoming her life partner following Wynne's divorce. Both were women of means with wide-ranging social connections. Putnam and Wynne shared a Boston studio, where they practiced metalwork and jewelry making, among other crafts. After 1885, Putnam spent her summers with Wynne in Deerfield, where they restored the historic Willard

122. Henry Hunt Clark. (Courtesy Archives, Museum of Fine Arts, Boston) This photo appears in a scrapbook documenting the 1898 Boston Art Students' Association Festival.

123. Vase with relief-molded ornamentation, designed for the Grueby Pottery by George P. Kendrick, ca. 1900. (Courtesy Susan J. Tarlow and Donald Davidoff) The distinctive type of molded leaf ornamentation for which the pottery was known—attributed to Kendrick—complements Grueby's green "watermelon rind" glaze.

124a. Frank Gardner Hale. (Courtesy W. Scott Braznell)

124b. Jeweled scroll broach, by Frank Gardner Hale, ca. 1920. (Courtesy Museum of Fine Arts, Boston; Gift of Joseph B. and Edith Alpers, 1998.569) Gold, zircons, diamonds, sapphires, and peridots. 6.6 × 5 cm. (2 5/8 × 1 15/16 in.)

House, called "the Manse," filling it with an artistic mélange of salvaged architectural antiques—such as red wainscoting—family heirlooms, elegant light fixtures, and Putnam's collection of historic textiles and ethnic clothing (Fig. 125). Though she was a vocal member of the Jury, friends commented upon Putnam's charm, optimism, sense of humor, and reserve to the point of shyness. A passion for the crafts tempered all of these, which were valuable qualities for a Juror advocating in favor of Usefulness and Beauty.[10]

Another important Juror was Hermann Dudley Murphy (1867–1945). Educated in Boston, he subscribed to Denman Ross's theory of color harmony. After studying painting in Paris, he worked in the 1880s and 1890s as a book and magazine illustrator, eventually specializing in portraits, landscapes, and marine scenes. He founded the Carrig-Rohane Shop, which specialized in carved and gilded frames in a reformist style (Fig. 126). Well connected with the Boston art community, he included among his clients distinguished members of "the 10."[11]

Joseph Lindon Smith, Amy M. Sacker (1872–1965), Alice J. Morse (b. ca. 1872), and John Endicott Peabody all functioned broadly as designers in multiple media. Smith was a gifted painter (Fig. 127), who had studied at the School of the MFA (where he fell under the influence of Denman Ross) and in Paris at the Académie Julian. He began his career in Boston as a portraitist, taught briefly in Harvard's School of Architecture, and then became associated with the MFA's department of archeology. Under its auspices, he made frequent trips to Egypt, where he participated in excavations, producing careful renderings of artifacts, documenting their color and detail as they emerged fresh from the excavation site. He designed for the Dedham Pottery (Fig. 128)—creating its well-loved rabbit motif as well as those of fish and poppies—but was also known as a book artist, architect, actor, and participant in pageants. Funded by a donation made by A. A. Carey, Smith was among a distinguished group of muralists who embellished the interior of the new Boston Public Library. A member of the Tavern Club, Smith was part of a broad social/artistic network—counting among his friends John Ruskin, Henry and William James, Bernard Berenson, John Singer Sargent,

125. Studio of Madeline Yale Wynne and Annie Cabot Putnam. From George Sheldon, *The Little Brown House on the Albany Road* (Deerfield: Published by the Author, 1915), p. 2. (Photograph courtesy Pocumtuck Valley Memorial Association, Memorial Hall Association, Deerfield) Describing this room in the Williard House, Sheldon comments upon its Oriental rugs, "stuff, rich and rare," "elegant lamps," a "red wainscoted wall," and the "pictures and works of art [that] fill every 'coigne of vantage.'" The long-case clock and turned rush-seat chair add a Colonial touch to the eclectic mix.

Edward Burne-Jones, William Morris, and Isabella Stewart Gardner. His wife, Corinna, documented the breadth and scope of his accomplishments and social circle in her book *Interesting People: Eighty Years with the Great and Near-Great* (1962). A memorial tribute by a fellow Taverner said of Smith: "His days were spent, not with political or economic affairs, but with beauty, —not, however, as an escapist but as one completely absorbed in what to him were more important matters. He did indeed love beauty in all its manifestations, ... and consciously avoided what was ugly or mean." With such credentials he was well qualified to serve on the SACB Jury.[12]

Sacker, who had studied under C. Howard Walker, was "one of the most prolific" book artists in Boston, who "worked easily in a variety of styles," as she produced covers, illustrations, and bookplates (Plate 10, Fig. 129). A pupil at the School of the MFA, who had experimented in leatherworking early on, she eventually started her own school of design. Later, in the 'teens and 'twenties, she may have tried her hand at art direction for the Hollywood film industry.[13]

Alice J. Morse was a former director of the Department of Design and Decoration at Philadelphia's Drexel Institute of Art, Science and Industry. Morse also had a penchant for textiles; she organized an extensive display of weavings, lace, and embroideries shown at the SACB's important decennial exhibition of 1907. Though SACB records, and such directories as the *American Art Annual*, always list her middle initial as "J," she may have used a second middle initial, "C." Alice Cordelia Morse was a noted designer of trade bindings, who was active between 1897 and 1921. The latter showed work at the Chicago World's Fair, and contributed to the official catalogue documenting art and handicraft shown in

126. Self-portrait by Hermann Dudley Murphy, ca. 1900, oil on canvas. 101.6 × 76.2 cm. (40 × 30 in.) (Courtesy Museum of Fine Arts, Boston; Gift of Carlene Bowles Murphy Samoiloff, daughter of the artist, 1981.255) This three-quarter-length portrait shows Murphy against a textile backdrop. He often hung the walls of his studio—located in Winchester, Mass., overlooking the Mystic River—with old tapestries and embroideries.

127. "Apse of the Cathedral at Pisa," drawing, by Joseph Lindon Smith, from *Catalogue of the Architectural Exhibition* (Boston Architectural Club and Boston Society of Architects, 1899). (Courtesy Boston Athenaeum) Smith's sketches and renderings of Italian cathedrals and architectural details resemble those Ruskin completed for *Stones of Venice*. This study shows a firm command of perspective and value coupled with sensitivity to the portrayal of materials.

the Women's Building. In her essay "Women Illustrators," she called attention especially to the work of Sarah W. Whitman. Significantly, her designs for bindings often incorporate patterns or motifs adapted from historic textiles (Plates 11 and 12). Alice J. and Alice C. may have been the same person.[14]

John Endicott Peabody was born in Salem, on Boston's North Shore, and received his education in Cambridge, England, at Trinity College. In the 1870s, he worked abroad and at home in the mercantile and banking fields, but according to historian Walter Muir Whitehill, "had no taste for business." In 1878, he married Gertrude Lawrence (b. 1855) in a ceremony at which Phillips Brooks presided. Following his wife's untimely death in 1882—her parents gave the future site for Groton School in her memory—Peabody spent four years in Europe, traveling and studying painting and design. Upon his return to Boston, he established a business as a designer and decorator at 6 Beacon Street (Figs. 108a–c). A member of numerous social, sporting, and literary clubs, he enjoyed sailing and boating. Antiques, which he had displayed at the SACB 1899 loan exhibition, testified to his eclectic taste. These included an early seventeenth-century Portuguese chair of walnut and leather; an early nineteenth-century

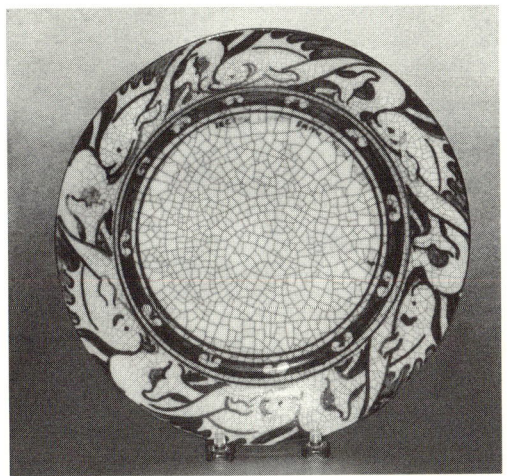

128. Plate, trial glaze design for the Dedham Pottery, by Joseph Lindon Smith, ca. 1898. (Courtesy Jim Kaufman.) This plate (measuring 8.5 inches in diameter) combines Dedham's typical gray crackle texture with a cobalt-blue border that features a dolphin motif. The Dedham Pottery did not adopt this dolphin design for regular production. The under-the-glaze inscription (along the border) reads "Joseph Lindon Smith trial plate … ?"

129. Illustration, "The Princess Who Never Laughed," by Amy Sacker. From Olcott and Pendleton, *The Jolly Book for Boys & Girls* (Houghton, Mifflin, 1915). (Boston Public Library/Rare Books Department. Courtesy of the Trustees) This black-and-white illustration recalls the work of Aubrey Beardsley. The details—a Dantesque chair, dado cloth with confronting and addorsing animals in the Byzantine manner, and floor pavers set into a guilloche pattern—reveal Sacker's knowledge of design history.

English lady's work box of painted satinwood; an eighteenth-century Dutch marquetry cabinet; a Jacobite embossed leather screen from Hampton Court Palace; and a Persian embroidery.[15]

As this brief overview indicates, Jury members included book artists, needleworkers, stained glass makers, leatherworkers, jewelry makers, metalworkers, wood-carvers, and architects, though most were multitalented designers. Several were already—or would become—design educators, whose insights and familiarity with the process of critiquing students' works proved to be particularly valuable. Many regularly published books and articles on the history and theory of their crafts (some contributing to *Handicraft*), adding to their credibility within the organization and extending their visibility in the city, region, and nation. In this way, the critics of the SACB Jury epitomized Ross's belief that "the real critic must have all the knowledge of the workman."

The Craftsman Constituents of the SACB Jury

A membership survey compiled in 1916, when the Society's membership had reached an all-time high of 911, suggests that the SACB attracted workers in a broad range of media, techniques, and trades (see Appendix B). Thus the Jury had to be equipped to evaluate a comprehensive range of products and skill levels. Some of these specialties—such as bookbinding, jewelry making, and weaving—fall within the standard repertoire of the arts and crafts. Others—carving of ships' models or toy making—are less typically associated with the movement. A few categories, such as the "colorist of plaster casts," are rare.[16]

Within the SACB, women dominated production in such categories as textiles, basketry, and pottery—crafts traditionally associated with their gender. A few practiced bookbinding, leatherwork, and jewelry making, following some historical precedents. Bookbinding was a trade at which even young women had made a subsistence living throughout the nineteenth century. A craze for more artistic bindings had created greater opportunities for women to design trade bindings as well as handcrafted, one-of-a-kind examples for collectors. A few rare women had functioned as goldsmiths in eighteenth-century London, but by the early nineteenth, apprenticeship of women had ceased completely, possibly because apprenticeship fees had increased prohibitively. The jewelers working in Boston in the late nineteenth century had a foundation—though distant—upon which to build. Within the SACB, such categories as stained glass, metalwork, and printing attracted equal numbers of male and female members.[17]

Photography also attracted both men and women practitioners to the SACB. From its inception, the organization welcomed this new medium as one requiring both artistry and craftsmanship. Prominent male photographers who exhibited with the SACB included F. Holland Day, W. B. Post, and Bertrand H. Wentworth. Women who received recognition for the quality of the work included Sarah C. Sears, Alice Kendall, Alice Austen, Mary Allen, Lois L. Howe, and Lillian M. Small. Several couples, such as Karl and Florence Maynard, or Mr. and Mrs. Irving Kimball, belonged to the organization, working and exhibiting together. Many of these photographers utilized the soft-focus approach promoted by F. Holland Day's "New School" of American photography, an approach that built upon the early training many photographers had received as painters in oil or watercolor. Some of these women pursued photography seriously as a profession—Frances and Mary Allen, and Alice Austen come to mind. Others chose photography to complement their primary interests in painting (Sarah C. Sears) or architecture (Lois L. Howe). Still others were skilled amateurs attracted to a novel craft requiring a relatively modest financial investment (ten dollars or less), and one that fit easily into their already full lives as wives, mothers, and caretakers. While most SACB members sought to work in traditional media and perfect age-old craft techniques, photographers struggled to master the latest technology while presenting images that were nostalgic, idealized, and anti-urban.[18]

The phenomenon of the craftswoman figured prominently in publications such as *The Woman's Book* (1894), which devoted its first chapter to a discussion of "Occupations for Women," addressing women's inroads as art workers, architects, and photographers. Within the SACB, men dominated the areas of glass blowing, woodworking, cabinet-making, and ecclesiastical work. Physically demanding crafts to practice, these were also among the most lucrative.[19]

While identifying the major categories that define the arts and crafts, the SACB's 1916 survey also makes distinctions among craft categories that appear arbitrary. What, for example, were the differences among the decorators (29), designers (143), interior decorators (3), and china decorators (34)? (Some of these may have been "industrial designers," those who provided designs for "textiles, wallpaper, floor coverings, and book-covers," a field infiltrated by women as early as the 1880s.) Was there a hierarchy that might explain divisions among the metalworkers (96), silversmiths (42), chasers (4), ironworkers (3), brass workers (3), and pewter workers (2)? What fundamental distinction separated a cement worker (1) from a concrete worker (2), and, more important, what exactly did each do, as that related to the arts and crafts? And how did a modeler, a sculptor, and a wood or stone carver differ? This survey suggests that the Arts and Crafts movement attracted many individuals whose expertise fell outside the five traditional craft categories of clay, glass, metal, wood, and fiber. For that reason, the members of the Jury had to be prepared to evaluate a little bit of everything.[20]

The Jury's Mission and Procedures

How the Jury functioned within the larger Society is evident from a brief overview of its mission and procedures. Some of these Whiting addressed in short bulletins or notices. Others the Council articulated in its annual reports. A summary of the actual opinions rendered by the Jury follows. This discussion of the Jury's approach and operations makes clear how Whiting, the Jury, and the Council worked side by side, sometimes independently, at other times as a unified team, and occasionally in opposition.

The Jury's philosophy of Usefulness and Beauty evolved alongside policies and procedures for conducting its work. From the start, Jurors found it necessary to determine how best to go about their business, even as they rendered opinions on work presented for examination. Not surprisingly, minutes from their first four meetings, which took place in November 1900, were copious and detailed. Eventually, the minutes became economical to the point of being cryptic, as members agreed upon a streamlined modus operandi and forged ahead with their work.

Initially, the Jury planned to record each member's vote—to accept, accept with criticism, or reject—in the minutes, along with written comments that might be shared with the contributor. These comments were especially important in the case of a rejection. Within the first month, however, the process was proving so time-consuming that an alternative was proposed. For each contributor whose works were rejected, a designated member of the Jury would prepare a written report with comments. After being approved by the Jury, this report would then be shared with the craftsworker, who could seek clarification in person or by letter. These reports, the minutes warned, were to be "courteous and careful."[21]

At the outset, the Jury established strict procedures to follow when reviewing members' works with the goal of ensuring fairness and impartiality. Members submitting work identified it by number to guarantee anonymity, and, for nearly a decade, the Jury met in secrecy behind closed doors. At first, its members were anonymous, their names listed only in confidential meeting minutes; later, the Society's annual reports published their names.[22]

Minutes of meetings and essays published in the Society's annual reports attest to the Jury's strictness. Both sources document opinions rendered as the Jury reviewed submissions by craftsmen wishing to sell work in the Society's salesroom or to exhibit under the SACB's auspices. In doing so, the Jury considered every aspect of a product's design or execution, as well as its price and relative salability, its cultural relevance, and conceptual validity. It insisted that each product reflect its maker's highest potential according to that individual's capabilities.

Before we consider those comments in detail, it is important to note that the Jury did more than simply vote on members' works. One activity in which they participated was to approve for reproduction by SACB members antiques from Jurors' collections. This was consistent with their goal of recommending models from the past that craftsworkers might emulate. Approved objects listed in the minutes include an "Italian Glass plate" and a small, presumably glass, vase "to be reproduced without engraving" by Julian de Cordova (b. 1857) of the Union Glass Works; "silver tankards" loaned by A. A. Carey, and "silver pitchers" loaned by D. W. Ross; a pair of andirons belonging to A. A. Carey; a "glass finger bowl (lent by Mrs. Whitman), to be reproduced by the Union Glass Co."; and "salts & creamer presented by Mr. Ross." Without further description, there is no way to know more about these approved models, but they may have been Colonial examples, since Colonial Revival reproductions or approximations were always among the salesroom's best sellers. Carey, Ross, and Whitman had far-ranging interests as connoisseurs and collectors.[23]

Another decision made by the Jury early on was to "recommend that the Council adopt a hallmark for approved silver," suggesting an equilateral triangle, filled with a capital A over another capital A and C.[24]

Though the group was in many ways secretive, the Jury's policies and procedures were of interest to the Council and SACB members as a whole. Thus, as early as 1903, the Society's annual reports made a habit of including information about the Jury's activities. That year there seems to have been some confusion regarding the role of the Jury versus that of the Society's Membership Committee, which admitted new applicants, but only after having seen an example of work by those persons. The Membership Committee, the report for 1903 explained, "does not pass upon the artistic value of the work submitted, nor does election to the Society guarantee or presuppose the Jury's acceptance of any work considered by the Membership Committee in reaching its decision. The Jury, on the other hand, only passes upon work which has been designed or executed (preferably both) by members of the Society. Each article submitted is either admitted or rejected solely according to its merits or defects, both in design and execution." This is, in essence, an early job description for the Jury, and an effort on the part of the Council to distinguish the Jury's activities—as the ultimate arbiter of taste within the organization—from those of other committees.[25]

130. Chestnut Street, looking west from River Street toward the embankment, Boston, 1917 (?). (Courtesy Historic New England) Metalsmith George J. Hunt ran a cooperative workshop at 79 Chestnut Street. Workers referred jokingly to this location as "Horse Chestnut Street," because of the plethora of horse-drawn carriages found there.

By 1905, the Council had begun openly commending the work of the Jury in the annual report, and it indicated that the scope of that work had increased. The SACB now allowed non-members to sell work in the salesroom, provided that it had received Jury approval. The decision to include outsiders—especially those from out of state—may have been driven by economic considerations, such as a need for more diverse and high-quality merchandise in the salesroom. Or it may be that the Council invited nationally known non-members to participate as a way of raising standards by providing outstanding examples.[26]

This raising of standards by example seems to have been on the mind of Jury members such as Sarah Wyman Whitman, who died in 1904 and left to the SACB "two excellent examples of pottery made by members of the Society. These form," the annual report noted, "the nucleus of a collection which will, it is hoped, be added to frequently, and soon become of sufficient size and variety to serve as a set of 'standards' to guide both Jury and craftsmen in judging the quality of new work." The Council envisioned this gift as the core of a Handicraft Museum collection, which may have been on permanent display in the Society's headquarters. In later years, the Committee on Exhibitions continued this practice.[27]

By 1905, contributions to the salesroom had increased to a point where "hundreds of articles [were] passing through the hands" of F. A. Whiting "each month," and he found it necessary to publish a small pamphlet, titled "To Contributors," outlining salesroom policies and procedures. Speaking of the Jury, Whiting noted: "The examining committee of the Jury will meet once a week to pass upon work submitted for sale." This confirms that (beginning in 1903) only a small group of rotating Jurors actually reviewed everything submitted, thus streamlining the process.[28]

Stressing the advisory nature of the Jury, Whiting also indicated: "The Jury is anxious to help contributors with criticisms and advice wherever possible; but the amount of work now considered at each meeting makes it impossible to supply special criticisms unless they are requested in submitting the work. When desired the Secretary will try to arrange for interviews between contributors and members of the Jury, for the personal criticism of rejected work." How many individuals actually took advantage of this service is unknown.

In 1906, the annual report suggested that the Jury process was of increasing importance to SACB members. It announced that Juror Henry Hunt Clark would begin offering a class in design criticism for members under the auspices of the SACB at 79 Chestnut Street, location of a new cooperative workshop with room for six benches, run by metalsmith George J. Hunt (1866–1947), formerly a Master in a similar sort of shop in Liverpool (Fig. 130). "A definite course in design," the Report of the Council stated, "is followed by criticism of designs prepared and of the execution of designs in materials." The "Fall Announcements," dated November 1, 1906, also indicated that Alice J. Morse (who would join the Jury in 1908) would begin offering a "class in design and criticism" at her studio at 4 Joy Street, charging five dollars for ten lessons. These classes were consistent with the SACB's belief in promoting design education. They also may have been developed in response to the Jury's recurring recommendations that members improve their knowledge of design fundamentals.[29]

It was also in 1906 that the first Report of the Jury appeared in an annual report. As a group, these reports are of such value that they will be addressed separately.

By 1908, the annual report included a section called Jury Advice and Criticism, calling attention to the fact that "members of the Jury will be present at the rooms from 12 until 1 o'clock on Thursdays from November 1 to June 1, to consult with members about proposed or rejected work." This illustrates the Jury's conviction that criticism was equally valuable at different stages of the design process—that is, at its beginning or end. Jurors may, in fact, have preferred to advise their constituents in the early stages, when mistakes might be avoided, rather than after the fact.[30]

This report also reflects upon the SACB's decennial exhibition (1907), arguing that it served as a way of "increase[ing] interest in the work of the Society and a wider appreciation of the standards of design and workmanship which it is striving to establish," through the work of the Jury. To that end, the annual report published in-house awards given to outstanding members at the time of the show, for individual entries or entire collections of work. This began a practice of listing work commended each year, as a way of calling attention to the most accomplished members, acknowledging them, and establishing them as role models for workers seeking inspiration. (See Appendix D.)[31]

The 1909 annual report was the first in which the Jury openly discussed its "regulations and aims," in response to a crisis in the salesroom—prompted by dissatisfaction among metalworkers—during the previous year. The report discussed the Jury's composition (eleven members with a chairman and vice-chairman), its meeting times, and availability. It stressed its willingness to "confer personally" with members and to offer "direct criticism if desired." It also indicated that it had received numerous suggestions from members on how best to conduct itself, but reminded readers that "its function is that of approval or disapproval," and that its ability to offer more services was limited. It also indicated that it was going to begin using a "form of acceptance and rejection, embodying criticism under headings such as construction, workmanship, design, line, color, surface, suitability and purpose, etc." These comments—unique among reports offered between 1900 and 1918—demonstrate the Jury's desire to be as helpful as possible, make its operations transparent, and assuage members' fears and frustrations.[32]

In the annual report for 1910, C. Howard Walker's name appeared for the first time as a key contact person for the Jury, who would provide "knowledge and advice," face to face or in writing. The report encouraged members to take advantage of his expertise.[33]

The annual report for 1911 further details the Jury's functions by stressing that C. Howard Walker now would act as its official spokesperson, explaining that "the criticism has thus acquired a unity which makes it much more efficient than under less advantageous circumstances." Presumably, Walker offered the final word on what constituted Usefulness and Beauty. He was the contact person for the Jury, charged with conveying its collective wishes clearly and forcefully. At this point, the Jury's annual report split into two sections, one giving a general overview of the year, and another offering Walker's more detailed and exacting comments.[34]

Reinforcing the comments of the Jury in the annual report for 1911 were those offered by the Council. Reminding SACB members of the "Principles of Handicraft" (Fig. 118), it asked: "How can the Society keep its pledge to 'develop craftsmen to their full capacity, that their work may become still more beautiful as it is more and more expressive of keen intelligence allied to greater skill of hand and finer perceptions of true beauty'?" The Council suggested that the salesroom, exhibitions, loan displays, meetings, and lectures would all contribute to achieving this goal. It implied that the Jury played an essential role in controlling the quality of most of these endeavors, a position asserted in an article, "Raising the Standards of Craftsmanship," published in the revitalized *Handicraft* (April 1911). The Council's query was important as well because it demonstrated that the Society's commitment to Usefulness and Beauty—achieved through the Jury process—remained unswerving.[35]

In evaluating an individual's work, the Jury consistently upheld the Society's mission "to develop and encourage higher artistic standards in the handicrafts." In addition, the Jury promoted the "Principles of Handicraft." Thus, they eagerly embraced the Society's pledge "to endeavor to stimulate in workmen an appreciation of the dignity and value of good design; to counteract the popular impatience of Law and Form, the desire for over-ornamentation and specious originality, [while] insist[ing] upon the necessity of sobriety and restraint, of ordered arrangement, of due regard for the relation between the form of an object and its use, and of harmony and fitness in the decoration put upon it." Such a conservative statement suggests that the Jury's chief concern was improving its members' understanding of design fundamentals without promoting any particular style.

The "Principles of Handicraft" are among the tools with which the Jury

131. Medal, the Society of Arts and Crafts, Boston. (Courtesy SACB Archives) The medal incorporated the Society's official seal on one side and provided dedicatory information on the reverse.

assessed work of SACB members. But they by no means constituted its sole criteria. Jurors cognizant of design theory were eager to apply their own principles to the evaluation process. Among these were Ross, author of *A Theory of Pure Design* (1907), and Walker, who regularly took time from his architectural practice (Walker and Kimball) to lecture on design fundamentals and history at several Boston institutions. Walker never wrote a volume articulating his design theory, but essays in the Society's annual reports (to be discussed) and articles in publications such as *Handicraft* elucidate his views. Members of the Jury actively promoted books written by well-known theorists. With such works at hand, they sought to convince their constituents that handicraft was less a craft than an art, and less the product of the hand than of the intellect. (For some of the books on design fundamentals that it promoted, see Appendix C.)[36]

In 1912, the Council reiterated its call for Beauty. "Our customers must realize that the objects they buy though us," it wrote, referring to the salesroom, "are more beautiful *because* they are produced under a greater personal expression than is possible under the modern factory system. Failing the attempt to point out this moral," it warned, "we are failing in an essential purpose of our existence." Reiterating a theme that it had voiced for nearly fifteen years, the Council sought to distinguish the SACB salesroom from retail stores in the city. It feared that the Society might devolve into "a business organization for the purpose of selling handicraft work selected by a Jury," unless it stressed its mission, and the uniqueness of what the SACB offered to the community.[37]

That same year, the Membership Committee wrote of a need for stricter membership standards in general, and of a greater demand for skill and taste among applicants. As the organization grew—its membership exceeded 900 in 1912—the work of the Jury became even more important. In 1912, the Council announced that it would begin awarding a select number of medals to those members whose work the Jury deemed superlative (Fig. 131). In 1913, the first of these medalists were Arthur J. Stone, John Kirchmayer, and Frederick Krasser.[38]

The Report of the Jury for 1914 was the first actually signed by C. Howard Walker, the "appointed Critic of the Jury." From then through 1918, the activities of the Jury as described in the annual report deviated very little from the pattern established during its first years. It provided a list of "work commended" that year. It designated one to three individuals as medalists. It highlighted Walker's availability to meet with members, and it offered his comments, filled with insight, humor, and a characteristic sardonic edge. It celebrated the members' accomplishments, but chided them for their failures. It increased its already high standards and kept raising the bar for new applicants.

The Report of the Council for 1916 summarized the Society's justification for pursuing excellence in Usefulness and Beauty. "If our 'infant' art industries are to hold their own in the intense competition which will follow the close of the world war," it began, "the American public must be educated, the American manufacturers must be educated, and American statesmen must be educated in the importance of art in industry. In the face of the remarkable industrial art renaissance throughout Europe before the war, America has shown a surprising apathy and disregard for the vitally important part the properly trained craftsman can and should play in furnishing models, ideals, and inspirations for arts industries. We have craftsmen in this country who are doing work of a very high standard in the various branches. This is recognized by foreigners, as the purchase of American craftswork for European and Japanese collections testifies. But," the report concluded, "to all too many Americans, the excellence of American handicraft and its importance and value are unknown." By approving works sold in the SACB salesroom, or exhibited locally and nationally, the Jury hoped to rectify this situation.[39]

By calling attention to the work of the Jury consistently in the annual reports, the SACB's administrators reinforced its importance. These reports clarified the Jury's role, justified its aims, offered praise for its work, and reiterated the necessity of maintaining high standards, as epitomized by the "Principles of Handicraft." They supported both F. A. Whiting and C. H. Walker, especially during times of adversity. The reports did more, however, than simply justify the policies and procedures from an administrative point of view. They also offered pep talks to the members (who may have questioned the roles of the Jury, Whiting, and Walker), while stressing how members might be proactive: by attending classes, reading appropriate books, participating willingly in critiques, or aspiring to become role models—whose works might ultimately receive commendations or medals.

Jury Recommendations: Highlights of Meeting Minutes, 1900–1905

The best indicator of how the Jury performed in its early days is evident in the minutes of its first meeting (11–07–00). On this occasion, Contributor No. 51 submitted eleven metal objects for consideration, of which the Jury rejected eight. This necessitated a detailed report, written by Sarah Wyman Whitman, and later shared with the contributor. The report is worth quoting at length:

REPORT OF MRS. WHITMAN AS FOLLOWS:

SET OF FIRE IRONS. NO. 7. Figure which holds the tools is wholly out of scale: not intelligently attached to wall: not conventionalized. Design on handle of tools eccentric and badly modeled. Idea not easily understood. Not harmonious with simple classic designs usually found in fire-places.

SCONCE. NO. 10. Shape of sconce eccentric and treatment of decorative lines inorganic. Varying colors in metals not required in effect.

SMOKING SET. NO. 6. Very good composition. The large flat tray, and distribution of parts excellent; but workmanship and treatment of detail unsatisfactory. The figure of Egyptian origin if used at all must be on fine lines and carefully wrought. The Cups which are large and important should have in design some relation to the central motive. Again, they are attached and detached in an insecure way which does not explain itself at sight, and which in effect is like a top spinning to keep its equilibrium. In a word the construction is not apparent in the design.

INK STANDS. 2A & 2B. There again the construction masks the purpose of the object. On looking at this solid metal base it is not evident that it is an inkstand. It looks like something that belongs to something else. With the solidity and strength which are good elements, one might equally well show design, and more delicacy of treatment; always necessary in a small object.

BOOK RACK. NO. 14: Totally inorganic.[40]

What this critique reveals is the breadth of the Jury's watchfulness. Members reviewed conceptual, aesthetic, and technical traits, paying attention as well to historical precedence and overall expression. They considered each design element and principle. And they were wont to use favorite descriptors, such as "eccentric," or "inorganic," in trying to convey their points. Their language often reiterated points made in earlier statements published by the SACB. Whitman's comments on behalf of the Jury are worth comparing to her articles published in *Handicraft*, such as one entitled "Cups" (June 1902), in which she revealed her personal philosophy of good design.

When Jurors addressed conceptual issues, they considered workers' interpretation of historical or natural models, often implying that a craftsperson failed to comprehend the original and thus could not apply it appropriately. Sometimes the Jury felt that an interpretation from history or nature was too realistic and might benefit from abstraction. Jurors often commented upon subject matter and its appropriateness, or lack thereof, to the particular application or medium. The Jury might remark upon a work's originality—whether it was truly innovative, or merely imitative. Occasionally, the Jury suggested that one member might be (inadvertently) plagiarizing from another. The word that recurred most often in their critiques was "design."

As they considered the ideas conveyed by a work, Jurors often raised the issue of complexity or simplicity. They recommended conventionalization as a key to making form or ornament sleeker, more economical, or more abstract. As they considered the ideas informing a work, the Jury also pondered broad craft categories, and whether or not a particular group of objects or type of material was truly appropriate for the Society and its salesroom. These included printmaking in general, monotypes and woodcuts in particular, magazine covers, photograph frames, rattan frames, and key rings, to name just a few.[41]

In terms of aesthetic issues, the Jury was obsessed with line and form. Jurors often dismissed works as "clumsy," or "crude." They argued that forms must convey a sense of strength or solidity without being overly heavy. Similarly, they preferred lightness and delicacy, but not to the point of weakness. As they pondered scale and proportion, they advised against an appearance of "stumpiness." They commented upon the modeling of three-dimensional forms or two-dimensional reliefs, expecting a degree of finesse and thoughtful composition. They scrutinized decorative details, especially edges, lips, bands, borders, and moldings.[42]

Comments pertaining to color, texture, and pattern were limited, but the Jury paid particular attention to surface and finish, always alert for signs of impatience on the part of the craftsman, or what it called "hurried workmanship." It might return a piece of jewelry or metalwork that seemed overly bright, recommending that it "be oxidized" to tone down the coloration, but it would not tolerate pieces that already appeared overworked in any way, having, for example, a "surface too much fussed over." It rejected products having either an "affectation of age" or of "rudeness," expressing particular dislike for "heavy hammer marks," and for any "imperfections that were too obviously intentional." The Jury insisted that every surface or finish must be *genuine*, a true reflection of the nature of the material and the technique employed to manipulate it. It disdained artificiality. In doing so, the Jury supported many of the points made by F. A. Whiting in his speech on the origins of the Arts and Crafts movement.[43]

The issue of surface finish is partly an aesthetic consideration and partly a technical one. In discussing technique, the Jury analyzed a variety of traits, including execution (or workmanship), construction, the connections of small parts to the larger whole, and their logic (in terms of either fabrication or material usage), selection and handling of materials, and rudeness or crudeness of finish. Refinement in all areas was important.

Often, the Jury's comments pertained less to conceptual, aesthetic, or technical issues, and more to overall expression. On February 12, 1902, for example, the minutes read: "Rejected: Miss [Jane] Carson's buckle. Design not delicate or sensitive enough, and lacks *good* conventionality. Omission of silver lines makes it less valuable and interesting work." Here the Jurors reacted less to tangible traits and more to qualitative issues. The Jury held certain expectations for work in expensive media, such as the metals, enamels, and jewelry. And when a piece failed to measure up, the Jury questioned the artist's intention versus achievement.[44]

For every specific recommendation offered, such as the suggestion that one distinct type of molding be substituted for another, or that a cool gray glaze be adjusted to "a *warm* to harmonize," there were others that seemed arbitrary or ambiguous. What did the Jury mean when it labeled a color "unfortunate," a glaze "odd," or a shape "inappropriate"? What did it hope to convey by suggesting that a piece of jewelry was "lacking in quality"? Such statements were well founded but lacked the specificity required to be helpful, especially to the novice.[45]

The Jury often overlooked weaknesses in one aspect of a work if it noticed strengths of another sort. "Accepted," it stated regarding article no. 1 of contributor no. 56, "the admirable workmanship rather than the design is commended." "[Approved]," it noted on another occasion, "design of chairs [by Mrs. Dennett and Mrs. Hill] with

132. Henry Chapman Mercer. (Courtesy Bucks County Historical Society) Though Mercer was an extraordinarily successful ceramic artist, the SACB Jury often negatively critiqued his work.

some criticism of workmanship. [Approved] tables in design; but construction criticized." As this last comment suggests, the Jury's tolerance for weakness in design generally surpassed its willingness to overlook flaws in craftsmanship.[46]

Another aspect of the Jurors' work might best be described as "career counseling." Throughout the minutes of the period 1900–1905 are instances where they aimed their criticism at workers and their progress professionally, rather than at an individual's work. Sometimes they accepted work "for exhibition purposes" only, but clearly did not believe that it was salable or had merit in the long term. Upon returning one such example to its maker, the Jury stated in the minutes: "Voted: That the blue-printed cloths be returned to the maker. Having been on exhibition for some time without attracting favorable attention or interest, they are returned so as to give place for other things. In the opinion of the Jury the process is one which is not likely to lead to any important results. The designs are sure to lose quality when so mechanically reproduced."[47]

On another occasion, the Jury attempted to counsel a new member, Mr. E. K. Butler, Jr., on the production of rattan frames. Jurors approved his submission "with the suggestion that the Jury does not consider that these frames have enough of art in them to make them appropriate for admittance hereafter." Evidently Mr. Butler objected to this criticism, and sent a letter to the Jury challenging the decision. The Jury responded on February 12, 1902, stating that the rattan frames "seem to contain no possibility of developing into something better—the work seems to lead nowhere." Such criticism was evidently discouraging to Mr. Butler, who failed to renew his membership in the SACB the following year.[48]

Jury approval on one occasion did not guarantee a craftsperson's fate on another. On July 11, 1901, for example, the Jury reviewed multiple works submitted by the Dedham Pottery and its founder Hugh C. Robertson. It approved about five items, but rejected many more with the "Comment: That while accepting some of the pieces presented, the Jury feels that there has been a distinct deterioration in the quality of the works and unless there is a decided improvement, the Jury doubts if it can accept in future work of similar quality—especially in the drawing of the designs." What is clear is that the Jury set increasingly high standards for its members, and especially for those designated as Masters. (Robertson became a Master in 1902, so evidently the chiding of the previous year was something that he had taken to heart.)[49]

Despite the Jury's exacting attention to detail, during 1900–1905, it was reticent on the issues of Usefulness and Beauty. Its definition of each was implied in

133. "The Apostles," stained glass window, by Margaret Redmond, 1927. (Courtesy of Trinity Church in the City of Boston)

its comments, but it only rarely commented upon either directly. Of the two, Usefulness received more attention than did Beauty; and Jurors were more inclined to speak out on issues that compromised Usefulness rather than to define it outright. On one occasion, the Jury wrote of a water heater "Not well adapted to its use. Frivolous." On another, it labeled a "shape [as] inappropriate for its use." Later on, it wrote of a "material not precious enough for the use," and, in a similar vein, it remarked upon the "unpleasantness of [an] affectedly hammered surface which is unsuitable for its use." It denounced a "handle [that] lacks delicacy and utility," and warned metalsmiths against "*any* decoration on bottom of milk bowl on account of cleanliness." On another occasion, it rejected reticulations in silver "fear[ing] the perforations are too small for practical use." Clearly, Usefulness incorporated myriad qualities, pertaining to form, ornament, material, and finish.⁵⁰

On the rare occasions when the Jury spoke of Beauty, it did so to point out where an object fell short of achieving it. A set of tiles submitted by Henry Chapman Mercer (1856–1930, Fig. 132), it wrote, "need[ed] more exquisite treatment owing to the beauty of the subject matter." It approved a tray "with criticism of pierced decoration—which makes it seem thin & mechanical, &, in this case, takes away from its beauty. The form is the tray['s] chief charm." Finally, it approved a "Green & blue circle of [stained] glass," submitted by Margaret Redmond (1867–1948, Fig. 133), with the recommendation that it "might be much better if [the] design were more positive and structural; shapes not beautiful & not organized into unity." For an artist like Redmond, educated in Philadelphia, New York, and Paris, such comments on beauty—or its lack—may have seemed gratuitous, if not irksome.⁵¹

The Jury's minutes from its first years of operation provide insight into its biases regarding conceptual, aesthetic, and technical considerations. Not surprisingly, their recommendations on Good Design parallel closely those offered by Langford Warren in his introduction to the *1899 Exhibition Catalogue*. Warren advocated usefulness, appropriate materials and methods, harmonious and fit decoration, simplicity, and quality. He disdained "eccentricity" and objects reflecting divided labor. The Jury promoted many of these same concepts, while parroting Warren's distaste for eccentricity. The qualities that Warren and the Jury sought in well-designed work were often time-honored, harkening back to those espoused by Hogarth, Hume, Burke, Gerard, Home, and key eighteenth-century pattern-book authors.

What is ironic is that some of the members to whom the Jury offered its harshest criticism—Hugh C. Robertson, Henry C. Mercer, and Arthur J. Stone are just three examples—are those whose work is most valued in the antiques and collectibles market today. Has their work achieved such prominence in the twenty-first century because of—or in spite of—the Jury's criticism?

The Reports of the Jury, 1906–1918

In 1906, as noted above, the Jury began contributing an essay to the Society's annual report. These reports generally appeared in the spring, and summarized activities from the previous twelve months, with emphasis on the period August through June. The Report of the Jury transformed informal observations recorded in meeting minutes during the previous year into a formal report to be shared with the entire SACB membership. These reports are invaluable: they highlight the general strengths and weaknesses of work submitted to the Jury, provide recommendations for improvement, and list the types of objects that the Jury believed would enhance the merchandise selection in the SACB salesroom. As such, they are part critique, part market research, and part rallying cry on behalf of Usefulness and Beauty.

The Report of the Jury for 1906 noted a "gradual improvement in the character of the workmanship and designs" submitted that year, while indicating "there is still much to be desired." It insisted that handwork must be superior to machine work, and that individual designers must produce examples that were original and unique. Faults compromising the quality of work submitted included a lack of "knowledge and study," of "proportions," and of "understanding of the expressive potential of materials," along with poor line quality and composition. As these suggest, many of the points made in this first Jury report reiterated comments that it had recorded in its minutes for the previous five years.[52]

Wishing to provide constructive criticism, the report went on to list potential remedies for the problems it had mentioned. The Jury advised improving drawing skills, learning the "skilful adaptation of old forms," avoiding "ambitious flights" of fancy, and studying appropriate use of materials. Continuing to stress design fundamentals, it suggested that members study the traditions associated with a particular medium, arguing: "They are the root methods of attack, so to speak, and should be known as thoroughly as are the letters of an alphabet." The

134. Exhibition of the Society of Arts and Crafts, Copley Hall, Boston, 1907. (Courtesy SACB Archives)

Jury concluded: "We desire each piece of work, however small, to be done with skill of hand, to be finished and not left crude, and for the designs to show study of the simple fundamental principles of applicability to material, scale of areas, and of organic planning." Jurors hoped that such a formula for "good design" might inspire SACB members in the coming year.

The Report of the Jury for 1907 was published in May though written in February. It appeared after the conclusion of the Society's decennial exhibition, which provided a focus for the Jury's comments (Fig. 134). The report began by noting that the work submitted was better—but still showed room for improvement. "There still exists apparently an idea that design is a casual, happy-go-lucky sort of amusement," the Jury noted, "and that workmanship means the apparent effect, not the finished product." As such, it did not reflect the degree of sobriety and thoughtfulness that the Jury expected.[53]

With that as a general introduction, the report went on to discuss the decennial exhibition specifically. Remarking upon the standards evidenced at the show, the report noted "much work that would have been gratefully accepted ten years ago was rejected at once." This was in keeping with the organization's desire to raise the bar continuously in terms of standards. Jurors complimented members on their "steady improvement and sanity," noting proudly that work produced by commercial manufacturers in Boston now copied the sorts of designs purveyed by the SACB. What is more, the report noted, "The Exhibition gave testimony that this attitude—[that Arts and Crafts work is self-consciously aesthetic, and exclusively novel]—has been outgrown." With this last point, the Jury suggested that the work it approved was becoming less avant-garde.

This did not mean that work shown at the decennial exhibition had the Jury's full approbation. "It was well done," the report indicated, "well designed, but seldom excited marked comment." The report indicated that workers seemed to have developed a good foundation upon which to build. It suggested that they must continue to produce the staple goods of the arts and crafts shop, but must

135a. Metalwork shown at the 1907 Exhibition, from the exhibition catalogue. (Courtesy SACB Archives) Frederick Krasser produced the iron grille and set of wrought iron and brass andirons after designs by A. W. Longfellow, Jr. Frank Koralewsky fabricated the door pull and lock after designs by Weston Underwood.

135b. Silver shown at the 1907 Exhibition, from the exhibition catalogue. (Courtesy SACB Archives) Arthur J. Stone executed the loving cups left (lent by Charles W. Eliot of Harvard University) and right (lent by Edward Hale Abbot) after designs by H. Langford Warren. George P. Kendrick designed and decorated the tankard (lent by A. P. Loring), and the loving cup center (lent by the Reverend James Reed). Karl F. Leinonen executed the silver tray and fluted punch bowl, both of which may have been produced under the auspices of the Handicraft Shop.

also challenge themselves to create "more and more special things done with superlative skill." In conclusion, it offered this observation: "It is generally interesting to note that strength in design was coincident with strength in skill of workmanship, and vice versa; so that those departments which needed the greatest improvement needed it both as Arts and as Crafts." In the Jury's opinion, the strongest areas were bookbinding, basketry, metalwork—especially silver and iron (Figs. 135a and b)—and pottery, while the weakest were leatherwork, jewelry—which it labeled "thoroughly crude and childish in idea"—and painted china. In the years following the decennial exhibition, these areas of strength and weakness remained consistent.

The Report of the Jury for 1908 began on a positive note, remarking upon a "better conception of the attributes of good design and of good workmanship," and "little of sensational or meretricious character." Yet, it concluded, "with the increase of technical ability and of restraint in expression there has not been coincident an increase of originality of idea or treatment." Like previous reports, it thus addressed conceptual, aesthetic, and technical traits, as well as the issue of expression.[54]

It focused upon material usage, stating: "in very few cases has advantage been taken of the full opportunities of materials." It offered as examples metalwork that showed "little variety . . . in the treatment of the surfaces, in the possibilities of contrast of brilliant and dull surfaces of enamels." It singled out rugs as "crude," "coarse," and "violent" in coloration, explaining that they, and other woven textiles, showed little "contrast in weaves, etc. Each workman, having started with one method of attack, continues it monotonously throughout the work, providing little or no modulation; in fact, no orchestration of the work. The result is, that while there are many examples of negatively good work, there are comparatively few of positively good work and fewer still of distinguished work." Using materials with both integrity and innovation was, evidently, a common problem.

The report went on to argue that to be competitive in the marketplace, an arts and crafts shop must be "like an exhibit of masterpieces." It challenged craftspeople to submit "work of distinction and individuality, even if that work is devoted to comparatively insignificant objects." Referring to the SACB salesroom and potential merchandise that workers might submit, the Jury wrote: "More and better enameled work is desired, as are also better examples of bookbinding, wood-carving, painted tiles, delicate china, printed fans, carved ivories, wrought fire-irons, silver and brass scutcheons, and doorplates, hinges, etc. . . . An especial effort needs therefore to be made to improve design, and to develop originality in design, an originality, however, of idea, not of sensationalism." As always, the Jury was conservative in its taste.

The Jury ended its report by commenting upon its varying roles in relation to the range of its constituents' abilities. "A number of craftsmen do excellent work," it noted, "at the head of whom stand those whose design and execution is so good as to command only admiration and about whose work any observations come in the nature of a suggestion rather than of criticism." These were the sorts of individuals for whom the Jury served as adviser or mentor. On the other hand, it indicated, "there are also workers who are striving to improve all the opportunities at hand, who are endowed some with more, some with less, artistic talent and the appreciation and fitness of things decorative. The Jury strives to enter into the point of view of these craftsmen, and to point out where the work deserves praise and where it falls short of excellence; and in doing so, must frankly acknowledge its own limitations and the difficulty it finds in applying to every case the proper and helpful comments which it merits." These are the sorts of individuals—Masters and medalists—for whom the Jury served alternately as midwife and tormentor. But, much as it tried, it could not be all things to all people.

The conciliatory tone of this report may have reflected an attempt on the Jury's part to counteract feelings of antipathy that arose in 1908 among dissatisfied metalworkers, who questioned Whiting's running of the salesroom and the Jury's actions. This schism, which threatened the Society's esprit de corps, may have been a natural letdown following the focus provided by the decennial exhibition. It also may have been the product of disappointment with the salesroom (Figs. 136 and 137), Whiting's administration, and overall sales for 1907 and 1908, following the financial "Panic of 1907." This economic downturn was national in scope and threatened the spirit of optimism that had characterized the new century.[55]

The Jury's report for 1909 indicated that it was continually raising its standards and would no longer accept works that it might have condoned previously. This report differed from earlier examples, since it focused upon its policies and procedures rather than on the work submitted to it. In the aftermath of the crisis of 1908, the functioning of the salesroom and the related work of the Jury were of increasing interest to the SACB members, who were as interested in how the Jury operated and its composition as they were in its comments, critiques, and recommendations.[56]

136. Exterior, salesroom of the SACB, 9 Park Street. (Courtesy SACB Archives) The salesroom was located on the ground floor of a section of the Amory-Ticknor Building, also occupied by the Thomas Strahan Decorating Co.

137. Interior, SACB salesroom. Photograph by Dorothy Jarvis. (Courtesy SACB Archives) This shows reproductions of furniture from the Rococo and Classical Revival styles.

Perhaps because of the brevity of the Report of the Jury for 1909, that for 1910 was substantive. It remarked that the work of the past year had ranged from "good" to "commended" to "worthy of the highest praise." Commenting upon its ever-rising standards, it noted: "It seems right that the standard of judgment of both Jury and Craftsmen should be higher and more exacting in proportion as the handicraft of thoughtful and earnest workers is high above the standard of tradework." It went on to make recommendations, arguing in favor of "a better appreciation of line; better ability to draw; better planning and spacing and arrangement of forms; more study and knowledge. To which might be added, that better appreciation of the qualities of related materials, of the treatment of metals, of metal and stone, of enamel, of wood and leather, still holds good." Such comments reiterated—to the point of repeating exactly—recommendations from previous years.[57]

These comments betray the growing conservatism of the Jury, which sought "for more knowledge and better understanding and appreciation of the conditions in hand, including more careful workmanship." It, therefore, continued "to recommend to that end association with good examples of ancient work." The justification for that recommendation epitomizes Walker's philosophy of design, as a professor of the history of ornament. "We are still suffering somewhat from the insecure foundations upon which the modern movement of the Arts and Crafts rested," the report notes, "when eccentricity and individualism played so large a part, and were accepted joyfully in exchange for the arid taste then existing in the Victorian period,—when even eccentricities and false sentiment were hailed with hope of promise of a renascence of the arts to come. Those days are happily past," the report continued, "but we are only now outliving a later pretentious and cheap mode of production called 'Arts and Crafts' which has brought discredit to the name, and is still practiced with some enthusiasm in parts of our country and of England and Germany. A better, healthier atmosphere is taking the place of this self-conscious, 'aesthetic' work which dies hard, and a more real and sincere knowledge and feeling exists, while the functions and limitations of objects produced are better felt. We have now settled into soberer frames of mind and work, with real promise of excellence in the future which beckons an encouraging hand to those who labor in this field."

The report went on to refer to procedural changes initiated in 1909, arguing that the Jury had established closer relations with Craftsman members in the year past as a result. What is more, it announced that C. Howard Walker would now be available on a weekly basis in the Society's rooms to offer "his knowledge and advice, either in person or by criticism written at length and usually illustrated." Walker may well have written comments following this announcement, even though the signature of J. Templeman Coolidge, Jr., Chair of the Jury, appears at the bottom. If so, the Report of the Jury for 1909 introduced a pattern followed in later annual reports, which contained a brief introduction by Coolidge, followed by a lengthy report written and signed by Walker.

These annual reports of the Jury produced between 1906 and 1909 were an important source of information for SACB members. They highlighted every trait of good design that the Jury specifically and the SACB generally hoped to promote: fine handwork, originality, and appropriateness of form, materials, and technique. They also suggested methods for improving the quality of design, through drawing or sketching, mastering design fundamentals, consulting historical prototypes, and experimentation with materials and techniques. They shed light on the Jury process. Occasionally they remarked upon the Society's efforts within the broader context of the Arts and Crafts movement. They called attention to strengths without avoiding weaknesses, some of which were repetitive to the point of being predictable. They reflected the Jury's collective struggle to ensure that the work of the SACB demonstrated a proper balance between workmanlike attention to detail and innovation, with results that were exciting and distinctive.

C. Howard Walker, Critic of the Jury

By 1909, the Jury had "raised the requirements for acceptance of work both in technical skill and design," something that they would continue to do as the abilities of members improved. The report for that year focused on changes made to the jury system: it revealed jurors' identities, discussed the review process, and listed criteria for evaluation. In November 1909, Howard Walker was appointed the official Critic of the Jury. As such, he agreed for a nominal fee to meet with craftsmen on a weekly basis and to provide a written or verbal critique of work submitted to the Jury. He also included his own written assessment of the state of the applied arts in subsequent annual reports. Though his influence upon the collective taste of the Society had always been present, it became more pronounced after this date.[58]

His appointment followed a crisis in 1908, when the Guild of Metalworkers challenged the running of the salesroom and the function of the Jury. This crisis led to the appointment of a new committee, the Committee on the Salesroom, which that spring reported to the Council: "In the opinion of the Salesroom Committee, it is inexpedient for the Secretary of the Society to take any part in the criticism by the Jury, or in the reports of the Jury to the contributive members, and that the relation between the contributor and the Jury should be direct." A year and a half later, C. H. Walker supplied that direct link.[59]

His willingness to function in this capacity demonstrates an evolution in his attitude over the years. A reminiscence from April 1912 speaks of his reluctance to become involved—in any but the most peripheral ways—with the SACB and the Jury in their formative years. "It was in the early days of the arts and crafts society, and I was invited to become a member and declined, and was invited again and declined. It was in the period," he noted, with his characteristic sardonic humor, "of the apotheosis of the one-inch salt cellar. I stated positively I did not think it was the act of a sane man to waste five minutes of his time on things of that sort." That he finally agreed to join, and to take on the role of official critic shows his willingness to be flexible, and to undertake the sort of scrutiny of minutiae required by that role. By the time of his death in 1936, he had become, in the words of a *Boston Herald* editorial, "one of Boston's most caustic critics and most affectionate defenders."[60]

That he enjoyed his work as Critic of the Jury is evident from a comment made in April 1912, during a speech at a farewell dinner for Whiting. Responding to a point made by H. L. Warren—who envisioned a time "when the public at large [would] demand the best kind of handicraft work in all things of that sort" to the point that "shopkeepers [would] recognize that they must get that sort of thing to please the public," Walker replied: "If we are getting to the point where shopkeepers will go direct to our workers and where we won't need our salesroom—what's going to become of the Jury? A fellow's occupation will be gone."[61]

The lengthy essay for 1911 began with a general overview authored by J. T. Coolidge, Jr., which noted how the tenor of the Reports of the Jury had changed over time. "Comment and recommendation have taken the place of criticism," the introduction stated, acknowledging the heightened standards that members had achieved. "There is little work now from people untrained in the knowledge of design and workmanship; there is little left of self conscious aestheticism; the bizarre has given place to what is saner and the pot boiling class of object is rising to higher ground. Greater effort combined with better understanding has led to results which are gratifying and in some cases admirable." Such high standards, the report continued, had brought the SACB national recognition. Yet, "a considerable amount of material passed by the Jury and sold in the rooms," it noted, "is distinctly poorer in quality than it should be." To rectify this situation, the Jury once again advised its constituents to study work from the past. It recommended that members visit local museums, and private collections, and view work provided by the SACB's Committee on Exhibitions, which was assembling a study collection of "kindred art of the past."[62]

Following this introduction were Walker's "comments and practical recommendations." He began by noting that the work accepted by the Jury during the past year reflected multiple standards—one for established craftspeople for whom expectations were high, and a second lower standard for "product[s] of new members but which show possibilities of better achievement, and which are accepted under the former standard in effect when the workers needed encouragement more than criticism. The fact accounts," Walker explained, "for the presence in the Salesroom of some articles which are no better than those shown several years ago." Such fluctuating standards clearly irked Walker, but he seems to have regarded them as a necessary evil, given the SACB's expanding membership.[63]

In making these comments, Walker was clearly as concerned with explaining how the Jurors operated as he was with summarizing their impressions and recommendations. "The work marked 'commended' by the Jury during the year has been often distinguished work," he indicated. "The Jury wishes to express its appreciation of the spirit in which its criticisms have been received." Here Walker was most likely speaking for himself, since he was the one who met members face to face and conveyed the Jury's recommendations regarding rejected submissions. "In many cases the criticisms," he continued with his characteristic honesty, "have been severe and stated in no hesitating terms, yet despite this fact, there appear to be not only greater confidence in the decisions, but a very sincere effort to meet the standards."

Walker then offered a compliment intended for the membership at large. "It is a pleasure to be able to state that there is now an agreeable amount of work being done by some of our contributors," he wrote, "which of its kind cannot be better done elsewhere and which has in addition to skill, elements of marked individuality. The character of dilettantism which has been so constantly associated with arts and crafts products is disappearing. This is a sign," he concluded, "of sanity and of health."

Such praise did not preclude Walker from making very specific recommendations regarding particular media categories. Silver and jewelry he proclaimed "much improved," while noting that the "most distinguished piece received" in 1911 was an example in wrought iron. Ceramics, he indicated, were good but static, having "not advanced materially in merit." Leatherwork he condemned for its "weak naturalistic" ornament, which often approached the "still worse convolutions of the so-called *art nouveau*." Textiles he dismissed as "not of great interest." Wood-carving was somewhat improved; yet enamels "left much to be desired." Work in glass he noted was rare, while the book arts, though various, were of "little importance." After this summary of strengths and weaknesses, Walker provided a list of objects that the Jury hoped to receive in the coming year. The list for 1911 is worth quoting at length, since it is representative of lists provided in ensuing years, and it gives a good impression of the merchandise that the Jury believed the SACB salesroom should offer:

> IN SILVER: Silver grill work or perforated silver for tea-urn stands, etc., lamp stands under blazers, etc., candle sticks which are ornamented, card cases, cigarette cases, tea caddies.
>
> CERAMICS: New and delicate forms, not to be found in the shops, for teapots, sugar bowls, cream pitchers, etc., with delicate painted decoration in one color, not in a dozen colors. An appreciation of the fact that delicate concave or convex flutings are effective is needed. Especial study should be given to handles and covers. In many cases, while the decorative painting is good the forms bought of dealers are uncouth. Finer forms, finer clays and finer bisques are desired.
>
> LEATHER WORK: Music rolls, portfolios, etc., playing card cases, rectangular mats as well as circular ones.
>
> TEXTILES: Woven work which has a pattern (not too large), not merely broken stripe; scarfs with embroidered ends; embroidered medallions for appliqué work, etc.
>
> WOOD CARVING: Decorated handles for useful objects; umbrella handles; knife and fork handles; salad spoons—bellows sides with detail that is not coarse in scale; boxes; small cabinets, panels that may be adapted to useful forms, such as cabinet doors, pillasters [sic], drawer fronts, etc., and for centers of chair backs; carved and perforated screens which can also be used as panels such as Japanese ramas [sic]; carved bed posts; posts for pier glasses; work of this kind can be made into interesting furniture by framing simply; carved turnings which can be used on furniture; inlays of wood, ivory, and metal, of mother of pearl, etc.; and of every class of work. Very little of this work has been done.
>
> ENGRAVED METAL, like East Indian, Burmese, Siamese or Cingalese work in character but with original design; See also Greek mirrors.
>
> IVORIES in useful shapes.
>
> ENAMELS: Cloisonnées and Champlevé enamels.
>
> GLASS: Delicate glass of the Murano type. Venetian glass is becoming a thing of the past; the modern work in Venice is meretricious, yet no finer art existed. There is no reason why this cannot be done here, also engraved glass.
>
> BOOK WORK: lithographic designs; copper plate engraving; plates for head and tail pieces; vignettes, etc.
>
> FIGURE WORK in all materials.

Walker used this list as a way of inspiring workers while pointing out inherent problems in most categories. He never missed an opportunity to offer criticism, even covertly.

The Report of the Jury for 1912 opened by stating: "There is nothing new to record about the work and methods of the Jury, which continue upon the lines already developed, and now fully known." It spoke of the "excellence and shortcomings" of the past year's work, making another plea for members to study "work done by the craftsmen of the past." The Jury's specific recommendations, viewed within the context of contemporary theories of "good design," will be addressed in Chapter Four.[64]

Following a brief introduction, the report of 1912 deferred to Walker's essay, indicating that he "represent[ed] fully the opinion and comments of the Jury." Despite the presence of "steady improvement" and "a gradually advancing standard," Walker found much to criticize in 1912. He began by questioning the excessive prices of handicrafts in the salesroom, "which could have been made equally well or better by machine." He insisted that all work representing the SACB must possess "some distinctive artistic or skilful character . . . which is not to be found in machine work." This led to a discussion of finish—always an obsession of the Jury—and problems that Walker had witnessed in the year past. He condemned "that imitation of the happy accidents of crude craftsmanship," which "in modern work is pure affectation, as is likewise the exaggeration of elementary design and workmanship." He condemned especially "glazes which do not cover and tool marks which should have been worked out." He dissuaded members from imitating the "rough" and "uneven" glazing of "peasant" ceramics, or the "slipshod" effects and textures achieved by an "unskilled workman." With this in mind, Walker warned, "A great deal of the work presented is of no especial interest, being merely a poor attempt to be original to the point of uncouthness, or else barely meeting the utilitarian requirements." Once again, the need for Usefulness informed his comments, while he carried on the attention to surface finish initiated by the Jury in its early years.

Despite these reservations, Walker remained positive about the quality of work being produced by SACB members. In April 1912, he spoke of a recent trip abroad: "I went last June through the arts and crafts work in London, and with the exception of the enamels which are very fine, we are doing just as good, and in many cases even better, work in silver, gold and jewels." Adding to that, he declared, "our work is better than the work I saw at the Paris exposition of decorative art," presumably referring to the 1900 world's fair. Finally, he commended the SACB craftsmen for being at a point where they finally accepted criticism objectively.[65]

The Report of the Jury for 1913 stressed, once again, the issue of standards. It indicated that the Jury regularly accepted "a larger portion" of works submitted to it "than is desirable," but admitted that it must take into consideration the "'living' side of the question." Hoping to distinguish the SACB salesroom from its competitors, the Jury noted: "Many of the shops in Boston cater to the undeveloped or poor taste of their customers, forgetting that the best in the end is sure to be the most profitable. . . . Success invariably overtakes real excellence, even if it takes time and entails considerable sacrifice." As a way of achieving "real excellence," the Jury imagined a day in the future "when only good work will be brought before it, and it calls upon the producing members of the Society to cooperate in securing this desirable end. It can only set a standard," it reminded its readers, "and is powerless to make it creative or productive."⁶⁶

This report is unusually short and does not include a section authored by Walker. (There is a possibility that he may have resigned from the SACB for one year.) Nevertheless, it reiterates many of the points that he had made in previous essays. It implores workers to "take more advice from the craftsmen of the past," particularly since "examples [are] so easy of access." It notes that silverware "stands first" among all productions made by members precisely because it "has absorbed many of the fine qualities of feeling and delicacy to be found in good examples of the past." It suggests that jewelry might be similarly improved if its makers were to study historical precedents.

The report ends by commenting upon the strong relationship of craftsmen and critics within the Society, noting "a gratifying improvement in the work of many of those who have come to it for guidance and have developed most profitably, sometimes from discouraging beginnings." Clearly, it implied, the jury system worked. "Our productions have a quality not to be found elsewhere in our city," it noted proudly, "while our few masterpieces would hold their own anywhere. The mere achievement of having produced these few examples of first class merit, even out of thousands of passable ones, is a matter of congratulation and encouragement and points the way to higher percentages in the upward path." If Walker did take a brief leave, these words may have been an attempt on the part of J. T. Coolidge, Jr. to impress upon members the worth of Walker's participation—his exacting standards notwithstanding.

The Report of the Jury for 1914 bore the signature of A. W. Longfellow, Jr., who served as Acting Chair of the Jury in Coolidge's absence. (Coolidge was serving in World War I.) "The work of the Society has been growing more interesting," he began, "and a refreshing sense of adaptation and feeling for beauty has from time to time lightened the hours spent in selection, and in commending objects of special merit." Having served as vice-chairman since the Jury's first meeting, Longfellow was in a position to make such a comment with authority. Perhaps because Walker had not contributed an essay to the previous year's report, Longfellow found it necessary to reiterate Walker's importance as the appointed Critic of the Jury: "The Jury feels that his critical report can be made more helpful to the craftsmen than the general report of the Jury made in previous years, if it is received in the spirit in which its is made."⁶⁷

Walker's ensuing report was defensive in tone. His lengthy essay—which bears his signature at the end—began by reiterating the purpose and the ideals of the SACB and calling for "the cooperation which should be forthcoming in this regard from the members of the Society." He viewed the "purpose of the Society as twofold—to encourage artists and to recognize and if desirable to exploit merit. Therefore, the work which is accepted is of a varying quality, from that which is merely adolescent to that which is skillful and masterly. It is natural and inevitable that most of the work should fall far below the best work," he noted, "and if it had not been proved in the past that guidance and suggestion at times stimulated an untrained craftsman into becoming at least a little master, much of this work would at once have been rejected as trivial. The Jury accepts work when it sees evidence of sincerity in the worker, in order to stimulate that worker to better work." Walker's perspective as a seasoned teacher pervades these comments. He believed in the educational merits of the jury process and its relevance to the Society's mission "to develop and encourage higher artistic standards in the handicrafts," and he stressed his willingness to accommodate different levels of skill and ability among SACB members.[68]

At the same time, he had little patience with members who questioned his decisions in the salesroom, particularly as they pertained to the installation of work. "The exhibition of work should be distinctly in proportion to achievement," he notes. "The reputation of the Society should be for quality and not for quantity, or even for variety. Each worker may be confident that if his work is of superior character, it will be pushed to the front, and each worker should be equally confident that inferior work, accepted without a unanimous vote of the Jury, rightly should be shown modestly." Some of these comments may have related to the unrest in the salesroom that had begun in 1908, and had led eventually to the resignation of Frederick Allen Whiting in 1912.

Walker also alluded to a hierarchy among the crafts. "The various classes of objects are different in intrinsic merit," he wrote, "because of the materials and the skill required in the workmanship. It should be obvious that jewelry and enamels, wood carving and illuminating can be expressed in higher terms than the usual china painting and leather working and coarse basket making." Metalwork and jewelry had always been among the leading sellers in the SACB salesroom, and the Jury demanded that work in these categories be exemplary. To that end, Walker recommended that jewelry makers improve their use of contrast, their knowledge of form, their textures, and their use of stones. "Abalone pearl blister and pink quartz," he wrote, cheapen otherwise creditable attempts.[69]

This bias—that a hierarchy existed among craft categories—was not exclusive to the SACB Jury, but shared by critics and theorists worldwide. Their attitude might have been an outgrowth of divisions originally established and enforced by medieval guilds. But, more likely, critics and theorists were simply reacting to the inherent distinctions among crafts based upon the value of the materials from which they were made, the degree of finesse required in their construction or finish, or their relative historical importance in the evolution of the applied arts.

This belief that some crafts were worthier than others affected the organizational structure of the SACB in subtle ways: jewelry makers, enamelists, and metalworkers—those practitioners of the so-called higher crafts—comprised fully one-third of the SACB's total membership, and typically their work contributed to more than half the income in the salesroom. This made them a strong force in terms of both presence and economics. They occupied more seats (six) on the Council than any other group of craftspeople, and one-quarter of those on the Jury. Thus they were more involved in decision-making than were representatives of any other craft category, with the exception of architects. When they complained—as they had in 1908, and again in 1912—their complaints brought results.[70]

Use of the phrases "classes of objects or "class of work" in Walker and the Jury's critiques reflects a practice that had evolved at international exhibitions, such as the Great Exhibition of 1851. Organizers divided entries into broad classifications with distinct subdivisions, just as scientists subdivided the animal, vegetable, and mineral worlds into distinct species and genera. Their adoption of that scientific approach shows the Jury's awareness of international trends and their desire to appear as objective as possible.

Basketry, leatherwork, and china painting had often ranked among the weakest of crafts in the salesroom, and Walker directed his critique of 1914 toward ways of improving them. He condemned basketry for its "coarse, loose weaving," and he recommended that basket makers pattern their work after Philippine, Indian, or Mexican examples. He drew similar conclusions about wood-carving, complaining about "crude" work "with no knowledge of texture backgrounds and again with slipshod naturalistic designs." Regarding carved frames, he complained about "too many of a gouged and smeared type, with some qualities of picturesqueness and none of distinction."[71]

He also spoke of missed opportunities for SACB craftsmen, listing myriad media and techniques that were not represented in the SACB salesroom: enamels, niello, carved ivory, metal inlay, and embroidery—other than cross-stitch—were among these. He advised workers to produce "delicate, slightly decorated glass," believing it had "an absolutely free field to itself. He encouraged them as well to produce "perforated and sawn" metalwork.

Walker concluded his remarks stating: "The Jury finds that among the best of the workers there is steady progress and better work being done, but among many of the members there is not sufficient appreciation that distinguished work is desired and necessary to maintain both the individual reputation and that of the Society."

Walker's short report for 1915 reiterated many of the same themes. In his general remarks, he complimented members on demonstrating "a better comprehension of the character of the work which is desired to put before the public as having intrinsic merit." He chided others, though, for work that "fail[ed] to show conscientious technical quality," for examples marred by "hurried and inferior finish," and for work that was "cheap" and "trite." Strong categories remained so; weak ones—such as china painting—were "slowly improving." Certain recommended categories for endeavor—enamels and ivories especially—still remained conspicuous by their absence.[72]

"There has been a constant tendency for the best craftsmen to do more and more important pieces, leaving others to do the lesser work," Walker wrote. "There is a marked difference between the best workers and the next best workers." Quality overall was improving, he suggested, but he seemed concerned that few new members—with different sorts of skills and fresh ideas—were joining the organization.

As always, Walker ended his essay with an assignment for his readers for the upcoming year. On this occasion, he scolded them for their lack of "knowledge of the best examples in the very work they [were] undertaking, probably from ignorance of the illustrated work upon each subject." He recommended, therefore, "a study of the literature." Here, once again, he implied that workers should use local libraries to good advantage.

Evidently, they chose not to do so. In his report for 1915–16, Walker noted among works accepted for the year "the usual exuberance of fancy, unassociated with knowledge of expression, especially in line." Equally concerning to him was a lack of understanding of form and ornament. "As this is readily available," he wrote, referring to models in local museums and images published in books in libraries, "it is to be regretted that it is absent." Few craft categories escaped his critical eye. He found aspects of jewelry, bronze work, and textiles to be "crude," carving of all sorts to be "weak," cabinetry to be "not especially good," and basketry to be "uninspiring." He continued his tirade against china painting, noting "the work usually lacks delicacy, outlines are not finely drawn, and designs are often too large for the objects upon which they are put. Colors are also poorly contrasted." He went on to recommend that "work be sent in that is skilful in design and in one color only."[73]

Bright spots, on the other hand, included "the color of articles sent in, whether in combination of jewels, textiles, decorative work or illuminations." Other successful categories included mirror frames—"improved both in design and carving"—and photography. "There have been," he wrote, "a number of unusually good photographs presented, excellent in composition and tone." He concluded his remarks succinctly, stating "These criticisms are not made of those members who have received commendation but of those who are working towards that point." Once again, the use of commendation slips in the salesroom, listing of workers commended for the year, and naming of medalists were all supposed to be inspirational.

The Report of the Jury for 1916–17 began with an introduction by the chairman, A. W. Longfellow, Jr. He noted with pride that sixty-three individuals had received commendations from the Jury that year, attributing much of their success to their receptivity to input received from Walker on the Jury's behalf. Improved quality and more sophisticated work, he suggested, have been "the aim of the criticisms written and given personally, with advice for sources of inspiration in study from accepted models." Despite the improvements evident in the past year, however, Longfellow challenged his readers to be creative and innovative, and to venture into new terrain.[74]

Walker began his Report of the Critic of the Jury by acknowledging that "the Jury's report from year to year is necessarily one which repeats itself, unless there is very great improvement or equally great lack of it, of which," he noted, "the latter has never thus far been the case." He went on to ponder his role as Critic of the Jury in relation to SACB members: "As usual, the workers who have been feeling their way have obtained a better idea of good design and good workmanship. As usual, there is work which is treated tenderly because it is artistically adolescent and gives indication of 'growing up.'" He suggested that he and other Jurors were more tolerant of such adolescent work than was the public, "especially the indiscriminating public, who insist that the Arts and Crafts Society shows a 'lot of bad things.'" They are, he insisted, "forgetful or ignorant of the fact that often the ingenuity of expression in bad things is more hopeful under training than the unanimity of the commonplace." He concluded this prefatory statement saying "encouragement of recognition to the beginner is as much a part of the Society as is the presentation of superlative work." Having thus explained some of the challenges of his job, he turned to his critique of the year past, noting instances of excellence as well as amateurism.[75]

In the midst of his recitation of strengths and weaknesses, Walker reiterated a point that he, and other members of the Jury, had stressed previously. "There is one very persistent fact which manifests itself to the Jury," he wrote, "and that is, the inability of the average worker to use a good library, and his ignorance of books of instruction in his own art. Often skill of hand exists, with not an even elemental idea of design," he lamented. "While this is excusable where a large library is not available, it is inexcusable in cities . . . where . . . a wealth of information and of illustrations upon any special subject is set before the student, who at present seems to imbibe ideas from the very second-rate sources of some so-called artistic columns in weeklies and magazines. A mere bibliography of works means little to workers, for titles do not give adequate information of contents, but the actual survey of the books themselves is always possible, and always inspirational." Here, Walker assumed the persona of professor, exhorting his students to open the covers of their textbooks and to read! "The Jury wishes therefore especially to advocate the study of Design. Skill is technique and necessary for expression. Design is the best achievement of the expression."

The Report of the Jury for 1918 took on a very different tone from reports of previous years, in light of the ongoing world war and the concurrent economic downturn. Walker's comments had little to do with trifles, *objets d'art*, and bibelots. Instead, he advised his constituents to produce work in two categories—that "connected with the war" effort, and that "to replace imported articles which can no longer be obtained." In the first category, he spoke of articles of clothing and textiles of the sort distributed by the Red Cross. He advised weavers and needleworkers to produce designs of "individual character" and "attractiveness," that "might well be cheerful or even humorous." In the latter category, he encouraged members to produce everything from wood or tin toys, to memorials, textiles, and illuminations "for special occasions." In keeping with the sober mood of the time, Walker concluded his essay with a brief proclamation. "Designing is an art, to be gained by careful, serious study," he wrote, "not a fantasy or amusement, excepting in so far as achievement gives pleasure."[76]

As a group, Walker's reports are important: they provide insight into the Jury's definition of Usefulness and Beauty that is specific and detailed. They also elucidate Walker's views as Critic of the Jury that are significant for their rarity: a practicing architect, Walker published little. What is more, few of his personal papers survive. Stylistically, these reports demonstrate Walker's forthright commentary, enlivened by his characteristic use of the *bon mot*. In terms of tone, they reveal that Walker was authoritative and inspiring, though he occasionally sounded defensive, or impatient to the point of scolding. Striving to make the jury process transparent, Walker critiqued the status quo, while offering lists of potential new opportunities for SACB craftsworkers. Always a booster of high standards, diligent study, historicism, and artistic collaboration—even between craftspeople and critics—he shunned affectation, arbitrariness, shoddiness, and other instances of dilettantism, while retaining a consistent distaste for *art nouveau*. Presumably, the views Walker expressed as Critic of the Jury were similar to those he passed along to his students, clients, and colleagues.[77]

Responses to Jury Recommendations: Craftsmen versus Critics

Walker and his colleagues did not render their opinions without craftsmen's protestations. Many regarded the Jury's relentless pursuit of excellence as a threat to their artistic integrity. While they appreciated the Jury's quest for quality, they also feared it would constrain their opportunities to experiment and to take risks.

One of these was Annie C. Putnam, an outspoken member of the Guild of Metalworkers, who was appointed to the Jury in 1908. "To me the Jury is trying to make all keys fit the same keyhole," she complained. "Therein lies the danger of '*Standards*.' The machine standard which stands for accuracy and perfect finish has to me disastrously affected the handiwork of today. I have seen many beautiful things in Museums that would never be accepted by the Boston Arts and Crafts Society. Draw some of the beautiful old borders on the metalwork of India and Persia accurately, and you destroy the beauty and vitality in them."[78]

Reminding the Jury that the "use of an article . . . determines its design and execution," Putnam encouraged Jurors to allow for greater variety of character among the work approved. She argued in favor of using vernacular models depending upon a product's end use: "A piece of Favrile glass is not in keeping with a bungalo whereas a rather primitive bowl might be. A buckle designed for an outing dress is not suitable with a reception dress. Nor would we desire the same design and execution for the setting of precious and semi-precious stones." With this challenge, Putnam raised an important issue—that of the Jury's limited aesthetic vision. Arts and crafts designers had expressed an abiding interest in vernacular models—those produced by anonymous craftspeople, using traditional materials and techniques passed down orally by previous generations—since the 1860s, but SACB members who chose to do so risked infuriating the

138. Plate, silver with enamel decoration, by Mary C. Knight, undated. (Courtesy of Chicago Silver) Note the conventionalized grapevine motif with bunches of grapes.

Jury if their designs appeared crude in technique or rough in aspect. The Jury's standards demanded a degree of refinement that discouraged reference to primitive or provincial sources, or to anything "commonplace."[79]

Craftsmen's responses to the Jury's recommendations varied. Some challenged the Jury openly, by meeting with its representatives directly, by sending letters of protest regarding rejected work to the Jury, or by directing their criticisms of the Jury to the Council. A few resigned from the organization altogether, believing that the jury process was inherently unfair.

Some offered the Jury constructive criticism on how best to operate. The Report of the Jury for 1909, for example, noted that it had "received from various sources a number of suggestions, many of which are excellent. Among them is a recommendation that workers should be encouraged by praise as well as helped by criticism, and that the Jury should do this by 'pointing out not only what is bad, but by indicating, as well, that which is good or indifferent.'" One step that encouraged such input was the addition of a suggestion box in the SACB salesroom, soliciting the ideas of members.[81]

One of those supplying such criticism may have been Mary Catherine Knight, mentioned earlier as a designer and metalsmith who worked in the Handicraft Shop (Fig. 138). In the spring of 1908, when the Guild of Metalworkers was being so outspoken, she wrote a letter to Associate member Frederick P. Cabot (1868–1932), an attorney and judge who served on the SACB Finance Committee. "I cannot help feeling, Mr. Cabot, that even when the salesroom is working orderly in its business arrangements," she began, "it will not be a really progressive salesroom—bringing the best work before the public all the time—unless efforts are made to develop the craftsman. There are men who need just a little encouragement to learn to express their ideas on paper as well as in material. A craftsman might work by himself indefinitely," she argued, "when just a little encouragement from one who has seen more and knows more would help such a lot. As it is now a few sketches may be handed in and receive a slashing criticism from Mr. Walker or someone else. A criticism that is ever so good, but only one person in two or three at most has the chance to appreciate it." It is significant that she refers directly to Walker, even though he had not yet been appointed the official critic. Her phrase "one who has seen more and knows more" was an apt description of him.[80]

178 ADVISER, PROMOTER, TORMENTOR, AND MIDWIFE

"How much better it would be and more productive of good work if the Salesroom had a corps of good workers ready to present their ideas simply and directly," Knight went on. ". . . . Members of the Council may frankly say that not one of the Craftsmen can draw or design. But the mere saying so does not help this matter, nor publishing it in the A[nnual] R[eport]. If some of the time of the Council was spent in knowing the Craftsman and his needs and in visiting the various shops—might not the movement hold together more firmly and there be a greater incentive to do good work?" Here, Knight underlined the feeling of disenfranchisement shared by the Craftsman members within the SACB.

Sometimes workers who took issue with the Jury approached it as a group. One such group was the Guild of Metalworkers, formed in 1908. They were unhappy with Whiting, his running of the salesroom, and the Jury system, and they formed a block to effect changes within the salesroom, in part because their livelihood depended upon it. In 1907, sales of metalwork had constituted 55 percent of the salesroom's income. The Guild of Metalworkers thus believed that they had a right to take an active role. Not surprisingly, many of the most vocal critics during that period were appointed to the Jury in the fall of 1908, or shortly thereafter. These included Carl Forssen, Annie C. Putnam, and F. G. Hale (in 1910).[82]

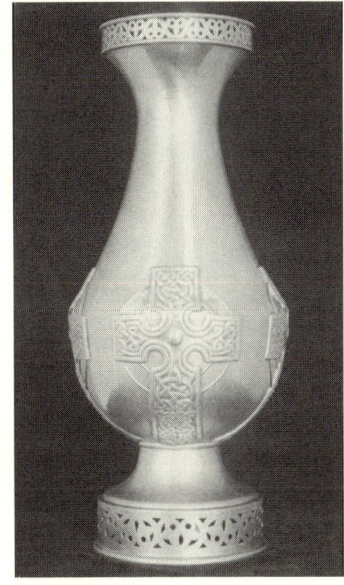

139. Altar vase, Grace Church, Providence, designed by Julia de Wolf. Addison, ca. 1890–1920. (Courtesy Massachusetts Historical Society) This design incorporates pierced and raised metalwork. Some areas are embellished with Celtic strapwork.

Another group was Saint Dunstan's Guild, composed of ecclesiastical workers who solicited funding from interested benefactors to "capitalize the production of a set of Ecclesiastical objects that would make a convincing demonstration of the capacity of the Society to compete with commercial houses in this field." It was the intention of guild members to mount a "complete exhibition of church articles, which would impress the clergy of the various denominations" with the potential of SACB members to supply local churches. The guild succeeded in attracting $2,000 out of the $5,000 they estimated that they would need for this venture. They invited craftsmen to submit preliminary designs so that they might secure funding for materials, but were disappointed by the "notable lack of enterprise in design" that they encountered. "We think," guild members reported, "there are those who have considerable ingenuity in design, but are unwilling to submit drawings to the Jury on account of its exacting standards." Given the character of these designs (Fig. 139) and the expense of the material involved, the Jury's standards would have been exceedingly high. "The officers [of the guild] feel," the report concluded, "that some concession might reasonably be made in work done under the direction of the Guild."[83]

A third group that took exception to the Jury's rigor was the Auxiliary

The Society of Arts and Crafts
Incorporated 1897
9 PARK STREET, BOSTON
7 WEST 56TH STREET, NEW YORK

GENERAL RULES FOR CONSIGNORS
(Please read carefully, as consignments are received only under these conditions)

1. Consignments.

All consignments must be sent to the *Boston address,* with delivery charges prepaid and articles accompanied by entry blank properly filled out, with article number, description and selling price. Duplicates should be numbered alike. The stock will then be distributed and rotated between the Boston and the New York shops at the discretion of the salesroom management. Consignors may indicate whether they wish a certain piece of work shown first in Boston or New York, but final action must rest with the Salesroom Committee, whose decision will be based on business expediency.

2. Jury Meetings.

Work submitted for sale should be delivered at 9 Park St., Boston, before five o'clock on Mondays to insure prompt attention of the Jury, which meets every Tuesday morning, except during July and August. *Articles delivered later must wait over until the next week.*

3. Criticism.

Mr. C. Howard Walker, representing the Jury, will generally be at Park St. on Wednesday mornings at nine o'clock, to criticise work not accepted by the Jury, to consult regarding new work under way, and to give any friendly advice members may desire. Appointments may be made by telephone the preceding day. Haymarket 4420.

4. Jewelry with Stones.

In submitting pieces of jewelry containing stones, the contributor should fully describe, on his entry slip, the stones and their condition.

5. Commission.

On articles sold, the Society deducts a regular commission of 33⅓% from the price fixed by the contributor on the entry blank, except in the case of greeting cards and calendars, on which the rate is 40%, and of all pieces of jewelry selling at $150 or over, on which the rate is 25%. When sales are made through the Society's introduction and the order is shipped and billed directly by the craftsman, the Society having no responsibility beyond the introduction, the commission is 10%.

In the case of any piece of jewelry where there is a diamond which has cost the worker $25 or more, the actual cost price of the diamond shall be stated on the entry blank, as well as the selling price of the piece of jewelry. In figuring the selling price of such pieces, the worker shall allow 10% commission on the cost of the stone, which shall go half to the Society and half to the worker. On the balance of the selling price, after deducting the above cost of stone and commission, the Society shall receive its regular commission.

6. Payments.

Payments by check are usually made during the first week of each month for the sales of the previous month. The war taxes are paid by the Society.

7. Removal of Articles.

Articles not accepted, or held for members, must be removed *within two weeks* after notice has been sent, otherwise they will be returned express collect.

Committee on Craftsman Membership (established ca. 1905). In 1913, this group expressed concern that the work of too few Craftsmen (as opposed to Masters) was represented in the salesroom. It complained that the showrooms were "too small and too crowded" to represent all members fairly. Encouraged by the Council to ascertain the feelings of Craftsman members on this issue, the committee reported as follows: "A considerable amount of attention has been given in this statement to the Jury and with good reason, for it is this committee which has maintained the high standards for which the Society is known. These standards could be raised at a more rapid rate than has been the case.... There is no question but that high standards are more demanding of Craftsmen and the results are better than when standards are reduced." (Here the report may have meant that lower standards allowed a greater number of Craftsmen to succeed in having their work accepted for display or sale.) "At the same time," the report continued, "we recognize that the majority of Craftsmen are not equal to the level maintained here and the Society has set a course which gives expression to the capabilities and ideals of the true Craftsman. Here the professional and the amateur may be found side by side, each contributing to the craft movement. Each learns from the other and the result is healthy." For workers of differing abilities to work side by side while neither giving the more skilled an undue advantage, nor compromising the salesroom's high standards was a challenge.[84]

One advantage offered by the membership categories within the SACB was the diversity that such variations in skill level provided. Allowing the professional to inspire the amateur and the amateur to take advantage of such mentoring fulfilled, in part, the Society's educational mission. The competitive nature of the jury process combined with limited space in the salesroom, however, put the amateur at a distinct disadvantage.

Contributors to the salesroom took issue with salesroom practices as well as Jury policies and procedures (Fig. 140). When the Jury began marking work "specially commended," it received diverse criticism. H. D. Murphy, who would become a Juror in 1908, believed that the practice encouraged favoritism. He argued at a meeting on March 11, 1908, that he didn't want the "specially commended" labels to have a deleterious effect upon the sale of others' goods. As Murphy predicted, those whose works were overlooked labeled the practice unfair, claiming that their work suffered by comparison with pieces bearing special labels, and complaining that this jeopardized their livelihood. But others approved of the practice. "It is an incentive to do extra fine work," wrote Hazel G. Collins, an embroiderer and designer from Brookline (b. ca. 1873), to the Committee on the Salesroom, "and helps a craftsman to become discriminating and appreciative in other crafts besides his own."[85]

Sometimes recommendations that Walker or other Jurors made fell upon deaf ears. In the 1910s, Walker frequently encouraged SACB enamelists to expand the scope of their craft, believing that they were among the Society's most gifted

140. (Opposite) "General Rules for Consignors," published by the Society of Arts and Crafts, Boston, 1924. (Courtesy Historic New England) In the 1920s, the SACB also operated a salesroom in New York City.

141. Studio of Arthur J. Stone in Gardner, Mass., about 1908. (Courtesy Museum of Fine Arts, Boston)

craftspeople. "The art of enameling has nowhere been revived more brilliantly than in Boston," Walker was quoted in the *Boston Herald* as saying at the time of a special show of enamels held in October 1915. Referring to one of Walker's trips to London a few years earlier, the author of the article reported that Walker had found "British practitioners of enameling—numerous and clever, but, in his judgment, doing less stimulating work than that produced" in Boston. In Paris, the reporter continued, Walker "found a certain vogue of enameling but of a weak, uninspired sort. Hardly anywhere but in Boston," had Walker "discovered workers who sense the true limitations of the medium, a form of colored glass whose color and translucence are to be heightened by a setting of gold, silver or copper. Here, in the past five years," the reporter concluded, "has been developed an art that is richer, more sensuous than any European school of enameling at any period of history, and that is inferior in finesse and design only to the best schools of the 14th, 15th and 16th centuries."[86]

Walker routinely urged the SACB enamelists to hone and perfect their work; yet clientele of the salesroom did not always respond. In his report for 1916–17, Walker noted with disgust, "Enamels have distinctly increased, but it is said that they are not appreciated by the public, in which case it might be well to adapt them to coloring backgrounds to gold or silver designs." This remark betrays a certain frustration. On the one hand, Walker faced craftsworkers who were slow to adopt his suggestions. On the other hand, he confronted a stubborn public, who did not always respond to his—or his constituents'—efforts.[87]

Most took the Jury's comments in stride because they believed that their livelihood depended upon conformity to its standards. Many craftsmen entrusted their life's work to the SACB salesroom, so they implemented the Jury's recommendations swiftly and without protest. Those who supported the jury process credited it with strengthening their professional development. "I think we can feel that the Society's success is our success," said metalsmith Arthur J. Stone of the benefits of mutual cooperation among craftsmen, the Jury, and the Society's administrators.[88]

142. Silver patch box with Celtic strapwork decoration, by Arthur J. Stone, ca. 1905–12, 2.1 x 4.3 cm. (1 3/16 x 1 11/16 in.). (Courtesy Museum of Fine Arts, Boston. Helen and Alice Coburn Fund, 1979.170)

Stone is one of those whom the Jury critiqued regularly throughout his career, despite his designations as master craftsman, and (in 1912–13) as a medalist—the Society's highest commendation (Figs. 141 and 142). The Jury offered Stone's silver hollowware and flatware as a model to novices and masters alike; yet, it persisted in finding fault with it, often to the point of nit-picking. By stating in its minutes for January 29, 1902, that certain pieces "might be varied a little," or that others might "possibly [be] a *trifle only* too wide and thick," the Jury established that even the most accomplished craftsmen must continually upgrade the quality of their work and demonstrated that no one within the organization could escape its discriminating eye.[89]

Despite such criticism, Stone enjoyed a sales record exceeding that of any other individual within the organization. "Mr. Stone is a veteran worker," the Committee on the Salesroom wrote in 1908, "whose experience is far greater than that of any other working member of the Society, and whose technical and artistic work has met the commendation of the Jury many times. It is fair to presume that patrons of the Society recognize this excellence." Stone welcomed input from the Jury graciously, agreeing with his wife and business partner, Elizabeth, "that no other jury system of equal intelligence exists" anywhere within the United States.[90]

Their vote of confidence did not, however, preclude the Stones from criticizing the Jury. They questioned salesroom policies, having a vested interest in its management, and even challenged the Jury's effectiveness, claiming that its abstract theories only frustrated and confused struggling craftsmen. Offering criticism that was consistently objective, constructive, and understandable was an art that sometimes eluded the Jury.[91] The reactions of members to its suggestions often trapped the group between its own goals and its constituents' conflicting needs and abilities. The imperative for craftsmen to earn a living caused the Jury to set aside its idealistic vision of what *might be*, and to promote instead a more realistic standard that a majority of members might achieve.

The relationship between craftsmen and critics depended upon willingness to compromise. Both groups had to view the creative process from the other's perspective and to balance individual agendas with the goals of the SACB. Ultimately, craftsmen accepted criticism as a vital part of their work process, while critics adjusted their principles to accommodate their constituents' practical needs. As a result, craftsmen expanded their conceptual horizons while critics witnessed their theories implemented with varying degrees of success.

Those theories are the focus of Chapter Four; it addresses historicism, naturalism, conventionalization, and the issue of expression as touted by SACB Jurors and critics who were influential nationally and internationally.

CHAPTER FOUR

Models and Methodologies

Guidelines for Achieving "Good Design"

Beauty and character—In these lie the gist of all design. While the technical conditions, if fully understood, fairly met, and frankly acknowledged, are sure to give character to a design, for whaterver purpose, beauty is not so easy to command.
—Walter Crane, *Line and Form* (1900)

True beauty could be discovered only by one who mentally completed the incomplete.
—Kakuzo Okakura, *The Book of Tea* (1906)

Advice offered by the SACB Jury reflected theories of "good design" that critics were espousing nationally and internationally. Of particular interest are those governing conceptualization, or the process by which craftspeople developed the ideas inherent in their work. The making of handicrafts, design reformers argued, must combine "doing" with "thinking," and it is the latter activity that is the focus of this chapter. It addresses the issue of models upon which craftsworkers might base their ideas—specifically history and nature. It considers the way in which craftspeople transformed those models into a statement that was both personal and original, through the process of conventionalization. (This was regarded both as a theory and as a methodology.) Finally, it explores the issue of expression, an intangible quality that transcends concept, aesthetics, and technique in such a way that the finished object communicates the maker's thoughts and appeals to the user. In doing so, this chapter places in a broader national and international context some of the advice offered by the SACB Jury to its constituents.

Critics and theorists were clear about which models designers and craftspeople might consult. Models "which never fluctuate as regards their popularity and approval," wrote one mid-century theorist, are "the masterpieces of ancient art themselves, of which every person agrees in testifying his approval. Works of nature ever hold with unvarying popularity the same pre-eminence." This sounds like William Morris, about to segue into his famous maxim, "For your teachers, they must be Nature and History." In fact, the words appeared well before Morris made that statement, in George Harris's *The Theory of the Arts . . .* , published in London in 1869.[1]

As Harris suggests, throughout the nineteenth century, history and nature were the two approved models from which designers might seek inspiration. These were not new ideas. Designers had been turning to history at least since the Renaissance, and nature was the driving force behind form and ornament during the Middle Ages, the Baroque, and the Rococo. Philosophers of aesthetics had defended historicism and naturalism as approved ways of working since the mid-eighteenth century. As schools and museums of applied arts flourished in the nineteenth century, along with publications written as texts and polemics—Owen Jones's seminal *The Grammar of Ornament* (1856) comes to mind—the continued championing of history and nature built upon past precedents, while offering conceptual antidotes to an increasingly technological world.

The lure of the past was partly romantic: "The secret of ancient triumph [in the arts]," wrote Lewis Day in *Ornament and Its Application*, "is commonly in the restricted means of the workman, which compel[led] him to simplicity.... The failures of modern times," on the other hand, "are as commonly to be accounted for by the multitude of facilities, leading [us] astray from [simplicity]." What was good about the old days and the old ways, Day suggested, was that workers had fewer options and distractions. They could focus upon form, ornament, material, and construction without falling prey to the eclecticism that influenced their nineteenth-century counterparts. Nor were they as distracted by a plethora of new machines and materials, as well as the dreaded "division of labor." The past was not only a source for ideas upon which the craftsworker might build; it was also the model for an idealized work environment. Turn-of-the-century craftsworkers could, thus, strive to work in a pre-industrial-type setting while emulating the form, ornament, materials, and construction of the past. If that setting were in the countryside, so much the better, as nature refreshed and restored the worker, while providing abundant opportunities to develop color schemes, motifs, and subject matter.[2]

The Past as Muse: History as a Conceptual Springboard

By the 1890s, history was an accepted model for Usefulness and Beauty. The job of critics was to point out which styles and time periods were best to emulate, to indicate where aspiring craftspeople might find such models, and to explain how to adapt those historical models in a way that was personal and original. Their recommendations varied.

A strong proponent of historical models was Clarence Chatham Cook. Writing *The House Beautiful* (Plate 5) in the aftermath of the American Centennial, he endorsed collecting antiques—particularly of the American Colonial period—as a way of introducing Usefulness and Beauty to the home; he urged his readers to study historic examples for the insight they might provide regarding the principles of "good design." Among the examples promoted in his book are a Savonarola-type chair (from the collection of the Boston Museum of Fine Arts), Windsor chairs, a seventeenth-century settlebench-table, a Louis XVI–period canapé, a William & Mary–period daybed, a Carolean-era flagged-seat chair, a Chippendale-type captain's corner chair, a seventeenth-century turned chair, and a Chippendale-type tilt-top, piecrust-edge, pedestal tea table. He also recommended textiles—"Turkey, Persian or Smyrna rugs, made by hand, of pure wool"—and blue-and-white ceramics of all sorts. Cook admired these pieces for the warmth and delight they could bring to an interior, especially if they could be purchased cheaply; but he offered them as well as forms that a contemporary craftsperson might adapt. "The wooden chairs, and chairs seated with rushes or cane of the old time, were as comfortable as the stuffed and elastic seats we are so fond of," he wrote. Many critics disparaged the latter—in the so-called Naturalistic style—as resembling "marshmallows on legs." Cook continued: "If we could consent to come back to something of the old-fashioned austerity, we should find it greatly to our profit in many ways." Aesthetes like Cook appreciated in particular the lean, skeletal forms of un-upholstered seat furniture—the more delicate the better—and those of lightly scaled tables and cabinets (Fig. 143).[3]

For this reason, he was particularly fond of late-eighteenth-century examples, especially if they were American. "The things we come upon in our own country are soon at home in our houses, because they were used by

143. T. Quincy Browne house, 98 Beacon Street, Boston, undated. Alterations made in 1882 by Herbert Browne, architect. (Courtesy Historic New England) This interior reflects a passion for recycled architectural antiques from the late Colonial/early Federal era that Clarence Cook might have approved. The fireplace mantle emanated from the Shirley-Eustis House (Roxbury), dating to the period of Governor Eustis. The cornice, door lintels, and dado came from the old Crafts House, Parker Hill. Note the lightly scaled Hepplewhite-type armchair (right of the fireplace) and the delicate, painted "fancy chairs." All reflect the influence of the Colonial Revival.

144. Bedroom, 200 Beacon Street, Boston, 1885. (Courtesy Historic New England) This charming room—with its Morrisian wallpaper, brass bedstead, chintz demi-celour, and aesthetic bric-a-brac incorporates a Chippendale-type side chair to the bedstead's right.

our own ancestors or our own people. They were to the manor born," he wrote. "They neither look affected, nor strange, nor pretentious, but native and natural." In this statement, Cook anticipates comments that the SACB Jury would make decades later, and expresses a bias that he shared with supporters of the Arts and Crafts movement, namely a preference for designs that were indigenous. Most design reformers rejected the foreign or imported in favor of models specific to their own culture or geographical region. "The furniture which was in use in this country at the time of our grandfathers," Cook wrote, "was almost always well designed and perfectly fitted for the uses it was to be put to." In other words, Colonial-era examples were Beautiful, Useful, and contextual (Fig. 144).[4]

145. Pulpit door from a mosque in Cairo, ca. 1382–98, Wood Carving Room, Museum of Fine Arts, undated. (Courtesy Historic New England)

Writing two decades after Cook, Arthur Wesley Dow (1857–1922) also found historic examples to be appropriate models. With his passion for Asia, Dow was less focused upon American Colonial models. But, like Cook's, his tastes were eclectic. As he advised readers on the best ways to study composition in his 1899 book by the same name, he recommended that they examine such varied examples as "old velvets of Japan, woven and printed textiles of all nations, marble floors, inlaid boxes and architectural ornament, church, mosque, temple, book covers and page borders, Aubrey Beardsley, [British painter and illustrator] R. Anning Bell." He advised "copying, under guidance, examples of acknowledged excellence, like Japanese prints, Oriental rugs, and reproductions of masterpieces." His book provided just the sort of "guidance" that he believed students of composition needed, by dictating a series of specific exercises that progressed in difficulty. Like many of his colleagues, Dow suggested that students of design "work from originals in museums" (Fig. 145), or consult his list of recommended reference books, employing line only, or a simple gray scale, before progressing to color studies.[5]

The SACB Jury similarly attempted to offer its constituents appropriate models, and methodologies for analyzing and then interpreting them. "The study of the work of the old masters can be urged as the most important influence in promoting good handicraft because the fundamental principles of design and execution were so well understood by them," it argued in one annual report. "We have examples of Greek, Gothic, Renaissance, Chinese, Persian, Japanese, and Moorish craftsmanship all around us, in our museums, our collections, our homes, in books and photographs to inspire and guide the worker" (Fig. 146). To learn from such examples, it advised, might require "copy[ing] directly as a painter copies an old picture, in order to acquire some of its feeling and skill," or studying such exam-

146. Greek Vase Room, Museum of Fine Arts, Copley Square, undated. Photograph by Baldwin Coolidge. (Courtesy Historic New England) Here a sarcophagus, sculpture, mural fragment, and myriad examples of pottery were available to educate consumers and craftspeople alike.

ples "to endeavor to reach the point of view of the old craftsman, with his exquisite sense of appropriateness in form and arrangement, in line and color, in surface treatment and the relation of materials." Note that such copying was not for the purpose of creating a line-for-line duplicate but, instead, of ascertaining something more nebulous—"its feeling" or "point of view."[6]

Here the writer—perhaps Walker or Coolidge—identifies what the contemporary craftsworker might glean from studying the past, namely guidelines regarding the use of design elements—line, form, color, and texture—as well as those pertaining to materials. He suggests that direct copying can influence technique or "skill," and that the process might reveal as well something about expression, or "feeling." He offers an eclectic range of models, listing myriad sources where a student might find actual examples or good reproductions locally. In doing so, the writer builds upon the works of Owen Jones, Christopher Dresser, and others writing during the third quarter of the nineteenth century.

One place was the Boston Museum of Fine Arts. In 1893, the *Boston Art Guide* described its collection as consisting of "minor arts of the ancients, bronzes, earthen and glass vessels, coins, Renaissance industrial arts and Medieval ceramics, enamels, textiles, carving, metalwork, etc." It also touted the Japanese collection of pottery, prints, and paintings assembled by Morse and Fenellosa. These were the sorts of models recommended by Walker, Dow, and to some extent Cook, consistently with their British counterparts, such as Crane and Day.[7]

147. Display featuring wrought iron work from Belgium, Metal Room, Museum of Fine Arts, Copley Square, undated. (Courtesy Historic New England) These historic strap hinges, brackets, locks, and keys may have inspired local metalworkers such as Frederick Krasser or his collaborator, Frank L. Koralewsky.

148. Illustration from trade catalogue, F. Krasser & Company, Roxbury, undated. (Courtesy Historic New England) In this photo, Krasser displays his artistry in the form of a gate, fireplace screen, strap hinges, and other artifacts, inspired perhaps by historic examples shown at the Museum of Fine Arts.

Despite such specific recommendations, SACB members were apparently slow to seize the Jury's advice. In 1911, a similar, but more general, recommendation appeared in the Report of the Jury. "There is no question that what is needed," it stated, "as much as qualities of brain and heart and skillful hand—is constant comparison and association with the best objects of the past; intelligent companionship with the productions of the master craftsman of old is surely the best means for advancement." Recommending "our Museums, our own libraries and collections," once again as resources, the report justified this historicist approach: "The workers of old faced the same problems which we do today, and the same difficulties; but with a simpler vision and a more direct understanding and deeper feeling." Here the Jury reiterated some of Day's argument, previously quoted. "We can at least, in studying their achievements, wring some of their secrets from them and acquire some of their qualities." Here the Jury was suggesting that consulting objects from the past required more than simply copying them line-for-line. It required analyzing them thoughtfully and critically to fathom some of their artistry and mystery (Figs. 147 and 148).[8]

With remarkable consistency, the Reports of the Jury built upon this theme in

149. Studio at the Massachusetts Institute of Technology, 1889. (Courtesy Massachusetts Historical Society) Pictured is a typical studio setting, filled with teaching aids. The young man second from the left is Walter H. Kilham, whose wife later joined the SACB. A caption reads: "Working on thesis, MIT, 1889."

subsequent years. In 1912, it chided its readers for "not taking advantage" of the "opportunities of studying fine examples" of "work done by the craftsmen of the past." It recommended specifically visiting the Museum of Fine Arts, the Public Library, and the Athenaeum as institutions whose collections might "answer many a puzzling problem and be of inestimable value to the worker." It reiterated its plea in 1913, 1915, 1917, and 1918.[9]

In making these repeated recommendations to study the past by consulting local models, Walker and the Jury were carrying on a tradition established at educational institutions in and around Boston, such as MIT, which in turn emulated pedagogy established in Paris at the École des Beaux Arts. Photos show Professor William Robert Ware (1832–1915) and his students in studios filled with books, casts, moldings, cornice fragments, pilasters, architectural drawings and models (Fig. 149). These may have been some of the thousands of examples he purchased in Britain and Europe in the 1860s, 1870s, and 1880s, during which time he headed MIT's Department of Architecture. His purchases included two- and three-dimensional artifacts, including "books and papers, 2,000 photographs, 500 prints, 400 plaster casts, 200 crayon drawings, 40 watercolors, architectural drawings, tiles, pottery, and stained glass." (Some Ware might also have obtained from local companies, such as P. P. Caproni & Bro. or A. Da Prato & Co., the latter of which advised its customers: "Good reproductions enable us to enjoy the work of the masters at a small price.") Ware believed that an understanding of historical principles was "the most efficient safeguard against the wild and wanton tendencies in American architecture," and that analysis of those artifacts might develop such an understanding. The SACB Jury felt similarly that familiarity with the finest craftsmanship of the past might check what Walker termed the "eccentricities and false sentiments" that threatened the integrity of American craft.[10]

In this regard, Walker echoed Professor A. D. F. Hamlin's theory of the "selective ideal," as espoused in his 1896 *Textbook of the History of Architecture* and his 1916–23 publication, *A History of Ornament*. Keith Morgan and Richard Cheek explain that Hamlin "stressed the importance of studying the finest styles and periods of history in order to understand fully the principles of their design and their appropriateness as models." Hamlin's theories built upon those of Ware, and may have influenced Walker through his connection to MIT.[11]

Such learning by copying extended as well into the classrooms at Wellesley College, where H. G. Wells reported in *The Future in America: A Search after Realities* (1906), "in a sunlit room . . . girls were copying the details in the photographs of masterpieces, and all around this room were cabinets of drawers, and in each drawer photographs. There must be in that room photographs of every picture of the slightest importance in Italy, and detailed studies of many." This activity paralleled one sponsored by the Architectural Society of MIT (founded 1886) in which students "trac[ed] plates from rare volumes that could be duplicated as blueprints and sold at cost. Each student," as Caroline Shillaber explains, "devoted three hours a week to tracing, until the early years of the twentieth century brought more rapid means of reproduction by photography and magazines began to publish illustrations of ancient buildings." Evidently, this pedagogy extended to students male and female, whether in a professional program or a liberal arts curriculum. It may be that some of them eventually transferred what they had learned at MIT and Wellesley into a greater appreciation for or practice of the crafts. Most likely, some later joined the SACB.[12]

This well-established approach was evident as well in the professional studio setting. Certainly, one of the best testimonies to its persistence beyond institutional walls was H. H. Richardson's Brookline studio. A period photograph of the architect's office (Fig. 83) shows walls with well-stocked, built-in bookcases surrounding a huge partners' desk standing in the room's center. Every surface overflows with books, folios, architectural fragments, and aesthetic bric-a-brac, which must have provided inspiration for Richardson, his apprentices, staff, and clients. Such personal reference collections were invaluable.

The SACB was at a disadvantage in trying to create a similar setting for its members; its headquarters were small, and the majority of its space was devoted to merchandise offered for sale. About 1906, it leased additional space, dedicating one room as "the Library. It will serve as Committee Room and Reading Room," the annual report stated, "and also for the use of members desiring facilities for correspondence, etc." (This may, by the way, have been the room in which the Jury met.) "The few books owned by the Society will be available for reference," the report continued. "It is hoped that others will be contributed and that funds will be given for the purchase of books. A small, carefully selected library on such subjects as economics, designing and the technical crafts would be of value to

150. Design for a silver with ebony sugar server, by Arthur John Stone, ca. 1914. (Courtesy SACB Archives) This drawing shows a form similar to eighteenth-century biscuit boxes. Historicist ornamentation—suitable for punchwork or bright-cutting—includes a rosette-and-leaf border and a central ellipse of bell flowers surmounted by a myrtle swag and ribbons. Delicate crisscrossed floral and foliate stems add elegant "S" curves.

many members and would help to center the life of the Society in the rooms." In addition to assembling the library, the SACB also gathered—on the advice of the Jury—a small study collection of contemporary crafts for members to consult, and often made available for study or duplication antiques from members' personal collections. Additionally, it brought in small traveling exhibitions of handicrafts from around the country and from abroad.[13]

Arthur Stone was one member who took seriously the Jury's recommendation to copy antiques. In 1914, he received permission from the Boston Museum of Fine Arts to copy several of the most noted of the Paul Revere silver pieces in the museum's collection. He was allowed to take exact measurements and to duplicate ornamental details, provided that he did so on a one-time-only basis, and that the copies were created solely for private ownership (Fig. 150).[14]

Three-dimensional objects were the best models for craftsmen desirous of learning from the past. Illustrations in books, however, served as an acceptable substitute. To that end, the Society's lending reference library included a "number of leading art journals" that had been contributed by members to "inspire and guide the worker." Magazines included *The International Studio*, *The Burlington Magazine*, *Die Kunst*, *Art et Décoration*, *The Keramic Studio*, *House and Garden*, and *The Manual Training Magazine*. Among the reference books were those devoted to design theory; a few were monographs on individual craftsworkers; others were purely technical in nature; and numerous volumes documented the historical evolution of particular crafts. The Society published a bibliography of its holdings in annual reports in 1907 and 1918 (see Appendix C) as an example for others wishing to develop their own reference libraries. Some of these may have been acquired by F. A. Whiting as part of his effort to establish a "bureau of information" in the 1900s. But the annual report for 1907–08 indicates that 40 of these volumes were on loan from the traveling reference library of the recently established National League of Handicraft Societies.[15]

The Jury often reminded craftsmen of the benefits of studying "the illustrated literature upon the class of work [they] produced," but it recommended publications selectively. It insisted that some were better than others and grew perplexed when SACB members chose to consult those not on its approved list. The best achievements in design, the Jury argued, drew inspiration only from approved models, and it questioned turning to what it deemed "second rate" sources.[16]

When he was not copying antiques directly to ascertain what he might learn from their design or construction, Arthur Stone also took to heart the Jury's recommendation to study "illustrated literature" in his discipline. Over the years, he amassed a personal reference library of 120 volumes (now part of the Stone Collection at the Boston Museum of Fine Arts). His annotations to these books demonstrate how closely he relied upon them for inspiration. In the front of his copy of Lewis Day's *Nature in Ornament* (1892) is his personal index of favorite motifs, including the "rosette or rose," "Tudor Roses," and a "Naïve Byzantine Vine." His copy of Ruskin's *Stones of Venice* (1873 reprint) similarly bears markings near favorite examples of ornamentation. Other books in his library include Ruskin's *Seven Lamps of Architecture* (1849) and his *Elements of Drawing and Elements of Perspective* (1907 reprint), Christopher Dresser's *Japan: Its Architecture, Art and Art Manufactures* (1882), Stewart Dick's *Arts and Crafts of Old Japan* (1912), A. W. N. Pugin's *Ornaments of the XVth and XVIth Centuries* (1836) and his *Designs for Iron and Brass Work in the Style of the XV and XVI Centuries* (1836), books on artists such as Albrecht Dürer, and numerous museum catalogues of silver and porcelain. Many of these still contain scraps of tracing paper tucked between pages onto which Stone copied the outlines of motifs that he planned to use in his own work. Significantly, many of the volumes in Stone's library are those on the recommended reading lists published by the SACB. Equally important, many of these motifs derived from historical sources, rather than from the countryside around Gardner, where Stone kept his studio. Always a proponent of naturalism, Stone nevertheless preferred a historicist approach.[17]

The Jury's advice to study historical models was consistent with theories of design that had evolved internationally since the 1840s. Though he wrote, "For your teachers, they must be Nature and History," William Morris added an important caveat indicating that historical understanding was only a means to a greater end. "Let us therefore study it wisely," he advised, "be taught by it, kindled by it; all the while determining not to imitate it or repeat it; to have either no art at all, or an art which we have made our own." This important point is one that most craftspeople seem to have overlooked. For that reason, C. H. Walker argued eloquently in "The Museum and the School" (1903) that workers must "constantly strive to improve upon precedents," or to adapt historical lessons to contemporary applications in a manner that was individual and distinctive.[18]

Catalogue entries from the Society's numerous exhibitions document the historical models from which craftsmen sought inspiration. Inspired by a broad range of cultures and time periods, they limited their reach only because of the inherent restrictions of the materials in which they worked, or according to the tenets of the craft tradition that they represented. When fabricating work for the Society's decennial exhibition (1907), for example, basketmakers turned to Native

American examples produced by the Washo, Pima, and Apache tribes. Glassmakers emulated Italian and French wares, while jewelers explored a wider range, including Egyptian, "Runic," Gothic, and Oriental. Leatherworkers were particularly catholic in their tastes, embracing Celtic, Old English, Elizabethan, Flemish, and Venetian models along with those from the Byzantine, Romanesque, Italian Renaissance, and Louis XVI periods. Woodworkers based their pieces on Florentine and Dutch sources, or upon the work of Thomas Chippendale (Fig. 151), while metalworkers, weavers, and embroiderers preferred to emulate their Colonial predecessors.[19]

151. Sketch for "Early Georgian" side chair in the Chippendale style, possibly by Samuel Hayward (b. 1844), ca. 1897. From "Things of Beauty—Masterpieces of Hand-work Put on Exhibition," *Boston Herald*, April 5, 1897. (Courtesy SACB Archives) Hayward spoke of the impact upon his work of "18th Century Reproductions" and the practice of "taking measured drawings of worthy examples."

The Colonial Revival became, in essence, the "house style" of the SACB, in part because of the preponderance of metalwork modeled after Colonial precedents and shown in the salesroom. At the 1907 decennial exhibition, it informed numerous craft categories on display in Copley and Allston Halls. According to reviewers, classicism—typical of the 1790s through the 1820s—prevailed throughout the departments of glassware, pottery and porcelain, printing, engraving and designing, metalwork, and woodworking. F. W. Coburn (an officer in the Winchester Handicraft Society and an independent journalist) wrote extensively of the classical and colonial influences evident in 1907, complimenting SACB craftsworkers for their "restraint, sobriety, logic, and style."[20]

Contemporary reactions to such historically based products were generally positive, in keeping with the conservative preferences of northeastern consumers. "Here," wrote Will Hutchins (a journalist and artist who eventually became president of the Greenfield Society of Arts and Crafts) regarding the decennial exhibition, "the complete absence of either the more brutal styles of 'crafts' furniture, or the more uncontrolled exuberance of the art-nouveau manner is conspicuous. Everything shown is refined and chaste and... carefully executed along the best traditions—for the most part of the eighteenth century." To those who accused the show of being either "too tame," or too "imitative and copied from the past," Walker replied, "Styles of art are so many that it is difficult to find any work which has not resemblance to antecedents, unless it be monstrous." Softening his tone, he added, "The intention certainly has been to avoid absolute copying, and to be grateful for a sense of appreciation of what is good in the past." What he failed to note was the difficulty most craftspeople experienced in extracting the spirit of the age from a particular model while avoiding line-for-line duplication of its form or ornament.[21]

What is striking about the historicism practiced by SACB members is the range of cultures and time periods to which they turned for inspiration. In the 1890s, and even during the first decade of the twentieth century, they cast their conceptual net broadly, in a fashion not too different from their precursors who had displayed works at the Great Exhibition of 1851. The difference between the historicism practiced at mid-century and that undertaken fifty years later, though, was one of interpretation. Mid-Victorians did not merely reproduce the past—they improved upon it, striving to outdo the originators, through a process of exaggeration to the point of caricature, all the while reinterpreting it using the latest—and often imitation—materials and new technologies. Design reformers were more inclined to an abstract historicism, which suggested—through form, ornament, material, and construction—the

152a and b. Living room, unidentified residence, undated. Photographs by William T. Clark. (Courtesy Historic New England) This interior utilizes abstract historicism in the manner of English architect Philip Webb. The fireplace uses the double-tapered, projecting hood common in the Middle Ages. Here the designer reduced the hood's scale and provided simplified—almost classical—moldings to create a form evocative of the past but appropriate for a room that emphasizes functionalism. The willow armchair, Morris chair, and table runner with Glasgow-style embroidery complete the eclectic look. The "AKX" monogram may indicate that this is a room in a fraternity house.

aesthetic of an earlier time period or exotic culture (Figs. 152a and b). Philip Webb (1831–1915), architect of William and Jane Morris's Red House (1859), was an excellent example of a designer who understood how to call to mind the Middle Ages and the Gothic in an innovatively spare way.

Design reformers evoked a historic period through a sensitive reinterpretation of selected elements. They strove to imagine how workers from the past might proceed were they still alive; then they tried to work accordingly. To study exemplary work from the past, and, more important, to understand the spirit that had led to its creation, were essential, the SACB Jury suggested, to producing contemporary products that might be both useful and beautiful while remaining technically competent and culturally relevant.

This is not to say that design reformers avoided line-for-line duplication of models from the past. Chief among those manufacturing reproductions were craftspeople, like Arthur Stone, working in the Colonial Revival style. But, even a Neo-Goth, such as Ralph Adams Cram (Fig. 153), preferred, Douglass Shand-Tucci argues, "careful reproduction" to "careless reminiscence."[22]

This enthusiastic embracing of historicism should not suggest that all design reformers regarded history as the ultimate muse. Even those who enjoyed living with antiques, such as Clarence Cook, questioned the effect upon originality and innovation that copying from the past might have. "The study of the work of former times,

153. Sketch of All Saints, Brookline, by Bertram Grosvenor Goodhue, undated. (Courtesy MIT Museum) This Gothic Revival–style structure expresses the dedication of Cram, Goodhue & Ferguson to careful reproduction.

so much in vogue today," Cook wrote, "whatever it may be doing for our higher art (and its usefulness in this regard may be reasonably questioned) is putting off indefinitely the day when we shall have originality in our own manufactures.... We weaken what we have of designing faculty by perpetually and persistently copying the designs of those who have gone before us." Readers of critics such as Cook must have been confused by the contradictory nature of his advice. He condoned historicism only as a means to an end. That end was the creation of a vital, living Art and Craft that reflected uniquely a place, society, and time.[23]

Others who disdained the "ancestor worship" that historicism inspired must have welcomed such comments. Many shared the opinion of the Asian critic Su Tung-p'o, quoted in Lawrence Binyon's 1911 primer, *The Flight of the Dragon: An Essay on the Theory and Practice of Art in China and Japan*, who stated: "To copy the masterpieces of antiquity is only to grovel among the dust and the husks." Clearly, they did not regard historical precedent as a source of freshness and vitality.[24]

Others were equally wary about just how far history should be allowed to influence contemporary craft. One of these was John Bascom (1827–1911), author of *Aesthetics. The Science of Beauty*. He speaks of the "warping power of previous association," and of the "mechanical" quality that results from what he termed "a stolid repetition of the past." He warns his readers against novelty on the one hand and habit on the other, preferring in the end "invention" to "the power of securing resemblance," especially exact reproduction of the form or ornament of the past. Clearly, many critics argued that learning from the past and applying its lessons effectively transcended mere duplication. It was the rare craftsperson who was able to realize such transcendence.[25]

Speaking bluntly in his 1935 *Silversmith's Manual*, Bernard Cuzner (who sold work through Liberty & Co.) stated: "It is as foolish to accept the works of the past as inevitably good as it is to condemn those of the present day solely because they are new." Cuzner suggested that every age had its merits. An editorial (possibly written by Langford Warren) published in *Handicraft* magazine (1902) indicates that designers should learn to think like the Greeks without imitating them, which led only to "lawless eccentricity" and "lifeless conventionality." Avoiding the eccentric had always been one of Warren's obsessions. And conventionality—though helpful to craftsworkers—could be carried to an extreme that deprived the creative process of its vitality.[26]

Prefiguring those sentiments, Day wrote in *The Planning of Ornament*: "A design is in harmony not when it is strictly according to Greek or Gothic precedent, but when all the parts fit." For Day, "fitness" was a prime criterion of "good design." In *Art in Needlework*, he and Mary Buckle suggested a way of adapting the past that applies equally to form and ornament in all media. "[Our] reference to old work must not be taken to imply," they begin, "that design should be in imitation of what has been done, or that it should follow on those lines. . . . One must study old work to see what has been done, and how it has been done, and then," they advised, "do one's own in one's own way. It is at least as foolish to break quite away from what has been done as to tether yourself to it. And in what has been done you will see, not only what is worth doing, but what is not." This, of course, implied a degree of critical thinking on the part of craftspeople; but few had the leisure time or the educational background to engage in it.[27]

Surveying these statements and others like them demonstrates the difficulty of the design reformers' task. What was right was relative, and dependent upon subtleties that were elusive. To create something in the spirit of the past—interpreted in a fashion that was both "fresh" and "fit"—required skillful maneuvering on the part of the craftsperson.

The Lure of Flora and Fauna: Nature as a Conceptual Springboard

For those not wishing to emulate history, nature offered an alternative. Following the recommendations of a host of internationally known theorist-practitioners, craftsmen turned to nature as the ultimate muse that inspired freshness and originality. "Nature," wrote Emerson, "is sanative, refining, and elevating." Emerson's belief in the restorative power of nature was tied especially to Transcendentalism (called "the most distinctly Boston 'ism'"). It may have influenced some members and patrons of the SACB; but even those who did not share its philosophy of antimaterialism could appreciate how nature provided an ever-changing source of inspiration.[28]

The beauty and abundance of the American landscape had inspired the arts of settlers since the Colonial era. From the aftermath of the Civil War through the era of the closing of the American frontier, artists, architects, designers, and craftspeople continued to celebrate the nation's seemingly inexhaustible bounties by depicting the sweep of great vistas or the particulars of a region's unique flora and fauna. "Nature had been the matrix that united various tenets within the American Arts and Crafts Movement," writes art historian Douglas Dreishpoon. "Nature signified a system that was grounded and holistic rather than compartmentalized and specialized, and architects and designers vehemently fought to preserve and perpetuate the notion of totality and unity."

154. Anonymous, Rookwood Pottery, "Corn Mug," 1903, whiteware, 4 x 3 7/8 in. (Collection of Arizona State University Art Museum; Gift of the ASU Ceramics Department) This ear-of-corn motif is a fitting reflection of midwestern regionalism, given Rookwood's location in Cincinnati.

That notion notwithstanding, they also focused upon those natural phenomena distinctive to their particular city, state, or region. Thus, exhibitions of the work of SACB members might feature such varied motifs as the California poppy, a midwestern ear of corn, Spanish moss–hung trees from the deep South, or acorns and roses found in a New England garden (Fig. 154).[29]

Naturalism depicted by arts and crafts designers was partly celebratory and partly prophylactic: As daily life at the turn of the century became compromised by hustle, bustle, noise, and soot, the lure of the countryside grew even stronger, providing an alternative lifestyle. Speaking of America's early settlers, New England architect and designer Charles Edward Hooper (1867–1920) wrote: "His descendents . . . spend the greater part of their lives in doors, and at the same time their children are sent to the hills to sleep in the open air, where the healing balm of nature shall restore them to the health seriously impaired under the false conditions of the modern home." For those unable to spend time in the country, however, household objects inspired by flora and fauna provided the next best thing.[30]

Nature was an alternative to history, but no less challenging. On the one hand, theorists made naturalism seem so simple: "We must not dictate to, but in meekness and lowliness, and with openness of heart, learn from nature," wrote the Scotsman W. Proudfoot Begg, in *The Development of Taste and Other Studies of Aesthetics*. We must, he continued, "listen to what she has to tell us and suggest to our spirit." This sounds easy. Yet, as Howard Walker cautioned, observing nature and then applying her lessons to one's work required discipline. "Naturalism requires great skill," he notes on one occasion. "It is the last work of the skilled designer," he warns on another."[31]

155. Illustration, by H. M. O'Kane, from *Sonnets from the Portuguese* (New Rochelle, N.Y.: The Elston Press [Clarke Conwell], 1900). (Boston Public Library/Department of Rare Books. Courtesy of the Trustees) Waterlilies, irises, daffodils, and other flowers so popular with designers of La Belle Époque figure prominently in O'Kane's work. Her black-and-white ink drawings echo elements found in Aubrey Beardsley's graphic designs, and her slender human figures anticipate those of Edward Gorey (see Fig 189).

The Jury was especially vigilant in evaluating works inspired by nature. On December 19, 1902, for example, the group critiqued a "small stained glass window [with] Poppy design" submitted by Margaret Redmond. "The order of the flower forms is missed in the drawing of them," the meeting minutes noted, "whereas the arrangement of them is absolutely symmetrical. The elements are too accidental for the perfect formality of the composition." The opinion was that Redmond's depiction of the poppy violated natural order, and that her careless rendition of the flower was not in keeping with the formal symmetry of the overall arrangement. Accordingly, the Jury rejected the panel. On the other hand, it approved a piece submitted by Arthur Stone "with criticism: wreath is heavy and lacks delicacy of treatment; & is not really quite in accordance with the law of growth which it figures." Earlier that year, it had rejected a "Lily Brooch [with] opal," by an unknown maker because of the "Inconsistency of lilies up & lilies down. Same effect could have been produced without inconsistency in matter of representation." This brooch's inconsistency with the laws of nature brings to mind an anecdote related by Cleveland Amory. "'Do you know,' [a Boston woman] said with quiet pride, 'that all lilies that grow north of Boston point South and all lilies South of Boston point North?'" Perhaps the maker of the brooch designed it with this observation in mind (Fig. 155).[32]

Although historicism dominated among the products displayed or sold under the SACB's auspices, naturalism informed every craft category. With varying degrees of realism, these crafts employed forms, ornament, motifs, and imagery adapted from flora, fauna, and countryside. And, in doing so, they were among the most innovative and progressive works that SACB members produced, while they reflected the sentiments of a host of international critics. "For the professional stylist, the confirmed conventionalist, an hour in his garden, a stroll in the embroidered meadows, a dip into an old herbal . . . ," wrote one of these, John D. Sedding in *Arts and Crafts Essays*, "is wholesome exercise, and will do more to revive the original instincts of a true designer than a month of sixpenny days at a stuffy museum. The old masters," he argued, "are dead, but 'the flowers', as Victor Hugo says, 'the flowers are always.'"[33]

Success at employing naturalism, however, depended upon the particular craft. According to the Jury, leatherwork frequently suffered from ornamentation that was either "of a weak naturalistic type, or of the still worse convolutions of the so-called art nouveau," a fault that it shared with china painting. "In both cases," stated the Jury in 1912, "the difficulty apparently is that each [craft] lends itself too readily to any type of design and there is not constructive necessity which tends to create any special type of design." Evidently the principles governing a naturalistic approach were more stringent than those controlling one that was historical. But, lacking a foundation in theory, as in history, few workers knew the underlying principles that dictated success, and thus could not make discriminating choices.[34]

156. Tenney (?) residence, Manchester, Mass., undated. Photograph by Mary Northend. (Courtesy Historic New England) The carving on the mantelpiece would have pleased design reformers. The repetitive leaf motif is simple, crisp, and rhythmic while recalling one element from the "tulip-and-leaf" motif found on seventeenth-century Hadley chests from western Massachusetts.

To benefit workers having difficulty, the Jury elucidated some of those principles. To improve leatherwork derived from "poorly drawn, naturalistic sketches," it advised, "The best leather designs of all time have been strongly conventional, with firm, true lines and forms, well suited for naturalistic work." Arguing that wood-carving also suffered from "slipshod naturalistic designs," it declared, "Naturalism requires great skill, and with the numberless fine examples of conventional wood carving upon the South Sea Island paddle blades and Dutch and Elizabethan and Jacobean furniture, it would seem wise for the wood carvers to study simpler forms than those they undertake." Ironically, in offering the model of South Sea Island paddle blades, the Jury was recommending a vernacular source. Evidently a model unsuitable in one medium, such as jewelry, might be appropriate in another, such as wood carving. This must have seemed paradoxical to SACB members seeking the Jury's advice (Fig. 156).[35]

As both statements suggest, the Jury regarded conventionalization as the key to transforming natural elements so that they might enhance an object's form. But even that approach was challenging. "If conventionalized naturalism is to occur, and it must occur in decorative pattern, especially upon small objects," the Jury warned, "it would be well to have a knowledge of the natural forms themselves before any conventionalism is attempted." Thus, looking to nature for inspiration, the Jury suggested, was as demanding as turning to history. Both approaches required close scrutiny of the chosen subject before transforming and then applying it—both originally and appropriately. Owen Jones offered a model

157. Illustration, from *Art-Studies from Nature, as Applied to Design: For the Use of Architects, Designers, and Manufacturers* (London: Virtue & Co., 1872), p. 34, featuring conventionalized treatments of the "Convolvulus." (Courtesy Boston Athenaeum) Flatness, repetition, geometricization, and value contrast contribute to this rhythmic border pattern.

for this approach. Plate 98, "Leaves and Flowers from Nature," in *The Grammar of Ornament* shows color studies of common garden flowers, flattened and viewed both in plan and in elevation.[36]

Conventionalizing nature was so difficult because it required close observation of a subject followed by its complete transformation. "It is not the wealth of available material—leaves, flowers, animals, etc.—that produces a good design," wrote Ernest Batchelder. "It is the [person] behind the material, and his grasp of fundamental principles." Batchelder went on to explain that a botanist should not be able to classify flowers or foliage according to their genus if properly conventionalized. Nature might be the "starting point," as Day put it, or "the font, the wellspring" as Voysey preferred, but an exact rendering of nature alone was insufficient. The designer's challenge was to interpret nature's creations freshly and fitly—with style and originality (Fig. 157). "Indeed it is not essential that the subject-matter should represent or be like anything in nature," wrote Binyon. "Only it must be alive with a rhythmic vitality of its own."[37]

Before we turn to the topic of conventionalization, it is worth noting that every critic did not advocate using nature as a model, just as everyone did not condone turning to history. Arthur Dow was one of these: "In times when art is decadent," he wrote in *Composition*, "the designers and painters lack inventive power and merely imitate nature or the creations of others. Then," he concluded, "comes Realism, conventionality, and the death of art." Here Dow was more con-

cerned with the manner of representation—
"mere imitation" versus innovation—and less
so with the actual model. He supported this
in commenting upon fallacies involved in
teaching students to draw: "In academic art
teaching representation is the starting point.
This means that one must first of all 'learn to
draw,' as power in art is thought to be based
upon ability to represent accurately and truth-
fully either nature's facts or historic ornament." But "drawing with such an end in view
is not strictly art-work. . . . The powerful
drawing of the masters is largely derived from
other masters, not from copying nature." It is
not "fact-statement." Dow also advised that a
student could not learn composition from
observing nature (Plate 13, Fig. 158). "The
sphinx," he wrote, "is not more silent than she
on this point." Dow's influence upon SACB
members was profound, in part because of his
summer school in Ipswich, discussed in an
article by Sylvester Baxter published in *Handicraft* (February 1903).[38]

158. Book cover, by Thomas B. Meteyard, for Bliss Carman, *A Winter Holiday* (1899). (Boston Public Library/Department of Rare Books. Courtesy of the Trustees) Both Arthur Wesley Dow's treatment of landscape and the flatness typical of Japanese woodblock prints may have influenced Meteyard's minimalist cover design.

Conventionalization: Theory and Methodology for "Good Design"

Critics' comments regarding the use of history and nature are rife with references to conventionalization—an important and complex topic. To understand it fully requires exploring its historical roots and discussing why critics advocated it between 1860 and 1920. This section offers selected definitions of conventional-ization, identifies several of its key traits, and indicates why it was difficult to achieve. Conventionalization was not just an aesthetic or technical concern. It was also conceptual. And there were certain concepts influencing arts and crafts orna-mentation that must be understood before one can fully comprehend the art and mystery of conventionalization.

Conventionalization is an outgrowth of the conventionalized ornamentation that was a product of the ancient world. But that ornamentation—including the fret, guilloche, the egg-and-dart, the palmette-and-anthemion, as well as the rosette and paired reverse-curves, to name just a few examples—is not necessar-ily what design reformers had in mind when they set out on their quest for the Useful and the Beautiful. Some arts and crafts designers used traditional borders and motifs, which by then had come to constitute part of their aesthetic heritage.

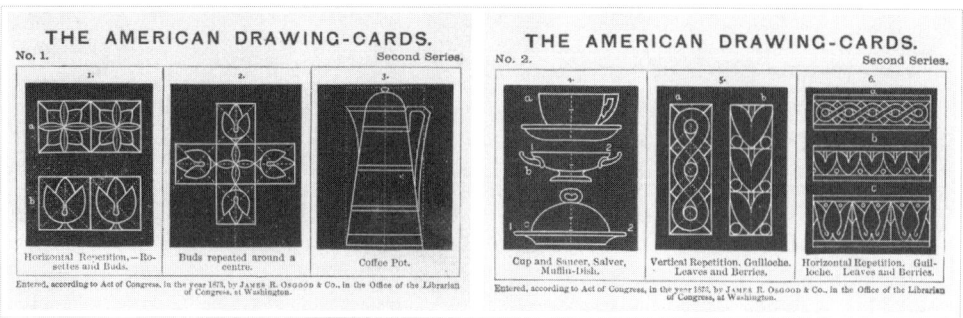

159. "The American Drawing-Cards," Nos. 1 and 2, Second Series, published by James R. Osgood & Co., 1873. (Courtesy Historic New England) The impact of functionalism, historicism, and conventionalization are all evident in this series of "drawing-cards" produced by a major American architectural publisher located in Boston. The small size and didactic quality of these cards suggest that they were made for students.

In the late nineteenth century, however, conventionalization had come to mean something more than simply reusing or adapting universal motifs from the past (Fig. 159).

How design reformers defined that something more is the crux of the problem: some viewed conventionalization as a theory, or an over-riding philosophy, while others regarded it more as a methodology, or a step-by-step approach. Both camps might agree that it was the key to "good design"—especially to good ornamentation—but every advocate seemed to have his or her own definition of what it was, along with advice on how to achieve it and a justification for why it was necessary in the first place. For every specific offered, there was a recommendation rife with ambiguity. For every rule, principle, or condition given, there seemed to be a disclaimer. Whether theory or methodology, conventionalization was both artful and mysterious.

This is evident in a statement by Lewis F. Day, one of the chief advocates of conventionalization, a recurring theme throughout his prolific writings on design. "Conventionality in ornament," he tells us in *Ornament and Its Application*, "is the natural consequence of reticence or self-restraint, of doing not all that the artist could have done, but just what is called for by the occasion." This assertion is an apt starting point. First, Day links conventionalization to ornament specifically, and it is clear in his and others' writings that conventionalization affects decoration more than it does shape, color, or texture. Second, he speaks of "natural consequence." Nature was a principal source of conventionalized ornamentation and "doing what comes naturally," that is, following a logical process, was very much a part of conventionalization as a methodology or way of working. Third, Day speaks of "reticence or self-restraint," words often used to summarize conventionalization in a nutshell.[39]

These were not the only definitions offered by Day or others, but they were among the most popular. They suggest why conventionalization is an important subject: it implied a process of design by subtraction, or what Frank Lloyd Wright called "the elimination of the insignificant." Reticence and self-restraint were truly proto-modern qualities, and through the use of conventionalization, design reformers of the 1860s and later laid the groundwork for the Modernism that dominated the twentieth century. (Reticence and self-restraint were also evident in Asian

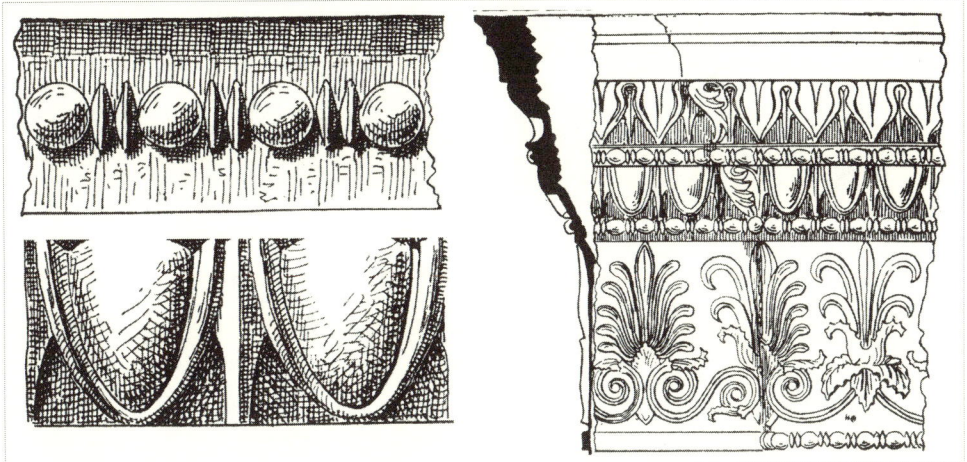

160. Examples of conventionalized ornament: border motifs showing the bead-and-reel, the egg-and-dart, and the palmette-and-anthemion. From Alexander Speltz, *The Styles of Ornament*, trans. David O'Connor (New York: Dover, rpt. of 1904 ed.), pp. 50, 52. (Courtesy Dover Pictorial Archives)

design at certain times and in certain places. The influence of *japonisme*—adopting Japanese conventions vis-à-vis the use of design elements and principles—and *japonaiserie*—borrowing Japanese motifs and subject matter—were evident in arts and crafts designs.) Lastly, when Day defines "reticence or self-restraint" as "doing just what is called for by the occasion," he indicates that his understanding may be more subjective and intuitive than scientific. It is just such instances of ambiguity—and downright self-contradiction—that make Day's and others' recommendations about conventionalization infuriating, and make the subject intriguing.[40]

With that as background, it is worthwhile considering what conventionalization meant historically. Webster sheds some light on this, defining "conventional" as: "of, sanctioned by, or growing out of custom or usage; customary." Thus conventionalized ornament tended to be that which appeared regularly in the artifacts and architecture of a culture or society, in part because it was based upon common knowledge, and in part because it conveyed accepted meaning. An obvious early example would be the conventionalized borders of ancient Greece, whether the bead-and-reel, the egg-and-dart, or the palmette-and-anthemion that graced certain architectural orders and styles of vase painting (Fig. 160). These conventionalized borders represented elements in the natural and human-made world. Some were naturalistic in treatment, while others were geometricized. All were symbolic.

Webster also indicates that "conventional" may also mean "depending on or conforming to formal or accepted standards or rules rather than nature," and thus "not natural, original, or spontaneous." The beauty of conventionalized ornament in the ancient world was that, once learned and memorized,—it was easily duplicable any time, anywhere. Even in the modern world, the convenience of conventionalization added to its charm. This may explain why classical orders and conventionalized borders and motifs were so popular at events such as the Chicago World's Fair of 1893. As architects struggled to build the White City on the shores of Lake Michigan efficiently, often supervising their crews long-distance and from diverse offices around the country, they counted on the fact that these ancient

161. Foyer, unidentified residence, ca. 1925. Photograph by William T. Clark. (Courtesy Historic New England) This room shows myriad influences, ranging from the exotic lantern and wicker teacart to the vernacular character of the rockers and rush-seat armchairs. The runner—possibly a Gustav Stickley Craftsman rug—combines the Greek fret motif with Islamic strapwork. The rug complements the crisp geometry of the interior architecture.

orders and ornaments were standardized—a known quantity. If every building and its ornamentation had been, by contrast, "original and spontaneous," it would have required more on-site supervision from the firm's principals to avoid logistical nightmares, and would *not* have ensured the aesthetic unity demanded by the "City Beautiful" movement. In Louis Sullivan's eyes, however, such dependence upon the past set back the pace of American architecture a hundred years.[41]

Adding to the claim that the "conventional" is neither original nor spontaneous, Webster goes on to state that it is neither "unusual" nor "extreme"; instead it is "ordinary." Thus, historic conventionalized ornament may be generic to the point of being universal. A border such as the Greek meander, fret, or key also appears in early Chinese ceramics. It resurfaces later, concurrent with the Greco-Roman Revival, and embellishes arts and crafts examples at the start of the twentieth century (Fig. 161).

A last synonym offered by Webster for "conventional" is "stylized," defined as "design[ed] or represent[ed] according to the rules of a style rather than according to nature." An excellent example might be strapwork, a type of conventionalized ornamentation having at least three distinct interpretations: the Islamic, the Celtic, and the Renaissance. All strapwork comprises an interlacing network of bands, straps, or strips. Islamic strapwork tends to be flat, angular, and geometric, in keep-

162. Examples of conventionalized ornament: strapwork, representing Moorish and Celtic variations. From Speltz, pp. 108, 210. (Courtesy Dover Pictorial Archives)

163. Book cover, by Theodore Brown Hapgood, Jr., for Jennie Hall, *Weavers and Other Workers* (1917). (Boston Public Library/Department of Rare Books. Courtesy of the Trustees) This illustrates strapwork in keeping with the Islamic approach, which often incorporates the star motif, and makes a striking comparison with the rug shown in Figure 161.

ing with that culture's fascination with both mathematics and astronomy. Celtic strapwork has a more curvilinear knot-like or plait-like quality, and was a favorite of British design reformers. Renaissance strapwork has more implied relief and auricular elements, resembling cut and curled leather bands riveted together. All examples of strapwork are conventionalized, yet each expresses a distinct stylistic quality (Figs. 162 and 163).

Conventionalized ornamentation produced during the era of the Arts and Crafts movement is often described as "stylized," meaning that it represents a unique personality or school of thought. This might be as specific as a design by Frank Lloyd Wright, or as broad as that of the Prairie School. It might, on the one hand, describe the idiosyncratic ornament of Charles Rennie Mackintosh, or that of the Glasgow School. A flat pattern by William Morris, such as that seen in his 1875 "Acanthus" wallpaper is, for example, as distinctly Morrisian as Louis Sullivan's acanthus leafage in the decoration of Chicago's Carson Pirie Scott Co. Building is characteristically

 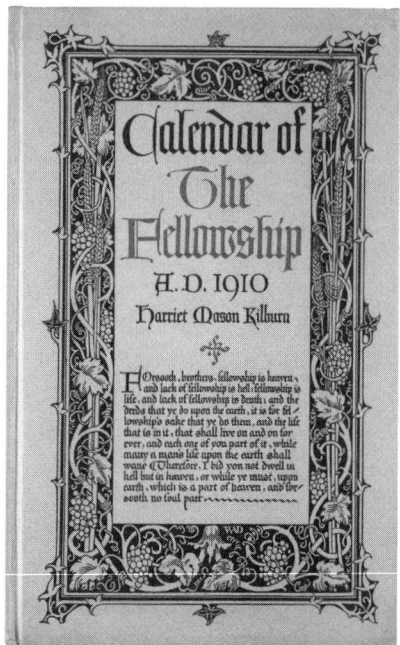

164. Detail of architectural metalwork, showing acanthus leafage, from the Schlesinger & Meyer/Carson, Pirie, Scott & Co. store, by Louis Sullivan, architect, 1889–1901, 1903–04. Photograph by Richard Nickle. (Courtesy of the Richard Nickle Committee, Chicago)

165. Graphic design, by Will Dwiggins, for Harriet Mason Kilburn, *Calendar of The Fellowship, A.D. 1910* (1909). (Boston Public Library/Department of Rare Books. Courtesy of the Trustees) Perhaps following William Morris's example, Dwiggins (1880–1956) used a variation upon the much-maligned running-vine-with-grapes motif. In this example, stalks of grass or wheat intermingle with the grapevine, possibly symbolizing the bread and wine of the Christian communion ritual.

Sullivanesque. To mistake one's approach for the other's would be difficult (Fig. 164). Each is instantly recognizable. Both reflect their particular designer, time, and circumstances at the same time that they represent a variation upon a theme derived from the acanthus borders and motifs designed in the ancient world.

This suggests that arts and crafts designers were aware of the rich history of conventionalized ornament upon which they might build. Certainly, the SACB Jury was quick to recommend that its constituents consult books of historic ornament available in the Society's lending library. Some made a conscious effort to adapt ancient historical motifs and borders to "reformed" artifacts, in keeping with a proto-modern or modern age. (H. H. Richardson, for example, interpreted egg-and-dart molding in the newel post of the Glessner House.) Others, however, cautioned against relying too much upon historical examples. "I would have every precedent stripped of its prestige, and scrutinized as carefully as the newest of recruits," wrote Day in *Nature in Ornament*. He warned design reformers against borrowing from historical conventions that were inherently inaccurate, such as the "running vine with grapes"—a border dating back to the ancient world and especially popular during the Middle Ages (Fig. 165). Even William Morris occasionally sinned, using this motif in designing initials for the *Kelmscott Chaucer*.[42]

Why was conventionality necessary in the first place? Why didn't designers simply look at the world around them and reproduce exactly what they saw? Lewis Day offers one possible answer. "With regard to ornament," he writes inimitably, "I have no hesitation in saying that more or less conventional it must be, or it would not be ornamental." In other words, by his standards, to be decorative required a natural motif's complete transformation into something new. If it were too realistic, it would be unsuitable to embellish any of the "useful arts." Realism and naturalism were not in themselves guarantees that ornamentation would be either Beautiful or Useful.[43]

In making this statement, Day was not trailblazing. His argument is a reiteration of those of his predecessors, one of whom was Ralph Nicholson Wornum. In his lengthy, often tedious essay, written at the time of the Great Exhibition, Wornum devotes the last section to "Ornament," and he explains why conventionalization was crucial. His thoughts are worth quoting at length. "The production and application of ornament," he begins, "are distinct processes, though they cannot be separated in applied design. A proper dis-

166. Illustration from trade catalogue, *Sterling Hollow Ware*, Reed & Barton, Manufacturer, ca. 1909, featuring "Deposit Ware," p. 241. (Courtesy Baker Library, Harvard Business School) This "Deposit Ware" uses a contrast of value and surface finish to create distinctive designs. Workers at Reed & Barton demonstrate their knowledge of conventionalization, using flatness, strong outlines, and repetition in their treatments of flowers, vines, and leaves.

tinction between a picture or model and an ornament, is of the utmost importance to the designer, for the mere power of imitation of natural objects, even their exact imitation, is perfectly compatible," he asserts, "with the total ignorance of Ornamental Art.... There is a *distinct study of ornament* wholly independent of the merely preliminary exercises of drawing, coloring, or modeling." What he is saying, in short, is that observing and then recording one's observations of the world around one is not designing. "He is a poor designer," Wornum goes on to say, "if he can do nothing more than imitate a few sprigs or leaves; he must give an ornamental motif character as well as beauty, and make it suggestive of something more than a cluster of weeds or flowers from the field." Popular "pattern books" such as Owen Jones's *Grammar of Ornament* or Christopher Dresser's *Studies in Design* (1874) build upon both history and nature, while demonstrating the principles of conventionalization (Fig. 166).[44]

Lamenting what he dubbed the "horticultural school of ornament" that prevailed at the 1851 Exhibition—in part because of the dominance of the naturalistic Baroque Revival and Rococo Revival styles—Wornum advocated conventionalization. "Natural floral ornament is a very beautiful kind of ornament, but it is but one kind.... In no popular style of ornament have natural details ever prevailed," he asserted. (In saying so, he flaunted his credentials as a historian of decorative

167. 348 Beacon Street, 1886 (?), Allen & Kenway, architects. (Courtesy Historic New England) Conventionalization plays an important role in suiting acanthus foliage to its use in a border ornamenting an arched doorway and pier capitals on the exterior of this Back Bay house. The strength and simplicity of the facade pay homage to H. H. Richardson. In no way does it prepare a visitor for the fanciful clutter of the interior (Fig. 66).

arts and ornament.) "The details of all great styles are largely derived from nature," he concluded, "but for the most part [are] conventionally treated, and theory as well as experience seems to indicate this as the true system." If design reformers promoted conventionalization, it was because they observed its absence all around them in most run-of-the-mill products. Theorists sought a "true system" that would ensure Usefulness and Beauty in form and ornament. Conventionalization, they argued, was the key.[45]

Theorists hoped to overcome the plague of "badness" that had beset design since the dawn of the Industrial Revolution. To repeat a remark of Arthur Clutton-Brock's: "We are more interested in art [read design] than any people of the past with the interest of a sick man in health." Conventionalization had the potential to make design good, whole, and healthy once again.[46]

How then did design reformers, theorists, and critics define conventionalization? Some did so outright: In *Nature in Ornament*, Day calls conventionalization "the degree and kind of modification calculated to render natural forms applicable to ornament and the various purposes to which it is put." But, he is often more comfortable defining what it is by telling us what it is not. Four pages later in the same book, he indicates: "Conventional treatment . . . is no mere stopping short of perfect rendering, no bald excuse for incompetence. . . . It does not consist . . . in the substitution of the diagram of a thing instead of its life and growth, neither does it mean the mere distortion of natural details nor yet that mechanical repetition of ancient conventions which is a weariness to everyone concerned in it. Our rendering of natural form must be our own, natural to us" (Fig. 167). A key to "good design," he suggested, was to create something personal and ingenuous.[47]

Some defined conventionalization without ever mentioning the word. Take, for example, Denman Ross in his *Theory of Pure Design*, who surely had conventionalization in mind when he wrote: "What we aim at is the Truth of Representation in a form of expression which will be simple, clear, reasonable, consistent, as well as true. The attention must be directed to what is important, away from what is unimportant. Objects, people and things represented must be brought out and emphasized or suppressed and subordinated, according to the Idea or Truth which the artist wishes to express." Here Ross refers to the artist's concept. "The irrelevant must be eliminated. The inconsistent and incongruous must be avoided." Ross sounds remarkably like Ernest Batchelder, who defined "good designs [as] invariably sane, regular, orderly, [and] consistent throughout." As both writers suggest, the traits that applied to "good design" often were those used to describe good people.[48]

These selected definitions begin to paint a broad picture of conventionalization in all of its complexity. Day first speaks of conventionalization as "calculated modification of natural forms." Next he says what it is not: a "stopping short," "incompetence," a "substitution," a "distortion," or a "mechanical repetition." Lastly, he indicates that it must be personal: "our own" interpretation, "natural to us." Ross builds upon this, asserting that conventionalized representations must be "simple, clear, reasonable, consistent, and true." Then he suggests that it is selective to the point of being subtractive. Batchelder reiterates that logic and predictability are key. From these three, a list of conventionality's traits begins to emerge.

The definitions of conventionalization offered by theorists, critics, educators, and practitioners were often as personal as the sorts of designs they hoped to inspire in themselves and others. But most share key words and phrases. Taken as a group, these reveal traits common to most, if not all, conventionalized ornament.

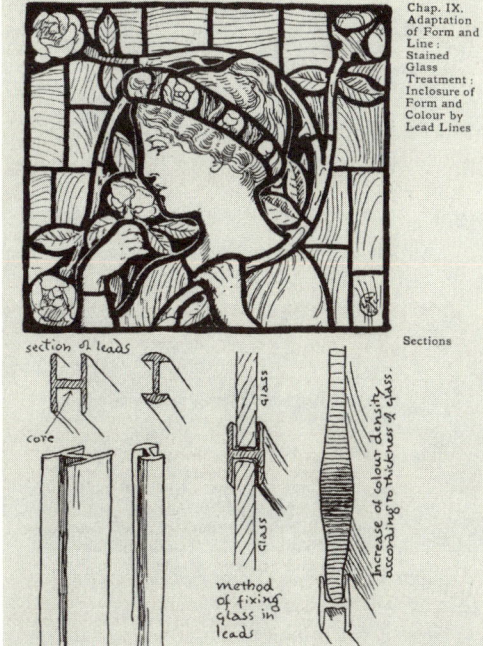

168a. Illustrations, from Walter Crane, *Line and Form* (1900), p. 247. (Courtesy Boston Athenaeum) Lead lines in stained glass work had both decorative and functional purposes.

168b. Stained glass and wrought iron fire screen, by Sarah Wyman Whitman, 1896. (Courtesy Historic New England) Whitman gave this to Richard Norton, son of Charles Eliot Norton, as a wedding present. This screen subscribes to many of the precepts of conventionalization—especially the use of strong outlines.

Achieving Conventionalization: Key Traits of "Good Design"

The first trait is line, specifically outline (Figs. 168a and b). Writers insist that it must be precise, crisp, and structural. Lines might be straight or curved, depending upon the form they embellished and the model that had inspired them. Batchelder

169a. Illustration, from *Art-Studies from Nature, as Applied to Design: For the Use of Architects, Designers, and Manufacturers*, p. 80, featuring conventionalized treatment of the "Sorrel." (Courtesy Boston Athenaeum) Flatness of elements—such as the tripartite, spear-tipped sorrel—enhanced abstraction and united naturalistic motifs with flat surfaces, such as the border of a plate or bowl.

169b. Living room, unidentified and undated. Photograph by William T. Clark. (Courtesy Historic New England) Flatness in rugs and carpets was an especially desirable trait, according to design reformers. They believed that flatness enhanced the apparent stability of the floor surface and thus contributed to a restful atmosphere. This may be a "Donegal" rug, attributed to C. F. A. Voysey and sold in the United States by Gustav Stickley's Craftsman stores. Few elements in this interior are as progressive as the area rug.

waxes eloquent on the "curve of infinity" evident "wherever nature wishes to express beauty," referring especially to vine-like borders. Day, on the other hand, advises: "You may take it as a sign of artistic demoralization to be afraid of a straight line." Here, in *The Planning of Ornament*, he's probably attacking the whiplash curves of Art Nouveau. "Hogarth," he writes, dismissing the author of the *Analysis of Beauty*, "who preached 'the line of beauty' [meaning the "S" curve], was not exactly an apostle of the beautiful." So important was line to conventionalization that Day asserts in *Ornament and Its Application*: "If it were true . . . that there are no lines in nature, the first business of the designer would be to invent them." (See, for example, Owen Jones's studies of "Leaves and Flowers from Nature" in *The Grammar of Ornament*.) Theorists also recommended that lines should conform to structure or material so that, for example, a woven design expressed obviously the warp and the weft.[49]

A second trait of conventionalization is flatness. Writers insisted that forms must be flat and unmodeled, or broad and deliberately shaded. Morris believed that flat blocks of color—especially in wallpaper—should emphasize the flatness of the plane upon which they lie, such as a wall or a screen (Figs. 169a and b). Dow argued, "In beginners' work and design, flatness is necessary." Even Voysey approximated the flatness of an old silhouette to suit human figures to their utilitarian purpose as decoration on a pierced strap hinge, ornamenting a desk-bookcase. Flatness was even more important when motifs were used over and over again. Day argued that "forms in order to be fit for reiteration must be abstract. The fact alone, therefore, that form is to be continually repeated demands departure from literal transcript in the rendering of it." Thus, the repetitive character of a flat pattern demanded that it not be overly realistic. And this was true for conventionalized ornamentation in general.[50]

As the previous quotations suggest, repetition was a third trait of conventionalization (Fig. 170). "The orderly repetition of parts frequently aids in the production of ornamental effects," writes Dresser in *Principles of Decorative Design* (1873). One of the basic design principles, repetition ensured unity and harmony. "Restraint is continually imposed upon the designer of ornament by the natural conditions of

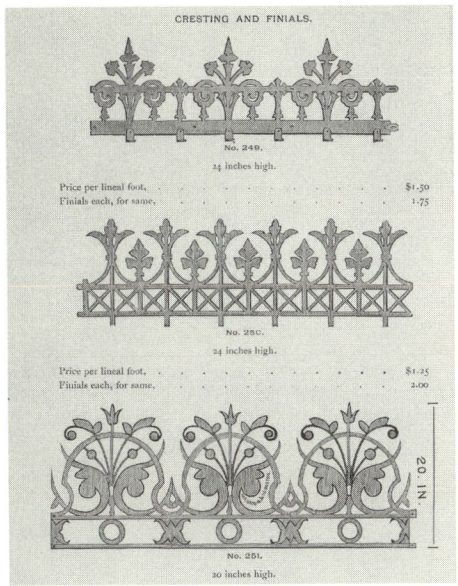  

170. Illustration of cresting and finials, from trade catalogue, W. A. Snow & Co., Boston. (Courtesy Baker Library, Harvard Business School) W. A. Snow & Co.—a purveyor of farm implements and equipment—seems an unlikely source for "good design" in Boston at the turn of the century. But the cast or wrought iron roof cresting and finials, along with weathervanes and other decorative metalwork, are stylish and up-to-date. They demonstrate a pleasing conventionalized naturalism, a strong linearity, flatness, and a rhythmic repetition.

171. Book cover, by Bertram Grosvenor Goodhue for Craigie's *An Old Man's Romance* (1895). (Courtesy MIT Museum) A gifted architectural illustrator—with a firm command of perspective drawing and an ability to convey a sense of depth and space—Goodhue was also skilled at designing flat patterns. This design, with its rhythmic repetition of flowers, foliage, and fruit, would be equally successful as a wallpaper or textile.

his work," wrote Day, "by the consideration of its place and purpose, by the means employed in doing it, and very especially in view of that repetition which becomes in these days more and more a necessity of [conventionalization's] very being." Repetition established a natural rhythm akin to walking or breathing—while contributing to unity (Fig. 171). Not everyone adhered to this organizing principle, however. A trade catalogue (1889) for the Boston-based Whitney's Linen Store, for example, advised customers purchasing needlework kits or patterns: "At the present time, conventional designs are greatly in demand, and the more carelessly they are scattered upon the material to be worked, the better the effect will be." Such dubious recommendations justified Day's need to keep publishing books on conventionalization.[51]

Repetition might be found in nature, as well as in historical examples. "From the rude patterns marked with sticks on Indian bowls and pots, or painted in earth colors on wigwam and belt, or woven on blanket," wrote Dow, "this form of space art [i.e., composition] has grown, through the complexities of Egyptian and Peruvian textile design to the splendors of Byzantine mosaic, the jewel patterns of the Moguls, and Gothic sculpture." He concluded his characteristically eclectic list by mentioning the "rock-cut pillars of cave temples" and the "colonnade of the Parthenon" as examples of rhythms found in architecture, and then recommended that repetition be used cautiously, noting that it "has come to be used in cheap and mean design where no regard is paid to the beauty of form."[52]

172a. Chimney detail, Popes Hill, 54 Boutwell Avenue (?), Dorchester, Mass. Cabot & Chandler, architects, ca. 1882. Photograph by Soule Photograph Company. (Courtesy Historic New England) *The American Architect & Building News* published this home in March 1882. It blends Queen Anne massing with an approach to texture and materials more in keeping with the Shingle style. These Japanese "pies" or rosettes in a grid pattern introduce a hint of the Aesthetic movement.

172b. Book cover, by Theodore Brown Hapgood, Jr., for Guy Wetmore Carryl, *Far from the Maddening Girls* (1904). (Boston Public Library/Department of Rare Books. Courtesy of the Trustees) Graphic designers recognized the effectiveness of the grid as a compositional framework. This crisp, flat pattern—reminiscent of ceramic tile work—contrasts with the more Morrisian approach that Hapgood took when designing the SACB's *Prospectus* in 1896.

A fourth trait of conventionalization was that it was often (although not exclusively) geometric, or at the very least geometricized: "The serious student of design," wrote Batchelder, "discovers sooner or later that his expression of an idea must conform to the requirements of mathematics and geometry." The ornament of American architects Frank Furness (1839–1912), Louis Sullivan, and Frank Lloyd Wright comes to mind. Emerson perhaps influenced them when he wrote: "Nature geometricizes . . . moon, plant, gas, crystal, are concrete geometry and number"—a sentence quoted in Claude Bragdon's influential book *Projective Ornament* (1915). But, as Bragdon notes, using geometry successfully required conventionalization, that is, "examin[ing], analyz[ing], and filter[ing it] through the consciousness of the artist." Repetition had mathematical properties, and geometry satisfied the desire for precise outlines and flat masses (Figs. 172a and b). Remarking on the beauty of Native American basketry, William H. Holmes notes the incidence of geometry in its conventionalized ornament, specifically "stripes, zones, rays, circles, ovals or rectangles." Other cultures and styles—Hindu, Chinese, Japanese, Moorish, and Gothic—relied on geometry as a basis for systems of ornament. The crisp, classic forms of so many arts and crafts vessels and containers lent themselves to geometric ornamentation.[53]

This leads to a fifth trait to which most writers alluded: that of the integration

173. Advertisement, from *Masters in Art: A Series of Illustrated Monographs*, December 1900 (Boston: Bates and Guild), p. 37. (Author's collection) Grueby pottery—which blended sleek forms with low-relief, molded, naturalistic ornament—exemplifies the integration of structure and decoration.

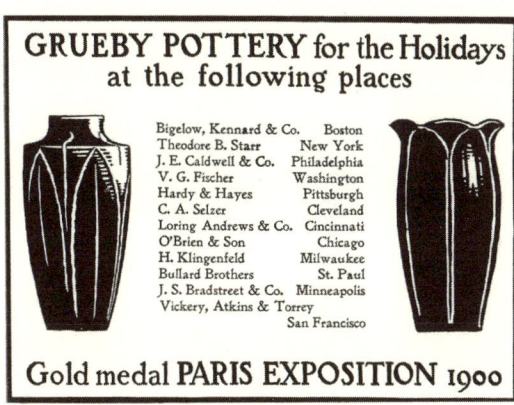

of conventionalized ornament with form (Fig. 173). In *Ornament and Its Application*, Day commented that ornament should "seem to be inseparable from the form that it graced," and that "it ought never look as if it could be removed." Similarly, Frank Lloyd Wright asserted: "In nature beauty is never applied to a thing—it is the thing." For that reason, Wright preferred structural ornamentation that was fully integrated into forms and planes.[54]

To say that conventionalized ornament must be linear, flat, repetitive, geometric (on occasion), and integrated was only a starting point. These recommendations were relatively easy for craftspeople to follow since they pertained to things they knew well: basic design elements—shape, color, texture—and fundamental principles—balance, rhythm, emphasis, harmony, unity. Other recommendations on what conventionalization should be were less comprehensible to the average craftsperson, since they were less specific. They dealt with issues such as "expression," or character, issues to which many critics and theorists devoted a lifetime of study and comment.

Theorists equated conventionalization with "reticence or restraint," and this explains why they often discussed simplicity as a sixth trait. "To conventionalize is in some cases scarcely more than to simplify," wrote Day in *Nature in Ornament*. Concurring with Frank Lloyd Wright, he concluded: "The omission of the superfluous in ornament is indisputably right." Denman Ross agreed, saying: "The rule of Pure Design, and it is the rule for all design is simplification rather than complication." Preceding both Day and Ross, Walter Crane argued similarly in *The Bases of Design*: "It is much better to do a simple thing well, than a complex or ambitious thing badly; and there is far more need in the world for well-designed and beautiful common things than for elaborate and exceptional things." Such emphasis upon simplicity reflected design reformers' desire to break away from the complexity that characterized mid- to late Victorian design. Complexity affected conceptual, aesthetic, and technical matters equally. It compromised not only the designer's approach but also the end product.[55]

To advocate simplicity was, however, easier said than done, since it flew in the face of the nineteenth-century belief that "more is more," that if a little of something beautiful is good, a whole lot more of it must be better. This was common despite Stickley's admonition that "Beauty does not imply elaboration or ornament." By contradicting the status quo, design reformers challenged conventional wisdom (Fig. 174).[56] To achieve simplicity required a subtractive approach, a stripping away of the superfluous to reveal a design's fundamental components. "There should be no

174. Example of a smoking-room from the Jordan Marsh Co.'s "Our House-furnishing Annex," Boston, ca. 1906. (Courtesy Historic New England). The stark simplicity visible in this suite demonstrates that design reform had infiltrated even established retailers. The room is functional and unified, a striking contrast to the cluttered eclecticism evident in so many Boston interiors of this era. This suite presents only one side of what Jordan Marsh could offer consumers, as the retailer also had a thriving antiques department.

175. Book cover, by Sarah Wyman Whitman, for Edna Dean Proctor, *Song of the Ancient People* (Boston: Houghton Mifflin, 1898). (Boston Public Library/Department of Rare Books. Courtesy of the Trustees) In comparison with most Victorian-era book covers, this design is notable for its simplicity to the point of bareness. The brown motifs, stamped on a brown suede leather binding, draw upon Native American sources. The "Z" border recalls the zigzag, representative of powerful natural forces. The lizard roundel encircling the title is akin to motifs found on Mimbres pottery (ca. 550–1150) that Whitman may have seen at Harvard University's Peabody Museum of Archeology and Ethnology.

suspicion of [ornament] having been an afterthought," wrote Day. "The test of artistic application is that [ornament] should not appear to be added." This was another way of saying that every part of a work should be integrated with the others (Fig. 175).[57]

Such ornament Day and others described as fit. "The fitness of fit ornament stands out as being the one condition of workmanlike design," he wrote. The turn-of-the-century era was obsessed with personal fitness; it was a time when shelter magazines promoted the benefits of fresh air, disciplined exercise, specialized equipment to enhance that exercise, and healthy eating. This sort of fitness regime, they argued, ensured a high quality of life. Functionalism of form—both in humans and in manufactured goods—became paramount. As it did, it seems only logical that "fit"—in essence suitable, logical, or in today's parlance "lean and mean"—ornament seemed increasingly desirable. But fit ornament was not necessarily ornament that had been placed on a strict diet. Day advised against "the substitution of the diagram of a thing instead of its life and growth." In other words, simple, fit ornament must never appear spare to the point of seeming emaciated.[58]

A last trait associated with conventionalization is perhaps one of the most difficult to explain. Repeatedly, writers on this subject identify as the desiderata of conventionalization such qualities as freshness, vigor, intensity, and immediacy. In advocating freshness, they hoped to avoid ornament that seemed "mechanical and perfunctory." Conventionalized ornament executed by hand must never, according

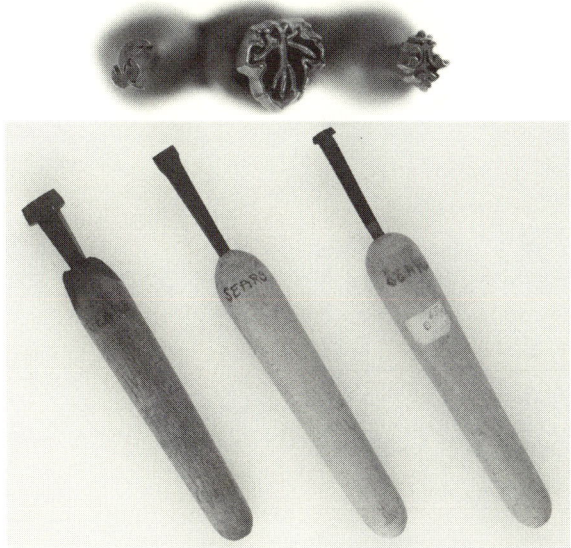

176a. Finishing tools used for book binding by Mary Crease Sears. Brass with wooden handles. (Courtesy Boston Athenaeum) For most craftspeople, the tools used on a daily basis served as an extension of the mind and the soul. These are among fourteen of Sears's finishing tools owned by the Boston Athenaeum. She used these to impress floral and foliate forms into the surface of the leather bindings.

176b. Book binding, designed and tooled by Mary Crease Sears, for the *Commonplace Book*, ca. 1917. (Courtesy Boston Athenaeum) This anonymous volume is entirely in calligraphic hand on glassine papers. Sears bound it in full brown morocco with gilt ornamentation.

to their standards, look machine-made. Freshness, critics argued, combated the "everyday soulless work turned out by the carload by the machine factories." It reintroduced the vitality of nature into the designed environment. In his *Principles of Decorative Design*, Christopher Dresser alludes to freshness when he opines: "With what power do the plants burst from the earth in Spring! What power do the buds develop into branches! . . . Our compositions, then, must be powerful."[59]

This list of key traits of conventionalization begins to make the point that it was not easy to define, or explain, or implement. Every recommendation varied subtly, based upon the type of application (three-dimensional or two-), medium, technique, or construction. For this reason, conventionalization remained the focus of critics' comments and theorists' writings for decades. It inspired the founding of schools and specific pedagogies. It remained the subject of an ongoing debate among critics, craftspeople, and consumers.

This is not to suggest that critics and educators were unsympathetic to the plight of craftspeople attempting to assimilate their advice. They knew that the art of conventionalization was difficult to master. Repeatedly, they spoke of the challenges of learning conventionalization specifically, and design generally. In 1887, in *The Planning of Ornament*, Day advised: "There is nothing careless or casual in the art of design—not even in the little art of ornament." Years later, in 1900, he and his co-author, Mary Buckle, asked in *Art in Needlework*: "How is it possible to take design seriously and yet think it is to be mastered without years of patient study, which few workmen can or will devote to it?" In 1918, C. Howard Walker reiterated Day and Buckle's point, when he argued: "Design is an art to be gained by careful, serious study." What they implied was that design required as much thought as did study of the fine arts and architecture. Yet, in the fast-paced

176c. Sanborn-Raymond House, 125 Magazine Street, Cambridge, undated. (Courtesy Historic New England) "Pleasant thought expressed in the speech of the tool" characterizes these exuberant fireplace andirons and tools by an unknown maker. The spiraling wirework functions simultaneously as form and ornament. A universal conventionalized element, the spiral is timeless in its dynamic appeal. An illustration in C. L. Eastlake's *Hints on Household Taste* (1868) of an "old Swiss Iron Candlestick" (fig. XXII) could have inspired these pieces.

world of the modern factory, time for reflection was a luxury afforded to few.[60]

In recommending conventionalization, critics did not fail to offer practitioners a lifeline: "The 'convention' which comes of obedience," wrote Day harkening back to Ruskin, "not to tradition, but to the conditions of the case at hand, is always right. We ask no more," he said, offering two specific examples, "of basket-work than ingeniously plaited pattern; no more of turning than the lathe will give." When Day and others spoke of "conditions," they indicated that medium, method, tool, and end use all influenced ornament: its size or scale, position, relief (or lack thereof), and its character. "A certain natural convention . . . ," wrote Walter Crane, "belongs to the conditions of material and method." Such conditions, he continued a few pages later, "influence every department of decorative design, and in proportion to the completeness with which they are satisfied will depend the success of designs; and any design which may have less actual beauty, perhaps, than another, but which completely fulfills the conditions of its existence, is likely to have a longer life." It was that longevity that allowed a good design possibly to become a "classic."[61]

In addition to satisfying conditions dictated by medium, method, tool, and end use, Crane and his colleagues listed other conditions—proportion, scale, composition, variety, rhythm, balance, harmony, and others—as rules that no worker should violate. Satisfying fundamental conditions and adhering to basic design principles were among the keys to achieving "good design."

There remain a few last points. Conventionalization may be primarily an aesthetic or a conceptual issue. But, in fact, much of conventionalization was technical, related to both medium and tool, and to executing a design in what many termed a "workmanlike" fashion. Kate Gordon, in her book *Esthetics*, wrote: "In designing we have something—our material—which we make into the likeness of something else—our idea." Making a parallel statement, architect William Lethaby wrote: "Proper ornamentation may be defined as a language addressed to the eye; it is pleasant thought expressed in the speech of the tool" (Figs. 176a–c). Both writers link concept to technique, expression to material or tool. They suggest that conventionalization would never be successful as merely "paper design." The test of its success lay in its materiality—its translation of an idea into a particular craft technique. "The way of technique," wrote Day, "is the straight way to success."[62]

Because conventionalization was dependent upon technique, every craft category had its own subset of rules. Myriad books of the period were devoted to a distinct medium or craft category. Specific rules governing conventionalization in clay contrasted greatly with those provided for metal or leatherwork. A sunflower executed in wood, for example, required a different approach altogether from one cut, stitched, and appliquéd in fabric.

This raises the issue of the ambiguous, if not downright contradictory, advice offered by experts on the subject of conventionalization. As a chief spokesperson on behalf of conventionalization, Lewis Day was one of the guiltiest in this regard. He may have advocated restraint as part of conventionalization; but he also wrote: "Ornament may be extremely rich and yet not 'overloaded,'" offering as an example "the exuberance of oriental ornament" in which "ornament [serves] as a foil to ornament." Though he advocated sincerity, he said conversely, that "fictitious detail, a fiction founded upon fact, when it is the development of some natural form or effect" was acceptable. On the one hand, he valued clarity and logic, but on the other, he conceded that good ornament might also be "fanciful" or "mysterious." In doing so, he anticipated Albert Einstein's claim that "the most beautiful thing we can experience is the mysterious." And, despite his own and others' claims that design was the result of "careful, serious study," Day called for his colleagues to, in today's parlance, "lighten up" occasionally. "A man must be allowed now and again to lay aside artistic dignity and be frolicsome," he wrote. "Playfulness is quite within the sphere of ornament," he insisted. "Frivolity itself is at times more to the purpose than an everlasting seriousness." Perhaps, he was simply stating in his own way Ruskin's belief that labor should be joyful, and building upon the work of Christopher Dresser, who included a section "Humour in Ornament" in his *Principles of Design*.[63]

Despite widespread support of conventionalization as a method for achieving "good design," there were some who were skeptical about its merits. Once was Clarence Cook, who characterized "bad design" variously as overcrowded, commonplace, tame, matter-of-fact—and conventional. Here, Cook might have been using the term as a synonym—in the Websterian sense—for "ordinary," a quality antithetical to that which he desired in *The House Beautiful*.[64]

But Arthur Dow was equally wary of conventionalization. "For a great while we have been teaching art through imitation—of nature or the 'historic style,'" he wrote, singling out the two approved sources that so many of his colleagues condoned, "leaving structure to take care of itself: gathering knowledge of facts but acquiring little power to use them. This is why so much architecture and decoration is only dead copies of conventional motifs." For Dow, emphasis upon realism, or what he called "nature-imitation," posed the greatest threat to creating art that was vital. "The picture-painter is led to think of likeness to nature as the most desirable quality for his work, and the designer talks of 'conventionalizing'; both judging their work," he warned, "by a standard of Realism rather than of Beauty." For Dow, achieving beauty in a work of art or craft superseded model or process of interpretation.[65]

It is these sorts of contradictions that must have made conventionalization infuriating and confusing to craftspeople at the time. Did Day and his colleagues

177. Thompson House, 161 Brattle Street, now 11 Kennedy Road, Cram, Goodhue & Ferguson, architects (?), undated. (Courtesy Historic New England) Designed in the Neo-Gothic style, this fireplace elevation shows remarkable restraint despite its historical allusions. Wainscot paneling recalls the Elizabethan age. The conventionalized carvings on the mantle face and repressed arch have Gothic overtones. The changing direction of the bricks provides structural ornamentation. But overall, the interior architecture is self-effacing, allowing the client's art and antiques to stand out.

obfuscate the issue on purpose, to guarantee that their services would be needed over decades? The ongoing debate about the character of ornament and the merits of conventionalization kept more than one writer busy for a lifetime. They may never have decided for certain whether conventionalization was a theory or a methodology. Perhaps, given the ambiguity and contradictions that surrounded it, it was a little bit of both.

The Power of Expression in "Good Design"

In addition to reinterpreting approved models—history and nature—through the process of conventionalization, critics argued that any successful work of art or craft had to convey expression, that is, a meaning that transcended mere Usefulness and Beauty. Expression might be intellectual or moral. It might say something about temperament, race, culture, or nation. Above all, it had to convey something about the maker that would resonate with the user. Arthur Dow alluded to the power of expression when he wrote: "Put together all the good points in [a] method and you have the qualities of the highest art; for what more do we require of the master"—a master of any art or craft—"than simplicity, unity, powerful handling, and that mysterious force that lays hold upon the imagination." That mysterious force was expression—the trait that distinguished the exceptional from the commonplace.[66]

As Dow's words suggest, a contributing factor to expression was simplicity. The simplicity that led to successful conventionalization, that is, simplicity of outline, of form, or of interpretation of a historical or natural model, also enhanced a work's expression by leaving out more than it put in, thereby allowing the viewer or user an opportunity for personal interpretation. The best works of the design reform movement display what one scholar has termed "ostentatious simplicity" (Fig. 177). Or, as Richard Guy Wilson explains, "Appreciation of simplicity requires sophistication; to reject the over-ornate, overstuffed emblems of 'Bozart' good taste required prior knowledge. There is about the Arts & Crafts a certain amount of

178. Book cover, by Sarah Wyman Whitman, for S. Weir Mitchell [M.D.], *In War-Time* (Cambridge: Riverside Press, 1884). (Boston Public Library/ Department of Rare Books. Courtesy of the Trustees) Some of Whitman's most effective book covers were remarkable for their "ostentatious simplicity." The rich, deep browns of title and sword hilt are striking and direct. The eloquent empty space of the overall composition is very Asian in character. The power of this design rests in its understatement.

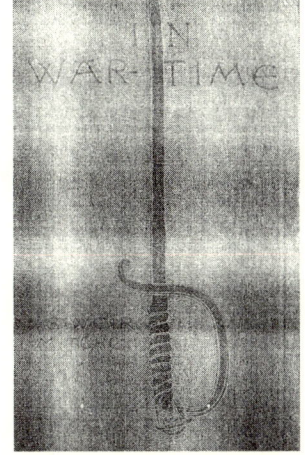 

179. Book cover, by Sarah Wyman Whitman, for Percival Lowell, *The Soul of the Far East* (Boston: Houghton Mifflin, 1888). (Boston Public Library/Department of Rare Books. Courtesy of the Trustees) A delicate prettiness contrasts this cover with that designed for *In War-Time*. The crane, elusive pearl, and cloud motifs derive from Asian porcelains and textiles. The lily bent into a "C" incorporates one of Whitman's signature motifs. This spare composition leaves much to the viewer's imagination.

snobbish simplicity or self-conscious unpretentiousness." These oxymorons perplexed the average worker and consumer, as this could be a simplicity—or lack of pretension—in narrative, composition, means, or even usage.[67]

Simplicity of narrative resulted from suggestion rather than reportage. "The [Gothic] stone-cutter was an artist as long as his restraint was self-imposed," wrote Dow in *Composition*, "as long as he held to a unity of the whole composition and kept details in their place—as long as he carved harmonies, not mere stories." That lack of literalism, critics argued, was something that engaged the viewer-user (Fig. 178). That simplicity of narrative was a quality adopted by Westerners from Asian art: "The Chinese and the Japanese, both in their literature and in their art," Lawrence Binyon argued, "make of evocation or suggestion an aesthetic principle. . . . So, in Chinese art and poetry we find an instinctive avoidance of display, a reliance on suggestion, a pregnant hint, which is to enter into the spectator's or the reader's mind and will be completed there." This quality meant that a user's appreciation of a maker's work became dialectic.[68]

In some cases, it was simplicity of composition (Fig. 179)—rather than simplicity of narrative—that contributed to a work's expression. Through exposure to Asian art, some design reformers incorporated eloquent empty space into their creations. In the late-Victorian era, when overcrowded, layered arrangements were the norm, such eloquent emptiness would have appealed to sophisticated consumers' sensibilities, simply by providing an alternative. Such a composition was "not filled," Binyon explains, precisely because "it is waiting for our imagination to enter into it." In such "emptiness," in "the blankness of great solitudes," Binyon argues, "the spirit could roam in freedom." For the fortunate consumers living with such works, the opportunity to complete the narrative according to one's intellect or to finish the composition in one's mind's eye must have been refreshing.[69]

Captivating expression might also be the product of simplicity of means: a work might convey a great deal, but economically. "With Chinese art, in its main

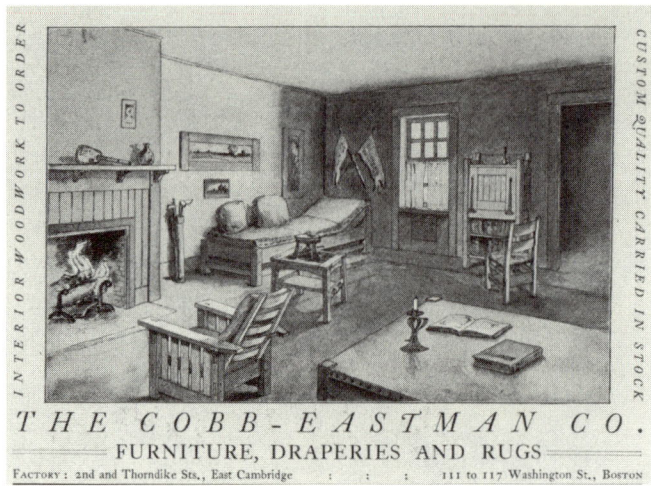

180. Advertisement, featuring a Craftsman-type interior, for the Cobb-Eastman Co., Boston, published in *Catalogue of the Architectural Exhibit, Boston Architectural Club* (Boston: B.A.C. 1902). (Courtesy Boston Athnaeum) "No false display" is evident in this room, which represents simplicity of usage in keeping with the design reform movement's ideals. It is worth noting that the Cobb-Eastman Co. sold copies of *The Craftsman* magazine in its Washington Street store.

tradition, there is . . . a powerful instinct for largeness and simplicity," writes Binyon. "Those artists were most praised who could give the utmost depth and distance in a small space and with few strokes." Conventionalization, combined with knowledge of medium, tools, and technique helped the designer to achieve a similarly powerful expression that seemed fit and effortless.[70]

These simplicities of narrative, composition, and means complemented simplicity of usage. Reformed wares often contributed most to a setting that was spare and functional (Fig. 180). Writing of the Japanese, Morse noted: "Their wants are few, and their tastes are simple and refined. They live without the slightest ostentation; no false display leads them into criminal debt." (Here he was contrasting the Japanese way of living with Western—specifically American—consumerism.) That sparseness appealed to select American consumers, who truly took to heart Morris's maxim regarding Usefulness and Beauty. It also appealed to American intellectuals. "Almost all the great men of this world," noted Clarence Cook, "have lived in an absolute independence of things," something that Cook admired in individuals such as Emerson and Thoreau, but ironically was incapable of achieving in his own surroundings.[71]

As Morse compared Japanese homes to their American counterparts, he often focused upon what archeologists term "negative evidence," that is, what was not there, or what he did not see. Often, features that were all-important in the late-Victorian American interior were absent from Japanese homes. Yet, the traits that remained in the Japanese home, and that Morse most admired—honest construction, refined finishes, embellishments placed strategically, and open, flowing space—were those very features that arts and crafts architects on both sides of the Atlantic prized most highly and sought to incorporate into their work (Fig. 181).[72]

Simplicity was not the sole manifestation of expression, although it may have been a favorite of design reformers. Handicrafts had the potential to satisfy physical needs of consumers, while appealing to their intellect, emotions, and spirit. Similarly, they had the potential to engage, as Batchelder stated eloquently, the "mind, eye, hand, heart and soul" of the worker. There was a spiritual aspect to handicrafts' expression that transcended Usefulness and Beauty. "For art is essentially a conquest of matter by Spirit," wrote Binyon, in a comment equally appli-

181. Fourth Presbyterian Church, Chicago, Cram, Ferguson & Goodhue, architects, ca. 1914. Cram & Ferguson Archives. (Boston Public Library/Department of Fine Arts. Courtesy of the Trustees) This sleek gathering place—modeled after a medieval Great Hall with balcony—is much simpler than the Neo-Gothic facade and sanctuary of the Fourth Presbyterian Church complex.

182. Edward Diers, "Landscape Vase," for Rookwood Pottery, 1919, earthenware, 8 × 5 3/8 in. (Collection of Arizona State University Art Museum; Gift of Gen. & Mrs. J. H. Rothschild) Diers may have had a particular landscape in mind when painting this vase, but the soft, tonalist treatment lends a degree of abstraction—and hence universality—to his composition.

cable to craft; "in Bacon's phrase, 'it is a subjecting of things to the mind as opposed to Science, which is a subjecting of the mind to things.'" Binyon might have concluded similarly that Art and Craft encouraged the "subjecting of things" to the psyche or the soul.[73]

One of the challenges faced by design reformers was to create works that appealed—on a fundamental level—to consumers' psyches. Their goal was to convey universal truths through their translation of a specific concept into design elements and principles, while responding to the particular demands of material and technique. To transform a common wildflower, tree, or bird—through a pattern or scene that conveyed a universal truth—was an achievement equally thrilling to maker and user (Fig. 182). "The artist must pierce beneath the mere aspect of the world," argued Binyon, "to seize and himself be possessed by that great cosmic rhythm of the Spirit which sets the currents of life in motion. We should say in Europe that he must seize the universal in the particular." A writer of short stories—Henry James, Hamlin Garland, and Sarah Orne Jewett come to mind—could appeal similarly to a broad audience by writing about particular persons or places that seem to resonate with any and every reader. So too could craftsworkers portray local flora and fauna, or a bit of historical ornament in a way that would appeal—intellectually, emotionally, or spiritually—to a broad range of consumers.[74]

Ultimately, expression was a matter of transcendence. It was a quality that exceeded or extended beyond mere Usefulness and Beauty. Richard Guy Wilson argues: "With most Arts & Crafts designers there is a sense of metaphysics, a recognition that the material or physical world is but one level of reality. How to

183. Howe residence, Manchester Cove, Mass., undated, Edmund M. Wheelwright, architect. Photograph by Soule Art Company. (Courtesy Historic New England) A perfect setting in which "to contemplate ... the order of the world." This covered porch, with its fieldstone piers, turned balustrade, and comfortable willow chairs, offers a vista—crisscrossed by a sinuous stream—that might have inspired graphic designs by A. W. Dow or T. B. Meteyard.

accomplish the transcendence to a higher reality varied," he explains, "ranging from nature to Christian mysticism, Swedenborgianism, and Theosophy. And assisting would be objects, whether a Roycroft vase or Harvey Ellis chair, that through their physicality and imagery would induce the participant to contemplate the essences of form and the order of the world" (Fig. 183). Simplicity and reticence in design revealed the essence of form. Careful composition and repetition ensured orderliness. As Wilson suggests, these were important to achieving design reformers' aesthetic ideals and to providing an alternative to Victorian over-elaboration and clutter. But they also appealed to consumers' more altruistic motives. The success of the design reform movement may be that its products satisfied consumers' physiological needs while enriching their intellectual, emotional, and spiritual desires. In their homes and workplaces, furnishings and decorative artifacts could become objects of contemplation that suggested how life might be.[75]

As I discussed in the Introduction, critics linked expression in design to that in language. They viewed design as a means of communicating that was as powerful as the spoken or the written word. Design reformers strove to democratize "good design," and willingly turned to vernacular models for inspiration. Indeed, the best critics of the era—just like the best designers—communicated their ideas simply, directly, and frankly, emulating in their words the qualities that they most admired in the designed environment. Similarly, they encouraged their constituents to design as they might speak, avoiding the complexities of high-toned rhetoric in favor of the simple language of everyday.

Advice offered by the SACB Jury regarding models and methodologies for achieving "good design" reflected the latest international theories. When the Jury discussed history or nature, conventionalization or expression, they promoted concepts that were *au courant*, understood by design reformers on both sides of the Atlantic. The works of their constituents may have differed stylistically from those produced in Chipping Camden, Glasgow, Dublin, Stockholm, Darmstadt, Vienna, or Barcelona. Yet, they reflected the impact of similar ideas linked to the quest for Usefulness and Beauty.

R.W.WINFIELD, CAMBRIDGE STREET WORKS, BIRMINGHAM.

1. Bedstead and hangings in Renaissance Revival style, by R. W. Winfield, Cambridge Street Works, Birmingham. From *Official Descriptive and Illustrated Catalogue of the Great Exhibition . . . , Part III* (London: Spicer Brothers and W. Clowes & Sons, 1851), color plate between pp. 638 and 639. (Courtesy Baker Library, Harvard Business School) The R. W. Winfield Company produced furnishings that epitomized British eclecticism and historicism at mid-century. It also experimented with innovative materials, such as tubular steel as a framework for furniture, though designs seldom shed historic ornament completely.

2. Interior of Wedgwood salesroom, London. From Rudolph Ackermann, *The Repository of the Arts, Literature, Commerce, Manufactures, Fashions, and Politics*, February 1809. (Courtesy Boston Athenaeum) The caption reads: "Wedgwood & Byerley, York Street, St. James Square [London]." This interior from the Greco-Roman Revival era illustrates a salesroom crowded with consumer goods produced by one of England's most admired entrepreneurial establishments.

3. Plate XXVIII, from Ackermann, *Repository of Arts, Literature, Commerce, Manufactures, Fashions, and Politics,* April 1811. (Courtesy Historic New England) One of the distinctive features of Ackermann's *Repository* was its inclusion of actual fabric samples, suitable for home furnishings or costume. Not only do these samples illustrate the popular hues, textures, and techniques of the era, but they also serve as testimony to the influence of England's textile manufacturers, who had led the Industrial Revolution.

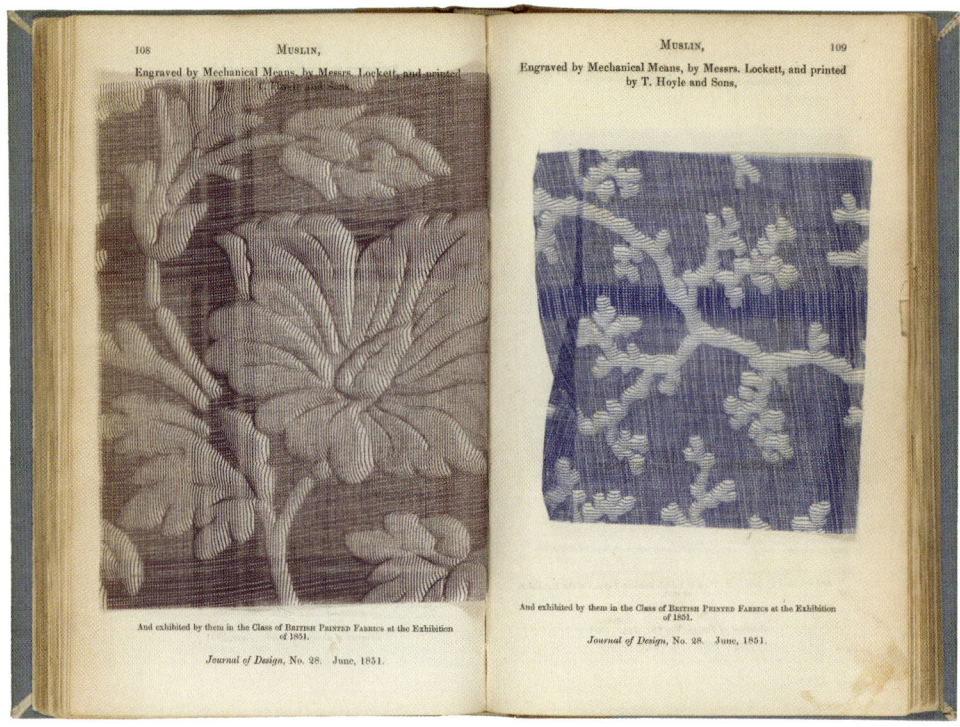

4. Plate, including "Engraved Muslins," from *The Journal of Design and Manufactures,* 5 (March–August 1851): 108–9. (Courtesy Baker Library, Harvard Business School) The *Journal* was published between 1849 and 1852. It argued the case for design reform and promoted the Great Exhibition. Like Ackermann's *Repository*, it included materials—textiles and wallpapers—exhibited at the Crystal Palace. In an era before color photography, few artifacts documented the colorful nature of such displays. Along with hand-colored engravings, these samples are an invaluable resource to design historians.

5. "My Lady's Chamber," frontispiece to Clarence Cook, *The House Beautiful* (rpt. 1881). (Courtesy Historic New England) Crane's illustration captures the essence of the tasteful home: furnishings hark back to the Colonial era; the heart motif implies that the hearth is the heart of the home; Japanese fans introduce exoticism; a cat lapping milk conveys peacefulness and contentment.

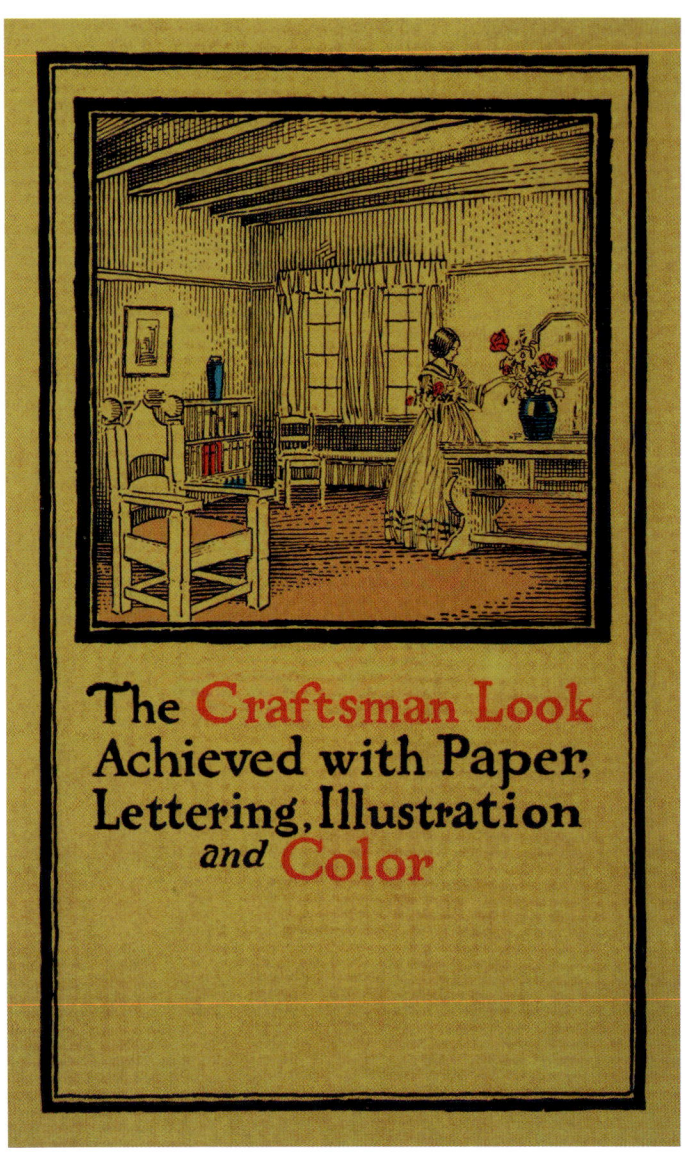

6. Illustration from advertising brochure for the Strathmore Paper Company, Mittineague, Mass., undated. (Courtesy Historic New England) Straight lines, right angles, and sturdy furniture contribute to the no-nonsense atmosphere of the Craftsman home. Yet the elegant young woman arranging flowers is not unlike the lovely aesthete pouring tea on the cover of Cook's *House Beautiful* (1877). The similarity between the two illustrations bespeaks the fascination of both the Arts and Crafts and the Aesthetic movements with Usefulness and Beauty.

7. Trade card illustrating "Aesthetic" vignette. Advertising Ephemera Box 13: 683. (Courtesy Baker Library, Harvard Business School) The plain, sturdy table demonstrates the influence of the Arts and Crafts movement, while the girl in Kate Greenaway–type attire, pouring tea into blue and white cups, shows popular Aesthetic touches. The spindly, rush-seat chair was evident in interiors of both movements.

8. Cover of a trade catalogue for Daniel Low & Co., Yearbook for 1927, cover signed by M. Woodbury (?), (published 1926). (Courtesy Historic New England) This delightful illustration caricatures an antiquarian examining the mark on the foot of a mug. Its composition mimics Cook's cover for *The House Beautiful*, even repeating the fireplace bellows with heart-shaped embellishment. The illustration documents the continuing importance of antiquarianism in New England, which Cook had promoted strongly in his book fifty years earlier.

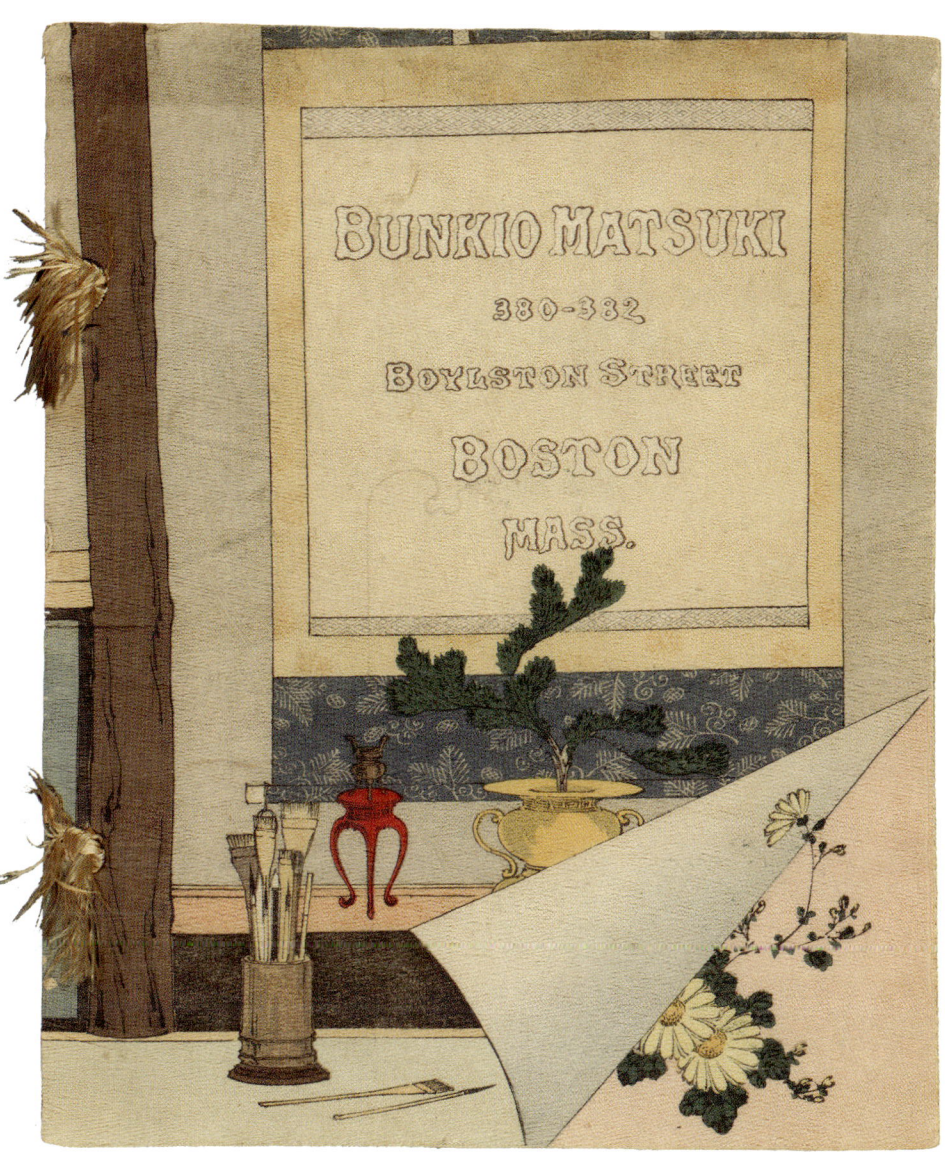

9. Cover of a trade catalogue for Buntio Matsuki, Boston. Bates Trade Card Collection, Box 9. (Courtesy Baker Library, Harvard Business School) This shows a recess, or "tokonoma," in a typical Japanese interior. A scroll features the store's name. Other important elements—discussed in E. S. Morse's *Japanese Homes and Their Surroundings*—include a rustic post, tripod table, incense burner, pot with bonsai plant, and bamboo brush holder. Bunkio Matsuki, aka The White Rabbit Store, was a key source for Japanese bric-a-brac and artists' supplies. Matsuki exhibited color woodblock prints under the auspices of the Society of Arts and Crafts.

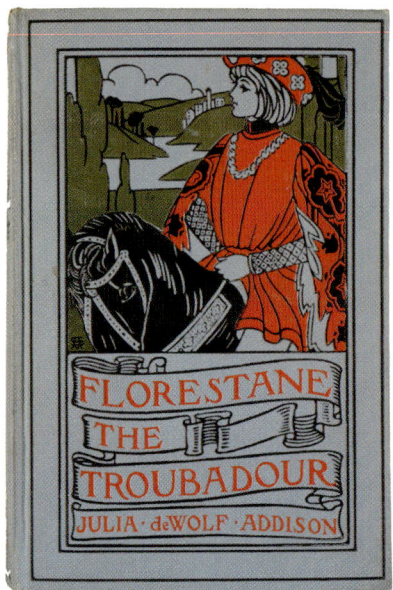

10. Book cover, by SACB Juror Amy Sacker, for Julia de Wolf Addison, *Florestane the Troubadour*, 1903. (Boston Public Library/Department of Rare Books. Courtesy of the Trustees) This joint effort between designer and author exemplifies the artistic collaboration that the SACB promoted among its members. Sacker's book covers were often narrative representations of the text, drawn with strong outlines, perspective depth, and attention to pattern and motif.

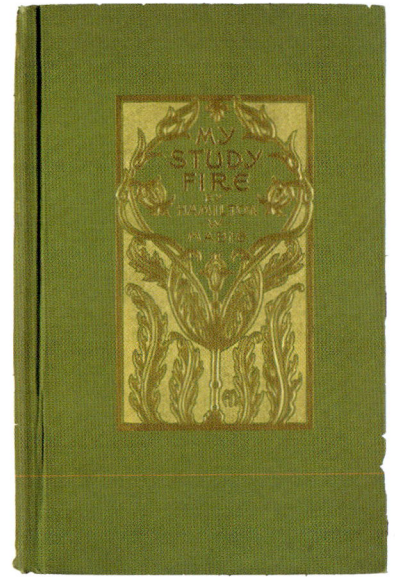

11. Book cover, by Alice Morse, for Hamilton W. Mabie, *My Study Fire* (Dodd, Mead & Company, 1899). (Boston Public Library/Department of Rare Books. Courtesy of the Trustees) This design demonstrates Morse's love of historic textiles. The central ogival motif appears frequently in Renaissance-era patterns, but the conventionalized poppy heads and sinuous stems owe more to Art Nouveau.

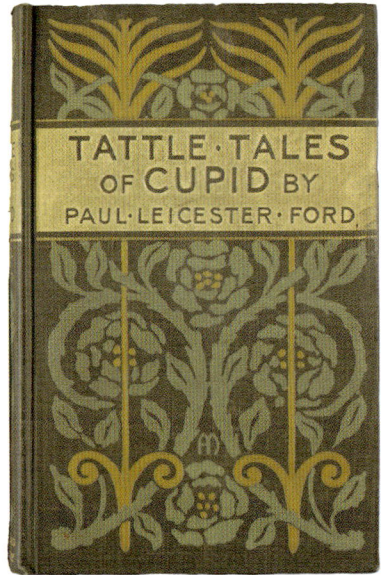

12. Book cover, by Alice Morse, for Paul Leicester Ford, *Tattle Tales of Cupid* (Dodd, Mead & Company, 1898). (Boston Public Library/Department of Rare Books. Courtesy of the Trustees) The scrolling stems, conventionalized roses, and palm fronds recall motifs from historic textiles, while the overall feeling of the composition is akin to flat patterns purveyed by Morris & Co.

13. Original study in oil of a marsh scene by Arthur Wesley Dow, undated. (Courtesy Historic New England) This flat plain, enlivened by a ribbon-like stream, is a favorite motif of Dow's, epitomizing the philosophy that he espoused in his book *Composition*.

14. Original study of a lily, by Arthur Wesley Dow, undated. (Courtesy Historic New England) Dow won a bronze medal at the Panama-Pacific Exposition for his wood engravings. Along with fine art prints, he also produced sets of more affordable "Ipswich Prints" that offered glimpses of flora and fauna along Boston's North Shore.

15. "Lily," by Arthur Wesley Dow (Ipswich Prints, Series F, Print 1), copyright 1901. (Courtesy Historic New England) The daylily was a ubiquitous feature of New England gardens, and the lily—in general—was one of the symbols of the Aesthetic movement.

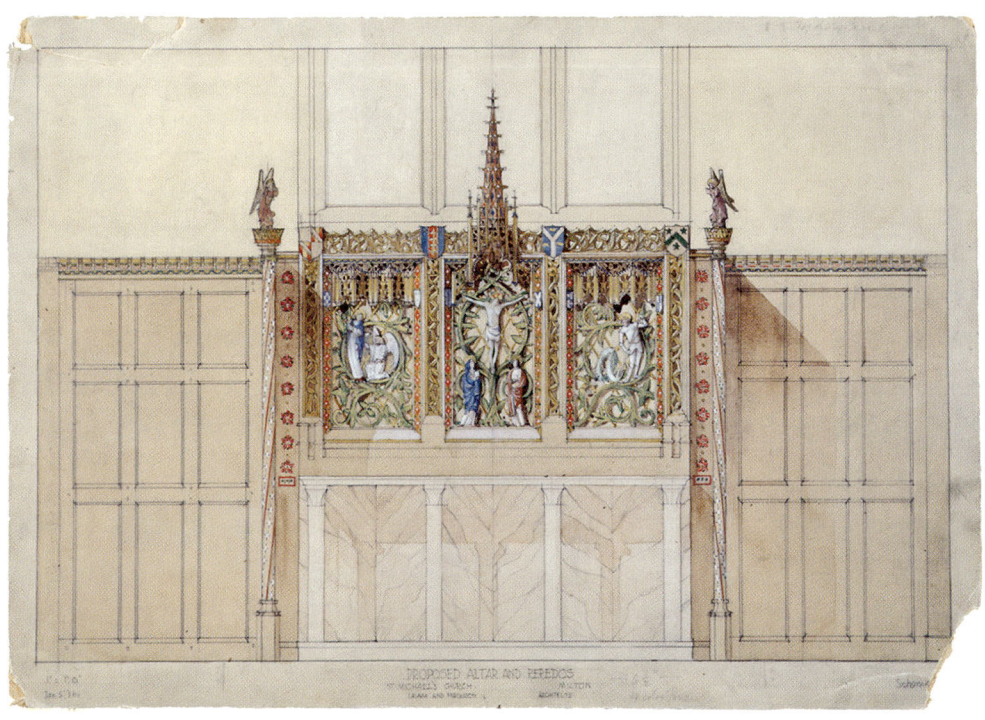

16. Architectural illustration in water media on tan board, by Alexander Hoyle, "Proposed Altar and Reredos," for remodeling of St. Michael's Church (Milton, Mass.), by Cram & Ferguson, ca. 1916. Cram & Ferguson Collection. (Boston Public Library/Department of Fine Art. Courtesy of the Trustees) This rendering reflects the firm's commitment to artistic collaboration, especially as it affected the finishing and furnishing of interiors. The design represents the firm's interest in the Gothic style, updated and simplified for the modern age.

17. Mr. and Mrs. Ralph Adams Cram's Christmas card, 1909. (Courtesy Historic New England) The card quotes the opening line from the carol "God Rest You Merry Gentlemen." The design combines a traditional diaper pattern that emphasizes the block "G," heraldic shields, and rows of tiny candles. Overall, it has the richness of a medieval illuminated manuscript.

18. "Willow Boughs," hand-blocked wallpaper, Morris & Co., ca. 1887. (Courtesy Special Collections, University Libraries, Arizona State University) "Willow," "Willow Bough," and "Willow Bough Minor" are all variations on a theme, incorporating stems and foliage in a subtle palette of yellow-greens and blue-greens.

19. Magazine cover, September 1994. (Courtesy *Home* magazine. Hachette Filipacchi Media U.S.) This quiet study, finished in a subdued palette of cream, green, and brown, incorporates straight-back Stickley chairs, blending an up-to-date attitude of environmental responsibility with nostalgia for the moralistic Arts and Crafts style.

CHAPTER FIVE

The Boston Diaspora
Promoting Boston's Standards of Usefulenss and Beauty Nationwide

> There is no excuse nowadays for anybody having ugly things. If they have them, they are themselves to blame, for they must have chosen ugliness and rejected, if not beauty and elegance, then simplicity.
> —Clarence Cook, *The House Beautiful* (1877)

The definitions of "Usefulness" and "Beauty" manifest in the work of SACB members resonated beyond Boston, the commonwealth, and the region. Within twenty years of its founding, the organization had attracted members from thirty states and nine foreign countries. By 1916–17, nearly 20 percent of members hailed from the Midwest, South, and Far West. Foreign members represented England, Ireland, Canada, Norway, Denmark, Mexico, and the Philippines, joining those from Italy and Switzerland who had become members at the start of the century. What began in 1897 as a small society with well-established Boston roots had grown by the time of the Great War into an organization of nearly a thousand members, spreading coast-to-coast and beyond. Though separated by distance, these members had a common dedication to promoting the gospel of "good design." Over the years, as the organization grew, some SACB members left Boston for other parts of the country or the world, either temporarily or permanently. As they traveled, lectured, or practiced beyond the city's confines, they constituted a diaspora, which gave the SACB national, and even international, influence. This scattering of members shared a common belief in Usefulness and Beauty, which proliferated as they dispersed.[1]

Members of this diaspora spread the gospel of "good design" in myriad ways. They participated in world's fairs, as visionaries, planners, architects, jurors, and exhibitors. Architects established wide reputations, designing buildings for diverse clients and uses. Educators indoctrinated students, who spread their respective philosophies as they moved across the United States. "He filled a great many vessels which were sent out into the world," William Fenwick Harris wrote of Charles Eliot Norton in 1908. But he was not the only SACB member and influential educator to do so. Many SACB members engaged in lecture tours that spread their influence from coast to coast, augmenting their written contributions to a plethora of publications. As societies of arts and crafts proliferated in America, the SACB served as a model, its members advising fledgling organizations firsthand.

184. Advertisement, from *Masters in Art: A Series of Illustrated Monographs*, April 1901 (Boston: Bates and Guild), p. 41. (Author's collection) Bigelow, Kennard & Co. specialized in jewelry, light fixtures, and gemstones, but it had one of the largest inventories of Grueby pottery. While it proudly purveyed local "art produce," it made certain—through ads such as this—that customers knew of Grueby's international reputation.

Craftsworkers showed their artifacts in exhibits around the nation and beyond, sold work in galleries across the country, and were honored to be included in museum collections here and abroad. Some SACB members remained in the Boston area despite frequent trips to other states or nations. Others relocated permanently, carrying the SACB's ideals into new communities.[2]

World's fairs—especially those taking place on American soil—were among the best opportunities for SACB members to promote the mission and ideals of their organization. Architects prepared site plans, designed exhibition halls, and exhibited renderings, models, and photographs of their work. Craftsworkers contributed works seen by thousands of visitors, gaining increased notoriety when they received grand prizes, gold, silver, or bronze medals, and coverage in the press. Visionaries helped with the planning, screening, and installation of works, while critics served on international juries-of-review. Those involved with selecting works beforehand or awarding prizes once the exhibition-competition had opened ensured that the standards upheld by the SACB, and its own Jury became influential within and beyond the nation.

The Louisiana Purchase Exposition

One event that illustrates the SACB's growing influence was the Louisiana Purchase Exposition, which took place in St. Louis in 1904. Members of the SACB were involved in the earliest planning stages of this world's fair, and, by the time of its conclusion, they had achieved international acclaim for their varied contributions. Many aspects of the Boston diaspora gained momentum as a result of the St. Louis world's fair; the event was a microcosm of the myriad ways in which SACB members achieved prominence across the United States and beyond.

This was not the first world's fair in which SACB members had participated. The Rookwood Pottery had contributed displays to the 1893 World's Columbian

185. Stereopticon slide, exterior, Palace of Fine Arts, Louisiana Purchase Exposition, 1904. (Author's collection) The Palace of Art, designed by Cass Gilbert, was one of the few fireproof buildings constructed at the time of the world's fair. It stands today at the core of the St. Louis Art Museum.

Exposition in Chicago. Several architects who later joined the SACB participated in that fair, including Lois Lilley Howe, Longfellow, Alden & Harlow, Edmund Wheelwright, C. Howard Walker, and Addison LeBoutillier, who "did some work in connection with the World's Fair" prior to moving from Chicago to Boston. Walker was responsible for designing several exhibition structures for the 1899 Trans-Mississippi Exposition in Omaha, and wrote an article about them for the *Century* magazine. The Grueby Pottery Co. exhibited its work—and won gold and silver medals—at the Paris (1900), St. Petersburg (1901), Buffalo (1901, Fig. 184), and Turin (1902) expositions. SACB members, including Rookwood and Grueby, participated in the Pan-American Exposition (1901), and Whiting attended it, although the SACB as an organization did not send work as "the cost proved greater than the probable results seemed to justify." C. Howard Walker designed the Massachusetts State Building in Buffalo.[3]

For American craftsworkers, the Louisiana Purchase Exposition was a particularly important event. For the first time at an international exhibition, the applied arts, or "original products of Art workmanship" as the catalogue described them, were segregated from machine-made goods. Their venue was neither the Manufactures nor Varied Industries buildings—locations where applied arts had been exhibited customarily—but rather the 224,000-square-foot Palace of Art, where they were intermixed with painting, sculpture, architectural renderings, photographs, and models (Fig. 185). Within the halls of this ivory temple, applied arts stood alongside fine arts, a testimony to the vision of the founders of the Arts and Crafts movement and the perseverance of its supporters. Organizers of the display were enthusiastic about its potential impact: they hoped that (as one of them quoted the words of Frederick A. Whiting) a "worthy and carefully selected" collection of applied arts would impress consumers and bestow a "new dignity" upon craftspeople, who would finally receive "proper recognition" for their work.[4]

During the first decade of the twentieth century, few cultural events in America overshadowed the Louisiana Purchase Exposition. In its eight-month lifespan, over twenty million visitors attended the fair, and most of those visited the display of American art. Captivating their attention were the fair's displays, its size, and its statistics: the expanse of the "Ivory City" encompassed more acreage than the earlier Chicago, Paris, and Buffalo expositions combined. Its fifty-million-dollar price tag exceeded by three times the cost of the event that the fair commemo-

186. Stereopticon slide, exterior, Electricity Building, Festival Hall, and Grand Basin, Louisiana Purchase Exposition, 1904. (Author's collection) The nine-acre Electricity Building (Walker & Kimball)—constructed of staff to resemble marble—housed displays documenting electrical technology and its application to modern-day appliances and transportation vehicles.

rated, the purchase in 1803 of the Louisiana Territory. The fair's two hundred fifty acres of displays, housed in some of the largest temporary exhibition structures ever built, comprised a veritable "encyclopedia of society."[5]

Organizers devised these displays to be as educational as possible, highlighting raw materials and works-in-progress alongside finished products, while celebrating the accomplishments of new technology. Critics compared the fair itself to an enormous "Machine, every part of which [was] interrelated with every other part, a tremendous moving picture of the art, the science and the industry of the age." In that progressive context, handicrafts were something of an anachronism.[6]

Major exhibition buildings were the products of "ten of the most distinguished architects [and firms] in the country," most of whom "had had experience in exposition work." Contributing architects included New Yorkers Carrère and Hastings (Manufactures Building), Cass Gilbert (Palace of Art and Festival Hall), and Chief of Design for the exposition E. L. Masqueray (Transportation and Agriculture Buildings). Local St. Louis practitioners were Eames and Young (Education Building), Barnett, Haynes and Barnett (Liberal Arts Building), Theodore C. Link (Mines and Metallurgy Building), and Widman, Walsh and Boiselier (Machinery Building). Boston's C. Howard Walker (Walker & Kimball) was responsible for the enormous Electricity Building, described by a critic for *Architectural Record* as "a scholarly performance," having a degree of "grandiosity" about it. "The building has a style of its own," Franz K. Winkler concluded, "and fills not unworthily its important space." Designing this impressive structure was only one of the many important contributions Walker made to the exposition (Fig. 186).[7]

The Division of Applied Arts: Classification and Selection

Using a scientific model, administrators "classified" all exhibits into categories, stressing commonalities among those within the same building, while acknowledging subtle distinctions from display to neighboring display. Within the Palace of Art, the unifying factor among all exhibits was that "Art [was] the predominating feature" and each object was "the original work of the artist, not a reproduction by another hand, [or] the result of any mechanical process." Beyond this commonality, organizers separated exhibits into six distinct categories and nineteen smaller classifications. This was not too different from the sort of classification system employed at the First Exhibition of the Arts and Crafts in Boston, or later alluded to by the SACB Jury.[8]

This classification system, more comprehensive than that used at any previous exhibition, reflected a perception on the part of administrators that "there should be no distinction between what commonly has been considered 'Fine Art,' and that which has been termed 'Industrial Art.' That all artwork—whether on canvas, in marble, plaster, wood, metal, glass, porcelain, leather, textile or other vehicle of expression—is equally deserving of respect in proportion as it is worthy from the standpoints of inspiration and technique." The system was intended by its breadth to correct "certain unjust conditions that [had] grown up in the art-world," such as the segregation of artists from craftspeople. By inviting contributions from American art workers, administrators for the Palace of Art acknowledged publicly the progress made in the previous decade by the design reform movement.[9]

187. Halsey C. Ives, chief, Department of Art, World's Fair, St. Louis, 1904. From Florence N. Levy, *American Art Journal, 1903–04*, vol. 4 (New York: American Art Annual, 1903). (Courtesy Boston Athenaeum)

The visionary behind the display of applied arts was Halsey Cooley Ives (1846/7–1911, Fig. 187), director of the St. Louis School of Fine Arts, and former chief of the Art Department at the World's Columbian Exposition. A champion of the arts and crafts, Ives had first tried to implement a similar classification system at the Chicago word's fair. But the apparent indifference of American craftspeople—who failed to submit handicrafts to the fine arts display—thwarted his efforts. In the fair's aftermath, Ives blamed their lack of participation on the fact that the American Arts and Crafts movement was yet in its infancy. American art workers, he explained, were unaware of the opportunity that such an exhibit offered.[10]

Ten years later, however, Ives felt encouraged when his call for entries for the Louisiana Purchase Exposition yielded a response far in excess of the capacity of the Palace of Art. To ensure that the final display would stress quality over quantity, he insisted that all entries undergo a strict selection process. Circulars for the Palace of Art emphasized that point. "In every department," they stated, "the aim is to secure productions of high character and to install them in a dignified, impressive manner." Above all, administrators wanted to avoid "crowd[ing] the structures with exhibits of inferior, average quality, with resulting indifferent effect." Ives knew enough about the current state of American arts and crafts to realize that standards of Usefulness and Beauty varied greatly.[11]

The Palace of Art, designed by architect Cass Gilbert (1859–1934), provided a noble setting for the collection that Ives sought to assemble. An ivory-colored Corinthian temple with elongated side pavilions (Fig. 185), it stretched along the brow of a hill, overlooking, and somewhat isolated from, the twelve-hundred-acre fairgrounds. (Following the overall concept of Chief of Design Emmanuel Louis Masqueray [1861–1917], C. Howard Walker was among those who had developed the site plan for the fairgrounds.) The main block of the U-shaped, classical palace was the only permanent, fireproof structure on the exposition grounds, a measure of its importance and that of its contents. Construction cost was approximately one million dollars. Its sober appearance, enlivened only by touches of pastel paint and hammered-copper giffin-shaped antefixae, reflected the conservatism of the displays within.[12]

Ives was the force behind the display of applied arts at St. Louis, but he chose Frederick A. Whiting to implement his ideas. This was a signal honor for the secretary of the SACB, and a reflection of his—and his organization's—growing national reputation. He was one of the most important links between the SACB and the exposition, a connection essential to the Boston diaspora. He served as "superintendent" of the applied arts division, taking a temporary leave-of-absence from the SACB. His strength was his network: he had contact with more contemporary American craftsworkers than possibly any other individual in the country.

Shortly after hiring Whiting, Ives advised him "to write to the leading art workers in the country at once, telling them if they have work in their possession of superior quality that has passed a jury of selection, you will be glad to make arrangements for its reception and installation." Stressing the importance of selectivity, Ives continued, "It is not our intention, to make an enormous collection of work, but rather a selected display of the good work—if there be such produced in this country." This last comment shows that Ives's confidence in the merits of the potential display was qualified.[13]

Whiting shared Ives's reticence. In an article published in the *International Studio*, he cautioned: "This awakened interest among both craftsmen and the public is a tremendous lever in safe hands, but, as in all such matters where untrained but well meant enthusiasm has to be dealt with, it can easily become an element of danger, if given too free a rein." Consequently, he and Ives exerted strong control over their division.[14]

Pressing deadlines warranted the urgency conveyed in their correspondence of late February. The fair was scheduled to open in early May, leaving Whiting only two months after being hired to gather a representative selection of arts and crafts from around the country. Complicating the job was the fact that few comprehensive directories of American craftsworkers existed at that time. Whiting's contacts through the SACB thus proved invaluable.

Whiting met Ives's challenge enthusiastically. He pledged "to do everything in my power" to make the display of applied arts "a credit to the Department and a matter of surprise and credit to the public." Ives encouraged him to "proceed in this manner as though you alone were responsible for the success of your Department." He also warned Whiting to be cautious in the undertaking. "There is so much fraud and froth indulged in under the heading of the Arts and Crafts," he wrote, "that one shudders at the mass of stuff that indiscriminate appeals might bring." With Ives's endorsement, Whiting had ultimate control over the applied arts display.[15]

The procedure for gathering work was far more complex than these early letters suggest. Striving to keep the selection process thorough and impartial, official regulations for the Palace of Art required that a regional "jury of selection" review each entry before it arrived at the exposition. Ives insisted that the jurors must be individuals "of acknowledged standing," and he assembled a distinguished group. The New York regional jury included sculptor William Couper (1853–1942), painter John La Farge, stained glass artist Frederick S. Lamb (1863–1928), designer Louis C. Tiffany, architect Stanford White, and painter and rugmaker Douglas Volk (1856–1935) of Center Lovell, Maine. Those for the Philadelphia region included Herbert E. Everett (1853–1935), a painter and professor of interior decoration at the University of Pennsylvania, the muralist Gustav Ketterer (1870–1953), and painter Emily Sartain (1841–1927). Sole juror for the West—defined at that time as California, Colorado, Utah, and Iowa—was painter and metalworker Charles Percy Davis (1858–1935), who worked at the St. Louis School of Fine Arts. Jurors for the Boston region were a subgroup of the SACB Jury: J. T. Coolidge, Jr., S. C. Sears, C. H. Walker, and Mrs. Frances C. Houston (1851–1906), a painter and jewelry maker. Whiting served ex officio on all regional juries.[16]

During the spring of 1904, jurors met in New York, Boston, Philadelphia, and St. Louis to review applications and rate accepted entries on a scale of one to three. Each accepted entry then went on to St. Louis, with the assurance that it would be displayed, space permitting. Should the total number of entries exceed space limitations, those designated "A. No. 1" would receive top priority during the installation process. Accompanying these items forwarded with regional jury approval were applications and "Information for Records" forms. On these, craftspeople listed each item submitted and described in detail processes used in its completion. Applicants noted with pride unique aesthetic or technical features for which they were known, and awards that they had won previously—especially at other world's fairs.[17]

The specific criteria used by jurors for accepting or rejecting entries are a matter of speculation. No record of their deliberations—such as meeting minutes or evaluation forms—exists, but articles written by Whiting, in which he described the review process, suggest that jurors serving on the regional selection committees modeled their procedures and standards after those used by the SACB Jury.

In his article "Arts and Crafts at the Louisiana Purchase Exposition" (*International Studio Supplement*, October 1904), Whiting argued that "the greatest weakness in the arts and crafts movement today" was its lack of a "recognized and uniform standard among the various societies." He explained that "work accepted by the jury of the Chicago Society" had been "rejected by the Boston Jury and *vice versa*." He mentioned how confusing this was to craftspeople, who tended to believe the less stringent jury to be the more accurate. Whiting used that anecdote to justify establishing a standard at St. Louis that was national and

188. Charles M. Kurtz, assistant chief, Department of Art, World's Fair, St. Louis, 1904. From Levy, *American Art Journal*, 1903–04, vol. 4. (Courtesy Boston Athenaeum) Kurtz famously referred to the handicrafts displayed in the Palace of Fine Arts as "art produce."

uniformly applicable. He suggested that such a standard was an outgrowth of the work of the SACB: "Those members of the Boston Society who have served on juries of selection which met in Boston, New York, Philadelphia and St. Louis have been gratified to notice how uniform the standard has been in the different cities and how nearly it coincides with that adopted by the Boston Society." He then quoted from the Society's statement of purpose to remind readers of its stringent conceptual, aesthetic, and technical standards.[18]

"Such restraints are irksome to many craftsmen," he continued, "who come to their work with no training, or very inadequate training in design, believing in their ignorance that, if they have the technical knowledge, inspiration will come for the design. They fail to realize," he noted, "that it is always the limitations imposed by materials and conditions, time and place, which mould the work; and the greater the restraints and limitations the more noble will be the result which rises superior to all difficulties and uses them to secure its own fair ends."

Challenges Facing Regional Juries-of-Review

Early in March, several members of the regional juries confessed disappointment at the quality of work submitted to date. One of these was the New Yorker Dr. Charles M. Kurtz (1855–1909, Fig. 188), Assistant-Chief to Ives, as well as Acting Secretary for the New York Commission on Fine Arts, and ex officio member of the New York regional jury for the applied arts division. In a letter, Kurtz summarized his impressions of the submissions that the New York jury had received. "The range of the exhibits," he wrote to Whiting, "covers a library table, designs for windows, clocks, boxes, tabourets, decorated porcelain, silk hangings, tapestry (1 piece with a modest valuation of $50,000 dollars,) [a] silk cushion, [a] looking glass frame, [an] electrolier, stenciled leather, embroidery, carved leather and other 'art produce.' I must say, the presentation is not particularly encouraging. I think you will find plenty to do if you undertake to form a creditable exhibit in this division." Months later, after Kurtz and his colleagues had worked vigorously to locate additional work from a broad range of New York–area artists, his enthusiasm increased.[19]

Motivated by such comments, Whiting initiated an aggressive personal campaign to locate suitable exhibits. In doing so, he violated the recommended procedures for the Palace of Art by becoming, in essence, a one-man jury and judge;

189. William Morris, *Pre-Raphaelite Ballads* (New York: A. Wessels Co., 1900), with illustrations by H. M. O'Kane. (Courtesy Special Collections, University Libraries, Arizona State University) Clarke Conwell ran the short-lived Elston Press (1900–1905), for which his wife, Helen Marguerite O'Kane, did illustrations in the spirit of Aubrey Beardsley. Occasionally—as in this case—Conwell sent his work to other presses to be printed.

but in this he had Ives's full support. Ives was as eager as Whiting to assemble a precedent-setting exhibit. Both were discouraged by the quality of entries submitted to date, but Ives encouraged Whiting "to go on and make the very best collection you possibly can within the space we have." Ives assured Whiting that he was "free to fill up the space . . . on invitation," and to approve and admit to the department "whatever [he] might deem of sufficient artistic value to justify its being shown." This was an opportunity for Whiting to apply everything he had learned by attending meetings of the SACB Jury and running the salesroom.[20]

This approach proved successful. By mid-March, the list of potential contributors to the applied arts division included printers, bookbinders, and potters with national reputations. Frederic W. Goudy (1865–1947) of the Village Press (Cambridge), Otto H. Zahn (1876–1952), bookbinder for S. C. Toof & Co. (Memphis), and representatives for the Grueby (Boston), Van Briggle (Colorado Springs), Newcomb (New Orleans), and Rookwood (Cincinnati) potteries all planned to contribute. Many of these craftspeople were personal acquaintances of Ives or Whiting. All but Otto Zahn were SACB members. Colleagues and officers of arts and crafts societies from around the country recommended others.[21]

Correspondence documents Whiting's use of flattery and peer pressure to solicit displays. He employed both to convince Clarke Conwell of the Elston Press (New Rochelle, N.Y.) to send in an exhibit for consideration (Fig. 189). Whiting assured Conwell that he would be part of "a fair representation of the best bookmaking being done in this country." He indicated that Conwell's work,

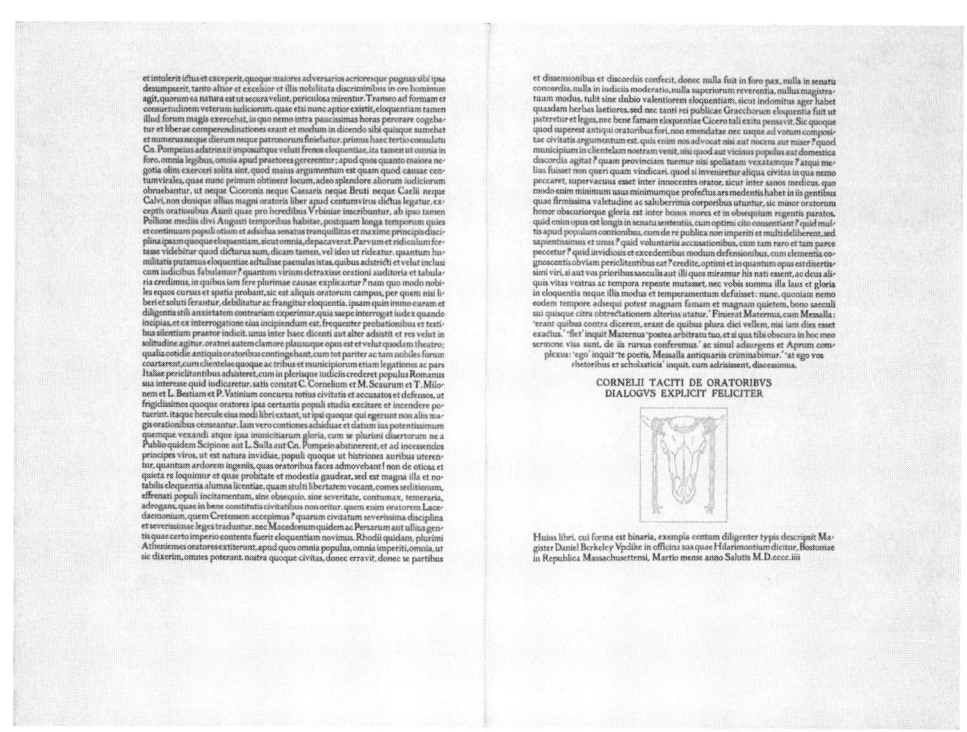

190. Pages from *Tacitus, Minor Works*, printed by Daniel Berkeley Updike at the Merrymount Press, 1904. (Boston Public Library, Department of Rare Books. Courtesy of the Trustees)

if accepted, would be in good company, since the display would include work representing three printers from Cambridge—"Mr. [D. B.] Updike [Merrymount Press], Mr. Bruce Rogers [Riverside Press] and Mr. Goudy of the Village Press." In his reply, Conwell explained that the Elston Press was "the only one in this country doing purely fine book work entirely by *hand*." He vowed to send to Whiting his "best" work.[22]

These four printers—all SACB members—contributed to an impressive display. Among the numerous volumes that D. B. Updike sent was a folio version of the *Minor Works* by the Roman historian Tacitus, described by Whiting as "a beautiful piece of work; the typesetting being perfect, and the margins, paper, and inking carefully studied and entirely satisfactory." This was a collaborative effort, including B. G. Goodhue, who had designed the "Merrymount" type, and the late Sarah Wyman Whitman, who was responsible for the cover (Fig. 190). Bruce Rogers displayed a collection of forty-one books and dummies including a "large folio Montaigne" that Whiting called "one of the most important achievements of modern printers." Goudy's display included the first three books produced by the Village Press, two of which featured writings by William Morris. The exhibition provided a rare opportunity for Conwell, who confessed: "A good deal of what I do is entirely unknown except to the comparatively limited number of those who buy the books." Whiting called several volumes by Conwell remarkable "for the excellent presswork."[23]

Work solicited "by invitation"—such as Conwell's—was nevertheless subject to review upon arrival in St. Louis. A special request from Whiting was no guarantee that a submitted piece would be among those objects ultimately installed in the Palace of Art. Predictably, this led to confusion and misunderstanding on the part of contributing craftspeople whose work was rejected in St. Louis. Responding to one such individual, Whiting wrote: "You can rest assured that you were not alone, in receiving unfavorable action by the Jury."[24]

Standards were especially severe in regard to ceramics. Early in February, Ives had complained to Whiting about "the great numbers of applicants for porcelain and various forms of pottery" that had deluged his office. He warned Whiting that ceramics, as a category, threatened to "overwhelm" the applied arts division unless regional juries were "rigid" in their evaluation. Ives's suggestion inspired

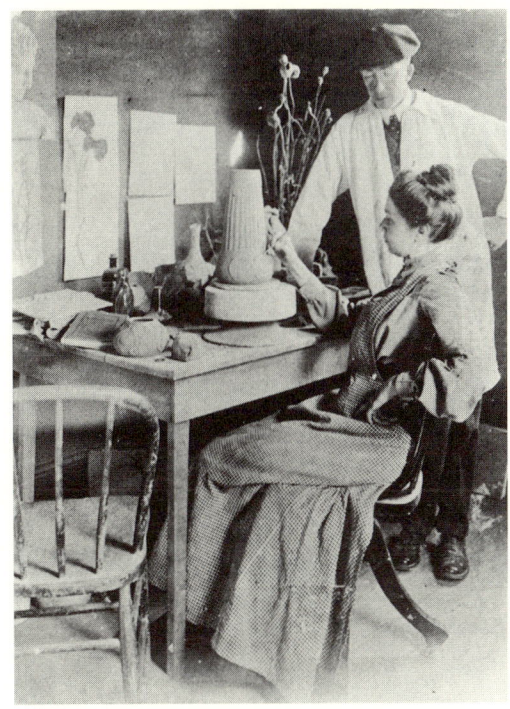

191. Portrait of Anne and Artus Van Briggle in their studio, ca. 1902–04. (Courtesy Colorado Springs Pioneers Museum) After Artus's death in 1904, Anne carried on their business.

Whiting to apply exacting standards to all entries regardless of source. As a result, he denied the Roseville Pottery Company (Zanesville, Ohio) a place in the Palace of Art altogether. Whiting justified this action by explaining that the "sample of pottery submitted [by Roseville] for consideration did not meet [jury] requirements." The Van Briggle Pottery—whose founders, Artus (1869–1904) and Anne (1868–1929), were SACB members variously from 1903 to 1926—was spared a similar fate, but had a much smaller showing than originally intended (Fig. 191). Whiting limited the number of pieces shown by the Van Briggles, since he felt that "their glazes and textures [were] often interesting, but in shape and decoration they seem[ed] . . . unusually bad or inappropriate."[25]

Even the Rookwood Pottery—whose prize-winning products were ubiquitous at international expositions—suffered near embarrassment because of Whiting's high expectations. He told Ives that he hoped to limit Rookwood's display to a group of "undecorated pieces" with "dull glazes," since he preferred them to the glossy "Indian head and flower vases which usually [made] up their exhibits" at most world's fairs. Accordingly, he wrote to the president of the company, William Watts Taylor (1847–1913), suggesting that he send for the jury's consideration "a collection largely made up of [such] undecorated pieces with lovely colors and textures."[26]

Taylor responded by assembling a varied group of sixty-three pieces that he deemed representative of the firm's best work. He was shocked subsequently to

192. Ernest Allen Batchelder, ca. 1918. (Courtesy Robert Winter)

learn that the jury had eliminated forty-eight examples upon their arrival in St. Louis. In exasperation, he wrote to Whiting and threatened to "withdraw the entire exhibit" from consideration. But he quickly changed his mind for fear that "it might in some way become public that Rookwood was rejected from the Fine Arts Dep[artmen]t and other potteries accepted." Eventually he and Whiting reached a compromise, but Rookwood had only a modest display in the Palace of Art. Whiting sent the bulk of the collection to the Palace of Varied Industries, the structure that housed manufactured objects "which have an artistic element in their composition." Rookwood was, consequently, one of several companies whose works appeared in multiple locations around the fairgrounds.[27]

Ernest Batchelder and Applied Arts of the West

The selection process was but one problem that Whiting encountered in securing exhibits for the applied arts division. Others were described by Ernest Batchelder (1875–1957, Fig. 192), a Boston-educated devotee of Denman Ross, ceramist, design educator, and founder of the Minneapolis Handicraft Guild (1902), whom Whiting appointed to gather entries from California and the Southwest. Though not an SACB member, Batchelder had strong ties to the organization. "I am sure there is very little good work in the state [of California] that has escaped inspection," he wrote to Whiting in April, but "the exhibit is not as notable as I had hoped." It "is typical of the work that is being done out here," he indicated, "and represents, with possibly two exceptions, the workers who are at all prepared for a display of handiwork." Among these were Isabel Austin, a leatherworker from Santa Barbara who showed an embossed and illuminated leather panel; May Mott-Smith (1879–1952), a painter, sculptor, and jewelry maker from San Francisco; Elizabeth Eaton Burton (b. 1869), who inlaid leatherwork with shell, or illuminated it with silver leaf; her father Charles F. Eaton (b. 1840s), whose "Arts and Crafts" shop in Santa Barbara submitted two small cabinets, illuminations, leatherwork, book bindings, and metal—some pieces trimmed with abalone; and Douglass Van Denburgh (b. ca. 1872), a metalsmith from Los Gatos and founder of the San Francisco Guild of Arts and Crafts. He submitted a brass candlestick. Burton, Eaton, and Van Denburgh, though not SACB members at the time of the St. Louis world's fair, joined the Society in later years. Writing of the impact of this group, Whiting said: "From California comes work which shows great promise and the possibility of new uses of materials."[28]

Another of Batchelder's assignments was to assemble a collection of Native American artifacts for the Palace of Art, in response to Whiting's argument that "some of the best crafts work done in the country is done among the Indians." Recognizing the uniqueness and quality of indigenous work, Whiting wrote to Batchelder: "Personally, I cannot see why the Indian should not be considered an artist craftsman as well as any other worker." Presumably Batchelder concurred, since he used illustrations of Native American artifacts in his books on design theory. A display of this type was an unusual addition to a turn-of-the-century art exhibit, but in character it was consistent with other displays scattered throughout the exposition grounds. Exhibits of Native American, Puerto Rican, Panamanian, and Philippine artifacts had been assembled to celebrate America's cultural heritage as well as its expanding, imperialist sphere of influence.[29]

The task of gathering Native American work proved less simple than either Whiting or Batchelder had anticipated. Pieces contained in private collections were subject to the conditions of protective owners, and merchants, who were unwilling to sacrifice potential sales for a period of twelve months, hesitated to contribute merchandise. "Collectors would not part with objects unless I would assume personal responsibility," Batchelder complained in a letter to Whiting, and "dealers were unwilling to deplete stock by sending away material for exhibition purposes." Batchelder finally found a merchant willing to contribute a sizable exhibit of "typical, contemporaneous Indian work." But he lamented to Whiting that "the best work in all lines of handicraft was done twenty to sixty years ago." This, he explained, had eliminated "many beautiful specimens of work which might otherwise have been secured," given an exhibition requirement that all work in the applied arts division must be contemporary.[30]

In the end, Batchelder obtained two collections of Native American artifacts for display. One stemmed from the noted ethnographer and collector George Wharton James (1858–1923). Many of the baskets sent by Wharton had served as illustrations in books, reports, and journal articles that he had written as founder and chief spokesperson for the "Basket Fraternity." The other came from the Wigwam Shop in Pasadena. Together they lent work of more than thirty-five individuals from the Hopi, Navaho, Zuni, and Pima tribes. Works consisted of eighty-five assorted textiles, baskets, and examples of jewelry. Visitors considered these to be among the highlights of the applied arts division.[31]

Batchelder's difficulties in gathering applied arts from California and the Southwest were typical of those that plagued Whiting on a daily basis. One problem was lack of participation because many craftspeople had already committed their best work to other shows and events taking place around the country. Another was withdrawal of approved entries by craftspeople who had a last-minute opportunity to sell their work prior to the opening of the exposition. Under such circumstances, a few sent substitutions to St. Louis, but the quality of these was often not up to the level of the piece originally approved. Of a substitute leather panel sent by Isabel Austin—described in the catalogue as an "illuminated and embossed leather panel, hand tooled over metal leaf and color"— Batchelder wrote disparagingly: "This panel is by no means as good either in design or workmanship as the one I selected, but [that,] unfortunately, found a purchaser. Mrs. Austin sent this one as her own next choice."[32]

Some craftsmen declined altogether Whiting's invitation to participate as his request for entries caught them off guard: they were unaware that an exhibit of handicrafts was to take place at St. Louis. They explained that they had on hand neither the type nor amount of work necessary to comprise a "creditable" display. The distinguished Chicago metalworker Robert R. Jarvie (1865–1941) was among those who declined to participate for this reason. Others were concerned about security within the Palace of Art. They were reluctant to submit work that might be stolen or damaged, especially if it had been borrowed from private collectors. None indicated outright that distance was a deterrent, but the collection overall was devoid of heavy, bulky items. The few examples of furniture listed in the official catalogue consisted of a desk and chair, representing William C. Codman (1839–1923) of the Gorham Company (Providence), a bridal chair carved after an antique Norwegian model by Karl von Rydingsvärd (New York), six pieces of oak furniture—in the Gothic and Elizabethan styles—sent by William L. Price (1861–1916) of the Rose Valley Shops (Pennsylvania), assorted carved wood picture frames by Boston's Hermann Dudley Murphy and Dawson Dawson-Watson of Winchester, Mass., and a jewelry casket—of cedar covered with sheepskin and trimmed with copper—by Charles F. Eaton (Santa Barbara). Price, Murphy, Dawson-Watson, and Eaton were all SACB members.[33]

The sheer size and duration of the exposition discouraged many artists from participating. Its scale might have delighted visitors and critics, but it intimidated artisans whose works were intended for quiet contemplation in intimate surroundings. Such was the case of bookbinders Ellen Gates Starr (1859–1940) and her apprentice Peter Verberg (b. ca. 1877), who were associated with Hull House in Chicago. Starr had helped Jane Addams to found Hull House, after returning from London, where she had studied bookbinding with T. J. Cobden-Sanderson. She justified their decision not to participate, explaining: "the St. Louis exhibition is so big and of so long duration that we, with our small numerical drawing [felt it would be] best not to do anything about it." Together, Starr and Verberg had "only about a dozen books now on hand which [they] could send to 'St. Louis,'" and they were concerned that such a small display would not be "enough to catch a wandering glance of people racing about such places" as the enormous Palace of Art. Like others, Starr and her partner—both SACB members at various times during their careers—were apprehensive about "the responsibility of borrowing books . . . sold or done to order" to augment their display. In addition, they admitted a general "weariness with the whole exhibition subject." They were involved continuously with shows "'til the end of May" and felt that "it [didn't] pay to keep one's things traveling about in [such a] way."[34]

Whiting regretted Starr's non-participation. He had struggled to assemble work representing the best "women bookbinders of the Country," and felt Starr would be conspicuous by her absence. Those he did interest in participating included Cordelia Taylor Baker (ca. 1868–1920s) of the St. Louis School of Arts and Crafts, Mary E. Bulkley (1856–1947) of Hillside, Missouri, Florence Foote (ca. 1870–1920s) of New York, Laura Hellman (b. ca. 1866) of St. Louis, Elizabeth Griscom Marot (1863–1930s) of Philadelphia, Emily Mott Shaw (b. 1848) of Boston, Gertrude Stiles (b. ca. 1875) of Chicago, and Mary H. Upton (1873–

193. *What Lies Beyond*, by Dawson Dawson-Watson, oil on canvas, 1936. (Courtesy Stark Museum of Art, Orange, Texas) Here Dawson-Watson interprets a desert landscape in a soft, impressionistic style.

1930s) of Philadelphia. Whiting was especially enthusiastic about the work of partners Mary Crease Sears and Agnes St. John, who, he explained, had "been working in Boston and London and Paris for several years, refraining hitherto from exhibiting their work, which [was] therefore known to comparatively few." He applauded their *Books of William Morris* for "both design and tooling (which is remarkable for its firmness and brilliance)," calling them "a shining example to the binders of this country."[35]

SACB member Ross Sterling Turner (1847–1915; Salem) echoed Starr's concerns. He sent a modest exhibit composed of just six specimen sheets from two illuminated manuscripts, though Whiting was evidently expecting something more substantial. Turner refused to send more work for several reasons: "I could not send my only copy of the Omar Khayyam Rubaiyat as I was not ready," he explained to Whiting. "Besides, I cannot hold it back from a possible sale for a year, and there is no possible hope—that anyone would buy it at a Great Exhibition—for all of these," he confessed, "I hold in little esteem as far as money goes—and one must *live*, if an artist." Though his display was small, Turner wished it to be shown to best advantage, and sent Whiting detailed installation instructions including a diagram, regarding the layout of his work in its assigned showcase, and proposed colors and construction details for mats. He also articulated concerns about lighting and atmospheric conditions that might affect his work.[36]

In contrast to those who had such reservations, other craftsworkers were eager to send work to St. Louis. "Thanks for my election," wrote Dawson Dawson-Watson (Fig. 193) upon learning that the jury had chosen two carved and gilded picture frames for display, "[and] may the Boston Section of the Arts & Crafts be a screaming success." These craftspeople believed that the benefits of exhibiting their work far outweighed any inconvenience or risk. They might be inspired by artistic ideals, but they were also motivated by the necessity of earning a living. They appreciated the widespread exposure they would receive as a result of participating at the Louisiana Purchase Exposition, believing it would benefit them as individuals as well as the organization that they represented.[37]

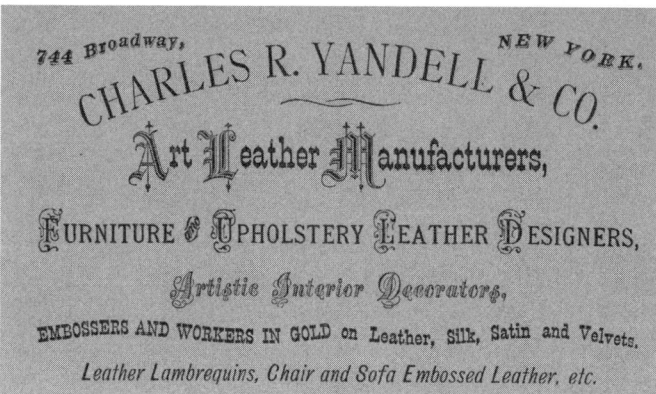

194. Stereopticon slide, Palace of Varied Industries, Louisiana Purchase Exposition, 1904. (Author's collection)

195. Trade card, Charles R. Yandell & Co., Art Leather Manufacturers, 744 Broadway, New York. (Courtesy Baker Library, Harvard Business School) As this card indicates, Charles Yandell manufactured a variety of household furnishings in embossed and gilded leather. Significantly, since she was studying the same craft, Mary Ware Dennett's sketchbook of her European tour, ca. 1898, made reference to Yandell in a note on the sketchbook's inside cover.

While most hoped to exhibit in the Palace of Art, others settled for showing their work in other locations. A few had displays in more than one exhibition structure, which proved confusing to visitors. These venues included the Manufactures, Varied Industries (Fig. 194), Mines and Metallurgy, and Education Buildings. The last was the first structure at a world's fair devoted exclusively to education. There Charles Fergus Binns showed student work from the New York State School of Clay-working and Ceramics. The Rookwood and Teco potteries had large displays in the Palace of Varied Industries, and the University Press (Cambridge, Mass.) exhibited in the Liberal Arts Building. Select objects of art workmanship were on view in the reception room of Ives's office suite, where they enlivened the interior decor. These "choice things"—such as a large leather panel by Charles R. Yandell (New York, Fig. 195)—were thus "available to the very class of people whom it [would] probably be the most profitable to have see [the] work."[38]

Usefulness and Beauty in the Palace of Art

When the doors to the Palace of Art opened—complications posed by a building contractors' strike notwithstanding—the American applied arts division boasted about one thousand examples of art workmanship. These represented the efforts of more than two hundred American craftsmen, including ninety-five women and about three dozen Native Americans. Despite the problems that Whiting encountered in gathering entries, critics praised the display as a "monument" to its organizers' "confidence in American genius to produce the beautiful and the useful."[39]

196a and b. Interior, Palace of Art, International Sculpture Hall. From Official Photographic Company of the Louisiana Pur-chase Exposition, *The Greatest of Expositions, Completely Illustrated* (St. Louis, 1904). (Author's collection) In these views, sculpture occupies the center section of the barrel-vaulted hall, while arched niches to either side display art objects in cases topped by architectural renderings and photographs.

The fireproof main block of the Palace of Art housed American arts and crafts, interspersed with paintings, sculpture, and architectural models, photographs, and renderings. "It has been made to embrace," wrote one journalist, "articles of virtue in which are manifest inspiration, reflection, and creative genius." Most of these sat in ebonized, illuminated cases, against backgrounds chosen to enhance their color or texture (Figs. 196a and b). Large items requiring natural side lighting hung near windows in corner galleries on the north side of the building. As a whole, the exhibit featured entries from every major craft category, including pottery, bookbinding, printing, leatherwork, woodworking, metalwork, jewelry, enamels, glass making, and fiber. To credit Whiting and his colleagues' efforts, the *Official Catalogue of Exhibitors* included a prominent footnote "acknowledg-[ing] the valuable services of the Society of Arts and Crafts of Boston in assisting to bring together the varied collection." Other publications included similar kudos.[40]

Stained glass windows were an important subgroup of the applied arts display.

197. Sarah Wyman Whitman, stained glass window, "America," or "Courage, Love, Patience," 1904. (Courtesy Schlesinger Library, Radcliffe Institute, Harvard University) The artist's description in the official catalogue for the St. Louis world's fair notes: "Conventional design—a Colonnade through which one looks out into the night. The decorative panels above represent, figuratively, America. The main part of the window is made of flat sheets of American glass, and is one, two and three thicknesses. The upper panels are made mainly of minute fragments of chipped glass; as many as 300 or 400 in each section. Paint is used nowhere in the window, except slightly in the heads and limbs."

198. Advertisement, The Harry Eldredge Goodhue Co., 23 Church Street, Cambridge, Mass., from *Exhibition of 1908, Galleries of the Boston Architectural Club*, 1908, p. 203. (Courtesy Boston Athenaeum) Harry Goodhue claimed to "despise opalescent glass." As his advertisement indicates, he based his work on Old World models, restricting himself to techniques used during the Middle Ages. This distinguished him from more avant-garde American stained glass painters and platers, who followed the lead of Louis C. Tiffany and John La Farge.

Those by the late Sarah Wyman Whitman, Harry E. Goodhue (b. 1873, younger brother of architect B. G. Goodhue), and others who were not SACB members—such as Peter Bell (New York), Frederick S. Lamb (1863–1928; New York), and Alfred Godwin (Philadelphia)—were built directly into the Art building's north, east, and west facades. Their permanency was a reflection of the "high standard" that they represented. Shipping these fragile windows to St. Louis—after constructing them to exacting specifications—was one of the many challenges weathered by these noted stained glass artisans. Mrs. Whitman's window—an allegorical representation of "America"—was the last completed before her death that year. (Today, it serves as a memorial to her within Radcliffe's Schlesinger Library; Fig. 197). Lamb's design evoked the "Spirit of the Revolution," while Bell's depicted "Loch Katrine." Goodhue (Fig. 198) showed two works, "The Presentation," and designs for the chancel decorations in Cram, Goodhue & Ferguson's Emmanuel Church (1902–04, Newport, R.I.). Godwin submitted four windows depicting the "Angel of the Annunciation," the "Virgin Mary," "Knights in Armour," and the "Angel Gabriel," described by the artist as incorporating "English antique glass painted with glass enamel, vitrified or fired." "The windows and panels by Mr. Godwin and Mr. Goodhue follow the English traditions," Whiting noted, "while those by Mrs. Whitman, Mr. Lamb, and Mr. Bell are in the American style, being varied enough in treatment to give an idea of its scope." He regarded the display as educational as well as aesthetically pleasing.[41]

Following the approach taken at the SACB's First Exhibition, documents for the applied arts division strove to identify everyone involved in the design or execution of works on display. In some cases this proved difficult, as when pieces were the product of workshops using a collaborative design and fabrication process. Some firms questioned why the name of individual workers took precedence over their company name in the catalogue. Keeping commercial interests—as well as artistic goals—in mind, several exhibitors wished to have brochures or circulars on hand, outlining where potential customers might purchase their goods in St. Louis, or how clients might order work in the future. Whiting discouraged this sort of commercialism, regarding the Palace of Art as an exhibition space—not a salesroom. "In the Department of Art," he explained, "we are trying in every possible way to dignify the product of individual artist's [sic] work." He promoted the applied arts first and foremost as works of art—not as consumer products.[42]

199. Vase, hand-thrown stoneware with drip-glaze, by Hugh C. Robertson, ca. 1896–1908. 7 1/4 in. tall and inscribed "Dedham Pottery HCR." (Courtesy Jim Kaufman) Robertson was a grand prize winner at St. Louis. This so-called Volcanic glaze has dramatic blood red and green coloration

As predicted, the collection of ceramics dominated the exhibition, despite Ives's campaign for selectivity. About four hundred examples of porcelain, pottery, and tiles illustrated the latest developments in the world's oldest craft. Objects came from New England, the Midwest, the South, the Rockies, and New York State. Contributors included the Grueby Pottery (Boston), and the Dedham, Merrimac (Newburyport), Marblehead, Rookwood, Gates (Terra Cotta, Ill.), Van Briggle, and Poillon Potteries (Woodbridge, N.J.). Newcomb College—directed by Ellsworth Woodward (1861–1939) in New Orleans—as well as the New York State School of Clay-working and Ceramics (Alfred, N.Y.) sent a large display of student work. Of the former, a critic for *The Chautauquan* wrote: "The achievements of the Newcomb College Pottery in New Orleans are in the highest degree an inspiration to other designers and a credit to the country." To the latter, Whiting offered a back-handed compliment, saying that many pieces would "appeal to those who care more for artistic feeling than for painstaking attention to technical perfection." Several individuals, including Louise McLaughlin (1847–1939) of Cincinnati, Henry C. Mercer (of Doylestown, Pa., Adelaide A. Robineau (1865–1929) of Syracuse, the English immigrant Louis M.

200. Anonymous, tile, Grueby Faience Pottery Company, 1900, white earthenware, 6 1/8 × 6 7/8 in. (Collection of Arizona State University Art Museum; Gift of Bellas Artes)

Solon (b. 1872) of New York, and Charles Volkmar (1841–1914) of Long Island, contributed exhibits regarded as superlative by critics and consumers alike. A majority of the displays had ties to the SACB.[43]

Significantly, this work attracted much attention in the press. Critics featured many of these individuals, schools, and potteries in articles that addressed their history, key personalities, and range of work, while providing a critical appraisal of items shown in St. Louis. Walter E. Gray discussed the Dedham display (Fig. 199), which included characteristic white crackleware with blue decoration, and select examples—called the "Twin Stars of Chelsea"—that featured a Chinese-inspired ox-blood glaze. "His crackle finish . . . is incomparable in its way, and the dragon's-blood effect of old Chinese pottery, so deep and rich in its tone, is to be regarded as one of the distinctive triumphs of American fictile art," Gray stated in his review for *Brush and Pencil*. "It is rather strange that a man so in love with the antique, and so bent on restoring to the world the secrets of antiquity, should yet have remained so closely in touch with the lovers of the beautiful to-day." Grueby's vessels, Whiting wrote, were notable for their "beautiful lines," "harmonious coloring," and "flowing texture of [their] surface." Ivan C. Waterbury, critic for *The Cosmopolitan*, added: "The most striking characteristics of the Grueby pottery are its dull mat glazes, in the greens, yellows, blues and grays observable in nature" (Fig. 200). Whiting commended Robineau and McLaughlin for showing "exquisite porcelains" that were "similar in body . . . but entirely different . . . in treatment and character." The Rookwood display featured designers Matthew Daly (1860–1937), Edward Diers, Magda M. Henermann, Edward T. Hurley (1869–1950), Frederick Sturgis Laurence (active 1895–1904), Laura E. Lindeman (1873–1967), Marianne Mitchell (active 1901–05), Fred Rothenbusch (1876–1937), and Harriet E. Willcox (1886–1930s). Most Rookwood vessels had floral or naturalistic subject matter, depicted in a variety of glazes. "The ware," wrote Waterbury, "has always been characterized by a mellowness of tone and a soft brilliancy." That the ceramic arts should attract such attention demonstrates the widespread appeal of the Arts and Crafts movement in 1904. That SACB members should be recognized as prominent contributors to this medium testified to the fundamental role played by the SACB at this world's fair.[44]

The collection of metalwork and jewelry rivaled the display of ceramics in both size and splendor. Exhibits included the decorative and utilitarian, the secular and ecclesiastical executed in a wide range of materials and techniques. Work represented individuals from different sections of the country who had sent just one or two choice pieces, as well as members of collaborative workshops such as

201. Writing table in Art Nouveau style, by William Christmas Codman, for Gorham Manufacturing Company, ebony, ivory, and silver, ca. 1904. From *The International Studio Magazine* (supplement), 23 (1904)

the Kalo Shop (Chicago), and Handicraft Shop (Boston). The main attractions, however, were three large displays featuring the work of William Christmas Codman of the Gorham Manufacturing Company (Providence); F. Walter Lawrence (New York), a worker in "rare stones, jewelry, and silverware"; and Paulding Farnham and Louis Comfort Tiffany of Tiffany & Co. (New York). None were SACB members, although Codman and Tiffany had exhibited in Boston 1897 and 1899.[45]

In an article titled "The Arts and Crafts" in *World's Work*, critic Herbert S. Houston noted enthusiastically: "The Gorham silversmiths . . . have again shown by their exhibits that their work is the standard for measuring what America is doing in combining art with craftsmanship." He went on to discuss Codman's "Martelé"—pieces reflecting the Art Nouveau style: "In the designs there is so much of artistic distinction, of quickening individuality—all bearing witness to the wisdom which has made the Gorham factories schools of freedom." Houston found especially captivating Codman's Art Nouveau–style writing table, chair, and assorted desk accessories. In his application, Codman had described the furnishings as "constructed of Ebony, Ivory and Silver mountings with Marquetrie panels composed of Ebony, Ivory, Pearl and Silver, Mahogany and boxwood, Chair; Ebony, Ivory and Silver with embossed leather seat" (Fig. 201). Accessories included a desk pad, check cutter, eraser, paper knife, pen wiper, paper rack, tray, seal, tape holder, match vase, letter clip, paper knife, and two pen holders. The splendor and comprehensiveness of this ensemble captivated the attention of visitors and the press.[46]

The display from Tiffany & Co. filled adjoining galleries near the northeast corner of the Art Palace, and was required viewing for any passer-by. Installers had hung the walls "with a brocade of neutral green," providing an elegant backdrop for five cases of jewelry, Favrile glass, pottery, enamels, and metalwork from the Tiffany Furnaces. These were the focus of each room, complemented by a few "watercolors, oil paintings and illustrations carefully selected to preserve the artistic impression of the room as a whole." A corps of armed guards—hired by Tiffany & Co.—protected a display exceeding $8,000 in value (in 1904 dollars), while supervising crowds that filled the gallery.[47]

Critics remarked especially upon Tiffany's Favrile glass. "In its grace and uniqueness of design, in the richness and iridescence of its colors, it represent[s] a refinement of taste and an attainment of the beautiful rarely if ever equaled in the art industries," noted James L. Harvey. Whiting pointed out the "delicious harmony" evident in Tiffany's lamps and shades, as well as their "practical use combined with tasteful form." He was not, however, as kind in his critique of Paulding Farnham's section of the Tiffany & Co. display: "The case of work . . . shows the extent of mechanical perfection to which such expert specialists as those employed by Tiffany and Company can go, and, in contrast with other silver work exhibited by individual workers, gives an excellent illustration of the loss which must result where work is passed through the hands of a number of workers, no matter how experienced. What is gained in mechanical perfection" through this division of labor, he pointed out, "is lost in the artistic 'feeling,'— that quality which cannot be described, but which is the most important element in a real work of art to those who value things from other than the commercial standard." In his critique of the exhibition, Whiting took every opportunity to educate visitors on the relative merits—or demerits—of each display.[48]

The Tiffany collection was but one of many costly exhibits in the applied arts division. The value (in 1904 dollars) of William C. Codman's inlaid silver desk, chair, and assorted silver desk accessories was around $25,000. F. Walter Lawrence's twenty-seven pieces of historicist gold jewelry—some set with two-thousand-year-old Cyprian glass fragments—were insured for over $3,000. Hugh C. Robertson's collection of Dedham pottery included the thousand-dollar pair of *sang-de-boeuf*-glazed vases known as the "Twin Stars of Chelsea." The late Sarah Wyman Whitman's stained glass window, "America," was valued at $3,000 and graced one of the Tiffany & Co. galleries.[49]

Bookbinder Otto Zahn (represented by S. C. Toof & Co., Memphis) contributed the single costliest exhibit. It featured twenty-five volumes on diverse subjects—poetry, philosophy, historic architecture, and politics—finished with French *levant* leather, tooled with gold leaf. Their collective value was $32,000. Zahn's private patrons—W. K. Bixby, F. W. Lehman, Judge Klein, and A. L. Hollingsworth— had loaned most of these, but the bookbinder willingly accepted the risk of exhibiting them in return for potential publicity. "The sole object a business firm can have in exhibiting at an Exhibition," he explained to Ives, "is the bringing of the product and the facilities of the exhibiting firm before the buying public. For them, an exhibition is to be a medium of advertising the excellence of their goods by ocular demonstrations." He reiterated this point in a letter written a few days later: "All the advertisement we care about consists in the bringing before the public's eye our best efforts in the way of art binding." His intention was to show "what we are doing," which, he argued, was far superior to merely "advertising to the world what we can, would or could do." Zahn argued with Ives and Whiting at

 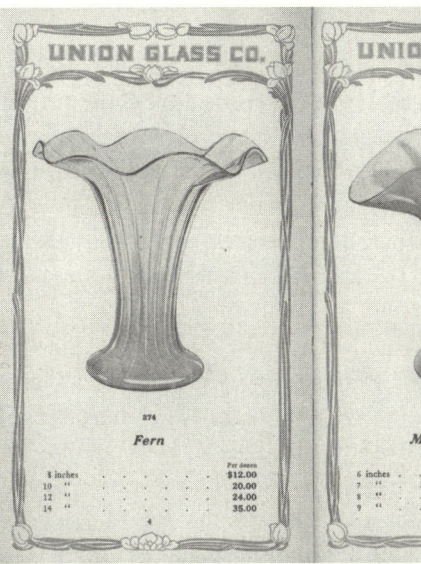 

202. Cover, trade catalogue, Union Glass Co., Somerville, Mass., undated. (Courtesy Historic New England) Many pieces of glassware from the Union Glass Co. showed the influence of Art Nouveau.

203. "Fern" and, "Morning Glory" vases, from a trade catalogue for the Union Glass Company, undated. (Courtesy Historic New England)

every turn regarding advertising, and using the company versus individual names in the catalogue. At the same time he questioned the proposed installation. Whiting ultimately gave in to some of Zahn's demands because of his firm's reputation for excellence and Whiting's wish that it be represented in the applied arts division.[50]

The value of such *objets d'art* suggests that they were unique masterworks, designed to illustrate a craftsperson's most advanced conceptual, aesthetic, and technical abilities. As such, they satisfied the public's preference for viewing at world's fairs only the "very novel" or the most "artistic effect." But their price was clearly beyond the reach of most visitors to the Palace of Art, who could do little more than admire from a distance the refined designs, expensive materials, and skilled craftsmanship. George Iles, writing for *World's Work*, looked forward to future exhibitions that would feature exhibits more suited to low-, or lower-middle-income families. He hoped to see completely furnished model homes, "adorned in good taste and with good sense," keeping in mind such necessities as "wholesomeness, durability, and maintenance."[51]

A few displays in the applied arts division featured items that the average consumer might purchase, and many took them home as souvenirs when the exhibition closed. Among these were "Empire" and "Italian" vessels and stemware from Julian de Cordova's Union Glass Company (Somerville, Mass.), which sold for just a few dollars each (Figs. 202 and 203); pottery and tiles representing Henry Chapman Mercer's Moravian Pottery, and "Teco" dishes and vases from the Gates Potteries that ranged in price from about two to twenty dollars. Of Mercer's tiles, Whiting wrote: "No one who has struggled to find something good in an ordinary tile wareroom can fail to be impressed by their charms." Mercer showed sixty cases of set tiles, along with mugs, sconces, and boxes, selling every piece of pottery by the exhibition's close. The Teco pottery exemplified the company's goal, "to produce a ware that in beauty of line and exquisite quality of color . . . conform[ed] to the highest art standard and still [came] within the range of the average purse." Displays like these inspired one writer to label the applied arts exhibit "democratic" in its appeal, and a true manifestation of William Morris's ideals.[52]

Consumers' and Jurors' Reactions

Visitors to the fair eagerly purchased such inexpensive "art produce," and sales demonstrated that arts and crafts exhibitions could be lucrative for participants. A few museums purchased pieces from the applied arts division for their permanent collections—a distinct honor for the craftspeople whose work they chose. In this way, the products and philosophy of the Art and Crafts movement remained before the public eye long after the exposition closed in November. And the work of SACB members found a new national and international audience.[53]

Sales were but one measure of success. There were some skeptics, but critics in general praised what they saw. Writing for *Scribner's*, Will Hickok Low—renown mural painter (1853–1932) and one of the administrators for the Palace of Art—admitted to being "surprised and charmed by the quantity and quality of the work" being produced by American craftsworkers. Frederic C. Howe (1867–1940), lawyer, economist, and journalist for *The Cosmopolitan*, viewed the exposition as an "expression of the West" and a reflection of the "disappearance of the frontier." He went so far as to predict that the display at the Palace of Art would prompt an eventual shift in artistic focus within the United States from the East Coast to the West.[54]

Like most world's fairs, the Louisiana Purchase Exposition was both an exhibition and a competition. SACB members participated as jurors, and fared well as competitors. Members of the international jury-of-review included C. Howard Walker (who served as chair), F. A. Whiting (secretary), Lockwood de Forest (New York), E. A. Batchelder (Pasadena), Charles Percy Davis (St. Louis), Mrs. Eugene Field (Buena Park, Ill.), and eight others who represented foreign countries. At their recommendation, SACB members from around the country received most of the major awards. Grand prizes winners were Henry Chapman Mercer (pottery and tiles), Hugh C. Robertson (ceramics), and Bruce Rogers (printing). Of the eight gold medal winners, five were SACB members: Agnes St. John (bookbinding), Mary C. Sears (bookbinding), D. Berkeley Updike (printing), Artus Van Briggle (ceramics), and William H. Grueby (ceramics). Of the sixteen silver medal winners, eleven were SACB members: Charles F. Binns (ceramics), Francis Barnum (metalwork and jewelry design), William Fuller Curtis (burned and carved wood), Harry W. Dudley (bookbinding), J. Samuel Hodge (bookbinding), Frederick Krasser (ironwork), Joseph F. Meyers (pottery), Thomas E. Nickerson (pottery), Arthur J. Stone (metalwork), William P. Kendrick (for collaborations with W. H. Grueby), and Addison B. LeBoutillier (ceramics). Of the twenty-one bronze medal winners, seven were SACB members: these included Clarke Conwell (printing),

Charles F. Eaton (mixed media), Frederick W. Goudy (designs for printing), Mary C. Knight (metalwork), Adolph C. Kunkler (metalwork), Elizabeth G. Marot (bookbinding), and Emily Mott Shaw (bookbinding). As a group, these prizewinners represented most media and every region of the country. Despite such diversity, however, these awards reflected the nationwide dominance of the SACB's standards for Usefulness and Beauty. F. W. Coburn noted "the Society of Arts and Crafts had to congratulate itself when the list of awards was published for the first time in the United States in the Boston *Herald*."[55]

Some craftsworkers protested their awards. One of these was Clarke Conwell. Unaware that the exhibition was also a competition, he declined accepting his third-prize bronze medal: "To my mind, the nature of the exhibits prohibits competition," he wrote Whiting in December 1904. "It would be quite as absurd to say that one man's productions in such a field are 'better' than another's as to say that Burne-Jones' woodcuts are 'better' than Whistler's etchings or vice versa." With that argument, he resigned from the SACB, saying "I can't see that it is doing me much good," a surprising conclusion given that he had won a medal and gained international exposure at his first major public exhibition. Had he not been a member of the SACB, Whiting might not have invited him to participate in the first place. Yet Conwell did not seem to value his connection with the organization.[56]

Another disgruntled participant was Ellsworth Woodward (of the Tulane University/Newcomb College Art Department), who lobbied Whiting to ensure that his assistant, Mary G. Sheerer, won a prize for her entry: a pottery lamp with a shade fabricated of "transparent beads upon brass gauze." Woodward regarded this lamp—which received extensive coverage in the press—as the "most distinguished product of the Newcomb Pottery to date," calling it "one of the most satisfactory and workman-like bits of handicraft that I have yet seen from any source." Though one of Sheerer's Newcomb colleagues, Joseph Meyers, won a silver medal for his "vase with red metallic glaze and modeled decoration," Sheerer was left empty-handed. Woodward rose to her defense, telling Whiting: "You know perfectly that Miss Sheerer's services to Ceramic art are such that coupled with her excellent exhibit, she deserves a handsome award." Despite such lobbying—"You simply must get her a medal"—Whiting could not or would not comply.[57]

Undaunted by these and other difficulties, Whiting remained convinced of the overall merit of the display of applied arts. He credited the regional review process with "set[ting] a standard which comes nearer to being national in its judgment than any which has heretofore existed." That standard, he argued, was one that "no section of the country can call local or provincial," one that would continue to ensure conceptual, aesthetic, and technical consistency among American arts and crafts in the aftermath of the exposition. It was a triumphant moment for the SACB.[58]

David R. Francis (1850–1927) concurred. The mayor of St. Louis, who went on to an international political career, he was responsible for bringing the fair to St. Louis. In his monograph devoted to the history and long-term implications of the world's fair, he emphasized that "the task of making selection of the best among those art works of various kinds offered for display was even more serious and more difficult than that of interesting prospective exhibitors." In an effort to assemble "a collection of art objects unparalleled in comprehensive and representative character," he credited the jury process with "preserv[ing] the highest standard of excellence among the accepted exhibits," and striving to "eliminate any possible shade of partiality."[59]

Other writers supported these points of view. Ives had predicted before the fair opened: "We believe that at St. Louis the American people will realize fully, perhaps for the first time, that the instinctive impulse for artistic expression in various forms of art work is a growing force in our land, and one likely to have no small part in our national development." In its aftermath, Will Low felt that the jury system had resulted in a breadth and depth in American art not seen before at an international exhibition. "Since freedom from tradition in the hands of men whose work is based on a sound technical foundation may be counted as an asset, the future would seem to be full of promise," he noted optimistically.[60]

Whether the standards set at St. Louis were uniform, objective, comprehensive, and national is questionable. Almost half of the exhibitors were from the northeastern part of the United States, and nearly 50 percent of these were members of the SACB. Rather than providing an impartial overview of the state of American craftsmanship in the year 1904, the applied arts exhibit featured costly masterpieces from a specific geographical region, produced by members of a single organization, and reflecting a very conservative approach. Nevertheless, it was a testimony to the strides made by the SACB in just seven years.[61]

The exhibit attracted critics' approbation regardless. Both the national and international press wrote about the applied arts division enthusiastically. Ceramics, metalwork, artistic printing, and stained glass, as well as portraits of individual craftspeople and companies were the subjects of feature articles in a wide variety of publications. David R. Francis made a point of including quotes from foreign critics in his discussion of the American art section: "The exhibit was, indeed, such as to excite extra ordinary comment, some of which may be considered of special significance as coming from the principle [sic] foreign experts in charge of competitive exhibits." A Dutch critic called the American section "the best displayed in the whole international collection of art," while a German professor noted the "great artistic advance . . . apparent . . . in every field of art achievement" throughout the United States.[62]

Writing of the applied art division specifically, Francis called its "educational value . . . second to none in the Exposition. It gave many thousands a first knowledge of what might be done in the way of beautiful handiwork and to many more a first realization of the great development of artistic quality of applied art productions reached during the past few years. The large scale upon which applied art objects were displayed and the constant expressions of appreciation and interest and pleasure by purchasers and those inquiring regarding exhibits," Francis stated, "constituted conclusive evidence of the important part conceded to the applied art exhibit by the most intelligent visitors to the United States section." Whiting and his SACB colleagues could claim responsibility for much of its success.[63]

204. Decorative sketch, "Jeanne D'Arc," George H. Hallowell, from *Catalogue of the Architectural Exhibi-tion*, Boston Architectural Club (1902), p. 55. (Courtesy Boston Athenaeum) Despite its realism, this portrait uses some of the traits of conventionalization—flatness and strong outlines—giving it a decorative quality suitable for a book illustration, stained glass window, or mural.

205. Book cover, by George H. Hallowell, for *Low Tide on Grand Pré, A Book of Lyrics by Bliss Carman* (Cambridge: Stone and Kimball, 1894). (Boston Public Library/Department of Rare Books. Courtesy of the Trustees) Relying almost entirely upon line, this scene of three irises, floating against a full moon, and above a tangle of sinuous stems and leaves, blends Asian and Art Nouveau sensibilities.

SACB Artists and Architects at St. Louis

The division of applied arts was not the only section of the fair to which SACB members contributed work. Several were accomplished artists and showed their paintings as well as crafts in the fine arts division. Hermann Dudley Murphy entered four works, including a portrait "distinguished by great subtlety of handling and dignity of pose," according to Boston artist Jean N. Oliver (1883–1946), who wrote a review for the *New England Magazine*. Such paintings complemented Murphy's collection of carved wood picture frames, representing the Carrig-Rohane Shop. Oliver described George H. Hallowell (1871–1926) and Joseph Lindon Smith (1863–1950) as "among Boston's young painters whose pictures are immediately notable in the present exhibition." (Hallowell also worked as a graphic designer; Figs. 204 and 205) Of Sarah Choate Sears Oliver stated: "[She] is represented by two portraits in pastel [one of which was illustrated in the article] and three watercolors, distinguished by broad sure qualities of color and drawing." Calling attention to Sears's versatility, Oliver noted: "Another field of endeavor in which she excels is that of decorative metalwork." Oliver described Frances C. Houston's painting "Indian Summer" as "perhaps the best of her later works . . . full of charm and poetic feeling," though she did not mention the silver buckle and pendant that Houston displayed as part of the jewelry exhibition. (The following year, Houston had a one-woman show at Boston's St. Botolph Club.) Like Houston, Harold B. Warren (brother of H. Langford Warren) and Dawson Dawson-Watson were also among those SACB members who showed works of fine art as well as applied art. Murphy, Sears, and Houston all participated on juries of review for the exposition.[64]

In addition to taking part in site planning and building design for the exposition,

SACB architect members displayed numerous drawings, renderings, models, and photographs of their work in the Palace of Art. A few—Robert D. Andrews, Guy Lowell, H. Langford Warren, Edmund M. Wheelwright—served on the Architecture Advisory committee. Of the seventy-two individuals or firms that contributed works to the architectural exhibit, ten were SACB members. These included principals in the following firms: Andrews, Jaques & Rantoul, Charles K. Cummings, George P. Fernald, Lois Lilley Howe, A. W. Longfellow, Jr., C. Howard Walker, Warren, Smith & Biscoe, Wheelwright & Haven, and Winslow & Bigelow. The renowned landscape architectural firm Olmsted Brothers (Frederick Law Olmsted, Jr., was an SACB member from 1908 through 1910) also participated.[65]

Francis summarized the exhibit's contents: "The collection of displays submitted embraced a large variety of designs, illustrating the different styles of architecture as applied to structures of varying character and size, and setting forth in faithful reproduction the details of exterior and interior treatment and decoration. A number of water colors as well as numerous superior photographs were presented in addition to drawings. Examples of public, private and commercial buildings, reflecting the latest achievements, were submitted," he noted, "also many examples of landscape architecture, all of which reported the marked progress made in the country since 1893." Architects who were also members of the SACB were not the only ones from Boston or Cambridge contributing to this display. Charles Collins, Kilham & Hopkins, Little & Browne, Parker & Thomas, Peters & Rice, Shepley, Rutan & Coolidge, and George T. Tilden augmented the group. Some of these practitioners—such as Little & Browne—were clearly influenced by the Aesthetic movement and the Arts and Crafts movement, but chose not to support the SACB. Their sympathy with the design reform movement, but lack of participation in the Society, is a topic deserving further research.[66]

Aftermath of the Exposition

The Louisiana Purchase Exposition was, clearly, an important forum for members of the SACB. It was an event that pushed them and their organization to the forefront of the American campaign for design reform. Visible as visionaries, planners, and architects for the fair's infrastructure, acclaimed for their contributions to the United States section in the Palace of Art and to exhibitions in other buildings, persuasive on juries-of-review, outspoken as critics, and opinionated as judges distributing prizes and medals, these individuals ensured that the gospel of "good design" manifested itself throughout the exposition.

One effect upon the SACB after the exhibition closed was an increase in membership of 30 percent. A majority of those who joined in the 1904–05 period—when membership increased from 335 to 472—were Craftsmen and Associates. With the increased membership came a need to expand the salesroom. In July 1904, the SACB moved from rooms leased from the Twentieth Century Club to a new headquarters located at 9 Park Street—the former home of the notable scholar George Ticknor (1830–1871)—which stood in close proximity to the

206. Decorated bowl, by Maud Masson, ca. 1907. (Courtesy SACB Archives) Maud Masson, who lived in New York City, was an SACB member between 1907 and 1927. This bowl conforms to the tenets of conventionalization informed by naturalism.

207. Candlestick, by Elizabeth Ethel Copeland, Boston, ca. 1917, silver with enamel decoration, 18.73 × 10.48 × 10.48 cm. (7 3/8 × 4 1/8 × 4 1/8 in.). (Courtesy Museum of Fine Arts, Boston; Gift of the Seminarians in honor of J. E. Robinson III, 1997.56)

Robert Gould Shaw Memorial, the Statehouse, the headquarters of Houghton, Mifflin & Co., the New-England Women's Club, the Union Club, and the Doll & Richards art gallery. "The wisdom of the step was shown," recalled Whiting in 1910, "by an immediate increase in the amount of sales," almost tripling from $13,298 (in 1904) to $37,150 (in 1905). "The reputation of Boston," wrote F. W. Coburn a few years after the St. Louis world's fair, "as a city where the arts and crafts are appreciated has given rise to a very general desire among craftsmen in all parts of the country to meet the conditions and become members, explaining this surge in membership."[67]

The St. Louis world's fair was not the last in which SACB members participated, though involvement at later events was relatively limited. Goodhue designed buildings for the Panama-California Exposition (San Diego, 1915), and others contributed to its sister fair, the Panama-Pacific Exposition, held that year in San Francisco. Whiting's successor, H. Percy Macomber, served on the international jury-of-review. Grand prize winners were A. A. Robineau (pottery) and L. Averill Howland (bookbinding); medals of honor were given to Laura C. Hills (1859–1952) for her miniatures and to the Fulper Pottery (Flemington, N.J.). Gold medals were awarded to Charles Connick (stained glass), F. Koralewsky (ironwork), Maud Masson (decorated china, Fig. 206), and Giovanni Battista Troccoli (1882–1940) for oil paintings. Silver medalists were Elizabeth Shippen Green Elliot (1871–1954) for watercolors and Philip Little (1857–1942) for oil paintings and watercolors. Bronze medalists included Elizabeth Colwell (1881–1954) for wood engraving, Elizabeth Copeland (enamels, Fig. 207), and Arthur Wesley Dow (wood engraving, Plates 14 and 15). Though cost prevented the SACB from sending a display representing the organization, it continued to be a player on a world stage, while expanding its national and international influence in myriad ways.[68]

Other Manifestations of the Diaspora
Architects and Craftsworkers

SACB members continued to spread the gospel of "good design" beyond the confines of the organization's home base using a variety of means. Some wrote articles, essays, and books, documenting their opinions on Usefulness and Beauty with a degree of permanency still appreciable today. R. A. Cram, A. W. Dow, and D. W. Ross were among those member-theorists whose works were printed and reprinted, and remain relevant. Some members undertook lecture tours with the particular goal of promoting the SACB and its mission throughout the region and across the nation. SACB secretary Whiting and his successor Macomber are two examples. A few of the SACB's more colorful personalities—such as Cram and Walker, to name just two—spoke regularly at national conferences, a testimony to their reputations as critics. Educators indoctrinated students, who left Boston and New England to practice elsewhere. These students comprised a second-generation diaspora, who carried their mentors' ideas to new locations, and may have subjected those ideas to reinterpretations along the way. Influential by means of word, thought, and deed, many educators were equally visible as practitioners.

Architect-members of the SACB formed a group that may have been more responsible than any other for promoting varying interpretations of Usefulness and Beauty nationwide. During its first two decades, the SACB attracted thirty-nine architects. (See Appendix E.) Many achieved national visibility by virtue of structures that they—or their firms—built around the country. Many were educators, writers, and lecturers. And most publicized the work of SACB craftsmen by specifying their handiwork as interior finishing materials, fittings, or furnishings in structures located from coast to coast.[69]

Chief among these were Ralph Adams Cram and Bertram Grosvenor Goodhue, often credited as SACB founders (although their names do not appear on the charter), and their associates Frank E. Cleveland (d. 1950), F. W. Ferguson (1861–1926), and Alexander E. Hoyle (d. 1969). Renown for ecclesiastical work, Cram, Goodhue, and Ferguson (partners between 1898 and 1913) epitomized the SACB's commitment to artistic cooperation (Plate 16), as they invited numerous artisans to embellish structures located across the United States and beyond. SACB members, including John Kirchmayer (wood-carving), Harry Goodhue and Charles Connick (stained glass), Frederick Krasser and Samuel Yellin (ironwork), John Evans (sculpture, carving), George Hallowell and D. B. Updike (book design and printing), Arthur Stone, James Woolley, George Germer, George Hunt, and George Gebelein (metalwork), and H. C. Mercer and Mary Chase Perry (ceramic tile). Perry's inclusion in this select group is significant, because few women were apparently invited to participate. Stained glass artist Margaret Redmond, for example, complained that Cram dismissed women as suited more for housework than for craftwork.[70]

Douglass Shand-Tucci summarizes the extent of Cram's oeuvre as embracing over seventy cathedrals and churches, built in thirty-five states and two of Canada's provinces, to accommodate congregations of numerous creeds and denominations, in a variety of historicist styles, especially the Gothic. But, his work did not stop there. He and his partners and associates—a group that changed and evolved over time—also undertook residential, commercial, and institutional (especially educational) commissions that testified to their breadth of interests, abilities, and belief in unifying the fine and applied arts.[71]

When Cram and Goodhue ended their partnership in 1913–14, Goodhue's influence spread increasingly westward. After designing structures for the Panama-California Exposition between 1911 and 1915, Goodhue became, according to Vincent Scully, "the architect most influential in Spanish colonial work on the West Coast" (Fig. 208). One of his many projects was designing the campus plan and buildings for the California Institute of Technology. A multitalented architect, artist, designer, and writer, whom Shand-Tucci labels "probably the best draughtsman in the country" at the time, Goodhue had a spreading influence well beyond Boston and the SACB.[72]

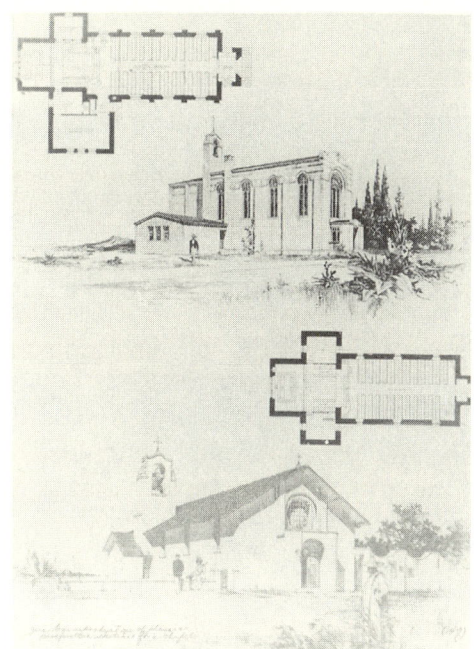

208. Architectural illustration, "Zinc line reproduction of plans & perspective sketches for a chapel," by Bertram Grosvenor Goodhue, undated. (Courtesy MIT Museum) Goodhue often provided two exterior schemes for the same plan. The lower perspective sketch is in the Spanish Colonial style, reinforced by the foreground figure wearing a serape and sombrero.

Like his partner, Cram was multitalented to the point that biographers and historians claim he defies categorization (Plate 17). A "founder or editor of five journals," a prolific writer devoted to history, theory, and criticism of the built environment specifically and of American culture in general, a passionate academic (associated with MIT in diverse roles between 1914 and 1922), Cram "exercised," Shand-Tucci argues, "a wider influence on diverse and important aspects of the national culture than any other architect in our history."[73]

While Cram, Goodhue, and Ferguson comprised an influential group within the SACB, so too did those trained in H. H. Richardson's office: Robert D. Andrews, Herbert Jaques, Alexander Wadsworth Longfellow, Jr., and Herbert Langford Warren.

Robert Day Andrews with his partners Herbert Jaques and Augustus Neal Rantoul (1865–1934) completed residences, schools, churches, and commercial buildings in New England, the Great Plains, and the Rockies from 1890 to 1917 (Figs. 209 and 210a and b). Andrews had essays and works published in such national journals as the *Producer & Builder*, *Architectural Review*, *American Architect & Building News*, and *Scientific American*. Authors featured the firm's work in anthologies. Though Jaques was also an SACB member, Andrews was the more visible.[74]

Another product of Richardson's Brookline studio was Alexander Wadsworth (Waddy) Longfellow, Jr., a principal in the firm Longfellow, Alden & Harlow

209. Architectural illustration, "House in Bar Harbor, Maine," by Andrews, Jaques & Rantoul, architects, from *Catalogue, Special Exhibition*, Boston Architectural Club (1897), p. 81. (Courtesy Boston Athenaeum) The rambling house with its circular drive is in the Colonial Revival style, but the firm also worked in the boulder-and-shingle style, a Voyseyan "roughcast" approach, and a modified Prairie style.

210. Houses at Cohasset and Milton, Mass.," by Andrews, Jaques & Rantoul, architects, from *Exhibition of 1908, Boston Architectural Club* (1908), n.p. (Courtesy Boston Athenaeum) In terms of massing, houses by this firm showed awareness of the English Domestic Revival and the Queen Anne. But it used a more limited selection of materials than its English counterparts.

211. Japanese Room, Longfellow House, Cambridge, Mass., undated. Photograph by J. F. Olsson & Co. (Courtesy National Park Service, Longfellow National Historic Site) Alexander Wadsworth Longfellow, Jr., wrote his mother about helping his cousin, Charley Longfellow, decorate the room in 1874. Notable elements include the Japanese fan ceiling treatment, the Morris and wicker chairs, and assorted Asian accessories.

(1888–96), whose major building project outside New England was the Allegheny Carnegie Library in Pittsburgh (1886–89). Longfellow, Alden & Harlow exhibited in the architecture displays at the Chicago and St. Louis world's fairs, and won awards. A devoted, long-term member of the SACB Jury and a supporter of numerous cultural institutions around Boston, Longfellow was a Fellow of the American Institute of Architects (Fig. 211).[75]

More visible than Andrews, Jaques, or Longfellow, Langford Warren had influence well beyond the SACB, where he served in numerous capacities until his untimely death at the age of sixty-one in 1917. A principal in the firms Warren, Smith & Biscoe (1900–1905) and Warren & Smith (1906–12), he undertook the design of "churches, institutions, and residences in New England, the West, and the South" (Figs. 212, 213a and b, and 214). His greatest contribution may have

212. Architectural illustration, "Renfrew Park Newport R.I., The Hall," by H. Langford Warren, architect, Boston, from *Catalogue of Exhibition, Boston Architectural Club* (1890). (Courtesy Boston Athenaeum) These low, rambling structures form part of a proposed resort complex. The round porches with their conical roofs and the shingled siding recall contemporary structures such as McKim, Mead, & White's Isaac Bell House (Newport, 1880s), but the shell-formed dormers are an idiosyncratic addition.

213a. Charles J. Page House, 90 Westland Avenue, Boston, H. Langford Warren, architect, ca. 1887. Photograph by Soule Art Company. (Courtesy Historic New England) The structural color and texture of this compact house near the Fenway reflects the "permanent polychrome" advocated by John Ruskin. Romanesque arches pay homage to H. H. Richardson.

213b. Dining room with inglenook, Charles J. Page House. Photograph by Soule Art Company. (Courtesy Historic New England) The arched fireplace inglenook with built-in seating was a planning convention beloved by design reformers and promoted by supporters of the English Domestic Revival. The round arch, heavy beamed and coffered ceiling, and wainscot paneling all recall interior treatments used by H. H. Richardson.

214. Residence in Brookline, Mass., undated, H. Langford Warren, architect. (Courtesy Historic New England) Though sided with clapboard, this house has a sleek continuity of surface more typical of Shingle style residences. The slender chimney, oblique gable, and latticework porch railing reflect knowledge of both the Queen Anne and the Aesthetic movement.

been his teaching at Harvard between 1893 and 1917. He established its program in architecture (ca. 1899) and took responsibility for its subsequent growth. At the time of his death, he was the Nelson Robinson, Jr., Professor of Architecture, Chairman of the Council of the School of Architecture, and Dean of the Faculty of Architecture. Though he was based in Cambridge, his reach extended throughout the United States by virtue of Harvard's students and alumni. Warren contributed articles to a broad range of publications including *Architectural Review*, *Architectural Record*, *American Architect & Building News*, *Picturesque and Architectural New England*, *Handicraft* (for which he served as an editor), *Progress*, and many regional journals. A Harvard edition of Vitruvius's *Ten Books on Architecture* (which Warren had edited), and his own textbook, *The Foundations of Classical*

215. Architectural illustration, "Store on Farnham St., Omaha, Neb.," by Walker & Best, architects, from *Catalogue of Exhibition, Boston Architectural Club* (1890). (Courtesy Boston Athenaeum) This facade utilizes tripartite composition also evident in commercial structures springing up in Chicago, New York, and Boston. The projecting cornice, ornamental top floor, sleek verticality of the central section, and broad display windows are conventions used by Adler & Sullivan and other "Chicago School" architects.

216. Edward Robinson residence, Manchester, Mass., C. Howard Walker, architect, ca. 1888. Photograph by Soule Art Company. (Courtesy Historic New England) This imposing residence in the Olde English style incorporates half-timbering in the manner of Richard Norman Shaw. Robinson was curator of classical antiquities at the Museum of Fine Art (ca. 1885–1906). Walker had traveled with him and his wife to the Mediterranean in 1881 on an archeological tour sponsored by the museum. The Olde English style seems an odd choice for a client with interests in classical archeology, but it was appropriate for a country house built along Boston's North Shore.

Architecture, appeared posthumously in the late teens and twenties. An obituary in the *Harvard College Gazette* concluded: "It is, then, not as a practitioner, keenly interested though he always was in this side of his work, that his memory will live; but as a scholar and teacher, and eminent authority on the historical development of Architecture." Warren's keen aesthetic sensibilities, diplomacy, and leadership were all invaluable to the SACB.[76]

To some degree, C. Howard Walker's career paralleled Warren's. Though he was a practicing architect (Walker & Best, Figs. 215 and 216), education was always Walker's forte. He had been a student of Charles Eliot Norton. In turn, and in the manner of Norton, Cram, and Warren, he influenced myriad students at diverse institutions. At the Lowell Institute, his own School of Fine Arts, Crafts, and Decorative Design, Harvard, and MIT, Walker lectured on design principles, theory, and criticism, and the history of ornament. He served on a variety of national boards and committees, becoming actively involved with the American Federation of Art, where he often spoke at annual meetings. He participated in numerous national and international expositions as a planner, architect, exhibitor, juror, and judge, designing buildings for the Trans-Mississippi Exposition (Omaha, 1899) and the Massachusetts State Building for the Pan-American Exposition (Buffalo, 1901), as well as the Electricity Building for the

217. Book plate, for (and possibly by) C. Howard Walker, 1922. (Courtesy SACB Archives) Walker's alter ego was a black bear, similar to the mascot of the Tavern Club, in which Walker held membership. The pediment above the bear reads: "Ars longa, vita brevis est," the same motto that William Morris incorporated above a fireplace in his home, Red House.

218. Frank C. Brown, undated. (Courtesy Historic New England) Brown was an SACB member between 1899 and 1908 and had an office at 9 Park Street, where the SACB salesroom was located, until about 1920. One business card presents him as a "Specialist in Dwellings, Alterations & English Domestic and Colonial Work."

Louisiana Purchase Exposition. He published in such national journals as *The White Pine Series of Architectural Monographs*, *Architectural Review* (for which he also served as editor), *The Brickbuilder*, *The Craftsman*, and *Handicraft*. He served as prefacer and essayist for books on all aspects of architecture and design. When he died in 1936, his obituary appeared in national and international journals. At that time, the *Boston Herald* called him "one of Boston's most caustic critics . . . who knew many of Boston's literary and artistic figures of the nineteenth century, and brought to the present era much of their devotion to classicism in thought and form." Walker's conservatism infused the SACB, its Jury, and its products. The nickname given to him by fellow members of the Tavern Club, "Howdy," belies the otherwise gruff persona that he cultivated as an arbiter of taste (Fig. 217).[77]

Cram, Goodhue, Longfellow, Warren, and Walker may have been the best-known SACB architects, but others were also multitalented and widely acclaimed. In addition to erecting new buildings and restoring old, Frank Chouteau Brown (1876–1947, Fig. 218) designed furniture, memorials, and stage sets. He was on the board of directors for the American Pageant Association (in which residents

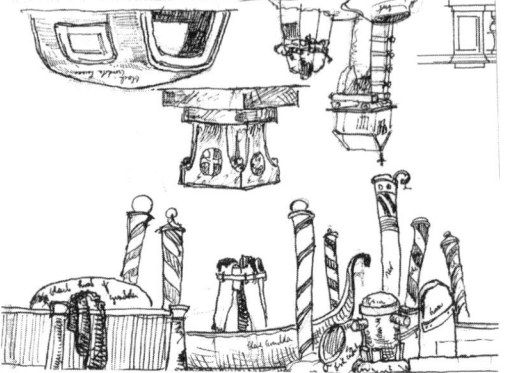

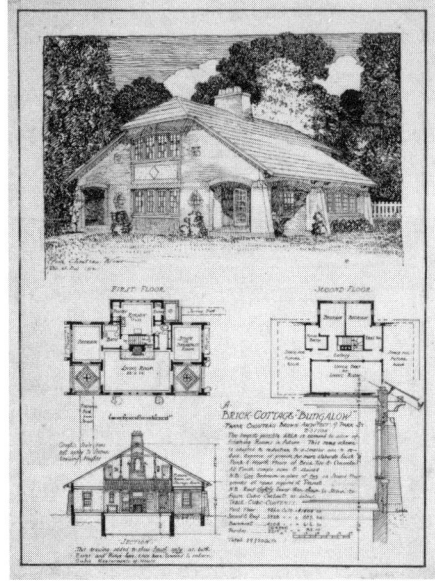

219. Business card for Frank C. Brown, illustrating his design for a home at Newton, Mass., ca. 1924. (Courtesy Historic New England) This perspective sketch features a house that derives from the work of both R. N. Shaw and C. F. A. Voysey. Battered walls, slender chimney stacks, and half-timbering are features of the Shavian Olde English style.

220. Architectural drawings including plans, sections, and exterior perspective sketch, titled "Proposal for a Brick Cottage Bungalow," by Frank C. Brown, architect, 1912. (Courtesy Historic New England) A two-story living room and towering central chimneystack add spaciousness and verticality to this otherwise snug bungalow. The battered piers and "cat slide" roof make the house seem rooted to its site, in a manner that design reformers approved.

221. Sketches for set design for *The Merchant of Venice*, by Frank C. Brown, ca. 1907. (Courtesy Historic New England) These ink sketches, labeled with color notations, have a facile cartoon-like quality and document Brown's fertile imagination. His penchant for drama and acting explains his presence on the board of the American Pageant Association.

of Deerfield actively participated). Editor of both *Old-Time New England* and *Architectural Review*, he published in the major architectural journals as well as *Country Life in America*, *The Craftsman*, *House Beautiful* (which moved to Boston and entered into a special arrangement with the SACB in 1915), *Pencil Points*, and the *International Studio*. A critic of broad interests, he wrote on all aspects of architecture and design (Figs. 219, 220, and 221).[78]

The reputation of Addison B. LeBoutillier (1872–1951) spread as a result of his association with the Grueby Pottery where he functioned as a designer, winning an award at the Turin (1902) Exposition. In addition to his architectural works and his interiors, which often featured Grueby tiles, he also produced advertisements, bookplates, and book covers (Figs. 222, 223, and 224). Lois Lilley Howe, a graduate of the MFA School and MIT's two-year degree program in architecture, won second prize for the Women's Building at the World's Columbian Exposition. In 1901, she was the first woman elected to the American Institute of Architects, and she became the first woman Fellow of the AIA in 1931 (Figs. 225 and 226a and b). A gifted photographer as well as architect, she published *Details from Old New England Houses* (1913) with Constance Fuller. Guy Lowell (d. 1927)

222. Fountain in Garden Room, in a house by Ripley, Fisher & LeBoutillier, architects, from *Current Architecture, Joint Exhibition, Architecture, Landscape Architecture, and the Allied Arts, 1916* (Boston: Boston Architectural Club, 1916). (Courtesy Boston Athenaeum) Given all his work in pottery design, it seems logical that LeBoutillier would specify ceramic tile as a finishing material for the firm's architectural commissions.

223. "Elevation of North End of Living Room in House at Winchmere for Cholmondelay Beauchamp-St. Leger, Esq.," by Fisher, Ripley & LeBoutillier, architects, from *Current Architecture, Joint Exhibition, Architecture, Landscape Architecture, and the Allied Arts, 1916*. (Courtesy Boston Athenaeum) This detailed elevation—particularly delightful in color—shows an attention to a client's personal possessions uncommon in later architectural illustrations of the modern era. Such concern for every aspect of an interior's finishes and furnishings distinguished the work of architects who joined the SACB.

224. Interior perspective rendering, "Chapel, Tabor Academy, Marion, Mass.," by Fisher, Ripley and LeBoutillier, architects, from *Current Architecture, Joint Exhibition, Architecture, Landscape Architecture, and the Allied Arts, 1916*. (Courtesy Boston Athenaeum) LeBoutillier captured the serene, light-filled atmosphere of this diminutive chapel in his sensitive rendering. Abstract historicism characterizes the style, which evokes the Elizabethan era while eliminating the inessential in a proto-modernist fashion.

constructed works throughout the Northeast, including the new MFA building in Boston, lectured on architecture and landscape architecture at MIT, and published two books on gardens (Figs. 227 and 228a, b, and c). Richard Clipston Sturgis—who, along with Edmund Wheelwright, collaborated with Lowell on the new MFA project—built the Cathedral of Manila in the Philippine Islands. He was a talented craftsman and designer of textiles, mosaic, and metalwork, taught at MIT, and succeeded Warren as SACB president in 1917 (Figs. 229, 230, and 231). His wife, Esther Mary Ogden Sturgis, wrote a spirited memoir of their life together, which he illustrated. As a group, the architect-members of the SACB were known far beyond Boston and Cambridge. Even as they expanded their professional horizons nationally, they maintained a close-knit network,

225. Country house, by Lois L. Howe, architect, undated, from *Catalogue of the Boston Architectural Club Exhibition, 1906.* (Courtesy Boston Athenaeum) This Shingle-style cottage incorporates a rustic porch railing and skirting to unite it with the site.

226. Two views in house, by Lois L. Howe, architect, undated, from *Catalogue of the Boston Architectural Club Exhibition, 1906.* (Courtesy Boston Athenaeum) Howe's interiors utilize traditional finishes combined with functional built-ins and Colonial antiques. Built-in or structural furniture was common in interiors designed by reformers, who sought to provide their clients with "a place for everything."

choosing to collaborate with other SACB members as appropriate, and using examples of their colleagues' work as illustrations when writing articles for national publication.[79]

National Outlets: Exhibitions, Galleries, Museums

In addition to gaining note through their collaboration with architects working across the United States, craftspeople continued to publicize their work through exhibitions. While international expositions facilitated the broadest exposure, other events were equally important. One of these was the SACB's decennial exhibition, intended to carry on the tradition established in 1897 and 1899. "It is hoped," stated the *Annual Report* for 1906, "to make this the most important exhibit of handicraft work ever held in this country," a tall order given the recent success of the St. Louis world's fair.[80]

The exhibition, held in Copley and Allston Halls, was smaller and more select than its predecessors owing to stringent "standard of merit" imposed by the Council and the Jury. A sober catalogue—the blue-gray cover unembellished save for a thin black border—seemed to reflect the organization's conservatism and the poor economic climate, epitomized by the Panic of 1907. Warren's intro-

227. Portrait of Guy Lowell, by John Singer Sargent, 1917. (Courtesy Harvard University Archives)

228. Three views of the Museum of Fine Arts, Boston. (a) Entrance facade, "Art Museum, Boston, Mass." Published by Mason Bros. & Co., Boston. (Author's collection) The caption for this postcard states with brevity and pride: "Located in Fenway on Huntington Avenue. One of the finest in America. Contains many unequaled collections." (b) The museum as seen across Fens from Fenway Studio, 1914. Photograph by Baldwin Coolidge. (Courtesy Historic New England) This moody vista shows the new museum's rear facade. Devoid of the Greek temple elements that distinguish the Huntington Avenue facade, the back is sleekly rectangular and functional, having more in common with the utilitarian smokestacks at right than the Gothic spires in the distance. (c) Museum entrance hall, as published in *The American Architect*, March 29, 1916. (Courtesy Historic New England) Guy Lowell attended the École des Beaux Arts between 1894 and 1896, and this stately entrance hall demonstrates his command of two concepts stressed there: rationalist planning and historicist detailing.

ductory essay and eight black-and-white photographs augmented descriptions of 1,200 items representing fourteen craft categories. Five hundred objects displayed in Allston Hall comprised a retrospective loan collection, the majority from the collections of Denman Ross, J. Templeman Coolidge, Jr., and Edward R. Warren.[81]

Frederick W. Coburn remarked on the "triumphant Gallic and classic" spirit

229a and b. Working-men's cottages at Bridgeport, Conn., R. Clipston Sturgis, architect, from *Catalogue of Exhibition, Boston Architectural Club, 1917*. (Courtesy Boston Athenaeum) Though the SACB shied away from politics—especially the socialism that influenced William Morris and his followers—Sturgis demonstrated an awareness of a need for affordable housing and "good design" for the working class.

230. Banking Room, First National Bank, Boston, by R. Clipston Sturgis, architect, from *Catalogue of Exhibition, Boston Architectural Club, 1908*. (Courtesy Boston Athenaeum) Equally adept at residential and commercial architecture, Sturgis designed this imposing bank interior, of vast proportions, in a formal historicist style.

that prevailed in Copley Hall. This contrasted with the "romantic, Gothic and reactionary" mood that had been evident in work shown in 1897 and 1899, in keeping with tendencies present in British work of the late 1890s. Coburn attributed the new spirit to the influence of SACB architect-members upon their craftsmen colleagues. He suggested that those architects' training in Paris or in American schools modeled after the École des Beaux Arts imposed a Greco-Roman sensibility and a "French solidity and constructiveness" upon SACB members. He did not deny an "English striving for delicacy and qualities of imagination" present in some work—especially that of Cram, Goodhue & Ferguson, and those with whom they collaborated—but he insisted that this "picturesque 'Gothic Camp'" was in the minority. Significantly, 1907 was the year of the ground-breaking for the new MFA building on Huntington Avenue, which reflected Boston's penchant for classicism in Guy Lowell's severe, white Greco-Roman facade.[82]

Another critic commented upon the SACB's assimilation of the past and the streak of conservatism that was apparent in the work in Copley Hall. "Instead of striving after 'mere odd or bizarre design,'" he wrote, "there is now apparent a striving after balance, proportion, dignity and the perfection of grace, all classic qualities, and sought with a truly classic warmth and not with the pseudo-Hellenistic coldness that has characterized periods of mere imitation."[83]

231. Book illustrations, R. Clipston Sturgis, for Mrs. R. Clipston Sturgis, *Random Reflections of a Grandmother* (Cambridge, 1917), beginnings of chapters 3 and 5. (Schlesinger Library, Radcliffe Institute, Harvard University) Sturgis, who worked at all scales and in diverse media, produced these charming sketches to illustrate his wife Esther's book. They provide an intimate glimpse into the Sturgis family's life, complementing his wife's revealing stories regarding the challenges of living with an often temperamental and opinionated architect.

As these two excerpts suggest, a majority of coverage of the 1907 exhibition appeared in the local and regional press. But other articles were wide-ranging, appearing in *Scribner's*, the *World Today*, the *Art Bulletin*, *Harper's Weekly*, and the *New York Times Literary Supplement*. Critic Frederick W. Coburn prepared press releases for the *American Art News*, the *New York Herald*, *Times*, *Sun*, *Tribune*, and *Globe*, along with papers in Philadelphia, Washington, D.C., and Chicago. Visitors came from as far away as New York, Rochester, and Chicago, adding to the 15,800 attendees.[84]

Another important forum was the Art Institute of Chicago, which began holding annual Arts and Crafts exhibitions in 1902. The Society's *Annual Reports* proudly noted members who participated in these exhibitions and listed those—and there were many—who won prestigious awards. Selected SACB members exhibited their work at the 1910 Handicraft League Exhibition in Cincinnati, and under the auspices of the Cleveland Decorative Arts Club (ca. 1908). Extending their visibility in the Midwest, members also showed work representing major craft categories at the Wisconsin State Fair in both 1911 and 1912.[85]

Members also took part in exhibitions sponsored by the American Federation of Arts. In 1913, one of these traveled to Pittsburgh, Greensboro, Nashville, and Rochester. In 1914, the show took place in Washington, D.C., concurrent with the Federation's annual conference, at which both Walker and Cram spoke. In 1915, a small exhibit took place at the Newark (N.J.) Museum. As this suggests, SACB members also joined other organizations that promoted the arts and crafts, holding memberships in groups including the National Society of Craftsmen (New York) and the Art Alliance of America (New York).[86]

Members also exhibited internationally. In 1913, the SACB sent a display to the Canadian National Exposition in Toronto, perhaps in response to an increased number of Canadian members. "The sales, however, were disappointingly small," the *Annual Report* for that year noted, "and so much difficulty and delay was experienced in getting the exhibition back into this country through the Boston Custom House that it is doubtful if the Society will care to send another exhibition to Canada." This may explain why individuals—rather than the organization as a whole—tended to show work at world's fairs. Though they acted independently, they still brought acclaim to the SACB by their association with it.[87]

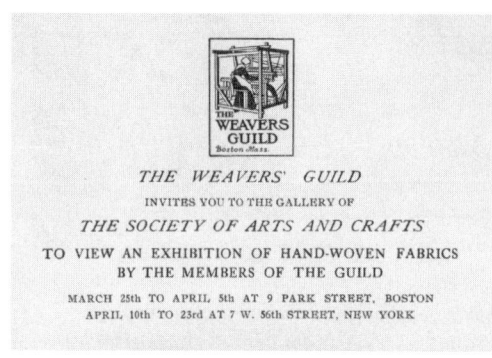

232. Invitation from The Weavers' Guild, 1922. (Courtesy Historic New England) This calls attention to the short-lived SACB salesroom that operated in New York City in the 1920s.

Craftsworkers also sold their work in galleries across the United States. These included the Taft and Belknap Galleries (New York), which represented A. A. Robineau and W. H. Grueby; Marcus & Co. (New York), advertising "Freedom from Cant in Design"; the Marshall Field & Co. Craft Shop (Chicago), a supplier for Morris & Co. and an important contributor of handicrafts to the St. Louis world's fair; Noonan-Cocian Co., and J. Kennard & Sons Carpet Co. (both in St. Louis), who were agents of Tiffany & Co. The SACB even took the step of opening its own New York gallery in 1923, which functioned on and off through 1928 (Fig. 232).[88]

Another recognition of the growing influence of SACB members was the acquisition of their work by museums, American and foreign, for permanent collections. In the aftermath of the 1904 world's fair, the St. Louis Art Museum, for example, purchased Mercer tiles and Newcomb vases. And, in 1916, an agent of a museum in Kyoto, Japan, purchased from the SACB "examples from fourteen different American potteries as well as examples of other craft work for the permanent collection of the museum." In this and other ways, the reputations of the SACB and its members grew increasingly widespread.[89]

Lecture Tours, Craft Societies, and Resettlement

Because of their organization's increasing visibility, SACB members often received invitations to speak around the United States. Following his successes in St. Louis, Whiting, for example, undertook a tour of the East, Midwest, and Plains states in 1907, traveling to Baltimore, St. Albans, Kansas City, Indianapolis, Detroit, Richmond, and Pittsburgh. On these occasions, he often presented a variation on his speeches "The Development and Meaning of the Arts and Crafts Movement," or "What the Arts and Crafts Movement Has Accomplished." Invited lectures took Whiting away from his duties at the SACB headquarters so frequently, in fact, that some members complained that he was shirking his responsibilities, but his tour of 1907 was indicative of his desirability as a speaker. The *Annual Report* summarized the impact of this tour: "These trips were full of encouragement, showing that throughout the country the demand for handicraft work and the understanding of the principles of handicraft are spreading. . . . This experience went far to show how generally the Boston Society is looked to as the center of the movement and the one to which the younger societies naturally turn for guidance and inspiration." This was an important accomplishment for the SACB after only ten years of operation, and Whiting deserves credit for serving as one of its chief promoters.[90]

Whiting's successor, H. Percy Macomber, a former employee of Houghton,

Mifflin, undertook a similar tour—which he called a "4000 mile trip of observation"—in 1914. He traveled to the South and West, visiting contributors to the salesroom and far-flung members. His itinerary took him to Baltimore, Washington, D.C., Tryon, N.C., New Orleans, St. Louis, Chicago, Detroit, Cleveland, Syracuse, and New York City. Upon his return, the *Boston Times* quoted him as saying "Chicago has 'gone in' very enthusiastically for Arts and Crafts, as for every form of art, and it is already evident that eastern institutions will have to be alive and alert to hold a position of leadership in competition with the western metropolis." Here Macomber may have been alluding to his own position at the SACB.[91]

This pressure from other arts and crafts societies may explain why the SACB was contemplating extensive renovations to its headquarters that year. An ad hoc building committee—comprised of Louis Newhall, Frederick P. Cabot, John Kirchmayer, Percy Macomber, and Howard Walker—concluded that the success of the Detroit, St. Louis, and Minneapolis societies might be related directly to their distinctive headquarters, while the lack of success of the New York and Philadelphia societies might be a result of their "inconspicuous, inadequate, and poorly located structures." Structure notwithstanding, in the aftermath of his tour, Macomber reported: "the severity of the Boston jury was everywhere quoted, sometimes with complete approval, sometimes with reservations. It was generally admitted that nowhere else is such strictness maintained as in this city." That strictness had first received national exposure at St. Louis in 1904, and craftsworkers were still commenting upon it a decade later.[92]

Another manifestation of the Boston diaspora was the founding of other organizations—arts and crafts societies, the National League of Handicraft Societies, the American Federation of Arts—that modeled themselves after the SACB, absorbing some of its structure, policies, and procedures. Whiting reported in a lecture delivered at the American Federation of Art, and later reprinted in *Handicraft* that, as of 1910, sixty-five organizations "for the advancement of handicraft work" had arisen around the United States in imitation of the SACB. Those in New York, Philadelphia, Baltimore, Detroit, Hartford, Columbus, Minneapolis, and St. Louis had organized retail shops in the manner of the SACB salesroom. This proliferation of arts and crafts organizations and retail shops throughout the country stands as testimony to how far the SACB's influence had spread.[93]

Many of those organizations banded together in 1907 to form the National League of Handicraft Societies (NLHS), which competed with the National Society of Craftsman founded in New York one year earlier. The initial meeting of prospective members—twenty-three of forty-five invited organizations sent representatives—took place in Boston, concurrent with the SACB's decennial exhibition. During the first few years, its headquarters were at the SACB, and Langford Warren served as its president. A. W. Dow was the vice-president (a position he held as well in the National Society of Craftsmen), while Whiting assumed the role of secretary/treasurer. The mission of the NLHS was: "to bring together the various Societies which are working for the same general purpose; to provide a small traveling exhibition, which could serve as a set of standards; to

233. Postcard, undated. Published by Mason Bros. & Co. (Author's collection) The small scale of the plantings suggests that the photograph was taken shortly after completion of the Charles River Basin, ca. 1916.

234. Postcard, "New England Views on Boston & Maine R.R., Deerfield Valley, Mass.," n.d. (Author's collection) This card illustrates the idyllic pastoral landscape and lovely farms along the Connecticut and Pocumtuck river valleys in the vicinity of Deerfield.

provide traveling libraries of technical hand-books and of photographs; to arrange, in cooperation with local societies, large exhibitions in various centers; to revive 'Handicraft' as an organ of the League; to arrange courses of lectures through cooperation, so that the various Societies can secure the leading lecturers at a minimum of cost, etc." As this mission suggests, activities undertaken by the NLHS paralleled those that the SACB had initiated during its first decade.[94]

Covering both the decennial exhibition and the initial meeting of what came to be called the NLHS, in Boston, critic Frederick W. Coburn claimed, "This city is now absolute leader in arts and crafts." Viewing its achievements as an extension of the city's socio-cultural resources, he argued, "Its success warrants the assertion that nowhere else in the United States are general conditions more propitious for the continued growth of the handicraft movement than in eastern Massachusetts," given "a gradual improvement in public taste," abundant educational facilities, and "the betterment of the whole district through park and recreational developments." The latter included the construction of the Back Bay Fens in the 1880s and 1890s, and subsequent development of the Fenway and Longwood areas, Franklin Park, creation of the Charles River Basin (Fig. 233), and eventual opening of Fenway Park (1912). The quest for Usefulness and Beauty in the handicrafts paralleled the City Beautiful movement, which introduced those concepts at a grand scale.[95]

Essential to the spreading of the gospel of "good design" across the United States were those SACB members who left Boston for other locations. They constituted a true diaspora. Their reasons for leaving varied, but their dispersal to other parts of the country and even to other countries enabled ideas forged in Boston under the auspices of the SACB to proliferate elsewhere. Some members—A. A. Carey, George E. Barton, Carl Purington Rollins, and Hartley Dennett, to name just a few—left to join utopian communities in rural areas. Several—Ashfield, Deerfield, and Montague—were clustered along river valleys in north-central Massachusetts (Fig. 234). In the manner of their early-nineteenth-century forefathers, these anti-urbanists "worshipped, and went apart for solitary thought." Because they were turning away and inward, their influence may have been limited. But others dispersed across the East, Midwest and Far West, and assumed positions in which they were highly visible.[96]

One of these was Whiting, who left the SACB in May 1912 to become director of the Museum of the John Herron Art Institute in Indianapolis. He had achieved international recognition at the St. Louis World's Fair, but he had encountered political problems within the SACB upon his return, especially in the aftermath of the decennial exhibition. This prompted him to explore alternatives.[97]

At a farewell dinner, Langford Warren spoke of the impact the Louisiana Purchase Exposition had had upon Whiting's career and the Society's development. "At the time of the World's Fair in St. Louis when this Society carried off most of the honors, it was Mr. Whiting efforts which made the Applied Arts Exhibit a success," he began, "extending in that way the influence of the Society to other parts of the country. That leads me to speak of another way in which the Society and the movement at large owes a great deal to Mr. Whiting. It has seemed to me that this Society, which is the first of its kind and has never been called the Boston Society of Arts and Crafts, but The Society of Arts and Crafts— is in a real sense a national organization." Warren credited Whiting with having contributed to its achievement of that status.[98]

Whiting's national visibility had led to his recruitment for the Indianapolis post. The new job offered him an opportunity to advance his career significantly, and he undertook an ambitious agenda from the start. In October 1912, shortly after his arrival, he welcomed a traveling exhibition of German decorative arts, organized by Karl Ernst Osthaus, a prominent promoter of the Deutscher Werkbund, and John Cotton Dana, director of the Newark Museum. Whiting would have been familiar with a similar display shown at St. Louis in 1904. There, in a special pavilion, Germany's eighty-thousand-square-foot installation of arts and crafts had attracted more attention than any other foreign exhibit. By hosting this exhibition, which appeared in museums around the United States, Whiting sought to expose his new constituents in Indiana to examples of the design reform movement as interpreted in Germany.[99]

In 1913, he left Indianapolis to become director of the newly established Museum of Art in Cleveland, recommended by individuals whom he had met as a result of working in St. Louis. He held that position until 1930, eventually serving as president of the American Federation of Art (AFA), an organization with which he had been involved since its inception. In his capacity as a museum director, Whiting continued to champion Usefulness and Beauty, by shaping museum collections, mounting exhibitions, lecturing, publishing—the *American Magazine of Art* was one focus for his efforts—and administering arts organizations, such as the AFA and the American Association of Museums.[100]

Another individual with ties to the SACB who moved to Indianapolis (1912) was metalsmith Janet Payne Bowles (1876–1948). She and her husband, the printer Joseph Bowles, had lived in Boston between 1895 and 1902. Joseph was briefly an SACB member, and the Bowleses had participated in SACB exhibitions in the late 1890s. Associating with printers, metalsmiths, and jewelry makers, they were part of the city's turn-of-the-century craft community and intelligentsia.

235. Cross pendant with chain, by Janet Payne Bowles, ca. 1907–11, tourmaline and silver. (Indianapolis Museum of Art, Gift of Jan and Mira Bowles in memory of their mother, Janet Payne Bowles) This cross design refers to such historical precedents as Celtic strapwork and the ancient grotesque motif.

Indicative of this was Joseph's invitation to lecture at the Greenacre Art Conference held in August 1898 in Eliot, Maine, along with Mary Ware, Hartley Dennett, A. W. Dow, and Frederick Eaton. Joseph had founded *Modern Art* magazine in 1893, a publication regarded, in Joseph Goddu's words, as "one of the most influential art journals to spread the Arts and Crafts message." One summer, Janet studied ceramics with Charles F. Binns in Alfred, N.Y. Another summer she traveled to Florence, where she attended a Bernard Berenson lecture. She was a proponent of William James's theory of pragmatism, and was "so impressed with James's essay on habit that she suggested it be printed in a special form for high school students." Payne Bowles collaborated with her husband on his magazine and books, and also published articles on her own. At Whiting's request, she wrote an article, "A Situation in Craft Jewelry," for *Handicraft* (December 1910).[101]

When the Bowleses separated in 1912, Payne Bowles returned to Indianapolis, where she and her husband had lived before moving to Boston. In his new post at the John Herron Institute, Whiting was instrumental in helping Janet to secure a teaching position at Shortridge High School, where she had a distinguished career. "Part of a tightly interconnected local arts network," Barry Shifman notes, "she also had a national impact as a designer, artisan, and educator. She and other individuals actively contributed to Indianapolis's participation in the Arts and Crafts Movement and to important advances in American Arts and Crafts ideology, aesthetics, and philosophy." Though her quirky metalwork (Fig. 235) did not epitomize the conservative definition of Usefulness and Beauty espoused by the SACB Jury, her work process—influenced by contemporary philosophy and psychology—betrayed an intellectual sophistication forged in Boston.[102]

Like Janet Payne Bowles, Madeline Yale Wynne (Figs. 236 and 237) was known for jewelry and metalwork that was idiosyncratic and bold. Her facility with metal may have been genetic, as her father was the inventor of the Yale lock. Wynne divided her time among Deerfield—where she was a driving force behind the restoration of Colonial-era houses and the founding of the Deerfield Society of Arts and Crafts, which evolved into the Society of Deerfield Industries—Chicago, and Tryon, N.C. An enthusiastic devotee of William Morris, Wynne was also an artist, writer, musician, teacher, and philanthropist. Though she never joined the SACB, she contributed three articles to *Handicraft*, knew Whiting and other SACB officers and administrators, and was a founding vice president of the National League of Handicraft Societies (which held its first annual meeting at

236. Madeline Yale Wynne. From "In Memory of Madeline Yale Wynne," 1918. (Photograph courtesy of Pocumtuck Valley Memorial Association, Memorial Hall Museum, Deerfield)

237. Box lid with rabbit motif, Madeline Yale Wynne, as featured in *Good Housekeeping* magazine, October 1903. (Photograph courtesy of Pocumtuck Valley Memorial Association, Memorial Hall Museum, Deerfield) Eight cabachon-cut, semi-precious stones complement the charming embossed rabbit figure.

Deerfield). Thus, she was a conduit for passing along ideas about the arts and crafts in New England, the Midwest, and the South.[103]

Ellen Gates Starr (1859–1940) also had ties to Deerfield. But, unlike Wynne, who discovered the town later in life, Starr had a connection through her family. Her father had been born there and was educated at the Deerfield Academy. Though Ellen was born and raised in Laona, Ill., she maintained a connection with Deerfield throughout her life, coming and going as her schedule permitted. From her father, Ellen had developed an appreciation for beauty and a sensitivity to labor issues and socialism. Studying bookbinding in London with T. J. Cobden-Sanderson was a manifestation of the former, while Ellen's work with Jane Addams at Hull House in Chicago built upon the latter. She limited her output to binding only a small number of books that she deemed to have "lasting value," and trained only three pupils at a time. In the early 1900s, Ellen

PROMOTING USEFULNESS AND BEAUTY NATIONWIDE

238. Ellen Gates Starr. Photograph by Frances and Mary Allen, ca. 1905. (Photograph courtesy of Pocumtuck Valley Memorial Association, Memorial Hall Museum, Deerfield). Starr was a cousin of the Allen sisters, accomplished art photographers who exhibited with the SACB. Mary was a member of the Society in the teens and twenties.

exhibited her work at Deerfield's annual display of art and craft, and served as a model for Deerfield's resident photographers, sisters Frances Allen and Mary Allen, who captured her in a thoughtful mood, writing at an eighteenth-century desk. The runner protecting its surface was probably made locally (Fig. 238). Traveling between Deerfield and Chicago, Starr carried strong New England values with her from place to place.[104]

Epitomizing the cosmopolitan nature of SACB members was Dawson Dawson-Watson. After receiving his education in England and France, he immigrated to the States, where he practiced painting—portraiture, landscape, and still life—graphic design, and frame making. He lived in Winchester, Mass., and then in Hartford, Conn., where he was a professor at the Hartford Art Society in the 1890s. After a brief stint at the Byrdcliffe Summer School (1903), he moved to St. Louis (1904) and exhibited at the world's fair, remaining until 1915, while teaching at the Museum of Fine Arts. As he moved, his influence spread to Springfield, Ill., and, ultimately, to San Antonio, where he died in 1939. By teaching and exhibiting his work widely, he carried English and northeastern concepts of Usefulness and Beauty into the Midwest and the Southwest. Despite his relocation from East to West, he maintained a connection with New England, summering in Scituate.[105]

California was also an attractive location for former Bostonians and Canta-

239. Fireplace with Batchelder tiles, and detail of corbel support, Charlevoix Public Library, Charlevoix, Mich., Warren S. Holmes, architect, ca. 1927. (Courtesy of Cynthia L. Postmus and the Charlevoix Public Library) Though Batchelder's influence was widespread, it is surprising to find these tiles in Michigan, since Detroit was home to the Pewabic Pottery.

bridgians, following the lead of such individuals as the Greene brothers, who had studied architecture at MIT, but chose to settle and practice in Pasadena. Another MIT alumnus, George Ellery Hale (1868–1938), went to Pasadena—the "Athens of the West"—to build an observatory. It was Hale who subsequently recruited Bertram G. Goodhue to develop a plan for a new campus and buildings at the California Institute of Technology, as it evolved from the earlier Throop Polytechnic Institute.[106]

The latter was the facility that had attracted Ernest Batchelder, who taught there between 1901 and 1909. Even after settling in Pasadena, Batchelder maintained connections elsewhere. He traveled to the Midwest in the summers to teach at the Minneapolis Guild of Handicrafts, which he founded in 1902 (Fig. 239). And, in 1901, he spoke on "A Theory of Color in Its Application to School Work" at the first annual meeting of the newly organized Council of Supervisors of the Manual Arts held in New Haven, Conn. In 1909, Batchelder considered establishing his own School of Handicraft in Pasadena, reportedly with funding from an anonymous Boston donor, but those plans never materialized. Helpmate to Whiting at the time of the Louisiana Purchase Exposition, author of books on design principles and theory (which appeared on the SACB recommended reading list in 1917–18), supportive of SACB members—such as H. C. Mercer whose tiles he selected for installation in his own home—Batchelder was an important link between the two coasts, whose attitudes toward Usefulness and Beauty complemented those espoused by the SACB.[107]

An even farther flung bearer of SACB influence was silversmith Albert Berry (active ca. 1899–1930). Associated with the Rhode Island School of Design (Providence), Berry exhibited with the SACB in 1899 and at the Chicago Art Institute in 1903. Eventually, he moved from his home in Auburn, R.I., to the wilds of Alaska. In 1918, he settled in Seattle, where he became proprietor of the eponymous Albert Berry's Craft Shop.[108]

Other SACB members and supporters migrated across the United States and abroad. Several book artists or graphic designers left Boston as other locations eclipsed its reputation as the center for fine publishing. Thomas Buford Meteyard—who had exhibited with the SACB in 1897—married and then moved to England in 1910, though he did not break his ties with New England's intelligentsia. He remained in contact with R. A. Cram, and, Nancy Finlay points out, one of his "closest neighbors in England was Henry James." Similarly, the printer Bruce Rogers, a native of Indiana and a devotee of William Morris, left the Boston area in 1911 to spend a few years in England, severing his connections with the magazine *Modern Art* and with Houghton Mifflin and the Riverside Press. Socialist Carl Purington Rollins, the longtime printer of *Handicraft* and the SACB's annual reports, left Montague, Mass. (a utopian community near Deerfield), in 1918 to take a position at Yale University. These relocations were advantageous to the individuals, but were disastrous for the book arts in Boston.[109]

Boston's losses of SACB members and supporters in this diaspora, however, were other cities' gains, as the latter benefited from an infusion of new ideas. In the history of the SACB, the effects of this scattering of people who shared a common devotion to the Arts and Crafts ideal were probably more positive than negative. By engaging in professional activities across the country, these individuals ensured that the definitions of Usefulness and Beauty enunciated by the organization's early founders became nationally influential. That they have remained so today is testimony to those founders' collective vision.

Afterword

> Our homes are overrun with things, encumbred with useless ugliness, and made to look more like museums or warerooms than like homes of thinking people and people of taste..
> —Clarence Cook, *The House Beautiful* (1877)

> Beauty is not attained by filling a room with beautiful things.
> —Herbert Spencer, *Facts and Comments* (1902)

The Great Exhibition and the criticism that it provoked fueled the ensuing international design reform movement. Influential publications that addressed that exhibition, including the *Art Journal* and the *Journal of Design and Manufacture*, epitomize the state of design criticism at the mid-point of the nineteenth century. These publications are an important nexus between the views of eighteenth-century philosophers of aesthetics who promoted Utility and Elegance and those of design reformers writing between 1860 and 1920 who went on to champion Usefulness and Beauty.

Similarly, the role of the exhibition—as tastemaker and trendsetter—is essential to the discussion of design reform. One would not have existed without the other. The exhibition brought together the multiple participants in the production/consumption cycle, while summarizing attitudes toward taste at a particular place and time.

Theories promoted by early critics linked Beauty inextricably with history and nature, while they connected Usefulness to function, materials, and construction. Theorists promoted conventionalization as ways of both thinking and doing. All figured prominently in the debate stimulated by the Great Exhibition and others about the direction design must take to serve as a positive force in an increasingly industrialized society.

Critics brought a diversity of background and experience to this discussion, and promoted varied points of view. While some critics worked in isolation—journalists might fall into this category—in other cases the craftsman and the critic were one. A critic's indirect or direct involvement with the creative process resulted in varied perspectives. Shifting levels of objectivity resulting from such involvement add richness to the discussion of craftsmen and critics.

Ideally, critics sought to do their jobs so well that they would, in essence, put themselves out of business. In reality, though, they knew that a certain *je ne sais quoi* would always distinguish truly great work, and that no amount of theory or number of guidelines would guarantee "good design." Its key was safe with them (if, in fact, they ever really knew what that key was). This ensured that critics would never truly become obsolete; their constituents would always need their help.

Boston's ascendancy as the seat of the "good design" debate was a result of serendipity: a blending of place, persons, and circumstances that led to the founding of the Society of Arts and Crafts. If any factor in that mix had been different, the resulting organization might have differed significantly. Many SACB members have already been the subjects of monographs—C. E. Norton, H. L. Warren, A. W. Longfellow, Jr., John Evans, and D. B. Updike, to name just a few—but others, such C. H. Walker, J. de W. Addison, and D. W. Ross, also deserve individual treatment.

Those who chose, for whatever reason, not to participate in the new organization also merit a large place in the story of the craftsman and the critic. Similarly, the range of individuals who left Boston and the SACB deserves scholars' consideration. Not the least of these is Frederick Allen Whiting, who was important nationally as well as locally. As essential as the Boston diaspora was to the spreading of the gospel of "good design" nationwide and internationally, what might have been the result locally and elsewhere if these individuals had stayed in Boston and remained involved with the SACB?

In the 1890s, Boston's intellectual milieu stimulated the critical discourse about "good design." Myriad aspects of Boston's turn-of-the-century culture and society that provoked that debate deserve further study. These include the links among the SACB and other Boston social and philanthropic clubs, which often had in common founders, members, and administrators; details regarding retailers in the city who satisfied a demand for "art produce" through their selection of merchandise and advertising campaigns; journalists who promoted the cause of design reform by means of exhibition reviews, interviews with craftsmen, and discussion of theories and ideas in the local press; and women who championed the cause of design reform—such as Mary Ware Dennett, Julia de W. Addison, Sarah W. Whitman, and Lois L. Howe. Some of these have already been subjects of individual biographies (published or unpublished). Exploring them as a "sisterhood" devoted to design reform might identify important connections among their backgrounds, education, training, and philosophical and philanthropic inclinations.

Architects played an especially important role in the evolution of the design reform movement in Boston. Without their participation as founders, administrators, jurors, and active members, the SACB would have been a different sort of organization. This raises the question: were architects as important to the evolution of craft organizations in other key American cities? Did societies in Minneapolis, Chicago, and Detroit, for example, involve architects to the same extent? What was architecture's impact as a profession upon the evolution of the movement nationwide?

A related topic is the evolution of the design reform movement in Canada. Who were its champions? Did architects also play an important role in arts and crafts organizations? What were the Canadian movement's links to both England

and America? How was Canadian design reform both similar to and different from its counterpart to the south? The fact that SACB members participated in Canadian exhibitions of handicraft and that Canadians joined the SACB makes this topic ripe for exploration.

The story of the craftsman and the critic in Boston is as much a tale of time as of place. The year 1897 was an unusually dynamic one. Innovation and experimentation abounded in all aspects of the built environment. A portrait of that year as a context for design reform—in Boston and internationally—could prove to be a fascinating study.

The SACB was one organization in a city of joiners, where clubs, associations, and societies proliferated. If the SACB succeeded (and its existence today attests to that success), it was in part because its members were comfortable in such a context. They supported the SACB's structure and its mission, and they welcomed the constraints and limitations that such an organization provided. Though the Society was exclusive, members sought to spread their gospel of "good design" throughout the community and were not content to keep innovative ideas behind closed doors. Under the SACB's auspices, they promoted a theory of "good design" by means of their statement of purpose, public exhibitions, their headquarters at 9 Park Street, and *Handicraft* magazine. All were efforts to reach out to the community, to spread ideas, ascertain a reaction, and fuel a debate about the role of design and craft in contemporary society.

While they were willing to argue over what constituted "good design," they discouraged haggling over politics. Strongly in favor of design education and trade schools, they nevertheless avoided run-ins with local trade unions. In an organization in which many members were strongly religious, they steered discussions away from Socialism, utopianism, and alternative approaches to spirituality. They pondered the advantages that their urban setting offered, but recognized the benefit for their members of living and working away from the city's hustle and bustle. Though a democratic organization, the SACB struggled with issues of class as they affected membership, income, and patronage. Much of the drama evident during the SACB's first twenty years might be attributed to its striving to attract members, to find commonalities among those members, to debate important issues without alienating large sections of that membership, and to remain united—despite their differences—around a common cause. A study of the institutional evolution of the SACB in comparison with that of other prominent arts organizations might shed light upon Boston's club culture.

In this discussion of the craftsman and the critic, the role of the SACB Jury is key. This was a multivalent and fluid group of individuals (in terms of background, beliefs, and participation) that adjusted its methodology even as it defined Usefulness and Beauty for its constituents. As it strove to do so, it considered conceptual, aesthetic, and technical issues; the existence of a craft hierarchy and all that it implies; how to implement differing standards for diverse media; and whether to promote conservatism, innovation, or a little bit of both. The Jury served as internal arbiter to a Society whose actions attracted increasing levels of external criticism.

The Jury had to strike a balance between theory and practice, between striving to reach an ideal versus accepting the reality of a worker's need to earn a living. It stood poised between its mission to raise standards from year to year, and the individual worker's capacity—and desire—to improve over time. Ultimately, Jury members had to compromise, among themselves and with their constituents, without also compromising the ideals and the mission of the Society. Their ability to do so is a reflection of their background as strong and talented individuals, whose influence increased exponentially when they came together as a group.

Most members of the SACB Jury represent the "practicing critic" or the "critical practitioner." Some have received scholarly attention; but most have not yet been the subjects of theses, dissertations, biographies, or monographs. An especially compelling subject is C. Howard Walker, despite the lack of a comprehensive archive of personal papers.

As a small group within a larger organization, the Jury faced a dilemma: whether to work anonymously or openly. How much should they expose regarding their own identities, work process, and decisions? How much should they ask members to reveal about themselves? Did anonymity throughout the jury process encourage objectivity and equal opportunity for all, or did it foment plagiarism or other sorts of misrepresentation on the part of craftsmen? How did the challenges facing the SACB Jury parallel that of juries working within other Boston institutions, such as clubs catering to the artistic and literary crowd?

The Jury's critique often extended beyond considerations of the object *per se* to issues affecting makers and their work processes. Access to workers' letters, diaries, sketchbooks, job books, and exhibition entry forms might document their reactions to the jury process. This might also bring to light important details regarding the relationship of craftsman to critic and the impact of that relationship upon their conceptual, aesthetic, and technical decision-making.

The story of the craftsman and the critic in arts and crafts–era Boston stands within the broader context of international design theory. Theorists advocated models as well as methods, suggesting what to consult as well as how to work. When members of the SACB prescribed turning to such models as history, nature, and language; when they advocated conventionalization; when they considered expression, they acknowledged internationally recognized theories, standards, and methodologies. The SACB's reference (and lending) library is a testimony to its awareness of broad intellectual trends brought home by means of contemporary literature.

International theories of "good design" supported those SACB members who argued in favor of strong schools, libraries, museums, collecting, and connoisseurship. Such theories justified Bostonians' investment in the "City Beautiful," leading to development of an expansive park system, the Fenway, tree-lined boulevards, and the Charles River embankment. All of these gave designers and consumers an opportunity to commune directly with nature. If the SACB Jury advocated copying from history or nature as a way to achieve originality, it did so with the blessing of international design theorists, whose recommendations transcended time and place. The arguments that the SACB promoted were both timely and aware, elevating its positions from what might have been parochial to what became *au courant*. Boston design reformers—C. Howard Walker comes to mind—were as concerned with the broad urban fabric as they were with small-scale objects of daily use, testimony to their multidisciplinary interests at every level, from macro to micro. In this regard, their concerns paralleled those of some British and European reformers and demonstrated the all-encompassing vision that they hoped to promote.

The Boston diaspora ensured that the definitions of Usefulness and Beauty promoted by Boston's critics had national and even international visibility. The St. Louis world's fair, in many ways, marked the moment when the SACB had its greatest influence upon American craft. By exhibiting handicrafts in the same venue as painting and sculpture, the fair raised important questions about the interrelationship of the fine and the applied arts in the context of the "City Beautiful." That debate regarding the distinctions among art, craft, and design still rages today, although the breadth and depth of design criticism as an art form has waned. The fair demonstrated at once the regional nature of American arts and crafts and their governance by a national standard of Usefulness and Beauty and by international theories. It highlighted especially the strength of American art pottery, while calling attention to importance of Native American craft within an evolving national craft tradition.

Just as the 1851 Great Exhibition had inspired vibrant criticism, so too did the fair of 1904. The diversity of critics' backgrounds and the range of publications to which they contributed reflect the appeal of American handicrafts to a broad audience. At the time of the fair, Halsey Cooley Ives called such handiwork "a growing force in the land." Is craft still such a force today, in the twenty-first century, and does it continue to inspire the level and intensity of debate that it once did? How does the relationship of craftsman to critic compare today to that of the past? Is Morris's admonition to seek the "Useful" and the "Beautiful" still relevant? The Epilogue that follows strives to address some of those important questions.

EPILOGUE

Usefulness and Beauty in the New Millennium

The Legacy of the Society of Arts and Crafts, Boston

Have nothing in a room in the way of furniture that is not needed—that has not a real use, whether for work or play; and hang nothing upon the walls that does not need a wall to show it, and that is not worth being shown.

—Clarence Cook, *The House Beautiful* (1877)

Have nothing in your house that you do not know to be useful, or believe to be beautiful.

—William Morris, as paraphrased in *Classic American Home* (September 2001)

The quest for Usefulness and Beauty, as espoused by William Morris, and promoted by the Society of Arts and Crafts, Boston, is still relevant today. Much quoted by scholars and connoisseurs, Morris's maxim resonates as well with the general public who read shelter magazines such as *Classic American Home*, but may be altogether unfamiliar with the origins of the Arts and Crafts movement. Morris's advice still seems timely at the beginning of the twenty-first century, when consumers regard their homes as refuge from the exigencies of daily life, global terrorism, and overwhelming natural disasters. Little could the editors of *Classic American Home* have anticipated the events of September 11, 2001, when they chose to include Morris's quote as an epigraph to their publication of the same month. In the post-9/11 era, the need for a home to be a refuge is ever more important—physiologically and psychologically. Yet, Morris's words imply some degree of control over one's environment on the part of consumers that is at best idealistic, and at worst futile. Such futility does not, however, dissuade us from dreaming of the better life that the design reform movement promised.

The Arts and Crafts movement is thus now "big business." The obscure darling of devoted scholars and perspicacious collectors in the 1970s, it has achieved a level of visibility over the past thirty-five years that is remarkable. Today, the Arts and Crafts movement has insinuated itself into myriad aspects of culture and society, spawning a full-blown Arts and Crafts Revival that shows no sign of dying out. Most likely, it will outlast the handful of scholars and collectors who first rediscovered the original movement in the late 1960s and early 1970s, and who have worked tirelessly to bring it to light.[1]

Interest in the original Arts and Crafts movement, and the Arts and Crafts Revival that it spawned is truly international. Similarly, awareness of the movement in Boston and of the contributions of its members grows broader, deeper, and increasingly sophisticated. Brought to light by the important exhibition "The Art That Is Life" (1987), the SACB was later the focal point of an in-depth, traveling exhibition, "Inspiring Reform: Boston's Arts and Crafts Movement," held in 1997, the centenary year of the Society's founding. Monographs on individuals and companies that supported the SACB appear regularly, and artifacts made by members are consistent inclusions in art, architecture, design, craft, and shelter magazines.[2]

Another outlet for these artifacts is the popular public television series *Antiques Roadshow*. Though guest hosts have come and gone since the show first aired in the United States in 1996, objects produced by SACB members have remained a staple of the series, a testimony to their usefulness, their beauty, and the impressive prices that they now command in the antiques and collectibles market. Their creators—who more often than not struggled to make ends meet—would be amazed to see those prices, and to learn of their own widespread recognition.[3]

Price guides to antiques and collectibles attest to the inflated values that American Arts and Crafts have achieved in the current market, with prices for goods linked to the SACB often at the lead. Numerous objects produced by SACB members figured prominently in the first edition of Bruce Johnson's *Official Identification and Price Guide to Arts and Crafts* (1983). The appearance alone of this specialized tome attests to the movement's widespread visibility. The work of even more SACB members augmented Johnson's third edition, compiled in 2003 with co-author David Rago, the latter a frequent *Roadshow* consultant. Just a few examples demonstrate how greatly these items have appreciated. While prices for Grueby pottery, for example, shown at the St. Louis world's fair ranged from $10 to $175 each (these figures—in 1904 dollars—were provided in application forms for insurance purposes), by 1983 average prices at auction ranged from $75 to $6,000. Those increased values pale by comparison to averages given in 2003, ranging from $500 to a staggering $92,000, a record price for a 17 3/4 in.–tall vase by Wilhemina Post.[4]

Rookwood Pottery has experienced similar price inflation, despite being much maligned by Frederick Allen Whiting in 1904. Pieces displayed at St. Louis had values ranging from $10 to $60. By 1983, average prices at auction for Rookwood had risen into the $100 to $3,250 range—a healthy increase; by 2003, those prices had escalated into the $300 to $20,000 range. Always more plentiful than work representing the Grueby Pottery, Rookwood appeals to novice and advanced collectors alike.[5]

Art pottery predominates as a category in contemporary price guides just as it once threatened to overwhelm the display of American Arts and Crafts at St. Louis. But metalsmiths have also fared well in the contemporary marketplace. Take, for example, the work of silversmith Arthur J. Stone. At St. Louis, values for insurance purposes were listed at $50 or less per piece. By 1983, Stone's work had appreciated into the $150 to $1,250 range. By 2003, values at the high end of the continuum approached $4,300. These examples demonstrate the high regard that collectors hold for artifacts emanating from the SACB. And they prove that the definitions of Usefulness and Beauty formulated in 1897 and honed over time by the SACB Jury still attract collectors more than a hundred years later. What is delightfully ironic is that William Grueby and Arthur Stone were among those SACB Masters to receive the harshest ongoing criticism from the SACB Jury, while Whiting nearly excluded Rookwood from the display in the Palace of Art at the 1904 world's fair. This begs the question: have these individuals and companies achieved such acclaim today because of, or in spite of, the pointed criticism offered by their colleagues during their careers?[6]

Our fascination with the Arts and Crafts ideal generally, and the quest for Usefulness and Beauty specifically is not limited to the products and propaganda of the SACB. "The best design from the Arts & Crafts period," write Michael Fitzsimmons, Anne Yaffe Phillips, and James L. Reinish in their foreword to the catalogue *From Architecture to Object*, "has a special resonance which echoes through the intervening decades to the present day." Their comments pertain to a broad selection of American handicraft, including interior architectural elements, furnishings, lighting, objects, textiles, and graphic design, as well as to products of the SACB, which comprise a substantial number of illustrations in the book. The movement's appeal has shaped museum holdings—as institutions have competed to acquire important archival collections and one-of-a-kind artifacts. The movement's cachet has influenced tastes among the glitterati, the most notable being Barbra Streisand, who demonstrated just how far the Arts and Crafts movement had come when she famously paid $362,000 for a 1902 Gustav Stickley sideboard. The Arts and Crafts movement today is "big business" precisely because it has attracted the attention of thoughtful scholars and venerable institutions, even as it has permeated all aspects of popular culture, material culture, and the media.[7]

Today those wishing to immerse themselves in the fine points of the Arts and Crafts can peruse any number of specialty periodicals, including expensive, limited-edition quarterlies printed by hand on creamy paper in the manner of Morris's Kelmscott Press (such as *Tiller, a Bi-monthly Devoted to the Arts & Crafts*, and *The Tabby, a Chronicle of the Arts & Crafts Movement*) as well as glossy publications with a broad readership, epitomized by David Rago's *Style: 1900*. Scholars and collectors can attend specialized conferences, symposia, and study tours that focus on aspects of the design reform movement from broad to narrow. Some of these take place in restored period hotels and inns, allowing conference participants to live the Arts and Crafts lifestyle while attending lectures, buying the latest publications, or perusing exhibition halls filled with antiques and sympathetic reproductions. Consumers can attend museum exhibitions—permanent, temporary, traveling—and analyze the details of carefully crafted period rooms. In the same visit, they can patronize museum stores offering a wide variety of books and magazines, and purchase pseudo–Arts and Crafts jewelry, scarves, tea tiles, and desk accessories based upon coveted period examples. Sales in museum stores have become a lifesaver to these beleaguered institutions' bottom lines, and the continuing presence of Arts and Crafts reproductions attests to their popularity (with both the public and the museums' accounting departments).[8]

For those unable to shop directly at a major museum, the mail-order catalogue and website have come to the rescue. Knock-offs of famous Morris & Co. products have, for example, become such a fixture of both that the newsletter of the William Morris Society includes a special section, "The Morris Marketplace," just to help its readers keep track of what's available and where. Recognizing the appeal of Arts and Crafts products to serious collectors, myriad specialty shops, galleries, and studios have proliferated since the 1980s. As period artifacts escalate in price and there seem to be fewer authentic pieces available to an ever-increasing number of cognoscenti, these pieces have become the subject of thefts, forgeries, and misrepresentations. Here, the irony is pointed, given the spirit of integrity and ingenuity in which the originals were conceived.[9]

The laws of supply and demand have contributed to today's Arts and Crafts Revival. Large-scale manufacturers and retailers, along with individual craft-artists working in tiny studios have filled the marketplace with a broad array of reproductions, in part because few consumers can afford to furnish a home or office in the Arts and Crafts manner using rare and costly originals. And where have average consumers learned enough about the Arts and Crafts movement to warrant incorporating aspects of it into their personal environments? Production designers for film and television are partially responsible. Network news anchors function amidst Arts and Crafts sets and props; an advertisement for Florida orange juice implies that it tastes best if sipped while one is perching on a high-back C. R. Mackintosh chair; television series—such as *Thirtysomething*, *Mad About You*, and *The Forsyte Saga*—along with movies as diverse as *My Fair Lady*, *Sleepless in Seattle*, *A River Runs Through It*, *Lord of the Rings*, and *Seabiscuit* have utilized Arts and Crafts furnishings and architecture in their sets. Seeing these examples, consumers cannot help but seek something similar.[10]

Shelter magazines have been equally influential, promoting the movement both overtly and covertly in cover stories, editorials, features, ads, and even advice columns. These publications include *House Beautiful* (a descendant of the original nineteenth-century magazine that catered to aesthetes and design reformers), *House and Garden*, *Architectural Digest*, *Elle Décor*, *Martha Stewart Living*, *Metropolitan Home*, *Traditional Home*, and *Old-House Interiors*, to name just a few. In 1994, *House Beautiful* collaborated with the Chrysler Corporation and the Frank Lloyd Wright Foundation to celebrate Wright's work and legacy. Retailers—sometimes working with shelter magazines—reinforce the casual consumer's desire to know more by offering no-cost, in-store seminars. Even cooking magazines have touched upon the Arts and Crafts. In its September 1999 issue, *Bon Appétit* surveyed the evolution of the twentieth-century place setting, starting with examples of Roycroft china.[11]

Responding to print advertisements and television commercials (or shows on the cable television Travel channel), consumers may choose to take a family vacation in California. There they can indulge in a simulated Arts and Crafts environment at Disney's Grand Californian Hotel. Throughout the resort, Disney icons blend with exemplars of Usefulness and Beauty, resulting in such hybrids as a laminated doorknob sign that features a wand-bearing, apron-clad mouse, requesting "Housekeeping Please" in an Arts and Crafts font and color scheme. Parents might read their children to sleep from Charles Perrault's *Cinderella* (2001)—a favorite Disney subject—whose cover also features an Arts and Crafts font.[12]

Today, consumers desirous of living "in the manner of" can purchase houses modeled after the Bungalow-type, Shingle style, or Prairie style, clustered in master-planned communities ripe with manufactured nostalgia. They can provide their homes with state-of-the-art thermal windows (purchased from Andersen or Hurd), paint both exterior and interior in appropriate period color schemes (courtesy of Sherwin Williams and Benjamin Moore), contrast such paint schemes with sympathetic wallpapers and textiles (produced by Bradbury & Bradbury, Schumacher, Scalamandré, or Sanderson), and accent their floors with carpets hand-crafted in the Far East (imported by PIR International or Tufenkian). Consumers can select interior architectural elements to complement the overall theme, including ceiling fans (Hunter or Casablanca), lighting (Rejuvenation Hardware, Arroyo Craftsman, LightingUniverse.com, or Lumature), hammered copper sinks for bath or kitchen (Waterworks), and ceramic tile (Country Floors). They can even outfit their kitchens with ultra-efficient appliances (Jenn-Air, Sub-Zero) that blend with Arts and Crafts–influenced custom cabinetry. They can choose furniture in every price range and for every room in the house (along with patio or garden) from Bassett, Bernhardt, Cassina, Ethan Allen, Henredon, Hickory Chair Co., Kincaid, Lexington, McGuire, Sander Woodworking Co., Stickley, Thomasville, Thompson, and Workbench. They can even find a pseudo–Arts and Crafts timepiece (offered by Howard Miller or Bulova) perfect for mantle or entry hall.[13]

Retailers assisting consumers in finishing and furnishing their Arts and Crafts dream homes vary from high-end department stores to such middle-American mainstays as Pottery Barn, Crate and Barrel, Target, Montgomery Ward, K-Mart (sometimes with the assistance of Martha Stewart), Home Depot, and The Great Outdoors. Even companies that once established their reputations in the fashion and textile industries (Ralph Lauren, Nautica) have not been unbitten by the Arts and Crafts bug, as they have expanded into selling lines of chic home furnishings. At art galleries and craft fairs, homeowners can purchase tasteful, handmade accessories that blend with their Craftsman-type interiors. They can even dress the part, wearing scarves, shawls, ties, and jewelry modeled after one-of-a-kind, vintage pieces. As they munch on Mauna Loa–brand Macadamia Nuts (whose 2001 advertisement in *Travel + Leisure* appears in an Arts and Crafts font), they can peruse specialty magazines featuring graphic designs inspired by period publications.[14]

So insidious is the infiltration of the Arts and Crafts aesthetic into daily life that it appears routinely in advertisements for products having no direct connection with the movement. These use backdrops, props, patterns, borders, and fonts derived from the movement—without identifying the source or the influence. Since 1990, companies as diverse as Minwax, Lexus, Ace Hardware, and

Benjamin Moore have used subtle Arts and Crafts references to make their products appeal on a subliminal level to a certain demographic.[15]

Similarly, icons of the movement appear regularly in advertisements and magazine articles, demonstrating their longevity and classic appeal. One of these is William Morris's "Willow" pattern (Plate 18), which is still available as a wallpaper and printed textile. Sometimes this pattern appears unidentified, as in an advertisement for Waterford Crystal (1992), where it upholsters an overstuffed armchair, upon which a barefoot, party dress–clad toddler sits daintily, reaching for fruit held in a crystal bowl, illuminated by a crystal lamp. The implication in this advertisement is that both Waterford Crystal and the "Willow" pattern are classics, destined to endure for decades, even after the charming little girl reaches maturity. "Part of the pleasure of owning beautiful things," the text reminds us, "is feeling at home with them." "Willow" wallpaper appears again on the cover of *House and Garden* magazine (July 1993), predominating in a bathroom interior (whose showcasing there is itself an iconoclastic break with the norm), though the cover text does not mention the pattern by name. Presumably, the editorial staff chose it deliberately, knowing the power of the right cover to sell a magazine. Here, "Willow" subtly sells this particular issue, and the lack of identification implies that savvy readers will recognize it regardless. *House Beautiful* also acknowledges the power of the "Willow" pattern, incorporating it (or its variations) in feature articles and advertisements on a regular basis (February 1997, March 1999, October 1999).[16]

If imitation is, indeed, the sincerest form of flattery that may explain why knock-offs of "Willow" are also widespread. In the June 1997 issue of *House Beautiful*, York Wallcovering Co. advertises its "Posie 'n Ivy" fabric, which resembles "Willow" in color, composition, and motif. In March 2000, Target advertises patio furniture whose umbrella and seat cushions illustrate an interpretation of this popular, leafy-green pattern, suitable for "a shady corner for curling up with a book or journal . . . vines and plants in every shade of green." That nothing is sacred, however, is evident from a September 1998 issue of *Martha Stewart Living*. In it, a "how-to" article on the topic of glazing wallpaper uses "Willow" as its victim, demonstrating the effect of a translucent whitewash applied to its surface, toning down what the writer terms an "overpowering" pattern. Such travesties notwithstanding, author Elizabeth Wilhide best explains the enduring popularity of this Morris & Co. product. "A perennial favorite," she writes, "it works as well flat on the wall or upholstering plain upright pieces as it does draped or gathered into simple curtains. The pattern has a timeless vitality and freshness." Note her use of the same descriptors that theorists such as Lewis F. Day employed at the turn of the nineteenth century to describe "good design."[17]

The Arts and Crafts Revival would have waned by now—it has been going strong for at least thirty-five years—were it not for its intellectual and emotional appeal. Today's consumers vary greatly in their knowledge of the movement's underlying philosophy, but most recognize that its attraction is more than skin-deep. The ideals that fueled the movement in its heyday still excite today's consumers who hope to imbue their homes—authentic or recreated—with meaning.

Like their Victorian predecessors, today's consumers are searching for surroundings that are easy to live with, that will age gracefully, and that seem both timeless and enduring. The sensuous appeal of handcraftsmanship—or a simulation thereof—in the early-twenty-first-century digital age is as strong as it was 150 years ago, when industrialization threatened the comfortable status quo. Today, an increasing number of once-leading American industries—producing textiles, furniture, and blown glass—have died out entirely, or moved overseas due to globalization. As a result, consumers lament the loss of products proudly "Made in America" that they can wear, touch, and use, and that remind them of the nation's rich handicraft tradition. As the United States suffers an inexorable transition to an information-based economy, the strong materials and rugged textures of Arts and Crafts products epitomize the "can-do" spirit of America's pioneers. They transformed a wilderness into a livable environment through determination, innate know-how, and a willingness to use their bare hands. Today, the hand-hewn, hand-forged, hand-thrown, and hand-woven appeal especially to someone who has spent a long day staring at a computer screen, manipulating mouse and keyboard. The genuineness, honesty, and integrity of such materials are reassuring; they are something to "hang on to" in an era of breathtaking change. "It's a pretty difficult life to live, this of the serious nineteenth Century," wrote Sarah W. Whitman in January 1885, a sentiment that seems apropos at the start of the twenty-first.[18]

Today's Arts and Crafts Revival parallels two contemporary movements that celebrate slowing down, turning off, and eliminating the inessential. David Shi's *In Search of the Simple Life* (1986) chronicles the role that simplicity has played in the intellectual life of the nation, from the 1600s to the present day. Sarah Ban Breathnach's popular daybook, *Simple Abundance* (1997), and Janet Luhr's *Simple Living Guide* (1997) provide consumers with strategies for disconnecting—both literally and figuratively—from the pressure and stress of modern life. In a Ruskinian tone, Luhr advises her readers to cultivate "more joyful living" by making do with less. *Real Simple* magazine promotes the attributes of moderation throughout the home including the kitchen. Even the trendy Slow Food movement reflects a desire to handcraft delicious family meals, using a time-tested *batterie de cuisine* in an atmosphere divorced from microwave and drive-through window. In a similar vein, alternative grocery stores advertise seminars in "Voluntary Simplicity" in their informative—if obsessive—newsletters.[19]

The "Simple Living" trend harkens back to the anti-urbanism of the Arts and Crafts era, as well as to its goal of stripping away the superfluous. Surely, a leaflet such as Mary Brown's *Simplification of Life* (1899) served as a model, by advising readers to "minimize wants" and "learn to do without." Yet, "Simple Living" does not imply a simplistic result. The original Arts and Crafts movement blended simplicity with a visual richness of effect, just as the Slow Food movement recreates time-honored comfort foods that offer varied textures, layered tastes, and complex aromas.[20]

As these examples suggest, the Arts and Crafts Revival is not just a "look"; it is a lifestyle. This neo-design reform movement is as much about home improvement as it is about self-improvement. Just as "fitness" fascinated design reformers at the turn of the nineteenth century (linking "fit" designs to "fit" individuals), health and wellness—whether aesthetic, physiological, or financial—are obsessions today. A convenient, well-equipped, tastefully appointed home and office that help inhabitants to feel good about themselves are the *desiderata* of the Arts and Crafts Revival.[21]

Other aspects of the Arts and Crafts movement that resonate with today's consumers are the values that its founders and supporters upheld. These values were broad, quintessentially American (and not restricted to "family values" touted during the 2004 presidential election).

"For your teachers, they must be Nature and History," Morris wrote, advice that still seems relevant today. In the postmodern era, consumers venerate tradition and historical precedent. They are as concerned for the state of local flora and fauna as they are for that of the global environment. While history provides a touchstone to the past and offers a contrast to today's frenetic pace, nature provides an antidote to an increasingly artificial, virtual world. Consumers thrive in homes and communities modeled after the best of the past, even as they incorporate aspects of so-called Green Design and sustainability into those environments. Just as design reformers turned to the Middle Ages, the Georgian or Colonial eras, and the Orient for inspiration, today's consumers look nostalgically at the post–Civil War to pre–First World War period, imagining it to have been a slower paced, more genteel, and visually rich time. They turn to history to provide a sense of rootedness, even as they embrace nature for its freshness and regenerative powers.[22]

This desire to feel both rooted to the past and attuned with nature inspired many homes constructed ca. 1860–1920. These blended sympathetically with their sites, incorporated local materials and time-honored construction techniques, and conveyed an earth-bound, sheltering quality by means of line and form. Contemporary architects and builders duplicate such qualities in homes representing the Arts and Crafts Revival. Fireplaces and hearths are just as much the heart of the home today as they were in Morris's Red House, or Voysey's Orchard. The steeply pitched roof still connotes protection, while a flat roof with broad overhanging eaves makes a house appear connected to and integrated with its site. Designers of Arts and Crafts Revival homes imbue entry doors, windows, chimneys, and terraces with much of the same symbolism employed by their turn-of-the-century counterparts. They strive to create houses that exude a comfort, welcome, and strength (Fig. 240).[23]

A connection to both local traditions and immediate surroundings resulted in period Arts and Crafts homes that varied widely from region to region across the United States. American architects produced structures in myriad styles—Olde English, Queen Anne, Colonial Revival, Shingle, bungalow-type, Prairie School, log-and-boulder, Spanish Colonial, Craftsman, and Mission. Yet the values that these homes represented were universal. Love for nation as well as region permeated these houses at the turn of the century in a manner that parallels the patriotism and pride of place that have resurfaced in the post-9/11 era.[24]

240. Contemporary residence in the Arts and Crafts Revival style, by Rick Neumann, architect (Petoskey, Mich.), 2004. Photograph by John Wooden. (Courtesy Rick Neumann) Here the large doors and windows convey welcome, while the coarse boulders of terrace and chimney stacks project solidity.

Regardless of regional variations, period Arts and Crafts architects sought to infuse homes with character, believing that a house's demeanor reflected that of its inhabitants. Today, in an era of broken families and corporate scandals, we continue to ponder the link between character and environment. This may, in part, explain the attraction of the Arts and Crafts Revival to today's consumers. "Nowadays, when affluent collectors furnish their homes with Mission Oak, and a Gustav Stickley sideboard brings thousands of dollars at auction," writes historian Bret Walker, "the links between hard work, personal character, and the redemptive quality of a well-designed chair are perhaps harder to credit than they were when the [twentieth] century was young. The belief that making and using simple, honest, straightforward domestic objects would inculcate parallel ethical and moral virtues sounds like wishful thinking. And yet," he concludes, "it is a continuing strain in American life and thought." So, too, is faith in a well-conceived floor plan, a sheltering roof, a welcoming front door. The moralism of model homes created in the nineteenth century by design reformers is equally evident today in those of the Arts and Crafts Revival.[25]

A sense of social responsibility inspired period architects to create environments intended to enhance the well-being of their clients. A similar sense of social responsibility inspires their contemporary counterparts. Some preserve or renovate period structures; others use gleaned or recycled building materials in new construction. Many are drawn to natural products that regenerate easily or can be produced without harming the environment. Exemplifying this trend is the "eco-friendly house, in harmony with nature" that graces the cover of *Home* magazine (September 1994, Plate 19). Editors describe this "harmony house" in a feature article, calling it "an innovative new house in Portland, Oregon, that combines a timeless Craftsman heritage and up-to-the-minute eco-sensitivity." The cover image shows a quiet study, finished in a subdued palette of cream, green, and brown and furnished with straight-back Stickley chairs.[26]

Those who collaborated on the realization of this dream house include an architect, a builder, an interior designer, and a host of national and international manufacturers and professional associations. The interdisciplinary nature of this project—in which the clients, too, actively participated—epitomizes the value of teamwork prized by both the original Arts and Crafts movement and its revival. Then as now, the close interaction of everyone involved in the creative process ensures a unified end product in which every part relates seamlessly to the whole. Today, businesses and institutions encourage their employees to engage in inter-, trans-, and cross-disciplinary efforts. The "artistic collaboration" and atmosphere of "mutually helpful relations" promoted by the SACB specifically, and by design reformers generally, have come full circle.

Another value prized in both 1908 and 2008 seems contradictory to this collaborative impulse; yet individualism is a part of the Arts and Crafts Revival. "It is a common trait that we believe our personal taste is infallible," writes David Dewing in Charlotte Gere's *The House Beautiful* on the assertion of the self, "as a result of which the design reform movement is still going strong, still trying to persuade people what to like and what to reject, albeit," he concludes, "in slightly less patronizing terms." Morris's advice on Usefulness and Beauty still resonates with consumers today because it bespeaks empowerment to make their own decisions about how to live. They may subscribe to the broader tenets of the Arts and Crafts Revival, but they insist upon interpreting its traits and values in their own, individualistic way.[27]

That the Arts and Crafts Revival can prize collaboration and individualism simultaneously only strengthens its ties with the original movement, which was ripe with duality. The Arts and Crafts movement promoted interdisciplinary interaction even as it nurtured the efforts of isolated craftspersons working alone in their respective studios. It stressed the importance of historical precedent as it searched simultaneously for freshness and originality. "While crediting its progressive aspects," Wendy Kaplan notes, "the conservative nature of much Arts and Crafts production can also be recognized as an integral part of it—which has significantly affected how we judge good design today." If the movement was bourgeois (or conservative), emphasizing homely virtues, strength, solidity, and what the Danes term *hygge*, or a "comfortable coziness," it was also bohemian (or progressive), delighting in "art for art's sake," iconoclasm, and innovation. It contrasted simplicity with a richness of visual effect.[28]

Even the movement's quest for Usefulness and Beauty demonstrates duality. Theorists as diverse as Italian Renaissance architect Andrea Palladio and nineteenth-century aesthetes Walter Pater, Oscar Wilde, and James A. M. Whistler were not alone in regarding these concepts to be mutually exclusive. Leaders in the Arts and Crafts movement acknowledged the difficulty of merging the two successfully: Charles Sumner Greene (of the Pasadena-based architectural firm Greene & Greene) confessed: "I seek till I find what is truly useful and then I try to make it beautiful." His use of the word "try" implies that he was not always able to achieve that lifelong goal.[29]

Some interpret the duality of Usefulness and Beauty along gender lines. Historian Michael Brooks suggests that both the nineteenth-century writer Henry Adams and the architect/theorist Eugène-Emanuel Viollet-le-Duc shared a theory that Usefulness epitomized the masculine while Beauty equaled the feminine. That theory was still influential in 1905, when architect Charles Hooper published a treatise on the American country house (which, by the way, included numerous works representing SACB architects). "The den is apt to be the most homelike room in the house," he writes, because "the man is apt to select furniture with a view to its use, and it is thus more likely to be comfortable than handsome. The woman, on the other hand, has a fairly good eye for the beautiful, with perhaps less of the practical." Though some might bristle at these stereotypes, they persist even to this day. In his column "Love & Money" in the *Wall Street Journal*, Jeff D. Opdyke comments upon a nearly identical situation existing in 2005. "It may be true . . . that many men have different criteria when it comes to picking furniture. Judging from the people I talk to," he begins, "women are more likely to look at furniture and see something that's 'beautiful' or 'goes perfectly with the antique pine ballfoot chest in the living room.' Men, on the other hand, seem to look at furniture and see pain, as in, 'that is the most uncomfortable couch I've ever sat on. I don't care how pretty it is.' A friend of mine admits that the only thing he has ever cared about when it comes to furniture is comfort." Opdyke ends by quoting an unidentified husband. "I didn't care what it looks like," the husband says, "I only care about sinking into it. If I could imagine falling asleep in it, then it passed the test." Opdyke explains that this man's "wife, meanwhile, 'wants it so that someone who visits will see it as beautiful.'" The husband concludes, regarding "good design": "We have two completely different tests."[30]

The presence of such dual tendencies—collaborative/individualistic, traditional/innovative, conservative/progressive, bourgeois/bohemian, simple/rich, masculine/feminine—may be the key to explaining the persistence of the Arts and Crafts ideal into the twenty-first century. The design reform movement did not present consumers with an "either/or" proposition. It did not frustrate its proponents by offering limited choices. If anything, the Arts and Crafts ideal valued a "both/and" attitude that encouraged eclecticism. Makers and users could choose from a wide variety of traits and values. Even critics could make strong pronouncements regarding "good design," while being, at times, vague, arbitrary, and even contradictory. By contrast, modernism was far more dictatorial, defining "good design" according to restrictive parameters. As its theories have given way to the more forgiving and inclusive attitudes of postmodernism, the duality that characterized the original Arts and Crafts movement continues to appeal to scholars, collectors, and consumers today. "The movement," argues Wendy Kaplan, "is no longer valued only in the context of a continuum which reached its zenith in modernism, but can be evaluated on its own merits." Essential to a thorough evaluation and determination of those merits is an understanding of dualities—not the least of which are Usefulness and Beauty—that characterized the movement. The process requires as well that we continue to ponder the way in which design reformers, whether craftsmen or critics, defined those enigmatic concepts at the time.[31]

APPENDIX A

MEMBERS OF THE SACB JURY, 1900–1917

NAME	DATES	OCCUPATION	SERVICE AS JUROR[1]
Carey, Arthur Astor	1857–1923	social reformer	1900–1902
Clark, Henry Hunt	1875–1962	book artist, illuminator	1900–1902
Coolidge, J. Templeman, Jr.	1856–1945	designer	1900–1903, 1908–17
Dennett, Mary Ware	1872–1947	leatherworker	1900–1903
Forssen, Carl G.	n.a.	metalworker	1908, 1910
Hale, Frank Gardner	1876–1945	jewelry maker	1910–16
Kendrick, George Prentiss	1850–1919	designer	1903–08
Kjellstrom, Nils	b. 1852	wood-carver	1900–1903
Longfellow, Alexander Wadsworth, Jr.	1854–1934	architect	1900–1903, 1908–17
Martin, Laurin Hovey	1875–1939	jewelry maker	1900–1903
Morse, Alice J.	b. ca. 1872	designer, textile artist	1908–17
Murphy, Herman Dudley	1867–1945	frame maker	1908–09
Peabody, John Endicott	1853–1921	designer	1909–17
Putnam, Annie Cabot	1850–1924	metalworker	1908–12
Ross, Denman Waldo	1853–1935	design educator	1900–03
Sacker, Amy M.	1872–1965	designer, educator	1903–14[2]
Sears, Mary Crease	1880–1938	designer, book artist	1908, 1910–17
Sears, Sarah Choate	1858–1935	designer, artist	1900–1903
Smith, Joseph Lindon	1863–1950	designer	1902, 1911–13
Sturgis, R. Clipston	1860–1951	architect, educator	1900
Walker, Charles Howard	1857–1936	architect, educator	1901, 1903, 1908–17
Warren, Herbert Langford	1857–1917	architect, educator	1900–1903, 1908, 1911
Whiting, Frederick Allen	1873–1959	administrator	1900–1903, 1908–12
Whitman, Sarah Wyman	1842–1904	stained glass maker	1900–1903

Sources: 1900–1903: AAA/SACB Papers: 316: 002, 009, 028. 1908: AAA/SACB Papers: 319: 464. 1909–1912: AAA/SACB Papers: 316: 036–049. 1913: AAA/SACB Papers 319: 817. 1914: AAA/SACB Papers: 318: 864. 1915–17: *Annual Report* for those years.

1. No records of jurors' names exist for the years 1904–07, but Coolidge, Kendrick, Longfellow, Ross, Sacker, Walker, H. L. Warren, and Whiting probably served during that time.

2. The *Annual Report* for 1914 calls attention to Sacker's retirement from the Jury after twelve years of service.

APPENDIX B

SURVEY OF THE SACB MEMBERSHIP BY CRAFT CATEGORY, 1916

Architect	22	Lace maker	8
Basketry	21	Leaded glass	2
Bead worker	2	Leather	37
Book plates	12	Metalworker	96
Brass worker	3	Modeler	22
Cabinet worker	12	Needleworker	7
Cement worker	1	Painter	8
Ceramic worker	1	Pewter	2
Chaser	4	Photographer	23
China decorator	34	Porcelain decorator	1
Color printer	2	Potter	29
Colorist of plaster casts	1	Printer	5
Concrete worker	2	Pyrographer	6
Crocheter	1	Sculptor	4
Decorator	29	Ship modeler	1
Designer	143	Silversmith	42
Draughtsman	2	Stained glass	5
Dyer	4	Stenciler	7
Embroiderer	33	Stone cutter	1
Enameler	22	Tapestry weaver	4
Frame maker	6	Tatting	1
Gem carver	1	Textiles	1
Illuminator	17	Toys	12
Illustrator	1	Weaver	19
Interior decorator	2	Wood block	2
Iron worker	3	Wood-carver	50
Jeweler	129	Wood engraver	1

Source: Survey of the Membership, Conducted by the Committee on Entertainment of the Society of Arts and Crafts, Boston, 1916. AAA/SACB Papers: 316: 074.

APPENDIX C

LIST OF BOOKS IN THE SACB LIBRARY, COMPILED 1917–1918

Arts and Crafts Essays, by Members of the Arts and Crafts Exhibition Society, with a preface by William Morris.
Art and Its Producers, and *The Arts and Crafts of Today*, by William Morris.
Hopes and Fears for Art, by William Morris.
Lectures on Art, by John Ruskin.
Smithsonian Institution Papers, Vol. I. Illustrated.
1. Japanese Wood-Cutting and Wood-Cut Printing. 2. Two Persepolitan Casts in the United States Museum. 3. The Golden Patera of Rennes. 4. Directions for Collectors of American Basketry. 5. Pewter and the Revival of Its Use. 6. A Primitive Frame for Weaving Narrow Fabrics. 7. A Collection of Hopi Ceremonial Pigments. 8. Museum Collections to Illustrate Religious History. 9. Report of the Exhibit of the United States National Museum at the Pan-American Exposition.
Smithsonian Institutions Papers, Vol. II. Illustrated.
1. The Graphic Art of the Eskimos, by Walter J. Hoffman.
Smithsonian Institution Papers, Vol. III. Illustrated.
1. A Sketch of the History of Ceramic Art in China, with a Catalogue of the Hippisley Collection of Chinese Porcelains, by Alfred E. Hippisley.
Smithsonian Institution Papers, Vol. IV. Illustrated.
1. Archeological Field Work in North Eastern Arizona. 2. Contributions of American Archeology to Human History.

Arts and Crafts of Old Japan, by Steward Dick. 30 illustrations.
Légendes Curiosités des Metiers, by Paul Sebillot. (In French.) 220 illustrations.
Les Arts et Metiers au Moyen Age: L'Ancienne France, by Paul la Crois. (In French.) 181 illustrations.
Mediaeval Art—312 to 1350, by W. R. Lethaby. Illustrated.

Donatello, by Lord Balcarres. Illustrated.
Great Masters of Decorative Art: Sir Edward Burne-Jones, by Aymer Vallance; William Morris, by Lewis F. Day; Walter Crane, by himself. Illustrated.
The Life of William Morris, by J. W. MacKail. In 2 volumes. Illustrated.
The Art Work of Louis C. Tiffany. Fully illustrated.

The Bases of Design, by Walter Crane. Illustrated.
Composition, Part I, by Arthur W. Dow. 6th edition. Illustrated.
Line and Form, by Walter Crane. Illustrated.
Nature and Ornament, Vol. I, by Lewis F. Day. 87 illustrations.

Nature in Ornament, by Lewis F. Day. 315 illustrations.
Practical Designing, edited by Gleeson White. A Handbook on the Preparation of Working Drawings. Illustrated.
The Principles of Design, by Ernest A. Batchelder. Illustrated.
The Principles of Ornament, by James Ward. Illustrated.
A Theory of Pure Design, by Denman W. Ross. Illustrated.
The Training of a Craftsman, by Fred Miller. Illustrated.

Les Armes, by Maurice Maindron. (In French.) Illustrated.
Art-Enamelling upon Metals, by H. H. Cunynghame. 3rd edition. Illustrated.
Gems and Gem Minerals, by Oliver C. Farrington. Illustrated.
Gems, Jewelers' Materials, and Ornamental Stones of California, by the California State Mining Bureau. Illustrated.
The History of Mount Mica, Maine, by Augustus Choate Hamlin. Illustrated.
Old Plate: Its Makers and Marks, by J. H. Bucks. New and enlarged edition. With numerous illustrations.
The Old Silver of American Churches, by E. Alfred Jones. With 145 photogravure plates.
Silverwork and Jewelry, by H. Wilson. Illustrated.
Details of Decorative Sculpture. French Renaissance. 50 plates.
Woodcarving, According to the Japanese Method, by Charles Holme. Illustrated.
Woodcarving, Design and Workmanship, by George Jack. Illustrated.

American Glassware, Old and New, by Edwin Atlee Barber. Illustrated.
English Table Glass, by Percy Bate. Illustrated.
Stained Glass Work, by C. W. Whall. Illustrated. (2 copies.)

The Decoration of Leather, by Maude Nathan, translated from George de Lecy. Illustrated.

Embroidery and Tapestry Weaving, by Mrs. Archibald H. Christie. Illustrated. (2 copies.)
Hand Loom Weaving, by Mattie Phipps Todd. 57 illustrations.
Needlework as Art, by Lady M. Alford. Illustrated.

Aboriginal American Basketry, by Otis Tufton Mason. 670 illustrations.
Indian Basketry, by George Wharton James. 360 illustrations. 2nd enlarged edition.

Bookbinding and the Care of Books, by Douglas Cockerell. Illustrated.
Twentieth Century Cover Designs, by Victor H. and Ernest L. Briggs. Illustrated.
Grammar of Lettering: A Handbook of Alphabets, by Andrew W. Lyons. Illustrated.
Letters and Lettering, by Frank Chouteau Brown. Illustrated.
Writing and Illuminating and Lettering, by Edward Johnston. Illustrated. (2 copies.)

The Little Passion of Albert [sic] Durer. Reproduced in fac-simile [sic]. Illustrated.

The Encyclopedia of Ceramics, by W. P. Jervis. Illustrated.

The Pottery Industry. Prepared by the Bureau of Foreign and Domestic Commerce, Washington.

Japanese Pottery. Catalogue of the Morse Collection of Museum of Fine Arts, Boston, by Edward S. Morse. 68 photogravure plates.

Old English Churches, by George Clinch. (2nd and enlarged edition.) Illustrated.

European and Japanese Gardens: Italian Gardens, by A. D. F. Hamlin; English Gardens, by R. Clipston Sturgis; French Gardens, by John Galen Howard; Japanese Gardens, by K. Honda. Edited by Glenn Brown. Illustrated.

The A B C of Photo-Micrography, by W. H. Walmsley. Illustrated.

Photographic Lenses, by Conrad Beck and Herbert Andrews. (2nd edition.) Illustrated.

American Art Annual, 1898–1903–1916, edited by Florence N. Levy. Illustrated. (3 vols.)

Annual Reports of The Society of Arts and Crafts, Boston, 1903–1913.

Art and Industry: American Education in the Industrial and Fine Arts in the United States, by Isaac E. Clarke. Vol. I. Drawing in the Public Schools. Vol. II. Industrial and Manual Training in the Public Schools. Vol. III. Industrial and Technical Training in Associations and Institutions. Vol. IV. Industrial and Technical Training in Schools of Technology, etc.

The Craftsman. Vol. I. (1901), Vol. II. (1902). Illustrated.

Handicraft. Vol. I. April 1902–March 1903. By The Society of Arts and Crafts. Illustrated. (2 copies.)

Industrial Education. Report of the Commissioner of Labor, 1901, Washington.

Official Catalogue of International Exhibition, Philadelphia, 1876.

Trade and Technical Education. Report of the Commissioner of Education, 1902, Washington.

Who's Who in America. Vol. IV. 1906–1907.

Any of these books may be borrowed by members for a period of two weeks, either by calling for them personally or by writing and paying the postage both ways. Apply to the Secretary.

The Society will be very glad to have donated to this library any books relating to the industrial arts.

Source: *The Annual Report of Society of Arts and Crafts, Boston, Massachusetts, for the Year* 1917 (Boston: Stetson Press, April 30, 1918), Section 9, "Library and Entertainment," pp. 20–23.

APPENDIX D

WORKS COMMENDED BY THE SAC'B JURY AS LISTED IN THE *Annual Reports*, 1913–1918

DATE OF ANNUAL REPORT	INDIVIDUAL	COMMENDATION CATEGORY[1]	MEDIUM	AWARD
1913	Isaac (John) Kirchmayer	Medallist	Wood-carver	Medal
	Henry C. Mercer	Medallist	Potter	Medal
	Arthur J. Stone	Medallist	Metalworker	Medal
1914	Julia de Wolf Addison		Embroiderer and illuminator	Commendation for 1913
	Fayette Barnum		Designer	
	Margaret A. Blair		Jeweler and designer	
	Lucretia McM. Bush		Jeweler	
	Elizabeth E. Copeland		Jeweler and metalworker	
	Eda Lord and L. B. Dixon		Jewelers and metalworkers	
	Mary H. Frye		Designer	
	Frank G. Hale		Jeweler and enameler	
	Edith Penman and E. R. Hardenbergh		Potters	
	Mary A. Kinsman		Embroiderer	
	Margaret Rogers		Metalworker and jeweler	
	Josephine H. Shaw		Metalworker and jeweler	
	Arthur J. Stone		Silversmith	
	John Verberg		Metalworker and jeweler	
	Mary P. Winlock		Metalworker and jeweler	
	Josephine H. Shaw	Medallist	Metalworker and jeweler	Medal
	Mary C. Sears	Medallist	Bookbinder	Medal
	Frank L. Koralewsky	Medallist	Ironworker	Medal

USEFULNESS AND BEAUTY IN THE NEW MILLENIUM

DATE OF ANNUAL REPORT	INDIVIDUAL	COMMENDATION CATEGORY[1]	MEDIUM	AWARD
1915	W. Cole Brigham		Maker of marine mosaics	Commendation for 1914
	Amy F. Dalrymple		China decorator	
	Onata Fitts		Porcelain decorator	
	George E. Germer		Chaser, silversmith, and ecclesiastical worker	
	Ellen Gilman		Designer	
	Clara S. Grierson		Needleworker	
	Marian Hague		Needleworker	
	Frank G. Hale		Jeweler and enameler	
	Marion Hardy		Designer	
	Mrs. R. H. Hicks		China decorator	
	Alice Kendall		Photographer	
	Elinore Klapp		Jeweler	
	Frank J. Marshall		Enameler	
	Max Peinlich		Modeler	
	W. B. Post		Photographer	
	Annie F. Pratt		China painter	
	Adelaide A. Robineau		Potter	
	Margaret Rogers		Jeweler and enameler	
	Elgia M. Ryder		China painter	
	Josephine H. Shaw		Metalworker and jeweler	
	E. E. Soderholz		Concrete worker	
	Arthur J. Stone		Silversmith	
	Caroline P. Ward		Maker of braided rugs	
	Bertrand Wentworth		Photographer	
	Arthur S. Williams		Metalworker, jeweler, and frame maker	
	Helen Wurlitzer		Needleworker	

302 APPENDIX D

DATE OF ANNUAL REPORT	INDIVIDUAL	COMMENDATION CATEGORY[1]	MEDIUM	AWARD
	Marion A. Youngjohn		China painter	
	Frank G. Hale	Medallist	Jeweler and enameler	Medal
	Adelaide A. Robineau	Medallist	Potter	Medal
1916	Alice Austen	Masters[1]	Photographer	Commendation for 1915
	Sidney T. Callowhill		China decorator	
	Carrig-Rohane Shop		Artistic frames, mirrors	
	Sarah R. Comer		Enameler and silversmith	
	Elizabeth E. Copeland		Jeweler and metalworker	
	Jessie A. Dunbar		Jeweler	
	George E. Germer		Silversmith	
	Arthur G. Grinnell		Lacquer worker	
	Ellen A. Gilman		Decorator	
	Frank G Hale		Jeweler and enameler	
	Marion C. Hardy		Decorator	
	Grace Hazen		Jeweler	
	Mary M. Hicks		China decorator	
	George J. Hunt		Goldsmith, silversmith, and ecclesiastical worker	
	Herbert Kelly		Jeweler	
	Frank J. Marshall		Metalworker and enameler	
	Reginald Pearce		Jeweler	
	Adelaide A. Robineau		Potter	
	Margaret Rogers		Metalworker and jeweler	
	Josephine H. Shaw		Metalworker and jeweler	
	Arthur J. Stone		Silversmith	
	Walford Thulin		Wood-carver	
	Harriet J. Timlin		Basket maker	

APPENDIX D   303

DATE OF ANNUAL REPORT	INDIVIDUAL	COMMENDATION CATEGORY[1]	MEDIUM	AWARD
	Robert T. Walker		Designer	
	James T. Woolley		Silversmith	
	Ellsworth Woodward		Potter	
	Elizabeth E. Copeland	Medallist	Jeweler and metalworker	Medal
	Eda Lord and l. B. Dixon	Medallist	Jewelers and metalworkers	Medal
	Ellsworth Woodward	Medallist	Silversmith	Medal
	Leander Anderson	Craftsman	Cabinet maker	Commendation for 1915
	Gertrude P. Ashley		Basket maker	
	Lucretia McM. Bush		Jeweler	
	George E. Buzza		Designer	
	Mabel P. Cook		Needleworker	
	Margaret Blair Dean		Jeweler	
	Nina B. Forsythe		Weaver	
	Mrs. James T. Garland		Needleworker (Old Colony Union)	
	Robert W. Hyde		Illuminator	
	William B. Luce		Cabinet maker	
	Karl Maynard		Photographer	
	Mary Morison		Needleworker (Handicraft Workers of Peterboro)	
	Augusta V. Norcross		Designer	
	W. B. Post		Photographer	
	George L. Scheidemantel		Leather worker	
	Rose Whitney Smith		Designer	
	Marion P. Weniger		Toy maker	
	Bertrand H. Wentworth		Photographer	
1917	Mary Allen	Masters	Photographer	Commendation for 1916

304 APPENDIX D

DATE OF ANNUAL REPORT	INDIVIDUAL	COMMENDATION CATEGORY[1]	MEDIUM	AWARD
	Lucretia McM. Bush	Masters	Jeweler	Commendation for 1916
	Jessie L. Burbank		Jeweler	
	George E. Buzza		Designer	
	Sydney T. Callowhill		China decorator	
	Kathryn E. Cherry		China decorator	
	Mable C. Dibble		China decorator	
	Jessie A. Dunbar		Jeweler	
	George C. Gebelein		Silversmith	
	Ellen A. Gilman		Bookbinder	
	John F. Grabau		Bookbinder	
	Clara S. Grierson		Needleworker	
	F. J. R. Gyllenberg		Silversmith	
	Frank G. Hale		Jeweler and enameler	
	Grace Hazen		Jeweler	
	Lois Lilley Howe		Architect and photographer	
	Mrs. L. Averill Howland		Bookbinder	
	George J. Hunt		Goldsmith, silversmith, and ecclesiastical worker	
	Mrs. Francis S. Kershaw		Weaver	
	Adolphe C. Kunkler		Silversmith	
	Karl F. Leinonen		Silversmith	
	Eugene W. Manchester		Silversmith	
	Marblehead Pottery		Potter	
	Florence and Karl Maynard		Photographers	
	William R. Mercer		Potter	
	Paul Revere Pottery		Potter	
	W. B. Post		Photographer	
	Margaret Rogers		Metalworker and jeweler	
	Josephine H. Shaw		Metalworker and jeweler	

APPENDIX D   305

DATE OF ANNUAL REPORT	INDIVIDUAL	COMMENDATION CATEGORY[1]	MEDIUM	AWARD
	Mary C. Sears	Masters	Designer, bookbinder, and pyrographer	Commendation for 1916
	L. B. Smith		Pewter smith	
	E. E. Soderholtz		Potter	
	Arthur J. Stone		Silversmith	
	Eleanore I. Sweringen		Bookbinder	
	Arnold G. Talbot		Weaver	
	Herbert A. Taylor		Silversmith	
	Robert T. Walker		Designer	
	Bertrand H. Wentworth		Photographer	
	James T. Woolley		Silversmith	
	Herbert A. Taylor		Silversmith	
	John Armstrong	Craftsmen	Weaver	
	Emma Bush		Ecclesiastical embroiderer	
	Faith B. Caruthers		Silversmith	
	Mabel P. Cook		Embroiderer	
	Winifred M. Crawford		Illuminator	
	A. M. Davis		Designer	
	Mrs. D. Brooks Garnsey		Weaver	
	Stanford A. Harding		Silversmith	
	Harriet R. Johnson		Weaver	
	Mr. and Mrs. Irving Kimball		Photographers	
	Mary V. McAbee		Enameler	
	Mrs. W. B. Nye		Weaver	
	Edward E. Oakes		Jeweler	
	Handicraft Workers of Peterboro		Needleworkers	
	Clarice Petremont		Designer	
	Clara L. Poillon		Potter	

DATE OF ANNUAL REPORT	INDIVIDUAL	COMMENDATION CATEGORY[1]	MEDIUM	AWARD
	Hope Rathbun		Tapestry weaver	
	Lillian M. Small		Photographer	
	Florence B. Todd		Needleworker	
	Maria G. Webber		Jeweler	
	Ellen A Webster		Weaver	
	Mrs. William Halsey Wood		Ecclesiastical embroiderer	
1918	M. Lamont Brown	Masters	Wood engraver	Commendation for 1917
	Lucretia McM. Bush		Jeweler	
	Sidney T. Callowhill		China and glass decorator	
	T. M. Cleland		Designer	
	Mabel P. Cook		Embroiderer	
	Elizabeth E. Copeland		Jeweler and metalworker	
	Winifred M. Crawford		Illuminator	
	Douglas Donaldson		Metalworker	
	Arthur W. Dow		Book designer, color printer, engraver	
	William H. Fulper		Potter	
	George C. Greener		Potter	
	Clara S. Grierson		Needleworker	
	Frank G. Hale		Jeweler and enameler	
	Marion C. Hardy		Decorator	
	Frank L. Koralewsky		Ironworker	
	F. W. Kulkmann		Cabinet maker	
	Florence and Karl Maynard		Photographers	
	Henry C. Mercer		Potter	
	Edward E. Oakes		Jeweler	
	Clarice Petremont		Designer	
	Adelaide A. Robineau		Potter	

APPENDIX D   307

DATE OF ANNUAL REPORT	INDIVIDUAL	COMMENDATION CATEGORY[1]	MEDIUM	AWARD
	Margaret Rogers	Masters	Jeweler	Commendation for 1917
	Josephine H. Shaw		Metalworker and jeweler	
	Lawrence B. Smith		Pewter worker	
	Arthur J. Stone		Silversmith	
	Mrs. John T. Timlin		Basket maker	
	Robert T. Walker		Designer	
	Bertrand H. Wentworth		Photographer	
	James T. Woolley		Silversmith	
	Douglas Donaldson	Medallist	Jeweler and metalworker	Medal
	Karl F. Leinonen	Medallist	Silversmith	Medal
	Bertrand H. Wentworth	Medallist	Photographer	Medal
	Mary Adams	Craftsmen	Needleworker (Handicraft Workers of Peterboro)	Commendation for 1917
	A.H. Andersen		Jeweler	
	Gustav Baumann		Block printer	
	E. Wenonah Brenan		Silversmith	
	Emma T. Bush		Ecclesiastical embroiderer	
	Julia S. Carpenter		Weaver	
	Florence Chase		Needleworker (The Denison House)	
	Elsie M. Dearborn		Needleworker	
	W. E. Hentschel		Leather worker	
	Mary I. Husted		Weaver (The Tide-Over-League)	
	Parker H. Kemble		Photographer	
	George R. King		Photographer	
	Ethel M. Lowell		China decorator	
	Marion C. Maercklein		Block printer	
	Sister Magdalen		Illuminator	
	Florence E. McLaughlin		Tatting maker	

308   APPENDIX D

DATE OF ANNUAL REPORT	INDIVIDUAL	COMMENDATION CATEGORY[1]	MEDIUM	AWARD
	John Murdoch	Craftsmen	Photographer	Commendation for 1917
	Mrs. Herbert A. Newhall		Needleworker (Child Welfare League)	
	Mary Patten		Photographer	
	Miriam B. Pearce		Leather worker	
	Gladys S. Ricker		Decorator	
	Elmer F. Senior		Silversmith	
	Emma A. Sylvester		Bead worker	
	Lester H. Vaughn		Pewter worker	
	Charles W. Warner		Basket worker	
	Mrs. William H. Wood		Ecclesiastical embroiderer	
	Marie Zimmermann		Metalworker	

1. Beginning with the *Annual Report* for 1916, commendations were broken down into two categories, "Craftsman" and "Master."

APPENDIX D   309

APPENDIX E

ARCHITECT MEMBERS OF THE SACB, 1897–1917

NAME	DATES	COMPANY OR FIRM	UNIVERSITY AFFILIATION			
			Harvard		MIT	
Allen, Francis R.	1843?–1931	Allen & Kenway Allen & Vance Allen & Collens	no		1876–77	Special Student
Andrews, Robert D.	1857–1928	Andrews & Jaques Andrews, Jaques & Rantoul	no		1875	Special Student
Barton, George E.	1880–1920	Sturgis & Barton	no		no	
Bigelow, Henry F.	1867–1932	Winslow, Wetherell & Bigelow Winslow & Bigelow Winslow, Bigelow & Wadsworth	n.a.		1888	Alumnus
Brown, Frank C.	1876–1947	Frank Chouteau Brown	no		no	
Chandler, Francis W.	1844–1926	Cabot & Chandler	no		no	
Cleveland, Frank E.	d. 1950	Cram, Goodhue & Ferguson	n.a.		n.a.	
Cram, Ralph Adams	1863–1942	Cram & Wentworth Cram, Wentworth & Goodhue Cram, Goodhue & Ferguson Cram & Ferguson	no		no	
Cummings, Charles K.	n.a.	Charles K. Cummings Cummings & Howard	no		no	
Dennett, W. Hartley	1870–1936	Hartley Dennett	1893	Alumnus	1892	Alumnus
Downer, Godfrey K.	d. 1955	Downer & Root	1910	Alumnus		
Dwight, Henry H.	n.a.	n.a.	n.a.		n.a.	
Eames, J. Henry	n.a.	n.a.	no		no	
Ferguson, Frank W.	1861–1926	Cram, Goodhue & Ferguson	no		no	
Fernald, George P.	d. 1920	Little & Browne	no		no	
Fisher, Richard A.	1868–1932	Fisher, Ripley & LeBoutillier (?)	no		no	
Goodhue, Bertrand G.	1869–1924	Cram, Wentworth & Goodhue Cram, Goodhue & Ferguson	no		n.a.	
Greeley, William R.	d. 1966	Kilham, Hopkins & Greeley Kilham, Hopkins, Greeley & Brodie	no		1902	Alumnus
Howe, Lois Lilley	1864–1968	Allen & Kenway Lois Lilley Howe Howe & Manning	no		1890	Alumnus

NAME	DATES	COMPANY OR FIRM	UNIVERSITY AFFILIATION			
			Harvard		MIT	
Hoyle, Alexander E.	d. 1969	Cram, Goodhue & Ferguson	n.a.		n.a.	
Ingraham, George H.	Ca. 1870–1950	George Hunt Ingraham; Ingraham & Hopkins	no		1892	Alumnus
Jaques, Herbert	1857–1916	Andrews, Jaques & Rantoul	no		1877	Alumnus
LeBoutillier, Addison B.	n.a.	Fisher, Ripley & LeBoutillier	no		no	
Longfellow, Alexander Wadsworth, Jr.	1854–1934	Longfellow & Harlow; Longfellow, Alden & Harlow	1876	Alumnus	1878	Alumnus
Loud, Joseph P.	d. 1942	Joseph P. Loud	no		1887	Alumnus
Lowell, Guy	1870–1926	Guy Lowell	1892	Alumnus	1894	Alumnus
Maginnis, Charles D.	1867–1955	Charles D. Maginnis; Maginnis, Walsh & Sullivan	no		no	
Newhall Louis C.	1869–1925	Newhall & Blevins	no		1891	Alumnus
Nichols, Edward H.	1864–1933	Edward Hall Nichols	1886(?)		1882	Alumnus
Putnam, William E.	d. 1947	Putnam & Cox; Putnam, Cox & Saltonstall(?); Putnam, Griswold, Wylde & Ames	1896		1898	Alumnus
Reed, Frederick F.	n.a.	n.a.	no		no	
Shaw, George R.	1848–1937	Shaw & Shaw; Shaw & Hunnewell	1869		1871	Alumnus
Sturgis, Richard C.	1860–1951	Sturgis & Cabot; Sturgis & Barton	1881		n.a.	
Swan, Walter D.	n.a.	n.a.	no		1895	Alumnus
Sylvester, Edmund Q.	1869–1942	n.a.	no		1892	Alumnus
Taylor, Bertrand E.	1855–1909	Rand & Taylor; Rand, Taylor, Kendall & Stevens; Kendall, Taylor & Co.	no		no	
Walker, C. Howard	1857–1936	Walker & Best; Walker & Kimball	1890		1899	?
Warren, H. Langford	1857–1917	Warren & Bacon; H. Langford Warren; Warren, Smith & Biscoe	1902		1879	Alumnus
Wheelwright, Edmund	1854–1912	Wheelwright & Haven; Wheelwright, Haven & Hoyt	1876		1875	Alumnus

Sources: Henry F. Withey and Elsie Rathbun Withey, *Biographical Dictionary of American Architects (Deceased)* (Los Angeles: New Age Publishing Co., 1956); Adolf K. Placzek, ed., *Macmillan Encyclopedia of Architects*, 4 vols. (New York: Free Press, 1982); Nancy Carlson Schrock, ed., *A Guide to Architectural Research in Boston* (New York: Garland, 1983); Harvard University Archives, Pusey Library; MIT Alumni Records, MIT Historical Collections.

NOTES

Preface

1. "Top 10 Home and Garden Events of the Century," *San Francisco Chronicle*, December 29, 1999: Section 3, pp. 1, 4.

2. David Shribman, executive editor, *Pittsburgh Post-Gazette*, as quoted in an interview on the PBS television show *Washington Week in Review*, January 28, 2000.

3. William Morris, "The Beauty of Life" in *Labour and Pleasure versus Labour and Sorrow*, pamphlet (Birmingham, 1880). This also appeared in *Hopes and Fears for Art* (London: Ellis & White, 1882), n.p.

4. "Men do not attain perfection by striving to do something out of the common. Perfection is acquired by doing common things uncommonly well." Anonymous quote in Ernest A. Batchelder, *The Principles of Design* (Chicago: The Inland Printer Company, 1904), p. 53.

5. Sloyd, which developed in the 1860s, was the prototype for programs in manual training and industrial arts education that evolved during the early twentieth century. Many thanks to Mary Jane Doerr for calling my attention to this important movement, to the arts and crafts classes taught at Bay View, and to the *Bay View Magazine*.

6. Fanny L. Armstrong, *To the Noon Rest: The Life, Work, and Addresses of Mrs. Helen M. Stoddard* (Butler, Ind.: L. H. Higley, 1909), pp. 164–65. Published in Detroit by John M. Hall, the *Bay View Magazine* was required reading for the "Bay View Reading Courses" and the Bay View Reading Club, both of which had national subscribers.

7. I would like to thank my former Arizona State University undergraduate students Cheyenne Harris and Heather Hanak for introducing me to this phrase.

Introduction

1. For background information on Wornum, see Simon Jervis, *The Penguin Dictionary of Design and Designers* (1984), p. 525; *Dictionary of National Biography* 21: 946–47; and www.lib.duke.edu/lilly/artlibry/dah/wornumr.htm. For a brief biography of Merrifield, see: www.lib.duke.edu/lilly/artlibry/dah/merrifieldm.htm.

2. For general information on the Great Exhibition, see Jeffrey A. Auerbach, *The Great Exhibition: A Nation on Display* (New Haven: Yale University Press, 1999); Herausgegeben von Franz Bosbach, John R. Davis, Susan Bennett, Thomas Brockmann, and William Filmer-Sankey, *The Great Exhibition and Its Legacy* (Munich: K. G. Saur, 2002); and John Tallis, *History and Description of the Crystal Palace and the Exhibition of the World's Industry in 1851* (London: John Tallis, 1851).

3. The Art-Journal, *The Great Exhibition, London 1851*, Illustrated Catalogue, (London: George Virtue, 1851;. Facsimile, New York: Bounty Books, 1970).

4. "History of the Great Exhibition," in The Art-Journal, *The Great Exhibition*, pp. XI–XXVI. *Nota Bene*: Each essay in this collection is paginated with Roman numerals, beginning with page I. To distinguish the page numbers for each essay, the Art-Journal augmented the Roman numerals with small symbols, such as a plus sign or asterisk.

Rather than including those symbols, I have referred to each essay either by title or by author, and page numbers are given just in Roman numerals.

5. Ibid., p. XII.

6. Ibid., pp. XIV, XIII.

7. *Punch* 19 (1851): 183. On the architecture of the Crystal Palace, see "History of the Great Exhibition," in The Art-Journal, *The Great Exhibition*, pp. XXI–XXIV; Nikolaus Pevsner, *The Sources of Modern Architecture and Design* (New York: Oxford University Press, 1968; rpt. 1981), pp. 10–11; Henry-Russell Hitchcock, *Architecture: Nineteenth and Twentieth Centuries* (New York: Penguin, 1975 rpt.), pp. 184–86. On Paxton, see John Anthony, *Joseph Paxton* (London: Shire Publications, 1973). On Jones, see Jervis, *Penguin Dictionary of Design*, pp. 256–60.

8. "History of the Great Exhibition," p. xxv. Ralph Nicholson Wornum, "The Exhibition as a Lesson in Taste," in The Art-Journal, *The Great Exhibition*, p. V. On the history of the *Art-Journal*, see the "Preface," in *The Great Exhibition*, p. VI.

9. Even the section on vegetables addressed Usefulness and Beauty. It begins: "Beauty and utility are equally the attributes of the vegetable kingdom." Edward Forbes, "On the Vegetable World as contributing to the Great Exhibition," in the Art-Journal, *The Great Exhibition*, p. I.

10. "History of the Great Exhibition," p. XXVI.

11. [Mary Philadelphia] Mrs. Merrifield, "The Harmony of Colors as Exemplified in the Exhibition," in The Art-Journal, *The Great Exhibition*, p. I. In addition to her essay of 1851, Merrifield published articles in the *Art-Journal*, and books including: *The Art of Fresco Painting* (London, 1846); *Original Treatises . . . on the Arts of Painting* (London, 1849); and *Dress as a Fine Art with Suggestions on Children's Dress* (Boston: John P. Jewett, 1854). During its short lifespan, *The Journal of Design & Manufactures* critiqued some of her books. *Original Treatises* paired texts in their original languages with Merrifield's translations. Commissioned by Queen Victoria to undertake the study in 1845, Merrifield wrote a thoughtful collaborative effort with other scholars and advisers, and addressed such crafts and techniques as gilding, embossing and gilding leather wall hangings, painting on glass, enameling, and intarsia. *Dress as a Fine Art* was inspired partly by poor examples shown at the Crystal Palace in 1851. A work of design criticism applied to fashion, it espouses a need for design education—especially for women—equal pay, a shorter workday, and the health benefits of eliminating corsets. It is significant that the latter volume was published in Boston. On Owen Jones, see Moncure D. Conway, *Travels in South Kensington . . .* (New York: Harper & Bros., 1882), pp. 150–59. On Chevreul, see Jervis, *Penguin Dictionary of Design*, pp. 109–10.

12. Merrifield, "Harmony of Colors," p. I.

13. Ibid., pp. I, VII.

14. Ibid., p. VIII.

15. Wornum, "The Exhibition as a Lesson in Taste," pp. I–XXII.

16. Ibid., pp. I, II.

17. Ibid.

18. Ibid., p. IV.

19. Ibid.

20. Ibid., p. V.

21. Ibid.

22. Ibid., passim, especially section III, pp. V–VIII.

23. Ibid., pp. VI, VII.

24. Ibid., p. XI.

25. For a biography of Hogarth, see: http://www.britainexpress.com/History/bio/hogarth.htm.

26. William Hogarth, *The Analysis of Beauty* (London, 1753; rpt. New York: Garland, 1973) pp. xv, 3.

27. For a biography of Hume, see: http://www.cooperativeindividualism.org/humebio.htm. David Hume, *Of the Standard of Taste and Other Essays*, with an introduction by John W. Lenz (Indianapolis: Bobbs-Merrill, 1965), pp. xi, 5. Dabney Townsend, *Hume's Aesthetic Theory, Taste, and Sentiment* (London: Routledge, 2001), p. 158.

28. Hume, from "Essays Moral, Political, and Literary," as quoted in Townsend, p. 183.

29. Edmund Burke, *A Philosophical Enquiry into the Origin of Our Ideas of the Sublime and the Beautiful*, ed. James T. Boulton (Oxford: Basil Blackwell, 1987, rev. ed.). See Part Two. section I, and Part III, section I.

30. Boulton, "Editor's Introduction," and Burke, "Introduction on Taste," in *A Philosophical Enquiry*, pp. x and 22.

31. Townsend, *Hume's Aesthetic Theory*, pp., 3, 193. For biographical information on Burke, see: http://odur.let.rug.nl/~usa/B/eburke/burke.htm.

32. Alexander Gerard, *An Essay on Taste* (London: A. Kincaid, and Edinburgh: J. Bell: 1759), p. 181. I would like to thank Christina K. Lindeman, a former ASU graduate student, for calling attention to these essays by Gerard, Shanhagan, and Home.

33. Ibid., pp. 182, 185, 183, 186.

34. Henry Home, *Elements of Criticism*. This essay appears with a range of publication dates in the 1760s. The date 1762 appears most consistently. For information about Henry Home, see Roger L. Emerson, "Home, Henry (Lord Kames)," in E. Craig, ed., *Routledge Encyclopedia of Philosophy* (London: Routledge, 1998), or www.rep.routledge.com. See also Henry Home, "An Original Life of the Author," in *Introduction to the Art of Thinking* (1761; New York: W. B. Gilley, 1818), pp. 1–24.

35. Home, *Elements of Criticism*, p. 442.

36. Ibid., pp. 442–43.

37. Ibid., p. 459.

38. Ibid., p. 460.

39. Ibid., pp. 481, 484.

40. Ibid., pp. 486, 488. See as well W. Proudfoot Begg, *The Development of Taste and Other Studies in Aesthetics* (Glasgow: James Maclehose and Sons, 1887), especially the section titled, "Can there Be a Standard of Taste?" pp. 140–57.

41. Home, *Elements of Criticism*, p. 490.

42. Ibid., pp. 492, 494.

43. Ibid., pp. 495–96, 497.

44. Ibid., pp. 495–96. One of these was Bostonian Mary Ware Dennett, discussed below in Chapter Two.

45. Roger Shanhagan [pseudo. William Porden, Robert Smirke, and Robert Watson], *The Exhibition or a Second Anticipation: Being Remarks on the principal Works to be Exhibited next Month, at the Royal Academy* (London: Richardson and Urgumart, 1779). Shanhagan's essay was a satire, written in the style of Richard Tickell's *Anticipation*. Porden (1755–1822) was an English architect who trained under James Wyatt between 1774 and 1779 and worked as Surveyor to the Grosvenor Estate (London) between 1783 and 1821. Smirke (1752–1845) was a painter and book illustrator. Robert Watson, a painter, remains a

mystery. For information about Porden and Smirke, see the *Grove Dictionary of Art online*. Many thanks to Deborah Husted Koshinsky, Head, Design Library, Arizona State University, for tracking down this obscure information.

46. Shanhagan, *The Exhibition*, p. 3. It is worth noting in this discussion of credentials that Smirke first exhibited with the Royal Academy of Arts in 1786 and became a member in 1793.

47. Ibid., p. 8. For biographical information on the Adam brothers, see Jervis, *Penguin Dictionary of Design*, pp. 19–21.

48. Shanhagan, *The Exhibition*, p. 36.

49. Ibid.

50. Ibid., p. 9.

51. Ibid.

52. Sir Uvedale Price, "Introductory Essay on Beauty," in *A Dialogue on the Distinct Characters of The Picturesque and The Beautiful, in answer to the objections of Mr. Knight* (Hereford: D. Walker, 1801), p. 36.

53. Thomas Chippendale, *The Gentleman and Cabinet-maker's Director* (New York: Towse, 1938, facsimile of 1762 3rd ed., based upon the original of 1754), title page. For biographical information, see Jervis, *Penguin Dictionary of Design*, p. 111.

54. Chippendale, *Director*, Preface, n.p.

55. Ibid. Even in Federal America, turning to the ancients in matters of taste influenced advice literature. In her tome *Rudiments of Taste, in a Series of Letters* (Litchfield, Conn.: Collier [1795]), a Mrs. Peddle advised her readers: "If the Greek and Roman veterans displayed qualities which the heroes of the present day would be proud to imitate, their wives and daughters," her primary audience, "were often paragons of such virtue, as would be allowed to dignify a lady of the eighteenth century" (pp. 40–41).

56. Chippendale, *Director*, plate XLVII, "Design of a State-Bed."

57. George Hepplewhite, *The Cabinet-maker and Upholsterer's Guide* (New York: Towse, 1942, facsimile of 1788 ed.), Preface, n.p. For biographical information on Hepplewhite, see Jervis, p. 229.

58. Thomas Sheraton, *The Cabinet-Maker and Upholsterer's Drawing-Book in four parts* (New York: Towse, 1946, facsimile of 3rd ed., rev. in 1802), pp. 6, 8. See as well plates XIX, XXII, and XXXII, along with his descriptions of a "Cylinder Desk and Bookcase," and the "Harlequin Pembroke Table." Jervis, pp. 449–50.

59. Thomas Sheraton, *The Cabinet Dictionary* (New York: Towse, 1946, facsimile of 1803 ed.). See entries for the Bed, the Chair, Grecian Couch Sofa Squab, Writing Tambour Tables, etc. Jervis, p. 449.

60. Thomas Sheraton, *The Cabinet-Maker, Upholsterer, and General Artist's Encyclopedia* (New York: Towse, 1946, facsimile of 1804 ed.). See description of the Four-Post Bed, plate III. In his brief biographical entry for Sheraton, Simon Jervis (p. 450) writes: "The text of the Encyclopedia is decidedly eccentric, the entries ranging from Baptism to Balls of Fire, but its indiscipline and ambition [are] surely characteristic of the artisan autodidact, not of the mental collapse discerned by some in Sheraton's later works. All the evidence agrees to his ability and energy."

61. S.D., "A Walk in London," *The Director, A Weekly Journal: containing I. Essays on the Subjects of Literature, the Fine Arts and Manners . . .* 2 (1807),: 108–12. Alexander Walker, *Beauty; Analysis and Classification of Beauty in Women, preceded by a critical view of the general hypotheses respecting Beauty by Hume, Hogarth, Burke, Knight, Alison, etc. . . .* (London: Effingham Wilson, Royal Exchange, 1836). M. V. Cousin, *Lectures on the True, The*

Beautiful, and the Good, trans. O. W. Wight (New York: D. Appleton, 1861), first published in 1854?

62. "Directions for the Breeding and General Treatment of Canary-Birds," *The Repository of the Arts, Literature, Commerce, Manufactures, Fashions, Politics* 2, no. 7 (July 1809): 77.

63. "Fashionable Furniture," *The Repository of the Arts . . .* , September 1813, p. 232. On the awarding of medals, see 2, no. 7 (July 1809):109.

64. "A Lady of Distinction," *The Mirror of the Graces* (New York: Wiley for Rilley, 1813), p. 11.

65. Preface to Volume 1, *The Journal of Design and Manufactures* (March–August 1849): vii–viii. The quote appears in vol. 2, no. 7 (September 1849): 208–9.

66. See, for example, the review of Ruskin's *The Seven Lamps of Architecture* in *The Journal of Design and Manufactures* 2 (September 1849–February 1850): 72. The same volume reviews Wornum's lecture on the Gothic style, pp. 115–16.

67. "Competitions for Designs," *The Journal of Design and Manufactures* 4 (September 1850–February 1851): 37.

68. "Which Direction is Ornamental Art Likely to Take in this country, toward Elaboration or Simplicity?" *The Journal of Design and Manufactures* 6 (September 1851–February 1852): 137.

69. The phrase "sweetness and light" has been associated with the architecture of the Aesthetic movement in Mark Girouard's excellent *Sweetness and Light: The Queen Anne Movement, 1860–1900* (Oxford: Clarendon, 1977). The phrase is attributed to Jonathan Swift, who wrote: "The two noblest of things, which are sweetness and light," as well as to Matthew Arnold, who stated: "The pursuit of perfection, then, is the pursuit of sweetness and light. . . . He who works for sweetness and light united, works to make reason and the will of God prevail" (Justin Kaplan, ed., *Bartlett's Familiar Quotations*, 17th ed. [Boston: Little, Brown, 2002]). Beverly K. Brandt, "In Quest of Usefulness and Beauty: Changing Interpretations of the Arts and Crafts Ideal. Part II: The Aesthetic Movement," Designers West 36, no. 13 (October 1989): 168, 166–67. Clarence Cook, *"What Shall We Do With Our Walls?"* (New York. Warren, Fuller, 1881), p. 16. On Cook, see Florence Levy, *American Art Annual, 1900–01*, p. 58. Born in Dorchester, Mass. (1828), Cook attended Harvard and studied architecture. As art critic for the *New York Tribune* (1860s), author, and one-time editor of *The Studio*, he was an important tastemaker.

70. Home, *Elements of Criticism*, p. 460.

71. Ian Small, ed., *The Aesthetes* (London: Routledge & Kegan Paul, 1979), p. xii. See also Arthur Clutton-Brock, *Essays on Art* (New York: Scribner's, 1920), p. 56, on "philosophic" criticism.

72. Pater, as quoted in Small, *The Aesthetes*, p. 11. Wilde as quoted in ibid., p. xxv. Whistler speaks of "claptrap" in *The Gentle Art of Making Enemies*, Propositions, 2 (1890). On the Aesthetic interior, see David Dewing, Introduction, in Charlotte Gere, ed., The *House Beautiful, Oscar Wilde and the Aesthetic Interior* (London: Lund Humphries, in association with the Geffrye Museum, 2000), p. 8.

73. Clutton-Brock, *Essays on Art*, pp. vi–vii. See also Beverly K. Brandt, "The Critic and the Evolution of Early Twentieth-Century American Craft," in Janet Kardon, ed., *The Ideal Home, 1900–1920* (New York: Harry N. Abrams, in association with the American Craft Museum, 1993), pp. 46–54.

74. Augustus Welby Northmore Pugin, *Contrasts* (London: Charles Dolman, 1836, 2nd ed., 1841), and *The True Principles of Pointed or Christian Architecture* (London: J.

Weale, 1841); John Ruskin, *Seven Lamps of Architecture* (London: Smith, Elder, 1849, 2nd ed., 1855), and *Stones of Venice*, 3 vols. (Boston: Dana Estes, 1900). Ruskin is quoted from an essay, "The Nature of Gothic," published in vol. 2 of *Stones of Venice*, p. 166. See also Beverly K. Brandt, "In Quest of Usefulness and Beauty. Changing Interpretations of the Arts and Crafts Ideal. Part I: The Arts and Crafts Movement," *Designers West* 36, no. 12 (September 1989): 214, 211, 213. William Morris, "The Art of the People," from "The Beauty of Life" (ca. 1880), in G. D. H. Cole, William Morris (New York: Random House, 1934), p. 561.

75. Ruskin, as quoted in Robert W. Edis, *Decoration & Furniture of Town Houses* (London: C. Kegan Paul, 1881), n.p.

76. Gilbert and Sullivan (in *Patience*, Act 2) speak of: "A pallid and thin young man—, A haggard and lank young man—, A greenery-yallery, Grosvenor Gallery, Foot-in-the-grave young man," as quoted in Small, *The Aesthetes*, p. 181. Charlotte Gere indicates that, as early as the 1870s, English architect E. W. Godwin (1833–86) was utilizing palettes of greens, golds, and blues derived from the pineapple. Gere, *The House Beautiful*, p. 70. On W. S. Gilbert, see Moncure Conway, Autobiography, Memories and Experiences, 2 vols. (Boston: Houghton Mifflin, 1904), 2:161–62.

77. On health and aestheticism, see Gere, *The House Beautiful*, p. 79. Scholar Cheryl Robertson has documented the way in which reformist tendencies affected myriad aspects of the lives of supporters of the Arts and Crafts movement (including their fascination with healthy eating and exercise), drawing parallels between the 1890s and the 1990s: Cheryl Robertson, "Culture & Design: Contextualizing the American Arts & Crafts Movement, Then and Now," in Audrey B. Morris, ed., *Reflecting on Design (Symposium) 6 November 1998* (Tempe, Ariz.: Herberger Center for Design Excellence, 1999). Marian Burros, columnist and writer for the *New York Times*, has also explored the topic of food reform at the turn of the century. Even Edward Waldo Emerson mentions the fad of "extreme vegetarianism" in *The Early Years of the Saturday Club, 1855–1870* (Boston: Houghton Mifflin, 1918), p. 4.

78. John Ruskin, *The Stones of Venice*, 2: 169–70.

79. Charles Fergus Binns, "Introduction," in *The Potter's Craft*, 4th ed. (1897; Princeton: Van Nostrand, 1967), p. xi.

80. Ibid.

81. [Edith] Mrs. Nelson Dawson, *Enamels* (London: Methuen, 1906), pp. 1–2.

82. Clutton-Brock, *Essays on Art*, p. 53.

83. On museums of industrial art, see Hamilton A. Hill, ed., *Reports of the Massachusetts Commissioners to the Exposition at Vienna, 1873* (Boston, 1875), pp. 100–156.

84. For a summary of some of these theories, see Peter Collins, *Changing Ideals in Modern Architecture, 1750–1950* (Montreal: McGill-Queens University Press, 1965).

85. On the importance of drawing and design education, see Charles DeGarmo, *Aesthetic Education* (Syracuse, N.Y.: C. W. Bardeen, 1913), p. vi, and Denman W. Ross, *A Theory of Pure Design: Harmony, Balance, Rhythm* (1907; New York: Peter Smith, 1933), pp. 192–94.

86. On the relationship of the production/consumption cycle to design reform, see George Harris, *The Theory of the Arts: or Art in Relation to Nature, Civilization, and Man. Comprising an Investigation, Analytical and Critical into the Origin, Rise, Province, Principles, and Application of Each of the Arts* (London: Trubner, 1869), p. 6; and Clutton-Brock, *Essays on Art*, pp. 114–18.

87. On the importance of textbooks, see W. R. Lethaby, ed., "Editor's Preface," in Luther Hooper, *Hand-Loom Weaving Plain & Ornamental* (New York: Pitman, n.d., rpt.

1920), pp. v–vi. For other lists of recommended reading, see Bernard Cuzner, *A Silversmith's Manual: Treating of the Designing and Making of the Simpler Pieces of Domestic Silverware*, 2nd ed. (1935; London: NAG Press, 1949), p. 187. In her book *Esthetics* (New York: Henry Holt, 1909), Kate Gordon mentions theorists Ross and Batchelder in the text, and mentions books by Batchelder, Crane, Day, Ross, and Ethel Dench Puffer in her reading list. Maude Lawrence and Caroline Sheldon, in *The Use of the Plant in Decorative Design* (New York: Scott, Foresman, 1909), passim, recommend books by Batchelder, Crane, Day, Morris, Ross, and James Ward on design theory, and the writings of various American and English practitioners on design practice.

88. Ernest A. Batchelder, *The Principles of Design* (Chicago: Inland Printer Company, 1904), p. 53.

89. Harris (*Theory of the Arts*, p. 145) makes links among the moral, the intellectual, and the national.

90. The source of Morris's quote was Hippocrates, who wrote: "Life is short, art long, opportunity fleeting, experience treacherous, judgment difficult." As quoted in David Bayles and Ted Orland, *Art & Fear: Observations on the Perils (and Rewards) of Artmaking* (Santa Cruz: Image Continuum Press, 1993), p. 1. Similar mottoes were popular in children's rooms—a model bedroom design by Liberty & Co. (ca. 1897) states along the frieze above the brass bed: "Seven hours to work, to soothing slumber seven, ten to the world allot, and all to heaven." See a period photograph of this room in Stephen Calloway, ed., *Liberty of London, Masters of Style & Decoration* (London: Thames and Hudson, 1992), p. 79. Bed linens were often sites for inspirational phrases, bidding the sleeper peaceful dreams or an early energetic awakening. Many were mass-produced as do-it-yourself kits for the homemaker, featuring red-on-white embroidery. See "Illustrated Catalogue and Price List of Popular Goods, W. N. Swett & Co. manufacturers, wholesale and retail dealers, No. 71 1/2 Market Street, Lynn, Massachusetts," ca. 1888, Historical Collections, Baker Library, Harvard University.

91. The term "recipes" appears in Lewis F. Day, *Ornament & Its Application: A Book for Students Treating in a Practical Way of the Relation of Design to Materials, Tools and Methods of Work* (New York: Scribner's, 1904), p. 262. For discussions of theories of "pure Design," see Batchelder, *Principles of Design*, generally, and for particular terms, pp. 3, 34, 46, 142, and Ross, *A Theory of Pure Design*, pp. v, 192–94; Begg, *Development of Taste*, p. 152; and John Bascom, *Aesthetics. The Science of Beauty* (New York: G. P. Putnam's, 1886), p. 168. On Bascom, see *Memorial Service in Honor of John Bascom at the University of Wisconsin* (June 14, 1912).

92. See Harris, *Theory of the Arts*, p. 4. At the same time, critics accepted that theories could only go so far. Lewis F. Day writes: "Theory is much more available in discussion than when we come to put it into practice, and many of the principles that are logically invincible are found to work so unsatisfactorily that they eventually die of disuse.... In all probability neither the cautious man nor the adventurous man will be influenced materially by anything that is said or written on the subject.... All that words can well do is to strengthen him in his resolve, or awaken in him a suspicion that others too may be right from their point of view." Day, *Instances of Accessory Art* (London: B. T. Batsford, 1880; rpt. New York: Garland, 1977), n.p.

93. Day refers to "artistic anarchy" in *The Planning of Ornament* (London: B. T. Batsford, 1887; rpt. New York: Garland, 1977), 10. Morris speaks of "masses of sordidness" in *Art under Plutocracy* (1883).

94. DeGarmo, *Aesthetic Education*, 102.

95. See Batchelder, *Principles of Design*, passim. See Crane, *The Bases of Design* (London:

G. Bell, 1898; rpt. New York: Garland, 1977), pp. 127–30. Crane writes: "The substance of the following chapters originally formed a series of lectures addressed to the students of the Manchester Municipal School of Art during my tenure of the directorship of design at that institution."

96. In *Ornament & Its Application*, p. 36, Day writes: "How far shall [the designer] submit to the dictation of conditions, and especially of the materials and tools he works with?" On the feeling experienced when the weight of an object does not correspond with the user's perceptions, see Binns, *The Potter's Craft*, p. v. On ease of cleaning, see Wilton P. Rix, "Pottery," in Gleeson White, *Practical Designing* (London: George Bell, 1893), p. 74.

97. On "mechanical processes" affecting finish, see Russell Sturgis, *The Artist's Way of Working in the Various Handicrafts and Arts of Design* (New York: Dodd, Mead, 1910), pp. 9–10. Other authors addressing issues of finish include Cuzner, *A Silversmith's Manual*, p. 186; Vernon Lee [pseudo. Violet Paget], *Laurus Nobilis. Chapters on Art and Life* (London: John Lane, 1909), pp. 255–56; and Day, *Ornament & Its Application*, p.135. Crane devotes chap. 5 (pp. 155–84) in *The Bases of Design* (1898) to "The Climatic Influence in Design," arguing for regionalism and contextuality.

98. Batchelder, *Principles of Design*, p. 73, uses the phrase "novelty for novelty's sake" in reference to Art Nouveau. Day uses the word "smug" in *Ornament & Its Application*, p. 133.

99. William Morris, "The Lesser Arts of Life," Lecture (1882).

100. Lewis F. Day, with Mary Buckle, *Art in Needlework* (London: B. T. Batsford, 1900; rpt. New York: Garland, 1977), p. 236.

101. The "ripe flavor of antiquity" referred to a display at the Centennial, the "New England Farmer's Home and Kitchen." See James D. McCabe, *The Illustrated History of the Centennial Exhibition . . .* (Philadelphia: National Publishing Co., [1876]), p. 240.

102. Cuzner, *A Silversmith's Manual*, p. 186.

103. Lewis F. Day, *Nature in Ornament* (London: B. T. Batsford, 1892; rpt. New York: Garland, 1977), p. 84.

104. Day, *Ornament & Its Application*, p. 13.

105. Mark Twain with Charles D. Warner, *The Gilded Age* (Hartford, Conn.: American Publication Co., 1873). Thorstein Veblen, *The Theory of the Leisure Class* (1899; rpt. New York: Macmillan, 1905).

106. Thomas Babington Macaulay coined the phrase "ostentatious simplicity" in 1848, speaking of the Quakers: *Critical and Historical Essays* (London: Longmans, 1848), 1: chap. 16. Laurence Binyon, *The Flight of the Dragon: An Essay on the Theory and Practice of Art in China and Japan* (London: John Murry, 1911), p. 32. Clarence Cook, *The House Beautiful, An Unabridged Reprint of the Classic Victorian Style Book* (New York: Dover, 1995, rpt. of 1881 American ed., based on an earlier version from 1877), pp. 155–56. C. F. A. Voysey, "The English Home," *British Architect* 75 (1911): 70.

107. A. H. Church refers to "rules of iron" in Batchelder, *Principles of Design*, p. 126. Day, *The Planning of Ornament*, p. 49.

108. E. E. Soderholtz, "Garden Pottery," brochure (West Gouldsboro, Me., n.d.), Historic New England.

109. Voysey, "The English Home," p. 60.

110. Day, *Ornament & Its Application*, pp. 34–35.

111. Cuzner, *A Silversmith's Manual*, p. 186.

112. Clutton-Brock, *Essays on Art*, p. 53.

CHAPTER I
Boston in the Gilded Age

1. See the SACB Charter in Smithsonian Institution, Archives of American Art/ Society of Arts & Crafts, Boston Papers, microfilm roll #300, frame #002. Hereafter referred to as: AAA/SACB Papers: roll #: frame#. There is some discrepancy regarding the number of founders. Some published accounts—by Karen Evans Ulehla (1981), and May R. Spain (1924)—indicate that there were twenty-four founders, including Ralph Adams Cram, Bertram Grosvenor Goodhue, and Sarah Choate Sears. But, the articles of agreement microfilmed by the Archives of American Art list only twenty-one. An article in the *Boston Daily Advertiser* (ca. April 16, 1897) states that Cram and Goodhue, in fact, opposed both holding an exhibition in 1898 and forming a permanent organization, AAA/SACB Papers: 322: 216. Cram and Goodhue—unlike all other founders listed in the articles of agreement—did not serve as officers, Councilors, Jurors, or on committees during the SACB's formative years.

2. Cleveland Amory, *The Proper Bostonians* (New York: E. P. Dutton, 1947; Parnassus Imprints Editions, 1984). Amory quotes Emerson, p. 199. He devotes chap. 5 to a discussion of the "Boston Woman," pp. 95–118. He refers to "institution men," p. 318.

3. Martin Green calls Norton a "senator" in *The Mount Vernon Street Warrens, A Boston Story, 1860–1910* (New York: Scribner's, 1989), p. 201. On Walker as "watchdog," see Grant Hyde Code, "The Decorative Arts in Boston, 1880–1930," in Elisabeth M. Herlihy, ed., *Fifty Years of Boston: A Memorial Volume 1880–1930* (Boston: Tercentery Committee, 1932), p. 383.

4. Charles Kurtz uses the phrase "art produce" in a letter: Charles M. Kurtz to Frederick Allen Whiting, March 12, 1904. Smithsonian Institution, Archives of American Art/ Louisiana Purchase Exposition-Department of Art Papers: microfilm roll #1748, frame #174–76.

5. Edward S. Cooke, Jr., "The Aesthetics of Craftsmanship and the Prestige of the Past: Boston Furniture-Making and Wood-Carving," in Marilee Boyd Meyer, ed., *Inspiring Reform: Boston's Arts and Crafts Movement* (New York: Abrams, in association with the Davis Museum and Cultural Center, 1997), p. 48. An article in the *Boston Herald* calls Cairns "The Boston Sculptor," and notes that he had produced a model for the pediment for the New Bedford Institute for Savings. "Two Watercolor Collections," *Boston Herald*, April 10, 1897, AAA/SACB Papers: 322: 210. On John Evans, see Ann Clifford, "John Evans (1847–1923) and Architectural Sculpture in Boston," M.A. Thesis, Tufts University, 1992. See also Herlihy, *Fifty Years of Boston*, p. 378; and H. L. Warren, Secretary, "Minutes of meeting of December 4, 1891, *Transactions of The Boston Society of Architects*, 1891. On Kirchmayer, see H. I. Brock, "Old-World Wood Carver Practices His Art Here," *New York Times Magazine*, March 28, 1926, p. 6.

6. Epitomizing the connections among these individuals is All Saints' Church in Brookline, designed by Cram, Wentworth & Goodhue. Daniel Dulany Addison, Julia de Wolf Addison's husband, was minister of this congregation, and she designed the altarpiece for the church. On Addison, see Chris Petteys, *Dictionary of Women Artists* (Boston: G. K. Hall, 1985), p. 6. Addison was the author of *Art of the Pitti Palace* (1903), *Classic Myths in Art* (1904), *Art of the Dresden Gallery* (1906), *The Boston Museum of Fine Arts* (1910), and *The Spell of England* (1912). Her papers are at Houghton Library, Harvard University.

7. Nancy Finlay, *Artists of the Book in Boston, 1890–1910* (Cambridge: Harvard College Library, Department of Printing and Graphic Arts, Houghton Library, 1985). On S. W. Whitman, see Anne Stewart O'Donnell, "The Arts and Crafts Greeting Card, 1908–1925:

A First Look," M.A. Thesis, Cooper-Hewitt, National Design Museum, and Parsons School of Design, 2002, pp. 27–28; Erica Hirshler, *A Studio of Her Own* (Boston: Museum of Fine Arts, 2001), pp. 23–39, and "Women Artists at Trinity," in James F. O'Gorman, ed., *The Makers of Trinity Church in the City of Boston* (Amherst: University of Massachusetts Press, 2004), pp. 152–173; and Petteys, *Dictionary of Women Artists*, p. 752.

8. For further information on Sam Warren's life and work, see Green, *Warrens*, passim. On the *Warrens*' respective memberships in the SACB, see Karen Evans Ulehla, *The Society of Arts and Crafts, Boston Exhibition Record, 1897–1927* (Boston: Boston Public Library, 1981), p. 265.

9. On Sam Warren's connection with the MFA, see Green, *Warrens*, pp. 167–73. On his values, see A. T. Cabot, "Sketch of Samuel Dennis Warren," May 9, 1910, in S. D. Warren, Personal File, Tavern Club Records, Massachusetts Historical Society. On Carey and Gray's association with the Museum of Fine Arts, see W. M. Whitehill, *The Museum of Fine Arts: A Centennial History*, 2 vols. (Cambridge: Belknap Press, 1970), passim. I am grateful to Betty Smith for sharing information on Whitman's involvement with the MFA.

10. Those who did not hold degrees from Harvard or MIT were Barton, Cairns, Kirchmayer, and Evans. To learn more about this group, see membership information in the SACB Archives (in the Fine Arts Department of the Boston Public Library, hereafter referred to as BPL/FA/SACB Archives), alumni information available through the Harvard Libraries and MIT Historical Collections, and general biographical sources such as *Who Was Who in America*, *Who's Who in New England*, *National Cyclopedia of American Biography*, and *Index to Women*.

11. Amory, *Proper Bostonians*, quotes Cabot, p. 238. Green provides population statistics, *Warrens*, p. 102.

12. George S. Hale, "The Charities of Boston and Contributions to the Distressed of Other Parts," in Justin Winsor, ed., *The Memorial History of Boston, 1630–1880*. 4 vols. (Boston: J. R. Osgood, 1881): 4:641–674. Hale notes that the reform movement in Boston generated over 480 private charities between 1870 and 1880.

13. Others connected with this group included writers Sarah Orne Jewett, William Dean Howells, Celia Thaxter, Charles Dudley Warner, and John Greenleaf Whittier. Artists associated with SACB founders include John S. Sargent, John La Farge, John Twachtman, Childe Hassam, J. A. M Whistler, and Edwin Austin Abbey. Thanks again to Betty Smith for providing me with this information. Erica E. Hirshler ("Women Artists," p. 158) points out that: "late nineteenth-century Boston's art and literary community was a small, insular dominion where each person knew everyone else, if indeed they were not related by blood or marriage."

14. Verna Posever Curtis and Jan Van Himmen, *F. Holland Day: Selected Texts and Bibliography* (Oxford: Clio Press, 1995), pp. 3–14. C. Jane Gover, *The Positive Image: Women Photographers in Turn of the Century America* (Albany: State University of New York Press, 1988), p. 84.

15. Sharon Darling speaks of Boston's centrality in "From 'New Woman' to Metalsmith: A Voyage of Self Discovery," in Barry Shifman, *The Arts & Crafts Metalwork of Janet Payne Bowles* (Bloomington and Indianapolis: Indianapolis Museum of Art in Cooperation with Indiana University Press, 1993), pp. 30–31.

16. Green, *Warrens*, pp. 27–28, discusses the contributions of S. D. Warren & Co. to paper production and publishing, ca. 1870–1900. For further information on the book arts, see Finlay, *Artists of the Book in Boston*, passim. S. W. Whitman was chief designer for Houghton Mifflin in 1887–1904.

17. Emerson as quoted in Frederick Allen Whiting, "What the Arts & Crafts Movement Has Accomplished," *Handicraft*, 3, no. 3 (June 1910): 96–97. Reinforcing Emerson's link to the Arts and Crafts movement is Moncure Conway's comment that Morris & Co.'s famous dining room in the South Kensington Museum served as the site of a dinner honoring Emerson during a trip to London: *Travels in South Kensington . . .*, pp. 135, 137. That Emerson enjoyed a fifty-year-long friendship with Carlyle only enhanced Boston's connection with the English founders of the movement. Conway, *Autobiography*, 2:113.

18. Templeman Coolidge's article may have described some of the carvings sold by Bunkio Matsuki (January 16–18, 1903) at an auction held at the American Art Association in New York. *The American Art Annual* of 1903 indicates that the collection sold for over $18,000. In that same year, the sale of works from the estate of Mrs. S. D. Warren brought over $346,000. Florence N. Levy, *American Art Annual*, 4 (1903–04): 40–43 and 97.

19. George William Sheldon, *Artistic Country-Seats . . .* (New York: 1886–87; rpt. DaCapo Press, 1979), pp. 33–34. This mentions Coolidge's purchase of the Wentworth Mansion. John Templeman Coolidge was born in 1856 to Joseph Swett Coolidge and his wife, Mary Louisa. He was the grandson of J. T. Coolidge. His son, christened John Templeman Coolidge, Jr., was born in 1888—issue of Coolidge's first wife, Katherine Scollay Parkman, daughter of the famous historian. Another son, Templeman, was born in 1917 to his second wife, Mary Abigail Parsons. Clearly, J. T. Coolidge's namesake—who became an artist, like his father—would have been too young to have played a major role in the SACB in the 1890s. The elder J. T. Coolidge held numerous offices in the SACB, founder, Councilor, vice-president, chair of the Exhibitions Committee, and of the Jury (after 1909). He graduated from Harvard in 1879, as did his namesake in 1911. Adding to the confusion regarding names was the birth of a grandson, also christened John Templeman Coolidge, after his father and grandfather. See Emma Downing Coolidge, *Descendants of John and Mary Coolidge of Watertown, Massachusetts, 1630* (Boston: Wright and Potter, 1930). See also: *Archives of American Art*: microfilm role number N99: frame numbers 710–11 (obit.), the *National Cyclopedia of American Biography*, and *Who's Who in New England*, 2nd ed. (Chicago: Marquis, 1916). On the "Little Harbor" group, see Sarah L. Giffin and Keven D. Murphy, *A Noble and Dignified Stream: The Piscataqua Region in the Colonial Revival, 1860–1930* (Old York Historical Society, 1992), p. 116.

20. Elizabeth Stone's recollections appear in the "Memorial Bulletin for C. Howard Walker," The Society of Arts and Crafts, Boston, 19, no. 1 (May 1936), BPL/FA/SACB Archives. A testimony to the interconnections among this group of founders and Boston's larger artistic, literary, and cultural circle is Henry Adams's novel *Esther* (1884).

21. General overviews of Boston from this era include Winsor, *Memorial History of Boston*, Herlihy, *Fifty Years of Boston*, and Richard Herndon, *Boston of Today, A Glance into its History and Characteristics* (Boston: Post Publishing Co., 1892). For information about civic improvements of the period, see Sam Bass Warner, Jr., "A Brief History of Boston," in Alex Krieger and David Cobb, eds., *Mapping Boston* (Cambridge: MIT Press, 1999), pp. 2–14.

22. On the Pre-Raphaelite Brotherhood, see Isabelle Anscombe and Charlotte Gere, *Arts and Crafts in Britain and America* (New York: Rizzoli, 1978), p. 54; and Conway, *Autobiography*. Regarding the Boston Foreign Fair, see *Annals of the Massachusetts Charitable Mechanic Association, 1795–1892* (Boston: Rockwell and Churchill, 1892), p. 386. On the Morris & Co. exhibit, see "The Morris Exhibit at the Foreign Fair, Boston, 1883" (Boston: Roberts Brothers, 1883), pamphlet. There are copies of this at both the Boston Athenaeum and the Boston Public Library. The quote appears in: "The Morris Exhibit at the Foreign Fair," *Evening Transcript*, October 20, 1883, to be found in a scrapbook on the fair, com-

piled by [Gen.] Charles B. Norton, June 19, 1884, Boston Public Library, Rare Books and Manuscripts. On the poster exhibition, see Finlay, *Artists of the Book in Boston*, p. 22.

23. *An Account of the Proceedings, At the Dinner Given by Mr. George Peabody to the Americans connected with the Great Exhibition at the London Coffee House, Ludgate Hill, on the 27th October 1851* (London: William Pickering, 1851). This account indicates that twenty-one residents of Boston or the Commonwealth attended. Julia de Wolf Addison indicates that the core of the collection of Egyptian artifacts acquired by the museum came from the Crystal Palace Exhibition. See *The Boston Museum of Fine Arts* (Boston: L. C. Page, 1910), p. x; Hamilton A. Hill, ed., *Reports of the Massachusetts Commissioners to the Exposition at Vienna, 1873* (Boston: Wright & Potter, State Printers, 1875); James D. McCabe, *The Illustrated History of the Centennial Exhibition . . . with a full description of the Great Buildings and All the objects of interest exhibited in Them . . .* (Philadelphia: National Publishing Co., 1876); *Report of the Massachusetts Board of World's Fairs Managers* (Boston: Wright & Potter, 1894). Cole, using a pseudonym, founded "Felix Summerly's Art Manufactures" in 1847. See Lionel Lambourne, *Utopian Craftsmen: The Arts and Crafts Movement from the Cotswolds to Chicago* (Salt Lake City: Peregrine Smith, 1980), p. 37.

24. Cook, *House Beautiful*, pp. 70, 242, 291, 297. Many of these companies advertised in the SACB's 1897 and 1899 exhibition catalogues. See also *King's How To See Boston* (Moses King, 1895), which discusses businesses along Washington Street, p. 104. *Clark's Boston Blue Book* (1906) contains an advertisement for W. H. Davis & Co., which specialized in textiles for both furnishing and fashion. See Bigelow, Kennard & Co. Papers, 1880–1925, Historical Collections, Baker Library, Harvard University. These contain business records, store inventories, and a few measured drawings and sketches.

25. On Bunkio Matsuki, see Marshall B. Davidson, ed., *The American Heritage History of Antiques from the Civil War to World War I* (New York: American Heritage., 1969), p. 129. See also advertisement in *Handicraft*, 2, no. 5 (August 1903), as well as Frederick A. Sharf et al., *"A Pleasing Novelty": Bunkio Matsuki and the Japan Craze in Victorian Salem* (Salem: Peabody and Essex Museum, 1993). For general information on the impact of Japanese goods on American interiors, see the exhibition catalogue "Out of the East: Oriental Imports for the Victorian Home from 1860–1915" (Rochester, N.Y.: Margaret Woodbury Strong Museum, 1977). Bunkio Matsuki's Japanese-style house was built in Salem by Andrews, Jaques and Rantoul, a firm whose two principal architects were SACB members. The Historical Collections / Baker Library/ Harvard University houses a trade catalogue for the store during the period when it was located at 380–382 Boylston Street. See Bates Trade Catalogue Collections.

26. Green, *Warrens*, p. 160. See also Van Wyck Brooks, *New England: Indian Summer, 1865–1915* (New York: Dutton, 1940), pp. 148, 289, 310.

27. Amory, *Proper Bostonians*, p. 70.

28. Cook, *House Beautiful*, p. 161. On "retail penury" see Amory, pp. 187–206.

29. Brooks, *New England: Indian Summer*, p. 147.

30. On Dresser, see Gere, *The House Beautiful*, p. 41. On Wilde, see Lloyd Lewis and Henry Justin Smith, *Oscar Wilde Comes to America* (New York: Harcourt, Brace, 1936); Gere, *The House Beautiful*, pp. 11, 88, 92; and Hesketh Pearson, *Oscar Wilde, His Life and Wit* (New York: Harper & Brothers, 1946), pp. 143, 171, 173.

31. On Crane, see Corinna Lindon Smith, *Interesting Persons: Eighty Years with the Great and Near-Great* (Norman: University of Oklahoma Press, 1962), p. 201; H. L. Warren, Secretary, "Minutes of a meeting of December 4, 1891," *Transactions of the Boston Society of Architects, 1891*, Massachusetts Historical Society; and Finlay, *Artists of the Book in Boston*, pp. 4, 6, 8.

32. On Ashbee's visit, see Gillian Naylor, "Ashbee and The Craft of the Machine," chap. 6, in *The Arts & Crafts Movement* (Cambridge: MIT Press, 1971), pp. 166–72 passim. On Cobden-Sanderson, see the "Bulletin" listing lecture dates and topics, published by the SACB on November 27, 1907 (BPL/FA/SACB Archives); *A Survey of Twenty Years, 1894–1914* (Boston: The Twentieth Century Club, and Montague, Mass.: The Montague Press, 1914).

33. On the impact of women's magazines, see Helen Woodward, *The Lady Persuaders* (New York: Ivan Oblensky, 1960).

34. For biographical information about these individuals, see Meyer, *Inspiring Reform*, pp. 206–37.

35. William Morris, "The Art of the People," from "The Beauty of Life" (ca. 1880), in G. D. H. Cole, *William Morris* (New York: Random House, 1934), p. 561.

36. For biographical information on these individuals, see Herlihy, *Fifty Years of Boston*, passim, as well as the *Dictionary of North American Authors Deceased Before 1950, Journalists of the United States*, and *Who's Who in New England*, vol. 2 (1916). On Baxter, see Krieger, Mapping: 156, 158. W. H. Downes, "General Progress in the Fine Arts," in Herlihy, pp. 335–39.

37. Bainbridge Bunting, *Houses of Boston's Back Bay* (Cambridge, Mass.: Belknap Press, 1967), pp. 351–53. Vincent Scully, *The Shingle Style and the Stick Style*, rev. ed. (New Haven: Yale University Press, 1971), pp. 10, 34. Henry Russell Hitchcock, Jr. *American Architectural Books*, 3rd ed. (Minneapolis, 1946). Lawrence Dowler in Finlay, *Artists of the Book in Boston*, p. v. Eleanor Garvey in Finlay, p. vii. Keith N. Morgan and Richard Cheek, "History in the Service of Design: American Architect-Historians, 1870–1940," in Elisabeth Blair MacDougall, ed., *The Architectural Historian in America* (Hanover: University Press of New England, 1990), p. 64.

38. Finlay, "Introduction," p. ix.

39. Bunting, *Houses of Boston's Back Bay*, pp. 354–59; Scully, *Shingle Style*, pp. 58, 69, 155. Amory, *Proper Bostonians*, comments on the persistence of the Colonial, pp. 22, 180–81, 250, as does Green, *Warrens*, pp. 28, 50, 82. William B. Rhoads provides an excellent summary of the literature of the Colonial Revival in "The Discovery of America's Architectural Past, 1874–1914," in MacDougall, *Architectural Historian*, pp. 23–29. On the impact of the Colonial Revival on architecture education, see Caroline Shillaber, *M.I.T. School of Architecture and Planning: 1861–1961: A Hundred Year Chronicle* (Cambridge: MIT Press, 1963), pp. 6, 34. Another example of this interest in antiquarianism was the Massachusetts Charitable Mechanic Association, the first president of which had been Paul Revere. In the 1890s, the MCMA had established a "Historical Patriotic Department" to collect "relics" that had belonged to or been made by early members. Massachusetts Charitable Mechanic Association, Records, 1791–1995, Massachusetts Historical Society.

40. Krieger, Mapping, p. 204. Bunting, *Houses of Boston's Back Bay*, passim.

41. Alice Morse Earle, *Customs and Fashions in Old New England* (New York: Scribner's, 1899).

42. Amory, *Proper Bostonians*, p. 249. Wells is quoted in Green, *Warrens*, p. 160. On the taste for using antiques in interiors, see Cook, *House Beautiful*, pp. 77, 79, 81, 118, 158, 161, 163, 164, 222, and 243–49. See also Charles E. Hooper, *The Country House, A Practical Manual of the Planning and Construction of the American Country Home and Its Surroundings* (New York: Doubleday, Page, 1905), pp. 126, 154, 156, 294. Historical Collections/Baker Library/Harvard University has trade catalogues for these two companies.

43. Grant Hyde Code, "The Decorative Arts," in Herlihy, *Fifty Years of Boston*, p. 383. See p. 762 for biographical information.

44. Green Pamphlet, titled: "Boston . . . its Attractions" [July 1898], pp. 27–34. Massachusetts Charitable Mechanic Association, Records: 1791–1995, Ms. N. 361, Box 5, Series IV, Folder, Disbound Scrapbook, 1898 Jul.–Dec., Massachusetts Historical Society.

45. Edward Atkinson, "Boston as a Center of Manufacturing Capital," in Winsor, *Memorial History of Boston*, 4:95–96. "Industrial History of Suffolk County," in *Professional and Industrial History of Suffolk County, Massachusetts in Three Volumes* (Boston History Co., 1894), 3:486–489.

46. Beverly K. Brandt, "The Essential Link: Boston Architects and The Society of Arts and Crafts," *Tiller* 2, no. 1 (September–October 1983): 7–32. An excellent firsthand account of such travels abroad is the journal kept by Edmund March Wheelwright in 1881, when he visited England and Europe, traveling with Robert D. Andrews, Alexander Wadsworth Longfellow, Jr., J. Templeman Coolidge, and others. The journal records, among other impressions, his reactions to Aestheticism, the Pre-Raphaelites, and the work of Morris & Co. Wheelwright Family II, E. M. Wheelwright Diary, 1881, vol. 3, Massachusetts Historical Society.

47. On 9 Park Street, see Frederick Allen Whiting, "Arts and Crafts In Boston," *Art Bulletin*, 6, no. 18 (March 2, 1907): AAA/SACB Papers: 320: 022. Elizabeth Cumming and Wendy Kaplan, chap. 4, "Regionalism in America," in *The Arts and Crafts Movement* (London: Thames & Hudson, 1991), p. 132.

48. William Austin, "A History of the Boston Society of Architects," unpublished manuscript (Boston Athenaeum, 1942). On the Boston Architectural Club, see *Sketchbook of the Architectural Association of Boston* (Boston, 1883). Walter H. Kilham, Personal Reminiscences, 1868–99, vol. 1, Massachusetts Historical Society. Kilham did not join the SACB, but his wife, Jane Houston Kilham, was a Craftsman member. SACB members who also belonged to the Tavern Club included R. D. Andrews, G. E. Barton, H. F. Bigelow, J. T. Coolidge, Jr., H. Jaques, A. W. Longfellow, Jr., Guy Lowell, J. L. Smith, R. C. Sturgis, C. H. Walker, S. D. Warren, and C. E. Norton. See *Clark's Boston Blue Book* (1906), pp. 676–77.

49. On education as a "regional specialty," see Warner, *Mapping*, p. 4. On the Massachusetts Charitable Mechanic Association, see *Professional and Industrial History of Suffolk County*, 3:521–42. On educational programs at the Massachusetts Charitable Mechanic Association, see ibid. SACB members involved with the activities of the MCMA included William H. Grueby, A. W. Longfellow, Jr., R. C. Sturgis, and M. Ware Dennett. *The Boston Art Guide and Artists' Directory* (Boston: Wheat Publishing, 1894) discusses numerous educational programs throughout the city, including the Cowles Art School, and the Massachusetts Normal School of Design. See also Herlihy, *Fifty Years of Boston*, p. 639. On the Lowell School of Practical Design, see "Our Native Talent. It Should Be More Thoroughly Developed," *Boston Herald*, ca. March 20, 1897, AAA/SACB Papers: 322: 188. For details about the Museum School, see H. Winthrop Pierce, *History of the School of the MFA, Boston, 1876–1930* (Boston: T. O. Metcalf, 1930). Pierce devotes chap. 7 to the Department of Design and Decoration, pp. 63–74. See also Hirshler, *Studio*, pp. 87–96. Finlay discusses the Eric Pape School in *Artists of the Book in Boston*, pp. xii and 98. Dow speaks of his summer school in *Composition*, p. 65, as does Finlay, pp. 76–77. On Amy Sacker, see O'Donnell, "The Arts and Crafts Greeting Card," pp. 25–39. "School of Fine Arts, Crafts and Decorative design, Boston" [(Boston: Merrymount Press, 1913).] This announcement discusses Walker's school; BPL/FA/SACB Archives. On the New England School of Design for Women, see J. Whitworth and G. Wallis, *The Industry of the United States in Machinery, Manufactures and Useful and Ornamental Arts* (New York: Routledge, 1854), pp. 153–56.

50. Descriptions of and membership lists for these clubs appear in *The Boston Club Book for 1888* (Boston: Edward E. Clark, 1888). Many of these organizations are listed in the *Boston Art Guide*, passim. On the Society of Printers, see Finlay, *Artists of the Book in Boston*, xiii. On the Dante Club, see Brooks, New England: Indian Summer, pp. 25–28. On the Decadents, see Finlay, p. ix. On the Pewter Mugs and the Visionists, see Douglass Shand-Tucci, *Ralph Adams Cram, American Medievalist* (Boston: Boston Public Library, 1975), p. 11, and Finlay, p. x. On the Saturday Club, see Brooks, p. 9, and various works by Edward Waldo Emerson. On social clubs at Harvard, see Amory, *Proper Bostonians*, p. 308. On the Twentieth Century Club, see Arthur Mann, *Yankee Reformers in the Urban Age, 1880–1900* (Cambridge: Belknap Press, 1954), p. 172; Edwin D. Mead, "Reminiscences: Boston Memories of Fifty Years," in Herlihy, *Fifty Years of Boston*, pp. 37, 752–53; and *A Survey of Twenty Years, 1894–1914*. On the St. Botolph Club, see Doris A. Birmingham, "Boston's St. Botolph Club, Home of the Impressionists," *Archives of American Art Journal*, 31, no. 3 (1991): 26–34. H. H. Richardson was a founder of this club. C. E. Norton and Denman Ross were members. S. W. Whitman was the first woman to have a one-person show here, in 1889.

51. Henry-Russell Hitchcock, *The Architecture of H. H. Richardson and His Times*, 2nd ed. (Hamden, Conn., 1961). Keith N. Morgan, "Introduction: From the Parish to the World: The Architectural Context of Trinity Church," in O'Gorman, *The Makers*, pp. 3–10. This volume also contains excellent essays on Trinity's furniture, stained glass, and the work of John La Farge. On Richardson's trip to Europe, see James F. O'Gorman, "On Vacation with H. H. Richardson: Ten Letters from Europe, 1882," *Archives of American Art Journal*, 19, no. 1 (1979): 2–14.

52. A. W. Longfellow, Jr., Letter to his Mother, Forest Hills, N.Y., March 5, 1882. Box 2, File 1, Personal Papers of Alexander Wadsworth Longfellow, Jr. Courtesy of the Longfellow National Historic Site, 105 Brattle Street, Cambridge. One year after the SACB was founded, Longfellow designed the Phillips Brooks House at Harvard.

53. On Norton's life and work, see Kermit Vanderbilt, *Charles Eliot Norton, Apostle of Culture in a Democracy* (Cambridge: The Belknap Press, 1959); "Charles Eliot Norton: The Aristocrat in a Plutocracy," in Martin Green, *The Problem of Boston* (New York: W. W. Norton, 1966); and James Turner, *The Liberal Education of Charles Eliot Norton* (Baltimore: Johns Hopkins University Press, 1999).

54. See the sources given in the preceding note and Mary N. Woods, "History in the Early American Architectural Journals," in MacDougall, Architectural Historian, p. 85. Nor was Moore entirely supportive of the SACB. In 1908, Waddy Longfellow wrote to Moore, inviting him to join the SACB. Moore declined. Asked to explain, Moore later wrote F. A. Whiting from abroad: "I think that something might be done to bring about right conditions; but in advance of this there appears to be little hope of developing capacity for producing what is beautiful. Certainly, the most of what is called artistic *handicraft*, both here and in America, seems to me far from beautiful." C. H. Moore to F. A. Whiting, May 20, 1910, AAA/SACB Papers: 429: 682–83.

55. Sara Norton and M. A. DeWolfe Howe, eds. *Letters of Charles Eliot Norton*, 2 vols. (Boston: Houghton Mifflin, 1913), 1:137–38 and 176.

56. Lambourne, *Utopian Craftsmen*, p. 146.

57. Norton, *Letters*, 1:420.

58. For other, local impressions of Carlyle, see Conway, *Autobiography*, 1:399; 2:97, 109–10, 112. On Carlyle's house, see Virginia Woolf, *The London Scene: Five Essays* (New York: Random House, 1975), pp. 23–26.

59. Norton, *Letters*, 1:173–75.

60. Ibid., pp. 341–48. A photographic portrait of an intense Burne-Jones and one of his wife—reading—were among Norton's personalia.

61. Ibid., pp. 309–10.

62. Charles Eliot Norton, *Historical Studies of Church Building in the Middle Ages, Venice, Siena, Florence* (New York: Harper & Brothers, 1880), pp. 30–31.

63. Virginia Chieffo Raguin points out that Norton's influence was evident in Trinity Church because he served as one of Boston's "chief figures at this intersection of art, culture, and religion. " See her essay: "Decorator: John La Farge," in O'Gorman, *The Makers*, pp. 129–130. That Trinity Church "pleased" Norton is evident in a letter of 1876 from James Russell Lowell to F. L. Olmsted. See O'Gorman, "On Vacation," p. 14, n. 20.

64. Johnson is quoted in "Moving to Newbury Street, Its Rich Heritage is Climaxed," ca. 1933, an unidentified clipping in the Arthur J. Stone Papers, BMFA. On the rarity of Norton's role, see his Letters, 2:5, where he also quotes Mill, referring to his "memorable address of 1867," during which Mill spoke of the purpose of education.

65. Morgan and Cheek, "History in the Service of Design" p. 64. Edward Waldo Emerson, "The Early Years of the Saturday Club, 1855–1870," in *Two Addresses by Edward Waldo Emerson and William Fenwick Harris* (Boston: Houghton Mifflin, 1912), pp. 247 (quoting Walker) and 239.

66. Charles Eliot Norton, "Dwellings and Schools for the Poor," *North American Review*, no. 75 (April 1852): 432, and *Letters*, 1:203–5.

67. Other settlement houses included Woods's South End House, which became Andover House (1891), and Parsons's Breadwinner's College (1903). For details, see Eva Whiting White, "Social Welfare, Social Agencies in Boston, 1880–1930," in Herlihy, *Fifty Years of Boston*, pp. 551–52; Mann, *Yankee Reformers*, p. 172; and Green, *Warrens*, pp. 109–11, 140–42, 190. On "Folk Handicrafts" exhibitions, see Ulehla, pp. 281, 284. On Denison House, see the brochure "Denison House, 93 Tyler Street, Boston, Directory of Clubs and Classes, 1903." p. 2, Schlesinger Library, Radcliffe Institute for Advanced Study, Harvard University. On the role of women in the settlement house movement, and for a listing of other settlement houses, see Mary C. Jones, "Women's Opportunities in Town and Country," in *The Woman's Book* (New York: Scribner's, 1894), 2:192–97. Norton's work paralleled philanthropic good works throughout Boston. See *A Directory of Charitable and Beneficent Organizations of Boston*, 4th ed. (Boston: Damrell & Upham, 1899).

68. The School of Practical Design for Women in Boston, and the Workingmen's College and Toynbee Hall in London were all manifestations of the same movement to introduce some form of design education at all levels of society, following the Great Exhibition. Toynbee Hall was founded the year following the death of Arnold Toynbee (1852–83), an English economic historian and reformer. The two London institutions are discussed in Naylor, "Ashbee and The Craft of the Machine," pp. 16–18, and Anscombe and Gere, *Arts and Crafts in Britain and America*, p. 12.

69. Michael W. Brooks, "New England Gothic: Charles Eliot Norton, Charles H. Moore, and Henry Adams," in MacDougall, *Architectural Historian*, pp. 113–23.

70. The Arts and Crafts Exhibition Society, "Its Origins and Aims," a pamphlet dated November 29, 1947; BPL/FA/SACB Archives. Lambourne, *Utopian Craftsmen*, pp. 32, 67–72. Naylor, p. 132. See also *Arts & Crafts Essays, by Members of the Arts & Crafts Exhibition Society, with a Preface by William Morris* (London: Rivington, Percival, 1893); Walter Crane, *Ideals in Art* (London: George Bell & Sons, 1905), pp. 1–34.

71. "Prospectus," AAA/SACB Papers: 320: 007. "The Boston Arts & Crafts Exhibition," *The Inland Printer*, March 1897, p. 692, AAA/SACB Papers: 322: 184.

72. *Professional and Industrial History of Suffolk County*, 3:530.

73. *Boston Herald*, January 9, 1897, AAA/SACB Papers: 322: 166. *The Metalworker* (New York), no date given, but probably March 1897, AAA/SACB Papers: 322: 180. Boston Globe, March 21, 1897, AAA/SACB Papers: 322: 187. *Boston Herald*, March 2, 1897. This article includes excerpts from Candace Wheeler's letter, AAA/SACB Papers: 322: 187. See also the *Boston Globe*, March 21, 1897, AAA/SACB Papers: 322: 189. The writer for the *Globe* demonstrated ignorance of Wheeler and her work, referring to her as "Mr. Wheeler." Wheeler notes that both Walter Crane and Oscar Wilde had visited the studio of Associated Artists during their respective trips to the United States. Candace Wheeler, *Yesterdays in a Busy Life* (New York: Harper & Bros., 1918), pp. 231–67.

74. See "Our Native Talent. It Should Be More Thoroughly Developed," *Boston Herald*, ca. March 20, 1897. This discusses in detail the Lowell School of Practical Design, AAA/SACB Papers: 322: 187–88. See also "Artists and Artisans: Effort to Encourage Better Work by Mechanics," *Boston Herald*, February 27, 1897, AAA/SACB Papers: 322: 178. This discusses design education in France and Germany. "American Decorative Art," *Boston Herald*, March 13, 1897, AAA/SACB Papers: 322: 185.

75. "Arts in the Crafts," *Commercial Bulletin* (Boston), February 13, 1897, AAA/SACB Papers: 322: 176.

76. "American Decorative Art." Clarence Cook offers insights about pertinent American "simplicity" in *"What Shall We Do With Our Walls?"* pp. 6, 12–14.

77. The work of Morris, Voysey, and the others was included in the exhibition; yet it is painfully obvious that many visitors were only vaguely familiar with their work. This is reflected in the understatement and inaccuracy of the following (*Boston Globe*, March 22, 1897): "Of special interest . . . will be the exhibits of wallpaper, carpets and rugs designed by the late Wm. Morris, who, up to the hour of his death, was very prominent in England for his applied art work, and also of the work of Mr. Chas. A Vesey [*sic*], who at the present is perhaps the most conspicuous designer of interior furnishings in England." AAA/SACB Papers: 322: 190. Otto Grundmann was the first instructor at the School of the Museum of Fine Arts, regarded by his students—both male and female—as professional and rigorous. See Hirshler, *Studio*, pp. 90–91. Approximately one-half of the architects who later joined the SACB exhibited in 1897 under the auspices of the BAC. See *Catalogue, Special Exhibition, Boston Architectural Club, Allston Hall, Grundmann Studio Building, From April 5th to 17th Inclusive, 1897* (Boston: Thomas P. Smith Printing, 1897), pp. 23–26.

78. On the role of women in Boston art, craft, and culture, see Hirshler, *Studio*. Of equal interest are the contributions of the women who ultimately comprised nearly half of the total membership of the SACB. Despite their numbers, however, they had limited effectiveness as decision-makers. They were under-represented as founders, officers, and administrators, but they presented a show of force at exhibitions. In 1907, for example, of the 450 individuals who displayed work in a huge tenth anniversary show, two-thirds were women.

79. Finlay, *Artists of the Book in Boston*, pp. 24–25, 51, 95, 98. Green, *Warrens*, p. 58.

80. Ednah D. Cheney, "The Women of Boston," in Winsor, *Memorial History of Boston*, 4:331–356. For more on Cheney and this essay, see Hirshler, *Studio*, pp. 4–21. On Cheney's life and work, see "Ednah Dow Cheney, Memorial Meeting, New England Women's Club, Boston, February 20, 1905" (Boston: George H. Ellis, 1905). See also The Ednah Dow Littlehale Cheney Papers, Schlesinger Library, Radcliffe Institute for Advanced Study, Harvard University.

81. Shillaber, *M.I.T. School of Architecture*, pp. 34, 43. Morgan and Cheek, "History in the Service of Design," p. 75.

82. Gover, *The Positive Image*, pp. 7, 31, 17, 20, 22.

83. Henry James, *The American Scene* (1907; rpt. Bloomington: Indiana University Press, 1968), pp. 65–66. Amory, *Proper Bostonians*, p. 96. Green, *Warrens*, p. 58.

84. On styles, see catalogue entries in *First Exhibition of the Arts and Crafts, Copley Hall, Boston, April 5–16, 1897* (Boston: Thomas P. Smith Printing, 1897), AAA/SACB Papers: 319: 707–29.

85. On the rose motif in graphic design in Boston, see Finlay, *Artists of the Book in Boston*, p. 70. Van Wyck Brooks speaks of many famous Boston-area men who grew roses, p. 179. On the pomegranate, see Finlay, pp. 20–21.

86. They weren't, however, entirely successful in banishing anonymity. See Finlay, pp. xi, xii.

87. [Untitled Article] in *The House Beautiful* (Chicago), AAA/SACB Papers: 322: 225. W. Henry Winslow, "The Arts & Crafts," *Boston Transcript*, April 5, 1897, AAA/SACB Papers: 322: 207–8.

88. "The Chatterer," *Boston Herald*, April 5, 1897, AAA/SACB Papers: 322: 206.

89. This notice is contained in a scrapbook of clippings and miscellany. Dated April 14, 1897, it includes endorsements by the following: A. W. Longfellow, Jr., R. Clipston Sturgis, General Charles G. Folsom, A. F. Sunergren, Alfred T. Waite, F. W. Chandler, A. J. Philpott, John Bianchi, Mabel C. Gage, Samuel Hayward, Charles E. Mills, George F. Newton, Walter R. Goodnow, Frank M. Mills, J. M. Bowles, G. P. Kendrick, C. Howard Walker, David Cronfield, Albert Haberstroh, Robert D. Andrews, J. C. Callowhill, J. Parker B. Fiske, Thomas P. Smith, Harry E. Goodhue, Theodore H. Pond, Henry Lewis Johnson, Otto Muller, and Amy M. Sacker (BPL/FA/SACB Archives). *Boston Herald*, April 16, 1897, AAA/SACB Papers: 322: 217.

90. "Permanent Society Formed with Many Members," *Boston Herald*, May 14, 1897, AAA/SACB Papers: 322: 201. Members of the "provisional governing committee," which the first council ultimately replaced, were H. Langford Warren, C. Howard Walker, D. B. Updike, Holker Abbott, Henry Lewis Johnson, John Kirchmayer, B. G. Goodhue, Hugh Cairns, Barton P. Jenks, George E. Barton, Joseph De Camp, J. T. Coolidge, Jr., John Bancroft, Prof. William T. Sedgewick, Mrs. J. Montgomery (Sarah Choate) Sears, and Mrs. J. de W. Addison.

91. *Boston Transcript*, May 14, 1897, AAA/SACB Papers: 322: 225. *Boston Journal*, May 20, 1897, AAA/SACB Papers: 322: 201.

92. Warner, *Mapping*, pp. 138, 214, 244–45.

93. Shillaber, *M.I.T. School of Architecture*, p. 49.

94. On the goals of these sewing circles, see '99 Sewing Circle, Minutes and Treasurer's Reports, 1901–22, Massachusetts Historical Society. Birmingham, "Boston's St. Botolph Club," p. 30. Amory, *Proper Bostonians*, pp. 354–55. Mann, *Yankee Reformers*, p. 172. Green, *Warrens*, p. 152. Clay Lancaster, Preface to Dover Edition, in Edward S. Morse, *Japanese Homes and Their Surroundings* (Boston: Ticknor, 1886; New York: Dover, 1961), p. vii. In 1897, Estabrook published *Some Slums* (Boston: Twentieth Century Club, 1898) under the club's auspices. See also *The Twentieth Century Club of Boston, 1894–1904* ([Boston]: Davis Press, [1904–05]). Finlay, *Artists of the Book in Boston*, p. 65.

95. Finlay, pp. 53, 47. On the Plimpton Press, see *The Plimpton Press Year Book, An Exhibit of Versatility* (Norwood, Mass.: 1911), p. 70. For more on Reed, see Hirshler, *Studio*, pp. 69, 71, 191; and Petteys, *Dictionary of Women Artists*, p. 588. Joseph Goddu, "Posters and Illustrated Books," in *From Architecture to Object* (New York: Dutton Studio Books, in association with Hirschl & Adler Galleries, 1989), p. 140.

96. Finlay, pp. 47, 65, and xi.

97. Anscombe and Gere, *Arts and Crafts in Britain and America*, p. 58. William A.

Coles quotes Edith Wharton in his introductory essay, "The Genesis of a Classic," in *The Decoration of Houses* (New York: W.W. Norton, rpt. 1978), xxvi. Coles mentions Updike's contributions on p. xxiv. On Gertrude Kasebier, see Gover, *The Positive Image*, p. 40.

98. Records of the Massachusetts Charitable Mechanic Association, 1791–1995, Massachusetts Historical Society. Press release in Scrapbook for 1907 SACB Exhibition, compiled by F. W. Coburn, rebound in 1988 and titled *Boston Society of Arts and Crafts*. This article is labeled: "Given to Sylvester Baxter as memorandum for *Boston Herald* article." January 15, 1906, BPL/FA/SACB Archives. Frederick Allen Whiting, "Arts and Crafts in Boston," *The Art Bulletin*, 6, no. 18 (March 2, 1907), AAA/SACB Papers: 320: 002.

99. Wharton and Codman, "Introduction," n.p.

100. Anscombe and Gere, *Arts and Crafts in Britain and America*, p. 58; Pevsner, *Sources of Modern Architecture*, p. 121; Lambourne, *Utopian Craftsmen*, p. 170. Pevsner is quoted in Daniel O'Neill, *Lutyens, Country Houses* (New York: Whitney Library of Design, 1981), p. 71. William Buchanan et al., *Mackintosh's Masterwork: Charles Rennie Mackintosh and the Glasgow School of Art* (San Francisco: Chronicle Books, 1995), p. 166.

101. Cummings and Kaplan, *The Arts & Crafts Movement*, p. 176. Anscombe and Gere, p. 58.

102. Naylor, "Ashbee and The Craft of the Machine," p. 184; Jervis, *Penguin Dictionary of Design*, p. 151; Hirshler, *Studio*, p. 76.

103. Naylor, p. 184. Görel Cavalli-Björkman and Bo Lindwall, *The World of Carl Larsson* (San Diego: Green Tiger Press, 1982), pp. 30–32, 55.

104. "For Good Craftsmanship," *Boston Transcript*, May 14, 1897, AAA/SACB Papers: 322: 225.

CHAPTER TWO

By Word, Deed, or Example

1. A bulletin printed by the Thomas P. Smith Printing Company (dated October 6, 1899) announced the meeting on October 13, 1897, at 8:00 p.m. at the Grundmann Studios Building (40 were printed). In a scrapbook in the SACB Archives, dated 1897–1904, BPL/FA/SACB Archives. "Permanent Society Formed with Many Members," *Boston Herald*, May 14, 1897, AAA/SACB Papers: 322: 201. On Sarah Choate Sears, see Petteys, *Dictionary of Women Artists*, p. 637.

2. *By-Laws of The Society of Arts and Crafts. Boston, Massachusetts* (Thomas P. Smith Printing Company, dated November 18, 1897). In a scrapbook in the SACB Archives, dated 1897–1904, BPL/FA/SACB Archives.

3. "Permanent Society Formed with Many Members." This article notes that Ralph Adams Cram "said he would be very glad to have it called the 'Guild of Artists and Artisans.' Mr. Fleischner [chief of the Fine Arts Department at the Boston Public Library] stirred applause by replying that a guild was an English thing and a close corporation, with peculiar government and management."

4. I want to thank Bruce Smith for offering this insight.

5. *[Prospectus Pamphlet.] The Society of Arts and Crafts, Boston Massachusetts, Incorporated A.D. MDCCCXCVII* (Thomas P. Smith Printing Company, December 9, 1897), AAA/SACB Papers: 316: 586. A hand-written note indicates that 250 copies were printed for $9.50.

6. "The Council Reports as Follows." Stamped January 21, 1903, AAA/SACB Papers: 316: 490–91. The usage of the capital T in the SACB's name was important to its founders. In 1912, Langford Warren stated: "It has seemed to me that this society—which is the first of its kind and has never been called the *Boston Society of Arts and Crafts*, but The

Society of Arts and Crafts—is in a real sense a national organization." See F. W. Coburn, Minutes taken at Farewell Dinner for Frederick A. Whiting, titled, "Addresses at Resignation Dinner," April 23, 1912, AAA/ SACB Papers: 300: 706–26.

7. *[Prospectus Pamphlet.] The Society of Arts and Crafts, Boston Massachusetts, Incorporated A.D. MDCCCXCVII* (Probably printed Fall 1898), AAA/SACB Papers: 300: 003. See the scrapbook in the SACB Archives dated 1897–1904 for examples of these announcements, BPL/FA/SACB Archives.

8. The first appearance of the concepts that would be formalized into the SACB statement of purpose is in the "Preliminary Report of the Committee," appointed by H. L. Warren on April 15, 1897. These minutes of a meeting held April 29, 1897, reflect the thoughts of Andrews, Sturgis, Frank W. Birchall, Harry E. Goodhue, and the chair, R. A. Cram. In these minutes, the committee outlines the purpose of the SACB roughly, identifying that it should promote interaction and equal treatment among members, provide education and assistance to them, improve and restore all branches of handicraft, and hold exhibitions, AAA/SACB Papers: 322: 218–19. These appear as the formal "statement of purpose" in a set of announcements for 1898, titled simply *The Society of Arts and Crafts. Boston*, Massachusetts. Incorporated, 1897. The pamphlet is undated. It lists members of the Council, committees, the statement of purpose, meetings, and classes. This serves as a model for the annual reports that follow, beginning ca. December 1898. See the scrapbook in the SACB Archives, dated 1897–1904, BPL /FA/ SACB Archives.

9. Carey married an Englishwoman, Agnes Whiteside, in 1889. He wrote three books: *New Nerves for Old* (1914), *The Scout Law in Practice* (1915), and *Boy Scouts at Sea* (1919). The latter two volumes reflected his work as founder of the Naval Division of the Boy Scouts in Massachusetts. *Who Was Who in America, Vol. 1, 1897–1942* (Chicago: A. N. Marquis Co., n.d.). Carey was a member of the Tavern Club. Russell Sturgis built his Cambridge house in 1882, partly modeled after the historic Hancock House. On Carey's association with the Boston Museum of Fine Arts, see Whitehill, *The Museum of Fine Arts: A Centennial History*, 1:157, 290.

10. May R. Spain, *The Society of Arts & Crafts, 1897–1924* (Boston: The Society of Arts and Crafts, 1924). Spain mentions Carey's financial support, p. 13. H. L. Warren alludes to Carey's support in his "Our Work and Our Prospects" *Handicraft*, 2, no. 9 (December 1903), (an address delivered to the Society on November 20, 1903). A note in the records of the SACB indicated that Carey "agreed to pay the Society $2,000 annually for five years so that the experiments planned were possible." AAA/SACB Papers: 300: 720.

11. "Another Arts & Crafts Exhibition to be Held," *Boston Transcript*, January 14, 1899, AAA/SACB Papers: 322: 228.

12. "Arts & Crafts Exhibition," *Boston Herald*, January 24, 1899, AAA/SACB Papers: 322: 229.

13. *Exhibition of The Society of Arts and Crafts, Copley Hall, Boston, Massachusetts, April 4–15, 1899* (Boston: George H. Ellis, 272 Congress Street) Exhibition catalogue, AAA/ SACB Papers: 319: 731. See section titled "Loan Collection of Old Arts and Crafts." On Macomber, see Whitehill, *Museum of Fine Arts*, 1:91, 241, 296, 310, 314–15, and 430.

14. H. Langford Warren, Introduction to the *1899 Exhibition Catalogue*, p. 5.

15. F. W. Coburn, An unidentified manuscript in a scrapbook documenting the SACB's 1907 Exhibition. Labeled "Sent to *The World Today*, January 28, 1907. F.W.C.," BPL/FA/SACB Archives. For more on Coburn, see Hirshler, *Studio*, pp. 94, 102.

16. "It Will Open Tonight," April 4, 1899, otherwise unidentified clipping, AAA/ SACB Papers: 322: 236. "One Woman's Chat," otherwise unidentified clipping, AAA/ SACB Papers: 322: 236.

17. "It Will Open Tonight." "Copley and Allston Halls Filled with Exquisite Specimens of Handiwork of the Past," *Boston Herald*, April 4, 1899, AAA/SACB Papers: 322: 166.

18. "Delayed Catalogue Will Be Ready for Distribution Today," ca. April 4–20, 1899, otherwise unidentified clipping, AAA/SACB Papers: 322: 248. On the prevalence of the poppy in graphic design in Boston, see Finlay, *Artists of the Book in Boston*, pp. 20–21. Ethel Reed and Sarah Wyman Whitman both employed this motif.

19. Warren, Introduction, p. 5.

20. Ibid., pp. 5–6.

21. Ibid., p. 6.

22. Ibid., p. 7.

23. "Adieu to the Arts & Crafts," April 21, 1899, otherwise unidentified clipping, AAA/SACB Papers: 322: 247. This article states that the exhibition closed on April 22, one week after the planned closing of April 15. "Great Crowd Sunday," *Boston Herald*, ca. April 4–20, 1899, AAA/SACB Papers: 322: 246. This report discusses students attending from the MFA School, the Cowles Art School, and the Rhode Island School of Design. "Commended by the Mayor," April 15, 1899, otherwise unidentified clipping, AAA/SACB Papers: 322: 248. This mentions Sarah Wyman Whitman's lecture. "Other Features of the Display in Copley Hall," ca. April 4–20, 1899, otherwise unidentified clipping, AAA/SACB Papers: 322: 244. This mentions live demonstrations.

24. "Arts & Crafts Exhibition," *Boston Transcript*, ca. April 4–28, 1899, AAA/SACB Papers: 322: 243. "Other Features of the Display at Copley Hall." "Arts & Crafts Exhibition," ca. April 4–28, 1899, otherwise unidentified clipping, *AAA/SACB Papers* 322: 245.

25. "Adieu to the Arts & Crafts."

26. On the decision to lease rooms at 14 Somerset Street, see AAA/SACB Papers: 300: 407 and 364. A letter, Morris Gray to Frederick P. Cabot, dated February 14, 1900, describes preliminary arrangements to rent rooms for $1,000 per year at 14 Somerset Street, from the Twentieth Century Club, in proximity to the Boston Society of Architects and the Boston Architectural Club. See *Record*, February 5, 1900, AAA/SACB Papers: 322: 250. Whiting refers to the move from 14 Somerset Street to 9 Park Street in his "What the Arts and Crafts Movement Has Accomplished," *Handicraft*, 3, no. 3 (June 1910): 103. The *Announcements for 1901* also describe these rooms. This pamphlet is in a vertical file in the Department of Fine Arts at the Boston Public Library. During this period, the Twentieth Century Club was located at 14 Ashburton Place. Its rooms were characterized by "simplicity in all that is outward and visible in the club's appearance": *The Twentieth Century Club of Boston, 1894–1904* ([Boston]: The Davis Press, [1904–05]). There is some confusion about the exact location of the Twentieth Century Club and hence the SACB headquarters. All publications give the Society's address as 14 Somerset Street. Yet F. W. Coburn speaks of the first salesroom as being "in one of the upper stories of the Twentieth Century Club's former building in Ashburton Place, reached by a creaky little elevator." F.W.C., "Sent to the World Today," *Scrapbook, 1907* (rebound in 1988 and titled *Boston Society of Arts and Crafts*), BPL/FA/SACB Archives. A perusal of street atlases shows that Somerset Street and Ashburton Place intersected, so a building on a corner might have borne dual addresses. The building stock in that neighborhood changed drastically during the 1890s and early 1900s.

27. On June 28, 1900, Henry Lewis Johnson sent a letter to Carey resigning from his position as Secretary. The following day, F. P. Cabot resigned from his position as Treasurer. Both did so in light of Whiting's recent hiring. AAA/SACB Papers: 316: 385–6. Walker mentions meeting Whiting in AAA/SACB Papers: 300: 708. That Mary Ware

Dennett and Hartley Dennett took credit for finding Whiting is evident in a notebook compiled in 1933 by then–SACB President Humphrey J. Emery, titled "Juried Craftsmen and Comments on Their Work," BPL/FA/SACB Archives. Whiting discusses his salary and terms of employment in a letter to Carey, August 4, 1903, AAA/SACB Papers: 300: 378. The Whitings married in 1903.

28. *[Announcement for 1900–1901.] The Society of Arts and Crafts: Boston, Massachusetts. Incorporated A.D. MDCCCXCVII. 14 Somerset Street: MDCCCC* [Boston: The Merrymount Press, 104 Chestnut Street, 1901]. This is in a vertical file in the Department of Fine Arts at the Boston Public Library.

29. Frederick Allen Whiting, pamphlet discussing the "Permanent Exhibition and Salesroom and the Bureau of Information," published by the SACB, 14 Somerset Street, ca. 1900–1904; Frederick Allen Whiting, "Salesroom and Permanent Exhibition of The Society of Arts and Crafts," 14 Somerset Street, ca. 1900–1904. Both pamphlets are in a vertical file in the Department of Fine Arts in the Boston Public Library.

30. Frederick Allen Whiting, text of a "Farewell Address," April 23, 1912, AAA/SACB Papers: 300: 722.

31. Elizabeth B. Stone, "Observations of an Onlooker," *Handicraft*, 3, no. 3 (June 1900: 79–89.

32. Frederick Allen Whiting to Arthur Astor Carey, July 3, 1901, AAA/SACB Papers: 300: 364–365. See also Whiting, pamphlet discussing the "Permanent Exhibition and Salesroom and the Bureau of Information."

33. Whiting to Carey, July 3, 1901.

34. Arthur Astor Carey, "The Past Year and Its Lessons, An Address Delivered to The Society of Arts and Crafts, November 22, 1901," *Handicraft*, 1, no. 1 (April 1902): 3–27.

35. Ibid. Ralph Radcliffe Whitehead (1854–1929) founded the Byrdcliffe Arts and Crafts Colony. There members devoted their time to painting, wood-carving, cabinetry, printing, and fabrication of picture frames. Elbert Hubbard (1856–1915) founded the Roycrofters, which promoted products made in bindery, leatherwork, and furniture shops. Architect William L. Price (1861–1916) established Rose Valley, known for furniture, pottery and publishing *The Artsman* magazine. Other utopian communities flourished in Montague, Mass. (New Clairvaux, 1902–08), and Arden, Del. (Arden). Even Charles Eliot Norton became involved in anti-urbanism, retiring to a country house in Ashfield, Mass., where he encouraged local children to develop appreciation for traditional handicrafts such as needlework, wood-carving, broom making, and basketry. He also sponsored the Ashfield Children's Labor and Prize Day. See Edward Waldo Emerson, "Charles Eliot Norton, The Man and the Scholar . . . ," in Charles Eliot Norton, *Two Addresses* (Boston: Houghton Mifflin, 1912), pp. 32–33.

36. Carey, "The Past Year and Its Lessons."

37. Ibid. Eileen Boris, *Art and Labor: Ruskin, Morris, and the Craftsman Ideal in America* (Philadelphia: Temple University Press, 1986), pp. 38–39. On the Handicraft Shop, see also the Annual Report and By-Laws MCMII. *The Annual Report of The Society of Arts and Crafts, Boston, Massachusetts, Inc. 1897, 14 Somerset Street. MDCCCCII* [Published ca. April 7, 1902].

38. Untitled article on the upcoming 1899 exhibition, in *The American Architect and Building News*, ca. February 4, 1899, AAA/SACB Papers: 322: 231. Walker also attacked trade unions in "The Museum and the School."

39. "Arts & Crafts Exhibit," *Boston Herald*, January 24, 1899, AAA/SACB Papers: 322: 229.

40. Frederick Allen Whiting, [*The Development and Meaning of the Arts and Crafts Movement,*] typewritten lecture, dated November 1, 1901, AAA/SACB Papers: 300: 26–34.

41. Ibid. Wright's phrase later influenced the title of a book by Henry-Russell Hitchcock regarding Wright's work, *In the Nature of Materials* (1942).

42. *Annual Report and By-Laws MCMII. The Annual Report of The Society of Arts and Crafts of Boston, Massachusetts, Incorporated MDCCCXCVII.* 14 Somerset Street. MDCCCII [Published ca. April 7, 1902]. See section 7 on "Monthly Magazine." On the availability of *The Craftsman,* see an advertisement in *The New England Magazine,* 32, no. 2 (October 1905): n.p.

43. "The Principles of Handicraft," *Handicraft,* 1, no. 1 (April 1902): n.p.

44. For general information about contributors, see the index for each issue and correspondence with Whiting. *Handicraft* was subsequently published by the National League of Handicraft Societies, from 1910 to 1912.

45. Ware Dennett received her education at the School of the Museum of Fine Arts, Boston. She studied with A. W. Dow and abroad. In 1894–97, she was director of the course in Design and Decoration at the Drexel Institute of Art, Science, and Industry in Philadelphia. She specialized in Cordova-type leatherwork, creating gilded wall hangings and tooled leather for screens, chairs, paneling, etc. She worked with her sister Clara, and together they attracted a wide range of clients from Boston as well as New York, Cleveland, Palm Springs, Los Angeles, and Washington, D.C. Ware Dennett may have heard Kropotkin speak at the Twentieth Century Club, which attracted speakers voicing myriad radical ideas. Kropotkin, Leo Tolstoy, Jacob Riis, and Jane Addams were among those on the speakers' roster during the club's first two decades: *A Survey of Twenty Years, 1894–1914,* pp. 38–47. A substantial number of Ware Dennett's personal papers are in the collection of the Schlesinger Library, Radcliffe Institute for Advanced Study, Harvard University. See also *Notable American Women, 1607–1950* (1971).

46. Mary Ware Dennett, "Aesthetics and Ethics," *Handicraft,* 1, no. 2 (May 1902): 29–47.

47. Ibid., p. 30.

48. Ibid., pp. 30–31.

49. Ibid., p. 32.

50. Ibid. This antipathy would evolve into a crisis in 1908, a topic developed further in Chapter Three.

51. Ibid., pp. 46–47.

52. *Catalogue of the Women's Department of the Twenty-First Exhibition of the Massachusetts Charitable Mechanic Association. Sept. 22–Nov. 1, A.D. MCMII, Boston.* Massachusetts Charitable Mechanic Association Records, 1791–1995. Ms N-361. (Massachusetts Historical Society).

53. Denman Waldo Ross, "The Arts and Crafts: A Diagnosis," *Handicraft,* 1, no. 10 (January 1903): n.p.

54. Mary Ware Dennett, "The Arts and Crafts: An Outlook," *Handicraft,* 2, no. 1 (April 1903): n.p.

55. Ibid. Gustav Stickley was among those who read and responded to her article. He sent a letter, indicating his wish to discuss its points with her directly: Gustav Stickley to Mary Ware Dennett, May 22, 1903, Mary Ware Dennett Papers, microfilm reel #9 (Schlesinger Library, Radcliffe Institute, Harvard University).

56. C. Howard Walker, "The Museum and the School," *Handicraft,* 2, no. 2 (May 1903): n.p.

57. Ibid. Chapter Four further explores Walker's views toward history.

58. *The Society of Arts & Crafts Annual Report and By-Laws, Boston, Massachusetts, MDCCCCIIII. 14 Somerset Street* [1904]. This announces Carey's resignation. Letter, A. A. Carey to E. G. Evans, March 18, 1902, Elizabeth Glendower Evans Papers, and Letter, A. A. Carey to M. W. and H. Dennett, April 19, 1904, Mary Ware Dennett Papers: Series III, 1909–1942 (inclusive) (Schlesinger Library, Radcliffe Institute, Harvard University). Despite her resignation, Ware Dennett maintained a connection with the SACB, later publishing "Arts and Crafts Problem and a Way Out" in *Handicraft*, 4, no. 6 (September 1911), 209–20. As her earlier essays had done, it attracted an impassioned debate, voiced in *Handicraft* (November 1911). Carl Purington Rollins of the Dyke Mill and Montague Press found her remarks "better than ever": C. P. Rollins to M. W. Dennett, September 18, 1911, Mary Ware Dennett Papers, Series II, 1894–1948 (Schlesinger Library, Radcliffe Institute, Harvard University) In view of the antipathy surrounding her resignation it seems surprising that Ware Dennett rejoined the SACB in the 1920s.

59. H. Langford Warren, "Our Work and Our Prospects, An Address Delivered to The Society of Arts and Crafts, Boston on November 20, 1903," *Handicraft*, 2, no. 9 (December 1903): n.p.

60. F. W. Coburn, "Ten Years of The Society of Arts and Crafts," press release sent to "The Field of Art," *Scribners Magazine*, January 17, 1907, BPL/FA/SACB Archives.

CHAPTER THREE
Adviser, Promoter, Tormentor, and Midwife

1. Denman Waldo Ross, "The Arts and Crafts: A Diagnosis," *Handicraft*, 1, no. 10 (January 1903): 229–48. Lloyd E. Hawes, *The Dedham Pottery and the Earlier Robertson's Chelsea Potteries* (Dedham: Dedham Historical Society, 1968), p. 32.

2. Charles Fergus Binns, Introduction, *The Potter's Craft*, 4th ed. (1897, rpt. 1910; Princeton, N.J.: D. Van Nostrand, 1967), p. xi.

3. "Anniversary Exhibit is a Notable One," February 6, 1907. This otherwise unidentified clipping is contained in a scrapbook documenting the SACB tenth anniversary exhibition. The author of most articles was F. W. Coburn. Rebound in 1988, this volume is now titled *Boston Society of Arts and Crafts*. BPL/FA/SACB Archives.

4. "A record of the meetings of the Jury of the Society of Arts and Crafts, Boston," AAA/SACB Papers: 316: 003–051. (Hereafter cited as "Jury Meeting Record.") For the years 1900–1903, see AAA/SACB Papers: 316: 002, 009, 016, 028. No records are available for 1904–7, but Coolidge, Kendrick, Longfellow, Ross, Sacker, Walker, H. L. Warren, and Whiting probably served during that time. An article discussing the Jury in *Handicraft* (4, no. 1 [April 1911]: 19–25) implies as much, stating: "Several of the present Jurors have been serving since the organization of the Jury in 1900." For 1908, see AAA/SACB Papers: 319: 464. For 1909–12, see AAA/SACB Papers: 316: 036–049. For 1913, see AAA/SACB Papers 316: 049, or 319: 817. For 1914, see AAA/SACB Papers: 318: 864. For 1915–17, see *Annual Reports* for those years.

5. On Walker's travel, see AAA/SACB Papers: 300: 708.

6. Whiting aspired to greater involvement, though. In August 1903, as he was negotiating with Carey at the time of his annual review, he mentioned in a letter that he would like to be in charge of the salesroom, even to the point of making all merchandise selections. In other words, he aspired to replace the Jury. Frederick Allen Whiting to Arthur Astor Carey, August 4, 1903, AAA/SACB Papers: 300: 378.

7. Jury Meeting Record, November 28, 1900; February 4, 1903.

8. Whiting kept files, ca. 1906, on SACB members. Note cards with biographical information on members are part of the BPL/FA/SACB Archives. For more on Martin, see Marilee Boyd Meyer, *Inspiring Reform: Boston's Arts and Crafts Movement* (Wellesley, Mass.: Davis Museum and Cultural Center in association with Abrams, Inc., 1997), pp. 222–23. On Clark, see Finlay, *Artists of the Book in Boston*, pp. 53–54, 86–87. See also "New Instructor at Museum School," *Boston Transcript*, April 12, 1913, AAA/SACB Papers: 322: 319. On Kjellstrom, see 1920 *United States Federal Census Records*, roll 625_742, Page 8A, ED 240; *Deaths for Massachusetts*, vol. 9, p. 309; *Cambridge City Directories*, 1887–90, and Ulehla, *The Society of Arts and Crafts, Boston, Exhibition Record*, p. 128. On Kendrick, see Susan J. Montgomery, *The Ceramics of William H. Grueby, The Spirit of the New Idea in Artistic Handicraft* (Lambertville, N.J.: Arts & Crafts Quarterly Press, 1993), p. 21.

9. This comment on Hale appears in a notebook on SACB membership, compiled between 1936 and 1939 by Humphrey Emery, Secretary and Treasurer for the SACB (1930–64), BPL/FA/SACB Archives.

10. On Putnam, see Mary W. Fuller, "Annie Cabot Putnam," in *History and Proceedings of the Pocumtuck Valley Memorial Association 1921–1929* (Deerfield: Pocumtuck Valley Memorial Association, 1929), p. 320. On Wynne, see Pamphlet, "In Memory of Madeline Yale Wynne" (ca. 1918). Pocumtuck Valley Memorial Association.

11. On Murphy, see the member cards compiled by F. A. Whiting, ca. 1906; "Carved and Gilded Wood," *Boston Transcript*, October 30, 1914, AAA/SACB Papers: 322: 326; Untitled Article, *Boston Transcript*, November 5, 1915, AAA/SACB Papers: 322: 332. On Murphy's adoption of Ross's theory, see Lockwood de Forest to F. A. Whiting, January 6, 1910, AAA/SACB Papers: 300: 625. *Boston Advertiser* (November 21, 1900) discusses the relationship of Murphy to "Boston School" painters. The Smithsonian Institution/Archives of American Art holds the papers of the Carrig-Rohane Shop. See also Meyer, *Inspiring Reform*, pp. 224–25.

12. On Smith, see Lawrence Dame, "Joseph Lindon Smith, Now 85, Awaits New Egypt Adventure," *Boston Sunday Herald*, November 28, 1948, n.p. The Smithsonian Institution/Archives of American Art holds some of Smith's papers. On his work for the Dedham Pottery, see "For Arts and Crafts. Exhibit of Work at Boston," *The Herald* (Chicago), April 11, 1897, AAA/SACB Papers: 322: 322. C.M.F. (possibly Claude Moore Fuess), "Memorial Tribute." *Tavern Club Records*, Massachusetts Historical Society. Smith, *Interesting People*.

13. On Sacker, see Anne Stewart O'Donnell, "The Arts and Crafts Greeting Card, 1908–1925: A First Look," M.A. thesis, Cooper-Hewitt, National Design Museum and Parsons School of Design, 2002, especially pp. 25–39; Finlay, *Artists of the Book in Boston*, pp. 51, 59, and 103; and "A Boston Chance for Designing Women," *Springfield Republican*, ca. April 5–17, 1897, AAA/SACB Papers: 322: 221. Sacker lectured on "Experiences of an Art Director in the Motion Picture Studios of California" (February 19, 1924) at the R. H. White Co. Department Store in Boston. This was part of the "Open Door to Art" series, organized by R. C. Sturgis. Other SACB lecturers were C. Howard Walker and Charles J. Connick. Letter, R. C. Sturgis to Charles J. Connick and George Germer, February 6, 1924. See *North Bennett Street Industrial School 1879; Records, 1883, IIAix*, 104–16 (Schlesinger Library, Radcliffe Institute, Harvard University).

14. On Morse, see Ulehla, *The Society of Arts and Crafts, Boston, Exhibition Record*, p. 155. Alice J. Morse appears in Florence Levy, ed., *American Art Annual* (1898), p. 357; (1900–1901), p. 230; and (1903–04), Part II, p. 160. Census records list an Alice J. Morse who was a lodger living in Boston in 1920. Born in New Hampshire, she was 48 years of age, and her occupation was "School Teacher." *1920 United States Federal Census Records*, roll T625_742, p. 6A, ED 684, image 0433. Alice C. Morse contributed a section titled

"Women Illustrators," which includes examples of her book covers, in Maud Howe Elliott, ed., *Art and Handicraft in the Women's Building of the World's Columbian Exposition, Chicago, 1893. Official Edition* (New York: Goupil, 1893), pp. 68–79. Stuart Walker of the Boston Public Library identifies Morse's middle name as Cordelia.

15. On Peabody, see *Who's Who in New England*, vol. 2 (1916); S. H. Peabody, comp., Charles H. Pope, ed., *Peabody Genealogy* (Boston: Charles H. Pope, 1909), p. 420; Walter Muir Whitehill, *Captain Joseph Peabody, East India Merchant of Salem (1757–1844)* (Salem: Peabody Museum, 1962), pp. 42, 44, 49, 50, 176, 190; *Massachusetts Vital Records*, vol. 72, p. 244 (birth), vol. 300, p. 74 (marriage). On his antiques, see AAA/SACB Papers: 319: beginning at frame 751, passim.

16. "Survey of Membership, Conducted by the Committee on Entertainment of the Society of Arts and Crafts, Boston, 1916," AAA/SACB Papers: 316: 074. Trade catalogues provide insight into the craft of coloring plaster casts. Two local Boston businesses that sold statuary and bas-reliefs indicate that their products—though usually sold with a white or ivory finish—might be tinted by skilled artisans to match a client's interior décor. See *Catalogue and Supplement, P. P Caproni & Bro., Boston 1897* (Boston: Rockwell & Churchill, 1894), n.p., and *Catalogue of Reproductions in Plaster, A. Da Prato & Col, 12 and 14 Waverley House, Charlestown Dist., Boston, Mass.* (Cambridgeport: Louis F. Weston, [19—]), n.p. (Historical Collections, Baker Library, Harvard University).

17. Ivey Pinchbeck, *Women Workers and the Industrial Revolution* (London: Routledge, 1930), p. 293.

18. Janet Ruutz-Rees, *Home Occupations* (New York: Appleton, 1883), p. 123. Here the author discusses equipment and costs associated with amateur photography; Gover, *The Positive Image*, p. 46.

19. P. G. Hubert, Jr., "Occupations for Women," *The Woman's Book*, vols. 1, 2 (New York: Scribner's, 1894), p. 1–21.

20. Ulehla, *The Society of Arts and Crafts, Boston, Exhibition Record*, offers definitions for some of these craft categories, pp. 11–13. On "industrial designers," see *Work for Women* (New York: Putnam's, 1883).

21. Jury Meeting Record, November 7, 1900; November 9, 1900.

22. Jury Meeting Record, November 7, 1900.

23. Jury Meeting Record, December 19, 1900; January 16, 1901; January 29, 1902; October 1, 1902; December 12, 1902.

24. Jury Meeting Record, April 10, 1901. I don't know if this hallmark ever materialized.

25. *The Society of Arts and Crafts Annual Report and By-Laws. Boston Massachusetts, 1903.* See section: Membership. BPL/FA/SACB Archives. Annual reports are available at the Boston Public Library and on microfilm, filmed by the Smithsonian Institution/Archives of American Art, AAA/SACB Papers: microfilm roll 316.

26. *The Society of Arts and Crafts Annual Report & List of Members, Boston. 1905.* See section: Salesroom.

27. Ibid. See section: Handicraft Museum.

28. Frederick Allen Whiting, "To Contributors," The Society of Arts and Crafts, Boston, Incorporated 1897, No. 9 Park Street, Boston. (The Village Press, August 1, 1905.) See sections 5 and 6.

29. *The Society of Arts & Crafts Annual Report and List of Members. 1906.* See section: Workshops and Classes. Frederick Allen Whiting, "Fall Announcements," The Society of Arts and Crafts, No. 9 Park Street, Boston, Massachusetts. November 1, 1906. For more on 79 Chestnut Street, see Meyer, *Inspiring Reform*, pp. 75–76, n. 13.

30. *The Annual Report of The Society of Arts and Crafts, Boston, Massachusetts. 1908.* See section: Jury Advice and Criticism.

31. Ibid. See section: Awards.

32. *The Society of Arts and Crafts Twelfth Annual Report & List of Members: Boston 1909.* See the Report of the Jury, pp. 15–17. To date, I have not located one of these forms.

33. *The Society of Arts and Crafts Thirteenth Annual Report: List of Members Boston 1910*, p. 15.

34. *The Society of Arts and Crafts Fourteenth Annual Report and List of Members: Boston, 1911.* [The Merrymount Press, Boston.] See the Report of the Jury, pp. 14–19.

35. Ibid., Report of the Council.

36. For biographical information on Walker, see "Memorial Bulletin for C. Howard Walker," The Society of Arts and Crafts, 32 Newbury Street, Boston, 19, no. 1, May 1936; Obituary, *Technology Review*, 38 (February 1936), p. III; and Further Obituary, *Technology Review*, 38 (July 1936), p. II.

37. *The Annual Report of The Society of Arts and Crafts*, Boston, Massachusetts. 1912. See the Report of the Council.

38. Minutes from the meeting of the Council (February 16, 1911) state: "The Secretary suggested the advisability of having a medal made after the design of the Seal to be given to members producing work of very rare quality." AAA/SACB Papers: 316: 106. Minutes from the meeting of the Council (February 13, 1912) added to this discussion: "Voted: That hereafter at each annual meeting not more than three medals shall be awarded for excellence. These medals shall be awarded by the Council on the recommendation of the Jury." AAA/SACB Papers: 316: 111.

39. *The Annual Report of The Society of Arts & Crafts Boston Massachusetts for the Year 1916.* April 30, 1917. See the Report of the Council.

40. Jury Meeting Record, November 7, 1900.

41. See, for example, Jury Meeting Record, December 4, 1901, or November 21, 1902.

42. Jury Meeting Record, August 12, 1902; November 14, 1900.

43. Jury Meeting Record, November 9, 1900; July 11, 1901; March 5, 1902; April 2, 1902.

44. Jury Meeting Record, February 12, 1902.

45. Jury Meeting Record, April 10, 1901; October 22, 1902; December 19, 1902; November 9, 1900; February 13, 1901, or March 6, 1901.

46. Jury Meeting Record, November 9, 1900; December 19, 1900.

47. Jury Meeting Record, November 9, 1900; July 11, 1901.

48. Jury Meeting Record, January 29, 1902; February 12, 1902.

49. Jury Meeting Record, July 11, 1901. For more on Robertson, see Hawes, *Dedham Pottery*.

50. Jury Meeting Record, November 7, 1900; March 5, 1902; December 19, 1902; October 16, 1901; October 22, 1902; May 13, 1903.

51. Jury Meeting Record, October 16, 1901; December 12, 1902; December 19, 1902. On Redmond, see Erica Hirshler, "Women Artists at Trinity," in O'Gorman, ed., *Makers of Trinity Church*, pp. 168–70. See also Petteys, *Dictionary of Women Artists*, p. 588; and A. N. Hosking, ed., *The Artists Year Book . . . for 1905–06* (Chicago, 1905), p. 161. On Mercer, see Cleota Reed, *Henry Chapman Mercer and the Moravian Pottery and Tile Works* (Philadelphia: University of Pennsylvania Press, 1987).

52. Report of the Jury, in the *Annual Report* for 1906, pp. 18–21.

53. J. T. Coolidge, Jr., Report of the Jury, in *Annual Report of The Society of Arts and*

Crafts, Boston [May 1907], pp. 17–19. The year 1907 was a busy one. In Boston, the groundbreaking for the new Museum of Fine Arts building on Huntington Avenue took place. Nationally, it was the year of the Jamestown Exposition, which included a display of American handicrafts.

54. Report of the Jury, in *Annual Report* for 1908, pp. 19–21.

55. The Panic of 1907 began in the summer, with bankruptcies, business failures, a stock market plunge, and a subsequent run on the nation's banks. Government and business leaders—including the United States Treasury and J. P. Morgan—collaborated to stabilize the financial market. The Panic led to reform of the American banking system, and to such legislation as the Aldrich-Vreeland Act (1908). On the effects of the Panic in Boston, see Frederic H. Curtis, "Fifty Years of Boston Finance, 1880–1930," in Herlihy, ed., *Fifty Years of Boston*, p. 235.

56. Report of the Jury, in *Annual Report* for 1909, pp. 15–17.

57. Report of the Jury, in *Annual Report* for 1910, pp. 13–16.

58. Minutes of the Meeting of the Council, dated November 2, 1909 state: "Voted: That arrangements be made to secure Mr. Walker's services for criticisms etc. for one hour each week for a weekly honorarium of $5.00." AAA/SACB Papers: 316: 92.

59. Memorandum, Saleroom Committee to the Council, Spring 1908, AAA/SACB Papers: 317: 414.

60. Farewell Address for Frederick Allen Whiting, April 1912, AAA/SACB Papers: 300: 708; Bulletin. Memorial to C. Howard Walker, The Society of Arts & Crafts, 32 Newbury Street, Boston, 19, no. 1 (May 1936). This includes the *Herald* editorial as well as essays by Charles J. Connick, J. Templeman Coolidge, and Elizabeth B. Stone, and excerpts from principles of good design, written by Walker.

61. Farewell Address for F. A. Whiting, AAA/SACB Papers: 300: 716–718.

62. Report of the Jury, in *Annual Report* for 1911, pp. 14–19. For insight into Coolidge's definition of good design, see his article "A Few Considerations of Japanese Wood-Carving," *Handicraft*, June 1903. Here he discusses a collection recently acquired by the BMFA, and enumerates the qualities of good design throughout. That collection may have included examples from a recent sale of "Old Japanese Carvings," sold by Bunkio Matsuki in New York for $18,770.50. Levy, *American Art Annual*, 4 (1903–04): 97.

63. Report of the Jury, *Annual Report* for 1911, pp 14–19.

64. Report of the Jury, *Annual Report* for 1912, pp. 15–18.

65. Addresses at Resignation Dinner, C. Howard Walker's Remarks, April 23, 1912, AAA/SACB Papers: 300: 708–718.

66. "Report of the Jury," in *The Annual Report of The Society of Arts and Crafts, Boston*, 1913, [April 21], pp. 14–16.

67. A. W. Longfellow, Jr., Acting Chairman, Report of the Jury, in *The Annual Report of The Society of Arts and Crafts, Boston*, 1914 [April 2], p. 9.

68. C. Howard Walker, [Report of the Critic for the Jury] in *Annual Report* for 1914, pp. 9–12.

69. Ibid. Beverly K. Brandt, "'All Workmen, Artists and Lovers of Art': The Organizational Structure of The Society of Arts and Crafts, Boston," in Meyer, *Inspiring Reform*, pp. 38–39.

70. Brandt, "'All Workmen,'" pp. 38–39.

71. Walker, [Report of the Critic for the Jury], 1914.

72. C. Howard Walker, [Report of the Critic for the Jury] in *The Society of Arts and Crafts, Annual Report* [March 20, 1915], pp. 9–10.

73. C. Howard Walker, [Report of the Critic for the Jury] in *The Annual Report of The*

Society of Arts & Crafts, Boston, Massachusetts, for the Year 1915 [March 22, 1916 (?)]. Printed by C. P. Rollins. The Montague Press 1915–16], pp. 7–9.

74. A. W. Longfellow, Jr., Report of the Jury, in *The Annual Report of The Society of Arts & Crafts Boston Massachusetts for the Year 1916* [April 30, 1917], p. 6.

75. C. Howard Walker, Report of the Critic of the Jury, in *Annual Report* for 1916, pp. 6–9.

76. C. Howard Walker, Report of the Critic of the Jury, in *The Society of Arts and Crafts. Annual Report . . . for the Year 1917* [Stetson Press, Boston, April 30, 1918], pp. 6–9.

77. A synopsis of Walker's views appears in the Memorial Bulletin issued by the SACB at the time of his death. This offers five principles of good design pertaining to style, labor, materials, symbolism, and order—views that he reiterated in his work as Critic of the Jury. *Bulletin. Memorial to C. Howard Walker* (May 1936).

78. Letter, Annie C. Putnam to the SACB Jury, March 14, 1908, AAA/SACB Papers: 300: 515.

79. Ibid. Putnam may have been arguing subtly on her partner Madeline Wynne's behalf. Wynne's eccentric metalwork would probably not have fared well with the SACB Jury, which may explain why Wynne never joined the organization.

80. Report of the Jury, in *Annual Report* for 1909, p. 16. Memorandum, the Committee on the Salesroom to the Council, May 15, 1908, AAA/SACB Papers: 317: 412–413.

81. Letter, Mary C. Knight to Frederick P. Cabot, June 1908, AAA/SACB Papers: 317: 381. On Cabot, see Herlihy, *Fifty Years of Boston*, pp. 498, 538, 640. Cabot may have been related to metalworker and Juror Annie Cabot Putnam.

82. See correspondence and reports for 1908, passim, AAA/SACB Papers, microfilm rolls 300, 316, and 317, especially letters and reports written to or by the Committee on the Salesroom.

83. "Abstract of Guild Reports. St. Dunstan's Guild," in the *Annual Report* for 1910, pp. 16–17.

84. Untitled, two-page, typewritten statement, probably prepared by the Auxiliary Committee on Craftsman Membership, ca. 1913, AAA/SACB Papers, microfilm roll 300. This report follows "Section 2. Charter and Statements of Criteria."

85. Hermann Dudley Murphy's comments appear in the minutes of a meeting of the Council, March 11, 1908, AAA/SACB Papers: 316: 441. Letter, Hazel G. Collins to the Salesroom Committee, March 13, 1908, AAA/SACB Papers: 300: 510.

86. C. Howard Walker, as quoted in "Boston Develops Brilliant Enameling," *Boston Herald*, October 3, 1915, AAA/SACB Papers: 322: 331.

87. Walker, "Report of the Critic for the Jury," *Annual Report* for 1916–17.

88. Letter, Arthur J. Stone and Elizabeth B. Stone to Frederick P. Cabot, July 17, 1912, AAA/SACB Papers: 317: 671.

89. Jury Meeting Record, January 29, 1902, AAA/SACB Papers: 316: 019.

90. "Answer to Mr. Roger's Criticism," a response written by the Salesroom Committee, ca. June 4–8, 1908, AAA/SACB Papers: 300: 562. Letter, Elizabeth B. Stone to H. Langford Warren, February 22, 1908, AAA/SACB Papers: 300: 498.

91. Elizabeth B. Stone, "Observations of an Onlooker," *Handicraft*, 3, no. 3 (June 1910): 79. Mrs. Stone also presented these views to the SACB on November 10, 1909.

CHAPTER FOUR
Models and Methodologies

1. George Harris, *The Theory of the Arts: or Art in Relation to Nature, Civilization, and*

Man. Comprising an Investigation, Analytical and Critical into the Origin, Rise, Province, Principles, and Application of Each of the Arts (London: Trubner, 1869), p. 149.

2. Day, *Ornament and Its Application*, p. 154.

3. Cook, *House Beautiful*, pp. 35, 59, 62, 65, 66, 67, 71, 75, 78, and 52.

4. Ibid., pp. 161, 163.

5. Arthur Wesley Dow, *Composition* (1899; 13th ed. with new introduction by Joseph Masheck, Berkeley: University of California Press, 1997), pp. 119, 121, 161, 171. "Practice in simple harmonies gives control of the more complex relations, and enables one to create with freedom in any field of art. Such training is the best foundation for work in design, architecture, the crafts, painting, sculpture and teaching. After this should come special training; for the designer, architect, craftsman, study of historic styles, severe drill in drawing (freehand and mechanical), knowledge of materials" (p. 173).

6. Report of the Jury, in *Annual Report* for 1910, p. 15.

7. "Museum of Fine Arts," in *Boston Art Guide* (Boston, 1893), n.p.

8. Report of the Jury, in *Annual Report* for 1911, p. 15.

9. Report of the Jury, in *Annual Report* for 1912, p. 16.

10. Morgan and Cheek, "History in the Service of Design," in MacDougall, *Architectural Historian*, p. 62. Shillaber, *M.I.T. School of Architecture and Planning: 1861–1961*, p. 9. Ware, as quoted in Woods, "History in the Early American Architectural Journals," in MacDougall, p. 83. See *Catalogue and Supplement, P. P. Caproni & Bro., Boston, 1897* (Boston: Rockwell & Churchill, 1894), as well as *Catalogue of Reproductions in Plaster, A. Da Prato & Co., 13–14 Waverley House, Charlestown Dist., Boston, Mass.* (Cambridgeport: Louis F. Weston, [19—]) (Harvard University, Baker Library, Historical Collections).

11. Morgan and Cheek, pp. 66–67.

12. H. G. Wells, as quoted in Martin Green, *The Mount Vernon Street Warrens: A Boston Story, 1860–1910* (New York: Scribner's, 1989), p. 160. Shillaber, p. 50.

13. On the library, see *Annual Report* for 1906. In 1904, as noted earlier, Sarah Wyman Whitman bequeathed to the SACB two examples of pottery (made by SACB members) to serve as the core of a contemporary study collection, intended to be "standards" to guide the Jury and its constituents: *Annual Report* for 1905. On the study collection of "kindred art of the past," see *Annual Report* for 1911, p. 15. A Record of the Meetings of the Jury frequently mentions antiques from members' collections that the Jury approved for duplication by craftsmen. See, for example, minutes for December 19, 1900; January 16, 1901; January 29, 1902; October 1, 1902, and February 12, 1902. On the traveling exhibitions and technical library, see *Annual Report* for 1907.

14. Obituary, Arthur J. Stone, unidentified newspaper clipping, Gardner, Mass., 1938, in the Arthur J. Stone Collection, Department of American Decorative Art and Sculpture, Museum of Fine Arts, Boston.

15. *Annual Report* for 1907. "The League Libraries," *Handicraft*, 3, no. 4 (July 1910): 136. "List of Books in the Library of the Society," in *Annual Report* for 1916, pp. 20–23.

16. C. Howard Walker, Report of the Jury, in *Annual Report* for 1915, p. 10. Walker, Report of the Critic of the Jury, in *Annual Report* for 1916, p. 8.

17. For further information, consult the Arthur J. Stone Collection. See also Elenita C. Chickering with Sarah Morgan Ross, *Arthur J. Stone, 1847–1933, Designer and Silversmith* (Boston: Boston Athenaeum, 1994), p. 36.

18. William Morris, "The Lesser Arts," in Cole, *William Morris*, pp. 494–516. C. Howard Walker, "The Museum and the School," *Handicraft*, 2, no. 2 (May 1903): p. 41.

19. *Exhibition of the Society of Arts and Crafts: Copley Hall, Boston, February 5–26, 1907*,

Arts and Crafts Exhibition in Celebration of the Tenth Anniversary of Organization . . . (Boston: Heintzemann Press, 1907), passim.

20. Beverly K. Brandt, "'Sobriety and Restraint': The Search for an Arts and Crafts Style in Boston, 1897–1917," *Tiller*, 2, no. 5 [Fall 1985]: 50.

21. O.L.E. to Edward H. Clement, ed., "Listener," *Boston Transcript*, ca. February 27, 1907; Will Hutchins, "The Boston Arts and Crafts Exhibition in Copley Hall," *Republican* (Springfield), February 7, 1907; C. Howard Walker to the editor, *Boston Herald*, ca. March 7, 1907. (All of these articles are contained in a scrapbook of clippings, assembled at the time of the SACB's 1907 Decennial Exhibition, in the SACB Archives, Fine Arts Department, Boston Public Library.) In his essay "The Discovery of America's Architectural Past, 1874–1914," in MacDougall, pp. 23–39, William B. Rhoads indicates that the Colonial era was characterized by such terms as "gentility, elegance, sense, taste, good breeding, and aristocratic atmosphere," and such descriptors as "homely, dignified, courageous, determined" (p. 36). These were the sorts of qualities and terms used often by the SACB Jury in describing "good design."

22. Shand-Tucci, *Cram, American Medievalist*, p. 16.

23. Cook, *House Beautiful*, pp. 259, 261. Commenting on why original Colonial artifacts were far superior to revivalist copies, Cook stated: "No matter how superficially resembling the copies may be [of old American or English furniture], they will always be wanting in something,—in proportion, in delicacy, or in spirit. And even if copies could be cast in a mold, it is not good to wish for them, for we can put all their merits into original pieces, made for ourselves to-day, that will not only give us pleasure, but will show our children that we knew how to profit by what our fathers taught us" (p. 81). For an excellent illustration of Cook's points, see figure 75, "Old Colonial Days," p. 247.

24. Laurence Binyon, *The Flight of the Dragon: An Essay on the Theory and Practice of Art in China and Japan* (London: John Murry, 1911), p. 96. Binyon was for years the head of the print department at the British Museum, later serving as Norton Professor of Poetry. See Letter, R. Clipston Sturgis to James Lawrence, Jr., Acting Secretary of the Tavern Club, November 25, 1933, R. C. Sturgis Personal File, Tavern Club Records (Massachusetts Historical Society). Julia de W. Addison quotes Binyon frequently while writing on Asian art in *The Boston Museum of Fine Arts*, passim.

25. John Bascom, *Aesthetics. The Science of Beauty* (New York, 1886), pp. 153, 147–51.

26. Bernard Cuzner, *A Silversmith's Manual, Treating the Designing and Making of the Simpler Pieces of Domestic Silverware* (1935; 2nd ed., London: NAG Press, 1949), p. 185. Editorial, possibly written by H. Langford Warren, *Handicraft*, 1, no. 4 (July 1902): n.p.

27. Day, *The Planning of Ornament*, p. 34. Day and Buckle, *Art in Needlework*, pp. 239–40.

28. Alex Krieger and David Cobb, eds., *Mapping Boston* (Cambridge: MIT. Press, 1999), pp. 212, 196. For a period definition of Transcendentalism, see Edwin M. Bacon, *King's Dictionary of Boston* (Cambridge: Moses King, 1883), pp. 255–56. Here Bacon states: "The definition of Transcendentalism is somewhat vague; denoting certain general tendencies of thought and opinion, rather than distinctly formulated theories. In general, it may be said to be that which is opposed to materialism; seeking the origin of knowledge in the intuitions of the senses and experience as the source."

29. Douglas Dreishpoon, "Photographs," in *From Architecture to Object: Masterworks of the American Arts & Crafts Movement* (New York: Dutton Studio Books, in association with Hirschl & Adler Galleries, 1989), p. 150.

30. Charles Edward Hooper, *The Country House: A Practical Manual of the Planning and Construction of the American Country Home and Its Surroundings* (New York: Doubleday, Page, 1905), p. 183.

31. Begg, *The Development of Taste*, p. 149; Walker, in *Annual Report* for 1914, p. 11; Walker, Report of the Jury, in *Annual Report* for 1912, p. 17.

32. A Record of the Meetings of the Jury, December 19, 1902, and October 22, 1902. Boston woman as quoted in Amory, *Proper Bostonians*, p. 22.

33. For references to naturalism, see the *Exhibition of the Society of Arts and Crafts: Copley Hall, Boston, February 5–26, 1907*, pp. 1–108, passim. John D. Sedding, "Design," in *Arts and Crafts Essays, by Members of the Arts & Crafts Exhibition Society* (London: Rivington, Percival, 1893), pp. 412–13.

34. *Annual Report* for 1911, p. 17; *Annual Report* for 1912, p. 17.

35. *Annual Report* for 1914, p. 11.

36. *Annual Report* for 1915, p. 9.

37. Batchelder, *Principles of Design*, p. 34; Day, *Nature in Ornament*, p. 84. "An Interview with Mr. Charles F. Annesley Voysey, Architect and Designer," *The Studio*, 1 (April–September, 1893): 232. Binyon, *Flight of the Dragon*, p. 21.

38. Dow, *Composition*, pp. 97, 109, 103.

39. Day, *Ornament and Its Application*, p. 13.

40. Frank Lloyd Wright, *An Autobiography* (London: Faber & Faber, 1945), p. 196. Wright uses this phrase to describe the Japanese home.

41. Thomas S. Hines, *Burnham of Chicago, Architect and Planner* (New York: Oxford University Press, 1974), chapter 4, passim.

42. Day, *Nature in Ornament*, pp. 102, 108.

43. Ibid., p. 3.

44. Wornum, "The Exhibition as a Lesson in Taste," in *The Great Exhibition, London 1851*, p. XXI.

45. Ibid.

46. Arthur Clutton-Brock, *Essays on Art* (New York: Scribner's, 1920), pp. vi–vii.

47. Day, *Nature in Ornament*, pp. 6, 10.

48. Denman W. Ross, *A Theory of Pure Design: Harmony, Balance, Rhythm* (1907; New York: Peter Smith, 1933), p. 7. Batchelder, *Principles of Design*, p. 3.

49. Batchelder, p. 114. Day, *The Planning of Ornament*, p. 12. Day, *Ornament and Its Application*, p. 298.

50. Dresser, Principles, p. 23. Dow, *Composition*, pp. 143–44. Day, *Ornament and Its Application*, p. 280.

51. Day, *Ornament and Its Application*, p. 13. See Catalogue, Whitney's Linen Store, Household and Art Linens, 37–39 Temple Place, Boston, 1889 (Harvard University, Baker Library, Historical Collections).

52. Dow, *Composition*, pp., 84, 86.

53. Batchelder, p. 43; William H. Holmes, as quoted in George Wharton James, *Indian Basketry*, 2nd ed. (New York: Henry Malkan, 1902), p. 123. On the influence of geometry on these architects' ornament, see James F. O'Gorman, *Three American Architects* (Chicago: University of Chicago Press, 1991), and O'Gorman, *The Architecture of Frank Furness* (Philadelphia: Philadelphia Art Museum, 1973). Claude Bragdon, *Projective Ornament* (Rochester, N.Y.: Manas Press, 1915), pp. 6–7.

54. Day, *Ornament and Its Application*, p. 232. Frank Lloyd Wright website: http://users.erols.com/donald.chandler/flw.html.

55. Day, *Nature in Ornament*, pp. 52, 69. Ross, *Theory of Pure Design*, p. 188. Crane, *The Bases of Design*, p. 101.

56. Foreword, *The Craftsman*, 1, no. 1 (October 1901).

57. Day, *Ornament and Its Application*, p. 20.

58. Ibid., p. 129; Day, *Nature in Ornament*, p. 10.

59. Robert Brown, Jr., to the Editor, *Boston Transcript*, February 20, 1897, AAA/SACB Papers: 322: 176; Christopher Dresser, *Principles of Design* (London: Cassell, Petter & Galpin, n.d.), p. 17.

60. Day, *The Planning of Ornament*, p. 49; Day and Buckle, *Art in Needlework*, p. 234; C. Howard Walker, Report of the Jury, in *Annual Report* for 1917, p. 8.

61. Day, *Ornament and Its Application*, p. 130. Crane, *The Bases of Design*, pp. 111, 127.

62. Kate Gordon, *Esthetics* (New York, 1909), p. 193; William Lethaby, Editor's Preface, in Luther Hooper, *Hand-Loom Weaving Plain & Ornamental* (New York: Pitman, n.d.; rpt. 1920), p. vi; Day, *Ornament and Its Application*, p. 89.

63. Day, *Ornament and Its Application*, pp. 175–76, 291, 289; Day, *Nature in Ornament*, p. 78. Albert Einstein, from a contribution to *Living Philosophies* (1949), vol. 7, as quoted in George Seldes, *The Great Thoughts* (New York: Ballantine Books, 1985), p. 120. John Dewey and Ernest Batchelder may have shared a similar philosophy. In *Batchelder Tilemaker* (Los Angeles: Balcony Press, 1999), p. 44, Robert Winter notes: "Like Dewey, Batchelder perceived that in the process of creating, what he called 'The Play Impulse' takes over and the artist's imagination is let loose."

64. Cook, *House Beautiful*, p. 120.

65. Dow, *Composition*, pp. 63–64, 103.

66. Ibid., p. 156.

67. Richard Guy Wilson, Introduction, *From Architecture to Object*, p. 19.

68. Dow, p. 135; Binyon, *Flight of the Dragon*, p. 28.

69. Binyon, pp. 75, 32.

70. Ibid., p. 79.

71. Morse, *Japanese Homes*, p. 114. Cook, *House Beautiful*, p. 314. Cook also addressed the issue of "old-fashioned simplicity" in his pamphlet *"What Shall We Do With Our Walls?,"* pp. 12–14.

72. The concept of "negative evidence" also pertains to crime detection. The concept is associated with the controversial British medical missionary Dr. Henry Faulds (1843–1936), one of the first to consider the use of fingerprints in crime detection, who discussed his theories with Charles Darwin.

73. Batchelder, p. 53; Binyon, p. 11.

74. Binyon, p. 13.

75. Wilson, Introduction, *From Architecture to Object*, p. 16.

CHAPTER FIVE

The Boston Diaspora

1. A.W. Longfellow, Jr., Report of the Membership Committee, *Annual Report* for 1916, pp. 10–11.

2. William Fenwick Harris, "Charles Eliot Norton, An Address Delivered before a General Meeting of the Archaeological Institute of America in Toronto, December 1908," in Edward Waldo Emerson and William Fenwick Harris, *Charles Eliot Norton: Two Addresses* (Boston: Houghton Mifflin, 1912), p. 48.

3. See *Annual Report* for 1902, section 9A. Addison B. LeBoutillier, "The Early Wooden Architecture of Andover, Mass.," *The White Pine Monographs*, 3, no. 2 (April 1917): 3–14; see the editor's note for biographical information about LeBoutillier. Bruce Johnson, "Rookwood Pottery," and "Grueby Pottery," in *Arts and Crafts: The Early Modernist Movement in American Decorative Arts*, 1894–1923 (New York: House of

Collectibles, 1988), pp. 391, and 286 n. 4. Whiting mentions having seen the Rookwood display in Buffalo. Letter, Frederick Allen Whiting to William Watts Taylor, March 17, 1904, *The Louisiana Purchase Exposition—The Department of Art Papers (St. Louis World's Fair—1904)*, owned and filmed by the Archives of American Art, Smithsonian Institution (Gift of the St. Louis Art Museum, July 1975), microfilm roll number 1748, frame 272 (hereafter cited as AAA/LPE—DA Papers: roll#: frame#). The application form completed by the Grueby Faience Company at the time of the St. Louis world's fair listed where each entry had been exhibited previously: AAA/LPE—DA Papers: 1752: 529. See also Letter, William H. Graves to Whiting, April 11, 1904, AAA/LPE—DA Papers: 1752: 535. Grueby proudly indicated expositions in which the company had participated and medals received in magazine advertisements. See, for example, those in the *Masters of Art* series, passim. See also "The Craft of Rookwood Pottery," *World's Work*, 8 (May–October 1904): following p. 5210.

4. General information concerning the Palace of Art and its various displays is provided in "Circular No. 2 to Artists," dated August 21, 1903, AAA/LPE—DA Papers: 1753: 497-98. Will H. Low commented on the rarity of finding applied arts in art buildings at international expositions. "So recently as the Paris Exposition of 1900," he wrote, "the student of art was obliged to search in buildings devoted to various industries the different objects of original Art workmanship, which at St. Louis were most justly brought within the walls of the Art Palace. In St. Louis, by passing through successive galleries, one could follow this latest and extremely interesting phase of art effort as expressed by different nations": "The Field of Art," *Scribner's*, 37 (January–June 1905): 765-68. David R. Francis, *The Universal Exposition of 1904* (St. Louis: Louisiana Purchase Exposition Company, 1913), chap. 4: "Art," p. 354, quoting Frederick Allen Whiting, Superintendent of the Applied Arts Division. See also Walter B. Stevens, "General Plan of the Exposition," *The World Today*, 7, no. 3 (September 1904): 1131. Stevens writes: "Moreover the utilitarian finds expression here in an enlargement of the classification to couple applied arts with fine arts. This is the 'Department of Art' and it comprehends in high degree the application of art to things of use as well as to things of sentiment."

5. This description was used by several writers including Frederic C. Howe, "The World's Fair at St. Louis," *The Cosmopolitan*, 5 (July 1903): 284, and E. S. Hoch, "A Fifty-Million-Dollar Exposition," *National Magazine* (Boston), 18, (May 1903[?]): 178. For general information about the Louisiana Purchase Exposition, see Mark Bennitt, ed., *History of the Louisiana Purchase Exposition* (New York: Arno Press Reprint, 1976).

6. David R. Francis, "The Greatest World's Fair," *Everybody's Magazine*, 10, no. 4 (April 1904): 438.

7. Most guides to the exposition list and/or illustrate the major buildings. For descriptions (including one for the Electricity Building), see Franz K. Winkler, "The Architecture of the Louisiana Purchase Exposition," *Architectural Record*, 15 (1904): 357. For a scathing criticism of these structures, see Halsey Ricardo, "Architecture at the St. Louis World's Fair," *Architectural Review*, 16 (July–December 1904): 162. E. L. Masqueray, "Art and Architecture at the Exposition," *The Independent*, 57, no. 2902 (July 14, 1904): 82. For C. Howard Walker, see Marquis, *Who Was Who in America*, vol. 1 (1897–1942) (A. N. Marquis Co.), p. 1289.

8. Charles M. Kurtz, *The Saint Louis World's Fair of 1904 in Commemoration of the Acquisition of the Louisiana Territory. A Handbook of Information Profusely Illustrated* (Saint Louis: Gottshalk Printing, 1903), p. 45. *Official Catalogue of Exhibits, Department of Art. Revised Edition. Universal Exposition, Saint Louis, 1904* (St. Louis: The Official Catalogue

Company, 1904), p. 14. The six major groups were Painting and Drawings; Engravings and Lithographs; Sculpture; Architecture; a Loan Collection of works produced between 1803 and 1893; and Original Objects of Art Workmanship. The small classifications for the latter category included "Art work" in glass, pottery or porcelain, metal, leather, wood, textiles, bookbinding, and "Art work worthy of representation which is not covered by any of the preceding classes of this Group or other Groups in the Department of Art," p. 14.

9. "To Workers in the Applied Arts," AAA/LPE—DA Papers: 1753: 484–86. See also Francis, *The Universal Exposition of 1904*, p. 347.

10. For information about Ives, see *Who Was Who in America*, 1:622; Kurtz, p. 695; and AAA/LPE—DA Papers: 1734: 284. Halsey Cooley Ives, "The Art Exhibition at St. Louis," *The American Monthly Review of Reviews*, 29: 574.

11. "Circular No. 2 to Artists." Ives also served on a national advisory board to Florence N. Levy, publisher of *The American Art Annual*. Joining him in this capacity were William Howe Downes, John La Farge, Lorado Taft, Candace Wheeler, and Ellsworth Woodward, among others. Several of Levy's advisers would eventually be involved with the St. Louis world's fair. Florence N. Levy, *The American Art Annual, 1900–01*, vol. 3 (Boston: Noyes, Platt Co., 1900).

12. For further information about the architecture of the Palace of Art, see W. S. Bridgman, "The Art Palace at the Louisiana Purchase Exposition," *Munsey's Magazine*, 31 (1904): 421–26; "The Vast Palaces of the World's Fair," *Scientific American Supplement*, no. 1498 (1904): 24004–5; chap. 10, "Architectural Problems," in Francis, *The Universal Exposition of 1904*; Montgomery Schuyler, "The Architecture of the St. Louis World's Fair," *Scribner's Magazine*, 35, no. 4 (April 1904); and "General Information to U.S. Artists," AAA/LPE—DA Papers: 1753: 483. The main block of the Palace of Art is now part of the St. Louis Museum of Art.

13. Letter, Ives to Whiting, February 23, 1904, AAA/LPE—DA Papers: 1748: 126–27.

14. Frederick Allen Whiting, "The Arts and Crafts at the Louisiana Purchase Exposition," *International Studio Magazine Supplement*, 23 (October 1904), p. ccclxxxiv. Similar control was not exerted with the "fine" arts. In soliciting entries, Ives and his team apparently contacted "every American artist here and abroad listed in catalogues or directories for the past ten years." The response was, not surprisingly, overwhelming. See "Circular No. 2 to Artists."

15. Letters, Whiting to Ives, February 27, 1904, AAA/LPE—DA Papers: 1748: 128; Ives to Whiting, February 23, 1904, AAA/LPE—DA Papers: 1748: 127; Ives to Whiting, March 1, 1904, AAA/LPE—DA Papers: 1748: 130–33.

16. These groups functioned in addition to the National Advisory Committee that assisted Ives. Bostonians serving on this committee of twenty-one members included Holker Abbott, Robert Swain Peabody, and Edward Robinson: Letter, Ives to Whiting, March 1, 1904, AAA/LPE—DA Papers: 1748: 1304. Numerous catalogues for the Department of Art—and the exposition in general—list jury members. See also Halsey C. Ives, "The Art Exhibition at St. Louis," *American Monthly Review of Reviews*, 29 (May 1904): 574–76. On Herbert E. Everett, see Florence N. Levy, *American Art Annual 1903–04*, vol. 4 (New York: American Art Annual, Inc., 1903), part 2, p. 154.

17. The jury process is described in various sources including "Circular No. 2 to Artists." See also "Rules and Regulations Governing Domestic Exhibitors," AAA/LPE—DA Papers: 1748: 166.

18. Whiting, "The Arts and Crafts," pp. ccclxxxiv–ccclxxxv.

19. Letter, Charles M. Kurtz to Whiting, March 12, 1904, AAA/LPE—DA Papers: 1748: 174–76. Very few of the items mentioned by Kurtz were actually accepted. See also Letter, Whiting to Ives, March 10, 1904, AAA/LPE—DA Papers: 1748: 137.

20. Letters, Ives to Whiting, March 1 and March 10, 1904, AAA/LPE—DA Papers: 1748: 130–37.

21. See correspondence of the month of March, AAA/LPE—DA Papers: 1748: passim.

22. Letter, Clarke Conwell to Whiting, April 11, 1904, AAA/LPE—DA Papers: 1748: 52. Ulehla, *The Society of Arts and Crafts, Boston. Exhibition Record 1897–1927*, does not list Conwell as an SACB member, but he tendered his resignation in December 1904, so he must have joined at some point. For other correspondence between Conwell and Whiting, see AAA/LPE—DA Papers: 1748, 52–59. Dates for Clarke Conwell are elusive, but they might coincide roughly with those of his wife, graphic designer Helen Marguerite O'Kane (1879–1927), with whom he collaborated. The most complete account of Conwell is Herbert H. Johnson, *Notes on the History of the Elston Press of Clarke Conwell and Helen Marguerite O'Kane (1900–1905)* (Wilmington: Douglas M. Harris, 1997).

23. Whiting, "The Arts and Crafts," p. ccclxxxvi. Letter, Conwell to Whiting, April 21, 1904, AAA/LPE—DA Papers: 1748: 55–57.

24. Letter, Whiting to Miss Emily M. B. Boyden, April 28, 1904, AAA/LPE—DA Papers: 1748: 40.

25. Letter, Ives to Whiting, February 23, 1904, AAA/LPE—DA Papers: 1748: 126. Letter, Whiting to the Roseville Pottery Company, April 7, 1904, AAA/LPE—DA Papers: 1748: 283. Letter, Whiting to Ives, March 7, 1904, AAA/LPE—DA Papers: 1748: 133–34. See also "The Van Briggle Pottery," *Brush & Pencil*, 9, no. 1 (October 1901): 1–11.

26. Letter, Whiting to Ives, March 7, 1904, AAA/LPE—DA Papers: 1748: 133–34. Letter, Whiting to William Watts Taylor, March 17, 1904, AAA/LPE—DA Papers: 1748: 272.

27. Letter, Taylor to Whiting, April 9, 1904, AAA/LPE—DA Papers: 1748: 278–79. Letter, Whiting to Taylor, April 11, 1904, AAA/LPE—DA Papers: 1748: 280. Letter, Whiting to J. H. Gest, April 7, 1904, AAA/LPE—DA Papers: 1748: 277. It was not uncommon for a company like Rookwood to have similar displays in two different buildings. The "point of distinction," stated a guidebook for the fair, was that "in the Palace of Varied Industries the product [was] shown by the manufacturing firm, while in the Art Palace it [was] shown by the artist": *Official Guide to the Louisiana Purchase Exposition (St. Louis: 1904)*, p. 73. On the display within the Varied Industries Building, see W. F. Sanders, "The St. Louis Fair: What Everybody Will Wish to Know Before Going," *The Monthly Review of Reviews*, 29 (May 1904): 565–76. For a description of the display, see "The Craft of Rookwood Potters," *World's Work*, 8 (May–October 1904): following p. 5210.

28. Letter, Ernest A. Batchelder to Whiting, May 13, 1904, AAA/LPE—DA Papers: 1748: 8–10. At the time of writing, Batchelder was the president of the Pacific Manual Training Teachers Association in Pasadena. Unfortunately, he never identified the "two exceptions" who were unable to participate. Charles Sumner Greene and Henry Mather Greene, or Arthur and Lucia Mathews seem likely candidates. But the Greene brothers were represented only in the American architecture section (see catalogue numbers 2404–6), and the Mathewses' shop was not yet in full operation. Whiting, "Arts and Crafts," p. ccclxxxviii. The seminal work on the design reform movement in California is Kenneth R. Trapp, *The Arts and Crafts Movement in California: Living the Good Life* (New York: Abbeville Press, 1993). On May Bird Mott-Smith, see Petteys, *Dictionary of Women Artists*, p. 511.

29. Letter, Whiting to Ives, March 10, 1904, AAA/LPE—DA Papers: 1748: 137. John M. Thurston, "One Hundred Years After. The Louisiana Purchase Exposition in 1904," *The Cosmopolitan*, 34, no. 1 (November 1902): 5, 8, and 9.

30. Letter, Batchelder to Whiting, May 13, 1904. Here Batchelder refers to a condition that exhibits in the Palace of Art had to have been completed after 1893, the year of the World's Columbian Exposition in Chicago.

31. For a detailed description of these Native American artifacts, see the catalogue, numbers 232–287 and 918–945. Though not an SACB member, James contributed to *Handicraft*, vol. 4, and lectured at the SACB (November 14, 1902), and at the Women's Educational and Industrial Union (prior to 1903). For more information on these baskets, see AAA/ LPE-DA Papers: 1752: 199–224.

32. Letter, Batchelder to Whiting, May 13, 1904. Craftsmen whose work was committed to other exhibitions included Charles Binns, William Fuller Curtis, Gertrude Stiles, and Jessie M. Preston. As a result, some craftsworkers were not represented at St. Louis. Others sent more modest exhibits than they might have liked: AAA/LPE—DA Papers: 1748: 26, 69, 122 and 220. *Official Catalogue of Exhibits*, p. 75.

33. Though he did contribute, Charles F. Eaton was initially surprised to learn of the applied arts exhibition. Robert Jarvie knew about the exhibit, but chose not to contribute, as he was unenthusiastic about the pieces that he had planned to send: AAA/LPE—DA Papers: 1748: 76, 151. For a detailed description of these pieces, see the catalogue, nos. 65, 591–95, and 879. See also artists' applications: AAA/LPE-DA Papers: 1752: 176, 373.

34. Letter, Whiting to Ellen Gates Starr, April 15, 1904, and Starr to Whiting, April 12, 1904, AAA/LPE—DA Papers: 1748: 286, 294.

35. Letter, Whiting to Starr, April 15, 1904. Whiting, "Arts and Crafts," p. ccclxxxvii. To determine birth/death dates for some of these book artists, I consulted *Federal Census Records* for 1910, 1920, and 1930. Cordelia Taylor Baker was born in Carrollton, Mo. An early influence on her work was Otto Zahn. She studied in New York, and in London with T. J. Cobden-Sanderson. See *Allgemeines Lexikon der Bildenden Kunstler*, or the *General Cyclopedia of Artists*. Mary Ezit Bulkley was associated with Hull House (Chicago), and Neighborhood House (St. Louis). Active in women's issues, suffrage, and social reform, she worked variously as a governess, bookbinder, and editor/secretary. See her memoir: *Grandmother, Mother and Me* [1947]. Florence Foote was director of the Evelyn Nordhoff Bindery in Manhattan. She also taught classes in bookbinding. Levy, *American Art Annual* (1903–04), vol. 4:.288–89. E. G. Marot was an instructor of bookbinding at the School of the Worcester (Mass.) Art Museum and contributed an article on the subject, "Tools in Bookbinding," to *Handicraft*, 4, no. 9 (December 1911): 319–25. On that occasion, her name was misspelled Marat. Mary Haskell Upton was born in 1873 in Massachusetts. She married Harry C. Groome, a gentleman farmer, ca. 1905. They had one son, born ca. 1908–09. She and her husband collaborated on an anthology of verse, *Saddle and Song* (Philadelphia, 1905). Upton may have died ca. 1930–32, at which time her husband remarried. I would like to thank Christopher C. Child, of the New England Historic Genealogical Society, for unearthing this information.

36. Letter, Ross Turner to Whiting, April 4, 1904, AAA/LPE—DA Papers: 1748: 335. For correspondence, dated April 26, 1904, between Turner and Whiting, see AAA/LPE—DA Papers: 1752: 412–15.

37. Letter, Dawson Dawson-Watson to Whiting, April 2, 1904, AAA/LPE—DA Papers: 1748: 361.

38. Stevens, *World Today*, p. 1129. See "The Vast Exposition Palaces . . . ," *Scientific American Supplement*, no. 1498: 24004–5. Letter, Whiting to Charles Fergus Binns, April

22, 1904, AAA/LPE—DA Papers: 1748: 29. Letter, Ives to Whiting, March 17, 1904, AAA/LPE—DA Papers: 1748: 141. Letter, Whiting to Charles R. Yandell, June 18, 1904, AAA/LPE—DA Papers: 1748: 402.

39. The number of pieces in each craft category were as follows: ceramics (359), bookbinding (64), printing (71), leatherwork (74), woodcarving (19), furniture (9), stained glass windows (8), metalwork (139), jewelry (92), glass (63), textiles (10), Native American artifacts (85), bookplates (two frames of approximately ten plates each), china painting (10), ceramic tiles (60 sets), plasterwork (1), beadwork (4), and illuminations (6). The quotation is from Howe, "The World's Fair at St. Louis," p. 284. See Francis, *The Universal Exposition of 1904*, p. 348.

40. David R. Francis, "Attractive Features of the St. Louis Exposition," *The Century Magazine*, 68 (June 1904): 264–68. See also Francis, chap. 10, "Architectural Problems, in *The Universal Exposition of 1904*. Along with painting, sculpture and applied arts, the Palace of Art exhibited "drawings, models and photographs of completed buildings; designs and projects of buildings (other than of architectural or constructive engineering); drawings, models and photographs of artistic architectural details; and mosaics, leaded and mosaic glass": *Official Catalogue of Exhibits*, pp. 12, 14. The section on American Arts and Crafts begins on p. 75.

41. See forms completed by these artists for details on each entry, AAA/LPE—DA Papers: 1752: 169–73. Letter, Ives to Whiting, March 13, 1904, AAA/LPE—DA Papers: 1748: 139. Whiting, "The Arts and Crafts," ccclxxxvi. On Goodhue, see "Notes on the Crafts," *The International Studio Supplement*, October 1904, pp. ccclix–ccclxiii. This illustrates the window from Emmanuel Church. See also Kirk D. Henry, "Art Industries of America—III: Stained Glass Work," *Brush and Pencil Bulletin and Record*, 15, no. 5 (May 1905): 98–111. The Lambs provided comprehensive ecclesiastical designs—many in churches throughout Boston and Massachusetts—that were "artistically correct, *appropriate and churchly*, whether the work be simple or ornate": Trade catalogue, "Catalogue of Figure Glass Work" (1893), Harvard University/Baker Library/Historical Collections.

42. Letter, Charles F. Eaton to Whiting, May 16, 1904, AAA/LPE—DA Papers: 1748: 78. Letter, Yandell to Whiting, April 30, 1904, AAA/LPE—DA Papers: 1748: 399+. Letter, Daniel B. Updike to Whiting, June 7, 1904, AAA/LPE—DA Papers: 1748: 350. Letter, Whiting to Updike, May 7, 1904, AAA/LPE—DA Papers: 1748: 347. Letter, Whiting (or Ives) to Otto H. Zahn, February 24, 1904, AAA/LPE—DA Papers: 1748: 404.

43. For descriptions of these pieces, see catalogue entries. McBride, "The Arts and Crafts in Technical Schools," *The Chautauquan*, 39 (March–April, 1904): 71–75. Whiting, "The Arts and Crafts," p. ccclxxxvi. On his application form, T. J. Nickerson (Marblehead Pottery) indicated that several pieces on display were loaned by collectors, including J. T. Coolidge, S. W. Whitman, F. A. Whiting, and S. C. Sears: AAA/LPE—DA Papers: 1752: 319.

44. Walter E. Gray, "Latter-Day Developments in American Pottery, IV," *Brush & Pencil*, 10, no. 7 (April 1902): 34–35. Whiting, "The Arts and Crafts," ccclxxxvi. Ivan C. Waterbury, "Great Industries of the United States, IX, Pottery," *The Cosmopolitan*, 38 (1904–05): 594. See also "Notes on the Crafts," *The International Studio Supplement*, 23 (October 1904): xci+. On Laura E. Lindeman, see Petteys, *Dictionary of Women Artists*, p. 442, and *Artists in Ohio*, p. 529.

45. Letter, F. Walter Lawrence to Whiting, April 18, 1904, AAA/LPE—DA Papers: 1748: 188.

46. Herbert S. Houston, "The Arts and Crafts," *World's Work*, 8 (May–October 1904):

following p. 5210. "Packing List for William C. Codman Display," AAA/LPE—DA Papers: 1752: 176.

47. Letter, Whiting to Tiffany & Co., March 17, 1904, AAA/LPE—DA Papers: 1748: 302. For a sketched plan of the Tiffany installation, see AAA/LPE—DA Papers: 1748: 306.

48. James L. Harvey, "The Source of Beauty in Favrile Glass," *Brush and Pencil*, 9, no. 3 (December 1901): 167–76. Whiting, "The Arts and Crafts," p. ccclxxxiv–ccclxxxix, passim.

49. For a description of these pieces and their values, see AAA/LPE—DA Papers: 1752: 102, 176, 250, 367. Twenty-five thousand dollars was the combined value for all items that Codman exhibited, including the desk, chair, all desk accessories, a bronze table, a glass showcase, and boxes.

50. Letters, Zahn to Ives, March 7 and March 16, 1904, AAA/ LPE—DA Papers: 1748: 405, 407. For a list of books and their dimensions, see AAA/LPE—DA Papers: 1752: 407. See *The International Studio Supplement*, 23 (October 1904): cccxciv–cccxcvi, on the goals of the artistic bookbinder. See Whiting, "Arts and Crafts," passim. Bixby, Lehman, and Klein were also patrons of Mary E. Bulkley. See *Allegemeines Lexikon der Bildenden Kunstler*, or *General Cyclopedia of Artists*.

51. Eltweed Pomeroy, "The Louisiana Purchase Exposition. A Comparison and a Criticism," *The World Today*, 7, no. 3 (September 1904): 1157. George Iles, "Possible Exhibits of Model Homes," *World's Work*, 8 (May–October, 1904): following p. 5210. Howe, "The World's Fair at St. Louis," p. 284.

52. Applications completed by each exhibitor provide prices for insurance and/or sales purposes. "The pieces of pottery have all been sold, so there will be only tiles to go back," wrote Whiting to Henry C. Mercer, November 29, 1904, AAA/LPE—DA Papers: 1748: 207. "A New Uplift to American Pottery," *World's Work*, 8 (May–October, 1904).

53. The St. Louis Art Museum demonstrated its interest in American craftsmanship by purchasing two Mercer tiles and two Newcomb vases: AAA/ LPE–DA Papers: 1745: 197.

54. Low, "The Field of Art," p. 766. Howe, "The World's Fair at St. Louis," pp. 285–90.

55. "Jury of Awards Correspondence and Lists, 1904," passim, *AAA/LPE—DA Papers*: 1749: 749–97. For the list of medalists, see "Awards to Art-Workers, Group 14," AAA/ LPE—DA Papers: 1749: 811–12. F. W. C., "Given to Sylvester Baxter as memorandum for *Boston Herald* article. January 15, 1906 (?)," p. 7, In *[Reports of an exhibition celebrating the tenth anniversary of the founding of The Society of Arts and Crafts, Boston, Copied from various newspapers]* Scrapbook [Boston, 1907] rebound in 1988 and titled *Boston Society of Arts and Crafts*, BPL/FA/SACB Archives. Hereafter Coburn Scrapbook.

56. Letter, Conwell to Whiting, December 15, 1904, AAA/SACB Papers: 300: 444–45.

57. Letter, Ellsworth Woodward to Whiting, December 2, 1904, AAA/LPE—DA Papers: 1748: 393.

58. Whiting, "The Arts and Crafts," pp. ccclxxxiv–ccclxxxv.

59. See Francis, *The Universal Exposition*, pp. 347–48.

60. Ives, "The Art Exhibit at St. Louis," p. 574. Low, "The Field of Art," p. 768.

61. Approximately 208 craftsmen participated altogether. If the 35 Native American craft workers (who were admitted by special invitation) are eliminated from the total, the domination of the applied arts division by SACB members is especially evident. Of the 173 craftsmen remaining, 80—or close to half—were members.

62. Francis, *The Universal Exposition*, p. 348.

63. Ibid., p. 354.

64. Jean N. Oliver, "New England Artists at the St. Louis Exposition," *The New England Magazine*, 30, no. 3 (May 1904): 259–71. Murphy's connection to the Boston art world extended to his marriage to watercolorist Nelly Littlehale. On many of these artists, see Hirshler, *A Studio of Her Own*, passim. See Doris A. Birmingham, "St. Botolph's Club: Home of the Impressionists," *Archives of American Art Journal*, 31, no. 3 (1991): 32.

65. "United States. Group 12. Architecture," in *Official Catalogue of Exhibits*, pp. 63–69.

66. Francis, *The Universal Exposition*, p. 352.

67. SACB annual reports provide details on membership and sales. Frederick Allen Whiting, "What the Arts and Crafts Movement Has Accomplished," *Handicraft*, 3, no. 3 (June 1910): 103. Frederick W. Coburn, Press Release, "given to Sylvester Baxter as a memorandum for *Boston Herald* article, January 15, 1906," in Coburn Scrapbook. Doll and Richards showed—among other works—French Impressionist paintings. See Birmingham, "St. Botolph's Club," p. 31.

68. Report of the Council, in *Annual Report* for 1915.

69. See Brandt, "The Essential Link." For a summary of the careers of SACB architects who taught at Harvard, see Samuel Eliot Morison, ed., *The Development of Harvard University since the Inauguration of President Eliot, 1869–1929* (Cambridge: Harvard University Press, 1930).

70. Shand-Tucci, *Cram, American Medievalist*, p. 4. Ralph Adams Cram, "Allies in Art," in *My Life in Architecture* (Boston: Little, Brown, 1936), pp. 185–99. On the lack of women in Cram's circle of artists, see Hirshler, "Women Artists at Trinity," in O'Gorman, ed., *Makers of Trinity Church*, p. 170.

71. Shand-Tucci, pp. 4, 43–45.

72. Ibid., p. 28. Vincent Scully, Jr., *The Shingle Style and the Stick Style* (rev. ed., New Haven: Yale University Press, 1971), p. 157, n. 6. See also Richard Oliver, *Bertram Grosvenor Goodhue* (Cambridge: MIT Press, 1983).

73. Shand-Tucci, p. 4.

74. Robert D. Andrews, Obituary, *Boston Society of Architects*, October 1928; Robert D. Andrews, Obituary, *American Art Annual*, *1929*, vol. 26: 383; *Macmillan Encyclopedia of Architects*, 1:80.

75. For the most comprehensive overview of Longfellow's work, see Margaret Henderson Floyd, *Architecture after Richardson: Regionalism before Modernism—Longfellow, Alden, and Harlow in Boston and Pittsburgh* (Chicago: University of Chicago Press, 1994). See also the A. W. Longfellow, Jr. Papers held at the Longfellow National Historic Site, Cambridge.

76. "Faculty of Architecture. Minute on the Life and Services of Dean Herbert Langford Warren," *Harvard College Gazette*, December 1, 1917: 45–46. The most comprehensive work on Warren is Maureen Meister, *Architecture and the Arts and Crafts Movement in Boston: Harvard's H. Langford Warren* (Hanover: University Press of New England, 2003).

77. As quoted in *Memorial Bulletin for C. Howard Walker, The Society of Arts and Crafts, 32 Newbury Street, Boston, Massachusetts*, 19, no. 1 (May 1936). C. Howard Walker, Obituary, *Technology Review*, 38 (February 1936): III, and "Further Obituary," 38 (July 1936): II. Though Walker destroyed most of his personal papers, some archival materials are available at the Archives of American Art, the Boston Public Library, the Massachusetts Institute of Technology, and Historic New England. His personal file, among the records

of the Tavern Club (held at the Massachusetts Historical Society), contains a diary written in 1881, when Walker traveled to the Aegean. His comments on the challenges and pleasures of daily life among the natives of Ageassos and Mytilene are revealing.

78. For a brief biography of Brown, see Finlay, *Artists of the Book in Boston*, pp. 85–86. Historic New England has a variety of his drawings. *Who Was Who in America*, vol. 2 (1943–50), p. 83; and Herlihy, *Fifty Years of Boston*, pp. 771–72. "Pageant of Old Deerfield" (Montague, Mass.: The Montague Press, 1913), p. 24, Pocumtuck Valley Memorial Association Library. Judy Williams, "Frank Chouteau Brown and Measured Drawings as a Tool for Historic Preservation" (unpublished paper, Tufts University, 1983), Historic New England.

79. On LeBoutillier, see Neville Thompson, "Addison B. LeBoutillier: Developer of Grueby Tiles," *Tiller*, 1, no. 2 (November-December 1982). Addison B. LeBoutillier, "The Early Wooden Architecture of Andover, Massachusetts," *White Pine Monographs*, 3, no. 2 (April 1917): 3–14. See also Susan J. Montgomery, *The Ceramics of William H. Grueby* (Lambertville, N.J.: Arts & Crafts Quarterly Press, 1993). Howe's papers are at MIT, in the Institute Archives and Special Collections. The most comprehensive overview of her work is D. Cole, K. C. Taylor, and S. Moore, *The Lady Architects* (New York: Midmarch Arts Press, 1990). On Guy Lowell, see Shillaber, *M.I.T., School of Architecture and Planning: 1861–1961*, p. 41, and Scully, *Shingle Style*, p. 156, n. 5. MIT Historical Collections has photographs of, drawings by, and obituaries for Lowell, including that published in *Technology Review*, 29 (1916): 279 and 436. Julia de Wolf Addison notes the collaboration of Lowell, Sturgis, and Wheelwright in *The Museum of Fine Arts*, p. x. Edmund M. Wheelwright, "The American Schoolhouse," *The Brickbuilder*, ca. 1898. In this series of articles, Wheelwright illustrates his own work as well as images of school buildings by Andrews, Jaques & Rantoul, and Walker & Kimball. On Sturgis, see "New President Elected," *Boston Transcript*, November 24, 1917, and *Harvard College, Class of 1881, Fiftieth Anniversary* (Concord, Mass.: Rumford Press, 1931), pp. 413–14. For insights on Sturgis's life and work, see Mrs. R. C. Sturgis, *Reflections of a Grandmother* (1917).

80. See "Exhibition of 1907," in *Annual Report* for 1906.

81. *Exhibition of The Society of Arts and Crafts: Copley Hall, Boston, February 5–26, 1907. Arts and Crafts Exhibition in Celebration of the Tenth Anniversary of the Organization of The Society. Exhibition of The Society of Arts and Crafts Together with a Loan Collection of Applied Art. Copley and Allston Halls* (Boston: The Heintzemann Press, 1907).

82. F. W. Coburn. Press release, "Sent to *The Nation*. February 13, 1907." See also Coburn, Press release, "An Exhibition of American Handicraft. Sent to *Harper's Weekly*, February 10, 1907," Coburn Scrapbook. See also *Museum of Fine Arts, Boston, 1870–1920* (Pamphlet issued by the Museum), pp. 33–38, Massachusetts Historical Society.

83. E.L.C., "The Boston Exhibition," in Annie M. Jones, ed., "Arts and Crafts," *The Scrip, Notes on Art*, April 1907, AAA/SACB Papers: 320: 025.

84. See Coburn Scrapbook. The *Annual Report* for 1908 lists the number of paid admissions (13,000), membership tickets (1,700), and complimentary tickets (1,100).

85. The Art Institute of Chicago held craft shows prior to 1902, but they were not national in scope. They tended to feature one medium, or the work of a specific (usually local) club or association. See the "Exhibition History of The Art Institute," http://www.artic.edu/aic/libraries/musarchives/archhist01900-1904.html. The Pocumtuck Valley Memorial Association Library has a collection of catalogues for various arts and crafts exhibitions that list SACB members. See, for example, the *Annual Report* for 1914 regarding the 12th Annual Industrial Art Exhibition of the AIC, as well as the *Annual Report* for 1915.

86. *Annual Report* for 1913; *Annual Report for 1914 of The Society of Arts and Crafts, Boston, Massachusetts, Incorporated MDCCCXCVII*. [March 20, 1915.], and *Annual Report* for 1915. On these other organizations, see *Papers of the Society of Blue and White Needlework*, esp. the folder labeled "Exhibits," Pocumtuck Valley Memorial Association Library.

87. *Annual Report* for 1913. This report, printed in 1914, refers to the exhibition held in Toronto from August 23, 1913, through September 8, 1913. On the Arts and Crafts movement in Canada, see Women's Art Association, "Exhibition of Home Arts" (1902), an exhibition catalogue in the *Papers of the Society of Blue and White Needlework*, Pocumtuck Valley Memorial Association Library. This exhibit featured contemporary and historic work, representing Anglo, French-Canadian, and Native North American individuals.

88. Regarding Robineau and Grueby, see Letter, Henry N. Belknap to Frederick A. Whitney [sic], April 18, 1904, AAA/LPE—DA Papers: 1748: 296. Regarding Tiffany & Co., see Letter, W. H. Thomas to Whiting, May 28, 1904, AAA/LPE—DA Papers: 1748: 328. Regarding Marshall Field & Co., see "Applications to Applied Arts division and 'Information for Records' Forms," AAA/LPE—DA Papers: 1752: passim, especially items 1, 27, 67, 118, 119, 176, 177, 180, 230, 734, 839, 882–89. On the New York gallery, see Ulehla, The Society of Arts and Crafts, Boston. Exhibition Record, p. 9.

89. A rough list indicates items shown at the fair that may later have been purchased by, or given to the St. Louis Art Museum: AAA/LPE—DA Papers: 1745: 197. On acquisitions by the Japanese museum, see *Boston Transcript*, March 6, 1916, AAA/SACB Papers: 322: 334, and "Japan Turns to Boston for her Art," *Boston Herald*, March 19, 1916, AAA/SACB Papers: 322: 344. In the mid-1980s, I attempted to locate these pieces. But correspondence suggests that this museum no longer exists, and that the examples of American art pottery were probably sold.

90. *Annual Report* for 1907. Regarding complaints, see Letter, Elizabeth B. Stone to H. L. Warren, February 23, 1908, AAA/SACB Papers: 300: 498.

91. On hiring Macomber, see Letter, F. S. Kershaw to F. P. Cabot, July 18, 1912, AAA/SACB Papers: 300: 737. "Arts and Crafts Work throughout the West," *Boston Times*, May 9, 1914, AAA/SACB Papers: 322: 324. Macomber's invitation to visit the Chautauqua-type summer community at Tryon, N.C., may have come from Annie C. Putnam. Toward the end of their lives, she and Madeline Yale Wynn spent the summer there, and Wynne became leader of its artistic, musical, theatrical, and literary activities. See Michael J. McCue, *Tryon Artists: 1892–1942* (Columbus, N.C.: Condor Company for Michael J. McCue, 2001).

92. Report of the Building Committee, January 8, 1914. AAA/SACB Papers: 300: 770+. "Arts and Crafts Work throughout the West."

93. Whiting, "What the Arts and Crafts Movement has Accomplished," p. 102. Frederick Allen Whiting, "Arts and Crafts in Boston," *Art Bulletin*, 6, no. 18 (March 2, 1907), AAA/SACB Papers: 320: 022. F. W. Coburn, "Art Movements of Today, III, Revolt from the Machine," *The National Magazine* (Boston), May 1903, pp. 59–60. This article provides a list of arts and crafts organizations.

94. "Conference of Arts and Crafts Societies," in *Annual Report* for 1907. The League organized a traveling exhibition of work of members in 1907–08. Two-thirds of the items shown represented individuals who also belonged to the SACB. See Exhibition Catalogue (Boston: Heintzemann Press, 1907), *Papers of the Society of Blue and White Needlework*, folder labeled "Exhibits," Pocumtuck Valley Memorial Association Library.

95. F. W. Coburn, Press release, "Sent to Sunday Editor, *The Post*, Boston, March 1, 1907. F.W.C," Coburn Scrapbook. On expansion within Boston, see Krieger and Cobb, *Mapping*, 137, 244–45.

96. Edward W. Emerson, *The Early Years of the Saturday Club, 1855–1870* (Boston: Houghton Mifflin, 1918), p. 3.

97. Correspondence from 1912 provides detail regarding Whiting's resignation. For example, Letter, Whiting to Lockwood de Forest, February 2, 1912, AAA/SACB Papers: 300: 689–729, passim.

98. Warren, "Farewell Address for Frederick Allen Whiting," April 23, 1912, AAA/SACB Papers: 300: 706–26.

99. Bruce Robertson, "Frederick A. Whiting: Founding the Museum with Art and Craft," in Evan H. Turner, ed., *Object Lessons, Cleveland Creates an Art Museum* (Cleveland Museum of Art, 1991), n.p. "Frederick Allen Whiting," *National Cyclopedia of American Biography*, 43 (1961): 47. W. Owen Harrod, "Towards a Transatlantic Style," in *Studies in the Decorative Arts*, 12, no. 1 (Fall–Winter, 2004–05).

100. Robertson, "Frederick A. Whiting," Many thanks to Barry Shifman for sharing biographical information on Whiting and Janet Payne Bowles.

101. J. Goddu, "Posters and Illustrated Books," in *From Architecture to Object*, p. 139. Barry Shifman, *The Arts and Crafts Metalwork of Janet Payne Bowles* (Indianapolis Museum of Art in cooperation with Indiana University Press, 1993), pp. 22, 38, 40, 55–57, 65. On the Greenacre Art Conference—dedicated to the "spiritual, philosophical and fundamental" aspects of "real art reform"—see Levy, *American Art Annual, 1898*, p. 70.

102. Shifman, p. 22.

103. Sharon S. Darling, "From 'New Woman' to Metalsmith: A Voyage of Self Discovery," in ibid., p. 31. *Annual Report* for 1907. On Wynne, see Annie Cabot Putnam, "Necrology, Madeline Yale Wynne," *History and Proceedings of the Pocumtuck Valley Memorial Association, 1912–1920*, vol. 6 (Deerfield: Pocumtuck Valley Memorial Association, 1921), pp. 420–24. Other individuals with ties to both the SACB and Deerfield were Mrs. J. Templeman Coolidge, who belonged to the Deerfield Arts and Crafts Society, and Sarah Choate Sears, who owned a painting, "Winifred Dysart," done by Deerfield artist George Fuller, and valued in 1907 at $25,000. See *Deerfield Town Papers. Commercial Organizations*, Box 1, Category 2I, Folder #4, Pocumtuck Valley Memorial Association Library. "Deerfield Workers in Arts and Crafts," *Boston Sunday Globe*, February 17, 1907, p. 4.

104. Ellen Gates Starr, "Memorial, Caleb Allen Starr," *History and Proceedings of the Pocumtuck Valley Memorial Association, 1912–1920* (Deerfield: Pocumtuck Valley Memorial Association, 1921), p. 336. Ellen Gates Starr, "A Note of Explanation" (pamphlet undated), Pocumtuck Valley Memorial Association Library. On Ellen Gates Starr, see "Arts and Crafts at Deerfield. Yearly Show of Industries," *Springfield Republican*, July 11, 1905, p. 11.

105. Finlay, *Artists of the Book in Boston*, p. 88; Ulehla, *The Society of Arts and Crafts, Boston. Exhibition Record*, p. 227. See as well A. N. Hosking, ed., *The Artists' Year Book . . . for 1905–06* (Chicago, 1905), p. 161.

106. Winter, *Batchelder: Tilemaker*, discusses Hale, pp. 96–98.

107. Ibid., passim. On Batchelder, see also Anscombe and Gere, *Arts and Crafts in Britain and America*, p. 210, and Finlay, 97–98.

108. *From Architecture to Object*, p. 127. Bruce Johnson, *Arts and Crafts Price Guide*, pp. 464, 521.

109. Finlay, pp. 97–98. Shand-Tucci, *Cram, American Medievalist*, p. 11.

EPILOGUE

Usefulness and Beauty in the New Millennium

1. For a select bibliography of key works on the Arts and Crafts movement, especially those written since the early 1970s, see Elizabeth Cumming and Wendy Kaplan, *The Arts*

and Crafts Movement (London: Thames and Hudson, 1991), p. 208. For an overview of collecting Arts and Crafts artifacts since the 1970s, see David Rago, "Arts and Crafts Market Review," in Rago and Bruce Johnson, *Official Price Guide to American Arts and Crafts*, 3rd ed. (New York: House of Collectibles, 2003), pp. xv–xxx.

2. Wendy Kaplan, ed., *The Art That Is Life: The Arts and Crafts Movement in America, 1875–1920* (Boston: Museum of Fine Arts, 1987). Marilee Boyd Meyer, ed., *Inspiring Reform: Boston's Arts and Crafts Movement* (New York: Harry Abrams in collaboration with the Davis Museum and Cultural Center, 1997). The "Inspiring Reform" exhibition took place at Wellesley College and the Smithsonian Institution/Renwick Museum. Footnotes throughout *Inspiring Reform* cite books and articles pertaining to the SACB.

3. The fact that *The Antiques Roadshow* is produced in Boston by WGBH may have something to do with this phenomenon. A British series of the same name was the model for the show.

4. Bruce Johnson, *Official Identification and Price Guide to Arts and Crafts*, 1st ed. (New York: House of Collectibles, 1983), pp. 283–93. Rago and Johnson, pp. 64–74.

5. Johnson, pp. 389–401. Rago and Johnson, pp. 133–42.

6. Johnson, pp. 505–508. Rago and Johnson, pp. 353–55.

7. Michael Fitzsimmons, Anne Yaffe Phillips, James L. Reinish, Foreword, in *From Architecture to Object*, p. 7. "Streisand Spectacular at Christie's," *Architectural Digest*, October 1999: 43.

8. The Hotel Pattee (Perry, Iowa) and Grove Park Inn (Asheville, N.C.) offer such conferences. The Metropolitan Museum of Art (New York) and Museum of Fine Arts (Boston) regularly purvey such "art produce" in their catalogues.

9. Shannon L. Rogers, ed., "The Morris Marketplace: A Shopper's Guide," in *The William Morris Society in the United States Newsletter*, Summer 2004: 33–35. See: "Art Crimes," *Art and Antiques*, November 1999: 26, as well as "Tiffany Expert Judged Guilty" in the same issue, p. 30.

10. See, for example the set used by correspondent Bob Scheiffer on the television show *Face the Nation*, March 23, 2003. Both his desk and a round table were in the Mission style. I remember seeing a television commercial for Florida orange juice that used either the Hill House ladder-back chair or the "Argyle" chair, but I did not record the date. Sets for the 1964 production of *My Fair Lady* clearly predated the Arts and Crafts Revival (which began about a decade later). But the sets showed a sensitive interpretation of the Aesthetic movement, the Arts and Crafts movement, and the Glasgow style. *Sleepless in Seattle* used Craftsman-style furnishings selectively, as did *A River Runs Through It*. *Lord of the Rings—The Fellowship of the Rings* incorporated elements reminiscent of Voysey, Liberty & Co., and the Celtic Revival. A house in *Seabiscuit* and another in *Thirtysomething* were American Arts and Crafts examples. *Mad About You* included Morris & Co. Sussex-type chairs and Stickley-type dining chairs. *The Forsyte Saga* blended elements of both the American and the British Arts and Crafts movement in the house, Robin Hill, which harkened back to the work of both Frank Lloyd Wright and Charles Rennie Mackintosh.

11. In 1994, the Chrysler Corporation and *House Beautiful* sponsored a traveling exhibition, "The Legacy of Frank Lloyd Wright," and published a brochure by that name. The Arizona Lifestyles Store advertised a free seminar on the American Arts and Crafts movement and Stickley furniture, in *The Arizona Republic*, Sunday, January 16, 1994: A8. Randi Danforth, "Bon Vivant," *Bon Appétit*, September 1999: 135–40.

12. On the Grand Californian Hotel, see, for example, an advertisement in *Sunset*, January 2001: n.p. See also: "Hotels of the Disneyland Resort Place Guests in the Middle

of the Magic," *Disneyland Getaways*, May 2003: 6. The "Housekeeping/Privacy Please" sign was a gift from a former student.

13. My knowledge of these products—and this list is by no means complete—stems from years of compiling paper paraphernalia related to the Arts and Crafts Revival that comes through the mail. My notebooks of clippings cover the period 1983 to the present. The usefulness of this collection relates directly to the hard work of my research associate, John Turpin, during the first half of 2004. John compiled a detailed summary of approximately 14 lineal inches of eclectic material.

14. The Mauna Loa advertisement (copyrighted 2001) appeared in *Travel + Leisure*, ca. Fall 2001–Spring 2002. Nancy Finlay points out (*Artists of the Book in Boston*, p. 62) that the logo for Barnes and Noble Booksellers has been modeled after the personal bookplate of SACB member Theodore Hapgood, Jr.

15. Minwax included a Stickley cabinet in its ads in 1990. Lexus places an automobile in front of a building lit by a series of torchères with Frank Lloyd Wright–type stained-glass shades: *Martha Stewart Living*, August 1999: n.p. Ace Hardware incorporates green Grueby-type pottery on shelves in its ad in *Martha Stewart Living*, December 1999: 121. Benjamin Moore Paints uses a Craftsman-type bed with inlay in the manner of Harvey Ellis in its ad in *Quick and Easy Decorating*, Summer 2001: n.p.

16. "Willow," "Willow Bough," and "Willow Bough Minor" are all variations upon the same theme. For the sake of simplicity, I'm referring to all of these patterns simply as "Willow." The Waterford ad appears in Home, March 1994: n.p. *House and Garden*, July 1993, cover. *House Beautiful*, February 1997: 73, illustrates a chair upholstered in "Willow Bough." Christine Pittel, "Applied Artistry: Portraitist Comer Jennings, an admirer of William Morris, creates his own gentlemanly blend of Arts and Crafts in his 1920s house in Atlanta," *House Beautiful*, March 1999: 117–21. An ad for Sanderson, showing reproductions of Morris & Co. fabrics, features "Willow Bough" on a pair of loveseats: *House Beautiful*, October 1999: n.p.

17. York Wall Coverings and Borders advertisement, *House Beautiful*, June 1997: n.p. Target advertisement, *House and Garden*, March 2000: n.p. Glenn Peake, "Decorating. Glazing Wallpaper," *Martha Stewart Living*, September 1998: 170–72. Wilhide writes specifically of "Willow Bough," but her comments seem equally appropriate for describing the appeal of all of Morris's "Willow" variations: Elizabeth Wilhide, *William Morris Décor and Design* (New York: Abrams, 1991), p. 93.

18. *Letters of Sarah Wyman Whitman* (Cambridge: Riverside Press, 1907), pp. 225–26. These letters make clear Whitman's appreciation for the therapeutic qualities of both nature and handicraft as antidotes to the pressures of modern society.

19. The quote comes from the subtitle of Luhr's book. Her book complements the *Simple Living Journal*, published in Seattle. On Slow Food, see Jean Zimmerman, *Made from Scratch: Pleasures of the American Hearth* (New York: Free Press, 2003). Lynne Rosetto Kasper, host of the American Public Media radio show *The Splendid Table*, mentioned in 2004 her concern for her personal *batterie de cuisine* and her plan to bequeath her best kitchen knives to the next generation in her will. "Wild Oat Natural Marketplace, January 2003 Community Calendar" (Scottsdale, Ariz.) advertised a discussion group on "Voluntary Simplicity" (January 4, 2003). The Bay View Association (Petoskey, Mich.) offered an adult education course on the same subject during summer 2004.

20. Mary Brown, *Simplification of Life: Some Words to Women from an English Leaflet*, *Women's Educational and Industrial Union, Leaflet No. 10* (Cambridge, Mass.: The Cooperative Press, [1899]), n.p. Richard Guy Wilson argues that the Arts and Crafts movement, though "ascetic in appreciating simplicity" was simultaneously "profligate in

details": Introduction, *From Architecture to Ornament*, p. 11. Barbara Mayer speaks of the movement's "simple yet remarkably rich aesthetic": *In the Arts and Crafts Style* (New York: Running Heads, 1992), p. 80.

21. Cheryl Robertson, "Culture and Design: Contextualizing the American Arts and Crafts Movement, Then and Now," in Audrey B. Morris, ed., *Reflecting on Design (Symposium) 6 November 1998* (Tempe, Ariz.: Herberger Center for Design Excellence, 1999).

22. William Morris, "The Lesser Arts" (Lecture, 1882), in *Fearless Rest and Hopeful Work* (San Marino, Calif.: Printed for Tyrus G. Harmsen by Grant Dahlstrom at the Castle Press, 1954). On Green Design, see the website for the U.S. Green Building Council, www.usgbc.org; and "What Is Green Building?" Environmental Design Building News, www.buildinggreen.com. See also James Steele, *Sustainable Architecture: Principles, Paradigms, and Case Studies* (New York: McGraw-Hill, 1997).

23. On the formal and symbolic traits of Arts and Crafts architecture, see Beverly Brandt, "Architecture," in Wendy Kaplan, ed., *The Encyclopedia of Arts and Crafts: The International Arts Movement, 1850–1920* (New York: E. P. Dutton, 1989), pp. 31–51.

24. Ibid. The architecture and artifacts of the Arts and Crafts movement in Boston evoke both a sense of place and the national zeitgeist at the turn of the nineteenth century. That they are celebrated locally, while still having national and even international significance, is indicative of this trend.

25. Bret Walker, Foreword, in Shifman, *The Arts and Crafts Metalwork of Janet Payne Bowles*, p. 6. Gwendolyn Wright, *Moralism and the Model Home: Domestic Architecture and Cultural Conflict in Chicago, 1873–1913* (Chicago: University of Chicago Press, 1980).

26. "Harmony House," *Home*, September 1994: 81–93.

27. David Dewing, Introduction, in Gere, *The House Beautiful*, pp. 8–9.

28. Kaplan, *The Arts and Crafts Movement*, p. 207.

29. Charles Sumner Greene, as quoted in James Massey and Shirley Maxwell, *Arts and Crafts Design in America: A State-by-State Guide* (San Francisco: Chronicle Books, 1998), frontispiece.

30. Michael W. Brooks, "New England Gothic: Charles Eliot Norton, Charles H. Moore, and Henry Adams," in MacDougall, *The Architectural Historian in America*, p. 121. Charles E. Hooper, *The Country House: A Practical Manual of the Planning and Construction of the American Country Home and Its Surroundings* (New York: Doubleday, Page, 1905), p. 156. Jeff D. Opdyke, "Love & Money. Sofa vs. Sofa: Who Gets to Decorate?" *Wall Street Journal Sunday*, January 16, 2005, in the *Scottsdale Tribune*, B8.

31. Kaplan, *The Arts and Crafts Movement*, p. 207.

BIBLIOGRAPHY

ARCHIVAL COLLECTIONS AND RESOURCES

Historical Collections, Baker Library, Harvard University.
Charles Fergus Binns Papers Archives of American Art, Smithsonian Institution.
Boston Athenaeum.
Boston Building Department Collection. Historic New England.
Boston Public Library.
Building Inspectors Reports (1879–1903). Fine Arts Department, Boston Public Library.
City of Cambridge, Building Department.
Cambridge Historical Commission.
Fred Holland Day Papers. Archives of American Art, Smithsonian Institution.
Isabella Stewart Gardner Papers. Archives of American Art, Smithsonian Institution.
Houghton Library, Harvard University.
Alexander Wadsworth Longfellow, Jr., Papers, Longfellow National Historic Site, 105 Brattle Street, Cambridge.
Louisiana Purchase Exposition—Department of Art Papers, Archives of American Art, Smithsonian Institution.
Massachusetts Historical Society.
Massachusetts Institute of Technology Historical Collections.
North Bennet Street Industrial School Archives, Schlesinger Library, Radcliffe College.
Pusey Library, Harvard University.
Residential Interiors (1870–1920) Collection. Historic New England.
School of the Museum of Fine Arts Archives.
Society of Arts & Crafts, Boston Archives, Fine Arts Department, Boston Public Library.
Society of Arts & Crafts, Boston Papers, Archives of American Art, Smithsonian Institution.
Soule Art Photography Collection. Historic New England.
Samuel Yellin Papers, Archives of American Art, Smithsonian Institution.

WORKS BY MEMBERS OF THE SOCIETY OF ARTS & CRAFTS, BOSTON

BOOKS

Addison, Julia de W. *Arts and Crafts in the Middle Ages*. Boston: L. C. Page, 1908.
———. *The Art of the Dresden Gallery*. Boston: L. C. Page, 1907.
———. *The Art of the National Gallery*. Boston: L. C. Page, 1909.
———. *The Art of the Pitti Palace*. Boston: L. C. Page, 1904.
———. *The Boston Museum of Fine Arts*. Boston: L. C. Page & Co., 1910.
———. *Classic Myths in Art*. Boston: L. C. Page, 1904.
Binns, Charles Fergus. *The Potter's Craft; A Practical Guide for the Studio and Workshop*. New York, 1910; rpt. Princeton: D. Van Nostrand, 1967.
Brown, Frank Chouteau. An Architectural Monograph on *New England Colonial Houses*. St. Paul, Minn.: White Pine Bureau, 1915.

———. *Book Plate Designs*. Boston: Troutsdale Press, 1905.
———. *Modern English Churches*. Cleveland: J. H. Jansen, 1917.
———. *Modern English Country Houses*. Cleveland: J. H. Jansen, 1923.
Carey, Arthur Astor. *Nervous Prostration and Its Spiritual Cause*. Boston: Garden Press, 1904.
———. *New Nerves for Old*. Boston: Little, Brown, 1914.
———. *The Scout Law in Practice*. Boston: Little, Brown, 1915.
Chandler, F. W. *Construction Details*. Boston: Heliotype Printing, [1892].
Connick, Charles J. *Adventures in Light and Color: An Introduction to the Stained Glass Craft*. New York: Random House, 1937.
Cram, Ralph Adams. *Church Building*. Boston: Small, Maynard, 1901.
———. *Excalibur*. Boston: Richard C. Badger, The Gorham Press, 1909.
———. *The Gothic Quest*. Boston: Baker and Taylor, 1907.
———. *The Heart of Europe*. New York: Scribner's, 1915.
———. *Impressions of Japanese Architecture and the Allied Arts*. Boston: Marshall Jones Co., 1906.
———. *The Ministry of Art*. Boston: Houghton Mifflin, 1914.
———. *My Life in Architecture*. Boston: Little, Brown, 1936.
———. *The Ruined Abbeys of Great Britain*. New York: J. Potts, 1906.
———. *The Substance of Gothic*. Boston: Marshall Jones Co., 1917.
Dedham Pottery, formerly known as Chelsea Pottery, U.S. A Short History. [Boston: D. B. Updike, The Merrymount Press], 1898.
Dedham Pottery, formerly known to the Trade and to the Public as the Chelsea Pottery, U.S. but now newly established . . . . [Boston: The Merrymount Press], 1896.
Dwiggins, Will A. *Layout in Advertising*. New York: Harper and Brothers, 1948.
Exhibition of the Society of Arts and Crafts, Copley Hall, Boston, Massachusetts. April 4–15, 1899. Boston: George H. Ellis, 1899.
Exhibition of the Society of Arts and Crafts: Copley Hall, Boston, February 5–26, 1907. Boston: The Heintzemann Press, 1907.
First Exhibition of the Arts and Crafts, Copley Hall, Boston, April 5–16, 1897. Boston: Thomas P. Smith Printing Co., 1897.
Gray, Morris, *The City's Voice: A book of verse*. Boston: The Merrymount Press, [1923].
Johnson, Henry Lewis. *Historic Design in Printing*. Boston: The Graphic Arts Company, 1923.
———. *Printing Type Specimens: Standard and Modern Types with Notations on their Characteristics*. Boston: The Graphic Arts Company, 1924.
Kunz, George F. *The Book of the Pearl: the History, Art, Science and Industry of the Queen of Gems*. New York: Century, 1908.
———. *Rings for the Finger*. Philadelphia:. Lippincott, 1917.
———. *Shakespeare and Precious Stones*. Philadelphia: Lippincott, 1916.
Norton, Charles Eliot. *Considerations of Some Recent Social Theories*. Boston: Little, Brown, 1853.
———. *Facsimiles of Thirty-three Etchings of Turner*. Cambridge, Mass., 1878.
———. *Historical Studies of Church Building in the Middle Ages, Venice, Siena, Florence*. New York: Harper & Brothers, 1880.
———. *Notes of Travel and Study in Italy*. Boston: Ticknor and Fields, 1860.
———, ed. *Early Letters of Thomas Carlyle, 1814–1826*. London, 1886.
———, ed. *Letters of John Ruskin to Charles Eliot Norton*. 2 vols. Boston: Houghton Mifflin, 1904.
———, ed. *Reminiscences of Thomas Carlyle*. 2 vols. [S.I.]: Macmillan, 1887.

Report of the *Mayor's Committee on Proposed Monument to Boston Soldiers, Sailors, and Marines*. Note: This committee included C. A. Coolidge, R. A. Cram, F. W. Benson, C. E. Dallin, M. Gray, C. D. Maginnis, A. A. Shurtleff, R. C. Sturgis, and C. H. Walker.

Robineau, Adelaide A. *High-Fire Porcelains*. San Francisco: Panama-Pacific Exposition, 1915. Exhibition catalogue.

Ross, Denman Waldo. *On Drawing and Painting*. Boston: Houghton Mifflin, 1912.

———. *The Painter's Palette, A Theory of Tone Relationships, An Instrument of Expression*. Boston: Houghton Mifflin, 1919.

———. *A Theory of Pure Design. Harmony, Balance, Rhythm*. Boston, 1907; rpt. New York: Peter Smith, 1933.

Updike, Daniel Berkeley. *Notes on the Merrymount Press & Its Work*. Cambridge: Harvard University Press, 1934; expanded and republished by Alan Wofsy Fine Arts, San Francisco, 1975.

———. *Printing Types, Their History, Forms, and Uses*. Cambridge: Harvard University Press, 1922.

Walker, Charles Howard. *The Bookplates of Dorothy Sturgis Harding*. Boston: Graphic Arts Society, 1920.

Warren, Herbert Langford. *The Foundations of Classical Architecture*. New York: Macmillan, 1919.

———. *What May the Schools Do to Advance the Appreciation of Art?* Boston: The Museum of Fine Arts, 1924.

Wheelwright, Edmund March. *Lampy's Early Days, by an Old Lampooner*. Cambridge: The Harvard Lampoon Society, 1909.

———. *School Architecture: A General Treatise for the Use of Architects and Others*. Boston: Rogers and Manson, 1901.

Whitman, Sarah Wyman. *The Making of Pictures. Twelve Short Talks with Young People*. Chicago: Interstate Publishing, 1886.

———. *Robert Browning in his Relationship to the Art of Painting*. Boston: The Browning Society, 1889.

ARTICLES, ESSAYS, AND OTHER SHORT WORKS

Addison, Julia de W. "Notes on the Use of Gold Leaf in Illuminating." *Handicraft*, 3, no. 5 (August 1910): 171.

Andrews, Robert D. "The Changing Styles of Country Houses." *Architectural Review*, January 1904: 1–4.

Ashbee, C. R. "American Architecture." *Munsey*, 26 (October 1901): 1–9.

Bigelow, Henry Forbes. "A Town Hall in Massachusetts." *Brickbuilder*, January 1903: 13–15.

Brown, Frank Chouteau. "Beacon Hill." *Pencil Points*, 19 (March 1938): 177–92.

———. "Boston Suburban Architecture." *Architectural Record*, 21, no. 4 (April 1907): n.p.

———. "Early Boston Churches." *Pencil Points*, 18 (May 1937): 799–814.

———. "Historic Boston Massachusetts." *Pencil Points*, 18 (May 1937): 287–302.

Carey, Arthur Astor. "The Past Year and Its Lessons." *Handicraft*, 1, no. 1 (April 1902): 3–29.

Chandler, Francis W. "Professor Constant Desiré Despradelle." *Technology Review*, 14, no. 3 (November 1912): 527–29.

Cleveland, Frank P. "The Ecclesiastical Metal-Worker: A Plea for His Further Education." *Handicraft*, 3, no. 2 (April 1910): 29.

Connick, Charles J. "Stained Glass Windows: The Craft." *The Technology Monthly and Harvard Engineering Journal*, 3, no. 1 (April 1916): 1–7.

———. "Windows of Old France." *The International Studio*. (Series). 1923–24.

Coolidge, J. Templeman, Jr. "A Few Considerations of Japanese Wood-Carving." *Handicraft*, 2, no. 3 (June 1903): n.p.

Cram, Ralph Adams. "Have I a Philosophy of Design?" *Pencil Points*, 13 (November 1932): 729.

———. "The Influence of the French School on American Architecture." *The American Architect and Building News*, November 25, 1899: 65–66.

———. "John Kirchmayer, Master Craftsman." *Architecture*, 63 (February 1931): 87–92.

———. "Stained Glass: An Art Restored." *Arts & Decoration*, 20, no. 4 (February 1924): 11–13, 50.

Dean, Samuel B. "Art Enamels and Enameling." *Handicraft*, 1, no. 1 (July 1902): n.p.

———. "House Furnishing as an Art." *The House Beautiful*, 28 (October 1910): 133–34.

Dennett, Mary Ware. "Aesthetics and Ethics." *Handicraft*, 1, no. 2 (May 1902).

———. "The Arts and Crafts: An Outlook." *Handicraft*, 2 (?), no. 1 (April 1903): n.p.

———. "The Arts and Crafts Problem and a Way Out." *Handicraft*, 4, no. 6 (September 1911): 209.

Goodhue, Harry Eldredge. "Stained Glass." *Handicraft*, 2, no. 4 (July 1903): n.p.

Greeley, William Roger. "The Massachusetts Housing Demonstration." *American Architect and Building News*, May 15, 1918: 643–46.

Hodge, J. Samuel. "Bookbinding." *Handicraft*, 2, no. 5 (August 1903).

Koralewsky, Frank L. "A Little Talk on Ironwork." *Handicraft*, 3, no. 2 (May 1910): 57.

LeBoutillier, Addison B. "The Early Wooden Architecture of Andover, Massachusetts." *White Pine Monographs*, 3, no. 2 (April 1917): 3–14.

Low, W. H. "National Expression in American Art." *International Quarterly*, 3 (March 1901): 231–51.

Macomber, H. Percy. "Silversmiths of New England." *American Magazine of Art*, 25 (October 1932): 209–18.

Maginnis, Charles D. "Address to the Producers." *Architecture and Engineering*, 104 (February 1931): 129–31.

Norton, Charles Eliot. "A Criticism of Harvard Architecture Made to the Board of Overseers." *Graduate's Magazine*, March 1904: 3.

———. "Dwellings and Schools for the Poor." *North American Review*, no. 75 (April 1852): 482.

Pyle, Howard. "The Present Aspect of American Art from the Point of View of an Illustrator." *Handicraft*, 1, no. 4 (September 1902): n.p.

Rollins, Carl Purington. "A Principle of Handicraft." *Handicraft*, 4 (1911–1912): 91.

Ross, Denman W. "The Arts and Crafts: A Diagnosis." *Handicraft*, 1, no. 10, January 1903: n.p.

———. "The Arts and Crafts: A Diagnosis." *The Craftsman Magazine*, 7, no. 3, December 1904. (From *Handicraft* for January 1903.): 335.

Stone, Elizabeth B. "Making a Handforged Spoon." *Handicraft*, 4, no. 1 (April 1911): 1.

———. "Observations of an Onlooker." *Handicraft*, 3, no. 3 (June 1910): 79.

Updike, Daniel B. "Style in the Composition of Type." *Handicraft*, 1, no. 2 (May 1902): n.p.

Walker, Charles Howard. "L'Art Nouveau." *Architectural Review*, 1904: 13–20.

———. "Classical Architecture." In American Institute of Architects Committee on Education, *The Significance of the Fine Arts*. 1923.

———. "Competitive Designs for the Boston Atheneum." *American Architect*, August 2, 9, 16, and September 20, 1902: n.p.

———. Foreword to George Canning Wales, *Etchings and Lithographs of American Ships*. Boston: Goodspeed, 1927.

———. "The Influence of McKim." *The Brickbuilder*, 19, no. 2 (February 1910): n.p.

———. "The Master." [Bertram Grosvenor Goodhue.] In *Picturesque and Architectural New England*. 2 vols. Boston, 1899.

———. "Modern Architecture." *The Craftsman*, 9 (October 1905): 36–40.

———. "The Museum and the School." *Handicraft*, 2, no. 2, May 1903: 29–42.

———. *Parish Churches of England*. Introductory Text. Boston: Rogers and Manson, 1915.

———. "Some Old Houses on the Southern Coast of Maine." *White Pine Monographs*, 4, no. 2 (1918): n.p.

———. *Statement of the Plan for the Rearrangement of Copley Square*. Boston, 1907.

———. "What Colonial Architecture Really Is." *American Homes*, 6 (January 1909): 19–24.

Warren, Herbert Langford. "Architecture in New England." In *Picturesque and Architectural New England*. 2 vols. Boston, 1899.

———. "Architecture: Renaissance and Modern." *Progress*, 6, no. 3 (1900): 190–234.

———. "The Department of Architecture at Harvard." *Architectural Record*, 22 (August 1907): 135–50.

———. Illustrations and original designs prepared under the direction of. In Marcus Vitruvius Pollio, *The Ten Books on Architecture*. Trans. Morris Hicky Morgan. Cambridge: Harvard University Press, 1926.

———. "Our Work and Our Prospects." *Handicraft*, 2, no. 9 (December 1903): 179–202.

———. "The Qualities of Carving." *Handicraft*, 1, no. 9 (December 1902): n.p.

Whiting, Frederick Allen. "Arts and Crafts and the Louisiana Purchase Exposition." *The International Studio*, Supplement, 23 (October 1904): 384–89.

———. "The Arts and Crafts Movement." In Kenyon Cox, ed., *The Fine Arts*, 1911.

———. "On Exhibition Catalogues." *Handicraft*, 3, no. 1 (April 1910): 9.

———. "What the Arts and Crafts Movement Has Accomplished." *Handicraft*, 3, no. 3 (June 1910): 90–108.

PERIOD REFERENCES

BOOKS

An Account of the Proceedings, at the Dinner Given by Mr. George Peabody to the Americans Connected with the Great Exhibition at the London Coffee House, Ludgate Hill, on the 27th October 1851. London: William Pickering, 1851.

Adams, Henry. *Mont-Saint-Michel and Chartres*. Boston: Houghton Mifflin, 1904.

American Art Annual. 1891.

Annals of the Massachusetts Charitable Mechanics Association, 1795–1892. Boston: Rockwell and Churchill, 1892.

Barber, Edwin Atlee. *The Pottery and Porcelain of the United States, and Historical Reviews of American Ceramic Work from the Earliest Time to the Present Day*. Philadelphia: Allen, 1893.

Bascom, John. *Aesthetics. The Science of Beauty*. New York: G. P. Putnam's Sons, 1886.

Batchelder, Ernest A. *The Principles of Design*. Chicago: Inland Printer Company, 1904.

Begg, W. Proudfoot. *The Development of Taste and Other Studies in Aesthetics*. Glasgow: James Maclehose and Sons, 1887.

Bing, Samuel. *La Culture Artistique en Amerique*. 1893.
Binyon, Laurence. *The Flight of the Dragon, An Essay on the Theory and Practice of Art in China and Japan*. London: John Murry, 1911.
Boston Art Guide and Artists' Directory. Boston: Wheat Publishing, 1894.
Bowen, Abel. *Bowen's Picture of Boston*, 1833.
Bragdon, Claude. *Projective Ornament*. Rochester, N.Y.: Manas Press, 1915.
Burke, Edmund. *A Philosophical Enquiry. . . .* London, 1757.
Clutton-Brock, Arthur. *Essays on Art*. New York: Scribner's, 1920.
Coburn, Frederick W. *Individual Treatment of the Picture Frame*. New York: International Studio, 1906.
Coles, William A. *Hermann Dudley Murphy (1867–1954)*. Exhibition catalogue. New York: Graham Gallery, 1982.
Cook, Clarence. *The House Beautiful, Essays on Beds and Tables, Stools and Candlesticks*. New York: Scribner, Armstrong, 1877; rpt. New York: Dover, 1995.
Cook, E. T., and A. Wedderburn, eds. *Complete Works of John Ruskin*. London, 1903–12.
Cortissoz, Royal. *John La Farge: A Memoir and a Study*. New York: Houghton Mifflin, 1911.
Crane, Walter. *An Artist's Reminiscences*. New York: Macmillan, 1907.
Cutler, Thomas W. *A Grammar of Japanese Ornament and Design*. London: Batsford, 1880.
Cuzner, Bernard. *A Silversmith's Manual. Treating of the Designing and Making of the Simpler Pieces of Domestic Silverware*. 2nd ed., London: N.A.G. Press, 1949. First published 1935.
Dawson, Mrs. Nelson. *Enamels*. London: Methuen, 1906.
Day, Lewis F. *Enamelling. A Comparative Account of the Development and Practice of the Art*. London: Batsford, 1907.
———. *Instances of Accessory Art*. London: Batsford, 1880; rpt. New York: Garland, 1977.
———. *Nature in Ornament*. London: Batsford, 1892; rpt., New York: Garland, 1977.
———. *Ornament and Its Application. A Book for Students Treating in a Practical Way of the Relation of Design to Materials, Tools and Methods of Work*. London and New York: Batsford and Scribner's, 1904.
———. *The Planning of Ornament*. London: Batsford, 1887. Issued as No. 2 of *Textbooks of Ornamental Design*. Rpt. New York: Garland, 1977.
Day, Lewis F., with Mary Buckle. *Art in Needlework*. London: Batsford, 1900; rpt New York: Garland, 1977.
DeGarmo, Charles. *Aesthetic Education*. Syracuse, N.Y.: C. W. Bardeen, 1913.
Dewing, Maria R. *Beauty in the Household*. New York: Harper Brothers, 1882.
Dow, Arthur Wesley. *Composition*. 1899; rpt, Berkeley: University of California, 13th ed., with new introduction by Joseph Masheck, 1997.
Downing, Alexander Jackson. *The Architecture of Country Houses*. New York, 1850; New York: Da Capo Press, 1968, with new introduction by George B. Tatum.
Dresser, Christopher. *Japan, Its Architecture, Art and Art Manufactures*. London, 4th edition, 1882.
———. *Principles of Decorative Design*. London: Cassell Petter & Galpin, 1873.
———. *Studies in Design*. London, 1874.
Foster, Frank. *The Karma of Labor and Other Verses*. Boston, 1903.
Gardner, E. C. *Homes and How to Make Them*. Boston, 1974.
———. *The House That Jill Built*. New York, 1882.
———. *Illustrated Homes: a series of papers describing real houses and real people*. Boston: 1875.
Gilman, Charlotte Perkins. *The Home: Its Sphere and Influence*. [New York] Source Book Press [1970. Ca. 1903].

———. *Women and Economics*. Boston: Small, Maynard, 1915. Ca. 1898.
Gordon, Kate. *Esthetics*. New York: Henry Holt, 1909.
Grant, Robert. *The Chippendales*. New York: Scribner's, 1909.
Greenough, Horatio. *Form and Function*. Ca. 1853. Berkeley: University of California Press, 1944.
Hall, Dr. Herbert, and Metrice M. C. Buck. *Handicrafts for the Handicapped*. New York, 1916.
Harris, George. *The Theory of the Arts; or Art in Relation to Nature, Civilization, and Man, Comprising an Investigation, Analytical and Critical into the Origin, Rise, Province, Principles, and Application of Each of the Arts*. London: Trubner, 1869.
Hazlitt, William. *Criticism on Art*. London: C. Templeman, 1844.
Herndon, Richard. *Boston of Today, A Glance into its History and Characteristics*. Boston: Post Publishing, 1892.
Hill, Hamilton A., ed. *Reports of the Massachusetts Commissioners to the Exposition at Vienna*. Boston: Wright & Potter, State Printers, 1875.
Holden, Florence P. *Audiences. A Few Suggestions to Those who Look and Listen*. Chicago: A. C. McClurg, 1896.
Holly, Henry Hudson. *Modern Dwellings in Town and Country Adapted to American Wants and Climate*. New York: Harper, 1878.
Hooper, Charles Edward. *The Country House: A Practical Manual of the Planning and Construction of the American Country Home and Its Surroundings*. New York: Doubleday, Page, 1905.
Hooper, Luther. *Hand-Loom Weaving Plain & Ornamental*. New York: Pitman Publishing, n.d.; rpt. 1920 as part of the Artistic Crafts Series of Technical Handbooks, ed. W.R. Lethaby.
Howells, William Dean. *A Modern Instance*. Boston: Houghton Mifflin,189?.
———. *The Rise of Silas Lapham*. Boston: Houghton Mifflin, ca.1912.
James, George Wharton. *Indian Basketry. 2nd ed*. New York: Henry Malkan, 1902.
James, Henry. *The American Scene*. London: Chapman and Hall, 1907.
———. *The Bostonians*. London: Macmillan, 1921.
Jones, Owen. *The Grammar of Ornament*. London: B. Quaritch, 1868.
The Journals of Thomas James Cobden-Sanderson, 1879–1922. New York: Macmillan, 1926.
Kakuzo, Okakura. *The Book of Tea*. New York: Fox, Duffield, 1906.
Keeler, Charles. *The Simple Home*. San Francisco: P. Elder [1904].
Lawrence, Maude, and Caroline Sheldon. *The Use of the Plant in Decorative Design*. New York: Scott, Foresman, 1912.
Lee, Vernon [Violet Paget]. *Laurus Nobilis. Chapters on Art and Life*. London and New York: John Lane, Bodley Head and John Lane Company, 1909.
Mackail, J. W. *The Life of William Morris*. London: Longmans, Green, 1899.
Mackmurdo, A. H. *History of the Arts and Crafts Movement*. Unpublished manuscript in the William Morris Gallery, Walthamstow, U.K.
McCabe, James D. *The Illustrated History of the Centennial Exhibition . . . with a full description of the Great Buildings and All the objects of interest exhibited in Them. . . .* Philadelphia: National Publishing, 1876.
Mawson, Thomas H. *The Art and Craft of Garden Making*. Batsford, 1901.
Morris, William. Preface to *Arts and Crafts Essays*. London: Longmans, Green, 1899.
———. *Collected Works of William Morris*. 24 vols. London: Longmans, Green, 1910–15.
———, ed. *Arts and Crafts Essays*, by members of the Arts and Crafts Exhibition Society. London. 1893.

Morse, Edward S. *Japanese Homes and their Surroundings*. Boston, 1886; facsimile rpt., New York: Dover, 1961.
Norton, Sara, and M. A. DeWolfe Howe, eds. *Letters of Charles Eliot Norton*. Boston: Houghton Mifflin, 1913.
Official Catalogue of Exhibitors. St. Louis: The Official Catalogue Company, Inc., 1904.
Pater, Walter. *Marius the Epicurean*. London: Macmillan, 1888.
Professional and Industrial History of Suffolk County, Massachusetts. 3 vols. Boston: Boston History Company, 1894.
Pugin, Augustus W. N. *Contrasts*. London: C. Dolman, 1837.
Redgrave, Richard. "Class XXX: Supplementary Report on Design." In *Great Exhibition: Reports by the Juries on the Subjects of the Thirty Classes into which the Exhibition Was Divided*. London: Spicer Brothers, 1852.
Report of the Massachusetts Board of World's Fairs Managers. Boston: Wright & Potter Printing, 1894.
Ruskin, John. *The Seven Lamps of Architecture*. London, 1849; rpt, New York: Noonday Press, 1971.
Sheldon, George William. *Artistic Country Seats: types of recent American villas and cottage architecture, with instances of country club-houses*. 2 vols. New York: 1886–87.
Singleton, Esther. *The Furniture of Our Forefathers*. New York, 1901.
Slater, Joseph, ed. *The Correspondence of Thomas Carlyle and Ralph Waldo Emerson, 1834–1874*. New York: Columbia University Press, 1964.
Smith, Walter. *Examples of Household Taste, Illustrated*. New York: R. Worthington, 1877.
Soderholtz, E. E., and James M. Corner. *Examples of Domestic Colonial Architecture in New England*. Boston, 1891.
Sturgis, Russell. *The Artist's Way of Working in the Various Handicrafts and Arts of Design*. New York: Dodd, Mead, 1910.
———. *A Dictionary of Architecture and Building*. New York: Macmillan, 1901–02.
Thaxter, Celia. *An Island Garden*. Boston: Houghton Mifflin, 1894; rpt. 1988.
United States Art Directory. 1882, 1884.
Van Rensselaer, Mariana Griswold. *Henry Hobson Richardson and His Works*. Boston: Houghton Mifflin, 1888; rpt., New York: Dover, 1969.
Von Falke, Jacob. *Art in the House: Historical, Critical, and Aesthetical Studies on the Decoration and Furnishing of the Dwelling*. Ed. Charles C. Perkins. Boston: L. Prang, 1879. Authorized American edition, trans. from 3rd German Edition
Webb, Judson T. *Pottery Making: An Illustrated Text Book on Art Pottery Making for Teachers and Artists*. Chicago: Lewis Institute, 1914.
Wells, H. G. *New Worlds for Old*. London: Constable, 1908.
Whall, C. W. *Stained Glass Work: A Text-Book for Students and Workers in Glass*. London: John Hogg, 1905; new edition, introduction Peter Cormack, Bristol: M. & J. Venables, 1999.
Wharton, Edith, and Ogden Codman, Jr. *The Decoration of Houses*. New York, 1897.
Wheeler, Candace. *Development of Embroidery in America*. New York: Harper & Brothers, 1921.
———. *Principles of Home Decoration*. New York: Doubleday, Page, 1903.
White, Mary. *How to Make Baskets*. New York: Doubleday, Page, 1902; rpt. Detroit: Gale Research, 1972.
———. *More Baskets and How to Make Them*. Garden City, N.Y.: Doubleday, Page, 1912; rpt. Detroit: Gale Research, 1972.

Wigley, Thomas B. *The Art of the Goldsmith and Jeweller: A Treatise on the Manipulation of Gold in the Various Processes of Goldsmith's Work, and the Manufacture of Personal Ornaments, etc.* London: Charles Griffin, 1898.

Wilson, Henry L. *The Bungalow Book.* 4th edition. Los Angeles:, 1908.

Winsor, Justin, ed. *The Memorial History of Boston, 1630–1880.* 4 vols. Boston: J. R. Osgood, 1880–83.

Wornum, Ralph Nicholson. *An Analysis of Ornament.* London: Chapman and Hall, 1877.

PERIODICALS AND ARTICLES

"Adaptation of Public Architecture to American Needs, and the Development of a National Style." *The Craftsman*, 10 (April 1906): 32–45.

American Architect and Building News (Boston).

Architectural Record (New York).

Architectural Review (Boston).

"Arts and Crafts Exhibition, Boston, 1897." *American Architect and Building News*, 56: 13, 21.

"The Arts and Crafts House." *House Beautiful*, 25 (April 2, 1909): 102–4.

Atlantic Monthly (Boston).

Batchelder, E. A. "Carving as an Expression of Individuality: Its Purpose in Architecture." *The Craftsman*, 16 (April 1909): 60–69.

Boyd, John Taylor, Jr. "H. Langford Warren: Obituary." *Architectural Record*, 42 (December 1917): 588–90.

Bradley, Will. "Art of Illustration." *The Nation*, 97 (July 10, 1913): 42–43.

———. "Illustrators and Their Recent Work." *The Independent*, 73 (December 12, 1912): 1345–51.

———. "Two Houses for less than $2600." *The Ladies Home Journal*, 22 (June 1905): 20.

———. "Bradley's Ideas for a $1500.00 House." *The Ladies Home Journal*, 26 (April 1909).

———. "Bringing an Old New England Home Up-to-Date with Consummate Art Leaving Its Ancient Beauty Unmarred." *The Craftsman*, 29, no. 3 (November 1915): 180–91.

Brochure Series of Architectural Illustration.

Brush and Pencil (Chicago).

The Chautauquan (Chautauqua, N.Y.).

Coburn, F. W. "Arts Movements of Today." *The National Magazine (Boston)*, 18 (April 1903): 58.

———. "A Colonial Crafts Museum." *The Craftsman*, November 1904: 158–64.

———. "Wood Carving and Architecture—work by I. Kirchmayer and others." *International Studio*, 41 (September 1910): 63–65.

———. "Worker in Stained Glass. [Harry E. Goodhue.]" *International Studio*, 41, (August 1910): Supplement, 37–40.

Country Life in America.

Dagett, M. P. "Women: the larger housekeeping; the widening range of women's activities as exemplified in Boston." *World's Work*, 24 (October 1912): 664–70.

Day, F. Holland. "Art and the Camera." *Lippincott's Monthly Magazine*, 65 (January 1900): 83–97.

———. "Opening Address. The New School of American Photography." *Photographic Journal*, 25, no. 2 (October 31,1900): 74–77.

"Development of an American Style of Home Furnishing Founded upon Beauty, Comfort and Simplicity." *The Craftsman*, 27 (October 1914): 69–78.

DeWolfe, Elsie. "Reproductions versus Antiques." *Good Housekeeping*, 55 (November 1912): 644–48.
Eberlein, H. D. "Family Built House: The Home of Will Bradley at Short Hills, New Jersey." *American Homes and Gardens*, 11 (July 1914): 218–23.
Foster, E. D. "Dedham Pottery." *House Beautiful*, 36 (April 1912), Supplement: 47.
———. "William A. Robertson, Master Potter." *International Studio*, 51 (November 1913), Supplement: 95–96.
Foster, Frank. "Condition of the American Working-class: How Can It Be Benefitted?" *Forum*, 24 (February 1898): 711–22.
———. "Trade Unionism and Social Reform." *American Federationist*, 7 (March 1900): 64–67.
French, Henry Willard. "Paul Revere's Old North Church, Boston, Mass." *Architectural Record*, 19 (March 1906): 214–22.
Grey, Elmer. "The Architect and the 'Arts and Crafts.'" *Architectural Record*, 21 (January 1907): 131–34.
Hall, Dr. Herbert. "Marblehead Pottery." *Keramic Studio*, 10 (June 1908): 31.
"Handicrafts in Massachusetts." *The Nation*, 78 (June 23, 1904).
Haviland, E. "Development of the Arts-and-Crafts House." *American Homes and Gardens*, 7 (May 1910): 196–97.
Howe, J. W., and M. Howe. "Story of My Boston Drawing-room." *Women's Home Companion*, 37 (October 1910): 7–8.
"Influence on Our Architecture of the École des Beaux Arts." *Architectural Record*, 22 (November 1907): 333–42.
"John La Farge, The Craftsman," *The Craftsman*, 19, no. 4 (January 1911): 330–36.
Keiley, J. T. "American Pictorial Photographers. No. V.—F. Holland Day." *Photography*, 17, no. 806, (April 23, 1904): 347–50.
Littell's Living Age (Boston).
Lyman, C. B. "Market: Latest Things in the Way of House Furnishings." *Country Life in America*, 21 (November 15, 1911): 39–40.
Masters in Art (Boston).
Mather, F. J., Jr. "Decorative Arts in America." *The Nation*, 82 (April 19, 1906): 317–18.
"Modern Furniture from Antique Models." *The Craftsman*, 24, no. 2 (May 1913): 245–48.
Moore, D. "Fenway Court Art Museum." *The Century*, 45 (January 1904): 362.
National Magazine (Boston).
"New Development of English Furniture Based on Old Models." *The Craftsman*, 20 (June 1911): 335–38.
Northend, Mary H. "Paul Revere Pottery." *House Beautiful*, August 1914: 82–83.
———. "Where Women Work and Rest." *The Craftsman*, 8, no. 3 (June 1905): 339.
"The Paul Revere Pottery: An American Craft Industry." *House Beautiful*, January 1922: 50, 70.
Pendleton, Margaret. "Paul Revere Pottery." *House Beautiful*, 32 (August 1912): 74.
Pennell, E. R., and R. Sturgis. "English and French Movements in Decorative Art." *Scribner's Magazine*, 23 (February 1898): 253.
Picturesque and Architectural New England.
Pratt, Jane. "From Merton Abbey to Old Deerfield." *The Craftsman*, November 1911: 183–91.
Price, W. L. "House Furnishings and Home Furnishing." *The Craftsman*, 20 (May 1911): 125–29.

Price, Will. "Confession of Faith." *The Craftsman*, 19 (March 1911): 535–39.

———. "Democracy in American Domestic Architecture." *The Craftsman*, 16 (June 1909): 251–256.

Rawson, J. A. "Recent American Pottery." *House Beautiful*, 31 (April 1912): 148–150.

———. "Teco and Robineau Pottery." *House Beautiful*, 33 (April 1913): 151–152.

"The Regeneration of Beacon Hill: How Boston Goes About Civic Improvement." *The Craftsman*, April 1909: 92–95.

Robie, V. "Mission Furniture: What It Is and Is Not." *House Beautiful*, 27 (May 1910): 162–63.

"Rookwood Pottery; a woman's contribution to American Craftsmanship." *The Independent*, 77 (March 16, 1914): 377.

Sanbourn, A. F. "Scope and Drift of the American Arts and Crafts Movement." *Forum*, 40 (September 1908): 254–64.

Sargent, Irene. "A Recent Exhibition of Arts and Crafts." *The Craftsman*, 4 (May 1903): 69–83.

"A Social and Business Experiment in the Making of Pottery." *Handicraft*, February 1911: 411–16.

Stickley, Gustave. "Greater Sincerity Necessary for the True Development of American Art." *The Craftsman*, 16 (April 1909): 50–59.

———. "Story of Paul Revere Pottery," *The Craftsman*, 25, no. 2 (November 1913): 205–7.

Sturgis, R. "Tendency toward an American Style of Architecture: Its Development Traced." *The Craftsman*, 10 (April 1906): 3–17.

Taylor, Herbert Whyte. "F. Holland Day: An Estimate." *Photo Era*, 4, no. 3 (March 1900): 77–78.

Taylor, W. T. "Personal Architecture: The Evolution of an Idea in the House of H. C. Mercer, Esq., Doylestown, Pa." *Architectural Record*, 33 (March 1913): 242–54.

Teall, G. "The Modern Colonial House: what it holds of history and beauty in the development of an American architecture." *The Craftsman*, 24 (April 1913): 61–68.

Trower, L. L. "Wood carvings of I. Kirchmayer." *The International Studio*, 51 (November 1913), Supplement: 89–93.

Wright, Frank Lloyd. "The Art and Craft of the Machine." *Brush and Pencil*, May 1901.

SECONDARY REFERENCES

BOOKS AND CATALOGUES

Acton, David. *A Spectrum of Innovation: Color in American Printmaking, 1890–1960*. Worcester, Mass.: Worcester Art Museum, 1990.

Adams, Henry, et al. *John La Farge*. Pittsburgh and Washington, D.C.: Carnegie Institute with the Smithsonian Institution, 1987.

Adams, Russell B., Jr. *The Boston Money Tree*. New York: 1977.

Alland, Alexander, Sr. *Jessie Tarbox Beals, First Woman News Photographer*. New York: Camera/Graphic Press Ltd., 1978.

Amory, Cleveland. *The Proper Bostonians*. New York: E. P. Dutton, 1947; Parnassus Imprints Edition, 1984.

Anderson, Timothy, Eudorah Moore, and Robert Winter, eds. *California Design 1910*. [Pasadena, Calif.]: California Design Publications, ca. 1974.

Andrew, Jack. *Samuel Yellin Metalworker*. Ocean City, Md.: Skipjack Press, 1992.
Anscombe, Isabelle. *A Woman's Touch: Women in Design from 1860 to the Present Day*. New York: Viking Penguin, 1984.
Anscombe, Isabelle, and Charlotte Gere. *Arts & Crafts in Britain and America*. New York: Rizzoli, 1978.
Art-Journal. *The Great Exhibition London 1851, an illustrated catalogue compiled by The Art Journal*. London: George Virtue, 1851 (?). Facsimile ed., New York: Crown, 1970.
Aslin, Elizabeth. *The Aesthetic Movement*. London: Elek, 1969.
Ayre, William S., and Ann Barton Brown, eds. *A Poor Sort of Heaven, A Good Sort of Earth: The Rose Valley Arts & Crafts Experiment*. Chadds Ford, Pa.: Brandywine River Museum, ca. 1933.
Bates, Elizabeth Bidwell, and Jonathan L Fairbanks. *American Furniture: 1620 to the Present*. New York: Richard Marek, 1981.
Bell, Quentin. *The Schools of Design*. London: Routledge & Kegan Paul, 1963.
Bishop, Jo-Ann C. *Out of the East, Oriental Imports for the Victorian Home, 1860–1915*. Rochester, N.Y.: The Margaret Woodbury Strong Museum, 1977. Exhibition catalogue.
Blumenthal, Joseph. *Bruce Rogers, A Life in Letters*. Austin, Tex.: W. Thomas Taylor, 1989.
Bolger, Doreen, et al. *In Pursuit of Beauty*. New York: Metropolitan Museum of Art, ca. 1986.
Boris, Eileen. *Art and Labor: Ruskin, Morris, and the Craftsman Ideal in America*. Philadelphia: Temple University Press, 1986.
Bowman, Leslie Green. *American Arts and Crafts: Virtue in Design*. Boston: Bulfinch Press/Little, Brown in association with the Los Angeles County Museum of Art, 1990.
Brooks, Van Wyck. *New England: Indian Summer, 1865–1915*. New York: Dutton, 1940.
Bunting, Bainbridge. *Houses of Boston's Back Bay: An Architectural History, 1840–1917*. Cambridge, Mass.: The Belknap Press, 1967.
Callen, Anthea. *Angel in the Studio: Women Artists of the Arts and Crafts Movement, 1870–1914*. London: Astragal, 1979.
Calloway, Stephen. *Twentieth-Century Decoration: The Domestic Interior from 1900 to the Present Day*. London: Weidenfeld and Nicholson, 1988.
Carpenter, Charles H., Jr. *Gorham Silver, 1831–1981*. New York: Dodd, Mead, 1982.
Cathers, David M. *Furniture of the American Arts and Crafts Movement, Stickley and Roycroft Mission Oak*. New York: New American Library, 1982.
Chickering, Elenita C. *Arthur J Stone, 1847–1938: Designer and Silversmith*. Boston: Boston Athenaeum, 1994.
Clark, Robert Judson, ed. *The Arts and Crafts Movement in America, 1876–1916*. Princeton: Princeton University Press, 1972.
Cormack, Peter. *The Stained Glass Work of Christopher Whall, 1849–1924: "Aglow with Brave Resplendent Colour."* Boston: Boston Public Library and the Charles J. Connick Foundation, 1999.
Corn, Wanda M. *The Color of Mood: American Tonalism, 1880–1910*. San Francisco: DeYoung Memorial Museum, 1972.
Crawford, Alan. *C. R. Ashbee: Architect, Designer and Romantic Socialist*. New Haven: Yale University Press, 1985.
Crawford, Caroline. *Famous Families of Massachusetts*. N.p: N.d.
Crichton, Laurie W. *Book Decoration in America: 1890–1910*. Williamstown, Mass.: Williams College, 1979.

Cumming, Elizabeth, and Wendy Kaplan. *The Arts and Crafts Movement*. London: Thames and Hudson, 1991.

Curtis, Verna Posever, and Jan Van Nimmen, eds. *F. Holland Day, Selected Texts and Bibliography*. Oxford: Clio Press, 1995.

Darke, Rick. *In Harmony with Nature: Lessons from the Arts & Crafts Garden*. New York: Friedman/Fairfax, 2000.

Darling, Sharon S. *Chicago Ceramics & Glass*. Chicago: Chicago Historical Society, University of Chicago Press, 1979.

———. *Chicago Furniture: Art, Craft, & Industry, 1971–1983*. New York: Chicago Historical Society in association with W. W. Norton, 1984.

———. *Chicago Metalsmiths*. Chicago: Chicago Historical Society, 1977.

———. *Teco: Art Pottery of the Prairie School*. Erie, Pa.: Erie Art Museum, 1989.

Davey, Peter. *Arts and Crafts Architecture: The Search for an Earthly Paradise*. London: Architectural Press, 1980; rev. ed., 1998.

Davidson, Marshall B., ed. *American Heritage History of Antiques from the Civil War to World War I*. New York: Simon & Schuster, 1969.

Directory of Boston Architects, 1846–1970, Compiled from Boston City Directories and Related Works. Cambridge: Mass.: Committee for the Preservation of Architectural Records, 1984.

Donaldson, Christine Hunter. "The Centennial of 1876." Dissertation, Yale University, 1948.

Eaton, Allen. *Handicrafts of New England*. New York: Bonanza Books, 1946.

Finlay, Nancy. *Artists of the Book in Boston: 1890–1910*. Cambridge: Harvard College Library, Department of Printing and Graphic Arts, The Houghton Library, 1985.

Fleming, John, and Hugh Honor. *Dictionary of the Decorative Arts*. New York: Harper & Row, 1977.

Floyd, Margaret Henderson. *Henry Hobson Richardson: A Genius for Architecture*. New York: Monacelli, 1998.

Flynt, Suzanne. *The Allen Sisters: Pictorial Photographers, 1885–1920*. Deerfield, Mass.: Pocumtuck Valley Memorial Association, 2002.

France, Jean R. *A Rediscovery—Harvey Ellis: Artist, Architect*. Rochester, N.Y.: Memorial Art Gallery of the University of Rochester, 1972.

From Architecture to Object: Masterworks of the American Arts & Crafts Movement. New York: Dutton Studio Books, in association with Hirschl & Adler Galleries, 1989.

Girouard, Mark. *Sweetness and Light: The "Queen Anne" Movement, 1860–1900*. Oxford: Clarendon Press, 1977.

Gover, C. Jane. *The Positive Image: Women Photographers in Turn of the Century America*. Albany: State University of New York Press, 1988.

Gowans, Alan. *Images of American Living: Four Centuries of Architecture and Furniture as Cultural Expression*. Philadelphia: Lippincott, 1964.

Green, Martin. *The Mount Vernon Street Warrens: A Boston Story, 1860–1910*. New York: Scribner's, 1989.

———. *The Problem of Boston: Some Readings in Cultural History*. New York: Norton, 1966.

Handlin, Oscar. *Boston's Immigrants, 1790–1880: A Study in Acculturation*. Cambridge: Harvard University Press, 1959; rev. ed., 1968.

Harrington, Elaine. *Henry Hobson Richardson: J. J. Glessner House, Chicago*. Tubingen: Wasmuth, 1993.

Herlihy, Elisabeth M. *Fifty Years of Boston: A Memorial Volume*. Boston, 1932.

Hills, Patricia. *Turn-of-the-Century America: Paintings, Graphics, Photographs, 1890–1910*. New York: Whitney Museum, 1977. Exhibition catalogue.

Hirshler, Erica. *A Studio of Her Own: Women Artists in Boston, 1870–1940*. Boston: Museum of Fine Arts, 2001.

Hitchcock, Henry-Russell. *The Architecture of H. H. Richardson and His Times*. New York: Museum of Modern Art, 1936; rev. paperback, Cambridge: MIT Press, 1966.

———. *In the Nature of Materials, 1887–1941: The Buildings of Frank Lloyd Wright*. New York: Hawthorne Books, 1942.

———. *Modern Architecture: Romanticism and Reintegration*. London, 1929.

Hitchmough, Wendy. *Arts and Crafts Gardens*. New York: Rizzoli, 1997.

———. *C. F. A. Voysey*. London: Phaidon, 1995.

Howe, Margery. *Deerfield Embroidery*. Deerfield, Mass.: Pocumtuck Valley Memorial Association, 1976.

Huggins, Nathan. *Protestants against Poverty: Boston's Charities, 1879–1900*. Westport Conn.: Greenwood, 1971.

Hussey, Christopher. *The Picturesque: Studies in a Point of View*. New York: Putnam, 1927.

Hutner, Martin. *The Merrymount Press*. Cambridge and New York: The Grolier Club and the Houghton Library, 1993.

Jordy, William H. *American Buildings and Their Architects: Progressive and Academic Ideals at the Turn of the Twentieth Century*. New York, 1972.

Kaplan, Wendy. *Leading "the Simple Life": The Arts and Crafts Movement in Britain, 1880–1910*. Miami Beach: Wolfsonian-Florida International University, 1999.

———, ed. *"The Art That Is Life": The Arts and Crafts Movement in America, 1875–1920*. Boston: Museum of Fine Arts, 1987.

Kardon, Janet, ed. *The Ideal Home, 1900–1920: The History of Twentieth Century American Craft*. New York: Harry N. Abrams, in association with the American Craft Museum, 1993.

Karlson, Norman. *American Art Tile, 1876–1941*. New York: Rizzoli, 1998.

Keefe, John Webster, and Samuel J. Hough. *Magnificent Marvelous Martele: American Art Nouveau Silver: The Jolie and Robert Shelton Collection*. New Orleans: New Orleans Museum of Art, 2001.

Kidney, Walter C. *The Architecture of Choice: Eclecticism in America, 1880–1930*. New York: Braziller, 1974.

Koch, Robert. *Louis C. Tiffany: Rebel in Glass*. New York: Crown, 1964.

Krieger, Alex, and David Cobb, eds. *Mapping Boston*. Cambridge: MIT Press, 1999.

Lambourne, Lionel. *Utopian Craftsmen, The Arts and Crafts Movement from the Cotswolds to Chicago*. Salt Lake City: Peregrine Smith, 1980.

Lancaster, Clay. *The Japanese Influence in America*. New York: Abbeville, 1963.

Lane, Roger. *Policing the City: Boston, 1822–1885*. Cambridge: Harvard University Press, 1967.

Leighton, Margareth Gebelein. *George Christian Gebelein, Boston Goldsmith, 1878–1945*. Boston: by the author, 1976.

Lewis, Lloyd, and Henry Justin Smith. *Oscar Wilde Comes to America*. New York: Harcourt, Brace, 1936.

Lyndon, Donlyn. *The City Observed*. New York: Vintage, 1982.

MacCarthy, Fiona. *William Morris: A Life for Our Times*. New York: Alfred A. Knopf, 1995.

MacDonald, Stuart. *The History and Philosophy of Art Education*. London: University of London Press, 1970.

Maher, Thomas K. *The Jarvie Shop: The Candlesticks and Metalwork of Robert R. Jarvie.* Philmont, N.Y.: Turn of the Century Editions, 1997.

Mann, Arthur. *Yankee Reformers in the Urban Age: Social Reform in Boston, 1880–1900.* New York: Harper & Row, 1954.

Massey, James, and Shirley Maxwell. *Arts & Crafts Design in America: A State-by-State Guide.* San Francisco: Chronicle Books, 1998.

Mayer, Barbara. *In the Arts & Crafts Style.* San Francisco: Chronicle Press, 1992.

Meech, Julia, and Gabriel Weisberg. *Japonism Comes to America: The Japanese Impact on the Graphic Arts, 1876–1925.* New York: Harry N. Abrams, 1990.

Meister, Maureen, "Herbert Langford Warren: Architecture, Harvard, and the Organizations of the Arts and Crafts Movement." Dissertation, Brown University, 2000.

———, ed. *H. H. Richardson: The Architect, His Peers, and Their Era.* Cambridge: MIT Press, 1999.

Meyer, Marilee Boyd, et al. *Inspiring Reform: Boston's Arts and Crafts Movement.* Wellesley, Mass., and New York: Davis Museum and Cultural Center, distributed by Harry N. Abrams, 1997.

Michaels, Barbara L., and Gertrude Kasebier. *The Photographer and Her Photographs.* New York: Harry N. Abrams, 1992.

Montgomery, Susan J. *The Ceramics of William H. Grueby.* Lambertville, N.J.: Arts and Crafts Quarterly Press, 1993.

Morgan, Will. *The Almighty Wall.* New York: Architectural History Foundation/ Cambridge: MIT Press, 1983.

Morrison, Hugh. *Louis Sullivan: Prophet of Modern Architecture.* New York: W. W. Norton, 1935; rpt. 1962.

Mumford, Lewis. *The Brown Decades: A Study of the Arts in America, 1865–1895.* New York: Dover, 1931; rpt. 1955.

Naylor, Gillian. *The Arts and Crafts Movement in America: A Study of Its Sources, Ideals, and Influences on Design Theory.* London: Studio Vista, 1971; Cambridge: MIT Press, 1980; London: Trefoil, 1990.

Ochsner, Jeffrey Karl. *H. H. Richardson: Complete Architectural Works.* Cambridge: MIT Press, 1982.

O'Gorman, James F. *The Architecture of Frank Furness.* Philadelphia: Philadelphia Art Museum, 1973.

———. *H. H. Richardson: Architectural Forms for an American Society.* Chicago: University of Chicago Press, 1987.

———. *H. H. Richardson and His Office.* Cambridge: Department of Printing and Graphic Arts, Harvard College Library, 1974.

———. *Living Architecture: A Biography of H. H. Richardson.* New York: Simon & Schuster, 1997.

———. *Three American Architects, Richardson, Sullivan, and Wright, 1865–1915.* Chicago: University of Chicago Press, 1991.

Oliver, Richard. *Bertram Grosvenor Goodhue.* New York: The Architectural History Foundation; Cambridge: MIT Press, 1983.

Parry, Linda. *William Morris Textiles.* New York: Viking, 1983.

Pause, Michael. "Teaching the Design Studio, a Case Study: M.I.T.'s Department of Architecture, 1865–1974." Dissertation, MIT, 1977.

Pevsner, Nicholaus. *The Sources of Modern Architecture and Design.* London: Thames and Hudson, 1968.

Pierce, H. Winthrop. *History of the School of the Museum of Fine Arts, Boston, 1876–1930*. Boston: T. O. Metcalf, 1930.
Placzek, Adolf, ed. *Macmillan Encyclopedia of Architects*. 4 vols. New York: Free Press, 1982.
Reed, Cleota. *Henry Chapman Mercer and the Moravian Pottery and Tileworks*. Philadelphia: University of Pennsylvania Press, 1996.
Rhoads, William B. *The Colonial Revival*. 2 vols. New York: Garland, 1977.
Richardson, Margaret. *The Craft Architects*. New York: Rizzoli, 1983.
Saint, Andrew. *Richard Norman Shaw*. New Haven: Yale University Press, 1976.
Santayana, George. *Character and Opinion in the United States*. New York: W. W. Norton, 1967.
———. *The Last Puritan*. New York: Scribner's, 1936.
———. *Persons and Places*. New York: Scribner's, 1963.
Schrock, Nancy Carlson, ed. *Architectural Records in Boston: A Guide to Architectural Research in Boston, Cambridge, and Vicinity*. New York: Garland, in association with Mass COPAR, 1983.
Scully, Vincent J. *The Shingle Style and the Stick Style: Architectural Theory and Design from Downing to the Origins of Wright*. Rev. ed. New Haven: Yale University Press, 1971.
Shifman, Barry. *The Arts and Crafts Metalwork of Janet Payne Bowles*. Indianapolis: Indianapolis Museum of Art, 1993. Exhibition catalogue.
Shand-Tucci, Douglass. *Boston Bohemia, 1881–1900*. Amherst: University of Massachusetts Press, 1995.
———. *Built in Boston*. Boston: New York Graphic Society, 1978.
———. *Ralph Adams Cram, American Medievalist*. [Boston]: Boston Public Library, 1975.
———. *Ralph Adams Cram: Life and Architecture*. Amherst: University of Massachusetts Press, 1995.
Shillaber, Caroline. *M.I.T. School of Architecture and Planning, 1861–1961: A Hundred Year Chronicle*. Cambridge: MIT Press, 1963.
Solomon, Barbara Miller. *Ancestors and Immigrants: A Changing New England Tradition*. Boston: Northeastern University Press, 1956; rev. ed. 1989.
———. *In the Company of Educated Women*. New Haven: Yale University Press, 1985.
Stansky, Peter. *Redesigning the World: William Morris, the 1880s, and the Arts and Crafts*. Princeton: Princeton University Press, 1985.
———. *William Morris, C. R. Ashbee, and the Arts and Crafts Movement*. London: Nine Elms Press, 1984.
Thernstrom, Stephan. *The Other Bostonians: Poverty and Progress in the American Metropolis, 1880–1970*. Cambridge: Harvard University Press, 1973.
Thompson, Susan Otis. *American Book Design and William Morris*. New York: R. R. Bowker, 1977; rpt. Oak Knoll Press, 1996.
Trapp, Kenneth R., et al. *The Arts & Crafts Movement in California: Living the Good Life*. Oakland, Calif.: Oakland Museum; New York: Abbeville Press, ca. 1993.
Vanderbilt, Kermit. *Charles Eliot Norton, Apostle of Culture in a Democracy*. Cambridge: Belknap Press, 1959.
Venable, Charles. *Silver in America, 1840–1940: A Century of Splendor*. Dallas: Dallas Museum of Art, 1994.
Vogel, Morris. *The Invention of the Modern Hospital: Boston, 1870–1930*. Chicago: University of Chicago Press, 1980.
Volpe, Tod M., and Beth Cathers. *Treasures of the American Arts and Crafts Movement, 1890–1920*. New York: Harry N. Abrams, 1988.
Waddell, Roberta. *Bradley, American Artist and Craftsman*. N.d.

Warde, Frederic. *Bruce Rogers, Designer of Books.* Cambridge: Harvard University Press, 1926.

Ware, Norman J. *The Labor Movement in the United States (1860–1895).* 1929; Gloucester, Mass.: P. Smith, 1959.

Warner, Sam Bass. *Streetcar Suburbs: Process of Growth in Boston, 1870–1930.* Cambridge: Harvard University Press, 1962; 2nd ed., 1978.

Wecter, Dixon. *The Saga of American Society.* New York: Scribner's, 1937.

Weinstein, Frederick D. "Walter Crane and the American Book Arts Movement, 1880–1913." Dissertation, Columbia University, 1970.

Whitaker, Charles H., ed. *Bertram Grosvenor Goodhue, Architect and Master.* New York: Press of the American Institute of Architects, 1925.

Whitehill, Walter M. Boston: *Centenary History of the Museum of Fine Arts, Boston.* Cambridge: Belknap Press, 1970.

———. *A Topographical History.* Cambridge: Belknap Press, 1959. 2nd ed., 1968.

Who Was Who in America, I, 1897–1942. Chicago: A. N. Marquis Co., n.d.

Wickman, Kenneth R. "Historical and Locational Aspects of the Economic Decline in the New England Furniture Industry." Dissertation, Syracuse University, 1962.

Wilson, Richard Guy, Dianne H. Pilgrim, and Richard N. Murry. *The American Renaissance, 1876–1914.* New York: Brooklyn Museum, distributed by Pantheon Books, 1980.

Winship, George Parker. *Daniel Berkeley Updike and the Merrymount Press.* Rochester: The Printing House of Leo Hart, 1947.

Winter, Robert W. *Batchelder Tilemaker.* Los Angeles: Balcony Press, 1999.

Withey, Henry F., and Elsie Rathburn Withey. *Biographical Dictionary of American Architects (Deceased).* Los Angeles: New Age, 1956.

PERIODICALS, ARTICLES, ESSAYS, AND CHAPTERS

Adams, Ann Jensen. "The Birth of a Style: Henry Hobson Richardson and the Competi-tion for Trinity Church, Boston." *Art Bulletin,* 62, no. 3 (September 1980): 409–33.

Alofsin, Anthony. "Toward a History of Teaching Architectural History: An Introduction to Herbert Langford Warren." *Journal of Architectural Education,* 37, no. 1 (Fall 1983): 2–7.

Andrews, Wayne. "Random Reflections on the Colonial Revival." *Journal of the Archives of American Art, 4, no. 2* (April 1964): 1–4.

Athineos, Doris. "Arts and Crafts' Silver Lining: Turn-of-the-century Arts and Crafts Silver Outshines Much of the Movement's Furniture and Pottery." *Traditional Home,* July 1994: 104–9.

Ayers, Dianne. "A Primer on Arts and Crafts Textiles." *Arts and Crafts Quarterly,* April 1991.

Brandt, Beverly K. "'All Workmen, Artists, and Lovers of Art': The Organizational Structure of The Society of Arts and Crafts, Boston." In Marilee Boyd Meyer et al. *Inspiring Reform: Boston's Arts and Crafts Movement.* Wellesley, Mass., and New York: Davis Museum and Cultural Center, distributed by Harry N. Abrams, 1997.

———. "The Critic and the Evolution of Early Twentieth-Century Craft." In Janet Kardon, ed., *The Ideal Home, 1900–1920: The History of Twentieth-Century American Craft.* New York: Harry N. Abrams, in association with the American Craft Museum, 1993. Exhibition catalogue.

———. "The Essential Link: Boston Architects and The Society of Arts and Crafts, Boston, 1897–1917." *Tiller, a bi-monthly devoted to the Arts and Crafts Movement*, 2, no. 1 [September–October 1983]: 7–32.

———. "Foreword." In Donald A. Davidoff and Stephen Gray, *Innovation and Derivation: The Contribution of L. & J. G. Stickley to the Arts and Crafts Movement*. Morris Plains, N.J.: Craftsman Farms Foundation, 1995. Exhibition catalogue.

———. "In Quest of Usefulness and Beauty, Changing Interpretations of the Arts and Crafts Ideal, Part I: The Arts and Crafts Movement." *Designers West*, 36, no. 12 (September 1989): 211, 213–14.

———. "In Quest of Usefulness and Beauty, Changing Interpretations of the Arts and Crafts Ideal, Part II: The Aesthetic Movement." *Designers West*, 36, no. 13 (October 1989): 166–68.

———. "Introduction," "Interior Design," "Architecture," and "Afterword." In *The Encyclopedia of Arts and Crafts, the International Arts Movement, 1850–1920*. New York: E. P. Dutton, 1989; rpt. New York: Knickerbocker Press, 1998.

———. "'One Who Has Seen More and Knows More': The Design Critic and the Arts and Crafts." In Bert Denker, ed., *The Substance of Style: Perspectives on the American Arts and Crafts Movement*. Wilmington: Winterthur Museum, 1996.

———. "Overview: Gustave Stickley's *Craftsman Magazine*." *The Craftsman on CD-ROM*. New York: Interactive Bureau, 1998.

———. "'Sobriety and Restraint': The Search for an Arts and Crafts Style in Boston, 1897–1917." *Tiller, a bi-monthly devoted to the Arts and Crafts Movement*, 2, no. 5 (Fall 1985): 26–73.

———. "'Worthy and Carefully Selected': American Arts and Crafts at the Louisiana Purchase Exposition, 1904." *Journal of the Archives of American Art*, 28, no. 1 (1988): 2–16.

Braznell, W. Scott. Entries in Wendy Kaplan, ed., *"The Art That Is Life": The Arts and Crafts Movement in America, 1875–1920*. Boston: Museum of Fine Arts, 1987.

———. "The Influence of C. R. Ashbee and His Guild of Handicraft on American Arts and Crafts Movement Silver, Other Metalwares, and Jewelry." In Bert Denker and Onie Rollins, eds., *The Substance of Style: New Perspectives on the American Arts and Crafts Movement*. New York: W.W. Norton, 1996.

———. "Metalsmithing and Jewelrymaking, 1900–1920." In Janet Kardon, ed., *The Ideal Home, 1900–1920: The History of Twentieth-Century American Craft*. New York: Harry N. Abrams, in association with the American Craft Museum, 1993. Exhibition catalogue.

———. "The Metalwork and Jewelry of Janet Payne Bowles." In Barry Shifman, with contributions by W. Scott Braznell and Sharon S. Darling, *The Arts and Crafts Metalwork of Janet Payne Bowles*. Indianapolis: Indianapolis Museum of Art, 1993.

Bricker, Lauren Weiss. "The Writings of Fiske Kimball: A Synthesis of Architectural History and Practice." In Elisabeth Blair MacDougall, ed., *The Architectural Historian in America*. Hanover: University Press of New England, 1990.

Brooks, H. Allen. "Chicago Architecture: Its Debt to the Arts and Crafts." *Journal of the Society of Architectural Historians*, 30, no. 4 (1971): 312–17.

Brooks, Michael W. "New England Gothic: Charles Eliot Norton, Charles H. Moore, and Henry Adams." In Elisabeth Blair MacDougall, ed., *The Architectural Historian in America*. Hanover: University Press of New England, 1990.

Carpenter, Charles H., Jr. "The Tradition of the Old: Colonial Revival Silver for the American Home." In Alan Axelrod, ed., *The Colonial Revival in America*. A Winterthur Book. New York: W. W. Norton, 1985.

Clark, Robert Judson. "Aspects of the Arts and Crafts Movement in America." *Record of Art Museum, Princeton*, 34, no. 2 (1975).

Cunningham, Harry F. "Goodhue, the First True Modern." *Journal of the American Institute of Architects*, 15 (July 1928): 246–48.

Curran, Kathleen. "The Romanesque Revival, Mural Painting, and Protestant Patronage in America." *Art Bulletin*, 81, no. 4 (December 1999): 693–722.

Decker, Ellen Paul. "Women in the Arts and Crafts Movement: Artists, Consumers, Pioneers." *Arts and Crafts Quarterly*, 7, no. 1 (1994): 30–33.

Derby, Carol. "Charles Prendergast's Frames: Reuniting Design and Craftsmanship." In *The Prendergasts and the Arts and Crafts Movement*. Williams College Museum of Art, 1988: 28–43.

Dietz, Jean. "Extending the Bond of the Saturday Evening Girls." *Boston Globe*, May 12, 1991, n.p.

Falino, Jeannine. "Circles of Influence: Metalsmithing in New England." In Marilee Boyd Meyer et al., *Inspiring Reform: Boston's Arts and Crafts Movement*. Wellesley, Mass., and New York: Davis Museum and Cultural Center, distributed by Harry N. Abrams, 1997.

Fergusson, Peter. "Medieval Architectural Scholarship in America, 1900–1940: Ralph Adams Cram and Kenneth John Conant." In Elisabeth Blair MacDougall, ed., *The Architectural Historian in America*. Hanover: University Press of New England, 1990.

Frank Lloyd Wright Quarterly.

Greenough, Sarah. "'Of Charming Glens, Graceful Glades, and Frowning Cliffs': The Economic Incentives, Social Inducements, and Aesthetic Issues of American Pictorial Photography, 1880–1902." In *Photography in Nineteenth-Century America*. Fort Worth: Amon Carter Museum of Western Art, 1991.

Hall, Donald S. "Glaze Craze, Collectors Get Fired Up about Rookwood Pottery." *Art & Antiques*, November 1995: 42–44.

Harrington, Elaine. "International Influences on Henry Hobson Richardson's Glessner House." In John Zukowsky, ed., *Chicago Architecture 1872–1922: Birth of a Metropolis*. Munich: Prestel-Verlag, 1987.

Havinga, Anne E. "Pictorialism and Naturalism in New England Photography." In Marilee Boyd Meyer et al., *Inspiring Reform: Boston's Arts and Crafts Movement*. Wellesley, Mass., and New York: Davis Museum and Cultural Center, distributed by Harry N. Abrams, 1997.

Hubka, Thomas C. "H. H. Richardson's Glessner House: A Garden in the Machine." *Winterthur Portfolio*, 24 (Winter 1989): 209–29.

Kimball, Fiske. "Goodhue's Architecture: A Critical Estimate." *Architectural Record*, 62 (December 1927): 537–39.

Lancaster, Clay. "Japanese Buildings in the United States before 1900: Their Influence upon American Decorative Domestic Architecture." *Art Bulletin*, 35 (1953): 217–24.

———. "Synthesis: The Artistic Theory of Fenollosa and Dow." *Art Journal*, 28, no. 3 (Spring 1969): 286–87.

Meister, Maureen. "Observations of an Architect: Herbert Langford Warren's 1878 Sketchbook." *Nineteenth Century*, 21, no. 1 (Spring 2001): 3–9.

Meyer, Marilee Boyd. "Arthur Wesley Dow and His Influence on Arts and Crafts." In *Arthur Wesley Dow: His Art and His Influence*. New York: Spanierman Gallery, 1999.

———. "Saturday Evening Girls and the Children's Movement." *Antiques Journal*, January 1991: 14, 15, 34.

Molloy, Mary Alice. "Richardson's Web: A Client's Assessment of the Architect's Home and Studio." *Journal of the Society of Architectural Historians*, 54 (March 1995): 8–23.

Monkhouse, Christopher. "The Spinning Wheel as Artifact, Symbol and Source of Design." *Nineteenth Century*, 8, nos. 3–4 (1982): 155–72.

Montgomery, Susan J. "The Potter's Art in Boston: Individuality and Expression." In Marilee Boyd Meyer et al., *Inspiring Reform: Boston's Arts and Crafts Movement*. Wellesley, Mass., and New York: Davis Museum and Cultural Center, distributed by Harry N. Abrams, 1997.

Morgan, Keith N., and Richard Cheek. "History in the Service of Design: American Architect-Historians, 1870–1940." In Elisabeth Blair MacDougall, ed., *The Architectural Historian in America*. Hanover: University Press of New England, 1990.

Ochsner, Jeffrey Karl, and Thomas F. Hubka. "H. H. Richardson: The Design of the William Watts Sherman House." *Journal of the Society of Architectural Historians*, 51 (June 1992): 121–45.

O'Gara, Noreen. "Charles J. Connick." *Stained Glass*, 82, no. 1 (Spring 1897): 44–61.

Peacock, Molly. "Home Base. A Marriage of Taste. Geraldine and Kit Laybourne's Arts and Crafts apartment shows a genius for collaboration—and a serious sense of play." *House & Garden*, September 1996: 176–84.

Prisant, Carol. "Decorating the Century." *Art & Antiques*, September 1995: 50, 52 –53, 55, 58–59.

Seidler, Jan M. "A Tradition in Transition: The Boston Furniture Industry, 1840–1880." *Nineteenth Century*, 82, nos. 3–4 (1982): 76–84.

Skinner, Orin E. "Connick in Retrospect." *Stained Glass*, 70, no. 1 (Spring 1975): 17–19.

Sloan, Julie L. "The Rivalry between Louis Comfort Tiffany and John La Farge." *Nineteenth Century*, 17, no. 2 (Fall 1997): 27–34.

Sloan, Julie L., and James L. Yarnall. "Art of an Opaline Mind: The Stained Glass of John La Farge." *American Art Journal*, 24, nos. 1–2 (1992): [4]–42.

Smeaton, Suzanne. *The Art of the Frame: American Frames of the Arts and Crafts Period*. New York: Eli Wilner, 1988.

Stebbins, Theodore E. "Richardson and Trinity Church: The Evolution of a Building." *Journal of the Society of Architectural Historians*, 27 (1968): 281–98.

Stephens, Suzanne. "Architecture Criticism in a Historical Context: The Case of Herbert Croly." In Elisabeth Blair MacDougall, ed., *The Architectural Historian in America*. Hanover: University Press of New England, 1990.

Style 1900: The Quarterly Journal of the Arts & Crafts Movement.

Tankard, Judith B. "Arts and Crafts Gardens," *Old House Interiors*, Winter 1997.

Thompson, Susan Otis. "The Arts and Crafts Book." In Robert Judson Clark, ed., *The Arts and Crafts Movement in America 1876–1916*. Princeton: Princeton University Press, 1972.

Thomson, Neville. "Addison B. LeBoutillier: Developer of Grueby Tiles." *Tiller*, 1, no. 2 (November–December 1982): n.p.

Upton, Dell. "Outside the Academy: A Century of Vernacular Architecture Studies, 1890–1990." In Elisabeth Blair MacDougall, ed., *The Architectural Historian in America*. Hanover: University Press of New England, 1990.

Vilain, Jean-François. "Graphics." In *The Encyclopedia of Arts and Crafts: The International Arts Movement, 1850–1920*. New York: E. P. Dutton, 1989.

Weinberg, Helene Barbara. "John La Farge and the Decoration of Trinity Church, Boston." *Journal of the Society of Architectural Historians*, 33, no. 4 (December 1974): 323–53.

———. "John La Farge and the Invention of American Opalescent Windows." *Stained Glass*, 67 (Fall 1972): 4–11.

———. "John La Farge: Pioneer of the American Mural Movement." In Henry Adams et al., *John La Farge*. New York: Abbeville Press, 1987.

Wilner, Eli. *The Gilded Edge: The Art of the Frame*. San Francisco: Chronicle Books, 2000.

Wilson, Richard Guy. "Ralph Adams Cram and the Idea of Medieval Culture in America." In B. Rosenthal and P. Szarmach, eds., *Medievalism and American Culture* Binghamton: SUNY, 1988.

Yarnall, James L. "Classics for the Classes: John La Farge's Windows for Wellesley College." *Nineteenth Century*, 17, no. 2 (Fall 1997): 21–26.

———. *John La Farge: Watercolors and Drawings*. Yonkers, N.Y.: Hudson River Museum of Westchester, 1990.

INDEX

Note: Page numbers in *italics* refer to the illustrations and captions. For entries with multiple illustrations, page numbers are listed under the subentry "illustrations."

Ackermann, Rudolph, 26–27, Plate 2, Plate 3; *Repository of the Arts, Literature, Commerce, Manufactures, Fashions, Politics*, 25–27, Plate 3
Adam, Robert and James, 19–20, 22, 53
Addison, Julia de Wolf, 60–61, 64–65, 100, *179*, 276, 301, 321n. 6, Plate 10; *Arts and Crafts in the Middle Ages*, 61, 67
advertising, 78, 99, 113, 246–247, 260, 276, 284–86; illustrations, *35, 40, 45, 53, 59–60, 70, 72, 77, 80, 83, 97, 105, 215, 222, 226, 242, 260*, Plate 6, Plate 7, Plate 8, Plate 9
aesthetes, 33, 75, 90, 135–36, 187, 284, 290; and antiques, 28; and Asian art, 72; and Beauty, 28–29, 31, 33; and eclecticism, 29; illustrations, *42, 45, 79, 84,* Plate 5, Plate 6
Aesthetic Education (DeGarmo), 44–45, 47
aestheticism, 29, 31, 34, 72–73, 168, Plate 7
Aesthetic movement, 2, 72, 90, 317n. 69; architects and, 252; and Arts and Crafts Movement, 28, 31, 33–34, 270; and Beauty, 29, 31; Bostonians and, 55, 62, 69; and design criticism, 28–31, 33–34; illustrations, *30, 42, 49, 53, 59, 73, 81, 82, 187, 214, 257,* Plate 6, Plate 15
aesthetics, 3, 34, 38, 41, 139, 197–98, 200, 218; and design criticism, 28–31; eighteenth-century philosophy of, 1, 12–20, 31, 186–87, 275; and "good design," 31; and morality, 14; Morris and, 45; SACB Jury and, 158–59, 161, 177–78; Ware Dennett on, 132–33, 135
Albert, Prince of Wales, 3, 26

Allen, Frances S. and Mary E., *80*, 101, 150, 272, *272*
American Exhibition of Products, Arts and Manufactures of Foreign Nations, 69
American Federation of Art, 258, 267, 269
Amory-Ticknor House, 84, 252–53; illustrations, *84, 166*
Analysis of Beauty (Hogarth), 12, *13*, 18, 212
Analysis of Ornament (Wornum), 8
Analytical Inquiry into the Principles of Taste (Knight), 20
Andrews, Jaques and Rantoul, 145, 252, 256
Andrews, Robert Day, 58, 67, *86, 87*, 103, 109, 114, 255–56. See also Andrews, Jaques and Rantoul
antiquarianism, 48, 60, Plate 8
antiques, 48–49, 68, 73, 74, 81, Plate 8; and aesthetes, 28; approved by SACB Jury for copying, 152, 193; Cook and, 186–87, *187*; twenty-first-century demand for, 282–83; Peabody and, 115, *116*, 148; Stone and, 193, 196
Appleton, William Sumner, *45*, 67
architects, 19, 32, 48, 65, 75–76, 199, 254; and artistic cooperation, 83, 138, 144, 254, 262, 264; and Arts and Crafts movement, 34, 222, 289; and beauty, 19; Boston, 57–58, 67–69, 75, 77–88; at Chicago's Steinway Hall, 84; as critics, 34, 36; and design reform movement, 77–79, 83, 86, 107, 276; education for, 34, 36, 58, 76, 83–85, 94, 100, 104, 257; and exhibitions, 96, 98, 103, 114, 205–6, 226, 251–52,

381

architects (*continued*) 256; influence beyond Boston, 225–28, 251–52, 254–61, 272–73, 288; illustrations, *58, 63, 70, 79, 80, 87, 102, 148, 202, 210, 212, 214, 220, 223, 224, 255–58, 260–64*; professional organizations, 36, 84, 86; publications, 67, 77–78, 192–94, 255, 257–60; and quest for Usefulness and Beauty, 77–88, 254; and SACB, 57, 121, 173, 177, 225, 254–62, 264, 311–12; and SACB Jury, 149, women, 100, 150, 260. *See also* architecture

architecture, 2, 32, 34, 36, 67, 205; morality and, 54, 63; Orders of, 21, 25, 48, 205; and Usefulness and Beauty, 55. *See also* architects

art education, 4, 39, 84–86, *85*, 92–95, 98, 203

Art in Needlework (Day and Buckle), 198, 217

Art Institute of Chicago, 265, 353n. 85

artist, as critic, 33–34, 36

Art-Journal, 4–6

"art produce," 58, 69, 73, 276, 321n. 4

Arts and Crafts, ideal, xviii, 274, 283, 291

Arts and Crafts: A Diagnosis, The (Ross), 132, 134, 141

Arts and Crafts Exhibition Society (ACES) (Britain), xix, 96, 98, 101, 104

Arts and Crafts in the Middle Ages, 61, 67

Arts and Crafts movement, xvii, 1–2, 134, 159, 167, 187, 227, 229, 244, 248, 270; and Aesthetic movement, 28, 31, 33–34; and architects, 34, 222, 252, 289; Boston and, xix, 62, 69; British, 69, 89; 135; and conventionalization, 207–9; critics promoting, 34–39; and design reform, 2, 27–28, 31–34; foundations of, 166–67, 281; illustrations, *35, 42, 97, 102*, Plate 6, Plate 7; media divisions in, 10; and moralism, *35, 42*, 43, 47; naming of, 96; and Trinity Church, 86–87; and Usefulness and Beauty, 1, 47, 106; and Whiting, 122, 128, 139, 231, 266; women in Boston's, 99–101. *See also* Arts and Crafts Revival

Arts and Crafts Revival, xvii, xx–xxiii, 116, 281–82, 284, 286–90, *289*, Plate 19

Ashbee, Charles Robert, 75–76, 95

Asian influences, 11–12, 51–52, 69, 72–73, 105, 188, 205, 221–22; illustrations, *50, 53, 73, 221, 251, 256*, Plate 9

Austen, Alice, 150, 303

Austin, Isabel, 236–37

Babcock, Mabel Keyes, 100

Baker, Cordelia Taylor, 238, 349n. 35

Barton, George Edward, 58, *58*, 268, 311. *See also* Sturgis & Barton

Bascom, John, 197–98

Batchelder, Ernest Allen, 38, 41, *236*, 248, 273, *273*; on conventionalization, 214; on good design, 202, 211, 214, 222; and Louisiana Purchase Exposition, 236–40; *The Principles of Design*, 38

Baxter, Sylvester, 76, 132, 203

Beauty, 47, 52–54, 105, 108, 215, 275; aestheticism and, 28–29, 31, 33, 73; Architectural, 19; and Arts and Crafts movement, 31–32; Dow on, 219; eighteenth-century philosophers on, 14–18, 47; Emerson on, 66; and expres-sion, 17, 52–54; illustrations, *60, 195*; Morris on, 32; publications on, 25, 197; Ruskin on, 33; and SACB, 113, 156, 161; Shanhagan on, 19; and Taste, essays on, 12–13; and work environment, 33. *See also* Usefulness and Beauty

Beauty and Usefulness. *See* Usefulness and Beauty

Bell, Peter, 242–43

Berenson, Bernard, 65, 68, 75, 146, 270

Berry, Albert, 273

Bigelow, Kennard & Co., 70, *70*, 226

Binns, Charles Fergus, 36, 76, 107, 142, 240, 248, 270; *The Potter's Craft*, 36, 107

Binyon, Laurence, 51–52, 197, 202, 221–23, 343n. 24; *The Flight of the Dragon: An Essay on the Theory and Practice of Art in China and Japan*, 197

book artists, 105–106, 113, 147, 149, 274

book arts, 61–62, 66, 75, 105–6, 147; effect of diaspora on, 274; illustrations, *214, 216, 217, 234*, Plate 10, Plate 11, Plate 12; and Louisiana Purchase Exposition, 233–34, 238; Walker on the, 169; women and the, 150, 238

Boston Architectural Club, 84, 98, 103, 121; illustrations, *59, 70, 80, 99, 148, 242, 251, 256–58, 261–62, 264*

Boston Foreign Fair, 69, *69*, 85
Boston School of Design for Women, 100
Bowles, Janet Payne (Mrs. Joseph). *See* Payne Bowles, Janet
Bowles, Joseph M., 105, 269–70
Bradley, Will, 97, 105; *Bradley–His Book*, 105, *105*
Brown, Frank Chouteau, 259, 259–60, *260*, 311
Buckle, Mary, 198, 217
Bulkley, Mary E., 238, 349n. 35
Burke, Edmund, 12, 15, *15*, 20, 25, 162; *A Philosophical Enquiry into the Origin of our Ideas of the Sublime and the Beautiful*, 12, 15
Burne-Jones, Lady Georgina (Mrs. Edward), 89
Burne-Jones, Margaret, *91*
Burne-Jones, Sir Edward, 87, *89*, 89–91, 95, 147
Burton, Elizabeth Eaton, 236
Butler, E. K., Jr., 160

Cabinet Dictionary, The (Sheraton), 23–24
Cabinet-maker and Upholsterer's Drawing-Book (Sheraton), 20, 23
Cabinet-Maker and Upholsterer's Guide (Hepplewhite), 20, 22–24, 107
Cabot, Frederick P., 178, 267,
Cairns, Hugh, 59, 76, 87
Carey, Arthur Astor, 62, 62–64, 67, 132, 137–38, 146, 152, 268, 293; and *Handicraft*, 130–136; and Handicraft Shop, 126–27; in SACB, 103, 109, 114–15, 121, 123–25, 129, 136; on SACB Jury, 143
Carlyle, Thomas, 27, 75, 89–90, 120, 128
Carman, Bliss, 105, *203*, 251
Carrig-Rohane Shop, 146, 251, 303, 337n. 11. *See also* Murphy, Hermann Dudley
Centennial Exhibition (Philadelphia, 1876), 48, 73, 98
Chamberlin, Joseph Edgar, 76
Cheney, Ednah D., 95, *99*, 99–100
Chevreul, Michel Eugène, 6; *The Principles of Harmony and Contrast of Colors*, 6
Chicago World's Fair (1893), 147–48, 205
Chippendale, Thomas, 12, 21–25, 22, 48, *80*, 195; *The Gentleman and Cabinet-Maker's Director*, 12, 21–22, *22*, 48
Chippendale style, 186, *187*, 195
Clark, Henry Hunt, 143–45, *145*, 154, 293
classicism, 195, 259, 264; neo–, 19, 23, 48
Clement, Edward H., 76, *76*
Cleveland, Frank E., 254, 311
Clutton-Brock, Arthur, 32, 36, 55
Cobden-Sanderson, Thomas James, 75–76, 96, 238, 271
Coburn, Frederick William, 76; on First Exhibition, 116–17; on SACB, 195, 249, 253; and SACB decennial exhibition, 263–64, 265, 268; on SACB Jury, 143; on Warren, 139
Code, Grant Hyde, 76, 82
Codman, William Christmas, 238, *245*, 245–46
Coffin, Marian C., 100
college settlement house movement, 94–95, *95*
Collins, Hazel G., 181
Colonial Revival, 60, 101, 126, 132, 152, 195–97, 288; illustrations, *44*, *60*, *61*, *67*, *116*, *187*, *256*
Composition (Dow), 38, 72, 202–3, 221
connections, transatlantic, 67, 76, 88, 90, 107–8
Connick, Charles J., 253–54
Considerations of Some Recent Social Theories (Norton), 88
Consignors, General Rules for, *180*
consumer(s), 1, 32–33, 79, 92, 128–29, 195, 220–23, 243, 247, 278; and "art produce," 73, 248; choices, 12–13, 214; critics and, xvii–xviii, 11, 14, 20–21, 23, 31, 41, 44, 76; education, 41, 118, 128, 135, *189*; and exhibitions, 103, 118, 227, 244, 248; guidance for, 5, 12–14, 20, 23, 76–77, 119, 136; influences on, 21, 143; as lay critics, 39, 49; quality of life for, 28, 52; SACB and, 138; and social reform, 34; and taste, 98; twenty-first century, 281, 283–91
conventionalization, xx–xxi, 11, 75, 158, 203–20, 251; in Arts and Crafts movement, 207–9; Batchelder on, 211–12, 214; contradictions of, 219–20; Day on, 204, 208–19;

conventionalization (*continued*)
definitions of, 203–6, 209–11; design reformers and, 209; Dow on, 212, 219; and "good design," 203–12, 211–19; history of, 205–6; illustrations, *105, 204–9, 211,* Plate 11, Plate 12; methodology of, 50–52, 203–20; and nature, 204; Ross on, 210–11, 215; rules of, 217–19; and SACB Jury, 208; traits of, 211–17; and Wornum, 209–10;
Conwell, Clarke, 233–34, 248–49; illustrations, *200, 233,*
Cook, Clarence Chatham, 29, 31, 52, 71–73, 186–188, 189, 197, 219, 222. *See also House Beautiful, The*
Cook, Olive Elizabeth. *See* Whiting, Olive Elizabeth Cook (Mrs. Frederick)
Coolidge, J. Templeman, Jr., 60–61, *61,* 63–64, 67–68, 109, 323n. 19; and exhibit loans, 114–15, 263; on Louisiana Purchase Exposition jury, 231; on SACB Jury, 143–44, 167–68, 172, 189, 293
Cordova, Julian de, 152, 247
Cousin, M. V., 25
Cram, Goodhue & Ferguson, 242, 254, 264, 311–312; illustrations, *197, 220, 223,* Plate 16
Cram, Ralph Adams, 65, 197, 254–55, 258–59, 265, 274, Plate 17. *See also* Cram, Goodhue & Ferguson
Crane, Walter, 33, 37, 75, 96, 107, 189; *The Bases of Design,* 37, *37,* 129, 215; *Line and Form,* 51, 185, 211
critics. *See* design critics
Crystal Palace, 4–6, 27, 92; illustrations, *3, 4, 8, 9*
Cuzner, Bernard, 49, 54, 198; *Silversmith's Manual,* 198

Davis, Charles Percy, 231, 248
Dawson, Edith (Mrs. Nelson), 36
Dawson-Watson, Dawson, 105, 238–239, *239,* 251, 272
Day, F. Holland, 65–66, 101, 150
Day, Lewis Foreman, 33, 48, 50–51, 53–54, 186, 209; advocate of conventionalization, 204, 208–14, 217–19; 286; *Art in Needlework,* 198, 217; on fitness, 198, 215–16; and historicism, 48; *Nature in Ornament,* 194, 204, 210, 215; *Ornament and Its Application,* 186, 204, 212, 215; *The Planning of Ornament,* 198, 212, 217

Dedham Pottery, 142, 146, 160, 243–244, 246; illustrations, *149, 243*
DeGarmo, Charles, 44–45, *45,* 47; *Aesthetic Education,* 45, 47
Dennett, Hartley, 122, 132, 137, 268, 270, 311
Dennett, Mary Ware (Mrs. Hartley). *See* Ware Dennett, Mary
design criticism, 5–7; and Aesthetic movement, 28–31, 34; and Arts and Crafts movement, 31–34; British, 11; classes in, 154; and design reform movement, 25–28; at Great Exhibition, 5–12; literature of, 25–28, 31–34; profession of, 2–3, 16, 19, 25–26; and theory, 43
design critics, xviii–xix, 12, 25, 55, 185; and Arts and Crafts movement, 31–32; background of, xviii–xix, 34; on conventionalization, 211–19; credentials and guidelines, 39; defined, 6, 28, 36; and design reform, 11; in design reform movement, 39–43; education of, 38–39; eighteenth century, 18, 20–25, 33; entrepreneurs as, 21–25; and exhibits, 39; on expression, 220; Gerard on, 16; history of, 48; as jurors, 39; and language, 54–55, 67; and the media, 76–77; motives of, 41; 43; nineteenth century, 33; profession of, xxiii, 1–2, 16; promoting Arts and Crafts movement, 34–39; qualities of, 28, 36, 141; and SACB Jury, 142; and Taste, 21;
design education, 6, 84–85, 94–95, 97, 107, 112, 154, 225, 277; books for 156; Carey on, 125, 127; role of, 38–39; Ross and Ware on, 134–35; Warren on, 138. *See also* art education
design elements, 15, 47, 189, 215
design literature, 36–39, 49, 192–93
design principles, 15, 38, 43–44, 47
design reform, xvii–xviii, 11, 17, 90, 141, 215; and architects, 77–79, 83, 86–87, 107; Boston roots of, 68–77, 95, 97, 100, 276; and critics, 11, 32, 34, 55, 141; foundations of, 25–26, 32–33; and Great Exhibition, 3, 275; and *Handicraft,* 130, 134–35; international response to, 107–8, 277; literature of, 25, 33, 76, 107; and SACB, 57, 96, 104, 112–13, 115, 119, 124–30, 252;

and social reform, 34; Warren, 138; Whiting and, 122; women and, 276; and work environment, 41; 55, 57; Wornum on, 10–12

design reformers, 1, 17–18, 44, 47, 82–83, 135, 185–88, 187, 279, 291; challenges to, 51, 120, 198, 222–24; and conventionalization, 203–5, 209; and environment, 32–33; European, 108, 206–7; and fitness, 54, 288; and historicism, 67, 195–96, 208–9, 288; illustrations, *45, 46, 201, 202, 212, 257, 260*, Plate 6; moralism and, 289; publications for, 275, 284; and simplicity, 215, 221–22; speaking tours by British, 75–76;

design reform movement, xvii–xxiii, 222, 223–24, 229, 281, 283, 289, 291; and architects, 86, 252, 276; and design criticism, 39–43; and eighteenth-century criticism, 1; and First Exhibition, 103; foundations of, 25–28; international, 76, 107, 269, 275–76; and Great Exhibition, 2; influence of, 28–34; naming of, 96; and simplicity, 220–21; and women, 100

design theory, 38, 43–47, 58, 134, 156, 192–93, 209–10, 278

Dialogue on The Distinct Characters of the Picturesque and the Beautiful (Price), 20

Dow, Arthur Wesley, 188–89, 203, 253, 270, 307; Asian interests of, 72, 188–189; *Composition*, 38, 72, 202–3, 221; on conventionalization, 212, 213, 219; on expression, 220; and historicism, 188; illustrations, *203*, Plate 13, Plate 14, Plate 15; and National League of Handicraft Societies, 267; and SACB, 203; and theory, 38, 254

Downes, William Howe, xxiv, 76

Dresser, Christopher, 75, 189, 194, 209, 212–13, 217, 219; *Japan, Its Architecture, Art and Art Manufactures*, 194; *Principles of Decorative Design*, 75, 212–13, 217, 219; *Studies in Design*, 209

Eaton, Charles F., 236, 238, 249

eclecticism, 5, 10, 26, 29, 31, 41, 62, 82–83, 98, 186–89, 213, 291; and aesthetes, 29; and Arts and Crafts ideal, 291; illustrations, *3, 30, 41, 82, 87, 147, 196, 216*, Plate 1

Edis, Robert W., 33, *42*

Ek, Seth, 126

Elements of Criticism (Home), 16, 18

Elston Press, 233–34; illustrations, *200, 233*

English Domestic Revival (architecture), 2, 77, 79, 256–257

Essay on Taste, An (Gerard), 13, 15

Esthetics (Gordon), 218

Evans, John, 59, *60*, 76, 87, 103, 109, 254, 276

Exhibition of the Arts and Crafts, First (SACB, 1897), 96–98, 100–103, 113, 116, 119; illustrations, *58, 62, 97, 99, 102*

Exhibition of the Arts and Crafts (SACB, 2nd, 1899), 49, 113–123, 125, 133; illustrations, *118, 119*

exhibitions, international, 1–3, 39, 49, 69, 82, 92, 96–97, 108, 134, 140, 143, 174, 226, 253, 265. *See also* Exhibition of the Arts and Crafts; Great Exhibition of Works of Industry; Louisiana Purchase Exposition

expression, 17, 38, 164, 176, 185, 189, 215, 218; and "good design," 54–55, 220–224; and Usefulness and Beauty, 17, 52–54

Ferguson, Frank W., 254–255, 311. *See also* Cram, Goodhue & Ferguson

Fisher, Alexander, 76, 144

Fisher, Ripley & LeBoutillier, *261*

fitness, 6, 14, 25, 27, 113, 133, 155, 165, 198, 215–16, 288

Flight of the Dragon: An Essay on the Theory and Practice of Art in China and Japan, The (Binyon), 196–97

Foote, Florence, 238, 349n. 35

foreign goods shops, 70–72

Forest, Lockwood de, 126, 248

Forssen, Carl, 145, 179, 293

Francis, David R., 249–250, 252

functionalism, 38, 43, 47, 75, 216; illustrations, *30, 45, 196, 204*

Furness, Frank, 213

Gardner, Isabella Stewart, 115, 147

Gates Pottery, 243, 247

Gentleman and Cabinet-Maker's Director, The (Chippendale), 21–23, *22*

Gerard, Alexander, 13, 15–16, 20, 162; *An Essay on Taste*, 13, 15

Gilbert, Cass, 227, 228–229

Godwin, Alfred, 242–43

INDEX 385

good design: achieving, 48–50; aesthetics and, 31; Arts and Crafts movement and, 31; Batchelder on, 202, 211, 214, 222; and Boston, 276; and conventionalization, 51, 201–2, 203–4, 209–11, 219; critics and: 17–20, 38–39, 43–45, 48, 217, 276; and expression, 54–55, 220–224; fitness and, 198; history as model for, 21, 189–98; illustrations, 213, 264; Merrifield on, 7; models for, 10, 16, 21, 39, 50, 54; SACB and, 113–114, 116, 118–120, 128–130, 224, 252, 254, 268, 277–78; SACB Jury and, 123, 142, 155, 160–61, 163–64, 167, 185–86; spread of, 268; twenty-first century, 290–91; and Usefulness and Beauty, 20, 137; Warren on, 118–20, 137; Wornum on, 10–12
Goodhue, Bertram Grosvenor, 65, 96, 101, 106, 108, 113, 242, 254–55; illustrations, 102, 197, 213, 255
Goodhue, Harry E., 242–43, 242, 254
Gordon, Kate, 218
Gorham Company. *See* Codman, William Christmas
Goudy, Frederic W., 233–34, 249
Grammar of Ornament, The (Jones), 186, 202, 209, 212
Gray, Morris, 62, 62–63, 103, 109
Great Exhibition of Works of Industry (London, 1851), 1–8, 26–28, 44, 174, 275; design criticism at, 5–12
Grueby, William H., xviii, 248, 283
Grueby Faience Company, 145
Grueby Pottery Co. 227, 233, 243, 248, 260, 266, 282; illustrations, 14, 215, 226, 244

Hale, Frank Gardner, 145, 146, 179, 293, 301–3, 305, 307
Hale, George Ellery, 273
Hallowell, George H., 251, 251, 254
Hamlin, A. D. F., theory of "selective ideal," 191
Handicraft, 129–40, 143, 149, 198, 203, 259, 274; illustrations, 77, 126, 131; and Principles of Handicraft, 130–31; reform debate in, 132–36; revitalized, 155–57
Handicraft Shop (SACB), 126–27, 132, 134–35, 178, 245; illustrations, 126, 164
Hapgood, Theodore Brown, Jr., 96, 97, 101; illustrations, 207, 214

Hayden, Sophia, 100
Heintzemann, Carl H., 76, 105
Hellman, Laura, 238, 349n. 35
Hepplewhite, George, 12, 20–24, 107; illustrations, 23, 74; *Cabinet–Maker and Upholsterer's Guide*, 20–24, 107; style: illustrations, 80, 116, 187
Hills, Laura C., 253
Historic Design in Printing (Lewis), 67
historicism, 8, 10, 21, 39, 41, 43, 48–50, 58, 67–68, 158, 176, 185–86, 189–98, 200; illustrations, 50, 196, 204, 261, 263, 264, Plate 1
Hogarth, William, 12–15, 13, 18, 20; *Analysis of Beauty*, 12, 13, 18, 212
Home, Henry (Lord Kames), 16–18, 20, 29, 162; *Elements of Criticism*, 16, 18
Hooper, Charles, Edward, 199, 290
Houghton Mifflin & Co., 62, 84, 105, 253, 266, 274
House Beautiful, as concept, 33, 52, 75
House Beautiful, The, xvii, 31, 71–72, 76, 102, 106–7, 186–87, 196, 219, 260, Plate 5; contemporary, 284, 286. *See also* Cook, Clarence
Houston, Frances C. (Mrs.), 231, 251
Hovey, Richard, 105–6
Howe, Frederic C., 248
Howe, Lois Lilley, 78, 100, 134, 150, 227, 252, 260, 276; illustrations, 100, 262
Hume, David, 14, 20; *Of the Standard of Taste*, 12, 14–15
Hunt, George J., 153, 154, 254
Hurley, Edward T. 244

Industrial Revolution, 12
Ives, Halsey Cooley, 229, 229–33, 235, 246, 250, 279

James, George Wharton, xxiv, 237
Japan: Its Architecture, Art and Art Manufactures (Dresser), 194
Jaques, Herbert, 86, 87, 145, 252, 255–56, 256
Jarvie, Robert R., 238, 349n. 33
Jenkins, William Porter, 118, 119
Jenks, Barton P., 60, 60
Johnson, Henry Lewis, 62, 62, 67, 93, 96, 109, 114–15, 127; *Historic Design in Printing*, 67
Jones, Owen, 4, 4, 6, 26, 28, 75, 189; *The Grammar of Ornament*, 186, 202, 209, 212

Journal of Design and Manufactures, 26–28, *27*, 275, Plate 4

Kendall, Alice, 150, 302
Kendrick, George Prentiss, 60, 143–45, *145*, *160*, 164
Ketterer, Gustav, 231
Kimball, Mr. And Mrs. Irving, 150, 306
Kirchmayer, John (Johannes), 59, *60*, 76, 109, 114, 156, 254, 267
Kjellstrom, Nils, 143–144, 293
Knight, Mary Catherine, 126, *126*, 178–79, *178*, 249
Knight, Richard Payne, 20; *Analytical Inquiry into the Principles of Taste*, 20
Koralewsky, Frank, 253, 301, 307; illustrations, *164*, *190*
Krasser, Frederick, 156, 248, 254; illustrations, *164*, *190*
Kunkler, Adolph C., 249, 305
Kurtz, Charles M., *232*, 232

La Farge, John, 87, 231, 242
Lamb, Frederick S., 231, 242–43
Laurence, Frederick Sturgis, 244
Lawrence, Gertrude, 148
LeBoutillier, Addison B., 227, 248, 260, *261*, 311–312
Leinonen, Karl F., 76, 126, 305, 308; illustrations, *126*, *164*
Lethaby, William R., 96, 218
Lindeman, Laura, E., 244
Longfellow, Alden & Harlow, 227, 255–256, 312
Longfellow, Alexander Wadsworth (Waddy), Jr., *58*, 63, 64, 67–68, 227, 293, 312; illustrations, *58*, *164*, *256*; and Louisiana Purchase Exposition, 143, 226–52, 259, 269, 273; and Richardson, 87, 255–56; and SACB, 109, 114, 255, 259; as SACB Juror 143–44, 172, 175
Low, Will Hickok, 248, 250
Lowell, Guy, 63, 68, 252, 260–61, 308, 312; illustrations, *63*, *263*

Machine, the, 38–39, 75, 128, 137, 228
Macomber, Frank Gair, 115, *115*
Macomber, H. Percy, 253–54, 266–67
Mahoney, Marion L., 100
Marot, Elizabeth Griscom, 238, 249, 349n. 35
Martin, Laurin Hovey, 143–44, *144*, 293

Masqueray, Emmanuel Louis, 228, 230
Massachusetts Charitable Mechanic Association, 82, 85, 96, 106, 134
Masson, Maud, 253, *253*
Matsuki, Bunkio, 72, 73, 324n. 25, Plate 9
Maynard, Florence, *100*, 150, 305, 307
Maynard, Karl, 150, 304–5, 307
McLaughlin, Louise, 243–44
Mead, Edwin Doak, 94, 132
Mercer, Henry Chapman, *160*, 161–162, 243–48, 254, 266, 273, 301, 307
Merrifield, Mary Philadelphia, 1–2, 12, 18–19, 21, 27–28, 314n. 11; on Great Exhibition, 5–7; and social reform, 34
Merrymount Press, 61, 62, 234. *See also* Updike, Daniel Berkeley
Metalworkers, Guild of, 168, 177–79
Meteyard, Thomas Buford, 105, *203*, 224, 274
Mirror of the Graces, The, 26
models, for good design, 10, 16, 21, 39, 50, 54
modernism, 51, 204, 291
Moore, Charles H., 88, 327n. 54
moralism, and Arts and Crafts movement, 42, 43, 289
Morgan, William de, 96
Morris, May, 43
Morris, William, xvii–xviii, 32–33, 41, 67, 75, 87, 96, 98, 104, 108, 147, 207–8; and conventionalization, 212; and History and Nature, 48 50, 194; illustrations, *37*, *196*, *233*, *256*; and Norton, 89–91; and Trinity Church, 86–87; on Usefulness and Beauty, 44
Morris & Co., xviii, 44, 49–50, 69, 70–71, 87, 266, 284, 286; illustrations, *50*, *70*, *73*, *80*, Plate 18. *See also* William Morris
Morse, Alice Cordelia, 147–48
Morse, Alice J., 146–48, 154, 293, Plate 11, Plate 12
Morse, Edward S., 72, 105, 189, 222
Mott-Smith, May, 236
Murphy, Hermann Dudley, 146, *148*, 181, 238, 251, 293. *See also* Carrig-Rohane Shop
Museum of Fine Arts (MFA) (Boston), 68–69, 73, 75, 105, 189–90; connections with SACB, 62–64, 103, 114–15, 146, 193, 272; illustrations, *62*, *63*, *104*, *189*, *191*, *263*; new building, 68, 92, 264

Museum of Fine Arts, School of the, 63, 85, 92, 98, 114, 143–44, 146–47, 192–93
museums: beginnings of, 38–39, 49; and SACB crafts, 226, 266; twenty-first-century, 283–84; Whiting and, 269. *See also* Museum of Fine Arts

National League of Handicraft Societies (NLHS), 107, 193, 267–68, 270–71
Native American: artifacts, at Louisiana Purchase Exposition, 236–237; handicrafts in *Handicraft*, 131; influence on craftspeople, 194–95, 215, 279; baskets and conventionalization, 214
naturalism, 11, 39, 43, 49–50, 101, 185–187, 198–203, 204–5, 208–10; and conventionalization, 201–2; illustrations, *41, 213, 253*
Nature in Ornament (Day), 194, 208–10, 215
Newcomb College Pottery, 233, 243, 249, 266
Newhall, Louis C., 65, 267, 312
Norton, Charles Eliot, 88–96, 130, 225, 258; and art education, 93–95; and Burne-Jones, 90–91; and Carlyle, 90; and college settlement house movement, 94–95; and *Handicraft*, 130; illustrations, *56, 89, 211*; and Morris, 90–91; publications by, 67, 88; and Ruskin, 88–90, 92, 94; in SACB, 57–58, 63, 88, 91, 103–4, 109, 113–15; Norton, Susan Ridley Sedgwick (Mrs. Charles), *89,* 89, 92

O'Kane, Helen Marguerite (Mrs. Clarke Conwell): illustrations, *200, 233*
organizations, social, 65, 84, 86, 105–106, 276–78, 327n. 50
ornament, 8–12, 21, 23–24, 36, 51, 185–86, *213,* 219; conventionalized, 51, 75, 203–7, 209–11, 214–16; Day on, 50–51, 186, 197, 203–4, 208–9, 211–12, 215–19; and design criticism, 31; Dresser on, 75; illustrations, *23, 50, 126, 204, 206, 215, 218;* design reformers and, 75; and "good design," 113; and SACB Jury, 158, 161, 166, 169, 175; Walker on, 136, 166, 169, 175, 258; Warren on, 120; Whiting on, 129; Wornum on, 21, 208–9

Ornament and Its Application (Day), 186, 204, 212, 215
ornamentation, 32, 113, 137, 201–2, 203–10, 213, 214–15, 217; illustrations, 79, *145, 193, 217, 218,* 220

Palace of Art (St. Louis), 227–29, 247–48; as exhibit space, 228–29, 231–32, 235–36; illustrations, *227, 240, 241;* security and the, 238; and Usefulness and Beauty, 240–43
Parsons, Frank, 94, 132, 134
Partridge, Frederick, 76, 145
pattern book(s), 12, 20–23, *23,* 162, 209
Paxton, Joseph, 4
Payne Bowles, Janet, 269–270, *270*
Peabody, John Endicott, 115, *116,* 146, 148, 293
Philosophical Enquiry into the Origin of our Ideas of the Sublime and the Beautiful, A (Burke), 12–13, 15
photography: architectural, 78; reproduction, 192; and SACB 150, 175, 295; women in, 100–101, 150
Planning of Ornament, The (Day), 198, 212, 217
Porden, William (pseud. Shanhagan, Roger), 19–20, 53, 315n. 45
Post, W. B., 150, 302, 303–4
Potter's Craft, The (Binns), 36, 107
Pre-Raphaelite, 33, 90, 97, *233;* Brotherhood, 69, 87, 89–90, 99
Price, Sir Uvedale, 20; *Dialogue on The Distinct Characters of the Picturesque and the Beautiful,* 20
Price, William L., 238
Principles of Decorative Design (Dresser), 75, 212, 217, 219
Principles of Design, The (Batchelder), 38
"Principles of Handicraft," 130–31, *131,* 136–37, 155, 157
Principles of Harmony and Contrast of Colors, The (Chevreul), 6
Pugin, Augustus W. N., 27, 32–33, *41,* 194
Putnam, Annie Cabot, 145–46, *147,* 177, 179, 293

Rantoul, Augustus Neal, 145, 252, 255, 256
realism, 200, 202–3, 209, 219, 251
Redmond, Margaret, 87, *161,* 161, 200, 254
Reed & Barton, *44,* 209

reform, social, xxiv, 34, 57, 65, 75–76, 86, 94, 114, 127, 132, 134–35, 238, 271, 318n. 77
Repository of the Arts, Literature, Commerce, Manufactures, Fashions, and Politics (Ackermann), 25–27, Plate 3
revivalism, xviii, 8, 10, 41, 43, 68
Richardson, Henry Hobson (H. H.), 58–59, 86–88, 96, 192, 208; illustrations, *87, 102, 210*
Riverside Press, *221,* 234, 274. *See also* Rogers, Bruce
Robertson, Hugh Cornwall, 76, 142, 160, 162, *243,* 246, 248, 255
Robineau, Adelaide A., 243–44, 253, 266, 302–303, 307
Rogers, Bruce, 101, 234, 248, 274. *See also* Riverside Press
Rollins, Carl Purington, 268, 274
Rookwood Pottery, 226–27, 233, 235–36, 240, 243–44, 282–83; illustrations, *199, 223*
Roseville Pottery Company, 235
Ross, Denman Waldo, 38, 58, 63–64, 115, 123, 236, 254, 263, 293; "The Arts and Crafts: A Diagnosis," 132, 141, 156; on conventionalization, 210–11, 215; and debate in *Handicraft,* 132, 134–36; illustrations, *38, 56;* on SACB Jury, 141–45, 152, 156; *A Theory of Pure Design,* 38, 156, 210
Rossetti, Dante Gabriel, 89–90, 95. *See also* Pre–Raphaelite
Ruskin, John, 32–34, 37, 48, 58, 88–90, 92–95, 120, 146; on beauty, 33; critique of, 27; *Seven Lamps of Architecture,* 27, 32, 194; *Stones of Venice,* 27, 32, 34, 37, 148, 194

SACB (Society of Arts and Crafts Boston), xix–xx, 57, 59; architects in, 77–88, 225–26, 254–62; Boston background of, 57, 69–77, 86, 99–101, 104–8; and Boston diaspora, 225–26, 266–74; building committee, 267; and collaboration, Plate 10; craft categories and, 149–51; decennial exhibition, 262–65; design reform philosophy of, 124–30; and First Exhibition of the Arts and Crafts, 96–98, 101–4; first year, 109–113; founders, 57–68; and *Handicraft,* 130–140; headquarters for, 121–24; illustrations, *38, 106, 118, 156, 182;* and National League of Handicraft Societies, 193, 267–68; international exhibitions and members of, 225, 253, 265; international role of, 253; Library, 192–93; and Louisiana Purchase Exposition, 226–52; medal, 156; membership, 156, 225, 252–53, 277; and Norton, 88–96; and politics, 138, 264; and Second Exhibition of the Arts and Crafts, 113–21; speakers from, 266; and Usefulness and Beauty, 66, 109, 120, 131, 139–40, 249, 254, 281; women and, 100–101, 150
SACB Jury: membership, 142–49; constituents, 149–51; mission and procedures, 151–57; recommendations, 157–62; reports of, 162–67, 171, 175–78; responses to, 177–184; and conventionalization, 208; on "good design," 118–20, 185, 224; on models and methods, 188–92, 224; and naturalism, 200–203; on Usefulness and Beauty, 123, 142, 146, 151, 155, 157, 160–62, 176–77, 277, 283
SACB Salesroom, 121–124, 142, 156–57, 162, 165–66, 178, 181; Committee on the, 168, 183; crafts Jury wanted in, 169–70; in New York, 266
Sacker, Amy, 85, 134, 143, 146–47, *149,* 293, Plate 10
Saint Dunstan's Guild, 179
Sartain, Emily, 231
Sears, Mary Crease, 143, 217, 239, 248, 293, 301, 306
Sears, Sarah Choate, 109, 143, 150, 231, 251, 293; illustrations, *110, 111*
Seven Lamps of Architecture (Ruskin), 27, 32, 194
Shanhagan, Roger. *See* Porden, William; Smirke, Robert; Watson, Robert
Shaw, Emily Mott, 238, 249
Shaw, George R., 58, *59,* 64, 114, 312
Sheerer, Mary G., 249
Sheraton, Thomas, 12, 20–21, 23–25, 32; *Cabinet-maker and Upholsterer's Drawing-Book,* 20, 23; *The Cabinet Dictionary,* 23–24; *The Cabinet Encyclopedia,* 24, *24*
Silversmith's Manual, (Cuzner), 198
Small, Lillian M., 150, 307
Smirke, Robert (pseud. Shanhagan, Roger), 19–20, 53, 315n. 45, 316n. 46
Smith, Joseph Lindon, 115, 143, 146–47, 251, 293; illustrations, *116, 148, 149*

Society for the Preservation of New England Antiquities (SPNEA), *45*, 67, 86
Society for the Protection of Ancient Buildings (Britain), 67
Society of Arts and Crafts Boston (SACB). *See* SACB
Society of Arts and Manufactures, 3
Soderholtz, E. E., 53–54, 306
Solon, Louis A., 243
St. John, Agnes, 239, 248
Standard of Taste, Of the (Hume), 12, 14–15
Starr, Ellen Gates, 94, 238, 271–72, *272*
Stickley, Albert, 107
Stickley, Gustave, *206*, 283, 285, 289, 335n. 55
Stickley furnishings, 107, *206*, 283, 285, 289
Stiles, Gertrude, 238
Stone, Arthur J., xxiii, 76, 123, 196, 282–83, 301–3, 306, 308; and awards, 156, 248; critique of, by SACB Jury, 162, 183, 200; illustrations, *164*, *182*, *183*, *193*, *251*; library of, 193–194
Stone, Elizabeth Bent Eaton (Mrs. Arthur J.), 123–24, 183
Stones of Venice (Ruskin), 27, 32, 34, 37, *148*, 194
strapwork, 206–7; illustrations, *179*, *183*, *206*, *207*, *270*
Studies in Design (Dresser), 209
Sturgis, Esther Mary Ogden (Mrs. R. C.), 261–62, *265*
Sturgis, Richard Clipston, 63, 67, 143, 261–262, 312, *293*; illustrations, *63*, *70*, *264*, *265*

Taste, 5, 7, 12–20, 25
Taylor, William Watts, 235–36. *See also* Rookwood Pottery
Teco pottery, 240, 247–48
ten Kate, Lambert Hermanson, 13–14
"The 10," 65, 99, 105, 146
Theory of Pure Design, A (Ross), 38, 156, 210
Tiffany, Louis Comfort, 97, 126, 231, 245
Tiffany & Co., 245–46, 266
Toof & Co., S. C., 233, 246
Toynbee Hall, 94–95, 105
Trinity Church, 59, *63*, *85*, 86–87, *91*
Turner, Ross Sterling, 134, 239
Twentieth Century Club, 75, 86, 94, 105, *121*, *122*, 252. *See also* Mead, Edwin Doak

Union Glass Co., 152, 247, *247*
Updike, Daniel Berkeley, 62, 106, 113–14, 234, 248, 254, 276; illustrations, *38*, *234*; portrait, *61*; *Printing Types, Their History, Forms and Uses*, 67
Upton, Mary Haskell, 238–39, 349n. 35
Usefulness, xvii–xviii, 17, 29, 31, 47, 129, 161, 171. *See also* Usefulness and Beauty
Usefulness and Beauty, xvii–xix, 16–18, 31–33, 97, 132, 225, 229, 268, 272–275, 279, 285, 290–91, Plate 6; aesthetes and, 29; architects and, 77–88, 104, 254; and Arts and Crafts movement, 1, 31, 47, 106; and consumers, 20; and conventionalization, 209; criteria for, 20, 47–48; design criticism and, 31; eighteenth-century critics and, 20–22; and expression, 17, 52–54; and gender, 290–91; "good design" and, 20, 137; history as model for, 186; literature and, 25; Merrifield on, 5; Morris on, 44; at Palace of Art, 240–48; quest for, 1–2, 10, 12, 94, 106–8, 268, 281, 283; and SACB, 66, 109, 120, 131–32, 139–40, 249, 254; and SACB Jury, 123, 142, 146, 151, 155, 157, 160–62, 176–77, 277, 283; and Walker, 132, 136, 140, 155; Ware Dennett on, 132–33; Warren, 137; Whiting and, 128–29, 269; Wornum on, 5, 10
utopian communities, 58, 125–126, 268, 274, 334n. 35

Van Briggle, Anne and Artus, 235, *235*, 248
Van Briggle Pottery, 233, 235, 243
Van Denburgh, Douglass, 236
Verberg, Peter, 238
Victoria (queen of England), 3, 314n. 11
Village Press, 233–234. *See also* Goudy, Frederic W.
Volkmar, Charles, 244
Voysey, Charles F. A., xviii, 52, 54, 98, 107, 202, 212, 288; illustrations, *212*, *260*

Walker, Charles Howard, 58, 144, 147, 178, 267, 279, *293*, 312; career, 258–59; on design, 217; as Critic of the

Jury, 142, 167–77; and education, 63, 136, 258–59; and *Handicraft*, 132, 136; on historicism; 194–95, 199, 231, 276; illustrations, *56, 86, 228, 258, 259*; on naturalism, 199; and SACB, 109, 121; and SACB Jury, 143, 155–57, 166, 181–82, 188–92, 195, and Louisiana Purchase Exposition, 143, 228, 230–33, 248, 252; and Trans-Mississippi Exposition, 227; writings, 67, 132, 136, 259. *See also* Walker & Kimball
Walker, Emery, 96
Walker and Kimball, 156, *228, 228,* 312
Ware, William Robert, 191–92
Ware Dennett, Mary, 121–22, 126, 143, 159, 270, 276, 293, 335n. 45; and *Handicraft* debate, 132–39; illustrations, *37, 106, 132, 240*; and reform, 134
Warren, Fiske, 63, 105
Warren, Gretchen Osgood (Mrs. Fiske), 63, 100, 105
Warren, Harold Broadfield, 76, 251
Warren, Herbert Langford, 58, 67, 168, 251–52, 255–57, 269; and 1899 Exhibition Catalogue, 123, 125, 129, 137, 139, 162; and decennial exhibition catalogue, 262–63; on "good design," 118–20, 137; and *Handicraft*, 130, 132, 198; at Harvard, 58, 257–58; illustrations, *56, 164, 257*; and National League of Handicraft Societies, 267; and Richardson, 87; and SACB, 109, 113–14, 118–20, 123, 125, 137–39, 255–56, 267; and SACB founding, 63–64, 76; and SACB Jury, 143, 162; on Whiting, 269; writings by, 257–58
Warren, Mabel Bayard (Mrs. Samuel), 63, 100
Warren, Samuel Dennis II, 62–64, 94; illustrations, *62, 64, 66*
Warren family, 64
Watson, Robert (pseud. Shanhagan, Roger), 19–20, 53, 315n. 45
Webb, Philip, 196, *196*
Wedgwood, Josiah, 12, Plate 2
Wentworth, Bertrand H., 150, 302, 304, 306, 308
Wheeler, Candace, 97, 126
Wheelwright, Edmund March, 63–64, 68, 114, 227, 252, 261, 312; illustrations, *64, 224*

White, Stanford, 59, 231
Whiting, Frederick Allen, 121–24, *122*, 193, 227, 276, 282–83, 293; and Louisiana Purchase Exposition, 230–41, 243–50; and National League of Handicraft Societies, 267; SACB, 121–24, 131–32, 139–40, 173, 179, 253, 270; after SACB, 269–70; at on SACB Jury, 143–44, 151, 153, 157; and SACB Salesroom, 123–24, 153, 165; speeches by, 128–29, 159, 254, 266–67; on Usefulness and Beauty, 128–29, 269
Whiting, Olive Elizabeth Cook (Mrs. Frederick), 122, *123*
Whitman, Sarah Wyman, xxiv, 61, 63–64, 99, 246, 276, 287, 293; and 1899 Exhibition, 120; and book arts, 66, 234; illustrations, *61, 211, 216, 221, 242*; in SACB, 103, 109, 114–15; on SACB Jury, 143, 152–53, 157–58; stained glass windows by, 87, 242–43; at Twentieth Century Club, 121
Wilde, Oscar, 31, 33, 74, 75, 290
Willcox, Harriet E., 244
Winslow, W. Henry, 76, 102
Woman's Book, The, 150
women: architects, 100, 150, 260; and book arts, 150, 238; in Boston Arts and Crafts Movement, 99–101; and design reform, 26, 57, 103, 276; and Louisiana Purchase Exposition, 238, 240; photographers, 150; in SACB, 100, 111, 150–51, 254; workers, *125*
Woodward, Ellsworth, 243, 249, 304
world's fairs. *See* exhibitions, international
Wornum, Ralph Nicholson, 1–2, 7, 21, 25, 39, 41; *An Analysis of Ornament*, 8; critiqued by *Journal*, 27; on Great Exhibition, 5, 7–12, 18; on ornament, 8–10, 209
Wynne, Madeline Yale, 145–46, 270–71; illustrations, *147, 271*

Yellin, Samuel, 254

Zahn, Otto H., 233, 246–47

MD INSTITUTE COLLEGE OF ART
10076928

NK 1141 .B73 2009
Brandt, Beverly Kay.
The craftsman and the critic

Maryland Institute, College of Art
The Decker Library
1401 Mount Royal Avenue
Baltimore, MD 21217

WITHDRAWN